# Dictionary of Accounting Terms

## Sixth Edition

Jae K. Shim, Ph.D.
Former Professor of Accounting
College of Business Administration
California State University, Long Beach

Joel G. Siegel, Ph.D., CPA
Professor of Accounting
Queens College of the City University of New York

Nick Dauber, MS, CPA
Lecturer in Accounting
Queens College of the City University of New York

Anique A. Qureshi, Ph.D., CPA
Professor of Accounting and Information Systems
Queens College of the City University of New York

BARRON'S

**ACKNOWLEDGMENTS**
The authors would like to acknowledge the contributions made by reviewers John Downes, formerly of the New York City Office of Economic Development, and Dr. G. Thomas Friedlob, Professor of Accounting at Clemson University. Their in-depth evaluations have been of great importance to the technical accuracy of the manuscript. Gerald J. Barry suggested many meaningful insertions and deletions that greatly enhanced the authors' prose. Thanks also go to Roberta Siegel, Allison Shim, University of California at Irvine, Oleksiy Y. Duplinskyy and Therese Dayvit, both from California State University, Long Beach, and Dr. Qianyun Ivy Huang, Assistant Professor of Accounting at Queens College of the City University of New York, for their assistance with the computer terms, graphics, and word processing. Anna Damaskos, Don Reis, Sally Strauss, and Eileen Prigge of Barron's have been invaluable during the many stages of editing the manuscript into its bound book form.

Barron's books are available at special quantity discounts to use as premiums and sales promotions, or for use in corporate training programs. For more information, please write to the Special Sales Manager, Barron's Educational Series, Inc. at the mailing address indicated below.

*All inquiries should be addressed to:*
Barron's Educational Series, Inc.
250 Wireless Boulevard
Hauppauge, NY 11788
**www.barronseduc.com**

*Library of Congress Catalog Card No. 2013046910*

ISBN: 978-1-4380-0275-0

**Library of Congress Cataloging-in-Publication Data**
Shim, Jae K.
   Dictionary of accounting terms / Jae K. Shim, Ph.D., Professor of Accounting, College of Business Administration, California State University, Long Beach, Joel G. Siegel, Ph.D., CPA, Professor of Accounting, Queens College of the City University of New York, Anique Qureshi, Ph.D., CPA, Professor of Accounting and Information Systems, Queens College of the City University of New York, Nick Dauber, MST, CPA Lecturer in Accounting, Queens College of the City University of New York. — Sixth Edition.
      pages cm
   Includes bibliographical references and index.
   ISBN: 978-1-4380-0275-0 (alk. paper)
   1. Accounting—Dictionaries. I. Siegel, Joel G. II. Title.
HF5621.S54     2014
657.03–dc23                                            2013046910

PRINTED IN CHINA
9 8 7 6 5 4 3 2 1

# CONTENTS

# PREFACE

Whether you audit the records of a large corporation or balance your own checkbook, you will find Barron's *Dictionary of Accounting Terms* of immeasurable help. You may be a business person—a bookkeeper, a manager, or a proprietor. You may be a business student—an accounting major or an MBA candidate. You may *be* an accountant or you may have to *deal* with accountants. Whatever the case, this Dictionary provides the definitions, examples, and illustrations you need to know about all aspects of financial record keeping.

In class or at a business meeting, you are likely to hear an accounting term that is unfamiliar to you. You need to know what that term means and its application in order to follow the presentation intelligently. At home you may be puzzled by a reference in a text you are studying or by a direction in a form you are completing. You need to understand what is meant in order to proceed with the task efficiently. Keeping a copy of this volume by your side will provide the explanations and demonstrations that will enable you to handle all of these problems.

Accounting is a dynamic area with a vocabulary that is constantly changing. To talk its language, you have to keep up-to-date with the latest terms that have just emerged and with the latest definitions of older terms. It is this book's purpose to present the working vocabulary of accounting today—defining new terminology as it affects the accounting profession, while updating the traditional language of accounting and its related disciplines.

Entries have been drawn from all areas within accounting including financial accounting, managerial and cost accounting, auditing, financial statement analysis, and taxes. Definitions have also been provided for many terms from related business disciplines that the accountant must know about in order to perform his or her functions in the business world. Included are essential words from finance, international accounting, quantitative techniques, information technology and the Internet, and economics. In all, clear, concise definitions are provided for more than 2500 terms, and a further explanation of the term or a demonstration of its use is frequently given to amplify the definition. Thus, each entry is basic enough for the novice to grasp the essential meaning quickly, yet comprehensive enough for the professional to find additional detail when it is needed.

The authors sincerely hope that this dictionary will prove a handy reference for anyone involved with accounting—from the layman to the expert.

*Jae K. Shim*
*Joel G. Siegel*
*Nick Dauber*
*Anique A. Qureshi*

# HOW TO USE THIS BOOK EFFECTIVELY

**Alphabetization:** All entries are alphabetized by letter rather than by word, so that multiple-word terms are treated as single words. For example, **ACCOUNT FORM** follows **ACCOUNTANT,** and **AD VALOREM TAX** follows **ADMINISTRATIVE BUDGET.** In unusual cases (such as **BASIC**) abbreviations appear as entries in the main text, in addition to appearing in the back of the book in the separate listing of Abbreviations and Acronyms. This occurs when the short form or acronym, rather than the formal name, predominates in the common usage of the field. For example, **BASIC** is commonly used when speaking of the **"BEGINNER'S ALL-PURPOSE SYMBOLIC INSTRUCTION CODE";** thus, the entry is at **BASIC.** Numbers in entry titles are alphabetized as if they were spelled out. For example, **401(K) PLAN** follows **FORWARD RATE.**

Many words have distinctly different meanings, depending upon the context in which they are used. The various meanings of a term are listed by numerical or functional subheading. Readers must determine the context that is relevant to their purpose.

When terms are defined as different parts of speech, the grammatical forms are not labeled but the sequence is always nouns, followed by verbs, followed by qualifiers.

**Abbreviations:** A separate list of Abbreviations follows the Dictionary.

**Cross-References:** To add to your understanding of a term, related or contrasting terms are sometimes cross-referenced. The cross-referenced term will appear in SMALL CAPITALS either in the body of the entry (or subentry) or at the end. These terms will be printed in SMALL CAPITALS only the first time they appear in the text. Where an entry is fully defined by another term, a reference rather than a definition is provided—for example: **ALPHA RISK** *see* TYPE I ERROR.

**Italics:** Italic type is generally used to indicate that another term has a meaning identical or very closely related to that of the entry. Italic type is also used to highlight the fact that a word or phrase has a special meaning to the trade. Italics are also used for the titles of publications.

**Parentheses:** Parentheses are used in entry titles to indicate that an abbreviation is used with about the same frequency as the term itself; for example, **SECURITIES AND EXCHANGE COMMISSION (SEC).**

**Special Definitions:** Organizations and associations that play an active role in the field are included in the Dictionary along with a brief statement of their mission.

# A

## ABACUS

1. instrument of ancient origin used to perform arithmetic calculations by sliding counters along rods or in grooves.
2. semiannual accounting research journal (founded in 1965) published by the Sydney University Press, edited by the University of Sydney, Department of Accounting. The subject matter covers all areas of accounting including international accounting.

**ABANDONMENT** voluntary surrender of property, owned or leased, without naming a successor as owner or tenant. The property will generally revert to a person holding a prior interest or, in cases where no owner is apparent, to the state.

**ABATEMENT** complete or partial cancellation of a levy imposed by a governmental unit. Abatements usually apply to tax levies, special assessments, and service charges.

**ABC** *see* ACTIVITY-BASED COSTING.

**ABC METHOD** inventory management method that categorizes items in terms of importance. Thus, more emphasis is placed on higher dollar value items ("A"s) than on lesser dollar value items ("B"s), while the least important items ("C"s) receive the least time and attention. Inventory should be analyzed frequently when using the ABC method. The procedure for ABC analysis follows: (1) Separate finished goods into types (chairs of different models, and so on); separate raw materials into types (screws, nuts, and so on). (2) Calculate the annual dollar usage for each type of inventory (multiply the unit cost by the expected future annual usage). (3) Rank each inventory type from highest to lowest, based on annual dollar usage. (4) Classify the inventory as A—the top 20%; B—the next 30%; and C—the last 50% of dollars usage, respectively. (5) Tag the inventory with its appropriate ABC classification and record those classifications in the item inventory master records.

**ABNORMAL SPOILAGE** spoilage that is recognized as a loss when discovered. NORMAL SPOILAGE is inherent in the manufacturing process and is unavoidable in the short run. Abnormal spoilage is spoilage beyond the normal spoilage rate. It is controllable because it is a result of inefficiency. It is not a cost of good production, but rather it is a loss for the period. Costs are assigned to the spoiled units and then credited to WORK-IN-PROCESS inventory and debited to a loss account.

## ABSORB

1. to assimilate, transfer, or incorporate amounts in an account or a group of accounts in a manner in which the first entity loses its identity and is "absorbed" within the second entity. Examples

include the sequential transfer of expenditure account amounts to WORK-IN-PROCESS, finished goods, and COST OF SALES.
2. to distribute or spread costs by the process of proration or allocation. *See also* ABSORPTION COSTING.

**ABSORPTION COSTING** method in which all manufacturing costs, variable and fixed, are treated as PRODUCT COSTS, while nonmanufacturing costs (e.g., selling and administrative expenses) are treated as PERIOD COSTS. Absorption costing for inventory valuation is required for external reporting. *See also* VARIABLE COSTING.

A comparison between absorption and variable costing follows:

| Absorption Costing | Variable Costing |
|---|---|
| 1. Required for outside reporting | 1. Not accepted for outside reporting |
| 2. Includes fixed overhead as an inventoriable cost | 2. Does not include fixed overhead as an inventoriable cost |
| 3. Stresses gross profit | 3. Stresses contribution margin |
| 4. Has a higher net income when production exceeds sales | 4. Has a higher net income when sales exceed production |

**ABUSIVE TAX SHELTER** limited partnership the IRS believes is claiming illegal tax deductions. This type of shelter usually inflates the value of purchased property, thus providing a basis for higher depreciation write-offs. When the IRS disallows the write-offs, back taxes as well as interest charges and high penalties must be paid. *See also* LIMITED PARTNER.

**ACADEMY OF ACCOUNTING HISTORIANS** voluntary organization dedicated to the study of accounting history. This organization (http://accounting.rutgers.edu/raw/aah) publishes the ACCOUNTING HISTORIANS JOURNAL in addition to monographs, working papers, and a newsletter.

**ACCELERATED COST RECOVERY SYSTEM (ACRS)** system of depreciation for tax purposes mandated by the Economic Recovery Act (ERA) of 1981 and modified by the Tax Reform Act of 1986. The type of property determines its class. Instead of providing statutory tables, prescribed methods of depreciation are assigned to each class of property. For 3, 5, 7, and 10 year classes, the relevant depreciation method is the 200% declining balance method. For 15 and 20 year property, the appropriate method is the 150% declining balance method switching to the STRAIGHT-LINE method when it will yield a larger allowance. For residential rental property (27.5 years) and nonresidential real property (31.5 years), the applicable method is the straight-line method. A taxpayer may make an irrevocable election to treat all property in one of the classes under the straight-line method. Property is statutorily placed in one of the classes. The purpose of ACRS is to encourage more capital investment by businesses. It permits a faster recovery of the asset's cost and thus provides larger tax benefits in the earlier years. *See also* MODIFIED ACCELERATED COST RECOVERY SYSTEM (MACRS).

**ACCELERATED DEPRECIATION** method recognizing higher amounts of depreciation in the earlier years and lower amounts in the later years of a fixed asset's life. Some machines, for example, are more efficient early on and generate greater service potential; matching dictates higher depreciation expense in those years. Over time, depreciation expense moves in a downward direction and maintenance costs tend to become higher; thus the effect of accelerated depreciation is fairly even charges to income. Greatest tax benefits from depreciation are enjoyed in the earlier years. *See also* ACCELERATED COST RECOVERY SYSTEM; DOUBLE DECLINING BALANCE; SUM-OF-THE-YEARS'-DIGITS (SYD) METHOD.

**ACCELERATION CLAUSE** provision contained in a BOND INDENTURE requiring that in an event of default any remaining interest and principal become immediately due and payable.

**ACCEPTABLE QUALITY LEVEL (AQL)** a quality standard that allows a prespecified number of defects.

**ACCEPTANCE**
1. drawee's promise to pay either a TIME DRAFT or SIGHT DRAFT. Typically, the acceptor signs his name after writing "accepted" on the bill along with the date. Instead of "accepted," similar wording indicating an intention to pay would also suffice to show a desire to honor the bill at maturity. An acceptance of a bill in effect makes it a PROMISSORY NOTE: the acceptor is the maker and the drawer is the endorser.
2. BANKER'S ACCEPTANCE.
3. binding contract effected when one party to a business arrangement accepts the offer of another. Acceptance may be in written or oral form.

**ACCEPTANCE SAMPLING** statistical procedure used in quality control. Acceptance sampling involves testing a batch of data to determine if the proportion of units having a particular attribute exceeds a given percentage. The sampling plan involves three determinations: (1) batch size; (2) sample size; and (3) maximum number of defects that can be uncovered before rejection of the entire batch. This technique permits acceptance or rejection of a batch of merchandise or documents under precisely specified circumstances, thereby ensuring that the auditor does not reject too many acceptable batches. Acceptance sampling is of particular value to the internal auditor who wants continuous control on the quality of clerical work. From acceptance sampling tables, one can select a sampling plan to assure that errors will not be greater than a specified percentage of the batch (tolerable error rate), provided a full check of rejected batches is made. Acceptance sampling can also be used by the internal auditor to inspect the documents flowing through information channels of the organization. Items that can be checked include pricing and mathematical calculations. Acceptance sampling is basically an internal audit tool. It would be very difficult for the external auditor to devise a sampling plan that, while rejecting, say, 90% of unsatisfactory batches, does not also reject a high number of satisfactory batches.

**ACCESS CONTROLS** used to ensure that only authorized individuals are able to access certain resources. In a computer system, access controls are used to limit the individuals who are allowed to log in. This is often done through the use of passwords or a combination of passwords with smart cards. Other forms of authentication, such as fingerprint or retinal scan, and other biometric systems are also becoming popular.

**ACCESS DATABASE** a relational database management system within Microsoft Office with a graphical user interface. A database like Access can store and track virtually any kind of data, including textual and audio/video. The data is stored in an SQL database; this provides for security and scalability. Newly introduced in 2013 are Access Web apps that can be hosted on SharePoint servers.

**ACCESS POINT** sends and receives signals from other local wireless devices and allows these devices to connect to a wired Local Area Network (LAN). A router is similar to an access point device, but a router provides additional functionality, such as firewall and assignment of IP addresses. An access point may be used to extend coverage within a network to eliminate "dead spots." Also referred to as *wireless access point*.

**ACCESS TIME** length of time that a data storage device, associated with a computer, takes to process and return data from the time of the original request for the data.

**ACCOMMODATION ENDORSEMENT** written agreement to be liable made without consideration on a credit instrument (e.g., notes payable) to which another person or firm is a party, thus adding strength to the credit application. An example: a parent company *endorses* a note of a subsidiary payable to a bank or other lender.

**ACCOUNT**
1. systematic arrangement showing the effect of transactions and other events on a specific balance sheet or income statement item. An account is usually expressed in money. A separate account exists for each asset, liability, stockholders' equity, revenue, and expense. Accounts are the way in which differing effects on the basic business elements are categorized and collected. Accounts are in the ledger (ledger account). Examples are cash, accounts payable, and dividend revenue. *See also* CHART OF ACCOUNTS.

**2.** relationship between one party and another. Examples are a depositor or borrower with a bank or thrift institution or a credit relationship with a seller of goods or services.

**ACCOUNTABILITY** individual or departmental responsibility to perform a certain function. Accountability may be dictated or implied by law, regulation, or agreement. For example, an auditor will be held accountable to financial statement users relying on the audited financial statements for failure to uncover corporate FRAUD because of negligence in applying GENERALLY ACCEPTED AUDITING STANDARDS (GAAS).

**ACCOUNT ANALYSIS** way to measure cost behavior. It selects a volume-related cost driver and classifies each account from the accounting records as a variable or fixed cost. The cost accountant then looks at each cost account balance and estimates either the variable cost per unit of cost driver activity or the periodic fixed cost. Account analysis requires a detailed examination of the data, presumably by cost accountants and managers who are familiar with the activities of the company, and the way the company's activities affect costs. *See also* ENGINEERING ANALYSIS; HIGH-LOW METHOD; REGRESSION METHOD.

**ACCOUNTANCY** British term referring to the activities and theories comprising accounting including practice, research, and teaching. It includes the guidelines, principles, and procedures accountants are to follow in conducting their tasks. Accountants have legal and ethical responsibilities to their clients and public. *See also* ACCOUNTING.

**ACCOUNTANT** one who performs accounting services. Accountants prepare financial statements and tax returns, audit financial records, and develop financial plans. They work in private accounting (e.g., for a corporation), public accounting (e.g., for a CPA firm), not-for-profit accounting (e.g., for a governmental agency). Accountants often specialize in a particular area such as taxes, cost accounting, auditing, and management advisory services. A BOOKKEEPER is distinguished from an accountant as one who employs lesser professional skills. The bookkeeping function is primarily one of recording transactions in the journal and posting to the ledger. *See also* CERTIFIED PUBLIC ACCOUNTANT.

**ACCOUNTANT IN CHARGE** professional responsible for the field engagement associated with an audit. Duties include the general supervision of the engagement, distributing the workload to assistants, reviewing audit findings, and drafting required field reports.

**ACCOUNTANTS FOR THE PUBLIC INTEREST (API)** organization dedicated to serving the public welfare. API provides objective analysis of public policy questions in terms of their fiscal, accounting, or financial implications. Services include technical support to nonprofit organizations that do not have the resources to afford such services.

*ACCOUNTANTS' INDEX* bibliography of accounting books and articles of interest to accounting professionals. It is published quarterly and annually by the AMERICAN INSTITUTE OF CERTIFIED PUBLIC ACCOUNTANTS (AICPA). Included are publications on all phases of accounting, including auditing, tax, financial accounting, managerial accounting, and computer applications.

**ACCOUNTANTS INTERNATIONAL STUDY GROUP (AISG)** organization founded to examine and report on common interesting topics within the accounting discipline. This group consists of representatives from the AMERICAN INSTITUTE OF CERTIFIED PUBLIC ACCOUNTANTS (AICPA), CANADIAN INSTITUTE OF CHARTERED ACCOUNTANTS (CICA), and the INSTITUTE OF CHARTERED ACCOUNTANTS IN ENGLAND AND WALES.

**ACCOUNTANT'S LIABILITY** potential legal obligation of an accountant who commits fraud or is grossly negligent in the performance of professional duties. The term typically applies when an auditor conducting the ATTEST FUNCTION does not employ GENERALLY ACCEPTED AUDITING STANDARDS (GAAS) with sufficient care. To avoid liability, the accountant must be knowledgeable about the accounting profession's authoritative pronouncements such as FASB statements and AICPA STATEMENTS ON AUDITING PROCEDURE as well as SEC ACCOUNTING SERIES RELEASES. An accountant who violates the established rules and guidelines can be held legally liable to parties retaining him and those relying on work performed (e.g., investors, creditors). Most accounting practitioners carry malpractice insurance. *See also* NEGLIGENCE.

*ACCOUNTANT'S MAGAZINE, THE* journal founded in 1897, originally published monthly by the Aberdeen, Edinburgh, and Glasgow chartered accountants' societies. The INSTITUTE OF CHARTERED ACCOUNTANTS IN SCOTLAND, founded in 1951, later adopted this magazine as its monthly journal. Subject matter includes international accounting, accounting education, information systems, financial accounting, managerial accounting, and legal topics.

**ACCOUNTANT'S RESPONSIBILITY** ethical obligation to those relying upon the accountant's professional work. The accountant has a duty to management, investors, creditors, and regulatory bodies to exercise due care in performing the accounting and ATTEST FUNCTIONS. The accountant must follow with competence the promulgations of the ACCOUNTING PRINCIPLES BOARD (APB) and FINANCIAL ACCOUNTING STANDARDS BOARD (FASB), among others.

**ACCOUNT FORM** balance sheet structure showing assets on the left, liabilities and stockholders' equity on the right. The alternative form, called the REPORT FORM, positions assets above liabilities and stockholders' equity.

**ACCOUNTING**
1. umbrella term encompassing the multitude of disciplines including auditing, taxation, financial statement analysis, and managerial accounting. Accounting-related functions include financial accounting, cost accounting, not-for-profit accounting, and financial planning.
2. process of recording, measuring, interpreting, and communicating financial data. The accountant prepares financial statements to reflect financial condition and operating performance. Also, the accounting practitioner renders personal accounting services to clients such as preparing personal financial statements and tax planning.

**ACCOUNTING AND FINANCIAL WOMEN'S ALLIANCE (AFWA)** organization of women accountants who are primarily CPAs and corporate accountants in middle management positions. AFWA publishes *The Woman CPA*, which covers all aspects of accounting including information systems, accounting education, financial accounting, and auditing. The organization attempts to promote women's interests in the profession.

**ACCOUNTING CHANGE AND ERROR CORRECTIONS** change in (1) accounting principles (such as a new depreciation method); (2) accounting estimates (such as a revised projection of doubtful accounts receivable); or (3) the reporting entity (such as a merger of companies). A change in principle requires retrospective application to previous years' financial statements, a change in estimate is accounted for prospectively over current and future years, and a change in reporting entities mandates the restatement of previous years' financial statements as if both companies were always combined. Corrections of errors adjust the beginning balance of retained earnings. *Note:* The correction of an error in previously issued financial statements is not an accounting change. However, the reporting of an error correction involves adjustments to previously issued financial statements similar to those generally applicable to reporting an accounting change retrospectively. FASB Statement No. 154, *Accounting Changes and Error Corrections* (ASC, 250-10-05) provides for accounting changes in principle, estimate, and reporting entity. Correction of an error in a prior year is also briefly mentioned. Proper disclosure of accounting changes is necessary. *See also* ERROR CORRECTION.

**ACCOUNTING CONTROL** procedures used to assure accuracy in the record keeping function. Controls exist to make certain source data placed in the system are proper and correct.

**ACCOUNTING CONVENTION** methods or procedures employed generally by accounting practitioners. They are based on custom and are subject to change as new developments arise. A new accounting or tax requirement, such as an SEC ACCOUNTING SERIES RELEASE (ASR), may make a convention inappropriate. The accountant in performing the reporting function should follow existing accounting conventions that apply to the given situation. *See also* ACCOUNTING PRINCIPLES.

**ACCOUNTING CUSHION** overstating an expense provision. This provides a larger balance in the estimated liability or allowance account so as to minimize the amount of an expense provision for a later period. It understates the current period's profit and in effect overstates the earnings in the period when the anticipated event occurs. For example, a company's allowance for bad debts from accounts receivable may substantially increase even though the company's bad debt write-off experience has become much better. In this case, the overstatement of bad debt expense unjustifiably understates the present year's net income. Because less of a bad debt expense provision will be needed next year due to the overstated allowance account, net income will be higher next period. The auditor should upwardly adjust net income for the charges creating the accounting cushion. It should be noted, however, that for tax purposes companies must use the direct write-off method for bad debts. *See also* INCOME SMOOTHING.

**ACCOUNTING CYCLE** series of steps in recording an accounting event from the time a transaction occurs to its reflection in the financial statements; also called *bookkeeping cycle*. The order of the steps in the accounting cycle are: recording in the journal, posting to the ledger, preparing a trial balance, and preparing the financial statements.

**ACCOUNTING ENTITY** business or other economic unit (including subdivisions) being accounted for separately. A system of accounts is kept for the entity. An accounting entity is isolated so that recording and reporting for it are possible. Examples of accounting entities are corporations, partnerships, trusts, and industry segments. A distinction should be made between an accounting entity and a legal entity. For example, a proprietor's accounting entity might be the business whereas the legal entity would include personal assets. Also, in the corporate environment, affiliated companies can be differently organized for legal and accounting purposes (e.g., industry segments). *See also* CONSOLIDATED FINANCIAL STATEMENT.

**ACCOUNTING EQUATION** double entry bookkeeping where there is an identity of debit and credit elements of a transaction. For each transaction, the total debits equal the total credits. For example, the payment of $100 to a creditor requires a debit to accounts payable and a credit to cash for $100. The accounting equation can also be expressed as:

$$Assets = Liabilities + Equity$$

An increase (or decrease) in total assets is accompanied by an equal increase (or decrease) in liabilities and capital.

**ACCOUNTING ERROR** inaccurate measurement or representation of an accounting-related item not caused by intentional FRAUD. An error may be due to NEGLIGENCE or may result from the misapplication of

GENERALLY ACCEPTED ACCOUNTING PRINCIPLES (GAAP). Errors may take the form of dollar discrepancies or may be compliance errors in employing accounting policies and procedures. Errors can be minimized by diligently following accounting procedures and standards, and maintaining proper INTERNAL CONTROL.

**ACCOUNTING EVENT** transaction entered in the accounting records of a business. It can be an external transaction—that is, one with an outsider, such as recording a sale. It can also refer to an internal transaction such as making an adjusting entry (e.g., expense or revenue accrual).

**ACCOUNTING HALL OF FAME** organization honoring individuals who have made significant scholarly contributions to accounting since the beginning of the twentieth century. The Hall of Fame was founded at Ohio State University in 1950.

***ACCOUNTING HISTORIANS JOURNAL*** publication of the ACADEMY OF ACCOUNTING HISTORIANS, which first appeared in 1977. All aspects relating to the history of accounting thought are covered in the journal.

**ACCOUNTING INFORMATION SYSTEM (AIS)** subsystem of a MANAGEMENT INFORMATION SYSTEM (MIS) that processes financial transactions to provide (1) internal reporting to managers for use in planning and controlling current and future operations and for nonroutine decision making; (2) external reporting to outside parties such as to stockholders, creditors, and government agencies.

**ACCOUNTING INTERPRETATION** prepared by the AMERICAN INSTITUTE OF CERTIFIED PUBLIC ACCOUNTANTS (AICPA) while the ACCOUNTING PRINCIPLES BOARD was in existence (1959 to 1973). Interpretations gave guidance to practitioners about accounting issues. Unlike APB Opinions, Interpretations are *not* requirements subject to the AICPA Code of Professional Ethics.

**ACCOUNTING MANUAL** handbook containing policy guidelines, procedures, and standards for accounts of a company or an individual. The chart (or classification) of accounts is part of the accounting manual.

**ACCOUNTING MEASUREMENT** quantification of accounting values in the form of money or other units. Transactions are recorded in the accounts in dollars based on historical cost. Some accounting measurements have to be expressed in volume such as direct labor hours used to apply overhead in a cost accounting system.

**ACCOUNTING PERIOD** time covered by financial statements, which can be for any length but is usually annual, quarterly, or monthly. The annual financial statements may be on a calendar or fiscal year basis. Quarterly (interim) financial statements are common and required of publicly owned companies.

**ACCOUNTING POLICIES** reporting methods, measurement systems, and disclosures used by a specific company. The accountant should evaluate the appropriateness of accounting policies employed by management. A description of the company's accounting policies should be presented in a separate section preceding the footnotes to the financial statements or as the first footnote. Disclosure of accounting policies should include ACCOUNTING PRINCIPLES and methods of application that involve: (1) a selection from generally accepted alternatives; (2) those peculiar to the industry or field of endeavor; and (3) unusual or different applications of GENERALLY ACCEPTED ACCOUNTING PRINCIPLES (GAAP). Examples of disclosures are basis of CONSOLIDATION, depreciation methods, and inventory pricing. Disclosure of accounting policies assists financial readers in better interpreting a company's financial statements. Thus it results in fair presentation of the financial statements.

**ACCOUNTING POSTULATE** basic assumption or fundamental proposition regarding the economic, political, or social environment that accounting operates in. Examples of postulates are accounting entity and continuity. A postulate is pertinent to developing an ACCOUNTING PRINCIPLE. Accounting postulates may relate to the environment of accounting, accounting entity, measurement process, and accounting objectives.

**ACCOUNTING PRACTICE** manner in which accountants and auditors carry out their daily work. It is the day-to-day implementation of accounting policies. Accounting practice relates to the practical application of accounting to the financial accumulation and reporting needs of clients. Practice may differ from accounting theory.

**ACCOUNTING PRINCIPLES** rules and guidelines of accounting. They determine such matters as the measurement of assets, the timing of revenue recognition, and the accrual of expenses. The "ground rules" for financial reporting are referred to as GENERALLY ACCEPTED ACCOUNTING PRINCIPLES (GAAP). To be "generally accepted," an accounting principle must have "substantial authoritative support" such as by promulgation of a FINANCIAL ACCOUNTING STANDARDS BOARD (FASB) pronouncement. Accounting principles are based on the important objectives of financial reporting. An example of an accounting principle is accrual.

**ACCOUNTING PRINCIPLES BOARD (APB)** former authoritative body of the AMERICAN INSTITUTE OF CERTIFIED PUBLIC ACCOUNTANTS (AICPA). It issued pronouncements on accounting principles until 1973. Of the 31 APB opinions, several were instrumental in improving the theory and practice of significant areas of accounting. The APB was replaced by the FINANCIAL ACCOUNTING STANDARDS BOARD (FASB).

**ACCOUNTING PROCEDURE** method or technique used to uncover, record, or summarize financial data in the preparation of financial statements.

**ACCOUNTING RATE OF RETURN** *see* SIMPLE RATE OF RETURN.

**ACCOUNTING RECORDS** the category of audit evidence that consists of the records of initial accounting entries and supporting records. Accounting records include checks, records of electronic fund transfers, sales and purchase invoices, contracts, the general ledger, subsidiary ledgers, journal entries, worksheets and spreadsheets, computations, and reconciliations.

**ACCOUNTING RESEARCH BULLETINS (ARB)** publications containing recommended accounting procedures. While the Bulletins were not binding on American Institute of CPAs members, the SECURITIES AND EXCHANGE COMMISSION (SEC) typically required their use by corporations under their jurisdiction. The Bulletins were issued by the COMMITTEE ON ACCOUNTING PROCEDURE of the AICPA. The Committee was replaced by the ACCOUNTING PRINCIPLES BOARD (APB) in 1959.

*ACCOUNTING REVIEW, THE* publication of the AMERICAN ACCOUNTING ASSOCIATION (AAA) covering all aspects of accounting of a scholarly nature. Many articles deal with hypothesis testing and empirical work. It is published four times a year.

**ACCOUNTING RISK** *see* TRANSLATION RISK.

**ACCOUNTING SERIES RELEASES (ASRS)** issued by the SECURITIES AND EXCHANGE COMMISSION (SEC) as official accounting pronouncements. Releases include accounting requirements, disclosure mandates, auditing policies, and Commission activities regarding CPA firms filing financial statements with the SEC for publicly traded companies. The Accounting Series Releases are now codified as Financial Reporting Releases (FRRs).

**ACCOUNTING SOFTWARE** programs used to maintain books of account on computers. The software can be used to record transactions, maintain account balances, and prepare financial statements and reports. Many different accounting software packages exist, and the right package must be selected given the client's circumstances and needs. An accounting software package typically contains numerous integrated modules (for example, spreadsheet and word processing abilities). Some modules are used to account for the general ledger, accounts receivable, accounts payable, payroll, inventory, and fixed assets. Reviews of accounting software packages can be found in the *JOURNAL OF ACCOUNTANCY*, *PC Magazine*, and *Computers in Accounting*, among other journals.

**ACCOUNTING STANDARD** conduct to be followed by accountants as formulated by an authoritative body (e.g., AMERICAN INSTITUTE OF CERTIFIED PUBLIC ACCOUNTANTS (AICPA)) or law. *See also* ACCOUNTING PRINCIPLES.

**ACCOUNTING STANDARDS COMMITTEE** committee with members from six accounting bodies in the United Kingdom and Ireland who draft and approve Statements of Standard Accounting Practice.

**ACCOUNTING STANDARDS EXECUTIVE COMMITTEE (AccSEC)** committee whose members prepare Statements of Position on accounting issues not acted upon by the FASB. Since 1978, its promulgation functions have been integrated with those of the FASB.

**ACCOUNTING SYSTEM** methods, procedures, and standards followed in accumulating, classifying, recording, and reporting business events and transactions. The accounting system includes the formal records and original source data. Regulatory requirements may exist on how a particular accounting system is to be maintained (e.g., insurance company).

*ACCOUNTING TRENDS AND TECHNIQUES* annual publication of the AMERICAN INSTITUTE OF CERTIFIED PUBLIC ACCOUNTANTS (AICPA) containing a survey of the accounting and disclosure characteristics of corporate annual reports. It gives examples representative of financial reporting by 600 sampled companies (e.g., their treatment of leases and business combinations). Financial statistics are also given.

**ACCOUNTING VALUATION** valuation of assets in accounting. Correct valuation is important. If, for example, an asset is valued incorrectly, it is impossible to draw accurate conclusions about a firm's liquidity or its value in liquidation. Valuation is usually made in accordance with GENERALLY ACCEPTED ACCOUNTING PRINCIPLES (GAAP).

**ACCOUNTS PAYABLE** obligations to pay for goods or services that have been acquired on open account from suppliers. Accounts payable is a current liability in the balance sheet.

**ACCOUNTS RECEIVABLE** amounts due the company on account from customers who have bought merchandise or received services. Accounts receivable are presented as a current asset in the balance sheet. *See also* ACCOUNTS RECEIVABLE TURNOVER; AGING OF ACCOUNTS.

**ACCOUNTS RECEIVABLE DISCOUNTED** obligation assigned or sold with recourse. *See also* ASSIGNMENT OF ACCOUNTS RECEIVABLE; FACTORING.

**ACCOUNTS RECEIVABLE TURNOVER** degree of realization risk in accounts receivable. The lower the turnover rate, the longer receivables are being held—and the less likely they are to be collected. Also, there is an OPPORTUNITY COST of tying up funds in receivables for a longer period of time. The accounts receivable turnover equals:

$$\frac{\text{Annual Credit Sales}}{\text{Average Accounts Receivable}}$$

Assume annual credit sales are $100,000, beginning-of-year accounts receivable are $30,000, and end-of-year accounts receivable are $20,000. The turnover is:

$$\frac{\$100,000}{\left(\dfrac{\$30,000 + \$20,000}{2}\right)} = \frac{\$100,000}{\$25,000} = 4 \text{ times}$$

If sales vary greatly during the year, this ratio can become distorted unless proper averaging takes place. In such a case, quarterly or monthly sales figures should be used.

## ACCRETION

1. growth in assets through mergers, acquisitions, and internal expansion. Examples are timber, livestock, nursery stock, and aging of wine.
2. adjustment of the difference between the face value of a bond and the price of the bond bought at an original discount.

**ACCRUAL ACCOUNTING** recognition of revenue when earned and expenses when incurred. They are recorded at the end of an accounting period even though cash has not been received or paid. The alternative is CASH BASIS ACCOUNTING. An example of accrued revenue is dividend income earned on stock owned even though it has not yet been received. Accrued salary expense due employees at period-end is an example of an accrued expense.

**ACCRUED ASSETS** *see* ACCRUED REVENUE.

**ACCRUED EXPENSES** incurred at the end of the reporting period but not yet paid; also called *accrued liabilities*. The accrued liability is shown under current liabilities in the balance sheet. For example, assume the last payroll date was January 28. The next payroll date is February 11. For the last few days of the month (January 29–January 31) the company owes its employees $500 in salaries. The appropriate journal entry on January 31 is to debit salaries expense and credit salaries payable for $500.

**ACCRUED LIABILITIES** *see* ACCRUED EXPENSES.

**ACCRUED REVENUE** money that has been earned but not received as of the end of the reporting period; also called *accrued assets*. To accrue means to accumulate. The accrued asset is shown under current assets in the balance sheet. For example, assume a landlord has not received January rent of $500 from a tenant. The adjusting entry at the end of January is to debit rent receivable and credit rental revenue for $500.

**ACCUMULATED BENEFIT OBLIGATION (ABO)** actuarial present value of benefits. Whether vested or nonvested, they are attributed by the pension benefit formula to employee services rendered before a specified date and based on employee service and compensation up to that date using *existing* salary levels. *See also* MINIMUM PENSION LIABILITY; PENSION PLAN; PROJECTED BENEFIT OBLIGATION (PBO); VESTED BENEFIT OBLIGATION (VBO).

**ACCUMULATED DEPRECIATION** sum of depreciation charges taken to date on a fixed asset. Accumulated depreciation is a CONTRA ACCOUNT to the fixed asset to arrive at BOOK VALUE. For example, on 1/1/2014 an auto is bought costing $10,000, with a salvage value of $1000 and a life of 10 years. Using STRAIGHT-LINE DEPRECIATION the accumulated depreciation on 12/31/2017 would be $3600 ($900 × 4).

**ACCUMULATED EARNINGS TAX** penalty tax levied upon the unreasonable accumulation of corporate earnings and profits. The intent is to tax earnings retained to avoid personal income tax on dividends.

**ACCUMULATED INCOME**
1. cumulative profit that has been retained and not distributed in the form of dividends.
2. income amount used as the base for the computation of the accumulated earnings tax. *See also* ACCUMULATED EARNINGS TAX.

**ACCUMULATION**
1. cumulative retained profit.
2. investment of a fixed dollar amount regularly and reinvestment of dividends and capital gains.
3. process of compounding.
4. periodic addition of interests to the principal amount.

**ACCURACY** correctness of an accounting item (e.g., account balance, invoice, financial statement); also called *accurate presentation*. The concept refers to an accounting objective that the item fully reflects and valuates the set of facts involved, including all economic implications of the underlying transactions and events.

**ACCURACY-RELATED PENALTY** a civil penalty imposed on the amount of underpayment (understatement) of tax. The penalty, which is equal to 20% of the underpayment, may be based on negligence or nonfraudulent lack of compliance with laws and regulations.

**ACID TEST RATIO** stringent test of LIQUIDITY; also called *quick ratio*. The ratio is found by dividing the most liquid current assets (cash, marketable securities, and accounts receivable) by current liabilities. (Notice that some current assets are not in the numerator: Inventory is not included because it usually takes a long time to convert into cash; prepaid expenses are left out because they cannot be turned into cash and thus are incapable of covering current liabilities.) In general, the ratio should at least be equal to 1. In other words, for every $1 in current debt there should be $1 in quick assets. Assume cash is $100, marketable securities are $400, accounts receivable are $800, inventory is $3,000, and current liabilities are $1,000. The acid test ratio equals:

$$\frac{\text{Quick Assets}}{\text{Current Liabilities}} = \frac{\$1,300}{\$1,000} = 1.3$$

The acid test ratio for the current year should be compared to prior years to evaluate the trend. It should also be compared to the acid test ratio of a competing company to get a relative comparison.

**ACQUISITION COST** price paid to buy goods, services, or assets. It equals the list price plus normal incidental costs to acquire the item including preparation, transportation, and installation.

**ACQUISITION CYCLE** the flow of transactions and related internal controls concerning the purchase of goods and services. Steps in the acquisition cycle are authorization, placing orders (including the preparation of purchase orders), receipt of goods (including preparation of receiving reports), inspection of goods, authorizing payments (including preparation of vouchers), as well as making and recording related cash disbursements.

**ACQUISITION METHOD** the method of accounting that must be used to record the acquisition of one entity by another. Under this method, the acquiring entity records all acquired assets, liabilities, and any noncontrolling interest at fair value.

**ACTIVE PARTICIPATION** a taxpayer is required to actively participate in an activity in order to qualify for the offset of rental real estate losses against nonpassive income. The maximum offset is $25,000 ($12,500 in cases of married couples filing separately), but is reduced by 50% of the amount of adjusted gross income in excess of $100,000 ($50,000 in cases of married couples filing separately). Active participation involves making significant and bona fide management decisions such as approving new tenants, repairs, capital improvements, and lease terms.

**ACTIVITY** in PROGRAM EVALUATION AND REVIEW TECHNIQUE (PERT), the action that consumes time or resources. Activities are represented by arrows in a PERT network.

**ACTIVITY ACCOUNT** name for a specific and distinguishable line of work performed by one or more organizational components of a governmental unit. For example, sewage treatment and disposal, garbage collection, and street cleaning are activities performed in carrying out the function of sanitation; and the segregation of the expenditures made for each of these activities constitutes an activity account.

**ACTIVITY ACCOUNTING** *see* RESPONSIBILITY ACCOUNTING.

**ACTIVITY ANALYSIS** evaluation involving the determination of the combination of production processes that maximizes output (or profits), subject to the restrictions on the required resources (inputs).

**ACTIVITY ATTRIBUTES** characteristics of activities. Attributes can be organized, sorted, or summarized according to the attribute categories. For example, a measure of the elapsed time required to complete an activity is an attribute. *See also* COST DRIVER; PERFORMANCE MEASUREMENT.

**ACTIVITY BASE** applicable to the production activity used to relate factory overhead to production (e.g., units produced, direct labor hours, direct labor cost, machine hours).

**ACTIVITY-BASED BUDGETING (ABB)** approach to budgeting that involves quantitative expression of the activities/business processes of the organization reflecting forecasts of workload (quantity of drivers) and other financial requirements to achieve strategic goals or planned changes to improve performance. Activity-based budgeting provides greater detail, especially regarding overhead, because it permits the identification of value-adding activities and their drivers. After operations, it is useful for comparing actual costing rates and driver usage with the amounts budgeted.

**ACTIVITY-BASED COSTING (ABC)** costing system that identifies the various activities performed in a firm and uses multiple cost drivers (volume and nonvolume based cost drivers) to assign overhead costs (or indirect costs) to products. ABC recognizes the causal relationship of cost drivers with activities.

**ACTIVITY-BASED MANAGEMENT (ABM)** approach to the management of activities within business processes as the route to continuously improve both the value received by customers and the profit earned by providing this value. Causes of activities are identified, measured, and used along with other activity information for performance evaluation; emphasis is on the reduction or elimination of nonvalue-adding activities. ABM draws on ABC data as a major source for information.

**ACTIVITY-BASED SYSTEM** information system that provides quantitative information about activities in an organization.

**ACTIVITY CAPACITY** demonstrated or expected capacity of an activity under normal operating conditions, assuming a specified set of resources and a long time period. An example is the rate of output for an activity expressed as 500 cycles per hour.

**ACTIVITY CENTER** pool of costs of two or more activities.

**ACTIVITY COST ASSIGNMENT** process in which the costs of activities are attached to cost objects using activity drivers. *See also* COST OBJECT; ACTIVITY COST DRIVER.

**ACTIVITY COST DRIVER** best single measure of the frequency and intensity of the demands placed on activities by intermediate and final cost objectives. It is used to reassign activity costs to cost objects. It represents a line item on the bill of activities for a product or customer. An example is the number of part numbers, which is used to measure the consumption of material-related activities by each product, material type, or component. The number of customer orders measures the consumption of order-entry activities by each customer. Sometimes an activity driver is used as an indicator of the output of an activity, such as the number of purchase orders prepared by the purchasing activity. *See also* INTENSITY; COST OBJECT; BILL OF ACTIVITIES.

**ACTIVITY COST POOL** grouping of all cost elements associated with an activity. *See also* COST ELEMENT.

**ACTIVITY DICTIONARY** listing and description of generic activities. It can include activity, activity description, business process, function source, whether value-added, inputs, outputs, supplier, customer, output measures, and cost drivers.

**ACTIVITY DRIVER ANALYSIS** identification and evaluation of the activity drivers used to trace the cost of activities to cost objects. Activity driver analysis may involve selecting activity drivers with a potential for cost reduction. *See also* PARETO ANALYSIS.

**ACTIVITY LEVEL** description of how an activity is used by a cost object or other activity. Some activity levels describe the cost object that uses the activity and the nature of this use. These levels include activities that are traceable to the product (i.e., unit-level, batch-level, and product-level costs), to the customer (customer-level costs), to a market (market-level costs), to a distribution channel (channel-level costs), and to a project, such as a research and development project (project-level costs).

**ACTIVITY SEQUENCE-SENSITIVE** calculation of time-based process costs taking into consideration the sequential relationships among activities.

**ACTUAL COST** expenditure required to buy or produce an item. The actual cost of a purchased item includes the list price (net of discounts) plus delivery and storage. The actual cost to manufacture a product is the total of direct material, direct labor, and factory overhead.

**ACTUARIAL** relating to analyses involving compound interest and/or statistics. It is usually associated with computations involved in insurance probability estimates. *See also* ACTUARY.

**ACTUARIAL BASIS OF ACCOUNTING** used in computing the amount of contributions to be made periodically to a pension fund. Total contributions plus the accumulated earnings on it must equal the required payments to be made out of the fund. Factors that must be considered are the length of time over which each contribution is to be held and the return on investment. A "Trust Fund" for a public employee retirement system is an example of a fund set up on an actuarial basis.

**ACTUARIAL COST METHOD** technique used by actuaries to determine the periodic employer contribution to the pension plan; also called *actuarial funding method*. It is used to measure pension expense and related funding. Two general approaches are usually considered when selecting an actuarial funding method, the *cost* approach and *benefit* approach. The cost approach projects an estimated total retirement benefit and then determines the level cost that will be adequate (including expected interest) to furnish total benefits at retirement. The benefit approach determines the amount of pension benefits attributable to service to date and then determines the present value of these benefits. *See also* ACTUARIAL GAINS, LOSSES.

**ACTUARIAL FUNDING METHOD** *see* ACTUARIAL COST METHOD.

**ACTUARIAL GAINS, LOSSES** difference between estimates and actual experience in a pension plan. For example, if the actual interest rate earned on pension assets exceeds the estimated rate, an actuarial gain results. Actuarial gains and losses are deferred and amortized to pension expense of future periods. The amortization of the actuarial gain will *reduce* pension expense. Actuarial gains and losses applicable to a single event not related to the pension plan and not in the ordinary course of business are recognized immediately in earnings. Examples are plant closing and segment disposal. *See also* ACTUARIAL COST METHOD.

**ACTUARY** practitioner involved in mathematical computations and analyses of insurance probability estimates.

**ADDITIONAL PAID-IN CAPITAL** excess received from stockholders over PAR VALUE or STATED VALUE of the stock issued; also called *contributed capital in excess of par*. For example, if 1000 shares of $10 par value common stock is issued at a price of $12 per share, the additional paid-in capital is $2000 (1000 shares $\times$ $2). Additional paid-in capital is shown in the STOCKHOLDERS' EQUITY section of the balance sheet.

**ADEQUATE DISCLOSURE** comprehensive and clear disclosure in the body of financial statements, FOOTNOTES, or supplemental schedules so that readers of a company's financial position and operating results can make proper investment and credit decisions.

**AD HOC DSS** is designed to handle a one-time or infrequently occurring problem. The purpose of a decision support system (DSS) is to assist decision makers in the various phases of unstructured or semistructured business problem-solving.

**ADJUNCT ACCOUNT** one that accumulates either additions or subtractions to another account. Thus the original account may retain its identity. Examples include premiums on bonds payable, which is a contra account to bonds payable; and accumulated depreciation, which is an offset to the fixed asset.

**ADJUSTABLE RATE LOAN** *see* VARIABLE RATE LOAN.

**ADJUSTED BASIS** value used as a starting point to compute depreciation or gain on the disposition of fixed assets for tax purposes. The adjusted basis is similar to the concept of BOOK VALUE. It is the taxpayer's basis at the time of acquisition—usually cost—increased or decreased by certain required modifications such as capital improvements.

**ADJUSTED GROSS INCOME (AGI)** federal tax term applying to the difference between the gross income of the taxpayer and adjustments to income. Adjustments to income include deductions for IRA and Keogh pension plans. Adjusted gross income is the basis for determining the eligibility and limitations of other components in calculating the taxpayer's tax, such as for medical expenses (generally 10% of AGI) and miscellaneous expenses (2% of AGI).

**ADJUSTING JOURNAL ENTRY**
1. necessary entry at the end of the reporting period to record unrecognized revenue and expenses applicable to that period. It is required when a transaction is begun in one accounting period and concluded in a later one. An adjusting entry always involves an income statement account (revenue or expense) and a balance sheet account (asset or liability). The four basic types of adjusting entries relate to ACCRUED EXPENSES, ACCRUED REVENUE, PREPAID EXPENSES, and UNEARNED REVENUE.
2. correcting entry required at the end of the accounting period due to a mistake made in the accounting records; also called *correcting entry*. For example, if during the same year land was charged instead of travel expense, the correcting entry is to debit travel expense and credit land.

**ADJUSTMENT**
1. increase or decrease to an account resulting from an ADJUSTING JOURNAL ENTRY. For example, the accrual of wages at year-end will cause an increase in both salary expense and salary payable.
2. changing an account balance because of some happening or event. For example, a customer who returns merchandise will receive a credit adjustment to the account.

**ADMINISTERED PRICE** one determined by the pricing policy of a seller rather than by competitive forces of market supply and demand. It assumes the selling firm has sufficient control over the market of the item.

**ADMINISTRATIVE ACCOUNTING**
1. accounting that focuses upon management planning and control through a formal system of accumulating and reporting data to achieve administrative or management objectives.
2. accounting that involves internal decision-making with respect to prorations, valuations, and reporting. Controllership and internal auditor functions relate to administrative accounting.

**ADMINISTRATIVE BUDGET** formal and comprehensive financial plan through which management may control day-to-day business affairs and activities.

**ADOBE SYSTEMS** a computer software company headquartered in San Jose, California. Adobe is known for products such as Photoshop and Acrobat. Adobe also introduced the Portable Document Format (PDF), a technology that has been adopted worldwide for electronic documents.

**AD VALOREM TAX** levy imposed on the value of property. The most common ad valorem tax is that imposed by states, counties, and cities on real estate. Ad valorem taxes can, however, be imposed on personal property.

**ADVANCE**
1. prepayment received for goods or services to be rendered. Some contracts require an advance before completion (e.g., construction project). When the business receives an advance payment, it records it as a liability. For example, a utility receiving a deposit from a customer will record it as a liability. Assume a lawyer receives a retainer of $50,000 on 1/1/2014 for future services to be rendered for a four-year period. Thus, each year $12,500 will be recognized as revenue. The journal entries for 2014 follow:

| | | |
|---|---|---|
| 1/1/2014 | | |
| Cash | 50,000 | |
| Deferred revenue | | 50,000 |
| | | |
| 12/31/2014 | | |
| Deferred revenue | 12,500 | |
| Revenue | | 12,500 |

  *See also* DEFERRED CREDIT.
2. money given to an employee before it is earned (e.g., advance against salary). The advance appears on the company's books as a receivable from employee.

**ADVANCED MANUFACTURING ENVIRONMENT** an environment featured by intensive global competition, high-tech technology, TOTAL QUALITY MANAGEMENT (TQM), and continuous improvement.

**ADVERSE OPINION 1.** term used when an auditor reports that the company's financial statements do *not* present fairly the financial position, results of operations, or changes in financial position or are not in conformity with GAAP. The auditor must provide the reasons for the adverse opinion in the AUDIT REPORT. An adverse opinion is rare and usually results when the CPA has been unable to convince the client to amend the financial statements so that they reflect the auditor's estimate about the outcome of future events or so that they otherwise adhere to GAAP. **2.** under the Sarbanes-Oxley Act, an opinion that internal control over financial reporting is not effective, because of one or more material weaknesses. When one or more material weaknesses exist as of the assessment date, the auditor must express an adverse opinion on the effectiveness of the company's internal control over financial reporting. Auditing Standard No. 5 indicates that when expressing an adverse opinion on the effectiveness of internal control over financial reporting, the auditor should provide specific information about the nature of the material weakness and its actual and potential effect on the company's financial statements. The PCAOB has also stated that it expects disclosure sufficient to allow users to understand the weakness and its actual and potential implications on the financial statements.

**ADVERTISING COSTS** costs wherein advertising is expensed as incurred or when the advertising program first takes place. However, the cost of direct response advertising may be deferred if the prime objective of the promotion is to elicit sales to customers who respond specifically to the advertising and for which there is future benefit. The deferred advertising is amortized over the expected benefit period using the revenue method (current year revenue to total revenue). The cost of a billboard should also be deferred and amortized.

**ADWARE** programs installed on a user's computer without the user's permission. Adware differs from spyware in that most adware does not perform malicious acts or steal data. It does, however, watch user activity and produce pop-up ads.

**AFFILIATED COMPANY** entity holding less than a majority of the voting common stock of another related company, or in which both companies are subsidiaries of a third company. Often the same management oversees and operates both companies. Interrelationships exist between the activities of the entities.

**AGENCY** relationship between two individuals where one is a principal and the other is an agent representing the principal in transactions with other parties. For example, a trust officer in a bank can engage in activities on behalf of clients.

**AGENCY COSTS** reduction in the value of the organization when an agent (a subunit manager) pursues his interest to the detriment of the principal's (the organization's) interest.

**AGENCY FUND** assets held in a fund under an AGENCY relationship for another entity. In governmental accounting, the agency fund consists of resources retained by the governmental unit as an agent for another governmental unit. It is a FIDUCIARY relationship. An example: taxes retained by a municipality for a school district.

**AGING OF ACCOUNTS** classifying accounts by the time elapsed after the date of billing or the due date. The longer a customer's account remains uncollected or the longer inventory is held, the greater is its realization risk. If a customer's account is past due, the company also has an OPPORTUNITY COST of funds tied-up in the receivable that could be invested elsewhere for a return. An aging schedule of accounts receivable may break down receivables from 1–30 days, 31–60 days, 61–90 days, and over 90 days. With regard to inventory, if it is held too long, obsolescence, spoilage, and technological problems may result. Aging can be done for other accounts such as fixed assets and accounts payable. *See also* COLLECTION PERIOD; DAYS TO SELL INVENTORY.

**AGREED-UPON PROCEDURES** applies to engagements relating to agreed-upon procedures to specified elements or accounts. Agreed-upon procedures is when the accountant is hired to issue a report of findings based on specified financial statement items. The users of the report agree upon the procedures to be conducted by the accountant that the user believes are suitable. The user takes responsibility for the adequacy of the procedures. In this engagement, the accountant does not express an opinion or negative assurance. Instead, the report should be in the form of procedures and findings. A representation letter is prepared that depends on the nature of the engagement and the specified users.

**AIS** *see* ACCOUNTING INFORMATION SYSTEM (AIS).

**ALGEBRAIC METHOD** one of the methods used to solve linear programming problems, a trial-and-error technique. Pairs of constraints are solved algebraically to find their intersection. The values of the decision variables are then substituted into the objective function and compared to find the best combination. The basic rule is that the optimal solution will be at the intersection of two or more constraint equations. Thus, all intersections can be computed and each solution evaluated in the objective function to determine which solution is optimal.

**ALIMONY PAYMENT** term used in a divorce for payment from one spouse to another. For tax purposes, the party making the payments treats them as a deduction in arriving at ADJUSTED GROSS INCOME (AGI). Frontloading of payments (significantly higher payments in the earlier years) is not permitted. The recipient of the alimony payments treats them as income for tax reporting.

**ALL INCLUSIVE INCOME CONCEPT** change in equity for an accounting period from business transactions related to nonowner sources; also called *comprehensive income*. It excludes capital transactions and dividends. The income statement includes all items of profit and loss occurring during the period plus EXTRAORDINARY ITEMS. Inclusion of all items affecting earnings makes the profit and loss statement more informative and less subject to judgment. As per Financial Accounting Concept No. 5, comprehensive income items excluded from earnings include: (1) cumulative effect of a change in accounting principle; (2) foreign currency translation adjustments; and (3) unrealized losses on the write-down of a long-term investment portfolio from cost to market value.

**ALLOCATE**
1. spread a cost over two or more accounting periods usually based on time. An example is assigning the prepaid cost of a three-year insurance policy by one-third each year.
2. charge a cost or revenue to a number of departments, products, processes, or activities on some rational basis. For example, a cost may be assigned to divisions of a company based on sales.
3. distribute the cost associated with the acquisition of two or more items based on their relative fair market values. This relates to a LUMP-SUM PURCHASE.

**ALLOCATED COMMON COSTS** *see* CENTRAL ADMINISTRATION COSTS.

**ALLOCATION** process of partitioning a VALUATION ACCOUNT and assigning the resulting subsets to periods of time. Allocation includes the assignment of assets to expense as well as the assignment of liabilities to revenue over a time frame. Examples of the former are the depreciation of a fixed asset or the amortization of an intangible asset over the period benefitted. An example of the latter is reflecting unearned fee revenue (deferred revenue) into revenue over the period the services are performed. Allocations result from applying rules for the assignment of costs to products or period expenses and the assignment of the value of the product to specific periods as revenue.

**ALLOTMENT** part of an appropriation that may be encumbered or expended during an allotment period, which is usually less than one fiscal year. Bimonthly and quarterly allotment periods are most common.

**ALLOWANCE**
1. acceptable reduction in quantity or quality such as normal spoilage in a manufacturing operation.
2. reduction in the amount owed a supplier because of damaged goods received or delays encountered.
3. valuation account reducing the cost of an asset such as the allowance to reduce marketable securities from cost to market value.

**ALLOWANCE FOR BAD DEBTS** provision for possible uncollectibility associated with accounts receivable. In the balance sheet, accounts receivable, representing gross receivables, is reduced by the allowance account to obtain *net* receivables—the amount expected to be collected (realizable value). For example, if gross receivables are $100,000 and the allowance account balance is $5000, the current asset section of the balance sheet shows:

| | |
|---|---:|
| Accounts receivable | $100,000 |
| Less: Allowance for bad debts | 5,000 |
| Net receivable | $ 95,000 |

The two ways of accounting for uncollectible accounts are the ALLOW-ANCE METHOD and the DIRECT WRITE-OFF METHOD.

**ALLOWANCE FOR SAMPLING RISK (ASR)** also known as *precision*, ASR is typically a concern in attribute sampling. ASR is the difference between the upper occurrence rate (i.e., projected population deviation rate) and the sample deviation rate.

**ALLOWANCE METHOD** accepted way to account for bad debts. Bad debt expense may be based on the percent of credit sales for the period, an aging of the accounts receivable balance at the end of the period, or some other method (e.g., percent of accounts receivable). The allowance method results in a good matching of bad debt expense against sales. The journal entry at year-end to record *anticipated* uncollectibility of accounts receivable is to debit bad debts and credit allowance for bad debts. When it is known that a customer will *actually* not pay the balance, because of bankruptcy, for example, the entry is to debit allowance for bad debts and credit accounts receivable. If for whatever reason the customer does pay at a later date, there is a recovery; reverse the last entry and make a second entry debiting cash and crediting accounts receivable. It should be noted that firms other than small financial institutions are required to use the DIRECT WRITE-OFF METHOD for tax purposes.

**ALL-PURPOSE FINANCIAL STATEMENT** one that satisfies the needs of all financial statement users. The financial statements included in the ANNUAL REPORT and in SEC Form 10-K are intended for diverse parties such as stockholders, potential investors, creditors, employees, and suppliers.

**ALPHA RISK** *see* TYPE I ERROR.

**ALTERNATIVE COST**
1. cost that would pertain if an alternative set of conditions or assumptions were to prevail (as compared to a cost assumed or experienced under current conditions).
2. choosing the next best or highest valued alternative, compared to the chosen alternative, will result in benefits forfeited, and thus an alternative cost. *See also* OPPORTUNITY COST.

**ALTERNATIVE MINIMUM TAX (AMT)** levy designed with the intent that everyone should pay a fair share of tax. The AMT is imposed on regular taxable income, adjusted for tax preference items, in excess of a statutory exemption. The AMT exemption is periodically adjusted for inflation. The AMT is applicable to individuals and corporations.

**AMERICAN ACCOUNTING ASSOCIATION (AAA)** organization primarily of accounting academicians emphasizing the development of a theoretical foundation for accounting. Its research with respect to education and theory is distributed through committee reports and a quarterly journal, *THE ACCOUNTING REVIEW*.

**AMERICAN INSTITUTE OF CERTIFIED PUBLIC ACCOUNTANTS (AICPA)** (www.aicpa.org) professional organization of practicing Certified Public Accountants. The "Institute" develops standards of practice for its members and provides technical guidance and advice to both governmental agencies (e.g., SEC) and AICPA membership. The AICPA publishes the *JOURNAL OF ACCOUNTANCY* and *THE TAX ADVISER*. The AICPA puts out many publications in the areas of accounting, audit, tax, and management services. For example, the STATEMENTS ON AUDITING STANDARDS (SAS) are promulgated by the AICPA.

**AMERICAN OPPORTUNITY CREDIT** formerly known as the Hope Scholarship Credit, this may be claimed by individuals and is based on qualified college education expenses (i.e., tuition and fees). The credit is phased out ratably based on the taxpayer's modified adjusted gross income. The amount of qualified expenses and phase-out ranges are indexed annually based on inflation. The credit is applicable to the first four years of undergraduate education and is limited to $2,500 per eligible student.

**AMERICAN WOMEN'S SOCIETY OF CERTIFIED PUBLIC ACCOUNTANTS (AWSCPA)** professional organization of CPAs, consisting mostly of women, that aids women in their advancement within the accounting profession. Women are encouraged to take part in technical programs involving accounting, auditing, and tax. This organization in a joint effort with the AMERICAN SOCIETY OF WOMEN ACCOUNTANTS publishes *The Woman CPA*, a professional journal.

**AMERICANS WITH DISABILITIES ACT (ADA)** enacted in 1990 and later amended, the ADA is a group of laws prohibiting discrimination based on disability. The ADA includes provisions relating to employment, access to public entities and transportation, public accommodations, and telecommunications.

**AMORTIZATION** gradual reduction of an amount over time. Examples are amortized expenses on limited life intangible assets and deferred charges. Assets with limited life have to be written down over the period benefitted. The amortization entry is to debit amortization expense and credit the intangible asset. However, unlimited life intangibles are subject to an annual impairment test. *See also* ALLOCATION; DEPRECIATION.

**AMORTIZE** to write off a regular portion of an asset's cost over a fixed period of time. Examples are amortization expense on a limited life intangible asset and depletion expense on a natural resource. *See also* SALES RETURN.

**AMOUNT OF $1** decimal ratio of the future value of an accumulation at compound interest to each dollar of the original sum. The FUTURE VALUE (compound amount) and PRESENT VALUE tables are available for the amount of $1. Also available are the future value and present value tables for an annuity of $1.

**AMOUNT REALIZED** tax term applied to money obtained or the fair market value of property or services *received* upon sale or exchange of property. The initial step in computing the realized gain or loss on a sale is to figure out the amount realized.

**ANALYSIS OF VARIANCES** seeking causes for variances between standard costs and actual costs; also called *variance analysis*. A VARIANCE is considered favorable if actual costs are less than standard costs; it is unfavorable if actual costs exceed standard costs. Unfavorable variances need further investigation. Analysis of variances reveals the causes of these deviations. This feedback aids in planning future goals, controlling costs, evaluating performance, and taking corrective action. MANAGEMENT BY EXCEPTION is based on the analysis of variances, and attention is given to only the variances that require remedial actions.

**ANALYTICAL PROCEDURES** auditing process that tests relationships among accounts and identifies material changes. It involves analyzing significant ratios and trends for unusual change and questionable items. Included in the analytical review process are: (1) reading important documents and analyzing their accounting and financial effects; (2) reviewing the activity in an account between interim and year-end, especially noting entries out of the ordinary; (3) comparing current period account balances to prior periods as well as to budgeted amounts, noting reasonableness of account balances by evaluating logical relationships among them (i.e., relating payables to expenses, accounts receivable to sales). In essence, therefore, analytical procedures involves reading the FINANCIAL STATEMENTS, scanning the figures, making comparisons to prior periods, appraising logical relationships among accounts, tracing financial statement items to the financial statements, and analyzing the overall process. The degree of analytical procedures required depends on the MATERIALITY of the item, available supporting data, and the quality of the internal control system. Analytical procedures assist in assuring the accuracy and reliability of the accounts.

**ANALYTICAL TEST** procedure evaluating data relationships to derive substantive audit evidence. It identifies areas requiring additional audit attention. For example, auditors would compare actual financial statement figures against their professional expectations and the firm's experience. Discrepancies are noted and investigated. A comparison may also be made between figures of competing firms and industry norms. Further, financial information can be compared to nonfinancial information, where appropriate. An example is the relationship between sales and number of employees. Analytical tests can be conducted in measures other than dollars, if desired, such as in physical quantities and ratio percentages. If the tests uncover illogical relationships, the CPA will perform more detailed audit testing. *See also* SUBSTANTIVE PROCEDURES.

**ANALYZE** to evaluate the condition of an accounting-related item and possible reasons for discrepancies. For example, an auditor will analyze the makeup of an expense account to determine whether it is properly stated; has it been charged for proper items that are verified by source documents? Another example: appraising the financial health of a company by analyzing its financial statements as a basis for making investment or credit decisions. *See also* EVIDENCE; EXAMINATION; VERIFICATION.

**ANDROID OPERATING SYSTEM** an open-source Linux-based operating system, primarily for smartphones and tablets, from Google Inc. Since it is "open source," a large number of companies and developers are making upgrades to the system. While this openness allows for innovation from many different sources, at times, this also creates compatibility problems for app developers.

**ANNUAL BUDGET** one prepared for a calendar or fiscal year. *See also* LONG-RANGE BUDGET.

**ANNUALIZE** to extend an item to an annual basis. It is a procedure specified by the INTERNAL REVENUE CODE whereby taxable income for part of a year is multiplied by 12 and divided by the number of months involved. For example, if taxable income for 3 months is $20,000, it will be annualized as follows:

$$\$20,000 \times \frac{12}{3} = \$80,000$$

Annualizing is common in financial forecasting.

**ANNUAL REPORT** evaluation prepared by companies at the end of the reporting year which might be either on a calendar or fiscal basis. Contained in the annual report are the company's FINANCIAL STATEMENTS including FOOTNOTES, supplementary schedules, MANAGEMENT'S DISCUSSION AND ANALYSIS OF EARNINGS, president's letter, AUDIT REPORT, and other explanatory data (e.g., research and marketing efforts) helpful in evaluating the entity's financial position and operating performance. The annual report is read by stockholders, potential investors, creditors, employees, regulatory bodies, and other interested financial statement users. *See also* COMPREHENSIVE ANNUAL FINANCIAL REPORT (CAFR); 10-K.

**ANNUITY** series of equal periodic payments or receipts. Examples of an annuity are semiannual interest receipts from a bond investment and cash dividends from a preferred stock. There are two types of an annuity: (1) *Ordinary annuity,* where payments or receipts occur at the end of the period; (2) *Annuity due*, where payments or receipts are made at the beginning of the period.

**ANNUITY DUE** *see* ANNUITY.

**ANNUITY IN ARREARS** *see* ANNUITY.

**ANNUITY METHOD OF DEPRECIATION** focusing upon cost recovery and a constant rate of return on the investment in depreciable assets; also called *compound interest method of depreciation*. This method entails first obtaining the INTERNAL RATE OF RETURN (IRR) on the cash inflow and outflow of the asset. Then the asset's beginning book value is multiplied by the IRR and this amount is subtracted from the cash flow for the period to determine the periodic depreciation charge. If cash flow is constant over the determined life of the asset, it is then called the annuity method. This method is not used in practice and not recommended by GENERALLY ACCEPTED ACCOUNTING PRINCIPLES (GAAP).

**ANTEDATE** assignment of a date that precedes the date on which a particular contract or instrument was actually written or executed. For example, antedated insurance coverage would be effective before the date the policy is issued.

**ANTIDILUTIVE** practice of excluding a convertible security in the EARNINGS PER SHARE (EPS) computation when the effect would be to *increase* EPS. This is based on the CONSERVATISM principle. In the EPS, numerator interest expense (net of tax) is added back to net income. The denominator is increased by the number of shares the convertible bond would be converted into. If the impact of including the convertible bond increased EPS, an antidilutive effect would exist.

**ANTITRUST LAWS** federal laws designed to improve market efficiency, encourage competition, and curtail unfair trade practices. This is accomplished by reducing barriers to entry, breaking up monopolies, and preventing conspiracies to restrict production or raise prices. There are three major antitrust laws: the SHERMAN ANTITRUST ACT of 1890, CLAYTON ANTITRUST ACT of 1914, and Federal Trade Commission Act of 1914.

**ANTIVIRUS PROGRAM** designed to protect against and destroy computer viruses. A computer virus is a malicious software program designed to interfere with a computer's normal operations, such as by corrupting or deleting data. Viruses are capable of spreading themselves to other computers, often through the Internet.

**APB OPINION** authoritative accounting pronouncement issued by the Accounting Principles Board before it was replaced in 1973 by the FINANCIAL ACCOUNTING STANDARDS BOARD (FASB). There were 31 Opinions issued. *See also* GENERALLY ACCEPTED ACCOUNTING PRINCIPLES (GAAP).

**APPLICABLE FINANCIAL REPORTING FRAMEWORK** represents the set of criteria used in the preparation of financial statements. Applicable financial reporting frameworks include general purpose financial reporting frameworks (e.g., U.S. generally accepted accounting principles and INTERNATIONAL ACCOUNTING STANDARDS) and special-purpose financial reporting frameworks (e.g., cash basis and income tax basis).

**APPLICATION CONTROLS** ensure accurate and automatic processing of transactional data, from input to output. Application controls, unlike general controls, are controls specific to a software application. Application controls perform a variety of functions, such as completeness check and validity check. Completeness check controls ensure that all data was processed, and validity check controls ensure that only valid data was inputted or processed.

**APPLICATION PROGRAM** in accounting, computer program written specifically to process data in an information system. It performs tasks or solves problems applicable to an accountant's work. Spreadsheet programs such as EXCEL and various software programs such as QUICKBOOKS and SPSS (Statistical Package for Social Scientists) are examples of application programs.

**APPLICATION PROGRAM INTERFACE (API)** a set of routines and protocols to support requests for services. APIs facilitate inter-organizational collaboration and information exchange. API protocols specify how information can be requested or exchanged online. One example of an API would be a Web service interface provided by Google for its mapping service.

**APPLICATION SERVICE PROVIDER (ASP)** an external entity that delivers software application or services across a wide area network to multiple clients based on either a flat rental fee or utilization pricing. Essentially, ASPs are utilized by an entity to outsource its information technology needs. An ASP generally owns the software and the servers on which the software is deployed. An ASP's employees maintain the software and the servers and make its services available through the Internet, generally through a standard browser or a "thin client."

**APPLIED COST** one that has been assigned to a product, department, or activity. An applied cost does not have to be based on actual costs incurred. Factory overhead applied to a product is an example of an applied cost. To apply overhead, a predetermined overhead rate is developed; it is based on budgeted overhead and budgeted volume of activity. *See also* PREDETERMINED OVERHEAD RATE.

**APPLIED (ABSORBED) OVERHEAD** is factory (manufacturing) overhead that has been allocated to products, usually on the basis of a predetermined rate. Overhead is over- or underapplied (absorbed) when overhead charged is greater or less than overhead incurred, respectively.

**APPRAISAL**
1. estimate of the value of an asset. An asset may be a piece of property, a collectible, or a precious metal. In the case of property, for example, an appraisal is made for the purposes of: (1) allocating the purchase price to the assets acquired (e.g., land, building, equipment); (2) determining the amount of hazard insurance to carry; (3) determining the value at death for estate tax purposes; and (4) determining a reasonable asking price in a sale.
2. activities such as inspection and testing of materials, in-process items, finished goods, and packaging.

**APPRAISAL CAPITAL** very rare practice in the U.S. (more common in other countries) of writing up an asset when appraised value exceeds book value. The entry would be to debit the asset for the increased value and credit appraisal capital, which is a stockholders' equity account.

**APPRAISAL COSTS** a category of QUALITY COSTS incurred to determine whether products and services are conforming to customer requirements, such as inspection and field testing costs.

**APPRAISAL METHOD OF DEPRECIATION** method in which depreciation expense charged to a period is the difference between the beginning and end-of-period appraised value of the asset if the appraised value has decreased. If not, there is no depreciation expense for that period. This method is not generally recognized as an acceptable method.

**APPRAISAL VALUE** *see* APPRAISAL.

**APPRECIATION** increase in the value of an asset. The asset may be real estate or a security. For example, an individual sold 100 shares of XYZ company's stock for $105 per share that he bought 10 years ago for $25 per share. The amount of appreciation was $8,000 = ($105 − $25) × 100 shares.

**APPROPRIATED RETAINED EARNINGS** term used when setting aside UNAPPROPRIATED RETAINED EARNINGS, thus making them unavailable for dividends. These appropriations might be used, for example, for plant expansion, sinking fund, and contingencies. When the appropriation is no longer needed, it is reversed.

**APPROPRIATION**
1. authorization of a governmental unit to spend money within specified restrictions such as amount, time period, and objective. There must be prior approval for such expenditure.
2. distribution of net income to various accounts.
3. allocation of retained earnings for a designated purpose such as for plant expansion. *See also* APPROPRIATED RETAINED EARNINGS.

**APPROPRIATION ACCOUNT** in GOVERNMENT ACCOUNTING, account of an agency that is credited when the appropriation has been authorized. It is reduced by expenditures during the period. When a budget is adopted by the governmental unit, the entry is to debit estimated revenues, credit appropriations, and debit or credit fund balance for the difference.

**ARBITRAGE** profiting from price differences when the same asset is traded in different markets. For example, an *arbitrageur* simultaneously buys one contract of silver in the Chicago market and sells one contract of silver at a different price in the New York market, locking in a profit if the selling price is higher than the buying price. It is also the process of selling overvalued and buying undervalued assets so as to bring about an equilibrium where all assets are properly valued.

**ARITHMETIC MEAN** *see* MEAN.

**ARM'S LENGTH TRANSACTION** one entered into by unrelated parties, each acting in their own best interest. It is assumed that in this type of transaction the prices used are the fair market values of the property or services being transferred in the transaction.

**ARPANET** founded in the late 1960s as a wide area network by the United States Defense Advanced Research Project Agency (ARPA). Its use of packet switching technology and the TCP/IP protocol makes it the father of our modern Internet. ARPANET is responsible for major innovations, including the development of e-mail, file transfer protocol (ftp), and remotely controlling a computer (telnet).

**ARREARS** past due payments or other liabilities. An example is cumulative preferred stock dividends that have been declared but have not been paid following their payment dates. (Common dividends cannot be paid as long as cumulative preferred dividends are in arrears.)

**ARTICLES OF INCORPORATION** formal documents prepared by individuals wishing to establish a corporation in the United States. They must file these documents with the authorities in the state in which the corporation wishes to reside. One copy is returned, after being reviewed, and, together with the Certificate of Incorporation, becomes the corporation's charter formally recognizing the corporation as a business entity entitled to begin business operations. Rules governing the company's internal management are set forth in its *bylaws*.

**ARTICLES OF PARTNERSHIP** formal document drawn up by partners indicating significant and important aspects of the partnership. Items included are capital contributions, profit and loss ratios, name of the enterprise, duration of relationship, and individual duties.

**ARTICULATE** to describe interrelationship between elements of any operating financial statements that have a common basis.

**ARTIFICIAL INTELLIGENCE (AI)** a branch of computer science in which human intelligence is simulated using computers. The aim is to create machines that can think like a human, yet are capable of doing computations like a computer. AI applications are used extensively today. These applications, however, do not recreate the human brain. Rather, modern AI applications rely on computer learning algorithms, massive amounts of data, and sensors to perform discrete tasks. For instance, Google uses AI to interpret human search engine queries. Netflix uses AI to recommend movies to its viewers.

**ASC** *see* FASB ACCOUNTING STANDARDS CODIFICATION.

**ASCII (AMERICAN STANDARD CODE FOR INFORMATION INTERCHANGE)** computer term. The code converts a character into a binary number used by most microcomputers and information services (online databases) so that different makes of microcomputers may be able to communicate with each other.

**ASSEMBLY LANGUAGE** intermediate-level computer language that is less complex to use than a machine language. Assembly languages use abbreviations or mnemonic codes to replace the 0s and 1s of machine language (A for "add," C for "compare," and MP for "multiply"). A translator is required to convert the assembly language program into machine language that can be executed by the computer. This translator is the assembly program. Every command in assembly language has a corresponding command in machine language. The assembly language differs among computers, and thus these programs are not easily transferable to machines of a different type from the one on which they were written.

**ASSERTIONS** statements or representations made by management that are explicitly or implicitly embodied in the financial statements. Assertions pertain to account balances, classes of transactions and events, and presentation and disclosure items. Assertions relevant to account balances involve existence, rights (ownership) and obligations, completeness, as well as valuation and allocation. Assertions relevant to classes of transactions and events involve occurrence, completeness, accuracy, cutoff, and classification. Assertions relevant to presentation and disclosure items involve occurrence, rights and obligations, completeness, accuracy and valuation, and classification and understandability.

**ASSESSABLE CAPITAL STOCK**
1. capital stock subject to calls and not fully paid.
2. capital stock of banks, subjecting stockholders to liabilities in excess of the amount originally paid in or subscribed. The assessment would occur only in cases in which the corporation was insolvent.

**ASSESSED VALUE** value established by a government for real estate or other property as a basis for levying taxes. For example, an individual receives a statement that, in the judgment of the local tax assessor, the individual's property is worth $50,000. If by law properties in this jurisdiction are assessed at 80% of market value, the individual's assessed value then is $40,000 (80% of $50,000), and property taxes will be based on this assessed value.

## ASSESSMENT

1. process of making an official valuation of property for purposes of taxation.
2. valuation placed upon property as a result of this process. For example, an individual owns a parcel of land assessed on the tax roll for $50,000. The tax rate is $1.00 per $100 of value. The tax assessment for the land is $500.

**ASSET** economic resource that is expected to provide benefits to a business. An asset has three vital characteristics: (1) future probable economic benefit; (2) control by the entity; and (3) results from a prior event or transaction. Assets are expressed in money or are convertible into money and include certain deferred charges that are not resources (e.g., deferred moving costs). They can be recognized and measured in conformity with GENERALLY ACCEPTED ACCOUNTING PRINCIPLES (GAAP). Examples of ownership rights or service potentials are cash, automobiles, and land. An asset may be tangible or intangible. The former has physical substance such as a building. The latter lacks physical substance or results from a right granted by the government or another company such as goodwill and a patent. An asset may be current or noncurrent. A current asset has a life of one year or less (e.g., inventory) while a noncurrent asset has a life in excess of one year (e.g., machinery).

**ASSET DEPRECIATION RANGE (ADR)** range of depreciable lives allowed by the INTERNAL REVENUE SERVICE (IRS) for a specified asset. The ADR system was replaced by the ACCELERATED COST RECOVERY SYSTEM (ACRS) for properties placed into service after 1980. But it was revived under the 1986 Tax Reform Act as part of new ACRS rules to determine class lives.

**ASSET RETIREMENT OBLIGATION** FASB Statement No. 143 requires companies to record a liability at fair market value when a retirement obligation exists, provided fair value can be reasonably estimated even though it is years prior to the asset's planned retirement. The associated asset retirement cost is also recorded for the same amount when the initial obligation arises. After the initial recognition, the liability will change over time, so the obligation may be accrued to its present value each year. The long-term asset's capitalized cost is depreciated over its useful life.

**ASSET TURNOVER** ratio revealing the efficiency of corporate assets in generating revenue. A higher ratio is desired. What is considered a high ratio for one industry, however, may be considered a low ratio for another industry. If there is a low turnover, it may be an indication that the business should either utilize its assets in a more efficient manner or sell them. Asset turnover ratios can also be calculated for specific assets such as the ratios of sales to cash and sales to inventory. Higher ratios reflect favorably on the firm's ability to employ assets effectively.

**ASSIGNMENT METHOD** problem of determining how the assignments to machines or work centers should be made in order to minimize total costs. It is used to assign employees to jobs, jobs to machines, sales associates to territories, bidders to contracts, and so on.

**ASSIGNMENT OF ACCOUNTS RECEIVABLE** the process of writing a promissory note with accounts receivable as collateral. If the note is dishonored, the assignee can collect upon the accounts receivable. In a *general* assignment, all the receivables serve as collateral. New receivables can be substituted for those collected. In a *specific* assignment, the parties sign an agreement specifying who will receive collection (assignor or assignee), whether customers will be notified of the arrangement, specific accounts to be COLLATERALIZED, and the finance charges. *See also* FACTORING.

**ASSOCIATED WITH** designates the responsibility of an auditor for information in the footnotes to audited financial statements. Although the footnotes are not audited, the reasonableness of the disclosures should be reviewed by the auditor.

**ASSOCIATION OF CERTIFIED FRAUD EXAMINERS** an international, 25,000-member, professional organization (www.acfe.org) dedicated to fighting fraud and white-collar crime. With offices in North America and Europe—and chapters around the globe—the association is networked to respond to the needs of antifraud professionals everywhere.

**ASSOCIATION OF GOVERNMENT ACCOUNTANTS (AGA)** organization dedicated to the specific interests of accountants employed by a governmental entity. Its major publications include the GOVERNMENT ACCOUNTANTS JOURNAL. The association was originally founded in 1950 and was known as the Federal Government Accountants Association.

**ASSUMPTIONS UNDERLYING COST-VOLUME-PROFIT (CVP) ANALYSIS** assumptions that limit the usefulness of the basic BREAK-EVEN and COST-VOLUME PROFITS (CVP) models. They are: (1) The behavior of both sales revenue and expenses is *linear* throughout the entire relevant range of activity; (2) There is only one product or service or a constant SALES MIX; (3) Inventories do not change significantly from period to period; (4) Volume is the only factor affecting sales and expenses.

**ASSURANCE SERVICES** a CPA's examination of a contract, financial statement item (e.g., inventory), Web site, or loan terms being satisfied to provide assurance as to correctness or appropriateness. The engagement letter signed by the client must clearly specify what assurance is being provided.

**AT PAR** price that is the same as the FACE VALUE, or nominal amount, of a security. Bonds with a face value of $1000 that are bought or sold for $1000 are traded at par. If they sell for more than $1000 they would be traded at a PREMIUM; if less, at a DISCOUNT.

**AT-RISK RULES** tax term. A taxpayer can deduct losses for tax purposes only to the degree of risk. At-risk amounts are restricted to the cash investment and the debt for which the taxpayer is personally liable. Assume an individual incurs losses from real estate activities of $40,000. If the cash investment and personal debt incurred were $35,000, the most that could be deducted as losses is $35,000. Note there is an expansion of the at-risk amounts to real estate only to include certain nonrecourse loans from qualified lenders.

**ATTACHMENT** legally seizing property in order to satisfy a judgment.

**ATTEST** formal statement by an auditor after thorough examination and consideration, as to whether financial statements fairly present financial position and operating results. With an attest, the public accountant provides an objective evaluation to aid financial statement users.

**ATTEST FUNCTION** activity of the CERTIFIED PUBLIC ACCOUNTANT (CPA) in performing audit procedures. The accountant examines, tests, and verifies the accuracy of client accounting data as a basis for forming an audit opinion. In doing so, appropriate sampling of data is made. It is the process of an independent review of a company's financial statements including the rendering of an AUDIT REPORT.

**ATTESTATION (ATTEST) ENGAGEMENT** an assurance service provided by CPAs relative to subject matter or assertions about subject matter. Examples of subject matter include prospective financial information such as forecasts and projections, internal control, historical performance, and compliance with laws and regulations. In general, attestation engagements include examinations, reviews, and the application of agreed-upon procedures. Compilation of prospective financial information is also permissible.

**ATTORNEY'S LETTER** letter sent by the CERTIFIED PUBLIC ACCOUNTANT (CPA) to the client's lawyer to verify litigation information provided by management. The auditor is concerned that management has not revealed all lawsuits and claims. The auditor must assess the impact the contingencies may have on the client's financial position. This includes the possibility of the client losing the suit and suffering damages. The attorney's letter is a major audit procedure.

**ATTRIBUTE SAMPLING** statistical procedure used to study the characteristics of a population. Attribute is a qualitative characteristic that a unit of a population either possesses or does not possess. For example, an account receivable is either past due or not; proper authorization for a payment either exists or does not. Thus the population under consideration is composed of two mutually exclusive classes—

units possessing the attribute and units not possessing it. The statistical procedure used to estimate the occurrence of a particular attribute in a population is referred to as *attribute sampling*. This technique can be used by the auditor to substantiate such accounting populations as cash receipts, cash payments, payrolls, sales, and entries posted to the wrong account. In this analysis, the auditor usually determines the expected *occurrence rate* and the upper *precision* limit. The occurrence rate equals the percentage of the population having the attribute. Precision is the magnitude of deviation of a sample value from the population parameter being estimated.

Attribute sampling is particularly valuable in estimating the extent of compliance, such as the effectiveness of accounting controls using tests of transactions. Tables are used to determine sample size based on the desired confidence level, upper precision limit, and the expected rate of occurrence. Note that when analyzing a sample, the auditor may test for several different attributes. The exact definitions of attributes and occurrences should be contained in the working papers. *See also* VARIABLES SAMPLING.

**ATTRIBUTION** used in situations where the tax law assigns to one taxpayer the ownership interest of another taxpayer; also called *constructive ownership*. For example, under the law a father is considered to own constructively all stock actually owned by his son.

**AUDIT**
1. *financial audit*—examination of a client's accounting records by an independent certified public accountant to formulate an AUDIT OPINION. The auditor must follow GENERALLY ACCEPTED AUDITING STANDARDS (GAAS). Source documents are examined to substantiate legitimacy of transactions. A careful evaluation of INTERNAL CONTROL is necessary.
2. INTERNAL AUDIT—investigation of the company's procedures and operations by the INTERNAL AUDITOR to assure that they conform to corporate policy.
3. MANAGEMENT AUDIT—evaluation of management's efficiency.
4. COMPLIANCE AUDIT—ascertainment of the firm's compliance with specified rules and regulations such as the Sarbanes-Oxley Act.

**AUDITABILITY** environment in which the auditor performs the ATTEST FUNCTION. Consideration is given to such factors as the condition of the records and the cooperation of the client's accounting staff. The accounting records must allow for sufficient evidence gathering. There must exist a good system of INTERNAL CONTROL. Management must also be honest and have no intention of perpetrating FRAUD.

**AUDIT COMMITTEE** body formed by a company's board of directors to oversee audit operations and circumstances. It selects and appraises the performance of the CPA firm. In accordance with SECURITIES AND EXCHANGE COMMISSION (SEC) regulation, the Committee must be composed of outside directors. Besides evaluating external audit reports, the Committee may evaluate internal audit reports as well. Management representations under the realm of the FOREIGN CORRUPT PRACTICES ACT are also reviewed. The Committee may also get involved with public disclosure of corporate activities.

**AUDIT CYCLE** period of time in which the accountant conducts audit procedures. Different parts of the audit may be carried out at different times. For example, inventory may be counted in November while accounts receivable confirmation may be conducted in December. The audit cycle also relates to when a particular business unit is examined. For instance, Production Department X may be examined once a year, while Production Department Y is audited biyearly.

**AUDIT DOCUMENTATION** *see* WORK PAPERS.

**AUDIT GUIDE** booklets from the AMERICAN INSTITUTE OF CERTIFIED PUBLIC ACCOUNTANTS (AICPA) that supplement STATEMENTS ON AUDITING STANDARDS (SAS) and STATEMENTS OF POSITION (SOP). Typically, an audit guide is directed toward the accounting practices in a particular industry, such as brokerages, finance companies, and insurance companies. Some guides apply to technical topics, such as personal financial statements. These guides are usually deemed authoritative in nature.

**AUDITING EVIDENCE** proof the auditor uses to substantiate a recorded item so that proper reliance may be placed on financial statement figures. *Proof* of accounting data includes examining source documents in support of a transaction. The degree to which evidence gathering is necessary partly depends on the quality of the client's internal control system. Also, the trend in an account should be looked at over time as a basis for determining the extent of testing required. For example, if travel expense went from 2% of sales last year to 25% of sales this year, this inconsistency requires close examination. Test checks of accounts and transactions are necessary. Evidence can be obtained through various means such as physical verification of inventory records or confirmation letters sent to verify recorded amounts of accounts receivable. *See also* ANALYTICAL PROCEDURES; AUDITING PROCEDURE.

**AUDITING PROCEDURE** auditor technique in gathering AUDITING EVIDENCE to substantiate the reliability of the accounting records. The auditor evaluates whether the information presented is logical and reasonable. Examples of auditing procedures are observing assets to verify existence and amount (e.g., fixed assets), collecting independent confirmations from external parties (e.g., bank confirmation), evaluating internal control, appraising management's activities, and obtaining management representations. The audit procedures to be followed on an engagement are indicated in the AUDIT PROGRAM. The WORK PAPERS indicate what has been done on the audit.

**AUDITING PROCESS** sequential order of steps followed by the auditor in the examination of client records. The audit process may vary depending upon the nature of the engagement, its objectives, and type of audit assurance desired. The process includes understanding the particular client's environment, conducting the auditing procedures and tests, appraising the audit results, and communicating the results to interested parties.

**AUDITING STANDARDS** guidelines that auditors follow when examining financial statements and other data. Auditing standards are promulgated by authoritative bodies, such as the AMERICAN INSTITUTE OF CERTIFIED PUBLIC ACCOUNTANTS (AICPA), which issues GENERALLY ACCEPTED AUDITING STANDARDS (GAAS) applicable to audits of nonissuers, and the Public Company Accounting Oversight Board (PCAOB), which issues GAAS applicable to audits of issuers. The INSTITUTE OF INTERNAL AUDITORS (IIA) also sets standards for internal auditors. Further, standards exist for auditors filing for companies with governmental regulatory bodies.

**AUDITING STANDARDS BOARD (ASB)** authoritative body of the AMERICAN INSTITUTE OF CERTIFIED PUBLIC ACCOUNTANTS (AICPA). The ASB formulates, revises, and interprets GENERALLY ACCEPTED AUDITING STANDARDS (GAAS). It issues authoritative auditing pronouncements called Statements on Auditing Standards, applicable to audits of nonissuers.

**AUDIT OPINION** report rendered by the independent CPA at the end of an audit investigation. The auditor reports on the nature of his or her work and on the degree of responsibility assumed. In the audit opinion, the auditor states that he or she has examined the client's financial statements for the year then ended in accordance with GENERALLY ACCEPTED AUDITING STANDARDS (GAAS) including tests of the accounting records and other necessary auditing procedures. The auditor then indicates whether in his or her opinion the client's financial statements present fairly the financial position, results of operations, and changes in financial position for the year-ended in conformity with GENERALLY ACCEPTED ACCOUNTING PRINCIPLES (GAAP) applied on a consistent basis. The four types of audit opinions are UNQUALIFIED (unmodified in the case of a nonissuer's financial statements) OPINION, QUALIFIED OPINION, ADVERSE OPINION, and DISCLAIMER.

**AUDIT PLAN** includes the nature, extent, and timing of the audit procedures to be performed by the auditor. The audit plan will vary from client to client and from year to year, due to the need to tailor the audit plan to meet the applicable circumstances. An audit plan should document the planned risk assessment procedures and planned further audit procedures, including relevant tests of controls and substantive procedures.

**AUDIT PROGRAM** a detailed list of the audit procedures to be performed. The audit program is the means by which an auditor documents the audit plan.

## AUDIT REPORT

1. *short form* audit report expresses the CPA's *audit opinion* on whether the financial statements are presented fairly in all material respects in conformity with U.S. GAAP. There are instances when a modification to the standard format of the audit report is necessary. A QUALIFIED OPINION (or a disclaimer of opinion) must be given, for example, when audit scope limitations exist; an opinion partly based on the report of other auditors must be noted; the CPA wants to emphasize a key matter affecting financial position.

2. *long form* detailed audit report directed to the management or Board of Directors may supplement, include, or replace the short-form report. Typically, it includes audit scope particulars, makes explanatory comments on financial position and operating results, discusses trends in financial data along with reasons, and gives procedural suggestions.

**AUDIT RISK** possibility that the auditor will not uncover material misstatements in the financial records resulting from fraud, negligence, or other reasons. For example, the auditor's sampling techniques will not always uncover an improper item such as an overstated expense. Further, the evaluation of internal control and checks may not spot a deficiency. The auditor should try to protect against the adverse consequences of failing to uncover misstatements by obtaining REPRESENTATION LETTERS and adequate malpractice insurance.

**AUDIT SOFTWARE** computer programs designed to assist in examining and testing clients' accounting records. Different audit software packages accomplish varying objectives. Some packages assist in gathering evidence, conducting analytical tests, sampling data, evaluating internal control, documenting the audit, scheduling the audit, printing exception reports (e.g., employee salary exceeding a prescribed limit), preparing audit reports, sending out confirmations and management letters.

**AUDIT TEST** procedure applied to a sample within a population. For example, it might examine supporting evidence for half of promotion and entertainment expenses or send out confirmations for 75% of accounts receivable. The purpose of an audit test is to assure that no material exceptions are included in the sample. Audit tests are also applied in microcomputer applications to assure that the accounting software package is processing data correctly. A "dummy file" with predetermined manual results is processed by the computer to see if the computerized result is the same as the manually determined figure.

**AUDIT TRAIL** recorded flow of a transaction from initiation (e.g., source document) to finalization (e.g., financial statement), or vice versa. The auditor, assuring that data are processed correctly, appraises the material that forms the audit trail. An audit trail may be either visible or invisible (e.g., magnetic storage). Components of an audit trail include: (1) source records, (2) list of transactions processed, and (3) transaction identifiers so that reference can be made to the source of a transaction. An audit trail allows the tracing of transactions to control totals and from the control totals to supporting transactions. An audit trail is good when the tracing process is easy to accomplish.

**AUTHORITY** power to direct and exact performance from others. It includes the right to prescribe the means and methods by which work will be done. However, the authority to direct is only as good as one individual's willingness to accept direction from another. Moreover, with authority comes RESPONSIBILITY and ACCOUNTABILITY.

**AUTHORIZED CAPITAL STOCK** maximum number of shares of common stock that can be issued under a company's Articles of Incorporation. If a public issue of stock is involved, the SEC and the relevant state must approve it. Issued shares are usually less than the authorized shares.

**AUTOCORRELATION** term used in the statistical measurement of relationships within a series. It is one of the assumptions required in a regression in order to make it reliable, also called *serial correlation*. It means that the error terms are independent of each other [see (a) below]. That is, the deviation of one point about the line (i.e., the error $= \mu = y - y'$) is unrelated to the deviation of any other point. When autocorrelation exists [i.e., the error terms are *not* independent see (b) below], the standard errors of the regression coefficients are seriously underestimated. The problem of autocorrelation is usually detected by the DURBIN-WATSON STATISTIC. *See* illustration.

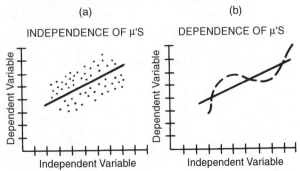

| (a) | (b) |
|:---:|:---:|
| INDEPENDENCE OF μ'S | DEPENDENCE OF μ'S |

**AUTOMATIC ERROR CORRECTION** method to uncover computer transmission data errors and permit the retransmission or correction of information by employing an error-correcting code.

**AUTONOMOUS** one of 12 criteria that must be met to account for a BUSINESS COMBINATION as a POOLING-OF-INTERESTS. Autonomous means that a combining company must not have been a subsidiary or division of any other corporation within two years prior to the *initiation date* of the business combination. If a combining company is *not* autonomous, then the PURCHASE (ACCOUNTING) METHOD must be used. The initiation date is the date that stockholders are notified in writing of an exchange offer.

**AVAILABLE FOR SALE SECURITIES** represent securities and other financial investments that are not held (1) for trading, (2) to maturity, or (3) for strategic reasons, and that have a readily available market price. Under U.S. GENERALLY ACCEPTED ACCOUNTING PRIN- CIPLES (GAAP), available for sale securities are carried on an entity's balance sheet at fair value.

**AVERAGE** *see* MEAN.

**AVERAGE AGE OF INVENTORY** number of days an average inven- tory item takes to sell:

$$\text{Average Age of Inventory} = \frac{\text{Average Inventory}}{\text{Cost of Goods Sold}} \times 365 \text{ days}$$

For example, assume that average inventory is $47,500 and cost of goods sold is $500,000. The average age of inventory is ($47,500/$500,000) × 365 days = 34.7 days. *See also* DAYS TO SELL INVENTORY.

**AVERAGE COST FLOW ASSUMPTION** one of the two cost flow assumptions used under PROCESS COSTING, more often called WEIGHTED AVERAGE COST flow assumption. The other is the FIRST-IN, FIRST-OUT (FIFO) cost flow assumption. *See also* WEIGHTED AVERAGE COSTING.

**AVERAGE COSTING** *see* WEIGHTED AVERAGE COSTING.

**AVERAGE COST OF CAPITAL** minimum desired rate of return on invested capital that is computed by taking an average of the cost of debt, cost of preferred stock, cost of common stock, and the cost of retained earnings.

**AVERAGE INVENTORY** amount equaling about half maximum inventory when demand is relatively constant. For example, if the maximum inventory is 500 units and depletion occurs at a fairly con- stant rate, the average inventory equals 250 units (500/2).

**AVERAGE LIFE** estimated useful-life expectancy of a depreciable group of assets. *See also* DEPRECIATION; ECONOMIC LIFE; USEFUL LIFE.

**AVERAGE RATE OF RETURN** *see* SIMPLE RATE OF RETURN.

**AVI FILES** stands for Audio Video Interleave, a file format created by Microsoft to store both audio and video data in a standard form to allow for simultaneous/synchronized playback of audio and video.

**AVOIDABLE COST** cost that will not be incurred if an activity is suspended; also called escapable cost. For example, it is the cost that can be saved by dropping a particular product line or department (e.g., salaries paid to employees working in a particular product line or department). All costs are avoidable, except (1) SUNK COSTS and (2) costs that will continue regardless of the decision.

**AZURE CLOUD** Windows Azure by Microsoft is an open and flexible cloud platform that enables one to build, deploy, and manage applications using any language, tool, or framework. One can store data using relational SQL databases, NoSQL table stores, or unstructured blob (binary large object) stores.

# B

**BACK CHARGE** item previously charged to an account but unpaid. The current invoice requests payment of the previous charge as well as of current charges.

**BACKFLUSH COSTING** product costing approach, used in a JUST-IN-TIME (JIT) operating environment, in which costing is delayed until goods are finished. Standard costs are then flushed backward through the system to assign costs to products. The result is that detailed tracking of costs is eliminated. The system is best suited to companies that maintain low inventories because costs then flow directly to cost of goods sold. Work-in-process is usually eliminated, journal entries to inventory accounts may be delayed until the time of product completion or even the time of sale, and standard costs are used to assign costs to units when journal entries are made, that is, to flush costs backward to the points at which inventories remain.

**BACK ORDER** customer's order that cannot be filled at the present time usually because the merchandise is not currently in stock. As soon as the product is available, it will be shipped to the customer. There usually exists a company policy of how long an unshipped order remains an order without some sort of confirmation or communication. An excessive amount of back orders may indicate to the accountant that poor inventory planning exists.

**BACK UP** to make a duplicate copy of original data or files usually stored on a separate data storage medium. Backup ensures the recoverability of files in the event of loss of the original data.

**BACKUP WITHHOLDING** procedure used to ensure that federal income tax is paid on earnings even though the recipient cannot be identified by a Social Security number. Banks, brokers, and other entities report nonwage earnings paid out on IRS Form 1099. When the form cannot be filed because it lacks the taxpayer's Social Security number, 20% of the interest, dividends, or fees is withheld by the payer and remitted to the federal government. For example, if interest earned on a bank account is $1,000 and there is no Social Security number on file for the account, the bank withholds $200. Financial institutions have account holders fill out a Federal W-9 form requiring the individual to certify that the Social Security numbers given are correct and that they are or are not subject to backup withholding. The information regarding interest payments is reported by the bank to the IRS for comparison with individual tax returns. Backup withholding is not an additional tax; the tax liability of persons subject to backup withholding will be reduced by the amount of tax withheld. The IRS Code Section 3406 (a)(1)(c) applies to backup withholding.

**BAD DEBT** account or note receivable that proves to be entirely or partially uncollectible despite collection efforts. If the allowance method of estimating bad debts is used, the entry at time of uncollectibility is to debit allowance for bad debts and credit accounts receivable. If the direct write-off method is employed, the entry is to debit bad debt expense and credit accounts receivable.

**BAD DEBT EXPENSE** account shown in the income statement representing estimated uncollectible credit sales for the current accounting period. *See also* ALLOWANCE METHOD; DIRECT WRITE-OFF METHOD.

**BAD DEBT RECOVERY** account receivable previously written off as uncollectible is now collected. The entry is to reverse the original write-off by debiting accounts receivable and crediting allowance for bad debts. A second entry is required for the collection by debiting cash and crediting accounts receivable. A high ratio of recoveries to write-offs may signify to the analyst that the firm writes off uncollected debts too quickly. *See also* ALLOWANCE METHOD.

**BAIDU** the market leader in paid online search engines in China with 62.1% market share in 2009, well ahead of Google China's 25.3% share.

**BAILMENT** contractual transfer of dollars or personal property for a specified objective. An example is the CONSIGNMENT of goods from the consignor to consignee. Another example is a bank holding an asset of a borrower as collateral. In a bailment, the deliverer is called the bailor and the receiver is termed the bailee.

**BAILOUT PAYBACK METHOD PAYBACK PERIOD** method incorporating the salvage value of the asset into the calculation. It measures the length of the payback period when the periodic cash inflows are combined with the salvage value.

**"BAIT RECORDS"** internal control device. Bait or dummy records may be in computer files so the auditor can see when these files are improperly used. Example: a nonexistent customer or inventory item with an assumed balance that should not be altered. Another example: a dummy record put into processing with an incorrect name and address file for an employee. When a mailing occurs, it will be returned.

**BALANCE**
1. difference between total debits and total credits in an account.
2. equality of total debits and total credits of all accounts in a GENERAL LEDGER in the preparation of a TRIAL BALANCE.
3. equality of a control account in the general ledger (e.g., accounts receivable) and the total balance of all accounts in the SUBSIDIARY LEDGER (e.g., customer accounts).
4. balance in a bank account.
5. balance of a loan.

**BALANCED BUDGET** one in which total expenditures equal total revenue. An entity has a budget surplus if expenditures are less than revenues. It has a budget deficit if expenditures are greater than revenues.

**BALANCED SCORECARD** a measurement and management system that suggests we view organization from four perspectives: financial, internal business processes, customer, and learning and growth.

**BALANCE OF PAYMENTS** record of the transactions of a country with the rest of the world. There are three main accounts in the balance of payments: (1) the current account, (2) the capital account, and (3) gold. The current account records trade in goods and services, as well as transfer payments. Services include freight, royalty payments, and interest payments. Transfer payments consist of remittances, gifts, and grants. The *balance of trade* simply records trade in goods. The capital account records purchases and sales of investments, such as stocks, bonds and land.

**BALANCE OF RETAINED EARNINGS** accompanies the balance sheet and shows the beginning balance of retained earnings, adjustments to it during the year, and the final balance. An illustrative statement format follows:

> Retained Earnings—1/1 Unadjusted
> Plus or Minus: Prior Period Adjustments
>
> Retained Earnings—1/1 Adjusted
> Plus: Net Income
> Minus: Dividends Declared
> Retained Earnings—12/31

**BALANCE OF TRADE** *see* BALANCE OF PAYMENTS.

**BALANCE SHEET** statement showing a company's financial position at the end of an accounting period; also called *Statement of Financial Position*. It presents the entity's ASSETS, LIABILITIES, and STOCKHOLDERS' EQUITY. It is classified into major groupings of assets and liabilities in order to facilitate analysis. Examples are current assets, fixed assets, current liabilities, and noncurrent liabilities. The accounting equation for the balance sheet is:

$$\text{Assets} = \text{Liabilities} + \text{Stockholders' Equity}$$

The balance sheet is useful to financial statement users because it indicates the resources the entity has and what it owes. *See also* INCOME STATEMENT.

**BALANCE SHEET ACCOUNT** appears in the balance sheet. Unlike income statement accounts that are NOMINAL ACCOUNTS, balance sheet accounts are REAL ACCOUNTS. A real account is not closed out at the end of the year but continues to exist into the next year.

Examples of balance sheet accounts are cash, accounts payable, and common stock.

**BALLOON** last loan payment when it is significantly more than the prior payments; also called *partially amortized loans*. For example, a debt agreement might provide for a balloon payment when future refinancing is anticipated.

**BANDWIDTH** the data transfer rate from one location to another in a given period of time, usually expressed in bits per second (bps) or kilo bits per second (kbps). Bandwidth is also used to refer to the width of the range of frequencies in electronic communication, often expressed in hertz (Hz).

**BANK BALANCE** amount in a bank deposit account, such as a checking or savings account, as of a certain specified time or date, indicated on a bank statement. Bank charges, deposits in transit, and outstanding checks usually are primary factors in reconciling an individual's or organization's books and the bank's statement, as of a particular date. *See also* BANK RECONCILIATION.

**BANKER'S ACCEPTANCE** time draft drawn by a business firm whose payment is guaranteed by the bank's "acceptance" of it. It is especially important in foreign trade, when the seller of goods can be certain that the buyer's draft will actually have funds behind it. Banker's acceptances are money market instruments actively traded in the secondary market.

**BANK RECONCILIATION** term used when settling differences contained in the BANK STATEMENT and the cash account in the books of the bank's customer. Rarely do the ending balances agree. To reflect the reconciling items, a bank reconciliation is required. Once completed, the adjusted bank balance must prove to the adjusted book balance. When it does, it indicates that both records are correct. Journal entries are then prepared to update the records and to arrive at an ending balance in the cash account that agrees with the ending balance in the bank statement.

The bank balance is adjusted for items reflected on the books that are not on the statement. They include OUTSTANDING CHECKS, DEPOSITS IN TRANSIT, and bank errors in charging or crediting the company's account.

The book balance is adjusted for items shown on the bank statement that are not reflected on the books. They include bank charges, not-sufficient funds checks, collections made by bank on the customer's behalf (e.g., collected notes receivable), interest earned, and errors on the books.

**BANK STRESS TEST** test that determines how much capital a bank needs to survive. For example, regulators may require that banks maintain a minimum 6% Tier 1 capital ratio, a common measure of financial health, and that at least half of that figure, or 3%, come from common stock. If a bank fails the test, its regulators will demand that it raise additional capital.

**BANK TRANSFER SCHEDULE** provides details of cash transfers between banks, including the dates and dollar amounts of transfers. Also known as an *interbank transfer schedule.*

**BANKRUPTCY (BUSINESS)** situation in which a business' debt exceeds the fair market value of its assets. It is also a court action under which a debtor may be discharged for unpaid debts, in whole or in part, and in which creditors receive distributions of assets from the debtor's property under the supervision of the court. CHAPTER 11 of the Bankruptcy Law provides for reorganization in which the debtor remains in possession of the business and in control of its operation, while the debtor and creditors are allowed to work together. *See also* BANKRUPTCY (PERSONAL).

**BANKRUPTCY (PERSONAL)** legal process that is available for an individual who is overextended financially and is unable to pay his debts. The individual can file for bankruptcy in order to seek to legally eliminate some or all of his debts. Under CHAPTER 7 of the Bankruptcy Law, often called straight bankruptcy, the intent is to liquidate assets to pay the debts. Should this method be elected, the bankrupt can claim certain property as "exempt" and this property can be retained to preserve the basic necessities of life (such as a certain amount of equity in the home, economical car, and personal clothing and effects). Once a person has declared bankruptcy, he cannot be discharged from debts again for six years. *Note:* The newest bankruptcy legislation, which came into effect in the fall of 2005, however, makes it difficult to file for Chapter 7 if their income is greater than the median for their state. As a result, more individuals are expected to file for Chapter 13.

Under CHAPTER 13, often called wage-earner plans, the assets are not liquidated. Instead, interest and late charges are eliminated and arrangements are made to pay off some or all of the debts over several years. Note that bankruptcy will not discharge all the debts. Debts that cannot be eliminated through bankruptcy proceedings include income taxes, child support, alimony, student loans, and debts incurred under false pretenses. Bankruptcy should not be taken lightly. One should be sure to consult an attorney on various decisions surrounding the issue and on how to get the greatest benefit from the new financial start. *See also* BANKRUPTCY (BUSINESS).

**BANKRUPTCY PREDICTION** ability of an auditor to project whether the client has a going-concern problem. If it does have a problem, this fact must be stated in the audit report and a QUALIFIED OPINION REPORT rendered. Failure to do so, if a client actually becomes bankrupt, will expose the CPA to lawsuits by financial statement users such as damaged investors and creditors. There are several ways to predict bankruptcy such as Altman's Z SCORE, trends in certain financial ratios (e.g., cash flow to total debt, net income to total assets), degree of FINANCIAL LEVERAGE, industry problems, poor economy, and low-quality management.

**BANK STATEMENT** form prepared by the bank and sent to the depositor to show transactions in the account. The bank statement reports the beginning balance, deposits made, checks cleared, charges to the account (e.g., bank service fees), credits to the account (e.g., interest earned on the account balance), and ending balance. Enclosed with the bank statement are the canceled checks, debit memoranda for charges, and credit memoranda for credits.

**BARGAIN PURCHASE** asset or goods acquired for materially less than fair market value. For example, a buyer may be able to get a bargain price on furniture from a seller in a liquidation situation.

**BARGAIN PURCHASE OPTION** one of the four criteria to be satisfied for a lessee to account for leased property under the CAPITAL LEASE method. A bargain purchase option exists if the lessee can buy the property at the end of the lease for a nominal (minimal) amount or renew at nominal rental payments. If this criterion exists, the leased asset is depreciated by the lessee over the life of the property. The PRESENT VALUE of the bargain purchase option payment is included in obtaining the present value of future payments as the capitalizable amount of the leased asset.

**BARGAIN RENEWAL OPTION** lessee's ability to renew a lease at subsequent minimal rental payments. Minimal rental payments are defined as those significantly below what typical rental payments on the property would be. This satisfies one of the criteria required for a CAPITAL LEASE. In effect, by doing so the lessee has acquired a property right.

**BARTER** exchange of products or services by two companies without cash involvement. The companies contract for a specified amount of the items and the proportions representing full payment. For financial reporting purposes, barter transactions should be reported at the estimated fair market value of the product or service received. This same requirement holds for tax purposes in that each party has to recognize as revenue the fair value of the exchange. For example, a barter takes place when an accountant renders services to a computer store in exchange for a personal computer.

**BASEL II** a new set of regulations designed by the Basel Committee on Banking Supervision to cover operational risk as well as financial risk for the global financial institutions. Set up in 1974, the Basel Committee on Banking Supervision is an international regulatory body for the world's financial institutions. In 1988, it introduced capital adequacy rules for banks in member countries, which required them to implement a financial risk measurement framework. The

Committee is currently creating a new set of regulations to replace the original rules that would cover operational risk as well as financial risk. The new framework, usually called Basell II, is based around three "pillars": the first determines minimum capital requirements, the second stipulates an effective supervisory review process, and the third sets out to strengthen market discipline by greater disclosure of banks' financial status.

**BASE PERIOD** selected period of time that serves as a basis for a comparison, a standard, or a mathematical construct to aid in financial computations. The base period selected should be the one that is the most typical of the business. The term base period applies to economic statistics (e.g., Consumer Price Index) and certain stock indexes (e.g., the base period of the Standard & Poor's 500 is 1941–1943).

**BASE STOCK** minimum inventory level necessary to maintain effective and continuous operations. *See also* BASE STOCK METHOD.

**BASE STOCK METHOD** inventory valuation method in which the base amount of goods is valued at acquisition cost; also called *normal stock method*. The base amount should be continually maintained. Additional quantities above the base level are valued on a LIFO basis. The method is *not* accepted.

**BASIC (BEGINNERS ALL-PURPOSE SYMBOLIC INSTRUCTION CODE)** high-level computer programming language written in an easy-to-understand English format; the language was first used at Dartmouth in 1967. It is one of the easiest languages to learn and is undoubtedly the best known of any high-level computer language today. However, it runs more slowly than some other languages, such as C.

**BASIC EARNINGS PER SHARE** net income available to common stockholders divided by the weighted-average number of shares outstanding. Net income available to common stockholders is net income less declared preferred dividends for the year. If the preferred stock is noncumulative, preferred stock dividends are subtracted only if they are declared during the year. If the preferred stock is cumulative, the dividends are deducted even if they are not declared in the current year. The weighted-average number of common stock shares outstanding is determined by multiplying the number of shares issued and outstanding for any time period by a fraction, the numerator being the number of months the shares have been outstanding and the denominator being the number of months in the period (e.g., 12 months for annual reporting).

**BASIC FEASIBLE SOLUTION** term in LINEAR PROGRAMMING (LP) used to designate a solution that occurs at the *corner point* of the feasible region in a graph. According to a theorem in LP, one or a linear combination of the basic feasible solutions will turn out to be an optimal solution. *See also* GRAPHICAL METHOD.

**BASING POINT** specific geographical location that is associated with a given price of a commodity. This price will then serve as a base price for the same commodity in a different geographical location. Freight costs between locations will account for the difference with respect to the base price.

**BASIS** figure or value that is the starting point in computing gain or loss, depreciation, depletion, and amortization. For example, in an asset sale, gain is proceeds minus basis, where basis is the amount on which depreciation is calculated.

**BASIS OF ACCOUNTING** method of recognizing revenues and expenses. Under the *accrual basis* of accounting, revenues are recognized as goods are sold and services are rendered regardless of the time when cash is received. Expenses are recognized in the period when the related revenue is recognized and the difference is the net income figure for a particular period. Under the *cash basis* of accounting, revenues are recognized only when money is received and expenses are recognized only when money is paid. Cash basis financial statements, however, distort financial position and operating results of an organization.

**BASKET PURCHASE** *see* LUMP-SUM PURCHASE.

**BATCH-LEVEL ACTIVITIES** activities performed each time a batch of goods is produced; such activities vary with the number of batches prepared.

**BATCH PROCESSING** term for a processing mode in which the work to be accomplished is done sequentially. Input such as transaction records is processed through the system in a predetermined order. *See also* REAL-TIME SYSTEM.

**BAYESIAN PROBABILITY** revised prior estimates of probabilities, based on additional experience and information. An example of Bayesian probability applied to accounting is when the estimated bad debt percentage has to be revised because of recent uncollectibility experience of customer defaults, sales to more marginal customers, or poor economic conditions.

**BEAR** one who believes that prices in the security and commodity markets will decline. A bear can profit from a declining stock market by selling a stock *short* or buying a PUT option. A BULL, the opposite of a bear, thinks prices will rise.

**BEARER BOND** unregistered bond that entitles the holder to payments of both principal and interest; also called a *coupon bond*, because whoever presents the coupon is entitled to the interest. With respect to transfers, bond endorsement is not a requirement.

**BEGINNING INVENTORY** balance at the start of the accounting period. The three types of inventory are RAW MATERIALS INVENTORY,

WORK-IN-PROCESS (WIP), and FINISHED GOODS INVENTORY. They are shown in the income statement in the analysis of cost of goods sold. *See also* ENDING INVENTORY.

## BEHAVIORAL ACCOUNTING

1. approach to accounting that stresses psychological considerations in decision making; also called HUMAN RESOURCE ACCOUNTING. For example, a budget should be participative so departmental managers who are involved with it will internalize the goals. Also profit centers engage a manager's ego because the financial results of the entity are a direct reflection of the manager's performance. In human resource accounting, a valuation is placed on people and reflected as an asset in the balance sheet.

2. theory that the management accounting function is essentially behavioral. The theory states that the nature and scope of accounting systems is materially influenced by the view of human behavior that is held by the accountants who design and operate these systems. PARTICIPATIVE BUDGETING is a simple application of behavioral accounting.

**BELLWETHER SECURITY** one that indicates the direction of the security market. General Electric is an example because much of it is owned by INSTITUTIONAL INVESTORS who influence supply and demand. In the bond market, the 20-year U.S. Treasury bond is a good indicator of the direction in which other bonds are moving.

## BENCHMARK

1. a standard, norm, or yardstick to judge one's performance as an individual or company.

2. a standard measurement or metric used to evaluate the performance of a portfolio. For example, an appropriate stock or bond index can be used to gauge the performance of an investment such as a mutual fund. An example is the EUROPE, AUSTRALIA, AND FAR EAST (EAFE) INDEX, a value-weighted index of the equity performance of major foreign markets, which is often used to evaluate the performance of international mutual funds.

**BENCHMARKING** learning from others; also called COMPETITIVE.

**BENCHMARKING (BEST PRACTICES)** the process of searching for new and better procedures by comparing your own procedures to that of the very best. The objective is to measure the key outputs of a business process or function against the best and to analyze the reasons for the performance difference. Benchmarking applies to services and practices as well as to products and is an ongoing systematic process. It entails both quantitative and qualitative measurements that allow both an internal and an external assessment. *Process benchmarking* is the process of assessing the quality of key internal processes by comparing them with those of other firms. In *results benchmarking*, a firm examines the end product or service of another company, focusing on product/service specifications and performance results.

**BENCHMARK RATES** interest or loan rates that other rates are pegged to. An example is the U.S. prime rate on which other loan rates are based.

**BENEFICIARY** individual who will receive an inheritance upon the death of another. The proceeds of an insurance policy may be in the form of a lump-sum or annuity.

**BENEFIT APPROACH TO PENSIONS** term used when determining the amount of pension benefits applicable for services rendered to date and present value of these benefits. The two benefit approaches are the accumulated benefits approach and the benefits/years-of-service (projected unit credit) approach. With the former, pension expense and related liability are determined each year based on years of service to date using *existing salary levels*. With the latter, pension expense and liability are based on *final salary*. *See also* PENSION PLAN.

**BEST PRACTICES** *see* BENCHMARKING.

**BETA** measure of systematic or undiversifiable risk of a stock. A beta coefficient of more than 1 means that the company's stock price has shown more volatility than the market index (e.g., Standard & Poor's 500) to which it is being related; usually, that indicates it is a risky security. If the beta is less than 1, it is less volatile than the market average. If it equals 1, its risk is the same as the market index. High variability in stock price may indicate greater business risk, instability in operations, and low quality of earnings.

The following presents betas for some selected companies:

**Betas for Some Selected Multinational Corporations**

| Company | March 23, 2009 |
|---|---|
| Boeing (BA) | 1.20 |
| Google (GOOG) | 1.26 |
| Best Buy (BBY) | 1.35 |
| Nordstrom (JWN) | 1.58 |
| Intel (INTC) | 1.25 |
| Wal-Mart (WMT) | 0.21 |

Source: MSN Money Central Investor (http://moneycentral.msn.com/investor/home.asp) and Google Finance (http://finance.google.com/finance)

**BETA ALPHA PSI** national accounting fraternity maintaining student chapters on more than 125 university campuses. Members discuss issues of interest to the accounting profession. Membership is gained by students demonstrating a high degree of scholastic achievement. It was founded in 1919.

**BETA DISTRIBUTION** probability distribution used to describe activity times.

**BETA RISK** *see* TYPE II ERROR.

**BETTERMENT** replacement of a major component of plant and equipment by another component that will result in *better* performance capability. The betterment increases overall efficiency of the asset. An example is a superior engine in an auto. Betterments represent CAPITAL EXPENDITURES.

**BID AND ASKED** term in the over-the-counter market for unlisted securities. Bid is the highest price an investor is willing to pay while asked is the lowest price a seller is willing to take. Together, the two prices represent a quotation in that stock. A spread is the difference between the bid and asked prices. Bid and offer are the more common terms in discussing listed securities.

**BIG 4 ACCOUNTING FIRMS** four major public accounting firms, from the original eight, with many regional and local firms as well. The four are: PricewaterhouseCoopers, Deloitte, Ernst & Young, and KPMG. The second-tier firms include BDO Seidman, Grant Thornton, and McGladrey & Pullen.

**BILLINGS ON LONG-TERM CONTRACTS** amount charged by a company (e.g., construction company, defense contractor) to the customer for work done or to be done on a long-term project. *See also* PROGRESS BILLINGS.

**BILL OF ACTIVITIES** listing of the activities and activity volumes and associated costs required by a product, service, process output, or other cost object.

**BILL OF EXCHANGE** *see* DRAFT.

**BILL OF LADING** written document issued by a carrier that specifies contractual conditions and terms (such as time, place, person named for receipt) for delivery of goods. It also evidences receipt of goods. Upon transfer of the bill, title is passed to the goods.

**BILL OF MATERIALS (BOM)** listing of all the assemblies, subassemblies, parts, and raw materials that are needed to produce one unit of a finished product. Thus, each finished product has its own bill of materials. The listing in the bill of materials file is hierarchical; it shows the quantity of each item needed to complete one unit of the next-highest level of assembly.

**BILL OF SALE** written document that transfers goods, title, or other interests from a seller to a buyer and specifies the terms and conditions of the transaction.

**BINOMIAL MODEL** the most commonly used LATTICE-BASED MODEL of option pricing. Unlike the BLACK-SCHOLES OPTION PRICING MODEL (OPM), the binomial method divides the time from the option's grant date to the expiration date into small increments. Because the share price may increase or decrease during any interval, the binomial model takes into account how changes in price over the term of the option would affect the employee's exercise practice during each interval. The binomial model can also consider an option grant's lack of transferability, its forfeiture restrictions, and its vesting restrictions—even for options with more complicated terms such as indexed and performance-based vesting restrictions.

**BIOMETRIC IDENTIFICATION** relies on specific information about an individual's biological characteristics, such as finger print, iris, retina, DNA, and voice print, to identify an individual.

**BIT** a contraction of binary digits. It refers to a basic unit in computing, which may be in a state of either "on" or "off." A bit can have only one of two values, and is commonly represented by a value of 0 or 1.

**BLACK-SCHOLES OPTION PRICING MODEL (OPM)** formula for valuing stock options designed in 1973 by Nobel laureates Fischer Black and Myron Scholes; also known as the Black-Scholes-Merton model. A model is used to determine the value of option securities prices based on the relationship between six variables—the current underlying asset price, the option strike price, the option time-to-expiration, the riskless return, the underlying asset payout return, and the underlying asset volatility.

**BLANKET APPROPRIATION** usually associated with governmental accounting, an expenditure that is authorized without specification of the individual project elements.

**BLANKET INSURANCE** policy covering several items of property. The insurance policy is allocated to the property items based on their fair market values.

**BLIND ENTRY**
1. entry that reveals only its classificatory identity, appropriate debit and credit amounts and does not include an explanatory description of the transaction. *See also* JOURNAL ENTRY.
2. posting to a ledger account not documented by a journal or other source record.

**BLOCK DIAGRAM** diagram using symbols to explain the interconnections and information flow between hardware and software.

**BLOCK SAMPLING** JUDGMENT SAMPLE in which accounts or items are chosen in a sequential order. After the initial item in the block is chosen, the balance of the block is automatically selected. *See also* CLUSTER SAMPLING; SYSTEMATIC SAMPLING.

**BLOG** a contraction for Web Log. A blog is a Web site where new content is added or updated on a continuous basis. Often, the content consists of an individual's opinion about a specialized topic. WordPress is a very popular blogging software.

**BLUE CHIP** common stock of high quality that has a long record of earnings and dividend payments. Blue chip stocks are often viewed as long-term investment instruments. They have low risk and provide modest but dependable return. Examples are International Telephone and Telegraph and Minnesota Mining and Manufacturing. Blue chip may also refer to a high-quality bond that is secure and stable in price and interest payments.

**BLUE SKY LAW** law providing for state regulation and supervision of the issuance of investment securities. The prevention of gross fraud is the primary purpose of these laws, which include procedures and regulations with respect to broker licensing, registration of new issues, and formal approvals by appropriate governing bodies.

**BLUETOOTH** the standard wireless Personal Area Network (PAN) for transmitting data over a 2.4 gigahertz (GHz) band frequency.

**BOARD OF DIRECTORS** group of persons elected by a company's stockholders to run the business according to the corporate charter. Senior management is appointed by the Board. Typically, the Board consists of top management executives (INSIDE DIRECTORS) and representatives external to the company (OUTSIDE DIRECTORS). The Board has significant influence over accounting and financial policies of the business entity.

**BOILERPLATE** standard legal language used in contracts, prospectuses, wills, and so on. Boilerplate typically appears in fine print. It contains important information rarely subject to modification between the parties.

**BOND**
1. written promise by a company, government, or other institution to pay the face amount at the maturity date. Periodic interest payments are usually required. Bonds are typically stated in $1,000 denominations. Bonds may be *secured* by collateral or *unsecured* (debenture). A *registered bond* has the name of the owner on the issuer's records, whereas the holder of a BEARER BOND presents coupons for interest payments. SINKING FUND bonds require the company to make annual deposits to a trustee. At maturity, the amount in the sinking fund (principal plus interest) is sufficient to pay the face of the bond. From the company's perspective, a bond issue has several advantages over a stock issue. Interest expense is tax deductible, whereas dividend payments are not. During inflation, debt is paid back in cheaper dollars. When bonds are issued at face value, the entry is to debit cash and credit bonds payable. When bonds are issued at a discount, such as with zero-coupon bonds, the entry is to

debit cash and bond discount and credit bonds payable. The entry to record the interest each period is to debit interest expense and credit cash. *See also* BOND CONVERSION; BOND DISCOUNT; BOND PREMIUM.

**2.** cash or property given to assure performance (i.e., contractor depositing a *performance bond* on a construction project to be completed by a specified date).

**3.** type of insurance compensating employer for employee dishonesty.

**BOND CONVERSION** exchange of a convertible bond for stock. While conversion is typically at the option of the investor, in some cases it may be at the option of the issuing company (e.g., forced conversion). The conversion may be accounted for under the BOOK VALUE METHOD or MARKET VALUE METHOD.

**BOND DISCOUNT** the amount below FACE VALUE at which a bond is issued. A bond may be issued at a discount when the interest rate on the bond is below the prevailing market interest rate, the company has financial problems, and the bond has a long maturity period. Bond discount is a CONTRA ACCOUNT to bonds payable to arrive at the CARRYING VALUE. Assume a $300,000 bond is issued at 93%. The bond discount is $21,000 ($300,000 × 7%). *See also* BOND PREMIUM.

**BOND ELECTRONIC TRANSFER FUNDS (ETFs)** fixed-income ETFs. Bond ETFs have several advantages: (1) They are well-diversified baskets of bonds with different maturities; (2) their expense ratio is low — 15 basis points, compared with an average of 39 for bond mutual funds; and (3) their greater transparency over individual bonds further lowers costs. Also, with bonds, individual investors can't get good prices, but institutions can.

**BOND FUND**

**1.** IN GOVERNMENT ACCOUNTING, a fund established for the receipt and distribution of monies received from the issuance of a bond.

**2.** a MUTUAL FUND that invests in bonds. *See also* SINKING FUND.

**BOND INDENTURE** agreement between a bond issuer and holder covering the terms of issue; also called *deed of trust*. The bond terms include such conditions as dollar amount of issue; PLEDGED ASSETS; COVENANTS (e.g., working capital requirement); events of default; and call privileges. It also provides for the appointment of a trustee. *See also* INDENTURE.

**BOND ISSUE COSTS** expenditures incurred in preparing and selling a bond issue such as legal, underwriting, accounting, commission, printing, promotion, and registration fees. These costs represent a DEFERRED CHARGE that is amortized using the straight-line method over the period the bonds are outstanding (date of issue to the maturity date). Note that the amortization starts from the date the bonds are sold and *not* the date of the bonds (which may be before the issue date).

Assume a five-year bond dated 1/1/2014 is sold on 9/1/2014. Bond issue costs are $10,000. Since there are 52 months between 9/1/2014 and 1/1/2019, the amortization per month is $192.31 ($10,000/52 months). The amortization expense for 2014 is $769.24 ($192.31 per month × 4 months from 9/1/2014 to 12/31/2014). *See also* AMORTIZE.

**BOND OUTSTANDING METHOD** method of amortizing bond discount or premium. This is a variation of the straight-line method that spreads bond discount or premium over the life of a bond issue by periodic charges to expense. The charges are determined by the ratio of the face value of bonds outstanding during the period to the total of such face values for all the periods during which the bonds are outstanding.

**BOND PREMIUM** the amount in excess of FACE VALUE (maturity value) at which a bond is issued. A BOND may be issued at a premium if the interest rate on the bond exceeds the market interest rate or it is from a financially strong company. For example, if a $100,000 bond was issued at 106, the bond premium is $6,000 ($100,000 × 6%). Bond premium is added to the bond payable account under noncurrent liabilities to arrive at the carrying value of the bond. The bond premium account is amortized each year so that at maturity the bond will equal its face value. The amortization entry each year is to debit bond premium and credit interest expense. When a bond is issued at a premium, the EFFECTIVE INTEREST RATE is less than the NOMINAL INTEREST RATE. *See also* BOND DISCOUNT; YIELD TO MATURITY.

**BOND RATINGS** calculations of the probability that a bond issue will go into default. They measure risk, and therefore have an impact on the interest rate. Bond investors tend to place more emphasis on independent analysis of quality than do common stock investors. Bond analysis and ratings are done by Standard & Poor and Moody's among other rating agencies.

**BOND SINKING FUND** represents cash that is set aside for the purpose of paying back bonds issued by an entity. The bond sinking fund, which may involve annual contributions, is typically administered by an independent trustee.

**BONUS METHOD** partnership accounting method in which a new partner contributing goodwill or intangible value is credited with capital in excess of the tangible assets contributed.

**BOOK**
1. used as a noun (usually plural), it refers to JOURNALS or LEDGERS.
2. used as a verb, it refers to the recording of an entry. *See also* BOOK VALUE.

**BOOK BALANCE** term used for the amount of an account balance at the end of an accounting period. For example, when preparing a BANK RECONCILIATION, the balance in the cash account at the end of the month is referred to as the book balance. In a similar vein, the auditor compares the book balance in ending inventory with the physical count to uncover any discrepancies.

**BOOK INVENTORY** inventory shown on the financial records. It is a book value as opposed to a physical count of inventory and is computed from the initial inventory plus purchases less requisitions or withdrawals. Book inventory typically differs from the physical inventory on hand due to SHRINKAGE (i.e., loss caused by such factors as evaporation and thefts).

**BOOKKEEPER** individual basically concerned with accounting support functions within the firm. Duties include recording journal entries in the various journals, posting and maintaining the ledger, preparing a trial balance, making up the payroll, and preparing a bank reconciliation. In a smaller firm, the bookkeeper often has a broader responsibility, such as accounts receivable collections.

**BOOKKEEPING** accounting support functions performed by the BOOKKEEPER. Bookkeeping is the most basic of the accounting duties and requires less education and experience.

**BOOKKEEPING CYCLE** *see* ACCOUNTING CYCLE.

**BOOK OF ORIGINAL ENTRY** JOURNAL in which transactions are *first recorded.*

**BOOK-TO-BILL RATIO** a ratio comparing new orders against shipments of specific goods. As an example, the Semiconductor Industry Association's book-to-bill ratio monthly movements are an indication of strength or weakness in the computer business because it shows the current demand for computer chips.

**BOOK VALUE**
1. net amount shown for an asset on the balance sheet. It equals the gross cost less the related valuation account. For example, the book value of an auto is its initial cost less the accumulated depreciation. Since book value is based on HISTORICAL COST, it will differ from market value. Book value is a going-concern value.
2. carrying value of a liability equal to its face value less unamortized discount.
3. the difference between total tangible assets and total liabilities, less the value of the preferred stock. This gives the book value of the common stockholders' equity. Book value of the net assets of a company may have little or no significant relationship to their market value. It was once used as a proxy for a company's intrinsic value. Especially with the new economy, book value is

a less relevant measure for a company's fair value for investors. For example, many new economy companies have assets that do not register significantly on their balance sheet, such as intellectual property, employees, strong brand, and market share. Book value per share of a stock is a company's books based on historical cost. It may differ significantly from current market price per share (as illustrated in the following table). Book value per share of common stock equals common stockholders' equity divided by outstanding common shares.

### Book Value and Market Value for Selected Companies (In billions) (March 23, 2009)

| Company | Book Value | Market Value |
|---|---|---|
| Microsoft (MSFT) | $34.53 | $162.96 |
| IBM (IBM) | 13.08 | 132.44 |
| Wal-Mart Stores (WMT) | 64.90 | 201.93 |
| General Electric (GE) | 105.26 | 110.15 |

Source: moneycentral.msn.com/investor/home.asp

**BOOK VALUE METHOD** manner of accounting for a BOND CONVERSION into stock. The entry is to debit bonds payable and premium on bonds payable (or credit discount on bonds payable) and credit common stock and premium on common stock. Note that the total credit is based on the bond's book value. No gain or loss is recognized. Other entries may also be involved such as recording the interest payment prior to the bond conversion. *See also* MARKET VALUE METHOD.

**BOOK VALUE PER SHARE** worth of each share of stock per the books based on historical cost. It differs from market price per share. Book value per share can be computed for common stock and preferred stock as follows:

Book Value Per Share (Common Stock):

$$\frac{\text{Total Stockholders' Equity} - \left(\begin{array}{c}\text{Liquidation Value} \\ \text{of Preferred Stock}\end{array} + \begin{array}{c}\text{Preferred Dividends} \\ \text{in Arrears}\end{array}\right)}{\text{Total Common Shares Issued and Subscribed at Year-End}}$$

Book Value Per Share (Preferred Stock):

$$\frac{\text{Liquidation Value of Preferred Stock} + \text{Preferred Dividends in Arrears}}{\text{Total Preferred Shares at Year-End}}$$

**BOOLEAN ALGEBRA** the algebra of logic. It is sometimes called symbolic logic. Boolean algebra is a method of expressing logic in a mathematical context. It is primarily concerned with binary operations and based on the cumulative, associative, and distributive laws of binary operations. Boolean algebra provides the theoretical concepts for computer design. It is not used to solve managerial problems directly.

**BOOT**
1. in *computers*, process of starting up a computer. The term *boot* derives from the idea that the computer has to pull itself up by its bootstraps, that is, load into memory a small program that enables it to load larger programs. There are two types of booting operations. One is *cold boot*, which is the operation of booting a computer that has been completely shut down. The other is *warm boot*, which is a restarting operation in which some of the needed programs are already in memory. In the case of the PC, for example, the warm boot is done by pressing the *ctr*, *alt*, and *del* keys simultaneously. On Macs, this can be done by pressing the Restart button.
2. in taxation, cash or property of a type not included in the definition of a nontaxable exchange. The receipt of boot will cause an otherwise tax-free transfer to become taxable to the extent of the smaller of the fair market value of such boot or the realized gain on the transfer. Examples of those types include transfers to controlled corporations.

**BOT** a computer program used to perform structured and repetitive tasks across the Internet. Bots are sometimes referred to as "spyders" or "crawlers" that access Web sites and collect data. A common use of bots is to index Web sites for use by search engines. Bots may also be used for malicious purposes, such as harvesting e-mail addresses from Web sites, to use for spamming.

**BOTTLENECK** an activity for which the work equals or exceeds the capacity of the activity.

**BOTTOM LINE**
1. net income after taxes.
2. expression as to the result of something. An example is the sales generated from an advertising campaign.

**BRAINSTORMING** the exchange of ideas. Brainstorming among CPA firm personnel is mandatory in the planning stage of a financial statement audit and should address the risk of material misstatement due to fraud.

**BRANCH ACCOUNTING** maintenance of a separate accounting system for each branch of one legal entity. The home office opens an account in its general ledger entitled Branch, Branch Control,

Investment in Branch, or some other similar name. Frequently, one account will be used to show the long-term investment in a branch while another account (such as Branch Current) will be used for more common accounts. In the home office ledger, this account or group of accounts is charged for everything sent to the branch or for services rendered to or for the branch, and it is credited for amounts received from the branch. In a similar manner, the branch ledger maintains an equity account entitled Home Office, Home Office Control, Home Office Current, or some other similar name. This account is credited for all assets received by the branch from the home office. It is also credited for all debts incurred for merchandise acquired or for services rendered by the home office for the branch. Such an account would also be credited as a result of expenses incurred by the home office for the benefit of the branch. It is debited for amounts sent by the branch to the home office. In operation, the branch account on the home office books will be debited when the home office account on the branch books is credited, and vice versa. Thus, the balances of such a pair of accounts should be equal in dollar amount, but the balances should be the opposite sides of the respective accounts. Two accounts that have such a relationship are often referred to as RECIPROCAL.

**BREAK-EVEN ANALYSIS** branch of COST-VOLUME-PROFIT (CVP) ANALYSIS that determines the break-even point, which is the level of sales where total costs equal total revenue. Thus, zero profit results. Breakeven sales is computed as follows:

Break-even sales in *units* = Fixed costs/Unit contribution margin.

Break-even sales in *dollars* = Fixed costs/Contribution margin ratio.

For example, assume:

Fixed costs = $15,000.

Unit contribution margin (selling price – unit variable cost) = $15, and

Contribution margin ratio (unit CM/selling price) = .6

Then, break-even sales in *units* = $15,000/$15 = 1,000 units *and* break-even sales in *dollars* = $15,000/.6 = $25,000.

A break-even chart is one in which sales revenue, variable costs, and fixed costs are plotted on the vertical axis while volume is plotted on the horizontal axis. The BREAK-EVEN POINT is the point at which the total sales revenue line intersects the total cost line. See the following sample chart.

**BREAK-EVEN CHART** chart where sales revenue, variable costs, and fixed costs are plotted on the vertical axis while volume is plotted on the horizontal axis. The break-even point is the point where the total sales revenue line intersects the total cost line.

**BREAK-EVEN EQUATION** equation that helps determine BREAK-EVEN SALES.

Let: $p$ = unit selling price
$v$ = unit variable cost
$FC$ = total fixed cost
$x$ = sales in units

Then, the break-even equation can be set up as follows:

$$px = vx + FC$$

For example, assume that $p$ = \$25, $v$ = \$10, $FC$ = \$15,000. The equation is:

$$
\begin{aligned}
\$25x &= \$10x + \$15,000 \\
\$25x - \$10x &= \$15,000 \\
\$15x &= \$15,000 \\
x &= 1,000 \text{ units}
\end{aligned}
$$

Therefore, break-even sales are 1000 units. Break-even sales expressed in dollars are \$25,000 (1,000 units × \$25).

**BREAK-EVEN POINT** *see* BREAK-EVEN SALES.

**BREAK-EVEN SALES** sales with no profit or loss, also called *break-even point*. It is the sales volume, in *units* or in *dollars*, where total sales revenue equals total costs. Thus, zero profit results. *See also* BREAK-EVEN ANALYSIS.

**BREAK-EVEN TIME** more sophisticated version of the payback method. It is the time required for the discounted expected future cash inflows on a project to equal the discounted cumulative cash outflows (usually the initial cost).

**BRIDGE LOAN** short-term loan that is made in expectation of intermediate- or long-term loans; also called a *swing loan*. The interest rate on the bridge loan is generally higher than on longer term loans. An example would be a temporary loan that is made to permit a closing on a building purchase prior to a closing on long-term mortgage financing.

**BROKERAGE FEE** commission paid to a broker who buys and sells securities. Fees vary depending on whether a full-service broker (e.g., one that provides recommendation reports) or a discount broker (e.g., one that just executes orders) is used. An example of a full-service broker is Prudential-Bache Securities. An example of a discount broker is Charles Schwab & Co. Fees also vary within each category so one full-service broker may charge you a different commission rate than another. Brokerage fees may depend on the market price per share and the number of shares traded.

**BROKER CALL LOAN** *see* CALL LOAN.

**BUDGET** quantitative plan of activities and programs expressed in terms of assets, liabilities, revenues, and expenses. Budget participants will be involved in carrying out the plan, or in other quantitative terms such as units of product or service. The budget expresses the organizational goals in terms of specific financial and operating objectives. Advantages of budget preparation are planning, communicating company-wide goals to subunits, fostering cooperation between departments, maintaining control by evaluating actual figures to budget figures, and revealing the interrelationship of one function to another. *See also* MASTER (COMPREHENSIVE) BUDGET.

**BUDGETARY ACCOUNTABILITY** in GOVERNMENT ACCOUNTING, process of recording budgetary amounts in the accounts of a fund. Recording the balances has a dual effect. (1) The control aspect of the budgetary function is stressed, and (2) recognition is given to the legal foundations of the budget. The need for such recording is consistent with the responsibility of fund accounting. It is concerned with performance in terms of authority to act and the action itself. Recording both the budget and actual transactions helps to fix responsibility. The journal entry at the adoption of a budget is:

| | | |
|---|---|---|
| Estimated revenue | $x$ | |
| Fund balance | $x$ or $x$ | |
| Appropriations | | $x$ |

The journal entry to close the budget at year-end is:

| | | |
|---|---|---|
| Appropriations | $x$ | |
| Revenue | $x$ | |
| Estimated revenue | | $x$ |
| Expenditures | | $x$ |
| Encumbrances | | $x$ |
| Fund balance | | $x$ or $x$ |

**BUDGETARY SLACK** intentional underestimation of revenues and/ or overestimation of expenses; also called *budget slack*. This must be avoided if a budget is to have its desired effects. Misstating projections of costs and revenues for this purpose is behavior that is both dysfunctional and unethical.

**BUDGET COMMITTEE** group, usually made up of top management and the chief financial officer, that reviews and approves, or makes appropriate adjustments to the budgets submitted from operational managers.

**BUDGET CONTROL** budgetary actions carried out according to a budget plan. Through the use of a budget as a standard, an organization ensures that managers are implementing its plans and objectives and that their activities are appraised by comparing their actual performance against budgeted performance. Budgets are used as a basis for rewarding or punishing managers, or perhaps for modifying future budgets and plans.

**BUDGETED BALANCE SHEET** schedule for expected assets, liabilities, and stockholders' equity. It projects a company's financial position as of the end of the budgeting year. Reasons for preparing a budgeted balance sheet follow: (1) discloses unfavorable financial condition that management may want to avoid; (2) serves as a final check on the mathematical accuracy of all other budgets; and (3) highlights future resources and obligations.

**BUDGETED INCOME STATEMENT** summary of various component projections of revenues and expenses for the budget period. It indicates the expected net income for the period.

**BUDGET INFORMATION** quantifiable information about an entity's future activities and the revenues or expenses associated with those activities.

**BUDGETING FUND** annual budgets of estimated revenues and estimated expenditures prepared for most governmental funds. The approved budgets of such funds are recorded in "budgetary accounts" in the accounting system to provide control over governmental revenues and expenditures.

**BUDGETING MODELS** mathematical models that generate a profit planning budget. The models help managerial accountants and budget analysts answer a variety of what-if questions. The resultant calculations provide a basis for choice among alternatives under conditions of uncertainty. Budgeting models are usually quantitative and computer-based. There are primarily two approaches to modeling in the corporate budgeting process: SIMULATION and OPTIMIZATION MODEL. *See also* FINANCIAL MODEL; SIMULATION MODELS.

**BUDGET MANUAL** collection of procedures that describe how a budget is to be prepared. Items usually appearing in a budget manual include a budget planning calendar and distribution instructions for all budget schedules. Distribution instructions are important because, once a schedule is prepared, other departments in the organization use the schedule to prepare their own budgets. Without distribution instructions, someone who needs a particular schedule might be overlooked.

**BUDGET PLANNING CALENDAR** schedule of activities for the development and adoption of the budget. It should include a list of dates indicating when specific information is to be provided to others by each information source. The preparation of a master budget usually takes several months. For instance, many firms start the budget for the next calendar year in September, anticipating its completion by the first of December. Because all of the individual departmental budgets are based on forecasts prepared by others and the budgets of other departments, a planning calendar is essential to integrate the entire process.

**BUDGET REPORT** report that provides the basis for controlling (monitoring and revising) activities of an organization by comparing actual performance (actual sales or costs) with budgeted performance (budgeted sales or costs). A budget report has columns for budgeted and actual amounts. The difference between the two is the VARIANCE.

**BUDGET VARIANCE**
1. any difference between a budgeted figure and an actual figure.
2. any difference between actual factory overhead costs and standard (flexible budget) costs, multiplied by the standard units of activity allowed for actual production. The budget variance is used in the TWO-WAY ANALYSIS of factory overhead. It includes the fixed and variable spending variances and the variable overhead efficiency variance that are used in the THREE-WAY ANALYSIS.

**BUFFER** area of a computer's memory set aside to hold information temporarily. The buffer compensates for the different rates that hardware devices process data. For instance, the buffer holds data waiting to be printed so that the central processing unit is free to perform other tasks. A buffer is also used to hold information received from a computer in a remote location when doing TELECOMMUNICATIONS. This is known as a *capture buffer*. A down-loaded ASCII file may be loaded into a word processing program and edited. Further, the ASCII data file may then be loaded into a smart telecommunications software program's *transmit buffer* and uploaded to another remote computer over the telephone lines.

**BUG**
1. mistake in a software program. Two types of errors are logic and syntax. A *logic error* is when the program does not conduct the process it was supposed to. A *syntax error* is where the rules of the programming languages are not followed.
2. hardware malfunctioning in the computer system. *See also* DEBUG.

**BULL** stock market jargon for an individual or institution that believes a given stock or the stock market in general will experience a price rise. It is also an adjective to describe an upward price stock movement. *Compare with* BEAR.

**BULLETIN BOARD (BB)**
1. a collection of message boards and files devoted to a particular topic.
2. properly known as the *OTC Bulletin Board*, an electronic quotation service that lists the prices of stocks that don't meet the minimum requirements for listing on a stock exchange or the NASDAQ stock-listing system.

**BUSINESS COMBINATION** alliance of a company and one or more incorporated or unincorporated businesses into a single accounting entity that then carries on the activities of the separate entities. A business combination must be accounted for under the PURCHASE (ACCOUNTING) METHOD. It does *not* cover the transfer of a business to a substitute corporation. The business combination date comes before the CONSOLIDATION date when consolidated financial statements are prepared.

**BUSINESS CONTINUITY PLAN (BCP)** identifies an organzation's exposures to vulnerabilities and how to resume functioning after a major calamity, such as a fire, hurricane, or earthquake. Sometimes referred to as a *Disaster Recovery Plan* (*DSP*).

**BUSINESS CYCLE** recurrence of periods of contracting and expanding economic conditions with effects on growth, employment, and inflation. The business cycle has an impact on corporate expansion, earnings, and cash flow.

**BUSINESS EXPENSE DEDUCTION** allowable reduction of business gross income, usually associated with expenses incurred that are reasonable and necessary for the production of business income. Examples include bad debts, depreciation, employee benefit programs, and insurance. Some business expenses are not deductible in the computation of taxable income (e.g., fines).

**BUSINESS INTELLIGENCE (BI)** software applications used to analyze an organization's raw data using techniques such as data mining, online analytical processing, and querying and reporting. BI is often used to identify inefficient processes that require dramatic reengineering.

**BUSINESS PROCESS** *see* PROCESS.

**BUSINESS PROCESS REENGINEERING (BPR)** the analysis and design of work flow within an organization. It is the key to transforming how people work in order to make an organization more efficient. BPR requires an organization to reexamine its core activity and implement a radical change.

**BYLAWS** self-imposed rules of a corporation. Unlike articles of incorporation, bylaws are not required to be filed with the Secretary of State. *See* ARTICLES OF INCORPORATION.

**BY-PRODUCT** item emerging from a single production process that has a relatively low sales value in comparison with the firm's main or JOINT PRODUCTS. Examples of by-products are sawdust or wood chips in lumber mill operations. Because the relative value of by-products is not very important, it is usually considered undesirable to use a refined accounting method in dealing with by-product costs. Generally, the sales value of by-products is used to reduce the cost of the main products. An alternative accounting approach is to treat the sales value of the by-products as "other revenue."

**BYTE** a basic unit of computing. A byte consists of 8 bits. Traditionally, an alphanumeric character has been represented by a byte. *See also* BITS.

# C

**CAFETERIA PLAN** one permitting employees to choose from a variety of fringe benefits. The tax code provides that, with minor exceptions, no amount shall be included in the gross income of the participant in a cafeteria plan solely because the participant may choose among the benefits (including cash) of the plan.

**CALL**
1. option to buy (or call) an asset at a specified price within a specified period.
2. right to buy 100 shares of stock at a specified price within a specified period. *See also* OPTION.
3. process of redeeming a bond or preferred stock issue before its normal maturity. A security with a CALL PROVISION typically is issued at an interest rate higher than one without a call provision. This is because investors demand it—they look at yield-to-call rather than yield-to-maturity.

**CALLABLE BOND** bond issue with a call (buy back) provision. *See also* CALLABLE SECURITY.

**CALLABLE SECURITY** bond or preferred stock issue with a CALL PROVISION. The provision in the indenture or preferred stock agreement allows an issuing company to redeem the security early. When interest rates are expected to decline, a call provision in the bond issue is desirable from an issuer's standpoint. Such a provision enables the firm to buy back the high-interest security and issue a lower-interest one. *See also* CALL.

**CALL LOAN** one that brokers make from banks to cover the securities positions of their clients; also called *broker call loan*. The rate is quoted daily in newspapers as a money market indicator.

**CALL PREMIUM**
1. amount in excess of par value that a company must pay when it calls a security. It is the difference between the CALL PRICE and the maturity value. The issuer pays the premium to the security holder in order to acquire the outstanding security before the maturity date. The call premium is generally equal to one year's interest if the bond is called in the first year, and it declines at a constant rate each year thereafter.
2. OPTION.

**CALL PRICE** price that must be paid when a security is called. The call price is equal to the par value plus the CALL PREMIUM.

**CALL PROVISION** feature of some bond indentures allowing the issuing company to redeem bonds prior to maturity by paying holders a premium above face value. An issuing company typically wishes to retire a callable bond when interest rates decline.

*CA MAGAZINE* journal published monthly by the Canadian Institute of Chartered Accountants. It is read by accountants in public practice, industry, and government. The subject matter includes information systems, international accounting, professional ethics, estate planning, and taxation. E-mail: camagazine@cica.ca.

**CANADIAN INSTITUTE OF CHARTERED ACCOUNTANTS (CICA)** primary national organization of chartered accountants in Canada. The CICA handbook is the principal authoritative reference for policy on accepted accounting practices in Canada. CICA was originally founded in 1902 as the Dominion Association of Chartered Accountants.

**CANCELED CHECK** draft paid by the bank on which it is drawn and returned to the depositor. The canceled check is in effect the depositor's receipt that the payee has cashed it.

**CAPACITY** ability to produce during a given time period, with an upper limit imposed by the availability of space, machinery, labor, materials, or capital. Capacity may be expressed in units, weights, size, dollars, man-hours, labor cost, etc. Typically, there are five different concepts of capacity.
(1) *Ideal capacity*—volume of activity that could be attained under ideal operating conditions, with minimum allowance for inefficiency. It is the largest volume of output possible. Also called *theoretical capacity*, *engineered capacity*, or *maximum capacity*.
(2) *Practical capacity*—highest activity level at which the factory can operate with an acceptable degree of efficiency, taking into consideration unavoidable losses of productive time (i.e., vacations, holidays, repairs to equipment). Also called *maximum practical capacity*.
(3) *Normal capacity*—average level of operating activity that is sufficient to fill the demand for the company's products or services for a span of several years, taking into consideration seasonal and cyclical demands and increasing or decreasing trends in demand.
(4) *Expected actual capacity*—similar to normal capacity, except it is a short-run level based on demand, it minimizes under- or overapplied overhead but does not provide a consistent basis for assigning overhead cost. Per-unit overhead will fluctuate because of short-term changes in the expected level of output. Also called *planned capacity*.
(5) *Operating capacity*—similar to planned capacity except the time period is within a small slice of a single year (i.e., daily, monthly, quarterly).

**CAPACITY COSTS** fixed costs incurred to provide facilities that increase a firm's ability to produce such as those relating to space, equipment, and factory buildings. They include rents, depreciation, property taxes, and insurance. *See also* DISCRETIONARY (FIXED) COSTS; FIXED COST.

**CAPACITY MANAGEMENT** management of a company's costs of unused (excess) capacity. The unused capacity in production facilities, distribution channels, marketing organizations, and so on are ordinarily not assigned to products or services on a cause-and-effect basis, so their inclusion in overhead rates may distort pricing decisions. Including the fixed costs of unused capacity in a cost-based price results in higher prices and in what is known as the downward (black hole) demand spiral.

**CAPACITY REQUIREMENTS PLANNING (CRP)** system for determining if a planned production schedule can be accomplished with available capacity and, if not, making adjustments as necessary.

**CAPITAL**
1. equity interest of the owner in the business that is the difference between ASSETS and LIABILITIES, also called EQUITY or NET WORTH. In a corporation, capital represents the stockholders' equity. Capital stock consists of common stock and preferred stock. *See also* CAPITAL ACCOUNT; LEGAL CAPITAL: PAID-IN CAPITAL.
2. goods purchased for use in production.
3. WORKING CAPITAL, which is the difference between current assets and current liabilities.
4. long-term assets that are not bought and sold in the ordinary course of business. The term usually refers to FIXED ASSETS such as machinery, equipment, building, and land.

**CAPITAL ACCOUNT** general ledger account describing OWNERS' EQUITY in a business. CAPITAL is the *equity interest*, which is the difference between assets and liabilities. In a sole proprietorship, there is only one capital account since there is only one owner. In a partnership, a capital account exists for each owner. In a corporation, capital represents the STOCKHOLDERS' EQUITY, which equals the capital stock issued plus paid-in capital in excess of par (or stated) value plus retained earnings. DONATED CAPITAL is added to and TREASURY STOCK is deducted from total stockholders' equity in the balance sheet.

**CAPITAL ADDITION**
1. *new* (as opposed to replacement) part added to an existing noncurrent productive asset (e.g., equipment) used for business purposes that increases the useful life and service potential of the asset.
2. in taxation, cost of capital improvements and betterments made to the property by a taxpayer.
3. anything added to long-term productive assets.

**CAPITAL ASSET**
1. asset purchased for use in production over long periods of time rather than for resale. It includes (a) land, buildings, plant and equipment, mineral deposits, and timber reserves; (b) patents, goodwill, trademarks, and leaseholds; and (c) investments in affiliated companies.

2. in taxation, property held by a taxpayer, except cash, inventoriable assets, merchandise held for sale, receivables, and certain intangibles.

3. FIXED ASSET usually consisting of tangible assets such as plant and equipment and intangible assets such as a patent.

**CAPITAL ASSET PRICING MODEL (CAPM)** theory of asset pricing used to analyze the relationship between risk and rates of return in securities. The return of an asset or security is the risk-free return plus a risk premium based on the excess of the return on the market over the risk-free rate multiplied by the asset's systematic risk (which cannot be eliminated by diversification). The model is given as follows:

$$r = r_f + b\,(r_m - r_f)$$

where $r$ = the expected (or required) return on a security, $r_f$ = the risk-free rate (such as a T-bill), $r_m$ = the expected return on the market portfolio (such as Standard & Poor's 500 Stock Composite Index or Dow Jones 30 Industrials), and $b$ = beta, an index of systematic (non-diversifiable, uncontrollable) risk. For example, assume that the risk-free rate ($r_f$) is 8%, and the expected market return ($r_m$) is 12%. Then if $b = 0$, $r = 8\% + 0\,(12\% - 8\%) = 8\%$. If $b = 2.0$, $r = 8\% + 2.0\,(12\% - 8\%) = 16\%$. This shows that the higher the degree of systematic risk ($b$), the higher the return on a given security demanded by investors.

**CAPITAL BUDGET** plan of proposed acquisitions and replacements of long-term assets and their financing. A capital budget is developed using a variety of CAPITAL BUDGETING techniques such as the *payback* method, the NET PRESENT VALUE (NPV) method, or the INTERNAL RATE OF RETURN (IRR) method.

**CAPITAL BUDGETING** process of making long-term planning decisions for capital investments. There are typically two types of investment decisions: (1) Selecting new facilities or expanding existing facilities. Examples include: (a) investments in long-term assets such as property, plant, and equipment; and (b) resource commitments in the form of new product development, market research, refunding of long-term debt, introduction of a computer, etc. (2) Replacing existing facilities with new facilities. Examples include replacing a manual bookkeeping system with a computerized system and replacing an inefficient lathe with one that is numerically controlled. As such, capital budgeting decisions are a key factor in the long-term profitability of a firm. To make wise investment decisions, managers need tools at their disposal that will guide them in comparing the benefits and costs of various investment alternatives. Many techniques used for evaluating investment proposals are widely available. They include *payback*, ACCOUNTING RATE OF RETURN, INTERNAL RATE OF RETURN, and the NET PRESENT VALUE method.

**CAPITAL DECAY**

1. quantification of the lost revenues or reduction in net cash flows sustained by an entity due to obsolete technology.

2. measure of noncompetitiveness.

**CAPITAL EXPENDITURE** outlay charged to a long-term asset account. A capital expenditure either adds a fixed asset unit or increases the value of an existing fixed asset. An example is a new motor for a truck. *See also* REVENUE EXPENDITURE.

**CAPITAL EXPENDITURE BUDGET** plan prepared for individual capital expenditure projects. The time span of this budget depends upon the project. Capital expenditures to be budgeted include replacement, acquisition, or construction of plants and major equipment. *See also* CAPITAL BUDGETING.

**CAPITAL GAIN** tax term involved with selling or exchanging a CAPITAL ASSET.
**Individual:** Maximum tax rate on capital gains is substantially less than the maximum tax rate on ordinary income.
**Corporation:** Capital gains are taxed as ordinary income. *See also* CAPITAL LOSS.

**CAPITAL INTENSIVE** term that describes a company with significant CAPITAL ASSETS (e.g., machinery), such as those in the automobile and airline industries. Capital intensive companies run a higher risk; if there is a downturn in sales, profits will decrease sharply because FIXED COST cannot be reduced in the short-term to meet declining demand. A diagram illustrating the downside risk potential follows:

CAPITAL INTENSIVE DIAGRAM

Downside Risk

Revenue
Fixed Cost
Earnings

*See also* LABOR INTENSIVE.

**CAPITAL INVESTMENT DECISIONS** management decisions about when and how much to spend on capital facilities for the organization.

**CAPITALIZATION**
1. total amount of the various securities issued by a corporation. Capitalization may include bonds, preferred and common stock.
2. a technique used by real estate appraisers to convert the income of a property into a value estimate for that property.

**CAPITALIZATION OF EARNINGS** concept of valuing a business by determining the NET PRESENT VALUE (NPV) of expected future profits. In an economic sense, a company is worth the discounted amount of its net income. The concept can also be applied to valuing a particular asset (e.g., machine), which should theoretically be worth the present value of future earnings to be derived from it.

**CAPITALIZATION OF INTEREST** process of deferring interest as an asset rather than an expense. Interest charges can be deferred only for interest incurred on borrowed funds for the self-construction of an asset or for discrete projects (e.g., real estate). The amount of interest capitalized is based on the company's actual borrowings and interest payments. The interest rate to be used is the rate on the specific borrowing associated with that self-constructed asset. If this cannot be achieved, the weighted-average interest rate on corporate debt is used.

**CAPITALIZATION RATE (CAP RATE)** a tool used by real estate people to determine a value of an investment. It is calculated by dividing a property's net operating income by its purchase price.

**CAPITALIZE** to charge an expenditure to an asset account because it benefits a period in excess of one year. For example, a betterment to a machine would be capitalized to the machinery account.

**CAPITAL LEASE** one in which the LESSEE obtains significant property rights. Although *not* legally a purchase, THEORETICAL SUBSTANCE governs over legal form and requires that the leased property be recorded as an asset on the lessee's books. The asset equals the present value of MINIMUM LEASE PAYMENTS. A capital lease exists if any *one* of the following four criteria is met: (1) the lease transfers ownership of the property to the lessee at the end of the lease term; (2) a BARGAIN PURCHASE OPTION exists; (3) lease term is 75% or more of the life of the property; (4) the present value of minimum lease payments equals or exceeds 90% of the fair value of the property.

**CAPITAL LEVERAGE** *see* FINANCIAL LEVERAGE.

**CAPITAL LOSS** federal tax term for the loss on the sale or exchange of a CAPITAL ASSET.
**Individual:** Capital losses are fully deductible to offset CAPITAL GAINS and can offset $3,000 of ordinary income.
**Corporation:** Capital losses are deductible only to the extent of capital gains.

**CAPITAL MAINTENANCE CONCEPT** principle in accounting stating that earnings can be realized only after an organization's capital has been maintained at a predetermined level.

**CAPITAL MARKET** trading center for long-term debt and corporate stocks. The NEW YORK STOCK EXCHANGE (NYSE), which trades the stocks of many of the larger corporations, is a prime example of a capital market. The *American Stock Exchange* and the regional stock exchanges are also examples. In addition, securities are issued and traded through the thousands of brokers and dealers on the OVER-THE-COUNTER market.

**CAPITAL PROJECTS FUND** in governmental accounting, a fund that accounts for financial resources to be used for the acquisition or construction of capital facilities. The total cost of a capital project is accumulated in a single expenditures account, which accumulates until the project is completed, at which time the fund ceases to exist.

**CAPITAL RATIONING** selecting the mix of acceptable projects that provides the highest overall NET PRESENT VALUE (NPV) when a company has a limit on the budget for capital spending. The PROFITABILITY INDEX is used widely in ranking projects competing for limited funds.

**CAPITAL RECOVERY ALLOWANCE** in *taxation*, term describing a cost recovery of capital. An example is depreciation expense taken over the expected life of the capital asset, although an ACCELERATED COST RECOVERY SYSTEM (ACRS) ignores such time-honored concepts as useful life and salvage value. A recovery allowance may also take the form of depreciation with shorter useful lives and immediate expensing (e.g., research and development). *See also* DEPRECIATION.

**CAPITAL STOCK** equity shares in a corporation authorized by its Articles of Incorporation and issued to stockholders. The two basic types of capital stock are COMMON STOCK and PREFERRED STOCK.

**CAPITAL STOCK SUBSCRIBED** shares acquired under an installment plan; also termed *subscribed stock*. In this way by making a down payment, a potential stockholder reserves shares that may be issued only when full payment has been received. The entry at the time of subscription is to debit cash and/or subscriptions receivable and credit capital stock subscribed and premium on capital stock, if any. Capital stock subscribed is shown under capital stock in the stockholders' equity section of the balance sheet. If a subscriber defaults on the subscription, the company must account for it in accordance with the laws of the states of incorporation.

**CAPITAL STRUCTURE** composition of common stock, preferred stock and the various classes thereof, retained earnings, and long-term debt maintained by the business entity in financing its assets. However, not everybody agrees that long-term debt is part of the capital structure. Proponents say it finances long-term assets. Opponents say it is debt—due to creditors—which means it has significantly different characteristics compared to any form of owners' equity.

**CAPITAL SURPLUS** paid-in capital not assigned to common stock. An example is the amount received from stockholders in excess of the par value of shares issued. Capital surplus is an archaic term. *Premium on capital stock* is preferred.

**CARRYING CHARGE** *see* CARRYING COSTS.

**CARRYING COSTS** expenses incurred because a firm keeps inventories, also called *holding costs*. They include interest forgone on money invested in inventory, storage cost, taxes, and insurance. The greater the inventory level, the higher the carrying costs.

**CARRYING VALUE** amount shown on an entity's books for assets, liabilities, or owner's equity, net of reductions or offsets such as for accumulated depreciation, allowance for bad debts, and bond discount; also called BOOK VALUE. It may refer to the entire firm's excess of total assets over total liabilities.

**CARRYOVER BASIS** method used in the valuation of property acquired from a decedent for tax purposes. The unified transfer tax of 1976 provides for the valuation of property to be the adjusted basis immediately preceding death. This adjusted basis is then further adjusted with respect to such aspects of a transfer as appreciated property, election of fair market value for personal items, and exceptions for small estates.

**CASH** money deposited in a bank and items that a bank will accept for immediate deposit (e.g., paper money, coins, checks, money orders). Items not included in the definition of cash are postdated checks, IOUs, and notes receivable. The cash on hand and cash on deposit in the bank are shown in the balance sheet as one figure. Cash is the most liquid of the current assets and is listed first. Note that *restricted* cash in a bank account is not considered a current asset. An example is cash held in a foreign country where remission restrictions exist.

**CASH BASIS ACCOUNTING** method of recognizing revenue and expenses when cash is received or disbursed rather than when earned or incurred. A service business not dealing in inventory has the option of using the cash basis or *accrual* basis. Individual taxpayers preparing their tax returns are essentially on the cash basis.

**CASH BUDGET** budget for cash planning and control that presents expected cash inflow and outflow for a designated time period. The cash budget helps management keep cash balances in reasonable relationship to its needs. It aids in avoiding idle cash and possible cash shortages. The cash budget typically consists of four major sections: (1) *receipts section*, which is the beginning cash balance, cash collections from customers, and other receipts; (2) *disbursement section* comprised of all cash payments made by purpose; (3) *cash surplus or deficit section* showing the difference between cash receipts and cash payments; and (4) *financing section* providing a detailed account of the borrowings and repayments expected during the period.

**CASH COW** a business or the segment of the business that generates tons of money.

**CASH DISBURSEMENT JOURNAL** book used to record all payments made in cash such as for accounts payable, merchandise purchases, and operating expenses; also termed *cash payments journal*. There are usually separate columns for the date, check number, explanation, cash credit, purchase discount credit, other credit, accounts debited, accounts payable debit, purchases debit, and other debt. *See also* CASH RECEIPTS JOURNAL.

**CASH DISCOUNT** *see* SALES DISCOUNT.

**CASH DIVIDEND** usual type of dividend paid to stockholders. It is typically expressed on a dollar-and-cents-per-share basis. However, with preferred stock, the dividend is expressed as a percentage of par value. Dividends are paid on outstanding shares. Assume on 11/15/2014, a cash dividend of $1.50 per common share is declared. Issued shares are 12,000 and treasury shares are 2000. The record date is 12/20/2014. Payment is to be made on 1/15/2015. The entry on 11/15/2014 is to debit retained earnings and credit cash dividends payable for $15,000 (10,000 shares × $1.50). Cash dividends payable is a current liability. No entry is made on the record date. On 1/15/2015, cash dividends payable is debited and cash credited for $15,000. Assume there are 30,000 shares of $10 par value, 8% preferred stock.

The cash dividend is:

$$
\begin{array}{rl}
30,000 & \text{shares} \\
\times \quad \$10 & \text{par value} \\
\hline
\$300,000 & \text{total par value} \\
\times \quad .08 & \text{dividend rate} \\
\hline
\$\,24,000 & \text{cash dividend}
\end{array}
$$

**CASH EQUIVALENT**
1. immediately realizable money that can be obtained in an exchange of goods or services.
2. financial instruments of high liquidity and safety. Examples are a TREASURY BILL and a MONEY MARKET fund.
3. in preparing the STATEMENT OF CASH FLOWS, a short-term, highly liquid investment having an original maturity of three months or less.

**CASH EQUIVALENT VALUE** funds that could be received upon the sale of an asset. It is the current realizable value for the item obtained in an exchange. *See also* FAIR MARKET VALUE; MARKET VALUE.

**CASH FLOW**
1. cash receipts minus cash disbursements from a given operation or asset for a given period. *Cash flow* and *cash inflow* are often used interchangeably.
2. in CAPITAL BUDGETING, monetary value of the expected benefits and costs of a project. It may be in the form of cash savings in operating costs or the difference between additional dollars received and additional dollars paid out for a given period.
3. *cash basis* net income. The procedures for converting an accrual basis net income amount to a cash basis net income figure are as follows:

|         | Accrual basis net income |
| :------ | :----------------------- |
| +       | Non-cash charges such as depreciation |
| + or –  | Changes in accounts receivable, inventory, prepaid expenses, accounts payable, and accrued liabilities |
| =       | Cash basis net income |

**CASH FLOW FORECASTING** future cash flow predictions including cash collections from customers, investment income, and cash disbursements.

**CASH FLOW RATIOS** ratios showing the cash position or change in cash of the business. Higher levels of cash flow indicate improved cash earnings and liquidity. Earnings are of higher quality if they are backed up by cash because cash can be used to pay debt, purchase fixed assets, and so on. Some cash flow ratios are (1) cash flow from operations/net income, (2) cash flow coverage equal to cash flow from operations/cash expenses, and (3) cash reinvestment ratio equal to cash used/cash obtained. A high cash reinvestment ratio indicates that more cash is being used in the business.

**CASH FLOW STATEMENT** statement showing from what sources cash has come into the business and on what the cash has been spent. The net result is reflected in the balance of the cash account as of a certain period of time. This is a valuable tool in FINANCIAL STATE-MENT ANALYSIS. *See also* STATEMENT OF CASH FLOWS.

**CASH FLOWS TO ASSETS** ratio of net cash flows from operating activities to average total assets. Used to measure the ability of assets to generate operating cash flows.

**CASH FLOWS TO SALES** ratio of net cash flows from operating activities to sales. Used to measure the ability of sales to generate operating cash flows.

**CASH-FLOW-TO-CAPITAL-EXPENDITURES RATIO** computation indicating a company's ability to maintain plant and equipment from cash provided by operations, rather than by borrowing or issuing new stock. The ratio equals cash flow from operations less dividends divided by expenditures for plant and equipment.

**CASH-FLOW-TO-TOTAL-DEBT RATIO** rate indicating a company's ability to satisfy its debts. It is useful in predicting BANKRUPTCY. The ratio equals cash flow from operations divided by total liabilities.

**CASH FLOW YIELD** ratio of net cash flows from operating activities to net income. Used to measure the ability of a company to generate operating cash flows in relation to net income.

**CASH-GENERATING EFFICIENCY** ability of a company to generate cash from its current or continuing operations.

**CASHIER'S CHECK** check drawn by a bank on its own funds and signed by its cashier. It is thus a direct obligation of the bank. A cashier's check is distinguished from a MONEY ORDER, which is an order for the payment of money, as one issued by one bank or post office and payable at another.

**CASH PAYMENTS JOURNAL** *see* CASH DISBURSEMENT JOURNAL.

**CASH RECEIPTS JOURNAL** book used to record all transactions involving the receipt of cash. Examples are cash sales, receipt of interest and dividend revenue, collections from customer accounts, and cash sale of assets. Typically, there are separate columns for the date, explanation, cash debit, sales discount debit, other debit, account credit, accounts receivable credit, and other credit. *See also* CASH DISBURSEMENT JOURNAL.

**CASH SHORTAGE AND OVERAGE** situation in which the physical amount of cash on hand differs from the book recorded amount of cash. When a business is involved with over-the-counter cash receipts, occasional errors may occur in making change. The cash shortage or overage is revealed when the physical cash count at the end of the day does not agree with the cash register tape. Assuming that the count is $600 and the cash register reading shows $620, the cash shortage and overage account would be charged for $20. It is shown in the income statement.

**CASH SURRENDER VALUE** portion of life insurance premiums paid that can be received if the policy is canceled. The beneficiary has the option of canceling the policy. Cash surrender value is classified on the balance sheet under Investments. As the company pays premiums, part represents an expense and part applies to the cash surrender value. The difference between the premium paid and the increase in cash surrender value represents an expense.

Cash surrender value of life insurance applies to ordinary life and limited payment policies. Term insurance does not have a cash surrender value.

**CASH-TO-CURRENT-LIABILITIES RATIO** computation that measures a company's ability to satisfy short-term financial obligations immediately and is therefore a good *liquidity measure*. The ratio equals cash plus near-cash and marketable securities divided by current liabilities.

**CASUALTY LOSS** loss arising from the partial or complete destruction of property resulting from circumstances of a sudden, unexpected or unusual nature, such as storms, floods, fires, and auto accidents. These circumstances must be identifiable as the proximate cause of such a loss for classificatory purposes. Individuals may deduct a casualty loss as an itemized deduction to the extent of any amount not compensated for by insurance or otherwise if: (1) the loss is incurred in a trade or business; (2) the loss is incurred in a transaction entered into for profit; and (3) the loss is caused by fire, storm, shipwreck, or other casualty or by theft. In a business, casualty losses are typically shown as an extraordinary item net of tax in the income statement. For example, if the casualty loss is $10,000 and the company is in the 34% tax bracket, the after-tax loss presented in the income statement is $6,600 = $10,000 (1 − .34).

**CDOs** *see* CORPORATE DEVELOPMENT OFFICERS (CDOS).

**CD-ROM (COMPACT DISK READ ONLY MEMORY)** an optical-disk format that is used for prerecorded text, graphics, and sound.

**CEILING** amount equal to the NET REALIZABLE VALUE. The market cannot exceed the ceiling (upper limit) when employing the LOWER OF COST OR MARKET method of inventory valuation. If market is greater than the ceiling, the ceiling is chosen. For example, if market is $12 and ceiling is $9, the inventory value would be $9. However, if market was below the ceiling, the market value would be used.

**CELL** point of intersection between a row and column in an electronic spreadsheet. The spreadsheet's cells can be related to one another, through arithmetic and logical formulas, to create financial data. When data in one cell is changed such as in "what-if" analysis, the software instantly calculates the effects of the change on all cells displaying the results.

**CELLULAR MANUFACTURING** groups of machinery that are closely associated with each family of parts.

**CENTRAL ADMINISTRATION COSTS** allocated common costs.

**CENTRAL BETA RISK** *see* TYPE II ERROR.

**CENTRALIZATION** situation in which decision-making power is at the top of an organization and there is little delegation of authority. It is the opposite of DECENTRALIZATION. Centralization and decentralization are really a matter of degree. Full centralization means minimum autonomy and maximum restrictions on operations of subunits of the organization. As an organization grows in size and complexity, decentralization is generally considered to be effective and efficient.

**CENTRAL LIMIT THEOREM** one of the most important theorems in statistics. It says: If a large number of random samples of size $\mu$ are chosen from virtually any population (with mean $\mu$ and standard deviation $\sigma$), the means ($\bar{x}$'s) of these samples will themselves follow a NORMAL DISTRIBUTION with a mean

$$\mu_{\bar{x}} = \mu$$

and a standard deviation $\sigma_{\bar{x}}$, called the standard error of the mean, given by

$$\sigma_{\bar{x}} = \frac{\sigma}{\sqrt{n}}$$

Two important implications of this theorem follow:

(1) Random samples can be drawn from any population, normally distributed or not. Thus, even if it is known that the dollar value of a certain inventory item is not normally distributed, the theorem can be invoked and the assumption made that the sample mean inventory dollar value will be normally distributed.

(2) The theorem allows statements to be made about the value of the population mean without looking at the entire population. Thus, interval estimates can be made about the true value of an inventory item. Such interval estimates are called CONFIDENCE INTERVAL.

**CENTRAL PROCESSING UNIT (CPU)** component of a computer hardware system that combines control unit, storage unit, and arithmetic unit. The control unit interprets the instructions given to the computer. *Internal* storage is where the program of instructions is kept and where data from the input devices are sent. *External* storage can consist of disk and tapes. The arithmetic unit actually does the calculation required by the program.

**CERTAINTY** situation in which there is absolutely no doubt about which event will occur, and there is only one STATE OF NATURE with 100% probability attached. *See also* DECISION MAKING UNDER CERTAINTY.

**CERTAINTY EQUIVALENT** amount of cash (or rate of return) that a decision maker would require *with certainty* to make the recipient indifferent between this certain sum and a particular *uncertain, risky* sum. Multiplying the expected cash inflow by the certainty cash equivalent coefficient results in an *equivalent certain* cash inflow. For example, given the expected cash inflows and certainty cash equivalent coefficients, the equivalent certain cash inflows are obtained as follows:

| Year | Cash Inflows | Certainty Equivalent Coefficients | Equivalent Certain Cash Inflows |
|------|--------------|-----------------------------------|---------------------------------|
| 1 | $10,000 | 0.95 | $ 9,500 |
| 2 | 15,000 | 0.80 | 12,000 |
| 3 | 20,000 | 0.70 | 14,000 |

**CERTIFICATE AUTHORITY (CA)** an independent trusted organization that issues digital certificates used for digital signatures and the creation of public and private keys. It is the CA's job to verify the identity of the individual or organization that is granted the certificate.

**CERTIFICATE OF DEPOSIT (CD)** special type of time deposit. A CD is an investment instrument available at financial institutions generally offering a fixed rate of return for a specified period (such as three months, six months, one year, or longer). The depositor agrees not to withdraw funds for the time period of the CD. If the funds are withdrawn, a significant penalty is charged. The fixed rate of return nominally increases with the amount or the term of the investment.

**CERTIFIED ACCOUNTANT** title given by the Association of Certified Accountants in the United Kingdom, Canada, Australia, India, and other British Commonwealth countries. They use the initials ACA (for member of the Association of Certified Accountants) or FCCA, which identifies a Fellow of the Association, one who has passed additional requirements. The accountant is authorized to provide an audit opinion on the propriety of a company's financial statements.

**CERTIFIED CHECK** depositor's check that a bank guarantees to pay. The funds are precommitted. When preparing a BANK RECONCILIA- TION, a certified check is *not* considered outstanding since both par- ties, the company and the bank, know about it.

**CERTIFIED FINANCIAL PLANNER (CFP)** professional designa- tion requiring a high level of skill and competence in the analysis of client financial conditions and the development of client-oriented personal financial plans. Candidates must pass a series of national examinations administered by the College for Financial Planning, Denver, Colorado (www.fp.edu). The CFP program consists of six separate parts, each of which is a three-hour written examination. The program includes the following parts: (1) introduction to financial planning; (2) risk management; (3) investments; (4) tax planning and management; (5) retirement planning and employee benefits; and (6) estate planning. Candidates must also meet other educational and work experience requirements of the college in order to obtain the right to use the college's designation of Certified Financial Planner (CFP). *See also* FINANCIAL PLANNER.

**CERTIFIED FINANCIAL STATEMENT** one that is accompanied by the independent CPA's AUDIT REPORT. *See also* AUDIT OPINION.

**CERTIFIED FRAUD EXAMINER (CFE)** a new designation offered by the Association of Certified Fraud Examiners (www.acfe.org), established in 1988 and based in Austin, Texas. Each member of the association is designated a Certified Fraud Examiner (CFE) who has earned certification after an extensive application process and upon passing the uniform CFE examination is trained in the highly spe- cialized aspects of detecting, investigating, and deterring fraud and white-collar crime.

**CERTIFIED INFORMATION SYSTEMS AUDITOR (CISA)** profes- sional designation in the area of information systems audits. It is con- ferred by the EDP Auditor Association to candidates who successfully pass the examination. The examination covers the following topics: (1) application systems controls; (2) data integrity review; (3) systems development life; (4) application development review; (5) maintenance review; (6) general operational procedures; (7) security review; (8)

systems software review; (9) acquisition review; (10) data processing resource management review; and (11) information systems audit.

**CERTIFIED INSOLVENCY AND REORGANIZATION ACCOUNTANT (CIRA)** another certification available to the forensic accountant. The CIRA's professional accounting experience includes insolvency and reorganizational accounting. There are three parts to the exam. The areas of concentration are financial reporting and taxes, managing turnaround and bankruptcy cases, and plan development and accounting.

**CERTIFIED INTERNAL AUDITOR (CIA)** recognition given by the Institute of Internal Auditors (www.theiaa.org) after a candidate has satisfied the organization's professional requirements. The INTERNAL AUDITOR verifies the accuracy of a company's record keeping and accounts as well as performing operational audits. The CIA must abide by a code of ethics.

**CERTIFIED MANAGEMENT ACCOUNTANT (CMA)** program requiring candidates to pass a series of uniform examinations covering a wide range of subjects. The examination consists of the following four parts: (1) Business Analysis, (2) Management Accounting and Reporting, (3) Strategic Management, and (4) Business Applications. The objectives of the CMA program are fourfold: (1) to establish management accounting as a recognized profession by identifying the role of the management accountant and financial manager, the underlying body of knowledge, and a course of study by which such knowledge is acquired; (2) to encourage higher educational standards in the management accounting field; (3) to establish an objective measure of an individual's knowledge and competence in the field of management accounting; and (4) to encourage continued professional development by management accountants. For more information, call IMA at (800) 638-4427, ext. 265 or (201) 573-6300 or visit its Web site: http://www.imanet.org/.

**CERTIFIED PUBLIC ACCOUNTANT (CPA)** title awarded in the United States to accountants who meet stringent professional qualifications. State authorities confer the title on those who pass the Uniform CPA Examination, administered by the AMERICAN INSTITUTE OF CERTIFIED PUBLIC ACCOUNTANTS (AICPA) (www.aicpa.org) and who satisfy the experience requirement of the particular state. The CPA is licensed to render an AUDIT OPINION on the fairness of a company's financial statements. A CPA in one state (e.g., New York) may be allowed to practice in another state (e.g., California) if reciprocal agreements exist.

**CHAIN LINKS** series of linked data items.

**CHANCE VARIANCES** *see* RANDOM VARIANCES.

**CHANGE IN ACCOUNTING ESTIMATE** restatement of an accounting assumption or forecast. Examples include changing the economic (useful) life or salvage value of a fixed asset. A change in accounting estimate is accounted for *prospectively* over current and future years. This will cause a change to the expense account in future years. Prior years are not restated. Note that a change in estimate coupled with a change in principle is accounted for as a change in estimate. Disclosure should be made of the particulars surrounding the estimate change.

**CHANGE IN ACCOUNTING PRINCIPLE** a change in principle justified by (1) a new FASB pronouncement, (2) a new tax law, (3) a new AICPA recommended practice, (4) a change in circumstances, or (5) the need to more readily conform to industry practice. A change in principle should be made only when necessary. Once an accounting principle is adopted, it is presumed that the principle should not be changed for events or transactions of a similar nature. A method used for a transaction that is being terminated or was a single, nonrecurring event in the past should not be changed. Retrospective application is required for all direct effects and the related income tax effects of a change in principle. Direct effects are changes in assets or liabilities necessary to effect a change in accounting principle. An example of a direct effect is an adjustment to an inventory balance to effect a change in inventory valuation method. Related changes, such as an effect on deferred income tax assets or liabilities or an impairment adjustment resulting from applying the lower-of-cost-or-market test to the adjusted inventory balance, also are examples of direct effects of a change in accounting principle. Footnote disclosure should be made of the nature of and justification for a change in principle, including an explanation of why the new principle is preferred. *See also* ACCOUNTING CHANGE AND ERROR CORRECTIONS.

**CHANGE IN REPORTING ENTITY** term used when two or more previously separate companies are combined into one. Changes in reporting entity are shown as the restatement of all comparative statements. The nature of the change in entity and the reasons for the change are described in the notes to the financial statements. In addition, the effects of changes on income before extraordinary items, net income, other comprehensive income, and related per-share amounts are disclosed for all periods presented.

**CHAPTER 7** statute of the 1978 Bankruptcy Reform Act that covers LIQUIDATION proceedings. As a general rule, any debtor subject to Chapter 7 is also subject to CHAPTER 11. Liquidation proceedings are used to eliminate most of the debts of the debtor. Chapter 7 provides for a court-appointed trustee to make management changes, secure additional financing, and operate the debtor business so as to prevent further loss. The fundamental assumption of the proceedings is that honest debtors may sometimes not be able to discharge fully their debts and that fairness and public policy both dictate that the debtor be granted a "fresh start" in both personal and business lives. *See also* BANKRUPTCY; CHAPTER 11.

**CHAPTER 11** statute of the 1978 Bankruptcy Reform Act. It covers the specific proceedings and provisions regarding REORGANIZATION and the execution of such a plan of an individual, partnership, corporation, or municipality. This statute provides possible solutions to insolvency and the difficulty of satisfying creditor claims. Under Chapter 11, unless the court rules otherwise, the debtor remains in control of the business and its operations. Debtor and creditors are allowed to work together, thus making possible the restructuring of debt, the rescheduling of payments, and even the granting of loans by the creditors to the debtor. *See also* BANKRUPTCY; CHAPTER 7.

**CHAPTER 13** court approved and coordinated plan that pays off an individual's debts over a period of three years; also called *wage-earner plan.* It is a plan for the repayment of debts that allows a credit user in serious financial difficulty to pay off credit obligations without declaring bankruptcy. *See also* BANKRUPTCY (PERSONAL).

**CHARGE**
1. term used to describe a debit to an account.
2. to debit an account.
3. to buy on credit.

**CHARGE AND DISCHARGE STATEMENT** summary accounting of the principal and income associated with a fiduciary responsibility such as that of an administrator or trustee of an estate. The statement usually first describes the *charge* as to principal, namely assets or gains, and the credit or *discharge* of debts, expenses, or legacies distributed. Next the statement describes the charges and discharges as to income, for example, interest received and discharges such as income taxes, administrative expenses, and distributions to income beneficiaries. Finally the form of the statement clearly states and reconciles both the principal and income balances as properly administrated as of a given date.

**CHARITABLE CONTRIBUTIONS DEDUCTION** itemized deduction for amounts given to qualified *domestic* organizations. A charitable contribution may be deductible even though all or some portion of the funds of the donee organization may be used in foreign countries for charitable or educational purposes. Generally, contributions made to foreign organizations are not deductible. Taxpayers not itemizing deductions cannot deduct charitable contributions. To the extent that untaxed appreciation of charitable contribution property is allowed as a regular tax deduction, the appreciation is a preference item for the alternative minimum tax rules.

**CHARTERED ACCOUNTANT (CA)** (www.icaew.co.uk) recognition given by the chartered institutes in present and former British Commonwealth countries including Australia, Canada, India, New Zealand, Nigeria, Pakistan, South Africa, and the United Kingdom to individuals meeting examination and practical experience requirements. The chartered accountant is authorized to render an audit opinion on a company's financial statements.

**CHARTERED FINANCIAL ANALYST (CFA)** title given by the CFA Institute (www.cfainstitute.org) to an individual meeting examination and experience requirements. A CFA is recognized as a specialist in analyzing companies for investment or credit purposes.

**CHARTERED FINANCIAL CONSULTANT (ChFC)** professional designation given by the American College, Bryn Mawr, Pennsylvania (www.theamericancollege.edu). It is conferred upon candidates who will provide financial planning services for clients. To earn the ChFC designation the candidate must complete ten courses, six required and four electives. The six required courses are: (1) financial services, (2) income taxation, (3) financial statement analysis/individual insurance benefits, (4) investments, (5) estate and gift tax planning, and (6) financial and estate planning applications. *See also* CERTIFIED FINANCIAL PLANNER (CFP); FINANCIAL PLANNER.

**CHARTERED MUTUAL FUND COUNSELOR (ChMFC)** a new designation offered by the National Endowment for Financial Education, showing a financial advisor's enhanced ability to advise clients on their mutual fund questions and concerns.

**CHARTING** method used by a technical analyst to evaluate market trends and price behavior of individual securities. Standard & Poor's *Trendline* is one publication providing charting information on many securities. In order to interpret charts the analyst must be able to evaluate chart patterns (e.g., head and shoulders) and detect buy and sell indicators. Three basic types of charts are line, bar, and point-and-figure. Charts can reveal whether the market is in a major upturn or downturn and help analysts predict whether the trend will reverse. The analyst can see what price may occur on a given stock or market average. Further, charts help to predict the magnitude of a price swing.

**CHART OF ACCOUNTS** a list of ledger account names and numbers arranged in the order in which they customarily appear in the financial statements. The chart serves as a useful source for locating a given account within the ledger. The numbering system for the chart of accounts must leave room for new accounts. A range of numbers is assigned to each financial statement category. For example, asset accounts may be assigned the numbers 1–100 and liabilities assigned 101–200. For large businesses, a wider range of numbers would be required for each grouping. In fact, some companies employ a three-digit numbering system for each account. In such a case, the first digit identifies the financial statement category and the remaining digits apply to the position of that account within that category. For example, 1 may be the first digit for Assets, and Cash, being the first asset account, would be identified as 101.

**CHATTEL MORTGAGE** mortgage on personal (as opposed to real) property. *See also* MORTGAGES.

**CHECK**
1. draft drawn upon a bank, payable upon demand to the person named upon the draft.
2. to determine an item's accuracy such as by retotaling charges on an invoice or auditing source documents.

**CHECK CLEARING FOR THE 21st CENTURY ACT** a federal law that went into effect in October 2004 allowing banks to process checks faster by making electronic copies of checks. People who write checks can no longer count on several days of "float" time and getting back canceled checks.

**CHECK DIGIT** numeric digit added to a number, such as an employee identification number or account number, for the purpose of detecting data entry errors. A check digit serves as a redundancy check. For instance, if an organization uses a nine-digit account number, a tenth digit is added as the check digit. This tenth digit's value is calculated based upon the nine-digit account number.

**CHIEF EXECUTIVE OFFICER (CEO)** the highest-ranking executive in an organization. The CEO is responsible for developing corporate strategy and setting its vision. The CEO is also responsible for the organizational culture and setting tone at the top. The CEO conveys values through his or her actions. The CEO leads the senior management of an organization and is responsible for hiring and firing senior management, as well as resolving conflicts among senior management. The CEO reports to the BOARD OF DIRECTORS. Sometimes, the CEO is a member of the board of directors and may even chair the board.

**CHIEF FINANCIAL OFFICER (CFO)** executive who directs all financial aspects of the business. Examples of functions performed are keeping accounting records, designing accounting systems and procedures, financial forecasting, and using funds. Large companies have financial vice-presidents (or vice-presidents of finance) and controllers and treasurers. A smaller company may have one officer responsible for the accounting and treasury functions; frequently that official has the title of controller. INTERNAL AUDIT responsibilities are often assigned to the controller.

**CHIEF INVESTMENT OFFICER (CIO)** an executive who is responsible for managing and monitoring the company's investment portfolio. Responsibilities include managing the investment portfolio, investing surplus funds, managing pension monies, maintaining liaison with the investment community, and counseling with financial analysts.

**CHIEF OPERATING OFFICER (COO)** a corporate officer in charge of the daily running of the business. He or she may be the president or executive vice-president. The COO reports directly to the chief executive officer.

**CIPHERTEXT** encrypted text. Text before encryption is called plaintext. Ciphertext is generated by performing encryption on plaintext.

**CIRCULATING CAPITAL** that part of an entity's investment that is continually used up and renewed to enable ongoing operations, such as materials, labor, and overhead costs.

**CIVIL PENALTY** a fine imposed by a taxing authority for failure to comply with tax laws and regulations. Civil penalties may be imposed on taxpayers and tax return preparers. Civil penalties, which are less severe than criminal penalties, include penalties for late filing of tax returns and late payment of taxes.

**CLASSICAL PROBABILITY** number of outcomes favorable to the occurrence of an event divided by the total number of possible outcomes. In order for this ratio to be valid, each of the outcomes must be equally likely. Distributions are gained from actual occurrences in long-run experience and experimentation. An example is repeated trials under a constant-cause situation. It is useful in estimating dollar value, quantity, or other characteristics of a given universe. For example, the probability of rolling a 4 on one die is 1/6.

**CLASSIFICATION AND UNDERSTANDABILITY** an assertion in an entity's financial statements made by management that (1) financial information is appropriately presented and described, and (2) disclosures are expressed in a clear and comprehensible manner.

**CLASSIFICATION OF ASSETS** process of grouping economic resources under appropriate categories. Asset categories include CURRENT ASSETS, FIXED ASSETS, INTANGIBLE ASSETS, INVESTMENTS, and DEFERRED COSTS. Assets are classified into major groupings to facilitate analysis of the entity's financial health. For instance, a company's liquidity can be appraised by concentrating on the current assets less prepaid expenses which are available to meet short-term debt.

**CLASSIFICATION OF LIABILITIES** process of grouping obligations by when they are due. The categories used are CURRENT LIABILITY and LONG-TERM LIABILITY. Liability classification assists financial statement users in evaluating the firm's financial position and ability to take on additional short-term or long-term debt.

**CLASSIFICATION OF STOCKHOLDERS' EQUITY** process of using group headings within the stockholders' equity section of the balance sheet. The headings include capital stock, paid-in capital, retained earnings, and treasury stock. Capital stock represents stock that has been issued (e.g., issued common or preferred stock) and stock to be issued at a later date (e.g., stock option). Paid-in capital consists of such items as contributed capital in excess of par and donations. Retained earnings are the accumulated earnings less cash dividends. Treasury stock is a deduction in determining stockholders' equity.

**CLASSIFIED STOCK** equity separated into different classes. For example, common stock may consist of Class A and Class B. Typically, Class A has greater voting rights. It may also contain dividend and liquidation privileges.

**CLAYTON ANTITRUST ACT** ANTITRUST LAW passed in 1914 as an amendment to the SHERMAN ANTITRUST ACT of 1890. The Act listed four illegal practices in restraint of competition. It outlawed price discrimination, tying contracts and exclusive dealerships, and horizontal mergers. It also outlawed interlocking directorates (the practice of having the same people serve as directors of two or more competing firms).

**CLEAN OPINION** *see* UNQUALIFIED (unmodified) OPINION.

**CLEAN SURPLUS CONCEPT** doctrine holding that entries to retained earnings are limited to record only periodic earnings and dividends.

**CLEARING ACCOUNT** usually a temporary account containing costs or amounts that are to be transferred to another account. An example is the income summary account containing revenue and expense amounts to be transferred to retained earnings at the close of a fiscal period.

**CLEARING HOUSE STATEMENT** report on a security or commodity broker's trading activity. This statement is submitted to the clearing house of the exchange by the broker, and through the reconciliation of other broker members' statements, amounts due or payable and net quantities of securities or commodities deliverable to or receivable by each broker are determined.

**CLOSED CORPORATION** *see* PRIVATELY HELD COMPANY.

**CLOSED-END MUTUAL FUND** one whose shares are limited and traded like the common stock of a corporation. Once shares are issued, the only way an investor can purchase or sell the fund shares is in the open market. An example of a closed-end mutual fund is Prudential-Bache Securities' Global Yield Fund. *See also* OPEN-END MUTUAL FUND.

**CLOSED SYSTEM** enterprise-wide scope of organization resource costs that are all reassigned through activities to final cost objects.

**CLOSELY HELD CORPORATION** firm that has only a few stockholders. It contrasts with a *privately held corporation* in that a closely held corporation is public although few of the shares are traded. The so-called "corporate pocket-books" may become subject to the additional personal holding company tax on income not distributed. For example, deductions and losses in transactions between a major stockholder and the corporation may be disallowed under certain circumstances.

**CLOSELY HELD STOCK** *see* CLOSELY HELD CORPORATION.

**CLOSING ENTRY** journal entry at the end of a period to transfer the net effect of revenue and expense items from the income statements to owners' equity. Entries are for NOMINAL ACCOUNTS and not REAL ACCOUNTS. At the end of the year, expenses are credited so that zero balances are left in them, and the total is debited to the INCOME SUMMARY account. Revenue accounts are debited to arrive at zero balances, and the total is credited to the income summary account. The net income or loss that now exists in the income summary account is then transferred to retained earnings. After the closing entries, the new year will start fresh in that no income statement account balances will exist.

**CLOUD COMPUTING** a way for an organization to add computing capacity on the fly without directly investing in new long-term infrastructure. The "cloud" is often used as a metaphor for the Internet. Cloud computing is based upon a subscription or pay-per-use model, where the computer processing ability of an organization can be expanded or contracted, in real time, over the Internet.

**CLUSTER SAMPLING** method of selecting groups of units. The first unit of each group is selected with the use of a random number table. This allows selection of more than one item at a time. In cluster sampling, the population is broken into groups of items, and a RANDOM SAMPLE is selected from all the clusters. Each cluster becomes a sampling unit. After determining the adequate number of clusters, the auditor has a choice of either examining all items in a cluster (one-stage) or only a random number of items in the cluster (two-stage). Cluster sampling requires computing the mean for the individual sampling unit and multiplying this by the number of units in the population to determine the population's estimated value. The precision limit on this estimate must also be computed. Cluster sampling lowers sampling cost and the cost to replace the sample. Sample selection is made easier; however, less statistical efficiency exists. Applications of cluster sampling measure variables such as inventory value and the balance in accounts receivable. It can also be used to measure attributes.

**CM** *see* CONTRIBUTION MARGIN (CM).

**CMA** *see* CERTIFICATE IN MANAGEMENT ACCOUNTING (CMA).

**CMA MAGAZINE** journal published by the Society of Management Accountants of Canada (www.cma-canada.org) on a bimonthly basis. Subject matter concentrates on managerial accounting and information systems.

**COBOL** *see* COMMON BUSINESS ORIENTED LANGUAGE (COBOL).

**COBRANDING** the linking of a credit card with a business trade name offering "points" or premiums toward the purchase of a product or service. Examples are Ford Motor Company's Citibank Visa and MasterCard and Nordstrom's cobranded Visa. Bankers are realizing that cobranded credit cards help build customer loyalty.

**CODE OF PROFESSIONAL ETHICS** authoritative statement regarding the rules of conduct for certified public accountants in performing their functions. THE AMERICAN INSTITUTE OF CERTIFIED PUBLIC ACCOUNTANTS (AICPA) and each state society prepares these ethical guidelines. For example, a CPA may not divulge confidential client information to the public.

**CODING OF ACCOUNTS** assignment of an identification number to each account in the financial statements. A CHART OF ACCOUNTS lists the account titles and account numbers being used by a business. For example, the numbers 1 to 29 may be used exclusively for asset accounts; numbers from 30 to 49 may be reserved for liabilities; numbers in the 50s may signify OWNERS' EQUITY accounts; numbers in the 60s may represent revenue accounts; and numbers from 70 to 99 may designate expense accounts. In large or complex businesses with many more accounts, a more elaborate coding system would be needed. Some companies use a four-digit coding system. The coding system is especially necessary for computerized accounting.

**COEFFICIENT OF DETERMINATION** statistical measure of GOODNESS-OF-FIT. It measures how good the estimated regression equation is, designated as $r^2$ (*read as* $r$-squared). The higher the $r$-squared, the more confidence one can have in the equation. Statistically, the coefficient of determination represents the proportion of the total variation in the $y$ variable that is explained by the regression equation. It has the range of values between 0 and 1. *See also* REGRESSION ANALYSIS.

*Example:* The statement "factory overhead is a function of machine-hours with $r^2 = .70$," can be interpreted as "70% of the total variation of factory overhead is explained by the machine hours and the remaining 30% is accounted for by something other than machine-hours." The 30% is referred to as the error term.

**COEFFICIENT OF VARIATION** measure of relative dispersion, or relative risk. It is computed by dividing the standard deviation ($\sigma$) by the expected value ($\bar{x}$). For example, consider two investment proposals, A and B, with the following data:

| Proposal | Expected Value ($\bar{x}$) | Standard Deviation ($\sigma$) |
|----------|---------------------------|-------------------------------|
| A | $230 | $107.07 |
| B | 250 | 208.57 |

The coefficient of variation for each proposal is:

For A: $107.70/$230 = .47
For B: $208.57/$250 = .83.

Therefore, because the coefficient is a relative measure of risk, B is considered more risky than A.

**COINSURANCE CLAUSE** provision in an insurance policy that limits the liability of the insurer. It specifies that the owner of property that has been damaged (e.g., by fire or water) must have another policy covering usually at least 80% of the *cash value* of the property at the time of damage in order to collect the full amount insured. This serves as an inducement for an individual to carry full coverage.

**COLD SITE** is an important aspect of disaster recovery planning, where the data center can operate for duration of the disaster from a backup location/site. An organization may have three types of backup locations: a cold site, a WARM SITE, or a HOT SITE. A cold backup site is least expensive. It generally consists of nothing more than an appropriately configured space in a building. All hardware and software must be acquired before the recovery process can begin. Often, there is a significant delay in resuming data center function to full operation from a cold backup site.

**COLLATERALIZE** to pledge assets to secure a debt. These assets will be given up if the borrower defaults on the terms and conditions specified in the debt agreement. An example is pledging inventory to collateralize a bank loan.

**COLLECTIBLES** art, stamps, coins, antiques, and other related items. They offer capital gains potential, inflation protection, and aesthetic enjoyment. Collectibles are acquired through dealers, at auctions, or directly from previous owners. Among the drawbacks are high security and insurance cost, poor liquidity, lack of income, and possible forgeries. Information about collectibles sometimes appears in magazines like *Money* and *Creditor/Investor*, and major categories of collectibles have magazines and newsletters devoted exclusively to them.

**COLLECTION PERIOD** number of days it takes to collect accounts receivable. The collection period should be or can be compared to the terms of sale. A long collection period may indicate higher risk in collecting the account; it ties up funds that could be invested elsewhere or used to make timely payments. It equals the number of days in a year divided by the ACCOUNTS RECEIVABLE TURNOVER. Assume a 360-day year and turnover rate of 10 times. The collection period is 36 days. *See also* AGING OF ACCOUNTS.

**COLLEGE FUNDS** term used in not-for-profit accounting. College funds consist of current funds, loan funds, endowment funds, annuity and life funds, agency funds, and plant funds.

**COLLUSION** exists when two or more people get together to perpetrate and conceal errors, fraud, or instances of noncompliance with laws or regulations. For example, collusion occurs when the TREASURER steals company funds and shares the stolen money with the CONTROLLER, who in turn covers up the theft by doctoring the company's books and records.

## COMBINATION
1. agreement between two entities to undertake a mutually beneficial action. An example is an agreement related to pricing.
2. BUSINESS COMBINATION.

**COMBINED APPROACH** involves performing both tests of controls and substantive procedures in a financial statement audit. The objective of a combined approach is to determine that the entity's internal controls are operating effectively, which in turn will enable the reduction of substantive procedures to be performed by the auditor.

## COMBINED FINANCIAL STATEMENT
1. presentation in which the balance sheet accounts or income statement accounts of a related group of entities have been added together so they are considered as one reporting entity. Intercompany transactions are eliminated in a combined statement.
2. in governmental accounting, statement in which the balance sheets of all fund and account groups are shown without interfund transfers being eliminated.

**COMFORT LETTER** term used when underwriters request "comfort" from an auditor about financial information in SEC registration statements not covered by the auditor's opinion and on subsequent events after the opinion date. Comfort letters are *not* filed with the SEC but are required by underwriters who have certain responsibilities under SEC regulations. Typically, comfort letters are mandated as part of the underwriting agreement. The adequacy of procedures conducted in the comfort review rests with the underwriter and not the auditor. Underwriting agreements typically provide for a closing date on which the agreement is to be consummated and a "cutoff date" shortly before the closing date. The comfort letter should specifically state that it does not cover the period between the cutoff date and the date of the letter. The contents of the comfort letter cover some or all of the following: compliance with SEC rules and regulations, audit procedures conducted, unaudited financial statements and schedules, statistics and tables, changes in certain financial statement items after the latest statement contained in the filing, auditor independence, and an understanding regarding the limited circulation of the letter. Note that comments on unaudited statements and subsequent changes should be restricted to NEGATIVE ASSURANCE since the auditor has not conducted an examination in accordance with GENERALLY ACCEPTED ACCOUNTING PRINCIPLES (GAAP). Any financial statement, schedule, or other information referenced in the letter should be clearly identified along with the auditor's responsibility regarding it. The auditor should not comment on matters involving management judgment (i.e., reasons for change in income statement items). Working papers should back up statements made in comfort letters and furnish evidence of procedures carried out.

**COMMERCIAL PAPER** short-term unsecured loan of a financially strong company having a maturity up to 270 days. It is typically issued on a discount basis meaning that the interest is subtracted immediately from the face of the debt to obtain the cash proceeds. Commercial paper interest rates are usually less than the prime interest rate (rate charged by banks to their best customers). Flexibility is another advantage; they can be issued at varying maturity dates when funds are needed.

**COMMITMENT**
1. expected expenditure backed by an agreement. A commitment may be disclosed in a *footnote* but generally is not given accounting recognition. Disclosure includes its nature and amount. However, a commitment can be recorded in the case of a loss commitment on a purchase contract where the market price has significantly declined below the agreed-upon delivery contract price. The entry for the difference is to debit loss on purchase commitment and credit estimated liability. But a gain on a purchase contract is not recognized because it violates CONSERVATISM. *See also* CONTINGENT LIABILITY.
2. bank commitment to lend a company funds when needed.

**COMMITTED COST** *see* CAPACITY COSTS; DISCRETIONARY (FIXED) COSTS.

**COMMITTEE OF SPONSORING ORGANIZATIONS (COSO) OF THE TREADWAY COMMISSION** an organization that prepares audit related reports. COSO includes representatives from the American Institute of CPAs, American Accounting Association, Institute of Internal Auditors, Institute of Management Accountants, and the Financial Executives Institute. The Committee's purposes are to establish a common definition of internal control serving the needs for different parties and providing a standard against which companies can evaluate their control systems and how to improve them.

**COMMITTEE ON ACCOUNTING PROCEDURE** former senior technical committee of the American Institute of CPAs that promulgated Accounting Research Bulletins from 1938 up to 1959. It consisted of accounting practitioners and professors. It was replaced by the Accounting Principles Board, which was, in turn, replaced by the FASB.

**COMMODITIES FUTURES** contracts in which sellers promise to deliver a given commodity by a certain date at a predetermined price. Price is agreed to by open outcry on the floor of the commodity exchange. The contract specifies the item, the price, the expiration date, and a standardized unit to be traded (e.g., 50,000 pounds). Commodity contracts may run up to one year. Investors must continually evaluate the effect of market activity on the value of the contract. While the futures contract mandates that the buyer and seller exchange the commodity on the delivery date, the contract may be sold to another party prior to the settlement date. This may occur when the trader wants to realize a profit now or limit the loss. Investors engage in commodity trading in the hope of high return rates and inflation hedges.

**COMMON BUSINESS ORIENTED LANGUAGE (COBOL)** programming language for business data processing. As compared to FORTRAN and BASIC, *COBOL* statements resemble English sentences and thus are long and wordy, but easy to read.

**COMMON COST** expense shared by different departments, products, or jobs, also called JOINT COST or INDIRECT COST.

**COMMON SIZE FINANCIAL STATEMENT** form of financial statement analysis in which the relative percentages of financial statement items as well as their dollar amounts are shown. *See also* VERTICAL ANALYSIS.

ABC Company
Common Size Income Statement
For Year Ended December 31, 2014

| | | |
|---|---|---|
| Sales | $100,000 | 100% |
| Less: Cost of goods sold | 20,000 | 20% |
| Gross profit | $80,000 | 80% |
| Operating expenses | 30,000 | 30% |
| Net income | $50,000 | 50% |

**COMMON STOCK** share in a public company or privately held firm. Common stockholders have voting and dividend rights. In the event of corporate bankruptcy, common stockholders are paid after bondholders and preferred stockholders. There is, however, a greater chance of capital appreciation by owning common stock.

The issuing company shows common stock at its total par value, or no-par value, or stated value in the capital stock section of stockholders' equity.

**COMMON STOCK EQUIVALENT** security that can be converted into common stock. It is *not* now in common stock form but has provisions enabling holders to become common stockholders. A common stock equivalent is included in PRIMARY EARNINGS PER SHARE if its effect is *dilutive*. Examples are stock options, warrants, two-class common stocks, and contingent shares (if related to the passage of time). Contingent shares are shares issuable upon the occurrence of a specified event. A convertible security is a common stock equivalent when its effective yield at the time of issuance is less than $66\frac{2}{3}\%$ of the average Aa corporate bond yield. *See also* EARNINGS PER SHARE; FULLY DILUTED EARNINGS PER SHARE.

**COMMUNICATION BETWEEN PREDECESSOR AND SUCCESSOR AUDITORS** provides guidance on communications between predecessor and successor auditors. The successor auditor is responsible for initiating the oral or written confidential communication. In the communication, the successor auditor should inquire of matters relevant to accepting the engagement such as management honesty, internal control, and accounting policy disagreements.

**COMPARABILITY** ability to rank companies so as to facilitate financial decisions. Comparability is aided when companies employ similar accounting procedures, measurement concepts, classifications, basic financial statement formats, and methods of disclosure. *See also* UNIFORMITY.

**COMPARATIVE STATEMENT** statement on which balance sheets, income statements, or statements of changes in financial position are assembled side by side for review purposes. Changes that have occurred in individual categories from year to year and over the years are easily noted. The key factor revealed is the *trend* in an account or financial statement category over time. A comparison of financial statements over two to three years can be undertaken by computing the year-to-year change in absolute dollars and in terms of percentage change. Longer-term comparisons are best undertaken by means of INDEX-NUMBER TREND SERIES.

**COMPARATIVE STATEMENT APPROACH** *see* TOTAL PROJECT APPROACH.

**COMPENSATED ABSENCE** expected payments to employees who miss work because of illness, vacation, or holidays. A liability is accrued for compensation for future absences if *all* of the following criteria are satisfied: (1) employee services have already been performed; (2) rights have already been vested; (3) there is probable payment; and (4) the amount is subject to reasonable estimation. If the amount is not determinable, accrual is not possible, but footnote disclosure should be given.

**COMPENSATING BALANCE** deposit that a bank can use to offset an unpaid loan. No interest is earned on the compensating balance, which is stated as a percentage of the loan. The compensating balance increases the EFFECTIVE INTEREST RATE on the loan. The compensating balance is usually 10%. Assume a company borrows $50,000 from the bank at a 10% interest rate with a 5% compensating balance. The loan is on a discount basis meaning interest is deducted immediately. The compensating balance is calculated at $2500. The effective interest rate is:

$$\frac{\text{Nominal Interest}}{\text{Proceeds}} = \frac{\$5,000}{\$50,000 - \$5,000 - \$2,500} = \frac{\$5,000}{\$42,500} = 11.8\%$$

**COMPENSATORY STOCK OPTION** option offered to employees as partial compensation for their services. Compensation for services is measured by the quoted market price of the stock at the measurement date less the amount the employee is required to pay (option price). The measurement date is the earliest date on which both the number of shares to be issued and the option price are known. Compensation involved in a compensatory stock option plan should be expensed in the periods in which the related services are performed. The entry is to debit compensation expense and credit deferred compensation.

**COMPETITIVE BENCHMARKING** *see* BENCHMARKING.

**COMPILATION** presentation of financial statement information by the entity *without* the accountant's assurance as to conformity with GEN-ERALLY ACCEPTED ACCOUNTING PRINCIPLES (GAAP). In performing this accounting service, the accountant must conform to the AMERICAN INSTITUTE OF CERTIFIED PUBLIC ACCOUNTANTS (AICPA) Statements on Standards for Accounting and Review Services (SSARS). For guidance on issues not covered therein, reference should be made to the STATEMENTS ON AUDITING STANDARDS (SAS). The engagement letter should set forth the type of services to be rendered, limitations of the service (such as nonreliance to disclose errors and irregularities), and nature of the compilation report. In undertaking a compilation assignment, the CPA should be familiar with the client and industry accounting principles and practices. The accountant should understand the client's accounting records, form and content of financial statements, and personnel qualifications. The accountant is *not* gathering evidence and does *not* verify client information provided. Rather, the CPA reads the compiled statements to assure that they are in appropriate form and without obvious material errors. Each page of the financial statement should refer to the compilation report. The accountant's report should indicate the completion of the compilation, the fact that the compilation is restricted to financial statement information presented by management, and that the statements have *not* been audited or reviewed. The accountant does not express an opinion on the financial statements nor does he or she give any other form of assurance on them. In the case where management omits needed disclosures, the CPA should state so in the report. *See also* REVIEW.

**COMPLETED CONTRACT METHOD** profit is recognized only when a long-term construction contract is completed. It should be used only when the conditions of the PERCENTAGE OF COMPLETION METHOD cannot be applied. However, if a loss on the contract is expected, it should be immediately recognized consistent with the CONSERVATISM principle. *See also* CONSTRUCTION-IN-PROGRESS; PROGRESS BILLINGS.

**COMPLEX CAPITAL STRUCTURE** financial structure with stock outstanding that has potential for DILUTION. *Dual presentation* of earnings per share by showing BASIC EARNINGS PER SHARE and DILUTED EARNINGS PER SHARE is required.

**COMPLIANCE AUDIT** special auditor's report covering compliance with contractual agreements, such as bond indentures and loan agreements, and regulatory requirements. The lender or agency wishes to obtain the auditor's assurance as to compliance with the terms of the agreement. The data need not be audited for compliance; however, if the financial statements have been audited, the auditor may provide NEGATIVE ASSURANCE on compliance. The compliance report may be separately issued or addended to the auditor's report on the financial statements. In the latter case, usually an explanatory paragraph appears below the opinion paragraph. An example of a compliance audit is one conducted for the trustee of bondholders to determine whether provisions of the bond contract (such as the maintenance of required financial ratios) are being adhered to.

**COMPLIANCE TEST** manner of furnishing reasonable assurance that internal accounting control procedures are being applied as prescribed so that the auditor is assured of the validity of underlying evidence. Any exceptions to compliance must be noted. Underlying evidence comprises an examination of the accounts themselves including reviewing the journals, ledgers, and worksheets. If the compliance tests provide evidence that controls are functioning properly, the underlying evidence is deemed reliable, and the CPA can reduce the degree of validation and analytical review procedures. The following three audit procedures are typically used in conducting compliance tests: (1) inquiry of personnel regarding the performance of their duties; (2) observing personnel actions; and (3) inspecting documentation for evidence of performance in conducting employee functions. An example is examining invoices to assure that receiving documents and proof of delivery are attached when the invoices are presented for payment. Tests of compliance should be applied to transactions throughout the year under audit since the financial statements reflect transactions and events for the whole year. Compliance tests may be conducted on a subjective or statistical basis. *See also* SUBSTANTIVE TEST.

**COMPONENT** an entity or business activity that prepares financial statements to be included in group financial statements. Components include subsidiary corporations, divisions of a business, and investments accounted for under the equity method of accounting.

**COMPONENT AUDITOR** an auditor who audits the financial statements of a component included in group financial statements. A component auditor may be part of the group engagement partner's firm, a network firm, or another firm.

**COMPONENTS OF INTERNAL CONTROL** the interrelated elements of an entity's internal control used by management to provide reasonable assurance that their objectives will be achieved. Components of internal control consist of the control environment, risk assessment, information and communication systems, monitoring, and control activities.

**COMPOSITE BREAK-EVEN POINT** term used to designate break-even sales when a company sells more than one product or service. A break-even point for all the products or services combined can be determined, based on the expected SALES MIX and the composite or weighted average unit contribution margin. For example, assume that

|                     | Baubles | Trinkets | Total   |
|---------------------|---------|----------|---------|
| Sales               | $1.00   | $1.250   | $2.250  |
| Variable cost       | 0.60    | 0.375    | 0.975   |
| Contribution margin | $0.40   | $0.875   | $1.275  |
| Fixed costs         |         |          | $7,600  |
| Sales mix           | 60%     | 40%      |         |

Then composite (or weighted average) unit contribution margin is ($0.40)(.6) + ($0.875)(.4) = $0.59. The break-even point for both products combined is $7600/$0.59 = 12,881 units. *See also* WEIGHTED AVERAGE CONTRIBUTION MARGIN.

**COMPOSITE DEPRECIATION** group depreciation of dissimilar assets with different service lives. Depreciation on all assets is determined by using the straight-line-depreciation method. Then, a composite depreciation rate is arrived at based on the ratio of depreciation per year to the original cost. Composite life equals the depreciable cost divided by the depreciation per year. In any given year, depreciation expense equals the composite depreciation rate times the gross cost balance in the asset account. The entry is to debit depreciation expense and credit accumulated depreciation. Under the method, when a particular asset is sold, the entry is to debit cash for the amount received and credit the asset for its original cost. The difference between the two is debited to accumulated depreciation. No gain or loss on the sale of a fixed asset is recognized under the composite method.

An illustrative schedule for composite depreciation is shown below:

| Asset | Original Cost | Salvage Value | Depreciable Cost | Life | Depreciation Per Year |
|-------|---------------|---------------|------------------|------|-----------------------|
| Autos | $100,000 | $10,000 | $ 90,000 | 10 | $ 9,000 |
| Trucks | 55,000 | 5,000 | 50,000 | 4 | 12,500 |
|  | $155,000 | $15,000 | $140,000 |  | $21,500 |
|  |  |  | $ 21,500 |  |  |
| Composite Rate | = |  | $155,000 | = | .139 |
| Composite Life | = |  | $140,000 | = | 6.512 |
|  |  |  | $ 21,500 |  |  |

**COMPOSITION** agreement designed to allow a debtor to continue to operate. It includes a voluntary reduction of the amount the debtor owes the creditor. The creditor obtains from the debtor a stated percent of the obligation in *full* settlement of the debt regardless of how low the percentage is. The advantages of a composition are that court costs are eliminated as well as the stigma of a bankrupt company. *See also* BANKRUPTCY.

**COMPOUNDING PERIOD** time during which compound interest is computed. Compounding means interest on interest and the period can be on a daily, monthly, annual, or other basis.

**COMPOUND INTEREST** rate that is applicable when interest in subsequent periods is earned not only on the original principal but also on the accumulated interest of prior periods. For example, assume that the initial principal is $1000 and annual interest rate is 10%. At the end of first year, the amount is the principal and interest, which is $1,000 + .1($1,000) = $1,000 + $100 = $1,100. At the end of second year, the amount is accumulated: $1,100 + .1($1,100) = $1,100 + $110 = $1,210. *See also* FUTURE VALUE.

**COMPOUND INTEREST METHOD OF DEPRECIATION** *see* ANNUAL METHOD OF DEPRECIATION.

**COMPOUND JOURNAL ENTRY** more than one debit or credit in a journal entry.

**COMPREHENSIVE ANNUAL FINANCIAL REPORT (CAFR)** official annual report of a government. In addition to a combined, combining (assembling of data for all funds within a type), and individual balance sheet, the following are also presented as appropriate: (1) statement of revenues, expenditures, and changes in fund balance (all funds); (2) statement of revenues, expenditures, and changes in fund balance, budget and actual (for general and special revenue funds); (3) statement of revenues, expenses, and changes in retained earnings (for proprietary funds); and (4) statement of changes in financial position (for proprietary funds).

**COMPREHENSIVE BUDGET** *see* MASTER (COMPREHENSIVE) BUDGET.

**COMPREHENSIVE INCOME** change in equity (net assets) arising from either transactions or other occurrences with nonowners. It excludes investments and withdrawals by owners. Comprehensive income is comprised of two elements: net income and other comprehensive income. Other comprehensive income relates to all items of comprehensive income except for net income. Other comprehensive income includes foreign currency translation gain or loss; unrealized loss or gain on available-for-sale securities; and changes in market value of a futures contract that is a hedge of an asset reported at fair value.

**COMPREHENSIVE TAX ALLOCATION** method of measuring the tax effects of all transactions includable in book income for the period irrespective of the fact that they may be shown in taxable income in another year. It is an INTERPERIOD INCOME TAX ALLOCATION.

**COMPTROLLER**
1. misspelling of CONTROLLER, caused by confusion about the word's Latin and French roots.
2. chief auditor in the government sector. For example, the COMPTROLLER GENERAL heads the GENERAL ACCOUNTING OFFICE.

**COMPTROLLER GENERAL** chief of the GENERAL ACCOUNTING OFFICE (GAO). The GAO assists the Congress in overseeing the executive branch and serves as the independent legislative auditor of the federal government. The General Accounting Office reports directly to Congress on operating results, financial position, and accounting systems of government agencies. It conducts audits of all branches of the government, both here and abroad.

**COMPUSTAT** database published by Standard & Poor's Corporation (www.compustatresources.com). The Compustat tapes are comprehensive, containing over 50 years of annual financial data for more than 88,000 global securities. Each year's data for the industrial companies include more than 120 balance sheet and income statement items and market data. There is also a file on utilities and banks. The annual file is updated weekly.

**COMPUTER-AIDED DESIGN (CAD)** use of a computer to interact with a designer in developing and testing product ideas without actually building prototypes.

**COMPUTER-AIDED DESIGN AND MANUFACTURING (CAD/ CAM)** computerized system to both integrate part design and to generate processing or manufacturing instructions.

**COMPUTER-ASSISTED AUDIT TECHNIQUES (CAAT)** used to simplify or automate the data analysis function in an audit. Auditors typically used specialized CAAT software, such as ACL's Data Analysis. However, CAAT may also be performed using a general purpose spreadsheet software like Excel or specialized statistical software such as SAS or SPSS.

**COMPUTER-INTEGRATED MANUFACTURING (CIM)** computer information systems utilizing a shared manufacturing data base for engineering design, factory production, and information management.

**COMPUTER SECURITY** method of protecting information, computer programs, and other computer system assets. *Hardware security*, which is the security of computer assets and capital equipment, refers to computer location, access control, fire protection, and storage procedures. Such measures as badges, electronic identification keys, alarm systems, and physical barriers at entries are used for this purpose. *Software security* entails the protection of software assets such as APPLICATION PROGRAMS, the OPERATING SYSTEM, and the DATA BASE MANAGEMENT SYSTEM and stored information. Special user numbers and passwords are typically used to prevent unauthorized access to software and data. In addition to security for hardware and software, good internal control also requires that measures be taken to prevent loss or accidental destruction of data.

**COMPUTER VIRUS** a program that replicates and spreads by attaching itself to other programs. When the infected program is run, the virus executes an event.

**CONCENTRATION BANKING** acceleration of cash collections from customers by having funds sent to several geographically situated regional banks and transferred to a main concentration account in another bank. The transfer of funds can be accomplished through the use of depository transfer checks and electronic transfers.

**CONCEPTUAL FRAMEWORK** study of the Financial Accounting Standards Board. It attempts to arrive at theoretical foundations for its Statements of Financial Accounting Standards. At this time, there are six Statements of Financial Accounting Concepts.

**CONCURRENT AUDIT TECHNIQUES** used to audit an entity on a continuous basis. Audit evidence is collected at the same time that an application system undertakes processing of its production. This is achieved by embedding the audit module into the application systems; the audit module is responsible for collecting and processing the audit evidenced.

**CONFERENCE BOARD, THE** not-for-profit group of business people that examines and studies economic and managerial issues to enhance business activities. The organization puts out such useful statistics as the help-wanted index. Recommendations are given to the business community regarding important business issues.

**CONFERENCE CALL** a valuable opportunity to hear senior management's take on the company's prospects of future earnings and new products in the pipeline. Institutional investors and financial analysts of brokerage firms call in to a special number to listen and ask questions. Yahoo Finance (http://finance.yahoo.com) maintains a calendar of upcoming conference calls. Enter a company's ticker to listen in on a current meeting or access an archive of a recent call.

**CONFIDENCE INTERVAL** estimated range of values with a given probability of including the population parameter of interest. The range of values is usually based on the results of a sample that estimated the mean and the sampling error or standard error. For example, for the population mean, the confidence intervals can be given by the interval whose lower ($L$) and upper ($U$) limits are as follows:

$$L = \mu - Z\sigma_{\bar{x}}$$

$$U = \mu + Z\sigma_{\bar{x}}$$

where $\mu$ is the *population mean, Z = standard normal variate, and* $\sigma_{\bar{x}}$ = *the standard error of the mean. See also* CENTRAL LIMIT THEOREM: NORMAL DISTRIBUTION.

**CONFIDENCE LEVEL** in statistical sampling, the degree of certainty that audit results are accurate. The sum of the confidence level (e.g., 95%) plus the risk of inaccurate results (e.g., 5%) totals 100%. Also known as *reliability*.

**CONFIRMATION**
1. verification of a condition or fact.
2. auditor's written or oral request to a third party to verify the existence or amount of a financial item related to the clients. A *positive* confirmation requests a reply in any event while a *negative* confirmation asks for a reply only in the event of disagreement. Examples are accounts receivable, accounts payable, and bank confirmations.

**CONFORMANCE COSTS (CONTROL COSTS)** category of QUALITY COSTS including costs of prevention and costs of appraisal, which are financial measures of internal performance.

**CONGLOMERATE FINANCIAL STATEMENT** *see* CONSOLIDATED FINANCIAL STATEMENT.

**CONGLOMERATE MERGER** combination of two or more firms with virtually unrelated activities. The key benefit claimed for conglomerates is the diversification of risk across various industries. *See also* MERGER.

**CONSERVATISM** accounting guideline that understates assets and revenues and overstates liabilities and expenses. Expenses should be recognized earlier than later, whereas revenue should be recognized later than sooner. Thus, net income will result in a lower figure. Conservatism holds that in financial reporting it is preferable to be pessimistic (understate) than optimistic (overstate) since there is less chance of financial readers being hurt by relying on prepared financial statements. One can argue that pessimism is needed to counteract the optimism of management. However, excess conservatism may result in misguided decisions.

**CONSIGNMENT** specialized way of marketing certain types of goods. The consignor delivers goods to the consignee who acts as the consignor's agent in selling the merchandise to a third party. The consignee accepts the goods without any liability except to reasonably protect them from damage. The consignee receives a commission when the merchandise is sold. Goods on consignment are included in the consignor's inventory and excluded from the consignee's inventory since the consignor has legal title.

**CONSISTENCY**
1. uniformity of accounting procedures used by an accounting entity from period to period.
2. uniformity of measurement concepts and procedures used for related items within the company's financial statements for one period.

It is difficult for financial statement users to make projections when data are not measured and classified in the same manner over time. A change in accounting principle should not be made unless it can be justified as being preferable. An example of a change is switching from the STRAIGHT-LINE DEPRECIATION method to the SUM-OF-THE-YEARS'-DIGITS method. A lack in consistency over time distorts the earnings trend and creates uncertainty in evaluating a company.

**CONSOLIDATED BALANCE SHEET** one that shows the financial position of an affiliated group of companies as though they constituted a single economic unit. The effect of intercompany relationships and the results of intercompany transactions will have been eliminated in the consolidation process. *See also* CONSOLIDATED FINANCIAL STATEMENT.

**CONSOLIDATED (CONSOLIDATION) GOODWILL** excess of cost over book value of the investment in a subsidiary. With consolidation, even when the assets and liabilities of the subsidiary are properly stated, and the net assets equal the values placed on them by the parent, an investor may still expect that the advantages of the combination will enable it to earn more than the two companies could earn separately. Therefore, the investor may be willing to pay an additional amount, which is, in effect, a bonus for control of the subsidiary. This bonus is an intangible asset, goodwill created as a result of consolidation. Consolidation has a special meaning in mergers because a new company is formed to own the stock of the companies being combined. In that type of reorganization, there is *no* goodwill. Goodwill arises from a PURCHASE METHOD merger and represents the difference between purchase price and book value of the acquired company. The meaning of the difference is theoretically the increased earning power of the companies as a result of their combination, but that value is not something superimposed on a balance sheet. It is what is actually paid less what is actually on the books.

**CONSOLIDATED FINANCIAL STATEMENT** statement that brings together all assets, liabilities, and operating accounts of a *parent* company and its subsidiaries. It presents the financial position and results of operations of the parent company and its subsidiaries as if the group were a single company with one or more branches. The technique for preparing consolidated financial statements is to take the individual statements to be consolidated and to combine them on a worksheet after eliminating all intercompany transactions and intercompany relationships. Most firms prepare consolidated statements when they hold more than 50% of the subsidiary's stock. *See also* COMBINED FINANCIAL STATEMENT; CONSOLIDATION.

**CONSOLIDATION** presentation as one economic entity of the financial statements of a parent and subsidiary (subsidiaries) subsequent to the date of acquisition. The parent company owns more than 50% of the voting common stock of the subsidiary, and is therefore in control. In consolidation, the reporting mechanism is the entire group and not the separate companies. Note that the entities that make up the consolidated group retain their separate legal entity; adjustments and eliminations are for CONSOLIDATED FINANCIAL STATEMENTS only.

**CONSTANT DOLLAR ACCOUNTING** method of measuring financial statement items in dollars of the same (constant) purchasing power. Historical cost is restated in units of constant purchasing power as follows:

$$\text{Historical Cost} \times \frac{\text{Average CPI for Current Year}}{\text{CPI at Time of Acquisition}}$$

Restating all accounts in constant dollars provides greater comparability among years because all assets appear in the same current year average dollars regardless of when the asset was bought. Constant dollar accounting also aids comparability among competing companies in the same industry because each company converts its accounts to the same CONSUMER PRICE INDEX (CPI) dollars.

**CONSTANT VARIANCE** *see* HOMOSCEDASTICITY.

**CONSTRAINED OPTIMIZATION** optimization with the restrictions imposed on the availability of resources and other requirements. Techniques such as linear programming (LP) and the Lagrangean multipliers are used for this purpose.

**CONSTRAINING (LIMITING) FACTOR** item that restricts or limits production or sale of a given product. Virtually all firms suffer from one or more constraining factors. Examples include limited machine-hours and labor-hours and shortage of materials and skilled labor. Other limiting factors may be cubic feet of display or warehouse space, or working capital.

**CONSTRAINT-BASED COSTING** method that assigns resource costs to products and services based on the existence and location of a capacity constraint. Often governed by revenue maximization, implying that pricing is combined with costing.

**CONSTRAINT EQUATION** *see* LINEAR PROGRAMMING (LP).

**CONSTRAINTS** explicit limitations that will be encountered in pursuing an objective. Examples of constraints are limitations in machine capacity, necessary materials, or skilled labor. In LINEAR PROGRAMMING (LP), constraints are typically expressed in terms of *inequalities*.

**CONSTRUCTION-IN-PROGRESS** inventory method used by construction companies. The inventory account reflects construction costs incurred using the COMPLETED CONTRACT METHOD and the PERCENTAGE OF COMPLETION METHOD. Under either method, when construction costs occur, the entry is to debit construction-in-progress and credit progress billings. Additionally, under the percentage of completion method, profit is recognized gradually each period when work is performed, requiring an additional entry to record the profit. The entry is to debit construction-in-progress and credit profit. Under either method, construction-in-progress is eliminated in the final year when the contract is completed. The entry is to debit PROGRESS BILL-INGS and credit construction-in-progress and profit. Under the percentage method, the profit is for the last year only. Under the completed method, the profit is the cumulative profit for all the years.

**CONSTRUCTIVE DIVIDEND** tax concept in which a stockholder is considered to have constructively received a dividend although it was not actually paid by the company. For example, a shareholder who used company property for personal purposes rent-free might be considered to have received a constructive dividend equal to the fair market rental value of that property.

**CONSTRUCTIVE OWNERSHIP** *see* ATTRIBUTION.

**CONSTRUCTIVE RECEIPT** tax concept in which income not actually received is considered to be constructively received by a taxpayer and thus must be reported. An example is a bond interest coupon. The interest is taxable in the year the coupon matures, even though the holder delays cashing it until a later year.

**CONSTRUCTIVE RETIREMENT** assumption used in consolidation procedures that allows the treatment of debt or equity securities as if they had been retired, thus allowing a consolidated entity to be viewed as a single reporting entity.

**CONSUMED COST** measure of expired benefits. Examples include cost of goods sold and periodic depreciation expense of a fixed asset. Income statement expenses are consumed costs in the generation of revenue.

**CONSUMER PRICE INDEX (CPI)** measure of price level computed by the Bureau of Labor Statistics on a monthly basis. It is the ratio of the cost of specific consumer items in any one year to the cost of those items in the base period, 1982–1984 = 100. Because the CPI includes things consumers buy regularly, it is frequently called the *cost of living index*. The so-called market basket, covered by the index, includes items such as food, clothing, automobiles, homes, and fees to doctors.

**CONSUMER'S RISK** probability of accepting a bad lot.

**CONSUMPTION TAX** levy charged directly on a specified item or commodity. It may be viewed as an indirect form of taxation in that it is not contingent upon income but on consumption of an item. Examples include excise taxes on cigarettes and alcohol, and sales taxes.

**CONTINGENCY PLANNING** a strategy to minimize the effect of disturbances and to allow for timely resumption of activities. The aim of contingency planning is to minimize the effects of a disruption on an organization. A disruption is any security violation, man-made or natural, intentional or accidental, that affects normal operations.

**CONTINGENT ASSET** item that depends on some future happening that may or may not occur. Its existence or value is not assured. A contingent asset may emanate from a CONTINGENT LIABILITY. An example of a contingent asset may be a successful lawsuit claiming damages of another party. It *cannot* be shown as an asset on the balance sheet because it violates conservatism. However, footnote disclosure may be made.

**CONTINGENT CONSIDERATION** a payment that is contingent upon specified future events or transactions.

**CONTINGENT LIABILITY** potential liability that may exist in the future depending on the outcome of a past event. Examples are an adverse tax court decision, lawsuit, and notes receivable discounted. Footnote disclosure is required of the circumstances for possible losses. Note that an ESTIMATED LIABILITY can be booked only if there is a probable loss.

**CONTINGENT RENTAL** payment based on factors other than the passage of time. For example, a rental is contingent when the lessee must pay an extra amount based on sales or profitability. Footnote disclosure is made of the contingent rental payment and terms.

**CONTINGENT RESERVE** appropriation of retained earnings for general loss possibilities; also called RESERVE FOR CONTINGENCIES.

**CONTINUING ACCOUNT** balance sheet account that is carried over from the previous accounting period (i.e., asset, liabilities, and equity accounts).

**CONTINUING INVESTMENT** one maintained on a continuous basis, according to some plan, across one fiscal period to the next.

**CONTINUING PROFESSIONAL EDUCATION (CPE)** credits required in some states for a CPA to continue in practice. New York initiated a CPE requirement beginning September 1987. CPE credits may be earned by attending courses and seminars, teaching, and doing research.

**CONTINUITY** accounting assumption that expects a business to continue in life indefinitely; also called GOING CONCERN. It is the basis for using HISTORICAL COST to value accounts rather than liquidation value since the company will remain in existence. SAS Number 59 deals with the auditor's consideration of an entity's ability to continue as a going concern. The auditor must appraise if significant doubt exists of a client's ability to continue as a going concern for a period not exceeding one year after the date of the financial statements. If significant doubt exists, there should be a separate explanatory paragraph of a going concern problem after the unqualified opinion paragraph.

**CONTINUOUS AUDIT** examination conducted on a recurring basis throughout the accounting period to detect and correct mistakes and improper accounting practices prior to the reporting year-end. A continuous audit also *spreads* the CPA's work throughout the year.

**CONTINUOUS BUDGET** budget that rolls ahead each month or period without regard to the fiscal year so that a twelve-month or other periodic forecast is always available.

**CONTINUOUS IMPROVEMENT (CI)** never-ending effort for improvement in every part of the firm relative to all of its deliverables to its customers; also called *Kaizen* in Japanese.

**CONTRA ACCOUNT**
1. reduction to the gross cost of an asset to arrive at its net cost; also called *valuation allowance*. For example, accumulated depreciation is a contra account to the original cost of a fixed asset to arrive at BOOK VALUE.
2. reduction of a liability to arrive at its CARRYING VALUE. An example is bond discount, which is a reduction of bonds payable.

**CONTRACT AUDITING** examination of contracts to provide assurance that the terms are being carried out such as with regard to the time and quality of work performed, and appropriation of billing.

**CONTRIBUTED CAPITAL** *see* PAID-IN CAPITAL.

**CONTRIBUTED CAPITAL IN EXCESS OF PAR** *see* ADDITIONAL PAID-IN CAPITAL.

**CONTRIBUTION APPROACH TO PRICING** manner of pricing a special order. This situation occurs because a company often receives a non-routine, special order for its products at lower prices than usual. In normal times, the company may refuse such an order since it will not yield a satisfactory profit. If times are bad or there is idle capacity, an order should be accepted if the incremental revenue exceeds the incremental costs involved. Such a price, one lower than the regular price, is called a contribution price. This approach is called the contribution approach to pricing, or the VARIABLE PRICING MODEL. For example, assume that a company with 100,000-unit capacity is currently producing and selling only 90,000 units of product each year with a regular price of $2. If the variable cost per unit is $1 and the annual fixed cost is $45,000, the income statement looks as follows:

|  |  | Per Unit |
|---|---|---|
| Sales (90,000 units) | $180,000 | $2.00 |
| Less: Variable cost | 90,000 | 1.00 |
| Contribution margin | $ 90,000 | $1.00 |
| Less: Fixed cost | 45,000 | 0.50 |
| Net income | $ 45,000 | $ 0.50 |

The company has just received an order that calls for 10,000 units at $1.20, for a total of $12,000. The acceptance of this special order will not affect regular sales. Management is reluctant to accept this order because the $1.20 price is below the $1.50 factory unit cost ($1.50 = $1.00 + $0.50). Is it advisable to refuse the order? The answer is no. The company can add to total profits by accepting this special order even though the price offered is below the unit factory cost. At a price of $1.20, the order will contribute $0.20 (CM per unit = $1.20 – $1.00 = $0.20) toward fixed cost, and profit will increase by $2000 (10,000 units × $0.20). Using the contribution approach to pricing, the variable cost of $1.00 will be a better guide than the full unit cost of $1.50. Note that the fixed costs will not increase because of the presence of idle capacity. *See also* INCREMENTAL ANALYSIS; RELEVANT COSTS.

**CONTRIBUTION MARGIN (CM)** difference between sales and the variable costs of the product or service, also called *marginal income*. It is the amount of money available to cover fixed costs and generate profits. For example, if sales are $15,000 and variable costs are $6,100, contribution margin is $8,900 ($15,000 less $6,100). Determining the contribution margin has many advantages. A company can sell an item below the normal selling price when idle capacity exists as long as there is a contribution margin since it will help to cover the fixed costs or add to profits. Also, the CM calculation requires the segregation of fixed and variable costs, which is needed in BREAK-EVEN ANALYSIS. Further, CM analysis is good in evaluating the performance of the department as a whole and its manager. However, the CONTRIBUTION (MARGIN) INCOME STATEMENT can only be used internally by management because it is not acceptable for external reporting in the annual report.

**CONTRIBUTION MARGIN ANALYSIS** *see* COST-VOLUME-PROFIT (CVP) ANALYSIS.

**CONTRIBUTION (MARGIN) INCOME STATEMENT** income statement that organizes cost by behavior. It shows the relationship of variable costs and fixed costs, regardless of the functions a given cost item is associated with. A contribution income statement highlights the concept of CONTRIBUTION MARGIN (CM). This format provides data that are useful for internal management. An illustrative format of the contribution margin income statement follows:

> Sales
> Less: Variable cost of sales
>         Variable selling and administrative expenses
> _____
> Contribution Margin (CM)
> Less: Fixed overhead
>         Fixed selling and administrative expenses
> _____
> Net income

**CONTRIBUTION MARGIN METHOD** variation of the EQUATION METHOD. It is used in COST-VOLUME-PROFIT (CVP) ANALYSIS or BREAK-EVEN ANALYSIS. The approach centers on the idea that each unit sold provides a certain amount of CONTRIBUTION MARGIN that goes toward the covering of fixed costs. Listed below are some formulas:

(1) Break-even Point *in units* = Fixed Costs/Unit Contribution Margin
(2) Break-even Point *in dollars* = Fixed Costs/Contribution Margin Ratio
(3) Target income volume *in units*:
   (Fixed Costs + Target Income)/Contribution Margin
(4) Target income volume *in dollars*:
   (Fixed Costs + Target Income)/Contribution Margin Ratio

**CONTRIBUTION MARGIN (CM) RATIO** computation showing CONTRIBUTION MARGIN (CM) as a percentage of sales.

**CONTRIBUTION MARGIN (CM) VARIANCE** difference between actual contribution margin per unit and the budgeted contribution margin per unit, multiplied by the actual number of units sold. If the actual CM is greater than the budgeted CM per unit, a variance is favorable; otherwise, it is unfavorable.

CM Variance = (Actual CM Per Unit − Budgeted CM Per Unit) × Actual Sales

**CONTRIBUTION PRICE** *see* CONTRIBUTION APPROACH TO PRICING.

**CONTROL ACTIVITIES** collectively constitute a component of internal control. Control activities are an entity's policies and procedures designed to reasonably ensure that management directives (i.e., orders) are carried out. Examples of control activities are physical safeguards to restrict access to assets and records and proper segregation of duties.

**CONTROL CHART** graphical means of depicting sample characteristics, such as means, ranges, and attributes, over time used for process control.

**CONTROL CONCEPT** one ensuring that actions are carried out or implemented according to a plan or goal.

**CONTROL (CONTROLLING) ACCOUNT** general ledger account. Its balance reflects the aggregate balance of related subsidiary ledger accounts. Most firms maintain subsidiary records for credit customers and for creditors, Accounts Receivable being the control account. The balance in a control account should not be changed unless a corresponding change is made in the subsidiary accounts. Subsidiary ledgers are often used for Accounts Payable, Inventory, Buildings, and Equipment. *See also* SUBSIDIARY ACCOUNT; SUBSIDIARY LEDGER.

**CONTROL ENVIRONMENT** the component of internal control that sets the tone of an organization by influencing employee consciousness of controls. The control environment provides discipline and structure and is the foundation for all other components of internal control. The control environment includes an entity's ethical values, its commitment to competence, participation of those charged with governance, and management's philosophy and operating style in connection with taking business risks.

**CONTROL PREMIUM** an amount paid to buy control of a business to set policies, direct operations, and make decisions for the business. This is the amount that an acquirer is usually willing to pay over the current market price of a corporation. This premium is justified by the expected synergies, such as the expected increase in cash flow resulting from cost savings and revenue improvements from the merger. This premium is typically 20–30% of the market capitalization of a corporation calculated based on a 20 trading days average of its stock price. For example, ABC Corporation has 2,000,000 shares outstanding. The 20 day average price per share is $2. Assume that the acquirer wishes to obtain 70% of the stock to gain control. The market price will be $1,400,000 \times \$2.00 = \$2,800,000$. If the buyer expects to realize 20% synergy from the merger, then the maximum price he/she is willing to pay is $\$2,800,000 \times 1.2 = \$3,360,000$. So the control premium is $560,000 ($3,360,000 − $2,800,000).

**CONTROLLABILITY** extent to which a manager can influence activities. Managerial performance theoretically should be evaluated only on the basis of those factors controlled by the manager. Thus, managers may control revenues, costs, or investment in resources. For example, a controllable cost is one that is directly regulated by a specific manager at a given level of production within a given time span. However, controllability and responsibility are rarely coextensive. One reason is that more than one manager may influence an activity.

**CONTROLLABLE COSTS** variable costs such as direct materials, direct labor, and variable overhead that are usually considered controllable by the department manager. Further, a certain portion of fixed costs can also be controllable. For example, certain advertising spent specifically for a given department would be an expense controllable by the manager of that department. Advertising expenses that benefit many departments or products are, however, NONCONTROLLABLE COSTS.

**CONTROLLABLE MANUFACTURING OVERHEAD VARIANCE** difference between actual manufacturing overhead costs incurred and the manufacturing overhead costs budgeted for the level of production reached.

**CONTROLLABLE VARIANCE** part of the total factory overhead variance not attributable to the volume variance in two-way analysis.

**CONTROLLED COMPANY** firm in which a majority of voting stock is held by an individual or corporation. The degree of control depends on the percentage of the voting stock owned.

**CONTROLLED FOREIGN CORPORATION (CFC)** foreign corporation in which more than 50% of the combined voting power of all classes of voting stock, or the total value of its stock, is owned by 10%-or-more U.S. shareholders on any day during its tax year.

**CONTROLLER** chief accounting executive of an organization. The controller is in charge of the Accounting Department. The principal functions of the controller are: (1) planning for control; (2) financial reporting and interpreting; (3) tax administration; (4) management audits and development of accounting systems; (5) internal audits.

In contrast with the controller, the TREASURER is concerned mainly with financial problems including planning the finances, managing working capital, formulating credit policy, and managing the investment portfolio. In a large firm, both the controller and treasurer report to Vice-President-Finance.

**CONTROL LIMITS** limits set for the purpose of effective quality control. Most commonly, *three-sigma* control limits are used. *See also* QUALITY CONTROL; THREE-SIGMA LIMITS.

**CONTROLLING** implementation of a decision method and the use of feedback so that the goals and specific strategic plans of the firm are optimally obtained. To do this, managers study accounting and other reports and compare them to the plans set earlier. These comparisons may show where operations are not proceeding as planned and who is responsible for what. The feedback that management receives may suggest the need to replan, to set new strategies, or to reshape the organizational structure.

**CONTROLLING COMPANY (PARENT) ACCOUNTING** method used in parent-subsidiary relationships. The holding of more than 50% of the voting stock of one corporation by another corporation generally creates a parent-subsidiary relationship. Control of a corporation may often be achieved with less than 50% of the subsidiary's voting stock, but this would not be regarded as a basis for preparing consolidated statements. In the latter situation, the investment would be accounted for under the EQUITY METHOD in an account called investment in investee. *See also* CONSOLIDATION; CONSOLIDATED FINANCIAL STATEMENT.

**CONTROL RISK** risk related to the effectiveness of a client's internal control structure policies and procedures. An ineffective internal control increases control risk.

**CONTROL RISK ASSESSMENT** risk that a material misstatement that could occur in an assertion will not be detected or prevented on a timely basis by an entity's internal controls.

**CONTROL TOTALS** in auditing, totals developed on "key" data fields in input records, and on the number of records processed to ensure that data have been properly transmitted, converted, and processed.

**CONVENTION** agreement or statement, expressed or implied, that is used to solve given types of problems. Conventions allow a standardized approach to problem solving and behavior in certain situations. An example of a convention is placing debits on the left side and credits on the right side of an account. The accountant performs daily functions by following conventions such as format guidelines in the preparation of financial statements.

**CONVENTIONAL COSTING** *see* ABSORPTION COSTING.

**CONVENTIONAL COST SYSTEM** a cost system that uses only unit- (or volume-) based COST DRIVERS to apply overhead costs to products and services.

**CONVERGENCE** the goal of establishing a uniform (worldwide) set of accounting standards in order to eliminate differences between U.S. GENERALLY ACCEPTED ACCOUNTING PRINCIPLES (GAAP) and the INTERNATIONAL FINANCIAL REPORTING STANDARDS (IFRS).

**CONVERSION**
1. act of exchanging one class of corporate security for another. An example is the conversion of convertible bonds into stock.
2. valuation substitution for another. An example is the restatement of historical cost for that of current cost. *See also* CONVERSION COST.
3. transfer of mutual fund shares from one fund to another in the same family.
4. switch from one currency to another using an exchange ratio.

**CONVERSION COST** sum of the costs of DIRECT LABOR and FACTORY OVERHEAD. *See also* PRIME COST.

**CONVERSION PRICE** effective price paid for common stock when the stock is obtained by converting either convertible preferred stock or convertible bonds. The face value of a convertible security divided by the CONVERSION RATIO gives the price of the underlying common stock at which the security is convertible. For example, if a $1,000 bond is convertible into 10 shares of stock, the conversion price is $100 ($1,000/10). An investor would usually not convert the security into common stock unless the market price was greater than the conversion price.

**CONVERSION RATIO (RATE)** number of shares of common stock that may be obtained by converting a convertible bond or share of convertible preferred stock:

Conversion Ratio (Rate) = Face Value/Conversion Price

For example, if the conversion price is $25 per share and the face value of a bond is $1,000, then an investor would receive 40 shares for each bond ($1,000/$25 per share).

**CONVERSION VALUE** value of the underlying common stock represented by convertible bonds or convertible preferred stock. This value is obtained by multiplying the conversion ratio (rate) by the per share market price of the common stock. For example, if the common stock is selling for $24 per share and the conversion ratio is 40 shares, the conversion value is $960 (40 shares × $24 per share).

**CONVERTIBLE DEBT** bond exchangeable for a specified number of common shares at a predetermined price, usually at the option of the holder. The investor in a convertible bond desires higher income than is available from common stock and the greater potential for capital appreciation than is possible with regular bonds. From the issuer's perspective the advantage of issuing a convertible bond is that its attractiveness results in greater marketability and a lower interest rate.

**CONVERTIBLE SECURITY** types of stocks and bonds that can be voluntarily converted into capital stock at a later date. Examples are convertible bonds and convertible preferred stock. The CONVERSION RATIO determines how many shares will be issued. For example, if a $100,000 convertible bond issue is convertible at 1 bond for 4 shares, 400 shares are involved calculated as follows:

$$\frac{\$100,000}{\$1,000} = 100 \text{ bonds} \times 4 \text{ shares} = 400 \text{ shares}$$

**COOKIE** a small file stored on a computer to facilitate interaction with a Web site. Generally, the information in a cookie is pretty innocuous. Web sites often use cookies to store personal preferences or track data.

**COOKIE JAR ACCOUNTING** accounting practice that inflates provisions for expected expenses and later reverses them to boost earnings—in many cases at very convenient times. This is traditionally abused when companies want to push reserves into future earnings. Reserves are set reserves to cover the estimated costs of taxes, litigation, bad debts, job cuts, and acquisitions. Company managers estimate reserves and the outside auditor judges whether the reserves are reasonable. Auditors rarely challenge company estimates because there are unclear guidelines for calculating reserves.

**"COOK THE BOOKS"** falsify financial records and statements to misrepresent the financial position and operating results of the entity.

**COOPERATIVE**
1. non-taxable entity that is formed to eliminate the middleman and gain profits or savings that would have been paid to it. Profit or savings is periodically distributed by the proportion of transactions and not in proportion to each member's investment.
2. an entity owned by members. For example, in terms of real estate, ownership shares in the apartment building are held by the occupants. They make decisions regarding the property.

**COORDINATING** process that involves a decision by management as to how best to put together the resources of the firm in order to carry out established plans. Coordinating also requires directing. In directing, managers oversee day-to-day activities and keep the organization functioning smoothly.

**COPYRIGHT** protection given by law to authors of literary, musical, artistic, and similar works. The copyright holder enjoys the following exclusive rights: (1) to print, reprint, and copy the work; (2) to sell, assign, or distribute copies; and (3) to perform the work. A copyright is recorded at its acquisition price. The legal life of a copyright is the life of the author plus 70 years. Rarely will the economic life of a copyright exceed its legal life. For example, some textbooks become obsolete in five years. As other limited life intangible assets, copyrights are amortized over the period benefited.

**CORNER (LP)** *see* GRAPHICAL METHOD.

**CORNER POINT** *see* BASIC FEASIBLE SOLUTION.

**CORPORATE DEVELOPMENT OFFICERS (CDOs)** the heads of in-house merger and acquisition (M&A) teams.

**CORPORATE GOVERNANCE** the system of checks and balances designed to ensure that corporate managers are just as vigilant on behalf of long-term shareholder value as they would be if it was their own money at risk. It is also the process whereby shareholders—the actual owners of any publicly traded firm—assert their ownership rights, through an elected board of directors and the CEO and other officers and managers they appoint and oversee. In the heels of corporate scandals including the Enron debacle in 2002, a series of sweeping changes are being sought, such as forcing boards to have a majority of independent directors, granting audit committees power to hire and fire accountants, banning sweetheart loans to officers and directors, and requiring shareholder's approval for stock option plans. More specifically, the following principles constitute good governance:

1. To avoid conflicts of interest, a company's board of directors should include a substantial majority of independent directors—*independent* meaning that directors don't have financial or close personal ties to the company or its executives.
2. A company's audit, nominating, and compensation committees should consist entirely of independent directors.
3. A board should obtain shareholder approval for any actions that could significantly affect the relationship between the board and shareholders, including the adoption of anti-takeover measures such as "poison pills."
4. Companies should base executive compensation plans on pay for performance and should provide full disclosure of these plans.
5. To avoid abuse in the use of stock options (and executive perquisites), all employee stock option plans should be submitted to shareholders for approval.

Institutional Shareholder Services, Inc. (http://www.issproxy.com/), an influential proxy advisor, started scoring companies on governance issues.

**CORPORATE JOINT VENTURE** cooperation between two or more corporations in which the purpose is to achieve jointly a specified business goal. Upon the attainment of the goal, the joint venture is terminated. An example is when two businesses agree to share in the development of a specific product. A joint venture, which is typically limited to one project, differs from a PARTNERSHIP that can work jointly on many projects. *See also* JOINT VENTURE.

**CORPORATE PLANNING MODEL** integrated business planning model in which marketing and production models are linked to the FINANCIAL MODEL. More specifically, it is a description, explanation, and interrelation of the functional areas of a firm (accounting, finance, marketing, production, and others), expressed in terms of a set of mathematical and logical equations so as to produce a variety of reports including PRO FORMA financial statements. Corporate planning models are the basic tools for risk analysis and WHAT-IF experiments. The ultimate goals of the model are to improve quality of planning and decision-making, reduce the decision risk, and, more importantly, favorably influence or even shape the future environment.

**CORPORATION** business organized as a separate legal entity with ownership evidenced by shares of stock. The corporation is formed by filing the ARTICLES OF INCORPORATION with the state authority, who returns it with a certificate of incorporation; the two documents together become the *corporate charter*. Each founding stockholder receives from the company a specified number of shares of capital stock. A stockholder may sell owned shares to other investors. The corporation is a *legal entity* separate from its owners. Advantages of a corporation are the ability to obtain large amounts of financing through a public issuance, ease of transferring shares, limited liability of owners, unlimited life, and professional management.

**CORRECTING ENTRY** *see* ADJUSTING JOURNAL ENTRY.

**CORRELATION** degree of relationship between business and economic variables such as cost and volume. Correlation analysis evaluates cause/effect relationships. It looks consistently at how the value of one variable changes when the value of the other is changed. A prediction can be made based on the relationship uncovered. An example is the effect of advertising on sales. A degree of correlation is measured statistically by the COEFFICIENT OF DETERMINATION ($r$-squared).

**CORRELATION COEFFICIENT ($r$)** measure of the degree of correlation between two variables. The range of values it takes is between $-1$ and $+1$. A negative value of $r$ indicates an inverse relationship; a positive value of $r$ indicates a direct relationship; a zero value of *r* indicates that the two variables are independent of each other; the closer *r* is to +1 and −1, the stronger the relationship between the two variables. For example, we may expect a negative relationship between the demand for a product and its selling price, because the higher the selling price charged, the lower the demand.

## COST

1. sacrifice, measured by the price paid, to acquire, produce, or maintain goods or services. Prices paid for materials, labor, and factory overhead in the manufacture of goods are costs.

2. an asset. The term cost is often used when referring to the valuation of a good or service acquired. When it is used in this sense, a cost is an ASSET.

   The concepts of cost and expense are often used interchangeably. When the benefits of the acquisition of the goods or services expire, the cost becomes an expense or loss. An EXPENSE is a cost with expired benefits. A LOSS is an expense (expired cost) with no related benefit.

**COST ABSORPTION** application of the costs to the physical units or other measures of output that pass through the process. First, costs must be accumulated by processing departments before applying the department costs to the units. An application of factory overhead costs to processing departments (or jobs), using a PREDETERMINED OVERHEAD RATE, is an example of cost absorption.

**COST ACCOUNTING** system for recording and reporting measurements of the cost of manufacturing goods and performing services in the aggregate and in detail. It includes methods for reorganizing, classifying, allocating, aggregating, and reporting actual costs and comparing them with standard costs. Determination of unit cost to make a product or render a service is needed to establish a selling price or fee to be charged. Also, costs for manufacturing a product for inventory valuation need to be known to prepare the balance sheet and income statement. Cost accounting systems include job order, process, standard, and direct costing.

**COST ACCOUNTING STANDARDS BOARD (CASB)** body established by Congress in August 1970 to promote consistency in cost accounting practices and to aid in the fair and accurate reporting of actual costs of governmental contracts. The board was authorized to promulgate standards and designed to achieve uniformity as to the application of cost accounting principles and concepts. The board ceased to exist in 1980, and its responsibilities are now handled by the Office of Federal Procurement Policy (OFPP).

**COST ACCUMULATION** collection of costs in an organized fashion by means of a cost accounting system. There are two primary approaches to cost accumulation: JOB ORDER and PROCESS COSTING. Under a job order system, the three basic elements of manufacturing costs—direct materials, direct labor, and factory overhead—are accumulated according to assigned job numbers. Under a process cost system, manufacturing costs are accumulated according to processing department or cost center.

**COST ALLOCATION** identification of costs with cost objectives, also called *cost apportionment*, *cost assignment*, *cost distribution*, and *cost reapportionment*. There are basically three aspects of cost allocation: (1) choosing the object of costing. Examples are products, processes, jobs, or departments; (2) choosing and accumulating the costs that relate to the object of costing. Examples are manufacturing expenses, selling and administrative expenses, joint costs, common costs, service department costs, and fixed costs; and (3) choosing a method of identifying (2) with (1). For example, a cost allocation base for allocating manufacturing costs would typically be labor-hours, machine-hours, or production units.

**COST APPLICATION** *see* COST ABSORPTION.

**COST APPORTIONMENT** *see* COST ALLOCATION.

**COST ASSIGNMENT** *see* COST ALLOCATION.

**COST ASSIGNMENT PATH** link between a cost and one of its two or more cost objects.

**COST-BASED PRICE** in a TRANSFER PRICING context, scheme in which the cost base can be either variable cost or full cost. It is easy to understand and convenient to use, but there are some disadvantages: (1) Inefficiencies of the selling divisions are passed on to the buying divisions with little incentive to control costs. The use of standard costs is recommended in such a case. (2) The cost-based method treats the divisions as COST CENTERS rather than PROFIT or INVESTMENT CENTERS. Therefore, measures such as RETURN ON INVESTMENT (ROI) and RESIDUAL INCOME cannot be used for evaluation purposes.

The variable cost-based transfer price has an advantage over the full cost method because in the short run it may tend to ensure the best utilization of the company's overall resources. The reason is that, in the short run, fixed costs do not change. Any use of otherwise idle facilities, without incurrence of additional fixed costs, will increase the company's overall profits.

**COST BEHAVIOR ANALYSIS** separating MIXED COSTS into their variable and fixed elements. Mixed costs are common to a wide range of firms. Examples of mixed costs include sales compensation, repairs and maintenance, and factory overhead in general. Mixed costs must be separated into the variable and fixed elements in order to be included in a variety of business planning analyses such as COST-VOLUME-PROFIT (CVP) ANALYSIS. There are several methods available for this purpose including the LEAST-SQUARES METHOD. *See also* COST BEHAVIOR PATTERN.

**COST BEHAVIOR PATTERN** manner in which a cost will react to changes in the level of activity. Costs may be viewed as variable, fixed, or mixed (semi-variable). A mixed cost is one that contains both variable and fixed elements. For planning, control, and decision purposes, mixed costs need to be separated into their variable and fixed components, using such methods as the HIGH-LOW METHOD and the LEAST-SQUARES METHOD. An application of the variable-fixed breakdown is a BREAK-EVEN and COST-VOLUME-PROFIT (CVP) ANALYSIS.

**COST-BENEFIT ANALYSIS** manner of determining whether the favorable results of an alternative are sufficient to justify the cost of taking that alternative. This analysis is widely used in connection with capital expenditure projects. An example of cost-benefit analysis is where the cost incurred to uncover the reasons for a variance outweigh the benefit to be derived. *See also* PROFITABILITY INDEX.

**COST CENTER** unit within the organization in which the manager is responsible only for costs. A cost center has no control over sales or over the generating of revenue. An example is the production department of a manufacturing company. The performance of a cost center is measured by comparing actual costs with budgeted costs for a specified period of time.

**COST CONTROL** steps taken by management to assure that the cost objectives set down in the planning stage are attained and to assure that all segments of the organization function in a manner consistent with its policies. For effective cost control, most organizations use STANDARD COST SYSTEMS, in which the actual costs are compared against standard costs for performance evaluation and the deviations are investigated for remedial actions. Cost control is also concerned with feedback that might change any or all of the future plans, the production method, or both.

**COST DEPLETION** method by which the costs of natural resources are allocated to depletion over the accounting periods that make up the life of the asset. Cost depletion is computed by (1) estimating the total quantity of mineral or other resources acquired and (2) assigning a proportionate amount of the total resource cost to the quantity extracted in the period. For example, assume that a company invests $50,000 in an oil well that contains an estimated 120,000 barrels of oil. The residual value is estimated at $6,000. In the first year, 12,000 barrels of oil are extracted and sold. The depletion for the first year is ($50,000 – $6,000) $\times$ (12,000/120,000) = $4,400. *See also* PERCENTAGE DEPLETION.

**COST DISTRIBUTION** *see* COST ALLOCATION.

**COST DRIVER** factor that has a direct cause-effect relationship to a cost, such as direct labor hours, machine hours, beds occupied, computer time used, flight hours, miles driven, or contracts.

**COST DRIVER ANALYSIS** examination, quantification, and explanation of the effects of cost drivers. The results are often used for continuous improvement programs to reduce throughput times, improve quality, and reduce costs.

**COST EFFECTIVE** among decision alternatives, the one whose cost is lower than its benefit. The most cost effective program would be the one whose cost-benefit ratio is the lowest among various programs competing for a given amount of funds. *See also* COST-BENEFIT ANALYSIS.

**COST ELEMENT** most disaggregated level of resource cost. For example, power cost, engineering cost, and depreciation may be cost elements in the activity cost pool for a machine activity. *See also* ACTIVITY COST POOL; BILL OF ACTIVITIES; RESOURCE COSTS.

**COST ESTIMATION** measurement of past costs for the purpose of predicting future costs for decision-making purposes. For example, a COST VOLUME FORMULA (such as $y = \$300 + \$5x$) can be used to estimate a cost item $y$ for any given value of volume $x$. *See also* COST PREDICTION.

**COST FLOW** *see* FLOW OF COSTS.

**COST FUNCTION** relationship between cost and activity. A cost function may be either linear or nonlinear. The general formula for a linear relationship is $y = a + bx$, where $y$ is the estimated value of a cost item for any specified value of $x$ (activity). The constant $a$, the intercept, is the fixed cost element; $b$, the slope, is the variable rate per unit of $x$. The possible measures of activity $x$ include:

> units of product
> machine-hours
> dollar sales volume
> direct labor-hours
> mileage driven

The coefficients $a$ and $b$ are estimated using such methods as the HIGH-LOW METHOD and the LEAST-SQUARES METHOD.

**COST HIERARCHY** framework for classifying production-related activities according to the level at which their costs are incurred.

**COST MANAGEMENT** management and control of activities to help set enterprise strategies and to determine an accurate product and service cost, improve business processes, eliminate waste, identify cost drivers, and plan operations.

**COST MANAGEMENT SYSTEM (CMS)** cost and management accounting, control, and reporting system that identifies, monitors, and maintains continuous, detailed analyses of a company's activities and provides managers with timely measures of operating results.

**COST MODULES** convention that is used to classify cost by point where incurred (resource module), its use (activity module), and its ultimate user (final cost object module). Activities also feed a process module.

**COST OBJECTS** intermediate and final dispositions of cost pools. Intermediate cost objects receive temporary accumulations of costs as the cost pools move from their originating points to the final cost objects. Final cost objects, such as a job, product, or process, should be logically linked with the cost pool based on a cause-and-effect relationship.

**COST OF CAPITAL** rate of return that is necessary to maintain market value (or stock price) of a firm, also called a *hurdle rate*, *cutoff rate*, or *minimum required rate of return*. The firm's cost of capital is calculated as a weighted average of the costs of debt and equity funds. Equity funds include both capital stock (common stock and preferred stock) and retained earnings. These costs are expressed as annual percentage rates. For example, assume the following capital structure and the cost of each source of financing for the XYZ Company:

| Source | Book Value | Percent of Total Weights | Cost |
|--------|-----------|--------------------------|------|
| Debt | $20,000,000 | 40% | 5.14% |
| Preferred stock | 5,000,000 | 10 | 13.40 |
| Common stock | 20,000,000 | 40 | 17.11 |
| Retained earnings | 5,000,000 | 10 | 16.00 |
| Totals | $50,000,000 | 100% | |

The overall cost of capital is computed as follows:

$$5.14\%(.4) + 13.4\%(.1) + 17.11\%(.4) + 16.00\%(.1) = 11.84\%$$

The cost of capital is used for CAPITAL BUDGETING purposes. Under the NET PRESENT VALUE METHOD, the cost of capital is used as the DISCOUNT RATE to calculate the present value of future cash inflows. Under the INTERNAL RATE OF RETURN method, it is used to make an accept-or-reject decision by comparing the cost of capital with the internal rate of return on a given project. A project is accepted when the internal rate exceeds the cost of capital.

**COST OF DEBT** interest rate times 1 minus the marginal tax rate because interest is a tax deduction—symbolically, $i(1 - t)$. Hence, an increase in the tax rate decreases the cost of debt.

**COST OF EQUITY CAPITAL** minimum desired rate of return on invested capital that is determined by calculating net income as a percentage of invested capital.

**COST OF GOODS MANUFACTURED BUDGET** detailed schedule that summarizes the costs of production for a future period.

**COST OF GOODS MANUFACTURED SCHEDULE** form showing the cost of producing goods during the accounting period. The cost of goods manufactured is an element in preparing the income statement. It consists of the cost of producing goods: DIRECT MATERIAL, DIRECT LABOR, and FACTORY OVERHEAD. Also considered is the change in the work-in-process inventory.

Assume work-in-process inventory was $30,000 on 1/1/2014 and $35,000 on 12/31/2013. During the year, manufacturing costs were direct material $20,000, direct labor $23,000, and factory overhead $40,000. The cost of goods manufactured schedule follows:

| | | |
|---|---:|---:|
| Work-in-process – 1/1/2014 | | $30,000 |
| Add: Manufacturing costs | | |
|     Direct material | $20,000 | |
|     Direct labor | 23,000 | |
|     Factory overhead | 40,000 | |
|     Total manufacturing cost | | 83,000 |
| Total | | $113,000 |
| Less: Work-in-process – 12/31/2013 | | 35,000 |
| Cost of goods manufactured | | $ 78,000 |

**COST OF GOODS SOLD** *see* COST OF SALES.

**COST-OF-LIVING ADJUSTMENT (COLA)** upward change in an employee's compensation because of inflation. The adjustment is typically based on a price index such as the Consumer Price Index, Wholesale Price Index, and Gross National Product Index. COLA is sometimes built into labor contracts.

**COST OF NEW EXTERNAL COMMON EQUITY** cost of newly issued common stock. This is higher than the cost of retained earnings because of stock flotation costs. Providers of equity capital are exposed to more risk than lenders are because the firm is not obligated to pay them a return. Also, in case of liquidation, creditors are paid before equity investors. Thus, equity financing is more expensive than debt because equity investors require a higher return to compensate for the greater risk assumed.

**COST OF PREDICTION ERROR** cost of a failure to predict a certain variable (such as sales, earnings, and cash flow) accurately. For example, assume that a company has been selling a toy baby doll having a variable cost of $.50 for $.90 each (a contribution of $.40 per doll). The fixed cost is $200. The company has no privilege of returning any unsold dolls. It has predicted sales of 1,500 units. However, unforeseen competition has reduced sales to 1,000 units. What is the cost of its prediction error—that is, its failure to predict demand accurately?

(1) Initial predicted sales = 1,500 units.
    Optimal decision: purchase 1,500 units.
    Expected net income (1,500 × $.40) – $200 = $400

(2) Alternative parameter value = 1,000 units.
Optimal decision: purchase 1,000 units.
Expected net income (1,000 × $.40 ) – $200 = $200

(3) Results of original decision under alternative parameter value.
Expected net income:

Revenue      Cost of Dolls    Fixed Costs
(1,000 units × $.90) – (1,500 units × $.50) –    $200    =
$900 – $750 – $200 = – $50

(4) Cost of prediction error, (2) – (3) = $250.

**COST OF PREFERRED STOCK** minimum desired rate of return on invested capital that is the stated dividend rate of the individual preferred stock issue.

**COST OF PRODUCTION REPORT** summary of the total manufacturing cost of an item. It involves charges to a processing department and the allocation of the total cost between the ending work-in-process inventory and the units completed and transferred out to the next department or finished goods inventory. The cost of production report generally consists of four sections: (1) *Physical Flow* accounts for the physical flow of units in and out of a department. (2) *Equivalent Production* is the sum of: (a) units in process, restated in completed units, and (b) total units actually produced. The computation of equivalent units of production depends on the flow of cost method-weighted average or FIFO. (3) *Costs to Account For* accounts for the incurrence of costs that were: (a) in process at the beginning of the period, (b) transferred in from previous departments, and (c) added by the department during the current period. (4) *Costs Accounted For* accounts for the disposition of costs charged to the department that were: (a) transferred out to the next department or finished goods inventory, (b) completed and on hand, and (c) in process at the end of the period. The total of the *Costs to Account For* must equal the total of the *Costs Accounted For*. *See also* PROCESS COSTING.

**COST OF RETAINED EARNINGS** cost of internally generated funds. It is an imputed or opportunity cost or the dividends given up by the common stockholders. It is the rate that investors can earn elsewhere on investments of comparable risk.

**COST OF SALES** price of buying or making an item that is sold; also called *cost of goods sold*. The difference between sales and cost of sales is gross profit. For a retail business, the cost of sale is the purchase price of the item. For a manufactured good, the cost of sale includes DIRECT MATERIAL, DIRECT LABOR, and FACTORY OVERHEAD associated with producing it. An example would be the cost to General Motors of making a car. An illustrative example of a gross profit calculation for a retail business follows:

| Sales | | | $100 |
|---|---|---|---|
| Less: Cost of Sales | | | |
| Beginning inventory | | $ 30 | |
| Add: Purchases | | 80 | |
| Cost of goods available | | $110 | |
| Less: Ending inventory | | 40 | |
| Cost of sales | | | 70 |
| Gross profit | | | $ 30 |

**COST-PLUS CONTRACT** form of contract that requires the customer to pay for all costs incurred plus a predetermined amount of profit.

**COST PLUS PRICING** clear and convenient way to establish a selling price. This method may be used in determining a contract price by a supplier seeking to avoid the uncertainty associated with predicting costs. Cost plus pricing may be found in developmental contracts for new products. Federal agencies deal with cost plus fixed fee contracts. In cost plus pricing, an item is priced at its cost (including direct material, direct labor, and factory overhead) plus some fixed fee or profit markup. For example, if the total cost of a contract is $325,000 and the fixed fee is $100,000, the contract price would be $425,000. If a profit markup is used, it should be based on the nature of the product and corporate considerations (e.g., marketing aspects). For example, if cost is $200,000 and a profit markup on cost of 30% is desired, the contract price is $260,000.

  When cost plus pricing is used to determine a transfer price for an internal transfer of a product within the organization, it closely approximates an outside market price. Thus, the resulting synthetic market price is considered a good practical substitute.

**COST-PLUS TRANSFER PRICE** transfer price computed as the sum of the costs incurred by the producing division plus an agreed-on profit percentage.

**COST POOL** grouping of individual costs. Subsequent allocations are made of cost pools rather than of individual costs. Costs are often pooled by departments, by jobs, or by behavior pattern. For example, overhead costs are accumulated by service departments in a factory and then allocated to production departments before multiple departmental overhead rates are developed for product costing purposes.

**COST PREDICTION** forecast of costs for managerial decision-making purposes. The terms cost ESTIMATION and *cost prediction* are used interchangeably. To predict future costs, a COST FUNCTION is often specified and estimated statistically. The cost function may be either linear (i.e., $y = a + bx$) or nonlinear. The estimated cost function must pass some statistical tests, such as having a high R-SQUARED and a high T-VALUE, to provide sound cost prediction.

**COST PRINCIPLE** *see* HISTORICAL COST.

**COST REAPPORTIONMENT** *see* COST ALLOCATION.

**COST-RECOVERY METHOD** revenue recognition method under which no gross profit is recognized until all the cost of the merchandise has been recovered. That is, the first payments received from customers are treated as a recovery of the cost of goods sold. Once the cost has been recovered, the remaining collections are recognized as gross profit. Like the *installment* method, this method may be used because of the uncertainty of collections, and is not generally accepted. *See also* INSTALLMENT (SALES) METHOD.

**COST REDUCTION PROGRAM** policy of cutting costs to improve profitability. It may be implemented when a company is having financial problems and must "tighten its belt." In some cases, the firm is initiating a policy to eliminate waste and inefficiency. A cost reduction program may detract from the QUALITY OF EARNINGS when significant cuts are made in DISCRETIONARY COSTS.

**COST REFERENCE** source to determine the price of a good or service, such as a supplier's price list.

**COST SHEET** form prepared for each job or department. It serves as a means of accumulating the manufacturing costs—direct materials, direct labor, and overhead costs—chargeable to the job or department and as a means of determining unit costs. A JOB (ORDER) COST SHEET is used for job order costing; a COST OF PRODUCTION REPORT is used for process costing. Cost sheets may serve as a subsidiary ledger supporting a Work-in-Process Control.

**COSTS OF CONFORMANCE** costs incurred to produce a quality product or service.

**COSTS OF NONCONFORMANCE** costs incurred to correct defects in a product or service.

**COSTS OF QUALITY** costs incurred in association with quality conformance. It must be assessed in terms of relative costs and benefits. Thus, an organization should attempt to minimize its total cost of quality. *See also* CONFORMANCE COSTS; PREVENTION COSTS; APPRAISAL; NONCONFORMANCE COSTS; INTERNAL FAILURE COSTS; EXTERNAL FAILURE COSTS.

**COST SUMMARY SCHEDULE** PROCESS COSTING schedule that is used to determine the costs to be transferred to the finished goods inventory account of a department or production process and the ending balance of the work in process inventory account.

**COST-TO-COST METHOD** in construction contracts, an estimate of completion in which the state of completion is the ratio of costs incurred as of a given date divided by the estimated total project cost. *See also* PERCENTAGE OF COMPLETION METHOD.

**COST-VOLUME FORMULA** cost accounting formula used for COST PREDICTION and FLEXIBLE BUDGETING purposes. It is a cost function in the form of:

$$y = a + bx$$

where $y$ = the semi-variable (or mixed) costs to be broken up
$\quad\quad x$ = any given measure of activity such as volume and labor-hours
$\quad\quad a$ = the fixed cost component
$\quad\quad b$ = the variable rate per unit of $x$

For example, the cost-volume formula for factory overhead is $y = \$200 + \$10x$ where $y$ = estimated factory overhead and $x$ = direct labor-hours, which means that the factory overhead is estimated to be $200 fixed, plus $10 per hour of direct labor.

**COST-VOLUME-PROFIT (CVP) ANALYSIS** analysis that deals with how profits and costs change with a change in volume. More specifically, it looks at the effects on profits of changes in such factors as variable costs, fixed costs, selling prices, volume, and mix of products sold. By studying the relationships of costs, sales, and net income, management is better able to cope with many planning decisions. For example, CVP analysis attempts to answer the following questions: (1) What sales volume is required to break even? (2) What sales volume is necessary in order to earn a desired (target) profit? (3) What profit can be expected on a given sales volume? (4) How would changes in selling price, variable costs, fixed costs, and output affect profits? (5) How would a change in the mix of products sold affect the break-even and target volume and profit potential? *See also* BREAK-EVEN ANALYSIS; TARGET INCOME SALES.

**COUNTERBALANCING ERROR** *see* OFFSETTING ERROR.

**COUPON BOND** *see* BEARER BOND.

**COUPON RATE** interest rate on the face amount of a debt security. For instance, the annual interest to be paid on a $1,000 bond with a nominal interest rate of 8% is $80. Typically, interest payments are made semiannually. The term derives from BEARER BONDS, once more common than now, which actually bore coupons to be detached and presented for payment as interest became due. Even with *registered bonds* the term survives and is distinguished from YIELD, which relates the coupon rate to the market price of the bond.

**COVENANT** promise, commonly found in the form of restrictions in a loan agreement imposed on the borrower to protect the lender's interest. Examples of typical restrictive provisions are a ceiling on dividends and the required maintenance of a minimum working capital. *See also* INDENTURE.

**COVERDELL EDUCATION SAVINGS ACCOUNTS** formerly known as education IRAs, these accounts permit nondeductible contributions for beneficiaries under the age of 18. Withdrawals made by beneficiaries for qualified education expenses are excluded from taxable income. The contribution limit is $2,000, but is phased out ratably based on modified adjusted gross income. Phaseout ranges are dependent on filing status and are periodically adjusted for inflation.

**COVERED OPTION** contract backed by owning the stock underlying the option. Assume the owner of 500 shares of XYZ writes (sells) 5 XYZ call options. The seller now has a covered option position. If the price of the stock rises and there is an exercise of the option, the seller has the stock to deliver to the purchaser. If the seller did not own the shares, he or she would be termed a naked writer.

**CPM** *see* CRITICAL PATH METHOD (CPM).

**CRASHING** process of reducing an activity time by adding resources and, hence, usually cost.

**CREATIVE ACCOUNTING** management's attempt to "fool around" with its accounting in order to overstate net income. Examples of income management include selling off low-cost basis assets to report gains, unjustifiably lengthening the expected life of an asset to reduce expense (e.g., depreciable life), and under-accruing expenses (e.g., bad debt provisions). To financial statement users, "creative accounting" has a negative connotation.

**CREDIT**
1. entry on the right side of an account. As a verb, to make an entry on the right side of an account. Under the DOUBLE ENTRY BOOKKEEP-ING system, credits increase liabilities, equity, and revenues and decrease assets and expenses.
2. to *enter* or *post* a credit.
3. the ability to buy an item or to borrow money in return for a promise to pay later.
4. in *taxation*, a dollar for dollar offset against a tax liability. *See also* TAX CREDITS.

**CREDIT AGAINST TAX** *see* TAX CREDIT.

**CREDIT ANALYSIS** process of determining, before a line of credit is extended, whether a credit applicant meets the firm's credit standards or those of a lender and what amount of credit the applicant should receive. It typically involves two steps: (1) obtaining credit information (such as financial statements, Dun & Bradstreet reports, etc.) and (2) analyzing the information in order to make the credit decision.

**CREDIT BALANCE**
1. balance in the right side of an account. According to DEBIT AND CREDIT CONVENTIONS, any asset and expense account will have

a normal debit balance, while any liability, equity, and revenue account will have a normal credit balance.
   2. overpaid customer account resulting in a credit amount in accounts receivable.

**CREDIT LINE** specified amount of money available to a borrower from a bank usually for one year. A credit line is a moral, not a contractual, commitment, and no commitment fee is charged. Compensating balances, though, are commonly required—10% of the line plus 10% of amounts borrowed under the line. There are confirmed lines of credit and guidance lines, the former being documented by a letter to the depositor, the latter being an internal limit observed by the bank. Credit lines contrast with revolving credits, which are contractual and involve a commitment fee.

**CREDIT MEMORANDUM**
   1. form or document used by a seller to notify the buyer of merchandise that the buyer's accounts payable is being credited (decreased) due to errors or other factors requiring adjustments.
   2. form given by a bank to a depositor to indicate that the depositor's balance is being increased due to some event other than a deposit, such as the collection by the bank of the depositor's note receivable.

**CREDITOR** business or individual that has extended credit and is owed money.

**CREDITORS' EQUITY** total amount of liabilities. The creditors' equity ratio equals total liabilities divided by total assets. This reflects the percentage of assets financed by creditors. In the event of corporate liquidation, creditors are paid before stockholders. *See also* STOCKHOLDERS' EQUITY.

**CRIMINAL PENALTY** fine or punishment imposed by a taxing authority for severe violations of tax laws and regulations. Criminal penalties, which may include imprisonment, include penalties for income tax evasion.

**CRITICAL PATH** longest path for a project. This is the minimum amount of time needed for the completion of the project. Thus, the activities along this path must be accelerated in order to speed up the project. On the other hand, delays in these activities would cause delays in the project. It is thus important to identify the critical path. *See also* PROGRAM EVALUATION AND REVIEW TECHNIQUE (PERT).

**CRITICAL PATH ACCOUNTING** method of accounting for costs and expenditures that must accompany the CRITICAL PATH METHOD (CPM) of project management. Costs for manpower, materials, and overhead must be accounted for by activities and paths of a given project. In many cases it is possible to shorten the project's total completion time by injecting additional money and labor. Critical path accounting should provide all the necessary cost data, including *indirect* costs such as facilities and equipment costs, supervision, and labor and personnel costs, and *direct* costs that are needed to speed up each activity or path. *See also* PROGRAM EVALUATION AND REVIEW TECHNIQUE (PERT).

**CRITICAL PATH METHOD (CPM)** technique in PROGRAM EVALUATION AND REVIEW TECHNIQUE (PERT) that uses a single time estimate for each activity, rather than three time estimates—*optimistic, most likely,* and *pessimistic.* The primary objective of CPM is to identify the CRITICAL PATH for a project.

**CROSSFOOT** procedure in which additions are made vertically as well as horizontally to assure the mathematical accuracy of totals. An example is verifying that the total debits equal the total credits in a journal (e.g., cash payments journal) at the end of the month.

**CROSS-SITE SCRIPTING (XSS)** a hacking technique that allows an attacker to embed malicious content into a dynamic Web page to fool the end user into executing that malicious code on his or her computer. Typically, a hacker attacks a legitimate Web site using XSS. When a user visits that legitimate Web site, the malicious code is downloaded and executed on the user's machine.

**CROSS-SUBSIDY** improper assignment of costs among objects such that certain objects are overcosted while other cost objects are undercosted relative to the activity costs assigned. For example, traditional cost accounting systems tend to overcost high-volume products and undercost low-volume products.

**CRYPTOGRAPHY** science of secret writing. It is a security safeguard to render information unintelligible if unauthorized individuals intercept the transmission. When the information is to be used, it can be decoded.

**CULMINATION OF EARNINGS PROCESS** method of recognizing revenue, usually at the time of sale or rendering of a service. A reasonable method for estimating collectibility must exist.

**CUMULATIVE ACTIVITY COST** cost of two or more activities added together. The buildup of activity cost so that each successive total includes activity costs that precede it.

**CUMULATIVE EFFECT OF A CHANGE IN ACCOUNTING PRINCIPLE** no longer allowed accounting treatment. Companies no longer will report a cumulative effect on the current year's income statement. Instead, they will report any necessary adjustment as an adjustment to the opening balance of retained earnings for the earliest period presented. FASB's retrospective approach eliminates all cumulative effect adjustments to current income and should greatly enhance the consistency and comparability of financial information over time and between companies. Because a change in principle is retrospectively applied to prior financial statements, there is a need to present pro forma information.

**CUMULATIVE PREFERRED STOCK** type of stock whose DIVI-DENDS, if not paid in a given period, accumulate. All preferred dividends in arrears must be paid before common stockholders can receive distributions. Assume 10,000 shares of $10 par 8% cumulative preferred stock has not paid dividends from 1/1/2011 to 12/31/2014. At the end of 2014, the cumulative dividend not paid is $32,000 ($100,000 × 8% × 4 years). *See also* PREFERRED STOCK.

**CUMULATIVE VOTING** method of voting that enables a minority group of shareholders to obtain some voice in the control of a corporation. Normally, shareholders must apportion their votes equally among the candidates for the board of directors. Cumulative voting allows them to vote all their shares for a single candidate. The number of shares required to elect a desired number of directors (*NR*) is calculated by the formula:

$$NR = [(DN \times TN)/(N + 1)] + 1$$

where *DN* = number of directors stockholder desires to elect, *TN* = total number of shares of common stock outstanding and entitled to be voted, and *N* = total number of directors to be elected.

For example, a company will elect six directors. There are fifteen candidates and 100,000 shares entitled to be voted. If a group desires to elect two directors, the number of shares it must have is:

$$[(2 \times 100,000 \text{ shares})/(6 + 1)] + 1 = 28,572 \text{ shares}$$

Note that a minority group wishes to elect one-third (two out of six) of the board of directors. It can achieve its goal by owning less than one-third (28,572 shares out of 100,000 shares) the number of shares of stock.

**CURRENT ACCOUNT**
1. running account, typically involving related companies, showing the movement of an item (e.g., goods, cash) between them. In most cases, a periodic settlement is not required.
2. partner's account showing salary withdrawals and other transactions.

**CURRENT ASSET** item having a life of one year or less, or the normal OPERATING CYCLE of the business, whichever is greater. For example, if a construction company's operating cycle is three years because it is engaged in long-term construction activities, it would show as current assets items having up to a three-year life. However, in almost all cases, the one-year cutoff is used. Examples of current assets are cash, marketable securities, inventory, and prepaid expenses.

**CURRENT COST** price of replacing an asset identical to an existing one. It should be of the same condition and age as well as have the same service potential. *See also* REPLACEMENT COST.

**CURRENT COST ACCOUNTING** method of measuring assets in terms of REPLACEMENT COST. One of the following techniques is applied: (1) the use of *indexing* based on price movements applied to homogeneous asset groups; or (2) direct pricing applicable to assets for which prices are determined from either price lists, manufacturers' quotes, and other direct price sources. Replacement cost cannot exceed recoverable amounts referring to cash recoveries from the sale or use of an asset via either NET REALIZABLE VALUE or the PRESENT VALUE of future cash flows. Assume land is acquired at the beginning of the year for $100,000. At year-end, it is appraised at $130,000. Thus, there is a holding (unrealized) gain of $30,000.

**CURRENT COST/CONSTANT DOLLAR** historical cost is first stated in terms of current cost which in turn is adjusted to constant purchasing power using the average CONSUMER PRICE INDEX (CPI) for the current year. In effect replacement cost and CPI are combined. This is accomplished as follows:

$$\text{Replacement Cost} \times \frac{\text{Average CPI for Current Year}}{\text{CPI at Time of Transaction}}$$

**CURRENT FILE** includes documentation applicable only to the year being audited. Items to include in the current file include the engagement letter, the audit plan, results of audit procedures, and the management representation letter.

**CURRENT LIABILITY** obligation payable within one year or the normal operating cycle of the business. A current liability requires payment out of a current asset or the incurrence of another short-term obligation. Examples are accounts payable, short-term notes payable, accrued expenses payable (e.g., taxes payable, salaries payable). *See also* CURRENT ASSET.

**CURRENT OPERATING CONCEPT** method of measuring the efficiency of a company. Net income is based on recurring and usual income statement items. Concern is with the effective utilization of the entity's resources in operating the business and making a profit. In computing income, special attention is placed on current and operating items. Specifically, earnings consist of value changes and events controllable by management and resulting from decisions of the *current* period. Included, however, are factors acquired in a previous period but used in the present one. Note that relevant changes arise solely from normal operations. Those advocating the current operating concept argue that the resulting current operating performance net income enhances interperiod and interfirm comparisons and facilitates predictions.

**CURRENT RATIO** measure of liquidity. Current assets are divided by current liabilities. Assuming current assets are $120,000 and current liabilities are $40,000 the current ratio is

$$\frac{\$120,000}{\$40,000} = 3$$

The higher the current ratio, the more assurance that current liabilities can be paid. Thus, there is greater short-term creditor protection. (A company's ratio can be compared with the average in its industry to see whether it is high or low.) An excess of current assets over current liabilities is a buffer against losses that may occur in selling inventory, collecting accounts receivable, or liquidating current investment (e.g., marketable securities). A high current ratio provides a margin of safety against uncertainty and random fluctuations (e.g., strikes, extraordinary losses).

In general, a business with less inventory and more collectible accounts receivable can operate safely with a lower current ratio than a company having a high percentage of current assets in inventory.

Creditors looking at a company's current ratio must consider the quality of the current assets and the nature of the current liabilities. For example, work-in-process inventory has a higher realization risk than finished goods.

**CURRENT VALUE** term for an asset shown at its present worth. Some measures that can be used are CURRENT COST, current exit value, and PRESENT VALUE. *See also* CURRENT VALUE ACCOUNTING.

**CURRENT VALUE ACCOUNTING** periodical revaluation of the CURRENT VALUE of assets and liabilities. Unlike CONSTANT DOLLAR ACCOUNTING, it requires the recognition of holding gains or losses prior to realization through sales or exchanges.

**CURTAILMENT IN PENSION PLAN** materially *reducing* the expected years of future services of current employees or eliminating for a significant number of employees the accrual of defined benefits for some or all of their future services. Immediate recognition is given to the gain or loss upon curtailment. The components of the gain or loss include (1) unamortized PRIOR SERVICE PENSION COST applicable to employee service no longer needed and (2) change in PROJECTED BENEFIT OBLIGATION occurring from the curtailment. *See also* SETTLEMENT IN PENSION PLAN; TERMINATION IN PENSION PLANS.

**CUSTOMER PROFITABILITY ANALYSIS** analysis that assigns revenues and costs to major customers or groups of customers rather than to organizational units, products, or other objects. The results may direct organizational resources toward more profitable uses. It is an application of segmented reporting in which a customer group is treated as a segment. It is especially helpful when combined with an activity-based costing approach that determines which activities are performed for each group and assigns costs based on appropriate drivers. For example, activities, their drivers, and their costs may be classified as order level, customer level, channel level, market level, or enterprise level.

**CUSTOMER RELATIONSHIP MANAGEMENT (CRM) SYSTEMS** the modern version of the old-fashioned Rolodex. A CRM system allows an organization to store customer and prospective contact information, accounts, leads, and sales opportunities in a centralized location, often in the cloud. It is used to automate customer service and support. CRM systems often have advanced features to assist the sales force in collaborating with colleagues and customers. For instance, Amazon.com uses CRM technology to make suggestions to customers based on their personal purchase histories.

**CUSTOMER RESPONSE TIME** delay from placement of an order to delivery of the good or service; also called DELIVERY CYCLE TIME. Response time is a function of time drivers, e.g., uncertainty about arrivals of customers in the queue and BOTTLENECKS (points at which capacity is reached or exceeded). It is another crucial competitive factor. *See also* ORDER RECEIPT TIME; MANUFACTURING CYCLE TIME; MANUFACTURING CYCLE EFFICIENCY.

**CUSTOMER RETENTION** important measure of service quality because loyal customers spend more, refer new customers, and are less costly to service.

**CUSTOMER VALUE** difference between customer realization and sacrifice. Realization is what the customer receives, which includes product features, quality, and service. This takes into account the customer's cost to use, maintain, and dispose of the product or service. Sacrifice is what a customer gives up, which includes the amount the customer pays for the product plus the time and effort spent acquiring the product and learning how to use it. Maximizing customer value means maximizing the difference between realization and sacrifice.

**CUTOFF DATE** audit procedure for determining whether a transaction took place before or subsequent to the end of an accounting period. It assures that the transaction has been recorded in the proper period. It is the date chosen to stop the flow of transactions, merchandise, cash, and so on for audit purposes. For example, in taking a physical inventory, there must be a cutoff date applicable to sales and purchases. This may require closing receiving and shipping rooms while the inventory count takes place. Transactions of one period must be distinguished from those of another. Cutoff errors must be diligently avoided when recording transactions.

**CUTOFF RATE** *see* COST OF CAPITAL.

**CUTOFF TEST** involves examining transactions a few days before and after year-end in order to determine that accounting transactions have been recorded in the proper time period.

**CVP ANALYSIS** *see* COST-VOLUME-PROFIT (CVP) ANALYSIS.

**CVP RELATIONSHIPS** *see* COST-VOLUME-PROFIT (CVP) ANALYSIS.

**CYBER INVESTING** investing such as on-line trading on the Internet.

**CYBERSPACE** Originally used in *Neuromancer*, William Gibson's novel of direct brain-computer networking, refers to the collective realms of computer-aided communication.

**CYCLE BILLING** method of billing customers at different time intervals. For example, customers with last names starting with A may be billed on the first of the month while those with last names beginning with B are billed on the second day.

**CYCLE TIME** time required to produce and deliver a product or service. Thus, total cycle time is the sum of value-added processing time and total nonvalue-added time. *See also* DELIVERY CYCLE TIME; CUSTOMER RESPONSE TIME.

**CYCLE TIME COMPRESSION** reducing the time required to produce and deliver a product or service, in order to increase throughput and become more flexible and responsive to customers.

**CYPHER** solve secret writing in a transmission based on a key to the code.

# D

**DATABASE** storehouse of related data records independently managed apart from any specific program or information system application. It is then made available to a wide variety of individuals and systems within the organization. In essence, it is an electronic filing cabinet providing a common core of information accessible by a program. An example is a database of inventory items.

**DATA BASE MANAGEMENT SYSTEM (DBMS)** software used to manage data in the database. It is a set of programs that provides for defining, controlling, and accessing the database. The database program allows accountants to enter, manipulate, retrieve, display, select, sort, edit, and index data. Advantages of a database management system include: (1) elimination of data redundancy, (2) improved efficiency in updating, (3) data sharing, (4) easy data access, and (5) reduced program maintenance cost. Major DBMs include Oracle, SQL Server, MySQL, and Access.

**DATA FLOW DIAGRAM (DFD)** graphically depicts the flow of data in an organization's information system. A DFD lets an organization visualize how its information system operates. The visual representation provided by DFD is generally preferable over narrative technical descriptions, making it easier to understand by technical and nontechnical users alike.

**DATA INTERCHANGE FORMAT (DIF) FILE** system to transfer computer files from one program to another. DIF files created on other systems (e.g., the client's) can be imported into the practitioner's spreadsheet or database. The DIF is produced as an output or export option by many of the existing spreadsheet programs and by some database programs. Various accounting packages can generate DIF files. An example of an application is extracting a spreadsheet from EXCEL and putting it into another spreadsheet program or a word processing program. It should be noted, however, a file written in DIF requires more storage space than the original it was built from.

**DATA MINING** the process of analyzing data, generally using specialized software, to increase revenue and cut costs. Essentially, data mining is the process of discovering correlations or patterns among muliple fields from a large database.

**DATA PRIVACY** security measures and devices employed by the accountant to assure that confidential information (e.g., client files) are not improperly accessed. For example, a password may be required to obtain access to electronic data files of clients.

**DATA PROCESSING** process that involves transformation of data into information through classifying, sorting, merging, recording, retrieving, transmitting, or reporting. Data processing can be manual or computer based.

**DATAQUICK** a national company that maintains a huge database that tracks 83 million properties. The firm provides information and analysis to clients such as newspapers, appraisers, mortgages and lending, and title insurance.

**DATA REDUNDANCY**
1. the storage of the same data in more than one field in a database. This repetition of data is generally discouraged since it can cause inconsistencies in maintaining the data; the value may be updated in one field, but not the other.
2. the backing up of data on multiple servers.

**DATA WAREHOUSES** designed to help an organization analyze its data, a data warehouse is a database that focuses on query and analysis rather than on transaction processing. Historical data from transactions and other sources is generally included. Its purpose is to consolidate data from multiple sources and to separate the transaction processing workload from the data analysis workload.

**DATE OF RECORD** date on which HOLDERS OF RECORD in a company's stock ledger are entitled to receive DIVIDENDS or STOCK RIGHTS. Stock usually trades EX-DIVIDEND or EX-RIGHTS beginning the fourth business day before the date of record. It is different from the DECLA-RATION OF DATE; that is, the date that the board of directors announces its intention to pay a dividend. Once this is done, the company has created a LIABILITY; it owes the dividend to the stockholders of record. For example, on July 5, the board of directors of XYZ Corporation declared a 25 cent cash dividend on its common stock payable on August 15 to stockholders of record on July 17. This creates a liability by the company to stockholders of record. The common stockholders on the company's list on July 17 will receive the 25 cent dividend on August 15.

**DAYBOOK** rarely used BOOK OF ORIGINAL ENTRY. It is basically a descriptive, chronological record of day-to-day business transactions, like a diary. Details formerly kept in daybooks are now represented by original documents such as invoices and supporting documents. If daybooks are kept, their detail must subsequently be entered into journals in bookkeeping form to enable posting to ledgers.

**DAYS PURCHASES IN ACCOUNTS PAYABLE** ratio measuring the extent that accounts payable represent current rather than overdue obligations. A comparison should be made to the terms of purchase. Accounts payable are divided by the purchases per day. The latter is determined by dividing purchases by 360 days. Assume accounts payable is $50,000 and purchases are $800,000. The ratio is:

$$\frac{\$50,000}{\$800,000/360} = \frac{\$50,000}{\$2,222.22} = 22.50$$

**DAYS TO SELL INVENTORY** ratio measuring the number of days inventory is held. As a general rule, the longer inventory is held, the greater is its risk of not being sold at full value. This ratio is crucial in the case of inventory that is perishable or prone to obsolescence, such as high technology and fashion items. Inventory also involves an OPPORTUNITY COST of funds. Days to sell inventory is one of the components in determining a company's OPERATING CYCLE. Assume an INVENTORY TURNOVER of 10 times. This means that the number of days inventory is held equals:

$$\frac{360}{10} = 36 \text{ days}$$

*See also* AVERAGE AGE OF INVENTORY.

**DEATH BENEFIT**
1. in *taxation*, a payment or receipt of proceeds to a specified beneficiary or beneficiaries by an employer, by virtue of the death of the employee. Under certain conditions, the first $5,000 of such a payment may not be subject to federal income taxes.
2. portion (tax exempt) of the proceeds of a life insurance policy representing protection as distinguished from investment value. Policy loans reduce the death benefit by the amount of the outstanding loan balance.

**DEATH TAX** tax imposed on property upon the death of the owner, such as an inheritance or ESTATE TAX.

**DEBENTURE** long-term debt instrument that is not secured by a mortgage or other lien on specific property. Because it is unsecured debt, it is issued usually by large, financially strong companies with excellent BOND RATINGS. There are two kinds of debentures: a senior issue and a *subordinated* (junior) issue, which has a subordinate lien. The order of a prior claim is set forth in the bond INDENTURE. Typically, in the event of liquidation, subordinated debentures come after senior debt.

**DEBENTURE CAPITAL** CAPITAL obtained through the sale of unsecured bonds, called DEBENTURE.

**DEBIT**
1. an entry on the left side of an account. As a verb, to make an entry on the left side of an account. Under the DOUBLE ENTRY BOOKKEEPING system, debits increase assets and expenses and decrease liabilities, equity, and revenues.
2. to *enter* or POST a debit.

**DEBIT AND CREDIT CONVENTIONS** rules for debit and credit to be followed under DOUBLE ENTRY BOOKKEEPING. The rules or conventions using the T-account form for the balance sheet and income statement accounts are as follows:

| Any Asset Account | |
|---|---|
| Dr. | Cr. |
| Increase | Decrease |
| + | − |
| Ending | |
| balance | |

| Any Liability Account | |
|---|---|
| Dr. | Cr. |
| Decrease | Increase |
| − | + |
| | Ending |
| | balance |

| Any Equity Account | |
|---|---|
| Dr. | Cr. |
| Decrease | Increase |
| | + |
| − | Ending |
| | balance |

| Revenues | |
|---|---|
| Dr. | Cr. |
| − | + |

| Expenses | |
|---|---|
| Dr. | Cr. |
| + | − |

**DEBIT MEMORANDUM**
  1. form or document used by a seller to notify a buyer that the seller is debiting (increasing) the amount of the buyer's accounts payable due to errors or other factors requiring adjustments.
  2. form or document given by the bank to a depositor to notify that the depositor's balance is being decreased due to some event other than payment of a check, such as bank service charges.

**DEBT** money or services owed to an outside party. It is a legal obligation of the business arising either from written or oral agreement. Debt may either be short-term or long-term. *See also* CURRENT LIABILITY; LONG-TERM DEBT.

**DEBT AND EQUITY SECURITIES** ways of financing a business through credit obligations (e.g., bond issue) and CAPITAL STOCK. Usually, a company finances with both rather than just one. The CAPITAL STRUCTURE of a company is commonly referred to as consisting of debt and equity securities. *See also* WARRANT.

**DEBT-EQUITY RATIO** measure used in the analysis of financial statements to show the amount of protection available to creditors. The ratio equals total liabilities divided by total stockholders' equity; also called *debt to net worth ratio*. A high ratio usually indicates that the business has a lot of risk because it must meet principal and interest on its obligations. Potential creditors are reluctant to give financing to a company with a high debt position. However, the magnitude of debt depends on the type of business. For example, a bank has a high debt ratio but its assets are generally liquid. A utility can afford a higher ratio than a manufacturer because its earnings can be controlled by rate adjustments. Usually, book value is used to measure a firm's debt and equity securities in calculating the ratio. Market value may be a more realistic measure, however, because it takes into account current market conditions. *See also* CAPITAL STRUCTURE.

**DEBT FINANCING** raising money by selling bonds, notes, or mortgages or borrowing directly from financial institutions. The presence of debt financing in a firm's capital structure provides FINANCIAL LEVERAGE, which tends to magnify the effects of increased operating profits on the stockholder's returns. Since debt is normally the cheapest form of long-term financing, due to the tax deductibility of interest, it is a desirable component of the firm's capital structure as long as the borrowed funds produce a return in excess of their cost. Also, during inflation, the company will be paying back the debt in cheaper dollars. However, too much debt can result in higher levels of FINANCIAL RISK in meeting the principal and satisfying interest payments. Excessive debt will make it more difficult to raise funds and will increase the COST OF CAPITAL. *See also* EQUITY FINANCING.

**DEBT LIMIT**
1. legal and maximum amount of debt that a governmental entity can undertake. This maximum debt amount minus the outstanding obligations is the legal debt margin.
2. provision often found in a COVENANT in a corporate loan agreement.

**DEBTOR** individual who has a legal obligation to pay money to another.

**DEBT RESTRUCTURING**
1. adjustment or realignment of debt structure reflecting concessions granted by creditors, to give the debtor a more practical arrangement for meeting financial obligations. Restructuring is needed when the debtor has severe financial problems. The agreement to restructure may result from legal action or simply be an agreement to which parties consent. *See also* CHAPTER 11; CHAPTER 7; TROUBLED DEBT RESTRUCTURING.
2. realignment of debt structure based on a voluntary financial management decision—for example, to replace short-term debt with long-term debt.

**DEBT SERVICE FUND** in governmental accounting, fund used to account for the accumulation of resources for, and the payment of, general long-term debt principal and interest except that payable from proprietary, fiduciary, or special assessment funds.

**DEBT TO NET WORTH RATIO** *see* DEBT-EQUITY RATIO.

**DEBUG** process of tracing and correcting flaws in a software program or hardware device. In a complex program, it may take longer to correct the errors than originally to write the program. Debug aids are prewritten sets of computerized routines that assist in finding the BUGS.

**DECENTRALIZATION** delegation of decision-making to the subunits of an organization. It is a matter of degree. The lower the level where decisions are made, the greater is the decentralization. Decentralization is most effective in organizations where subunits are autonomous and costs and profits can be independently measured. The benefits of decentralization include: (1) decisions are made by those who have the most knowledge about local conditions; (2) greater managerial input in decision-making has a desirable motivational effect; and (3) managers have more control over results. The costs of decentralization include: (1) managers have a tendency to look at their division and lose sight of overall company goals; (2) there can be costly duplication of services; and (3) costs of obtaining sufficient information increase.

**DECENTRALIZED ORGANIZATON** organization that has several operating segments; operating control of each segment's activities is the responsibility of the segment's manager.

**DECISION-MAKING** purposeful selection from among a set of alternatives in light of a given objective. Decision-making is not a separate function of management. In fact, decision-making is intertwined with the other functions, such as PLANNING, COORDINATING, and CONTROLLING. These functions all require that decisions be made. For example, at the outset, management must make a critical decision as to which of several strategies would be followed. Such a decision is often called a *strategic* decision because of its long-term impact on the organization. Also, managers must make scores of lesser decisions, *tactical* and *operational*, all of which are important to the organization's well-being.

**DECISION-MAKING UNDER CERTAINTY** term used in a situation when for each decision alternative there is only one event and therefore only one outcome for each action. For example, there is only one possible event for the two possible actions: "Do nothing" at a future cost of \$3.00 per unit for 10,000 units, or "rearrange" a facility at a future cost of \$2.80 for the same number of units. A decision matrix (or payoff table) would look as follows:

| Actions | State of Nature (with probability of 1.0) |
|---------|-------------------------------------------|
| Do nothing | \$30,000 (10,000 units × \$3.00) |
| Rearrange | 28,000 (10,000 units × \$2.80) |

Note that there is only one STATE OF NATURE in the matrix because there is only one possible outcome for each action (with certainty). The decision is obviously to choose the action that will result in the most desirable outcome (least cost), that is to "rearrange." *See also* DECISION THEORY.

**DECISION-MAKING UNDER UNCERTAINTY** term used in a situation that involves several events for each action with its probability of occurrence. The decision problem can best be approached using a payoff table (or decision matrix). *See also* DECISION THEORY.

**DECISION MATRIX** *see* DECISION THEORY.

**DECISION MODEL** formal or informal conceptualization of the relationship of the various factors that are relevant in decision-making and planning. OPTIMIZATION MODELS, MATHEMATICAL MODELS, and DECISION MATRIX are examples of a decision model.

**DECISION PACKAGE** procedure used in ZERO-BASE BUDGETING when a manager specifies recommended and alternative ways to undertake a proposed project (e.g., product). Dollars and time involved with the recommended and alternative means of accomplishing the project are specified. Thus, upper management has three possible choices: (1) not funding the project at all; (2) accepting the project as recommended; or (3) accepting the project in an alternative form. Note that an alternative means of performing the project may be chosen because it is less expensive than the recommended way. A decision package looks as follows:

DECISION PACKAGE
for Product X

Alternative A

Recommended Way in Dollars and Time

Alternative B

**DECISION RULE** designation of a specific condition or combination of conditions that may arise in the decision-making process and the appropriate action to take if the conditions exist. For example, in a CAPITAL BUDGETING decision, under the NET PRESENT VALUE (NPV) METHOD, a project should be accepted if its NPV is positive. Also, under the INTERNAL RATE OF RETURN (IRR) approach, a project should be accepted if the IRR of the project exceeds the cost of capital.

**DECISION SUPPORT SYSTEM (DSS)** branch of the broadly defined MANAGEMENT INFORMATION SYSTEM (MIS) that provides answers to problems and that integrates the decision maker into the system as a component. The system utilizes such quantitative techniques as *regression, linear programming,* and *financial planning modeling.* DSS software furnishes support to the accountant in the decision-making process. It analyzes a specific situation and can be modified as the practitioner wishes. Models are constructed and decisions analyzed. Planning and forecasting are facilitated.

**DECISION THEORY** systematic approach to making decisions especially under uncertainty. Although statistics such as EXPECTED VALUE and STANDARD DEVIATION are essential for choosing the best course of action, the decision problem can best be approached, using what is referred to as a *payoff table* (or *decision matrix*), which is characterized by: (1) the *row* representing a set of alternative COURSES OF ACTION available to the decision maker; (2) the *column* representing the STATE OF NATURE or conditions that are likely to occur and over which the decision maker has no control; and (3) the entries in the body of the table representing the outcome of the decision, known as *payoffs,* which may be in the form of costs, revenues, profits, or cash flows. By computing expected value of each action, we will be able to pick the best one.

*Example 1:* Assume the following probability distribution of daily demand for strawberries:

| Daily Demand | 0 | 1 | 2 | 3 |
|---|---|---|---|---|
| Probability | .2 | .3 | .3 | .2 |

Also assume that unit cost = $3, selling price = $5 (i.e., profit on sold unit = $2), and salvage value on unsold units = $2 (i.e., loss on unsold unit = $1). We can stock either 0, 1, 2, or 3 units. The question is: How many units should be stocked each day? Assume that units from one day cannot be sold the next day. Then the payoff table can be constructed as follows:

| Stock \ Demand (probability) | State of Nature 0 (.2) | 1 (.3) | 2 (.3) | 3 (.2) | Expected Value |
|---|---|---|---|---|---|
| Actions  0 | $0 | 0 | 0 | 0 | $0 |
| 1 | −1 | 2 | 2 | 2 | 1.40 |
| 2 | −2 | 1* | 4 | 4 | 1.90** |
| 3 | −3 | 0 | 3 | 6 | 1.50 |

*Profit for (stock 2, demand 1) equals (no. of units sold) (profit per unit) − (no. of units unsold)(loss per unit) = (1)($5 − 3) − (1)($3 − 2) = $1

**Expected value for (stock 2) is: −2(.2) + 1(.3) + 4(.3) + 4(.2) = $1.90. The optimal stock action is the one with the highest EXPECTED MONETARY VALUE, i.e., stock 2 units.

Suppose the decision maker can obtain a perfect prediction of which event (state of nature) will occur. The EXPECTED VALUE WITH PERFECT INFORMATION would be the total expected value of actions selected on the assumption of a perfect forecast. THE EXPECTED VALUE OF PERFECT INFORMATION can then be computed as:

Expected value with perfect information *minus* the expected value with existing information.

*Example 2:* From the payoff table in Example 1, the following analysis yields the expected value *with* perfect information:

| Stock \ Demand | State of Nature 0 (.2) | 1 (.3) | 2 (.3) | 3 (.2) | Expected Value |
|---|---|---|---|---|---|
| 0 | $0 | | | | $0 |
| Actions  1 | | 2 | | | .6 |
| 2 | | | 4 | | 1.2 |
| 3 | | | | 6 | 1.2 |
| | | | | | $3.00 |

With existing information, the best that the decision maker could obtain was select (stock 2) and obtain $1.90. With perfect information (forecast), the decision maker could make as much as $3. Therefore, the expected value *of* perfect information is $3.00 − $1.90 = $1.10.

This is the maximum price the decision maker is willing to pay for additional information.

**DECISION TREE** pictorial representation of a decision situation, normally found in discussions of decision-making under uncertainty or risk. It shows decision alternatives, states of nature, probabilities attached to the state of nature, and conditional benefits and losses. The tree approach is most useful in a sequential decision situation. For example, assume XYZ Corporation wishes to introduce one of two products to the market this year. The probabilities and present values (PV) of projected cash inflows follow:

| Products | Initial Investment | PV of Cash Inflows | Probabilities |
|---|---|---|---|
| A | $225,000 | | 1.00 |
| | | $ 450,000 | 0.40 |
| | | 200,000 | 0.50 |
| | | −100,000 | 0.10 |
| B | 80,000 | | 1.00 |
| | | 320,000 | 0.20 |
| | | 100,000 | 0.60 |
| | | −150,000 | 0.20 |

A decision tree analyzing the two products follows:

**DECISION TREE**

| | Initial Investment (1) | Probability (2) | PV of Cash Inflow (3) | PV of Cash Inflow $(2 \times 3) = (4)$ |
|---|---|---|---|---|
| | | 0.40 | $450,000 | $180,000 |
| | $225,000 | 0.50 | $200,000 | 100,000 |
| | | 0.10 | −$100,000 | 10,000 |
| Product A | | | Expected PV of Cash Inflows | $270,000 |
| Choice A or B | | | | |
| Product B | | 0.20 | $320,000 | $ 64,000 |
| | $ 80,000 | 0.60 | $100,000 | 60,000 |
| | | 0.20 | −$150,000 | 30,000 |
| | | | Expected PV of Cash Inflows | $ 94,000 |

For Product A:

Expected NPV = expected PV − I = $270,000 − $225,000 = $45,000

For Product B:

Expected NPV = $94,000 − $80,000 = $14,000

Based on the expected net present value, the company should choose product A over product B.

**DECISION VARIABLE** *see* LINEAR PROGRAMMING.

**DECLARATION DATE** date on which the dividend is voted and announced (declared) by the board of directors. At the declaration date, the dividend is a legal liability of the company. *See also* DATE OF RECORD.

**DECRYPTION** process of converting encrypted data back into its original form, so it can be understood. *See also* ENCRYPTION.

**DEDUCTIONS**
1. itemized deductions, which are deductions *from* ADJUSTED GROSS INCOME (AGI). Certain personal expenditures are allowed by the Tax Code as deductions from adjusted gross income if they exceed the STANDARD DEDUCTION (formerly the ZERO BRACKET AMOUNT). Examples include medical expenses in excess of the applicable AGI threshhold, interest on home mortgages, real estate taxes, and charitable contributions. Itemized deductions are reported on Schedule A of Form 1040.
2. deductions *for* adjusted gross income, such as employee business expenses and contributions to an IRA pension plan.
3. adjustment to an invoice.

**DEED OF TRUST** *see* BOND INDENTURE; INDENTURE.

**DEEP DISCOUNT BOND** bond that has a coupon rate far below rates currently available on investments and that consequently can be traded only at a significant discount from par value—usually more than about 20%. It may offer an opportunity for capital appreciation.

**DEFALCATION** unlawful and fraudulent misappropriation of property or funds under one's (e.g., cashier, trustee, administrator) control by breach of trust (e.g., EMBEZZLEMENT).

**DEFAULT** failure of a debtor to meet principal or interest payment on a debt at the due date. In the event of default, creditors may make claims against the assets of the issuer in order to recover their principal.

**DEFEASANCE**
1. to render null or void, or to terminate the interest in a property according to strictly stipulated conditions as in a deed. It may refer to the physical instrument itself stipulating the above conditions.
2. to discharge old, low-rate debt (without repaying it before maturity) by adding new securities paying high interest or having a higher market value. The object is to have a more debt-free balance sheet and increased earnings by removing the old debt and adding high-yielding new securities.

**DEFENSIVE INTERVAL RATIO** liquidity ratio revealing the ability of the business to meet its current debts. It indicates the period of time the entity can operate on its current liquid assets without needing revenues from next period's sources. The ratio equals defensive assets (cash, marketable securities, and receivables) divided by projected daily operational expenditures less noncash charges. Projected daily operational expenditures are determined by dividing cost of goods sold plus operating expenses and other ordinary cash expenses by 360. Assume cash of $30,000, marketable securities of $38,000, receivables of $46,000, projected daily expenditures of $450,000, and noncash charges of $20,000. The ratio equals:

$$\frac{\$114,000}{\left(\dfrac{\$450,000 - \$20,000}{360}\right)} = \frac{\$114,000}{\$1,194.44} = 95 \text{ days (rounded)}$$

**DEFERRED ANNUITY** annuity whose first payment or receipt does not begin until some time after the first period; for example, an annuity of $1,000 is not paid for the first three years and then commences payments at the end of each year from the fourth and continues through the end of that annuity.

**DEFERRED ANNUITY CONTRACT** agreement in which payments to the annuitant are postponed until a specified number of periods have elapsed. An example is when annuity payments begin at the age of 60.

**DEFERRED CHARGE** cost already incurred that is deferred to the future. The deferral is made because of anticipated future benefit or because the charge constitutes an appropriate allocation of costs to future operations. The basic accounting convention applicable is the matching of costs and revenues. Deferred charges are classified as noncurrent assets because their life extends beyond one year. Deferred charges have no physical substance. Examples of deferred charges are: (1) start-up costs in putting into operation new, better, or more efficient facilities; (2) plant rearrangement and reinstallation costs; (3) moving costs from one location to another; and (4) deferred income tax charges resulting from INTERPERIOD INCOME TAX ALLOCATION. Note that a company sometimes has discretion of whether to defer a cost and amortize or immediately expense it. An example is advertising expense, which is capitalized when the benefits to be gained will affect future years' income. Since deferred charges lack cash realizability and cannot be used to meet creditor claims, they are (when material) subtracted from assets in most ratio calculations. *See also* PREPAID EXPENSE.

**DEFERRED COMPENSATION** *see* STOCK OPTION.

**DEFERRED COST** expenditure incurred having future benefit in excess of one year that is capitalized to an asset account. An example is interest incurred on borrowed funds for the self-construction of an asset that is capitalized.

**DEFERRED CREDIT** income items received by a business, but not yet reported as income; also called *deferred revenue* and *deferred income*. An example is a consulting fee received in *advance* before being earned. The term also applies to revenue normally includable in income but deferred until earned and matched with expenses. For example, a magazine publisher might defer a 3-year subscription to match revenue against later publication expenses. The deferred credit is classified under noncurrent liabilities. When a portion of the deferred credit is earned, the entry is to debit deferred credit and credit revenue. *See also* INTERPERIOD INCOME TAX ALLOCATION.

**DEFERRED GROSS PROFIT** method of installment sales. Any profit not collected is deferred on the balance sheet pending cash collection from the customer. When collections are subsequently made, realized gross profit is increased via a debit to the deferred gross profit account. The deferred gross profit account is a contra account to accounts receivable as follows:

Accounts Receivable (Cost + Profit)

Less: Deferred Gross Profit (Profit)

Net Accounts Receivable (Cost)

**DEFERRED INCOME TAX CHARGE** asset resulting when taxable income exceeds book income as a result of a temporary difference in the recognition of income and expense items. Thus, the tax payable will be greater than the tax expense. In INTERPERIOD INCOME TAX ALLOCATION, this difference is reported as a deferred income tax charge. For example, warranty expense is deducted for book purposes in the year of sale but taken off on the tax return only when paid. The Deferred Income Tax Charge account will be classified partly as current (for the warranty period for the next year) and partly as noncurrent (for the warranty period in excess of one year). Assume income for both books and tax is $5000, warranty expense for books is $500, warranty expense for tax is $200, and the tax rate is 34%. Relevant computations and journal entry follow:

|  | **Book Income** | **Tax Income** |
|---|---|---|
| Income | $5,000 | $5,000 |
| Warranty expense | 500 | 200 |
| Income before tax | $4,500 | $4,800 |

| | | |
|---|---|---|
| Tax expense ($4,500 × 34%) | 1,530 | |
| Deferred income tax charge ($300 × 34%) | 102 | |
| Tax payable ($4,800 × 34%) | | 1,632 |

A deferred income tax charge results in a future deductible amount (for tax purposes), which can only be recognized as an asset in the current year if the entity is certain to have taxable income in the future. Thus, a deferred tax asset can only be booked for the amount of the certain future deductiblity of the item for tax purposes (e.g., resulting from temporary differences owing to DEFERRED INCOME TAX LIABILITIES already existing). A deferred income tax charge can also be recognized for the tax benefit of deductible amounts realizable by carrying back a loss from future years to reduce taxes paid in the current or a prior year.

**DEFERRED INCOME TAX LIABILITY** account showing estimated amount of future taxes on income earned and recognized for accounting purposes but not yet for federal income tax purposes. Thus, book income will exceed taxable income. In INTERPERIOD INCOME TAX ALLOCATION, this will result in tax expense being greater than tax payable. As a result, a deferred income tax liability will occur. It will eventually write itself off when the period for the temporary difference is fully reversed. Assume book income and taxable income are both $10,000. However, straight-line depreciation is used for book purposes amounting to a charge of $1,000 while an accelerated depreciation method is used for tax purposes amounting to $1,500. The corporate tax rate is 34%. Relevant computations and journal entry follow:

|  | Book Income | Taxable Income |
|---|---|---|
| Income | $10,000 | $10,000 |
| Depreciation | 1,000 | 1,500 |
| Income before tax | $ 9,000 | $ 8,500 |
| Tax expense ($9,000 × 34%) | $ 3,060 | |
| Tax payable ($8,500 × 34%) | | $ 2,890 |
| Deferred income tax liability ($500 × 34%) | $170 | |

*See also* DEFERRED INCOME TAX CHARGE.

**DEFERRED LIABILITY** debt where the payment made is postponed beyond the present date. An example is deferred taxes. *See also* DEFERRED CREDIT.

**DEFERRED MAINTENANCE**
1. maintenance that has been postponed and that may result in physical damage, lack of efficiency, decline in production, and other negative effects. If a company does not have an adequate repair program, future earnings potential of the assets are diminished.
2. factor in real estate appraisal. For example, deferred maintenance may produce broken windows and discolored paint that adversely affect the value of a piece of property.

**DEFERRED TAX ALLOCATION** procedure by which deferred taxes are computed with the tax rates in effect when the temporary differences between book income and taxable income originate; they are not adjusted for rate changes. The method is not acceptable for INTERPERIOD INCOME TAX ALLOCATION. It is income statement-oriented in that the deferred income tax liability or charge awaits future adjustment to tax expense in later years when the temporary difference starts to reverse. *See also* LIABILITY TAX ALLOCATION METHOD; NET OF TAX METHOD.

**DEFICIENCY** additional tax liability that the IRS deems to be owed by a taxpayer. A taxpayer can argue the correctness of a deficiency with the IRS. If unsuccessful, the taxpayer can appeal to the Tax Court.

**DEFICIENCY IN INTERNAL CONTROL** a deficiency when the design or operation of a control does not allow management or employees, in the normal course of performing their assigned functions, to prevent or detect misstatements on a timely basis. *See also* SIGNIFICANT DEFICIENCY; MATERIAL WEAKNESS.

**DEFICIENCY LETTER** IRS communication to a taxpayer explaining why the correct amount of tax is greater than shown on the tax return. *See also* DEFICIENCY.

**DEFICIT** debit balance in the Retained Earnings account resulting from accumulated losses.

**DEFINED BENEFIT PENSION PLAN** program stipulating the pension benefits employees will obtain when they retire. The pension benefit formula usually is based on the worker's salary level nearing retirement age and considers the employment years. The calculation must take into account the current year employer contribution to satisfy expected pension benefit payments at retirement. There must be an appropriate funding pattern to assure adequate funds are available to meet promised benefits. Considered in the funding level are such factors as turnover rate, mortality rate, and return on investment. Since the pension expense each year will typically be different from the amount funded, a deferred pension liability or asset will result. *See also* DEFINED CONTRIBUTION PENSION PLAN.

**DEFINED CONTRIBUTION PENSION PLAN** program under which an employer agrees to make a specified contribution each year based on the pension benefit formula. The formula may consider such factors as years of service, salary levels, and age. Note that only the employer's contribution is defined and that there is no guarantee regarding the future benefits to be received by employees. The entry each year for the funding contribution is to debit pension expense and credit cash for the same amount. *See also* DEFINED BENEFIT PENSION PLAN.

**DEFLATION** the opposite of inflation. A decline in general price levels, often caused by a reduction in the supply of money or credit. Deflation can also be brought about by direct contractions in spending, either in the form of a reduction in government spending, personal spending, or investment spending. Deflation has often had the side effect of increasing unemployment, since the process often leads to a lower level of demand in the economy. Other downside effects include possible pay cuts and more expensive repayment of consumer debts. The upside of falling prices is that mild deflation would assure working people (at least those who fend off pay cuts) of steadily rising real wages.

**DEGREE OF FINANCIAL LEVERAGE (DFL)** percentage change in earnings available to common shareholders that is associated with a given percentage change in net operating income. The greater the DFL, the riskier the firm; however, if the return on assets exceeds the cost of debt, additional leverage is favorable.

**DEGREE OF FREEDOM (DF)** number of data items that are independent of one another. Given a sample of data and the computation of some statistic (e.g., the mean), the degrees of freedom are defined as (number of observations included in the formula) minus (number of parameters estimated using the data). For example, the mean statistic for $N$ sample data points has $n$ DF, but the variance formula has $(n-1)$ DF because one parameter (the mean $X$) has to be estimated before the variance formula can be used.

**DEGREE OF OPERATING LEVERAGE (DOL)** change in operating income (earnings before interest and taxes) resulting from a percentage change in revenues. It measures the extent to which a firm incurs fixed rather than variable costs in operations. Thus, the greater the DOL, the greater the risk of loss when sales decline, and the greater the reward when sales increase.

**DEGREE OF RELATIVE LIQUIDITY (DRL)** percentage of a firm's cash expenditures that can be secured from (1) beginning fund and from (2) cash generated from its normal operation.

**DEGREE OF TOTAL LEVERAGE (DTL)** percentage change in net income that is associated with a given percentage change in sales. It is the product of DEGREE OF FINANCIAL LEVERAGE (DFL) and the DEGREE OF OPERATING LEVERAGE (DOL).

**DELINQUENT TAX** tax that is unpaid or remains unpaid as of or after the payment due date. Usually a penalty attaches to that sum. Any unpaid balance that may remain after a partial payment will still be considered delinquent. The penalty and the unpaid balance remain separately identifiable.

**DELIVERY BASIS** method of revenue recognition based on delivery instead of sale.

**DELIVERY CYCLE TIME** time period between acceptance of an order and final delivery of the product. *See also* CYCLE TIME.

**DELIVERY TIME** time period between product completion and customer receipt of the item.

**DELPHI METHOD** qualitative forecasting method that seeks to use the judgment of experts systematically to forecast what future events will be or when they may occur. It brings together a group of experts who have access to each other's opinions in an environment where no majority opinion is disclosed.

**DEMAND DEPOSIT** deposit from which funds may be drawn on demand and from which funds may be transferred to another party by means of a check. Demand deposits are the biggest component of the U.S. money supply. *See also* TIME DEPOSIT.

**DEMILITARIZED ZONE (DMZ)** in computer networking security, a computer inserted into a neutral zone between an organization's internal private network and outside public network. Its purpose is to prevent external users from accessing an organization's private network. When a request is received from the outside, only the computer in the DMZ is accessible. If a request is sent from the inside to access a public network, the computer in the DMZ will intercept that request and initiate a session with the public network on behalf on the internal user.

**DE MINIMUS FRINGE BENEFITS** fringe benefits provided to employees that are so minimal in value that they are impractical to account for and therefore are excludable from taxable income. Examples of de minimus fringe benefits include meal allowances, local transportation provided in connection with overtime work, and holiday gifts of property with a low fair market value.

**DENIAL OF SERVICE ATTACK (DOS)** an attack that essentially prevents a user from accessing some resource. Generally, a DoS attack does not result in a theft of data or other information, but rather a loss of availability of service. The attack is most commonly done by sending excessive data to a network address.

**DENOMINATOR LEVEL** *see* PREDETERMINED OVERHEAD RATE.

**DENOMINATOR VARIANCE** *see* FIXED OVERHEAD VOLUME (DENOMINATOR) VARIANCE.

**DEPARTMENTAL RATE** predetermined factory overhead rate for each production department. When products are heterogeneous, receiving different attention and effort as they move through various departments, departmental rates rather than a single plantwide rate are necessary to achieve more accurate overhead application to the products.

**DEPENDENT** person who derives primary support from another party. In order for a person to qualify as a dependent for federal income tax exemption purposes, five tests must be met: support test, gross income test, joint return test, citizenship or residency test, and relationship or member of household test.

**DEPENDENT VARIABLE** one whose value depends upon the values of other variables and constants in some relationship. For example, in the relationship $(y) = f(x)$, $y$ is the dependent variable. For example, market price of stock is a dependent variable influenced by various independent variables, such as earnings per share, debt-equity ratio, and beta. *See also* INDEPENDENT VARIABLE.

**DEPLETION** physical exhaustion of a natural resource (e.g., oil, coal). The entry for recording annual depletion is to debit depletion expense and credit accumulated depletion. Accumulated depletion is a contra account to the natural resource.

**DEPOSITS IN TRANSIT** cash receipts that arrived at the bank too late to be credited to the depositor's bank statement for the current month. Such deposits are added to the bank balance when preparing the BANK RECONCILIATION.

**DEPRECIABLE ASSET** certain types of assets (e.g., plant and equipment) that gradually lose their value over time. The law permits depreciation charges except when such assets are held by individuals as personal property.

**DEPRECIABLE COST** fixed asset cost that is subject to depreciation. Depreciable cost equals acquisition cost less salvage value.

**DEPRECIABLE LIFE** economic or physical life of a fixed asset. All fixed assets except land are depreciated over the number of years of expected use.

**DEPRECIATION**
1. spreading out of the original cost over the estimated life of the fixed assets such as plant and equipment. Depreciation reduces taxable income. Among the most commonly used depreciation methods are STRAIGHT-LINE DEPRECIATION and ACCELERATED DEPRECIATION such as the SUM-OF-THE-YEARS'-DIGITS and DOUBLE DECLINING BALANCE METHODS.
2. decline in economic potential of limited life assets originating from wear and tear, natural deterioration through interaction of the elements, and technical obsolescence. To some extent, maintenance (lubrication, adjustments, parts replacement, and cleaning) may partially arrest or offset wear and deterioration. *See also* DEPRECIATION ACCOUNTING.

**DEPRECIATION ACCOUNTING** amortization of fixed assets, such as plant and equipment, in order to allocate the cost over its depreciable life. It is a process of cost allocation and not valuation. DEPRECIATION reduces taxable income but does not reduce cash. Depreciation is recorded by debiting depreciation expense and crediting accumulated depreciation. There are several methods of computing depreciation: STRAIGHT-LINE DEPRECIATION, UNITS-OF-PRODUCTION, and ACCELERATED DEPRECIATION methods (e.g., SUM-OF-YEARS'-DIGITS and DOUBLE DECLINING BALANCE). Depreciation expense is deducted by a business on its federal income tax return. The depreciation amount on the tax return, however, may differ from the amount reported in the firm's income statement. In fact, the method used on the tax return need not be the same method used in the financial statements. Typically, a firm uses an accelerated depreciation for tax purposes and the straight-line method in its financial statements. ACCELERATED COST RECOVERY SYSTEM (ACRS) is a system that allows a specific accelerated write-off pattern of the asset for tax purposes.

**DEPRECIATION RECAPTURE** *see* RECAPTURE OF DEPRECIATION.

**DERIVATIVE** transaction or contract whose value depends on or, as the name implies, derives from the value of underlying assets such as stocks, bonds, mortgages, market indexes, or foreign currencies. One party with exposure to unwanted risk can pass some or all of that risk to a second party. The first party can assume a different risk from the second party, pay the second party to assume the risk, or, as is often the case, create a combination. The objectives of users of derivatives may vary. A common reason to use derivatives is so that the risk of financial operations can be controlled. Derivatives can be used to manage foreign exchange exposure, especially unfavorable exchange rate movements. Speculators and arbitrageurs can seek profits from general price changes or simultaneous price differences in different markets, respectively. Others use derivatives to *hedge* their position; that is, to set up two financial assets so that any unfavorable price movement in one asset is offset by favorable price movement in the other asset.

**DESK-TOP SOFTWARE** auxiliary program that operates in WINDOWS overlaying the accountant's principal application. When such a desk accessory is called up, the practitioner is temporarily exiting the main program. Some accessories let the accountant transfer information to and from the main application. Features of desk-top software may include an appointment calendar, a clock that can measure and record time spent with particular files, a notepad, a directory for mail and telephone, telephone dialing, card filing, and calculator functions.

**DETACHABLE STOCK WARRANT** certificate conferring the right to buy stock that is issued along with a *detachable* bond. The warrant has a market life of its own. The portion of the proceeds received for the bond and warrant that are allocable to the warrant should be accounted for as PAID-IN-CAPITAL. The allocation should be based on the relative fair market values of the two securities at time of issuance. Assume a $1000 convertible bond is issued for $1,050, with $50 applicable to stock warrants. The entry is to debit cash $1,050 and credit bonds payable $1,000 and paid-in-capital (stock warrants) $50. *See also* UNDETACHABLE STOCK WARRANT.

**DETAILED AUDIT** procedure in which all or most of a company's transactions and related record keeping are examined and verified. This is much more comprehensive than audit testing through a sampling process. It should be undertaken when wrongdoing is expected such as EMBEZZLEMENT. A detailed audit is more readily associated with INTERNAL AUDIT activity rather than audits made by an EXTERNAL AUDITOR.

**DETECTION RISK** the risk that an auditor will fail to detect a material misstatement that exists in a financial statement assertion. Detection risk is a component of the audit risk and can be controlled by performing sufficient appropriate audit procedures at the proper times.

**DEVELOPMENT STAGE ENTERPRISE** business devoting substantially all of its efforts to establishing itself. Either of the following conditions exist: (1) planned principal operations have not started or (2) there has been no significant revenue although principal operations are underway. GENERALLY ACCEPTED ACCOUNTING PRINCIPLES (GAAP) applicable to established companies apply equally to development stage enterprises. In the BALANCE SHEET, cumulative net losses are reported as "deficit accumulated during the development stage." In the INCOME STATEMENT, cumulative amounts of revenue and expense from inception of the enterprise are reported. The STATEMENT OF CHANGES IN FINANCIAL POSITION shows the cumulative amounts of sources and uses of funds from inception. The financial statements are identified as those of a development stage enterprise and include a description of the development activities. In the first year in which a development stage enterprise is no longer considered such, it must disclose that in prior years it had been.

**DEVIATION RATE** in statistical sampling, the number of times, stated as a percentage, that a prescribed internal control is not properly applied in a sample of items.

**DICTIONARY ATTACK** a method for learning the credentials of a password-protected system. An attacker generally has two choices when trying to break into a password-protected computer system. The attacker can use "brute force" and try every possible combination; this approach can be very time consuming. In contrast, with a dictionary attack, the attacker will try every word in a dictionary to try to learn the credentials. This approach often works, because most people use ordinary words contained in the dictionary as their password.

**DIF** *see* DATA INTERCHANGE FORMAT (DIF) FILE.

**DIFFERENCE ESTIMATION** a type of variables sampling that utilizes the average difference between audit and book values of items to project population values. Difference estimation is useful when an auditor expects a disproportionate relationship between differences and book values.

**DIFFERENTIAL**
1. difference in revenues and costs that change between two or more alternative courses of action to be undertaken or considered. *See also* INCREMENTAL COST.
2. in INVESTMENTS, the typical extra commission charge of ⅛ of a point for an ODD-LOT stock transaction.

**DIFFERENTIAL ANALYSIS** *see* INCREMENTAL ANALYSIS.

**DIFFERENTIAL BACKUP** copies all the files that have changed since the last full backup. The main advantage of differential backup is that to restore, only two files are needed: the full backup file and the differential backup file. The main disadvantage of differential backup is that the size of the differential backup file tends to keep on increasing with each backup until a new full backup is made. Please note that a differential backup is not the same as incremental backup. In an incremental backup, only files that have changed from the last backup, whether full or incremental, are copied. The main disadvantage of incremental backup is that all incremental backup files plus the full backup file are needed to do a restore. Of course, its biggest advantage is that each time the incremental backup is performed, only the files that have changed are backed up, resulting in significant time savings.

**DIFFERENTIAL COST** *see* INCREMENTAL COST.

**DIGITAL CERTIFICATE** used to establish one's credentials when engaging in a transaction on the Web. It is used to verify the identity of the sender. Digital certificates are issued by a Certificate Authority (CA) and signed by the CA's private key.

**DIGITAL SIGNATURE** a message signed with a special key. It is used to authenticate the sender or message integrity to the receiver. A secure digital signature process consists of (1) a method of signing a document that prevents forgery and (2) validating that the signature is the one it purports to be.

**DIGITAL VERSATILE DISK (DVD)** an optical disc storage media format. Its main uses are video and data storage. Most DVDs are of the same dimensions as compact discs (CDs) but store more than six times as much data. Variations of the term DVD include DVD-ROM (Read Only Memory), DVD-R, DVD+R, DVD-RW, DVD+RW, DVD-Video, DVD-Audio, and Blu-ray Disc. Also known as *digital video disk*.

**DILUTED EARNINGS PER SHARE** smallest figure that can be obtained by computing a common stock earnings per share that reflects the possible exercise of all convertible securities. It is based on a broader denominator in the earnings per share fraction than BASIC EARNINGS PER SHARE. Not only does the denominator include the weighted average of common stock outstanding it also includes those shares that may result from convertible securities and stock options. Diluted earnings per share equals:

$$\frac{\text{Net Income} - \text{Preferred Dividends}}{\text{Weighted Average Common Stock Outstanding} + \text{Diluted Securities}}$$

**DILUTION** decrease, loss, or weakening of a financial statement-related item. For example, if more common shares are issued, the equity interest represented by each common share is reduced. Another example is the inclusion of a convertible security that reduces earnings per share.

**DIRECT ACCESS** method of processing data so that it can be stored and retrieved without consideration being given to data stored in preceding or subsequent locations; also called *random access*.

**DIRECT ALLOCATION METHOD** method allocating costs of each service department directly to production departments; also called *direct method*. Under this method, no consideration is given to services performed by one service department for another. Assume the following data:

| | Production Departments | | Service Departments | |
|---|---|---|---|---|
| | A Machining | B Assembly | General Plant (GP) | Engineering (E) |
| Overhead costs before allocation | $30,000 | $40,000 | $20,000 | $10,000 |
| Engineering hours by Engineering | 50,000 | 30,000 | 5,000 | 4,000 |
| Direct labor hours by General Plant | 60,000 | 40,000 | 15,000 | 20,000 |

Using the direct method yields:

| | Service Departments | | Production Departments | |
|---|---|---|---|---|
| | GP | E | A | B |
| Overhead costs | $20,000 | $10,000 | $30,000 | $40,000 |
| Reallocation GP (60%, 40%)* | (20,000) | | 12,000 | 8,000 |
| E (⅝, ⅜) # | | (10,000) | 6,250 | 3,570 |
| | | | $48,250 | $51,750 |

\* Base is (60,000 + 40,000 = 100,000); 60,000/100,000 = .6; 40,000/100,000 = .4.
\# Base is (50,000 + 30,000 = 80,000); 50,000/80,000 = ⅝; 30,000/80,000 = ⅜.

**DIRECT COST** expenses that can be directly identified with the costing object such as a product and department. Examples are direct materials, direct labor, and advertising outlays made directly to a particular sales territory. *See also* INDIRECT COST.

**DIRECT FINANCING LEASE** method used by lessors in capital leases when both of the following criteria for the lessor are satisfied: (1) collectibility of minimum lease payments is assured and (2) no important uncertainties surround the amount of unreimbursable costs yet to be incurred. In a direct financing lease, the lessor is *not* a manufacturer or dealer in the item; the lessor purchases the property only for the purpose of leasing it. The lessor uses the interest rate implicit in the lease to discount the future payments from the lessee. The difference between the gross investment in the lease and the cost of the leased property is reported as unearned interest income. Unearned interest income is then amortized using the interest method thus resulting in interest income over the life of the lease. Initial direct costs of the lease are expensed. *See also* SALES-TYPE LEASE.

**DIRECT LABOR** work directly involved in making the product. Examples of direct labor costs are the wages of assembly workers on an assembly line and the wages of a machine tool operator in a machine shop. Direct labor is an *inventoriable* cost.

**DIRECT LABOR BUDGET** schedule for expected labor cost. Expected labor cost is dependent upon expected production volume (production budget). Labor requirements are based on production volume multiplied by direct labor-hours per unit. Direct labor-hours needed for production are then multiplied by direct labor cost per hour to derive budgeted direct labor costs. For example, assume budgeted production of 790 units, direct labor-hours per unit of 5, and direct labor cost per hour of $5. The expected labor cost equals:

| | |
|---|---:|
| Expected production | 790 units |
| Direct labor-hours per unit | $\times$ 5 |
| Direct labor-hours | 3,950 |
| Direct labor cost per hour | $\times$ $5 |
| Total direct labor cost | $19,750 |

**DIRECT LABOR EFFICIENCY VARIANCE** difference between standard direct labor hours allowed for the good units produced and actual direct labor hours worked, multiplied by the standard direct labor rate.

**DIRECT LABOR RATE VARIANCE** difference between the standard direct labor rate and the actual direct labor rate, multiplied by the actual direct labor hours worked.

**DIRECT LABOR TIME STANDARDS** expected time required for each department, machine, or process to complete production of one unit or one batch of output.

**DIRECT LABOR VARIANCES** difference between the standard direct cost and the actual direct labor cost. It is the sum of the DIRECT LABOR RATE VARIANCE and DIRECT LABOR EFFICIENCY VARIANCE.

**DIRECT MATERIAL** all the material that becomes an integral part of the finished product. Examples are the steel used to make an automobile and the wood to make furniture. Direct materials are charged to work-in-process as an *inventoriable* cost.

**DIRECT MATERIALS BUDGET** schedule showing how much material will be required for production and how much material must be bought to meet this production requirement. The purchase depends on both expected usage of materials and inventory levels. For example, assume expected production of 790 units, 3 lbs. of material needed per unit, desired ending inventory of material 216 lbs., beginning inventory of material 237 lbs., and unit cost per lb. of $2. Then lbs. of material to be purchased and purchase cost follow:

| | |
|---|---:|
| Material needed for production (790 units × 3) | 2,370 lbs. |
| Add: Desired ending inventory | 216 |
| Total need | 2,586 |
| Less: Beginning inventory | 237 |
| Purchases of material | 2,349 |
| × Unit cost | × $2 |
| Purchase cost | $4,698 |

**DIRECT MATERIALS PRICE STANDARD** careful estimate of the cost of a specific direct material in the next accounting period.

**DIRECT MATERIALS PRICE VARIANCE** actual price minus the standard price, times the actual quantity. The price variance may be isolated either at the time of purchase or at the time of transfer to WIP. The advantage of the former method is that the variance is identified earlier. Normal spoilage is considered in the calculation of standard direct materials cost per unit.

**DIRECT MATERIALS QUANTITY STANDARD** estimate of the amount of direct materials to be used, influenced by product engineering specifications, quality of direct materials, age and productivity of machinery, and quality and experience of the work force.

**DIRECT MATERIALS QUANTITY (USAGE, EFFICIENCY) VARIANCE** actual quantity minus standard quantity, times standard price. This variance is sometimes supplemented by the direct materials mix variance and the direct materials yield variance. These variances are calculated only when the production process involves combining several materials in varying proportions (when substitutions are allowable in combining materials).

**DIRECT MATERIALS VARIANCES** difference between the actual costs of materials and the standard costs of materials. They are usually divided into price and efficiency components. Part of a total materials variance may be attributed to using more raw materials than the standard and part to a cost that was higher than standard.

**DIRECT MATERIALS YIELD VARIANCE** weighted average unit standard cost of the budgeted mix multiplied by the difference between the actual quantity of materials used and the standard quantity. Certain relationships may exist among the various material variances. For instance, an unfavorable price variance may be offset by a favorable mix or yield variance because materials of better quality and higher price are used. Also, a favorable mix variance may result in an unfavorable yield variance or vice versa.

**DIRECT METHOD**
  1. *see* DIRECT ALLOCATION METHOD.
  2. procedure for converting the income statement from an accrual basis to a cash basis by separately adjusting each item in the income statement.

**DIRECTOR**
  1. head of a governmental agency.
  2. member on the board of directors of a corporation. The board of directors that is selected by the shareholders is the chief governing body of the corporation. It has the sole responsibility for the declaration of dividends. It also decides on major areas, including expansion, retraction, change of product, and selection of corporate officers.

**DIRECTORS' REPORT** financial report prepared for company directors. The report is typically prepared on a quarterly and annual basis. It includes detailed items such as the accountant's financial analyses and management recommendations. The report is usually unaudited.

**DIRECT TEST OF FINANCIAL BALANCE** substantive auditing procedure that is designed to validate or substantiate a recorded account balance, rather than the accounting treatment, errors, and irregularities associated with transactions.

**DIRECT TRACING** *see* TRACING.

**DIRECT WRITE-OFF METHOD** way of charging bad debt expense when an account receivable is actually deemed uncollectible. Thus, at the date it is certain that the customer will not be able to pay (in the most extreme instance, bankruptcy), the entry is to debit bad debt expense and credit accounts receivable. The advantage of this method is that it is based on *fact* rather than estimates. However, it is not accepted for financial reporting purposes because it fails to match bad debt expense against sales in the year of sale and does not show the realizable value of accounts receivable. It is the only method allowed for tax purposes (except for small banks and specified types of financial organizations).

**DISASTER RECOVERY PLAN** details the steps needed to recover an organization's IT system after a disaster. Recovery strategy should consider the loss of physical computer facilities, hardware, software, data restoration, and network connectivity.

**DISBURSEMENT** payment by cash or by check. *See also* EXPENDI-TURE.

**DISC** *see* DISK.

**DISCLAIMER**
1. rendered by the auditor when insufficient appropriate audit evidence exists to form an AUDIT OPINION. Examples are when audit SCOPE LIMITATIONS exist, or uncertainties (e.g., lawsuits) are such that the accountant cannot reasonably predict their ultimate outcome, which may have a devastating effect upon the firm. *See also* EVIDENCE.
2. under the Sarbanes-Oxley Act, a report stating that because of restrictions on the scope of the auditor's work, the auditor is unable to, and does not, express an opinion on the effectiveness of internal control over financial reporting.

**DISCLOSURE** information given as an attachment to the financial statements in footnote or supplementary form. It provides an elaboration or explanation of a company's financial position and operating results. Explanatory information concerning an entity's financial health can also be disclosed in the AUDIT REPORT. Anything that is material should be disclosed including quantitative (e.g., dollar components of inventory) and qualitative (e.g., lawsuit) information helpful to financial statement users. The SEC also requires special disclosures in filings with it. For example, any sudden significant happening affecting a company's financial position (e.g., Three Mile Island nuclear accident) must be disclosed in Form 8-K.

**DISCONTINUED OPERATION** sale, disposal, or planned sale in the near future of a business segment (i.e., product line, class of customer). The results of a discontinued operation are reported separately in the income statement as a separate line item after income from continuing operations and before extraordinary items. *See also* INCOME FROM DISCONTINUED OPERATIONS.

**DISCOUNT**
1. difference between the FACE VALUE (i.e., *future value*) and the PRESENT VALUE of a payment.
2. reduction in price given for prompt payment. *See also* SALES DISCOUNT; TRADE DISCOUNT.
3. excess of the *par value* (face value) of a financial instrument over the price paid for it. *See also* BOND DISCOUNT.

**DISCOUNTED CASH FLOW (DCF) TECHNIQUES** methods of selecting and ranking investment proposals such as the NET PRESENT VALUE (NPV) and INTERNAL RATE OF RETURN (IRR) methods where time value of money is taken into account.

**DISCOUNTED PAYBACK PERIOD** length of time required to recover the initial cash outflow from the *discounted* future cash inflows. This is the approach where the present values of cash inflows are cumulated until they equal the initial investment. For example, assume a machine purchased for $5,000 yields cash inflows of $5,000, $4,000, and $4,000. The cost of capital is 10%. Then we have

| Year | Cash Flow | PV Factor at 10% | PV of Cash Flow |
|------|-----------|------------------|-----------------|
| 1 | $5,000 | .909 | $4,545 |
| 2 | 4,000 | .826 | 3,304 |
| 3 | 4,000 | .751 | 3,004 |

The payback period (without discounting the future cash flows) is exactly 1 year. However, the discounted payback period is a little over 1 year because the first year discounted cash flow of $4,545 is not enough to cover the initial investment of $5,000. The discounted payback period is 1.14 years (1 year + ($5,000 − $4,545)/$3,304 = 1 year + .14 year).

**DISCOUNTED PRESENT VALUE** *see* PRESENT VALUE.

**DISCOUNT LOST** *cash discount* not taken because of the buyer's failure to pay within the specified time period. The discount lost occurs only when purchases are recorded *net* of the discount. If the discount is not taken advantage of, the gross amount will be paid. Assume a $1,000 purchase on terms of 2/10, net/60. The journal entry for the purchase is to debit purchases and credit accounts payable for $980. If payment is made after 10 days, the entry is to debit accounts payable $980 and purchase discount lost $20 and credit cash $1,000. Purchase discount lost is an expense account.

**DISCOUNT RATE**
1. interest rate charged by the Federal Reserve Bank to its member banks for loans; also called *rediscount rate*. The federal discount rate is less than the prime rate.
2. interest rate used to convert future receipts or payments to their present value. The COST OF CAPITAL (cutoff, hurdle, or minimum required rate) is used as the discount rate under the NET PRESENT VALUE METHOD.

**DISCOVERY SAMPLING** exploratory sampling to assure that the proportion of units with a particular attribute (i.e., error) is not in excess of a given percentage of the population. Three determinations needed to use discovery sampling are: (1) size of population; (2) minimum unacceptable error rate; and (3) confidence level. Sample size is provided by a sampling table. If none of the random samples has an error, the auditor can conclude that the actual error rate is below the minimum unacceptable error rate. Usually, discovery sampling is employed to identify batches of documents requiring detailed examination. Assume the auditor desires to determine the correctness of costing of documents from 20 branches. A discovery sample can uncover those batches having, for example, a 95% probability of an error rate below 1%. The auditor will accept those batches as satisfactory and examine in detail the remaining batches. It is a good procedure to follow in checking the quality of clerical work. When limited time exists, discovery sampling can reassure the auditor that the error rate is less then a certain percentage using a small sample size. Discovery sampling can also be used to test audit reliability ex post. Assume an error was not detected when the CPA used a random sample in examining the population. However, after the error is uncovered, the auditor can determine the probability of having found this error. The CPA may have checked random units giving him a 95% confidence level that the error rate in the population was below 1%. The incorrect units are, say .1% of the population, hence the method and assumptions used were appropriate. Assume the auditor looks at an inventory list comprising quantity, unit cost, and total cost. It would be impractical for auditors to examine each pricing and extension. They can utilize discovery sampling to derive a 90% confidence level that the error rate in pricing and extension is below 1%. The table indicates that for 2,000 inventory items, a random sample size of 220 is appropriate. If no errors are found, the accountant concludes the entire inventory list is correct. If one error is uncovered, the accountant ceases sampling and checks all of the extensions on the list. A problem with discovery sampling is the rejection of some acceptable batches. While discovery sampling may be used by the internal auditor as a final check, the external auditor should use it only as a *preliminary* scanning procedure to test the quality of data in a population.

**DISCOVERY VALUE ACCOUNTING** method of accounting for extractive enterprises (such as oil and gas). In this approach, the increase in value associated with the discovery of oil and gas reserves would be included in earnings. There are problems such as identifying the future market prices and the costs of production and making reliable estimates of the amount of resource (for example, number of barrels of oil that ultimately will be produced from the field). *See also* RESERVE RECOGNITION ACCOUNTING (RRA).

**DISCRETIONARY COST** cost changed easily by management decision such as advertising, repairs and maintenance, and research and development; also called *managed cost*. The analyst should note whether the current level of discretionary expense is consistent with previous trends and with the company's present and future requirements. Discretionary costs are often reduced when a firm is in difficulty or desires to show a stable earnings trend. A reduction in discretionary costs may cause a deterioration in the QUALITY OF EARNINGS since management is starving the firm by holding down necessary expenses (for example, a lack of repairs causing equipment breakdown). The trend in discretionary costs as a percent of net sales and related assets should be examined.

**DISCRETIONARY (FIXED) COST** fixed costs that change because of managerial decisions, also called *management (fixed) costs* or *programmed (fixed) costs*. Examples of this type of fixed costs are advertising outlays, training costs, and research and development costs. Management sometimes unjustly reduces these costs below normal levels in order to pad current net income, which may place the future net income of the company at risk.

**DISCUSSION MEMORANDUM** document published by the FASB to facilitate and encourage discussion of an issue or problem of current concern to the accounting profession and members of the interested public. It attempts to bring out all pertinent aspects of the subject under consideration both pro and con and provides a vehicle so that alternative solutions may be evaluated. It usually signifies that the FINANCIAL ACCOUNTING STANDARD BOARD (FASB) is considering the issuance of STATEMENTS OF FINANCIAL ACCOUNTING STANDARDS.

**DISINVESTMENT** opposite of capital budgeting decisions, because they concern whether to terminate rather than start an operation. In general, if the marginal cost of a project is greater than the marginal revenue, the firm should disinvest. Four steps should be taken in making a disinvestment decision. First, fixed expenses that would be curtailed by the disinvestment decision (e.g., depreciation and insurance on equipment used) should be identified. Second, the revenue needed to justify continuing operations (variable cost of production) should be determined. Third, the opportunity cost of funds that will be received upon disinvestment (e.g., salvage value) should be established. Fourth, if the book value of the assets is not equal to the economic value of the capital, the decision should be reevaluated using current fair value rather than book value. When a firm disinvests, excess capacity may exist unless another project uses this capacity immediately. The cost of IDLE CAPACITY should be treated as a relevant cost.

**DISK** (or disc) a small round plate on which data can be stored. A *disk* refers to magnetic media, while a *disc* refers to optical media.

**DISKETTE** disk that is usually 3½" in diameter; also called a *floppy disk*. The disk is made of a flexible piece of Mylar. When magnetized, it is able to store BITS on tracks (circles) on one side if a single-sided floppy disk or on two sides if it is a double-sided disk. A floppy disk has sectors that divide each track into sections.

**DISPOSABLE INCOME** personal income minus personal income tax payments and other government deductions. It is the amount of personal income available for people to spend or save; also called *take-home pay*.

**DISPOSAL DATE** date on which an asset is sold or discarded. A higher selling price may be realized if the asset is sold in the ordinary course of business than in a forced liquidation.

**DISPOSITION OF VARIANCES** closing of variances to cost of goods sold or income summary if they are immaterial. Variances that are material may be prorated. A simple approach to prorating is to allocate the total net variance to work-in-process, finished goods, and the cost of goods sold based on the balances in those accounts.

**DISTRESS PRICE** markdown that a firm should accept rather than discontinue its operation under distress conditions. Under these conditions, any contribution that can be obtained to help cover fixed costs may be preferable to ceasing operations altogether. If operations are discontinued, the company will have no contribution available to cover fixed costs and will end up with a huge amount of shutdown costs. A distress price typically would be a variable-cost-plus price. *See also* CONTRIBUTION APPROACH TO PRICING.

**DISTRIBUTED COMPUTER SYSTEM** system in which linked computers are at various locations instead of being centralized at one particular place.

**DISTRIBUTED PROCESSING** technique in which physically separate computers share resources in their respective information processing functions. This means that a number of computers can use the same disk drives, printers, and other peripherals. This becomes an important advantage when a large database is required by two different computers. Instead of using separate disk drives, the system is set up so that both computers can access the same database. Distributed processing is often implemented by linking microcomputers and minicomputers to mainframes, or by linking mainframes together, with each computer having a number of users.

**DISTRIBUTION COST** any cost incurred to fill an order for a product or service. It includes all money spent on warehousing, delivering, and/or shipping products and services to customers.

**DISTRIBUTION TO OWNERS** payment of earnings to owners of a business organization in the form of a DIVIDEND. A dividend is a distribution to a corporation's stockholders usually in cash; sometimes in the corporation's stock, called a STOCK DIVIDEND; and much less frequently in property (usually other securities), called a *dividend in kind*.

**DISTURBANCE TERM** *see* ERROR TERM.

**DIVERSIFIABLE RISK** portion of an asset's risk that can be eliminated through diversification, also called UNSYSTEMATIC RISK or *controllable* risk. It results from the occurrence of random events such as labor strikes, lawsuits, or loss of key accounts. This type of risk is unique to a given asset. Business, liquidity, and default risks fall into this category. It is assumed that any investor can create a portfolio in which this type of risk is completely eliminated through diversification.

**DIVERSITY** conditions in which cost objects place different demands on activities, activities place different demands on resources, or processes place different demands on resources. This situation arises, for example, when there is a difference in mix or volume of products that causes an uneven assignment of costs. Different types of diversity include: batch size, customer, market, product mix, distribution channel, and volume.

**DIVERSITY SEGMENTATION** recognizing varying levels of demand by using cost drivers.

**DIVIDEND** distribution of earnings paid to stockholders based on the number of shares owned. The most typical type of dividend is a CASH DIVIDEND. Dividends may be issued in other forms such as stock and property. Dividend reinvestment plans also exist where stockholders can reinvest the proceeds of the dividend to buy more shares of stock. *See also* LIQUIDATING DIVIDEND; STOCK DIVIDEND.

**DIVIDEND EXCLUSION** applied to the amount of dividends received that are exempt from tax. Dividend exclusion is not applicable to individual investors. A corporation that owns less than 20% of the stock in another company can exclude 70% of the dividends received from taxable income. When between 20% and 79% of the stock of another company is owned, 75% of the dividends received from that firm can be excluded from taxation. When 80% or more of another company's stock is owned, all of the dividends received from that firm can be excluded from taxation.

**DIVIDEND GROWTH MODEL** cost of internal equity using the next expected dividend per share, the expected growth rate in dividends or earnings, and the market price, also called *Gordon's Dividend Model*.

**DIVIDEND PAYOUT** ratio that measures the percentage of net income paid out in dividends. It equals dividends per share divided by earnings per share. Stockholders generally favor companies that distribute a high percentage of their earnings in the form of dividends. Some industries, such as utilities, are known for their stable dividend records. Assume net income is $100,000, cash dividends are $60,000, and common shares outstanding are 10,000. The dividend payout ratio is:

$$\frac{\$6,000}{\$10,000} = \underline{\underline{.60}}$$

*See also* DIVIDEND YIELD.

**DIVIDENDS IN ARREARS** amount of dividends on CUMULATIVE PREFERRED STOCK from past periods that have not been paid.

**DIVIDEND YIELD** ratio providing an estimate of the return per share on a stock investment based on the market price at the end of the reporting period. The ratio equals dividends per share divided by market price per share. A disadvantage of this ratio is the timing mismatch between the numerator, which is based on the dividend declaration date, and the denominator, which is based on the year-end market price of the stock.

Assume cash dividends are $80,000, market price per share is $10, and 80,000 shares are outstanding. The dividend yield is:

$$\frac{\$1}{\$10} = \underline{\underline{.10}}$$

*See also* DIVIDEND PAYOUT.

**DIVORCE** legal termination of a marriage. The tax benefits of the personal exemption claimed for a child are phased out as income increases. Thus only the lower income parent benefits from the personal exemption deduction. The party making an alimony payment can deduct it for tax purposes. The recipient reports it as taxable income. No gain or loss is recognized on a transfer of property incident to a divorce. Such transfers are treated as gifts, with the transferee taking the transferor's adjusted basis in the property. The gain on the property is taxed only when sold.

**DNS (DOMAIN NAME SYSTEM)** allows domain names, such as barronseduc.com, to be converted into its IP address. Using DNS allows users to substitute words (domain names) for numbers (IP address).

**DNS HIJACKING** redirecting Web traffic to a fraudulent Web site. With DNS hijacking, Web traffic is redirected to a different Web site, but no attempt is made to fool the user. In contrast, with DNS spoofing, the attacker is trying to fool the user into thinking that the user is connecting to the intended Web site. *See also* DNS (DOMAIN NAME SYSTEM), SPOOFING, DNS SPOOFING.

**DNS SPOOFING** making a DNS address resolve to a different IP address than the real one. DNS spoofing is often used to redirect Web traffic to a fraudulent Web site. In DNS spoofing, the attacker is trying to fool the user into thinking that the user is connecting to the intended Web site. In contrast, with DNS hijacking the Web traffic is simply redirected to a different Web site, but no attempt is made to fool the user. *See also* DNS (DOMAIN NAME SYSTEM), SPOOFING, DNS HIJACKING.

**DODD-FRANK WALL STREET REFORM AND CONSUMER PROTECTION ACT** more commonly referred to as Dodd-Frank, imposes major regulations on the financial industry. It is designed to (1) prevent the collapse of major financial institutions, and (2) protect consumers from abusive lending and mortgage practices.

**DOLLAR ACCOUNTABILITY** emphasis upon the flow of liquid assets in accounting for firms that have a not-for-profit purpose.

**DOLLAR UNIT SAMPLING (DUS)** procedure expressed in dollar amounts showing that a given attribute has been exceeded. The accountant combines a *probability proportionate to size sampling* of audit units, which have an upper level prediction of possible error based on dollar mistakes uncovered in the sample, with an attribute derived from a probability determination. For example, a supplier account with a book value of $100 constitutes 100 *dollar units*. The auditor undertakes a random sample of the dollar units with probabilities proportionate to size. Then the audit units applicable to the sampled dollars are audited. If a dollar mistake is uncovered in a sampled item, it is converted on a "per dollar" basis. Sample results are projected to the population.

**DOLLAR VALUE LIFO** inventory method computed in *dollars* (i.e., cost figures) rather than units. After dividing ending inventory into homogeneous "groupings" or "pools," each pool is converted to base year prices by means of appropriate price indices. The difference between beginning and ending balances, as converted, becomes a measure of change in inventory quantity for the year. An increase is recognized as an inventory layer to be added to the beginning inventory. It is converted at the current price index and added to the dollars identified with the beginning balance. Assume 12/31/2015 physical inventory is $130,000. The price index in 2015 is 1.30. The base inventory is $80,000 as of 12/31/2014 with a price index of 1.00. The dollar value inventory at 12/31/2015 is $106,000 as determined below:

| | | |
|---|---|---|
| 12/31/2015 inventory in base dollars | | |
| $130,000/1.30 | $100,000 | |
| 12/31/2014 base inventory | 80,000 | $80,000 |
| Increase in base dollars | $ 20,000 | |
| 2015 index | × 1.3 | |
| Increase in current prices | | 26,000 |
| 12/31/2015 dollar value LIFO inventory | | $106,000 |

The tax law allows a simplified dollar-value LIFO method for taxpayers having average annual gross receipts for the three preceding taxable years of $5,000,000 or less. Under this method, taxpayers keep a separate inventory pool for items in each major category in the applicable government price index. The adjustment for each separate pool is based on the change from the preceding taxable year in the component of that index for the major category. *See also* LAST-IN, FIRST-OUT (LIFO).

**DOMESTIC CORPORATION** company established under U.S. or state law. A FOREIGN CORPORATION, in one sense, is a domestic corporation organized in a state other than the one in which it does business.

**DOMESTIC INTERNATIONAL SALES CORPORATION (DISC)** in taxation, domestic corporations, usually subsidiaries, created by the Revenue Act (1971) to encourage exports and improve the balance of trade. A major benefit is the deferment of 50% of a DISC's income for a long period of time.

**DONATION** gift of assets to a company, usually by state or local governments, to induce a business to relocate. The item donated is recorded at its fair market value on the donation date. The donor does *not* have an owner's interest as a result of the donation. The recipient's entry is to debit the asset and credit contribution revenue. The donor debits contribution expense at fair value, credits the asset at cost, and the difference is a gain or loss.

**DOUBLE DECLINING BALANCE METHOD** ACCELERATED DEPRE-CIATION method in which a constant percentage factor of twice the straight-line rate is multiplied each year by the declining balance of the asset's book value. The straight-line rate is simply the reciprocal of the useful life in years, multiplied by 100. If the useful life is five years, the straight-line rate is $1/5 \times 100 = 20\%$. Therefore, the double declining rate is 40%.

To determine the annual depreciation expense, the asset's book value at the beginning of the period is multiplied by the double declining rate.

For example, assume that the asset costs $1,000 and has an estimated useful life of five years. The estimated salvage value at the end of the five-year period is $100. The calculations for this method follow:

| Year | Original Cost | Beginning Book Value | | Double Declining Rate | | Annual Dep. Expense |
|------|---------------|----------------------|---|-----------------------|---|---------------------|
| 1 | $1,000 | $1,000 | × | 40% | = | $400 |
| 2 | 1,000 | 600 | × | 40 | = | 240 |
| 3 | 1,000 | 360 | × | 40 | = | 144 |
| 4 | 1,000 | 216 | × | 40 | = | 86 |
| 5 | 1,000 | 130 | × | | | 30 |
| | | | | | Total | $900 |

Note that in the fifth year depreciation expense is only $30, the amount needed to reduce the asset's book value to the estimated salvage value of $100. An asset is not depreciated below its salvage value. Thus, even though salvage value was ignored in the initial computation, the depreciation in the last year(s) cannot bring the asset's book value to less than the salvage value.

**DOUBLE ENTRY BOOKKEEPING** record of transactions that require entries in at least two accounts. Every transaction is reflected in offsetting debits and credits. For instance, when a telephone bill is accrued at year-end, (1) telephone expense must be recorded and (2) accrued expenses payable must be increased.

**DOUBLE EXTENSION METHOD** approach used to get a price index for DOLLAR VALUE LIFO when broad inventory pools of similar items are unavailable. The method uses a *representative portion* of items to obtain an index.

**DOWNLOAD** transmit a file or program from a central computer to the accountant's computer. The accountant can retrieve information to be used in an application package such as spreadsheet, file information from a subsidiary, or file data or program from an online database. A BUFFER is the temporary storage area holding information. *See also* TELECOMMUNICATIONS; UPLOAD.

## DOWNSIDE RISK

1. an investment risk evaluation derived by estimating the total loss that could occur in a worst-case scenario. A variety of factors enter into such an evaluation including book value and net earnings as well as general market conditions.
2. a company's risk of loss in a downturn in business activity. For example, an auto manufacturer has downside risk in an economic downturn because it cannot slash its fixed costs, which results from the capital-intensive nature of the industry.

**DRAFT** instrument normally used in international commerce to effect payment; also called *bill of exchange*. It is simply an order written by an exporter (seller) requesting an importer (buyer) or its agent to pay a specified amount of money at a specified time. The person or business initiating the draft is known as the *maker, drawer,* or *originator*. The party to whom the draft is addressed is the *drawee*. *See also* ACCEPTANCE; SIGHT DRAFT, TIME DRAFT.

**DRAWING ACCOUNT** provision allowing a personal withdrawal of cash or other assets from a proprietorship by the owner. It is in effect a disinvestment in the firm and reduces owner's equity. The entry is to debit the owner's capital and credit cash. The drawing account of a proprietor or partner is equivalent to the dividend account used by a corporation.

**DSS** *see* DECISION SUPPORT SYSTEM.

**DUAL PRICING** TRANSFER PRICING scheme. For example, the seller could record the transfer to another segment at the usual market price that would be paid by an outsider. The buyer, however, would record a purchase at the variable cost of production. Each segment's performance would be improved by the use of a dual-pricing scheme, and the organization would benefit because variable costs would be used for decision-making purposes. In effect, the seller is given a corporate subsidy under the dual-pricing system.

**DUAL PROBLEM** one part of associated LINEAR PROGRAMMING (LP) problems called the *primal* and the *dual*. In other words, each maximizing problem in LP has its corresponding problem, called the dual, which is a minimizing problem; similarly, each minimizing problem has its corresponding dual, a maximization problem. For example, if the primal is concerned with maximizing the contribution from the three products A, B, and C and from the three departments X, Y, and Z, then the dual will be concerned with minimizing the costs associated with the time used in the three departments to produce those three products. An optimal solution to the dual problem provides a SHADOW PRICE of the time spent in each of the three departments.

**DUAL PURPOSE TESTING** involves performing tests of controls concurrently with substantive procedures (i.e., tests of details) on the same transaction. Dual purpose testing may be used by an auditor to increase audit efficiency.

**DUE DATE** promised delivery date.

**DUE DILIGENCE** a qualitative assessment of management's character and capability. Due diligence evaluation is like "kicking the tires" of the company by conducting plant tours, trade checks, and interviews with competitors, suppliers, customers, and employees. Comprehensive due diligence may also include an examination of the books and records, asset appraisals, reviews of the company's other debt obligations, legal and accounting affairs, internal controls, planned capital expenditures, and other matters that bear on the company's future success and profitability. Due diligence is a legal requirement before public offerings.

**DUMMY ACTIVITY** fictitious activity with zero activity time used to represent precedence or used whenever two or more activities have the same starting and ending nodes.

**DUMPSTER DIVING** in IT (information technology), refers to a technique where a hacker goes through someone else's trash to collect information that could be used to carry out an IT attack.

**DU PONT FORMULA** the breakdown of RETURN ON INVESTMENT (ROI) into margin and turnover.

$$\text{ROI} = \frac{\text{Net Profit After Taxes}}{\text{Total Assets}} = \frac{\text{Net Profit After Taxes}}{\text{Sales}} \times \frac{\text{Sales}}{\text{Total Assets}}$$

$$= \text{Net Profit Margin} \times \text{Total Asset Turnover}$$

For example, consider the following financial data:

| | |
|---|---|
| Total assets | $100,000 |
| Net income | $18,000 |
| Sales | $200,000 |

Then, ROI = $18,000/$100,000 = 18%

Margin = $18,000/$200,000 = 9%
Turnover = $200,000/$100,000 = 2 times

Therefore, ROI = 18% = 9% $\times$ 2 = 18%

The breakdown provides a lot of insights to enable managers to improve profitability of the company and its investment center.

**DURABLE GOODS** costly manufactured products expected to last at least three years, including appliances and automobiles. The Census Bureau of the U.S. Commerce Department keeps track of them. The bureau tracks the dollar value of new orders. Separately, it also tracks shipments, unfilled orders, and inventories. Orders for durable goods can help forecast future manufacturing activity, although the overall number needs to be used with care because it can be strongly influenced by large orders in a particular sector, such as defense spending. For more information, two Web sites are helpful: www.census.gov/ftp/pub/ and www.haver.com.

**DURBIN-WATSON STATISTIC** summary measure of the amount of AUTOCORRELATION in the error terms of the *regression*. Roughly speaking, if the statistic approaches a value of 2, there is no autocorrelation. If the error terms are highly positively correlated, the statistic would be less than 1 and could get near zero. If the error terms are highly negatively correlated, the statistic would be greater than 3 and could get near the upper limit of 4.

**DVD** *see* DIGITAL VERSATILE DISK (DVD).

**DYNAMIC PROGRAMMING** technique that divides the problem to be solved into a number of subproblems and then solves each subproblem in such a way that the overall solution is optimal to the original problem. For example, a company may wish to make a series of accounting and financial decisions over time that will provide it with the highest possible cash inflow.

# E

**EAFE** *see* EUROPE, AUSTRALIA, FAR EAST (EAFE) INDEX.

**EARLIEST FINISH TIME** in PROGRAM EVALUATION AND REVIEW TECHNIQUE (PERT), earliest time at which an activity may be completed.

**EARLIEST START TIME** in PROGRAM EVALUATION AND REVIEW TECHNIQUE (PERT), earliest time at which an activity may begin.

**EARLIEST TIME (ET)** in PROGRAM EVALUATION AND REVIEW TECHNIQUE (PERT), the time an event will occur if all preceding activities are started as early as possible.

**EARLY EXTINGUISHMENT OF DEBT** long-term debt called back by a company before the maturity date. This may occur when the interest rate on the debt exceeds the current prevailing interest rate. The difference between the cash paid and the carrying value of the bond is treated as an ordinary loss or gain.

**EARNED INCOME** income from personal services. Earned income generally includes wages, salaries, tips, and other employee compensation. Compensation includes items that can be excluded from gross income, such as lodging, or meals furnished for the employer's convenience. Earned income also includes any net earnings from self-employment. Pension and annuity payments are not included.

**EARNED INCOME CREDIT** tax credit available to certain low-income taxpayers. This is an amount that eligible individuals can use to reduce their tax liability.

**EARNED SURPLUS** archaic term referring to retained earnings, the accumulated net income over the life of a corporation *less* all dividends.

**EARNING POWER** *discounted present value* of future profit of a business.

**EARNINGS**
1. NET INCOME of a business. *See also* EARNINGS PER SHARE (EPS).
2. revenues earned by an individual such as compensation and passive income (e.g., interest, dividends).

**EARNINGS FORECAST** projection of EARNINGS or EARNINGS PER SHARE (EPS) frequently made by management and independent security analysts. Examples of forecast sources include (1) Thomson First Call and (2) Reuters and Zacks Investment Research.

**EARNINGS GROWTH** a weighted average of the one-year earnings growth rates of the stocks in the fund. This calculation excludes stocks whose earnings changed from a loss to a gain and stocks whose earnings gains exceeded 999.99%.

**EARNINGS MANAGEMENT** see MANAGED EARNINGS.

**EARNINGS MULTIPLE** *see* PRICE-EARNINGS RATIO.

**EARNINGS MULTIPLIER** *see* PRICE-EARNINGS RATIO.

**EARNINGS PER SHARE (EPS)** profit accruing to stockholders for each share held. In a SIMPLE CAPITAL STRUCTURE, basic earnings per share equals:

$$\frac{\text{Net Income} - \text{Preferred Dividend}}{\text{Weighted Average Common Stock Outstanding}}$$

In a complex capital structure, BASIC EARNINGS PER SHARE and DILUTED EARNINGS PER SHARE are presented.

**EARNINGS SURPRISES** a company's announced net income for the reporting period that is above or below that expected by analysts (i.e., the consensus forecast). Stock price will typically increase if the earnings report is better than anticipated with the opposite effect if the earnings report is less than that expected. In fact, if earnings reported are much lower than those being forecasted by securities analysts, a drastic falloff in stock price may occur because of the disappointment. An example of a company that closely monitors earnings surprises is *First Call* (www.thomsonreuters.com).

**EBIT** earnings before interest expenses; also called *operating profit* or *operating income*. It is net sales minus operating expenses. It represents the amount of cash that a company will be able to use to pay off creditors.

**EBITDA** earnings before interest, taxes, depreciation, and amortization. It is EBIT + depreciation expenses + amortization expenses. EBITDA is essentially the income that a company has free for interest payments.

**ECONOMIC GROWTH AND TAX RELIEF RECONCILIATION ACT OF 2001** tax legislation in the United States that made significant changes in several areas of the U.S. Internal Revenue Code, including income tax rates, estate and gift tax exclusions, and qualified and retirement plan rules. In general, the act lowered tax rates and simplified retirement and qualified plan rules such as those for Individual Retirement Accounts, 401(k) plans, 403(b) plans, and pension plans.

**ECONOMIC LIFE** estimated period that a fixed asset will provide benefits to the company. It is usually less than the physical life of an asset because an asset continues to have *physical life* despite inefficiency and obsolescence. Depreciation expense is typically based on the economic life. *See also* ACCELERATED COST RECOVERY SYSTEM (ACRS).

**ECONOMIC ORDER QUANTITY (EOQ)** size that minimizes the sum of carrying and ordering costs. At the EOQ amount, total ordering cost equals total carrying cost. *See also* ECONOMIC ORDER QUANTITY (EOQ) MODEL.

**ECONOMIC ORDER QUANTITY (EOQ) MODEL** mathematical model that determines the amount of goods to order to meet projected demand while minimizing inventory costs. In the original version of the model, demand is assumed to be known and constant throughout the year. Ordering cost is assumed to be a fixed amount per order, and carrying costs are assumed to be constant per unit. EOQ is computed as

$$EOQ = \sqrt{\frac{2 \, (\text{Annual Demand})(\text{Ordering Cost})}{\text{Carrying Cost Per Unit}}}$$

If the carrying cost is expressed as a percentage of average inventory value (say, 12% per year to hold inventory), then the denominator value in the EOQ formula would be 12% times the price of an item. *See also* ECONOMIC PRODUCTION RUN SIZE.

**ECONOMIC PRODUCTION RUN SIZE** particular quantity of production that will minimize the total annual cost of setting up and carrying inventory, if produced in one production run. *See also* ECONOMIC PRODUCTION RUN SIZE MODEL.

**ECONOMIC PRODUCTION RUN SIZE MODEL** one that determines optimum production run quantity. The way it is computed is exactly the same as ECONOMIC ORDER QUANTITY (EOQ), except that the ordering cost in the EOQ formula is replaced by the setup cost. *See also* ECONOMIC ORDER QUANTITY (EOQ) MODEL.

**ECONOMIC PROFITS** difference between the total revenue and the total opportunity costs.

**ECONOMIC VALUE ADDED (EVA)** variation of RESIDUAL INCOME (RI) that defines the variable in specific ways. EVA = After-tax Income − (Cost of Capital × Capital Invested). The major difference between RI and EVA is that RI uses the market value or book value of assets for the capital invested in the division or firm while EVA uses the market value of total equity and interest-bearing debt.

**EDGAR** *see* ELECTRONIC DATA GATHERING, ANALYSIS, AND RETRIEVAL (EDGAR)

**EDIT CONTROL** in auditing, an input control used to identify incomplete, misleading, or invalid input data.

**EDUCATIONAL TRAVEL DEDUCTION** costs of transportation between a taxpayer's place of work and school that are deductible *for* adjusted gross income as ordinary and necessary employee business expenses. For these costs to qualify for deductibility, they have to meet the following conditions: (1) the education maintains or improves skills required by the taxpayer in employment or other trade or business; or (2) the education meets the expressed requirements imposed by either the individual's employer or applicable law, and such requirements must be satisfied to retain the taxpayer's job, position, or rate of compensation. Travel that itself is the educational activity is not deductible.

**EFFECTIVE INTEREST METHOD** manner of accounting for bond premiums or discounts. The interest expense equals the carrying value of a bond at the beginning of the accounting period times the EFFECTIVE INTEREST RATE (yield); also called *scientific amortization*. This method is *preferred* over the straight-line method of amortizing bond discount or bond premium. Amortization of a bond discount or premium is the difference between the interest expense and the nominal interest payment. The amortization entry is:

Interest Expense (effective interest rate × carrying value)

Cash (nominal interest rate × face value)

Bond Discount (for the difference)

**EFFECTIVE INTEREST RATE**
1. YIELD TO MATURITY.
2. real rate of interest on a loan equal to the nominal interest divided by the proceeds of the loan. Assume a company took out a $10,000, one-year, 10% discounted loan. Discounted loan refers to interest being deducted immediately in arriving at proceeds. This effectively raises the cost of the loan. Further, assume a COMPENSATING BALANCE requirement of 5%. The effective interest rate equals:

$$\frac{\$1,000}{\$10,000 - \$1,000 - \$500} = \frac{\$1,000}{\$8,500} = \underline{11.8\%}$$

**EFFECTIVENESS** extent to which actual performance compares with targeted performance. For example, if a company has established a target sales plan of 10,000 units at the beginning of the year and the company's salespeople sell only 8,000 units during the year, the salespeople are appropriately considered "ineffective," as opposed to "inefficient." *See also* EFFICIENCY.

**EFFECTIVE TAX RATE** equals the tax divided by taxable income. For example, if the tax is $20,000 on taxable income of $80,000, the effective tax rate of the business is 25% ($20,000/$80,000). *See also* MARGINAL TAX RATE.

**EFFICIENCY** cost of inputs for each unit of output produced. For example, the assembly department spent 2,320 hours of direct labor in order to produce 2,000 actual units of output, while the budget allows only 2,000 direct labor-hours for that level of output. Then the department was clearly *inefficient* (or wasteful) in the use of labor since it spent 320 hours more than allowed. *See also* ANALYSIS OF VARIANCES.

**EFFICIENCY VARIANCE** difference between inputs (materials and labor) that were actually used (i.e., actual quantity of inputs used) and inputs that should have been used (i.e., standard quantity of inputs allowed for actual production), multiplied by the standard price per unit. Efficiency (quantity, usage) variance = (actual quantity – standard quantity) × standard price per unit of input. The efficiency variance is unfavorable if the actual quantity exceeds the standard quantity: it is favorable if the actual quantity is less than the standard. *See also* MATERIAL QUANTITY VARIANCE; LABOR EFFICIENCY VARIANCE.

**EFFICIENT MARKET HYPOTHESIS** controversial theory holding that a stock's price is the same as its investment value. In an efficient market, all data are fully and immediately reflected in a stock price. Price changes in an efficient market are equally likely to be positive or negative. The hypothesis applies most directly to large companies trading on the major securities exchanges. The forms of the efficient stock market are weak, semi-strong, and strong.

In the weak form, no relationship exists between prior and future stock prices. The informational value of historical data is already included in current prices. Hence, studying previous stock prices is of no value.

In the semi-strong version, stock prices adjust immediately to new data; thus action after a known event results in randomness. All public information is reflected in a stock's value. Therefore, fundamental analysis is not usable in determining whether a stock is overvalued or undervalued.

In the strong form, stock prices reflect all information—public and private (insider). A perfect market exists. No group has access to information that would enable it to earn superior risk-adjusted returns.

**8-K** form a public company files with the Securities and Exchange Commission when an event deemed material requires public disclosure. Examples: a sudden and drastic lawsuit contingency or a change in auditors. *See also* 10-K.

**ELECTRONIC COMMERCE (EC)** the buying and selling of goods and services on the Internet. In practice, this term and a new term, "e-business," are often used interchangeably. For online retail selling, the term *e-tailing* is sometimes used. It is also called e-commerce for short, online commerce, Internet commerce, e-business, or CYBERSPACE commerce. E-commerce can be divided into: (1) e-tailing or "virtual storefronts" on Web sites with on-line catalogs, sometimes gathered into a "virtual mall." The gathering and use of demographic data through Web contacts; (2) Electronic Data Interchange (EDI), the business-to-business exchange of data; (3) e-mail and fax and their use as media for reaching prospects and established customers (for example, with newsletters); (4) business-to-business buying and selling; and (5) the security of business transactions.

**ELECTRONIC DATA GATHERING, ANALYSIS, AND RETRIEVAL (EDGAR)** service that the Securities and Exchange Commission uses to transmit company documents to investors. Those documents, which are available via Smart Edgar service, include 10-Qs (quarterly reports), 8-Ks (significant developments such as the sale of a company unit), and 13-Ds (disclosures by parties who own 5% or more of a company's shares).

**ELECTRONIC DATA INTERCHANGE (EDI)** transmission of business transactions from one company's computer to another company's computer. Transmission is achieved through an electronic communication network that uses translation software to convert transactions from a company's internal format to a standard EDI format. Companies that participate in EDI are referred to as trading partners. Trading partners may be involved in online banking, online retailing, and electronic funds transfer. There are paperless transactions in an electronic format. In the case of EDI, the auditor should be cognizant of the possible impact on the gathering of evidential matter.

**ELECTRONIC FUND TRANSFER SYSTEM (EFTS)** system for electronically transferring funds among sellers, buyers, and other parties without the need to write checks. The cost of processing a large number of checks has motivated financial institutions to develop a system of this kind. A typical example of EFTS is the payment of payroll. An employer deposits the payroll checks of its employees directly to their checking accounts. The company then sends to the bank a magnetic tape coded with the appropriate payroll data.

**ELECTRONIC MAIL (e-mail)** document transmitted electronically from the user's computer or terminal to an information service. Accountants and their clients can take advantage of electronic mail to transmit essential messages. With electronic mail, each user in the system has a "mailbox," which receives, holds, and sends information to others. The information sent may be spreadsheets, reports, memos, and so forth.

**ELECTRONIC TRANSFER FUNDS (ETFs)** equity indices that were introduced in 1993 as a way for investors to buy into a liquid, transparent, and diverse basket of stocks while paying less than for a mutual fund. The shares are priced in real time, tracking the value of their underlying index, and can be held as long-term investments, flipped for a quick profit or sold short to hedge equity risk.

**ELEMENTS OF BALANCE SHEET** items or accounts that appear on the balance sheet. They are various assets, liabilities, and equity accounts. A list of specific or detailed accounts is provided in the company's CHART OF ACCOUNTS. *See also* SETS OF ACCOUNTS.

**ELIMINATIONS** accounting entries used when preparing CONSOLIDATED FINANCIAL STATEMENTS between a PARENT COMPANY and a SUBSIDIARY COMPANY. Examples of eliminations are the elimination of intercompany profit, receivables, payables, sales, and purchases. Thus the consolidated entity reports financial statement figures applicable to outsider transactions. Where many eliminations are involved, an *eliminations ledger* may be used. Eliminations are also involved in preparing combining financial statements. *See also* CONSOLIDATION.

**EMBEDDED AUDIT MODULE** a program code that is added to a computer application that enables an auditor to collect data during processing of transactions.

**EMBEZZLEMENT** theft of money or property from a business by an individual in whose custody it has been placed. An example is a bookkeeper who steals from the petty cash fund. Proper INTERNAL CONTROLS can restrict or disclose such fraudulent activity.

**EMPLOYEE EMPOWERMENT** placing the authority to make critical decisions with those closest to the problem, for example, those in the work area directly affected. *See also* DECENTRALIZATION.

**EMPLOYEE RETIREMENT INCOME SECURITY ACT OF 1974 (ERISA)** federal legislation enacted to ensure that pension/retirement plans of employers are fair and secure. Provisions cover participation, vesting, funding, transferability, contributions, benefits, responsibilities, and termination procedures.

**EMPLOYEE STOCK OWNERSHIP PLAN (ESOP)** program that encourages employees to invest in the employer's stock. Employees may participate in the management of a company and even take control to save it from bankruptcy. The ESOP, however, is an inappropriate instrument for retirement savings. Because most of the funds are concentrated in the stock of one company, it does not provide any safety through diversification.

**EMPLOYMENT COST INDEX (ECI)** the most comprehensive and refined measure of underlying trends in employee compensation as a cost of production. Measures the cost of labor and includes changes in wages and salaries and employer costs for employee benefits. ECI tracks wages and bonuses, sick and vacation pay plus benefits such as insurance, pension and Social Security, and unemployment taxes from a survey of 18,300 occupations at 4,500 sample establishments in private industry and 4,200 occupations within about 800 state and local governments. This index can be obtained free from the Bureau of Labor Statistics' Internet site (www.stats.bls.gov). *See also* INFLATION.

**ENCODING** putting a message into a certain code, often as a control to assure confidentiality. *See also* CODING OF ACCOUNTS.

**ENCRYPTION** computer term relating to the process of concealing transmitted data from unauthorized users. For example, only the sender and receiver will be able to understand the transferred information because it is in a secret code. *See also* DECRYPTION.

**ENCUMBRANCE**
1. in government accounting, commitments related to unfilled contracts for goods and services including purchase orders. The purpose of encumbrance accounting is to prevent further expenditure of funds in light of commitments already made. At year-end, encumbrances still open are not accounted for as expenditures and liabilities but, rather, as reservations of fund balance. When an estimated or contractual liability is entered into, the entry is to debit encumbrances for the estimated amount and credit RESERVE FOR ENCUMBRANCES. When the actual expenditure of an amount previously encumbered is known, there are two entries. The first entry is to *reverse* the original encumbrance. The second entry is to record the expenditure by debiting expenditures and crediting VOUCHERS payable. At year-end, the encumbrance account is closed out against fund balance.
2. debt secured by a lien on assets.

**ENDING INVENTORY** goods on hand at the end of the accounting period. Ending inventory shows up in the income statement in the calculation of cost of goods sold and in the balance sheet. *See also* BEGINNING INVENTORY.

**ENDORSEMENT** signature on a draft or check by a payee before transfer to a third party. A payee provides such an endorsement when transferring this draft to the payee's bank. Checks can be endorsed in three different ways. In a *blank endorsement*, once signed, it becomes a negotiable instrument and can be used as such by anyone. A *restrictive endorsement* limits the use of the check to a single purpose. "For deposit only" is written on a check when it is deposited by mail. If the check is lost in the mail and subsequently found, it cannot be cashed. A *special endorsement* is used to pay someone else. All that is required is to indicate the payee and sign.

**ENGAGEMENT LETTER** letter written by the CPA or public accountant to the client citing the accounting functions to be performed, responsibilities assumed, the basis for billing, expense reimbursement, and so on. Typically, the CPA requests that the client sign the engagement letter showing agreement with the terms. The purpose of the engagement letter is to have a clear agreement among the parties regarding the accounting work to be done and related particulars.

**ENGINEERED CAPACITY** *see* IDEAL CAPACITY.

**ENGINEERED COSTS** costs having a clear relationship to output. Direct materials cost is an example.

**ENGINEERING ANALYSIS** way to measure cost behavior (or develop a COST-VOLUME FORMULA) according to what costs *should be*, not by what costs *have been*. It entails a systematic review of materials, labor, support services, and facilities needed for product and services. Engineers use time and motion studies and similar engineering methods to estimate what costs should be from engineers' specifications of the inputs required to manufacture a unit of output or to perform a particular service. *See also* ACCOUNT ANALYSIS; HIGH-LOW METHOD; REGRESSION METHOD.

**ENROLLED AGENTS** income tax specialists who have passed the IRS's comprehensive, two-day Special Enrollment Examination on all aspects of tax law or who have had five years of audit experience with the agency. Enrolled agents are authorized by the Treasury Department to represent the taxpayer, at all levels of audit, review, and appeal when dealing with the IRS. The examination includes true-false and multiple-choice questions and covers the following tax topics: (1) individuals; (2) sole proprietorships and partnerships; (3) corporations (including Subchapter S Corporations), fiduciaries, and estate and gift tax; and (4) ethics, recordkeeping procedures, appeal procedures, exempt organizations, retirement plans, practitioner penalty provisions, and research materials.

**ENTERPRISE ACCOUNTING** accounting for the *entire* business rather than its subdivisions (e.g., department).

**ENTERPRISE FUND** in governmental accounting, fund that provides goods or services to the public for a fee that makes the entity self-supporting. It basically follows GAAP as does a commercial enterprise. An example is a government-owned utility.

**ENTERPRISE RESOURCE PLANNING (ERP)** latest phase in the development of computerized systems for managing organizational resources. ERP is intended to integrate enterprise-wide information systems. ERP connects all organizational operations (personnel, the financial accounting system, production, marketing, distribution, etc.) and also connects the organization with its suppliers and customers.

**ENTERPRISE RESOURCE PLANNING (ERP) SOFTWARE** system that grew out of MATERIAL REQUIREMENTS PLANNING (MRP) systems, which have been used for more than 20 years. MRP systems computerized inventory control and production planning. Key features included an ability to prepare a master production schedule and a bill of materials and to generate purchase orders. ERP systems update MRP systems with better integration, relational databases, and graphical user interfaces. Features encompass supporting accounting and finance, human resources, and various e-commerce applications including supply chain management (SCM) and customer relationship management (CRM).

**ENTERPRISE RISK MANAGEMENT (ERM)** a broad term for risk management system that:

1. makes each area manager responsible for documenting and evaluating financial controls in his or her own area. People closest to each business unit manage the data, which improves accuracy and completeness;
2. identifies areas with inadequate control measures so action plans can be initiated to resolve problems;
3. tracks the progress of outstanding action plans, describes who is responsible for those actions, and sets the expected time for resolution;
4. protects against fraud with systematic data management that ensures multiple reviews and verification;
5. raises the level and precision of reporting to management;
6. puts "localized knowledge" to work. Area managers become empowered to understand the impact of their roles on corporate results.

*See also* RISK MANAGEMENT.

**ENTERTAINMENT EXPENSE DEDUCTION** tax deduction allowed only if the expenses are directly related or associated with the active conduct of a trade or business and are reasonable and necessary. This area of business expense deductions is scrutinized heavily by the IRS, and documentation requirements are usually quite stringent to prevent taxpayer abuse. A business may write off only 50% of the cost of business meals and entertainment costs.

**ENTITY**

**Accounting:** separate economic unit subject to financial measurement for accounting purposes. Examples are a corporation, partnership, sole-proprietor, and trust.

**Legal:** individual, partnership, corporation, and so on, permitted by law to own property and engage in business. Affiliated legal entities such as those consolidated for financial reporting may exist. Here, two or more companies operate under common control.

**ENTITY ACCOUNTING** accounting and measurement process for an entity that may not be the same as the legal entity. Usually, it involves measuring financial condition and operating performance.

**ENTITY THEORY** view in which a business or other organization has a separate accountability of its own. It is based on the equation:

$$Assets = Liabilities + Stockholders' \ Equity$$

The entity theory considers liabilities as equities with different rights and legal standing in the business. Under the theory, assets, obligations, revenues, and expenses and other financial aspects of the business entity are accounted for separately from its owners. In other words, the company has an identity distinct from its owners or managers. The firm is viewed as an economic and legal unit. *See also* PROPRIETARY THEORY.

**ENTREPRENEUR** individual who has the initiative to start an *enterprise* with its associated responsibilities, obligations, and risks. The entrepreneur usually hires people to work for him.

**ENTRY** recording of a transaction in the books of account, such as the receipt of cash in the cash receipts journal.

**ENTRY VALUE** replacement cost. It is the current estimated fair market price or cost of acquiring an asset already on the books or of service that has already been received and accounted for.

**ENVIRONMENTAL COSTS** expenditures incurred to prevent, contain, or remove environmental contamination. Such costs are generally expensed. However, in the following cases only, the company may elect to either expense or defer the costs: (1) the expenditures either extend the life or capacity of the asset or increase the property's safety; (2) the expenditures are made to get the property ready for sale; and (3) the expenditures prevent or lessen environmental contamination that may result from *future* activities of property owned.

**EQUALIZATION** adjustment of the tax valuation of property in a county relative to other counties in the same state. To assure that all property owners in the state pay a fair and uniform share of the state tax, an *equalization factor* is established by the state. For example, property in a county that assesses property at 60% of market value would be adjusted relative to other counties in the same state that assess their property at 50% of market value.

**EQUALIZATION RESERVE** allowance or reserve account credited periodically to offset charges to cover expenditures made during an accounting period. Its purpose is to allocate the expense uniformly over a period's operations. Maintenance expenses are sometimes handled in this manner. As the expenditures are actually paid, the allowance is debited, and the asset (e.g., cash) expended is credited.

**EQUATION METHOD** method used to find the break-even point or target income volume in COST-VOLUME-PROFIT (CVP) ANALYSIS or BREAK-EVEN ANALYSIS. The equation is:

$$Sales = Variable\ Costs + Fixed\ Costs + Net\ Income$$

Let $p$ = unit selling price, $x$ = volume, $v$ = unit variable cost, and $FC$ = total fixed costs; the equation becomes

$$px = vx + FC + Net\ Income$$

At the break-even volume, $px = vx + FC + 0$. To find the break-even point in units, simply solve the equation for $x$. Assume $p = \$250$, $v = \$150$, and $FC = \$35,000$. Then the equation is:

$$250x = \$150x + \$35,000 + 0$$
$$\$100x = \$35,000$$
$$x = 350 \text{ units}$$

**EQUIPMENT TRUST CERTIFICATE** debt instrument used to provide funds for the acquisition of equipment. The holder of the certificate has a secured interest in the asset in the event of corporate default. The trustee (usually a bank) has title to the equipment until the bond is paid. These certificates are sometimes issued by transportation companies (e.g., shipping company).

**EQUITY**

1. assets minus liabilities, also called NET WORTH. In a sole proprietorship, it is the owner's equity. In a corporation, it is STOCKHOLDERS' EQUITY.

2. any right to assets; property right; a liability. An equity holder may be a creditor, stockholder, or proprietor.

**EQUITY FINANCING** method of obtaining funds by issuing common or preferred stock. Receipts may be in the form of cash, services, or property. It is in the company's best interest to issue shares at a time when the market price of the stock is at its highest.

**EQUITY METHOD** means of accounting used by an investor who owns between 20% and 50% of the voting common stock of a company. It can also be used instead of the MARKET VALUE METHOD when the investor owns less than 20% of the company but has *significant influence* over the investee. Further, it is employed instead of CONSOLIDATION, even though more than 50% is owned, when one of the negating factors for consolidation exists (e.g., parent and subsidiary are not economically compatible, parent is not in actual control of subsidiary, parent has sold or contracted to sell subsidiary shortly after year-end). Under the equity method, the investor recognizes the percentage interest in the profit of the company by debiting investment in investee and crediting equity in earnings of investee. Dividends received by the investor are debited to cash and credited to the investment in investee account. *Permanent* declines in the market price of the investee are recognized by debiting loss and crediting investment in investee. However, temporary declines in market price are *not* reflected in the accounts. INTERPERIOD INCOME TAX ALLOCATION will arise because investee profits are recognized for book purposes but investee dividends are reflected for tax purposes. Assume investor company buys 10,000 shares of investee company for $10 per share acquiring a 30% interest. Investee's net income is $20,000 and dividends are $5000. The investment in investee account would look as follows:

**Investment In Investee**

| Investment | 100,000 | Dividends | 1,500 |
|---|---|---|---|
| Profit | 6,000 | | |

**EQUITY SPREAD** calculation of equity value creation by multiplying beginning equity capital by the difference between the return on equity (net income/equity) and the percentage cost of equity.

**EQUITY TRANSFER FUNDS (ETFs)** equity indices that were introduced in 1993 as a way for investors to buy into a liquid, transparent, and diverse basket of stocks while paying less than they would for a mutual fund. The shares are priced in real time, tracking the value of their underlying index, and can be held as long-term investments, flipped for a quick profit or sold short to hedge equity risk.

**EQUIVALENT PRODUCTION** measure of the number of equivalent whole units produced in a period of time; also called EQUIVALENT UNITS.

**EQUIVALENT TAXABLE YIELD** method of comparing the taxable yield on a taxable bond such as a corporate bond to the tax-free yield on a municipal bond. The magnitude of difference, assuming equal credit quality, depends on the individual's tax rate. Of course, on an after-tax basis, the tax-free interest rate on a municipal bond can be less than the taxable interest rate on a corporate bond depending on the tax bracket of the taxpayer. Assume a taxpayer in 2000 is in the 28% tax bracket. A 6% municipal bond has the equivalent taxable yield of 8.3% (6%/.72) on a corporate bond. Thus the taxpayer would have the same after-tax return on a 6% municipal bond or an 8.3% corporate bond. To gain a higher after-tax return, the investor would therefore have to invest in a corporate bond paying in excess of 8.3%.

**EQUIVALENT UNIFORM ANNUAL COST** annualized sum of all relevant costs. It is like the amount of an installment loan payment.

**EQUIVALENT UNITS** number of fully completed units considered to be equivalent to a greater number of partially completed units. For example, if 1000 units are in WORK-IN-PROCESS at the end of the period and are considered 80% complete, the equivalent production is 800 units. The equivalent unit cost of manufacturing an item equals the total cost divided by the equivalent units. If the total cost of manufacturing the item was $2,400, the unit cost would be $3 ($2,400/800). Equivalent units are determined separately for DIRECT MATERIAL and CONVERSION COST. If 3,000 units in ending work-in-process are 70% complete as to direct material and 90% complete as to conversion, the equivalent units are 2,100 for direct material and 2,700 for conversion. *See also* PROCESS COSTING.

**ERROR** difference between a correct item or amount and an incorrect item or amount. Errors may be due to inaccurate measurement, representation, or mathematical mistake. An example of an error is charging to an expense account the wrong amount. Material errors can result in erroneous financial decisions. Proper safeguards such as a good system of internal checks can minimize the incidence of errors. An error may also occur in applying GAAP. *See also* PRIOR PERIOD ADJUSTMENT.

**ERROR CORRECTION** a change from an accounting principle that is not generally accepted to one that is generally accepted or a bookkeeping correction. This is shown as a restatement. Error corrections are distinguished from changes in accounting principles, which are considered retrospective applications. Thus, although error corrections, like changes in principles, are reflected by restating comparative financial statements along with a prior-period adjustment to the opening retained earnings balance, the term *restatement* is reserved for error changes. *See also* ACCOUNTING CHANGE AND ERROR CORRECTIONS.

**ERROR TERM** deviation of the actual value of an observation from the true regression line; also called *disturbance term* and *residual term*.

**ESCAPABLE COST** *see* AVOIDABLE COST.

**ESTATE ACCOUNTING** record keeping involved in and the preparation of reports by the one administering an estate of a deceased under the jurisdiction of a probate court.

**ESTATE PLANNING** manner of minimizing estate taxes at death. It involves deriving the most favorable tax treatment of wealth. Inheritance is passed on to beneficiaries with the smallest amount given over to taxes. Tax planning aspects for estates include: (1) determining what financial strategy could be developed taking into account the particular assets being considered; (2) the transfer of assets before the taxpayer's death (i.e., transfer title of property to those in low tax brackets); (3) drafting a will considering the tax and asset transfer ramifications (i.e., property can be transferred between spouses without any tax because of the unlimited marital deduction); and (4) having appropriate terms in life insurance policies.

**ESTATE TAX** levy paid to the federal government or state on a deceased person's assets that have been left to heirs. The estate pays the tax, not the recipients. No estate tax exists for property going from one spouse to another. *See also* INHERITANCE TAX.

**ESTIMATED COST**
1. cost that has been estimated or projected for a particular decision alternative or contract.
2. expenditures to be made after a sale. For example, expenditures for after-service repairs under product warranty are *estimated costs*. Proper matching of revenue and expenses requires that the estimated costs of providing these warranties be recognized as an expense in the period of sale rather than of a later period when the warranty costs may actually be paid.

**ESTIMATED LIABILITY** obligation or service that actually exists but the amount requires estimation. Examples are estimated taxes payable and warranties payable. *See also* CONTINGENT LIABILITY.

**ESTIMATED TAX** quarterly payments for estimated tax liability on income that is not subject to employer withholding.
   **Individual:** must pay 90% of the estimated tax liability for the year in quarterly installments. Further, estimated tax payments made under the SAFE-HARBOR RULE provision must be based on 90% of annualized taxable income. An underpayment penalty can be avoided by paying 100% or more of last year's tax liability.
   **Corporation:** must remit 90% of the tax to be shown on the return for the taxable year in quarterly estimated tax payments to avoid a non-deductible underpayment penalty.

**ETFs**
   1. mutual funds that change hands all day long on an exchange, just like stocks—which is very different from the once-a-day trading of ordinary mutual funds. *See also* EXCHANGE-TRADED FUNDS (ETFS).
   2. *see* ELECTRONIC FUND TRANSFER SYSTEM (ETFS).

**EUROPE, AUSTRALIA, AND FAR EAST (EAFE) INDEX** compiled by Morgan Stanley Capital International (MSCI), the Morgan Stanley Europe, Asia, and Far East Index is a value-weighted index of the equity performance of major foreign markets. The EAFE index (it is pronounced EE-feh) is, in effect, a non-American world index of over 1000 stocks. It is considered the key "rest-of-the-world" index for U.S. investors, much as the Dow Jones Industrial Average is for the American market. The index is used as a guide to see how U.S. shares fare against other markets around the globe. It also serves as a performance benchmark for international mutual funds that hold non-U.S. assets. Morgan Stanley also compiles indexes for most of the world's major stock markets as well as for many smaller, so-called "emerging" markets. In addition, there are Morgan Stanley indexes for each continent and the entire globe. The index is quoted two ways: one in local currencies and two in the U.S. dollar.

**EVALUATION OF INTERNAL CONTROL** study and appraisal of the system of internal control within a company. The study aids in determining the extent of testing and other audit steps that must be performed. The auditor's evaluation concentrates on the nature of the internal controls, whether the controls are adequate in reducing to a minimum errors and irregularities, and whether the controls have been properly maintained and operated effectively. Evaluation steps include: (1) ascertaining the procedures and controls established by the client and their effectiveness; (2) determining which ones the auditor will rely on; (3) deciding which audit procedures must be expanded or curtailed; and (4) recommending to the client ways to improve internal controls. In evaluating the client's internal control, items to be considered are segregation of duties, internal checks and verifications, quality of personnel, duties and relationships of employees, quality and characteristics of the accounting system, and the effectiveness of the internal audit function. The Sarbanes-Oxley Act requires a company auditor to report on management's internal control assessment.

**EVENT**
1. in PROGRAM EVALUATION AND REVIEW TECHNIQUE (PERT), point in time that represents the start or completion of a set of activities.
2. in probability theory, one or more of the possible outcomes of doing something. For example, if a coin is tossed, getting a tail would be an *event*, and getting a head would be another event.
3. happening indicating a business transaction requiring a JOURNAL ENTRY has occurred.

**EVIDENCE** something that provides substantiation of the existence or amount of an item. The third standard of field work for a certified audit requires the auditor to obtain sufficient competent evidential matter as a basis for formulating an opinion on the financial statements. Evidence is more reliable when obtained from an independent source. Further, the stronger the internal control system, the more reliable the evidence. Finally, evidence obtained directly by the auditor through physical examination, observation, computation, and inspection is more persuasive than information obtained indirectly. For example, the accountant needs "backup" to support an entry made in the CASH DISBURSEMENTS JOURNAL. The cancelled check would serve as that evidence.

**EXAMINATION**
1. AUDIT of a company's financial records.
2. review of documents, procedures, and personnel to assure accuracy.
3. test administered by a professional organization to measure competence in an area, such as the CPA or CMA examinations.

**EXCEL** popular SPREADSHEET software by Microsoft.

**EXCEPT FOR OPINION** the only type of *qualified opinion* that an auditor can render. The auditor attests that the financial statements present the financial position fairly *except* for repercussions caused by conditions requiring disclosure. There may be a SCOPE LIMITATION in the auditor's work due to factors beyond the auditor's control or due to client restrictions that prevent the CPA from gathering objective and VERIFIABLE evidence in support of transactions and events. An example is the inability to confirm accounts receivable. There may exist a lack of conformity of the financial statements to GAAP.

**EXCEPTION**
1. EXCEPT FOR OPINION.
2. notification by a supervisor to a subordinate disagreeing with the subordinate's action. An example is where the supervisor questions

an employee's expense reimbursement request. Such request may not be fully honored.

3. negative response to a confirmation request, such as when a customer disagrees with his or her account balance as per the confirmation request.

4. variance between actual and standard. *See also* EXCEPTION REPORT.

**EXCEPTION REPORT** material deviation between actual occurrence and expectation in a performance report, which warrants management investigation. Undesirable performance is identified, and corrective action is taken on a timely basis. If the variance is favorable, the reasons therefore are also searched out, so further advantage can be taken of the situation. An example is a variance between actual cost and standard cost for labor in a standard cost accounting system. In the area of data processing, an exception report may reflect those transactions not meeting the standards or requirements for the program being run. *See also* FLASH REPORTS.

**EXCESS CAPACITY** machinery and equipment kept on standby. *See also* IDLE CAPACITY.

**EXCESS ITEMIZED DEDUCTION** broad class of deductions for the computation of tax liability. They are deductions from ADJUSTED GROSS INCOME in excess of the STANDARD DEDUCTION (previously referred to as the ZERO-BRACKET AMOUNT or ZBA) and the personal and dependent exemption deductions.

**EXCESS PRESENT VALUE INDEX** *see* PROFITABILITY INDEX.

**EXCHANGE**
1. reciprocal transfer of goods or services from one entity to another.
2. market for securities or commodities, such as the NEW YORK STOCK EXCHANGE (NYSE) or the Chicago Mercantile Exchange.
3. EXCHANGE RATE.

**EXCHANGE GAIN (LOSS)** a gain (loss) on the exchange of one currency for another due to appreciation (depreciation) in the home currency (for receivables).

**EXCHANGE OF NONMONETARY ASSETS** exchange based on the fair market value of the asset given or that received, whichever is more clearly evident. As a result, a gain or loss on the exchange is recorded because there is commercial substance to the transaction. The gain or loss equals the difference between the book value of the asset given up and the fair market value of the asset received. There is commerical substance when future cash flows change because of the transaction arising from a change in economic positions of the two companies. However, if the exchange lacks commercial substance, we record at book value the asset given up with *no* recognition or gain of loss.

**EXCHANGE RATE** *see* RATE OF EXCHANGE.

**EXCHANGE-TRADED FUNDS (ETFs)** index portfolios that you buy or sell just like stocks. The best of them are super-cheap—iShares S&P 500 Index (IVV) costs 0.09% a year, half the price of the Vanguard 500—and they can be traded instantly, sold short, or bought on margin. And ETFs track an astonishing variety of indexes, from biotech to Brazilian stocks.

| Index Fund | Expense Ratio | Typical Commission |
|---|---|---|
| Vanguard 500 index | 0.18% | None |
| iShares S&P 500 index | 0.09% | $4 to $30 per trade* |

*The commission on an automatic investment plan is $4; the top base rate for one national discount brokerage is $30.

**EXCISE TAX** one levied on specific products or services, for specific purposes. For example, an excise tax on gasoline might be used to fund road construction and repair. Excise taxes are levied at all levels of government, primarily federal and state. They are normally a percentage of the purchase price.

**EX-DIVIDEND** term used to indicate that a stock is selling without a recently declared dividend. The ex-dividend date is four business days prior to the date of record, according to rules applicable to NEW YORK STOCK EXCHANGE (NYSE)-listed companies and observed generally by other exchanges. *See also* DATE OF RECORD.

**EXECUTIVE GAMES** *see* MANAGEMENT GAME.

**EXECUTORY COST** cost excluded from MINIMUM LEASE PAYMENTS to be made by the lessee in a CAPITAL LEASE. The lessee reimburses the lessor for the lessor's expense payments. Examples are maintenance, insurance, and taxes.

**EXEMPT INCOME** income not subject to tax. Examples are interest on certain municipal bonds, employee achievement awards (length of service or safety achievement) up to a certain amount, scholarships and fellowship grants received from a college and used by degree candidates for qualified tuition and related expenses, and certain military benefits.

**EXEMPTION** deduction allowed in computing taxable income. There are basically two types: personal exemptions and dependency exemptions. There are three categories of exemptions, including personal and dependency types: (1) exemption for the taxpayer; (2) exemption for the taxpayer's spouse; and (3) exemption for dependent children and other dependents where more than one-half of the dependent's support is provided. *See also* DEPENDENT.

**EXEMPTION ORGANIZATION** one that is exempt from federal income taxes. An example is a not-for-profit corporation organized for religious, charitable, scientific, literary, educational, or certain other purposes.

**EXERCISE PRICE** price at which each share of stock underlying a call or put option can be bought or sold, also called *strike price*. It is standardized in trading at $5 intervals for stock between $50 and $100, $10 intervals for those between $100 and $200, and $20 for those over $200.

**EXHIBIT** formal statement prepared primarily for the dissemination of information. It may be of a financial or other nature. An example is a listing of product costs. Financial statements often make reference to accompanying exhibits.

**EXISTENCE** term used to refer to two audit objectives: (1) the verification that amounts in a company's financial statements do indeed exist and are proper; and (2) the verification that all events and amounts that do exist are duly recorded.

**EXIT VALUE** proceeds that would be received if an asset were sold or a liability terminated in an ARM'S LENGTH TRANSACTION. It may be expressed in terms of net realizable value, current selling price, or present value. *See also* ENTRY VALUE.

**EXPECTED ACTUAL CAPACITY** *see* CAPACITY.

**EXPECTED ANNUAL ACTIVITY** anticipated level of production for the coming year. If the total sales volume does not change from year to year, expected annual activity and NORMAL ACTIVITY would be the same, which is not usually the case. For example, normal activity, which reflects long-run average consumer demand is, say, 20,000 units of output or 100,000 direct labor-hours, while expected annual activity, which represents annual demand, fluctuates from year to year.

**EXPECTED MONETARY VALUE** expected value of PAYOFFS, measured in monetary terms. *See also* DECISION THEORY.

**EXPECTED TIME FOR AN ACTIVITY** in PROGRAM EVALUATION AND REVIEW TECHNIQUE (PERT), a weighted average time that is widely used in a real life application of PERT to a complex project, where the completion times for activities are not certain. First, estimate three possible duration times for each activity: an optimistic, a most likely, and a pessimistic time. A weighted average of these three time estimates is then calculated to establish the *expected time* for the activity. The formula applies to a weight of one to both the optimistic and the pessimistic estimates and a weight of four to the most likely estimate.

**EXPECTED VALUE** weighted average using the probabilities as weights. For decisions involving *uncertainty*, the concept of expected value provides a rational means for selecting the best course of action. The expected value $(E(x))$ is found by multiplying the probability of each outcome by its *payoff*.

$$E(x) = \Sigma x_i \, p_i$$

where $x_i$ is the outcome for $i$th possible event and $p_i$ is the probability of occurrence of that outcome. *See also* DECISION-MAKING UNDER UNCERTAINTY; DECISION THEORY.

**EXPECTED VALUE OF PERFECT INFORMATION** maximum amount a decision maker is willing to pay for perfect information. It is the difference between expected profit under conditions of UNCERTAINTY and EXPECTED VALUE WITH PERFECT INFORMATION. For example, assume that the expected value of perfect information is calculated as $2.50. There is no sense in paying more than $2.50 for the perfect forecast; to do so would lower the expected profit. *See also* DECISION THEORY.

**EXPECTED VOLUME** estimated volume of activity for a future period based on forecasts of sales of product or service, adjusted for planned changes in inventory levels. For example, assume on June 30 there are 10,000 finished units on hand. Sales for July are expected to be 50,000 units, and management wishes to have an inventory of 20,000 units on hand on July 31 in order to fill a growing demand. Then the expected production volume for July is 60,000 units (50,000 planned sales + 20,000 desired inventory − 10,000 beginning inventory). *See also* PRODUCTION BUDGET.

**EXPENDITURE**
1. payment of cash or property, or the incurrence of a liability to obtain an asset or service.
2. in GOVERNMENT ACCOUNTING, the incurrence of an actual liability in accordance with governmental authority.

**EXPENSE** results from or measures the using up of an asset (e.g., depreciation) or incurrence of a liability (e.g., warranty expense) to *obtain revenue* in the *current period*. An expense can apply to the cost of merchandise sold or services rendered. Expenses apply to the ordinary course of business (e.g., salary expense) rather than to incidental transactions (e.g., fire loss). Expenses are deducted from revenue to derive net income. An expense account is maintained for each type of expense for control purposes. *See also* COST; LOSS.

**EXPERT SYSTEMS** computer software involving stored reasoning schemes and containing decision making processes of human experts in an area. This is the area of ARTIFICIAL INTELLIGENCE (AI) that has received great attention from business decision makers. Recent advances have been made in this area of software systems that are designed to mimic the way human experts make decisions, providing computerized consultants. In effect, the expert system evaluates and solves problems requiring human imagination and intelligence that involve known and unknown information. The components of the systems include a knowledge base, inference engine, user interface, and knowledge acquisition facility.

**EXPIRED COST** a cost that will not provide any future benefit.

**EXPONENTIAL SMOOTHING** forecasting technique that uses a weighted moving average of past data as the basis for a forecast. The procedure gives heaviest weight to more recent information and smaller weight to observations in the more distant past. The reason for this is that the future may be more dependent upon the recent past than on the distant past. The method is effective when there is random demand and no seasonal fluctuations in the data. It is a popular technique for short-run forecasting by business forecasters. Each new forecast is based on the previous forecast *plus* a percentage of the difference between that forecast and the actual value of the time series at that point. That is:

New Forecast = Old Forecast + $\alpha$ (Actual – Old Forecast)

where $\alpha$ is a percentage, known as a smoothing constant and (Actual – Old Forecast) represents the prediction error. More concisely, we have

$$F(t + 1) = F(t) + \alpha (A(t) - F(t))$$

where $F$ = forecast, $A$ = actual, and $t + 1$ = forecast period. For example, assume that cash collections from credit sales are forecast by exponential smoothing using a smoothing constant of $\alpha$ = .30. Suppose that the previous forecast for the latest period was $20,000 and that actual cash collections were $21,000. What is the forecast for the next period?

$F$ (next period) = $20,000 + (.30)($21,000 – $20,000) = $20,300

**EXPOSURE DRAFT** proposed Statement of Financial Accounting Standards or Concepts issued by the FINANCIAL ACCOUNTING STANDARDS BOARD (FASB). Exposure gives the public an opportunity to comment upon the draft before it is finalized and issued as an FASB pronouncement.

**EX-RIGHTS** term used to indicate that a stock is selling without a recently declared stock right. As with dividends, the ex-right date is generally four business days prior to the DATE OF RECORD.

**EXTENDED NORMAL COSTING** costing method that assigns direct costs to cost objects using budgeted rates and actual quantities of inputs. It assigns overhead based on budgeted rates and the actual quantity of the base used for cost assignment. This approach is prevalent in the service sector. Accordingly, overhead is assigned under normal costing to each job through a predetermined overhead rate equal to the budgeted overhead divided by the budgeted amount of the appropriate denominator measure. In a traditional system, a single overhead rate might be established for an entire department, e.g., $3 of overhead for every direct labor-hour. If ABC is used, however, the multiple activities that use resources classified as overhead will be identified, a cost pool will be established for each activity, and the costs in each pool will be assigned based on the driver specific to the activity. If a driver cannot be easily identified, overhead is assigned to products or services using an allocation procedure; that is, it is determined using some indirect measure.

**EXTENSIBLE BUSINESS REPORTING LANGUAGE (XBRL)** formerly code named XFRML, a freely available electronic language for financial reporting. It is an XML-based framework that provides the financial community a standards-based method to prepare, publish in a variety of formats, reliably extract, and automatically exchange financial statements of publicly held companies and the information they contain. XBRL is not about establishing new accounting standards but enhancing the usability of the ones that we have through the digital language of business. XBRL will not require additional disclosure from companies to outside audiences. This new language allows the financial community to communicate in a universal language.

**EXTENSIBLE BUSINESS REPORTING LANGUAGE** On May 30, 2008, the SEC issued a proposal that would require companies to provide XBRL financial statements, as well as posting such statements to company Web sites. The SEC approved this proposal at their December 17, 2008, open meeting. The final rules will initially apply to domestic and foreign companies using U.S. GAAP and, eventually, to foreign private issuers using International Financial Reporting Standards (IFRS) as issued by the International Accounting Standards Board (IASB). The XBRL financial statements will be required, as an exhibit, with a company's traditionally filed (ASCII or HTML formatted) annual and quarterly reports, transition reports, and Securities Act registration statements. The information produced in an XBRL format will include companies' primary financial statements, footnote disclosures, and financial statement schedules.

**EXTENSION OF TIME FOR FILING** time period for filing a tax return that is extended beyond the due date. The typical extension granted to individuals and corporations is six months. Partnerships, estates, and trusts usually get a five-month extension. The taxpayer must file an application requesting the extension by the due date of the return. Interest will be charged for deficient estimated tax payments.

**EXTERNAL AUDIT** audit conducted by an *independent public accountant*. It refers to the type of audit and not the place of the audit. The entity's records may be subject to an audit by a CPA with an audit opinion rendered. *See also* INTERNAL AUDIT.

**EXTERNAL AUDITOR** independent public accountant who examines a business entity's books. The external auditor is not an employee of the company. *See also* INTERNAL AUDITOR.

**EXTERNAL DOCUMENT** term applies to documents needed for the company record keeping that has somehow been handled by outside individuals. Vendor invoices and cancelled checks are examples. The

auditor can place much more reliance on external documents than
INTERNAL DOCUMENTS because of the greater independence and verifiability associated with them.

**EXTERNAL FAILURE COSTS** a category of QUALITY COSTS incurred
because products fail to conform to requirements after being sold to
customers. They include warranty costs, returns, and lost sales.

**EXTRANET** private network that uses the Internet protocols and the
public telecommunication system to securely share part of a business's information or operations with suppliers, vendors, partners,
customers, or other businesses. An extranet can be viewed as part of
a company's INTRANET that is extended to users outside the company.

**EXTRAORDINARY ITEM** one that is *both* unusual in nature and
infrequent in occurrence. Extraordinary gains and losses are presented
NET OF TAX separately in the income statement. They appear between
INCOME FROM DISCONTINUED OPERATIONS and cumulative effect of a
CHANGE IN ACCOUNTING PRINCIPLE. Examples of extraordinary items
are casualty losses, losses from expropriation of assets by a foreign
government, gain on life insurance, gain or loss on the early extinguishment of debt, gain on troubled debt restructuring, and write-off
of an intangible asset.

Write-down and write-off of receivables and inventory are *not*
extraordinary because they relate to normal business operational
activities. They would be considered extraordinary, however, if they
resulted from an Act of God (e.g., casualty loss arising from an earthquake) or governmental expropriation.

**EXTRAORDINARY REPAIRS** work that extends the life of a fixed
asset more than one year and that is capitalized rather than expensed.
An example is a new motor for a truck. Extraordinary repairs are
charged to the accumulated depreciation account, thus increasing the
book value of the asset. The asset is then depreciated over the new
life. Assume on 1/1/2014 a truck costing $20,000 with a 10-year life
is purchased. The book value on 12/31/2017 is $12,000 ($20,000 –
$8,000). On 1/1/2018, an extraordinary repair of $6000 is made. The
entry is to debit accumulated depreciation and credit cash for $6,000.
The new book value on 1/1/2018 is thus $18,000 ($20,000 – $2,000).
As a result of the expenditure, the *new* remaining life is 8 years rather
than 6 years. The depreciation expense each year starting in 2018 is
$2,250 ($18,000/8 years).

# F

**FACE VALUE** nominal amount of a debt obligation (e.g., note, bond, mortgage) or equity security as stated in the instrument. It excludes interest and dividends. The face value of an instrument is often different from its issuance price; for example, a bond may be issued at a BOND DISCOUNT or BOND PREMIUM. Also, after issuance the going market price of an instrument will typically differ from its face value. At MATURITY, the debt instrument will be redeemed at its face amount. The nominal amount of a share of stock represents its PAR VALUE or stated value. *See also* MATURITY VALUE.

**FACILITY LEVEL ACTIVITIES** activities performed to support a facility's general manufacturing process.

**FACTORING** outright sale of a firm's accounts receivable to another party (the factor) *without recourse*, which means the factor must bear the risk of collection. Some banks and commercial finance companies factor (buy) accounts receivable. The purchase is made at a discount from the account's value. Customers either remit directly to the factor (notification basis) or indirectly through the seller (non-notification basis).

**FACTORY BURDEN** *see* FACTORY OVERHEAD.

**FACTORY LEDGER** group of accounts used to record factory-related transactions and to keep track of various manufacturing costs such as direct materials, direct labor, and factory overhead costs. It is a record kept by a factory.

**FACTORY OVERHEAD** total of all costs of manufacturing except direct materials and direct labor, also called *manufacturing overhead*, *indirect manufacturing expenses*, *factory expenses*, and *factory burden*. In addition to INDIRECT MATERIALS and INDIRECT LABOR, it includes such items as depreciation, setup costs, quality costs, cleanup costs, fringe benefits, payroll taxes, and insurance. It is an inventoriable cost charged by allocation to WORK-IN-PROCESS.

**FACTORY OVERHEAD BUDGET** schedule of all expected manufacturing costs except for direct material and direct labor. Factory overhead items include indirect material, indirect labor, factory rent, and factory insurance. Factory overhead may be variable, fixed, or a combination of both.

**FAILURE COSTS** quality control costs that are associated with products or services that have been found not to conform to requirements, as well as all related costs (such as that of the complaint department); they may be internal or external. *See also* EXTERNAL FAILURE COSTS; INTERNAL FAILURE COSTS.

**FAILURE TO FILE PENALTY** at the federal level is equal to 5% of the tax due for each month (or part thereof) that the tax return is not filed. The failure to file penalty is limited to 25%. The failure to file penalty is reduced by the FAILURE TO PAY PENALTY.

**FAILURE TO PAY PENALTY** at the federal level is equal to one-half of 1% of the unpaid tax for each month (or part thereof). The failure to pay penalty is limited to 25%.

**FAIR AND ACCURATE CREDIT TRANSACTIONS (FACT) ACT OF 2003** a law that mandates the public's access to free copies of their reports, which track the amount of debt consumers have and whether they pay their bills on time. The law is better known as the FACT Act.

**FAIR LABOR STANDARDS ACT (FLSA)** act enacted in 1938 that applies to workers involved in interstate commerce. It sets standards with respect to working conditions, including such aspects as minimum wage and working hours. It has been periodically amended and adjusted to keep the standards relevant to the current working environment.

**FAIR MARKET VALUE** amount that could be received on the sale of an asset when willing and financially capable buyers and sellers exist and there are no unusual circumstances such as liquidation, shortages, and emergencies. *See also* LIQUIDATION VALUE.

**FAIRNESS** term indicating that an entity's financial condition and *operating results* are presented in a way that is understandable, appropriate, and comprehensive. Fairly presented financial statements are *not* slanted to favor one party over another and are not subject to management influence and limitations.

**FAIR TRADE PRICE** one that is mandated or fixed by a manufacturer for a specific product to decrease or remove any competition between wholesalers and retailers on the basis of price. In 1975 Congress repealed federal laws upholding the power of states to protect manufacturers through fair trade legislation.

**FASB** *see* FINANCIAL ACCOUNTING STANDARDS BOARD (FASB).

**FASB ACCOUNTING STANDARDS CODIFICATION** the FASB's Codification (http://asc.fasb.org/home) that is intended to simplify user access to all authoritative U.S. generally accepted accounting principles (GAAP) by providing all the authoritative literature related to a particular topic in one place. The Codification is organized into approximately 90 accounting topics. The Accounting Standards Codification (ASC) is not intended to change existing U.S. GAAP, but rather integrates existing accounting standards by multiple standard-setters within the current GAAP hierarchy. The Codification is the single official source of authoritative, nongovernmental U.S. GAAP, superseding existing FASB, AICPA, EITF, and related literature. Going forward, U.S. GAAP will no longer be issued in the form of an "accounting standard," but rather as an update to the applicable "topic" or "subtopic" within the Codification. As such, accounting guidance will be classified as either "authoritative" or "nonauthoritative" based on its inclusion or exclusion from the Codification.

The Codification content is arranged within (a) Topics, (b) Subtopics, (c) Sections, and (d) Subsections, as follows:

- Topics. Topics represent a collection of related guidance and reside in four main areas: (1) presentation (e.g., income statement, balance sheet); (2) financial statement accounts (e.g., assets, liabilities, equity); (3) broad transactions (e.g., business combinations, derivatives); and (4) industries (e.g., airlines, real estate).
- Subtopics. Subtopics represent subsets of a "Topic" and are generally distinguished by type or by scope. For example, "Operating Leases" and "Capital Leases" are two Subtopics of the "Leases" Topic.
- Sections. Sections represent the nature of the content in a "Subtopic" (e.g., recognition, measurement, disclosure).
- Subsections. Sections are further broken down into subsections, paragraphs, and subparagraphs.

The following is the structure of the classification system: XXX-YY-ZZ-PP, where:

$$XXX = \text{Topic}$$
$$YY = \text{Subtopic}$$
$$ZZ = \text{Section}$$
$$PP = \text{Paragraph}$$

For example, Statement of Financial Accounting Standards No. 141R (FAS-141R), *Business Combinations,* is now ASC 805-10, *Business Combinations-Overall.*

**FAULT TOLERANCE** a system that is able to continue in the event of a hardware failure. This is achieved by having multiples of all critical components, such as CPUs, memories, storage devices, and power supplies, into the same computer. If one component fails, another one automatically takes over. Hardware redundancy is the key to a fault tolerant system; of course, this redundancy in hardware results in a significant cost increase. Note that the processing capability of the computer system remains the same after hardware failure.

**FAVORABLE VARIANCE** excess of standard (or budgeted) costs over actual costs. *See also* STANDARD COST SYSTEM; VARIANCE.

**FBAR** the abbreviation for Report of Foreign Bank and Financial Accounts. An FBAR is required to be filed electronically (on or before June 30 of the year following the calendar year reported) with the Department of Treasury if (1) a U.S. taxpayer had a financial interest in or signature power over at least one financial account located outside of the U.S., and (2) the total value of all foreign financial accounts exceeded $10,000 at any time during the calendar year. Taxpayers subject to FBAR filing requirements include individuals, corporations, partnerships, and limited liability companies.

**FEASIBILITY STUDY** evaluation of a contemplated project or course of action, according to preestablished criteria (such as NET PRESENT VALUE, INTERNAL RATE OF RETURN, and *payback*) to determine if the proposal meets management requirements. An analysis is also made of alternative means of accomplishing the task. *See also* CAPITAL BUDGETING.

**FEASIBLE SOLUTION** values of decision variables that simultaneously satisfy all the restrictions of a LINEAR PROGRAMMING (LP) problem. Feasible solutions are found in the feasible region. The OPTIMAL SOLUTION is usually found at the corner of the region. *See also* GRAPHICAL METHOD.

**FEDERAL INCOME TAXES** levies by the federal government on personal and corporate income. Personal income taxes are government revenues collected from the earnings of individuals and unincorporated businesses, after allowance for certain exemptions and deductions. Corporate income taxes are revenues collected on a corporation's computed profits. Most federal tax revenues come from these sources.

**FEDERAL INSURANCE CONTRIBUTION ACT (FICA)** law dealing with SOCIAL SECURITY TAXES and benefits. The taxes withheld from the employee's wages for Social Security are called FICA taxes. The FICA taxes depend upon the tax rate and the base amount of the wages subject to the tax.

**FEDERAL RESERVE BANK** district bank of the Federal Reserve System. *See also* FEDERAL RESERVE BOARD (SYSTEM).

**FEDERAL RESERVE BOARD (SYSTEM)** organization created by an act of Congress in 1913. The System is made up of twelve *Federal Reserve District Banks*, their 24 branches, and many national and state banks throughout the nation. It is headed by a seven-member Board of Governors. The primary function of the Board is to establish and conduct the nation's monetary policy. The System manages the nation's monetary policy by exercising control over the money stock. It controls the money supply primarily in three ways: (1) by raising or lowering the reserve requirement; (2) by setting the DISCOUNT RATE for loans to commercial banks; and (3) through its open market operations by purchasing and selling government securities, mainly three-month bills and notes issued by the U.S. Treasury. The System also serves as the central bank of the United States, a banker's bank that offers banks many of the same services that banks provide their customers. It performs many other functions. It sets margin requirements, regulates member banks, and acts as Fiscal Agent in the issuance of U.S. Treasury and U.S. Government agency securities.

**FEDERAL TRADE COMMISSION (FTC)** organization created by the Federal Trade Commission Act in 1914. It is responsible for thwarting "unfair methods of competition" and preventing monopolies and activities in restraint of trade. It also investigates cases of industrial espionage, bribery for the purpose of obtaining trade secrets or gaining business, and boycotts.

**FEDERAL UNEMPLOYMENT TAX ACT (FUTA)** Social Security legislation affecting labor costs and payroll records. Unlike the FEDERAL INSURANCE CONTRIBUTION ACT (FICA), which is strictly a federal program, FUTA provides for cooperation between state and federal governments in the establishment and administration of unemployment insurance. Under FUTA, an employer must pay an unemployment insurance tax to the federal government. While the federal act requires no employee contribution, some states levy an unemployment tax on the employee.

**FEEDBACK** term used to refer to information concerning actual performance, particularly in comparison with the plan. The feedback process is a critical part of a management control system in order to test a given system or model to see if it is performing as planned. Timely feedback enables quick corrective action when things get out of hand.

**FEES** charges billed for services rendered. They are tied into the monetary value of those services. Professional fees apply to accounting, tax, and legal work. They may be on a flat basis or an hourly one. For example, the accountant may charge a client $5,000 per year for all services or $100 per hour times the hours worked.

**FICO CREDIT SCORE** an acronym for Fair, Isaac & Company. A computer-generated credit score that predicts a lender's risk in doing business with a borrower. Any company or individual that issues mortgage loans, home-equity loans, car loans, insurance policies, or health care services (even the IRS) bases much of its lending decisions and terms on the applicant's FICO score. FICO scores are determined by computers and released through the three credit bureaus to their subscribing members. At Experian, the scores are called Experian/Fair, Isaac; at Equifax, they are called Beacon scores; at Trans Union, they are called Empirica scores. FICO scores five main kinds of credit information. Listed from most important to least important showing the percentage of the score based on the category, the categories are: (1) payment history (approximately 35% of score); (2) amount owed (approximately 30%); (3) length of credit history (approximately 15%); (4) new credit (approximately 10%); and (5) types of credit in use (approximately 10%). Credit scores range from 300 to 850. Scores provide an extremely valuable guide to future risk based solely on credit report data. The higher the consumer's score, the lower the risk to lenders when extending new credit to a consumer.

**FIDELITY BOND** insurance coverage against specified losses that occur from the dishonest acts or defalcations of employees. This bond may be applied to persons or positions.

**FIDUCIARY** individual or institution responsible for holding or administering property owned by another. An executor, guardian, trustee, and administrator are examples of a fiduciary. The PRUDENT MAN RULE is one way states ensure that fiduciaries invest responsibly.

**FIDUCIARY ACCOUNTING** proper accounting for property that is entrusted to the fiduciary acting under the conditions set forth in a deed. *See also* CHARGE AND DISCHARGE STATEMENTS.

**FIDUCIARY FUND** term used when a governmental unit acts in a fiduciary capacity such as a trustee or agent. The government unit is responsible for handling the assets placed under its control.

**FIELD** group of adjacent characters. For example, in a company's payroll system, separate fields can exist for an employee's name, employee's Social Security number, and hourly rate. *See also* RECORD.

**FIELD AUDITOR** individual who conducts audits at locations other than central headquarters such as in distant divisions and branches. *See also* TRAVELING AUDITOR.

**FIFO** *see* FIRST-IN, FIRST-OUT.

**FILE** collection of information stored as *records*. For example, the records for all charge customers at the local department store collectively form the *accounts receivable file*. Thus Mr. Smith's account is an *accounts receivable record*. A record that describes a single business activity is called a transaction record. Thus, when Mr. Smith buys a new suit on credit, the sales clerk writes up a credit sales ticket as a *transaction record*. The total set of credit sales tickets for that day would collectively comprise a *daily credit sales transaction file*.

**FILE TRANSFER PROTOCOL (FTP)** a standard TCP/IP for transmitting files between computers on the Internet. Using FTP, one can also copy, delete, rename, and move files on a server.

**FILING STATUS** one of four basic categories for taxpayer filing: (1) married, filing a joint return; (2) married, filing separately; (3) head of household; and (4) single. The filing status determines the tax rate schedules to be used to compute tax liability. Tax rates generally increase in each category with the respective order listed above.

**FINANCIAL ACCOUNTING** information developed in conformity with GENERALLY ACCEPTED ACCOUNTING PRINCIPLES (GAAP). It involves the recording and summarization of business transactions and events. Financial accounting relates to the preparation of financial statements for external users such as creditors, investors, and suppliers. The financial statements include the balance sheet, income statement, and statement of changes in financial position. These statements, including related footnotes, President's letter, management's discussion of operations, etc., appear in the annual report. *See also* MANAGEMENT ACCOUNTING.

**FINANCIAL ACCOUNTING FOUNDATION (FAF)** institution that funds the FINANCIAL ACCOUNTING STANDARDS BOARD (FASB) and appoints its members. Founded in 1972, the FAF is composed of nine trustees chosen by the board of directors of the AMERICAN INSTITUTE OF CERTIFIED PUBLIC ACCOUNTANTS (AICPA). They are the president of the AICPA, four CPAs who are accounting practitioners in public practice, two financial executives, one financial analyst, and one academician. Organizations that sponsor the FAF are AICPA, Financial Executives Institute, Financial Analysts Federation, National Association of Accountants, Securities Industry Association, and American Accounting Association.

**FINANCIAL ACCOUNTING STANDARDS BOARD (FASB)** (www.fasb.org) nongovernmental body with the authority to promulgate U.S. GENERALLY ACCEPTED ACCOUNTING PRINCIPLES (GAAP) and reporting practices. These are published in the form of FASB Statements. Practicing CPAs are required to follow the FASB pronouncements in their accounting and financial reporting functions. The FASB is *independent* of other companies and professional organizations. The AMERICAN INSTITUTE OF CERTIFIED PUBLIC ACCOUNTANTS (AICPA) and the SECURITIES AND EXCHANGE COMMISSION officially recognize the Statements issued by the Financial Accounting Standards Board. The FASB was established in 1973 to succeed the Accounting Principles Board (APB). *See also* FINANCIAL ACCOUNTING FOUNDATION.

**FINANCIAL ANALYSIS** use and transformation of financial data into a form that can be used to monitor and evaluate the firm's financial position, to plan future financing, and to designate the size of the firm and its rate of growth. Financial analysis includes the use of FINANCIAL STATEMENT ANALYSIS and FUNDS FLOW ANALYSIS.

**FINANCIAL ANALYSIS SOFTWARE** software capable of taking financial data from an online database to perform ratio and trend calculations. Investment and credit decisions are based on the analysis results.

*FINANCIAL ANALYSTS JOURNAL* bimonthly publication of the CFA Institute (www.cfapubs.org). Its readership includes financial analysts and executives. Subject matter covers security analysis, portfolio management, financial accounting theory, professional ethics, financial management, financial planning, and taxation.

**FINANCIAL BUDGET** one that embraces the impacts of the financial decisions of the firm. It is a plan including a BUDGETED BALANCE SHEET, which shows the effects of planned operations and capital investments on assets, liabilities, and equities. It also includes a CASH BUDGET, which forecasts the flow of cash and other funds in the business. Cash budgeting (cash planning) is a critical part of budgeting because it is essential to have the right sums of cash available at the right times.

## FINANCIAL CRISIS

1. a situation in which the supply of money is outpaced by the demand for money. This means that liquidity evaporates quickly because available money is withdrawn from banks (called a run), forcing banks either to sell other investments to make up for the shortfall or to collapse.

2. the global financial crisis of 2008–2009 emerged in September 2008 with the failure, merger, or conservatorship of several large U.S.-based financial institutions, such as investment banks, insurance firms, and mortgage banks, consequent to the subprime mortgage crisis, and spread with the insolvency of additional companies, and of governments in Europe, recession, and declining stock market prices around the globe.

**FINANCIAL DECISIONS** decisions that involve: (1) determining the proper amount of funds to employ in a firm; (2) selecting projects and capital expenditure analysis; (3) raising funds on the most favorable terms possible; and (4) managing working capital such as inventory and accounts receivable.

**FINANCIAL DERIVATIVE** *see* DERIVATIVE.

**FINANCIAL ENGINEERING** application of economic principles to the dynamics of securities markets, especially for the purpose of structuring, pricing, and managing the risk of financial contracts.

*FINANCIAL EXECUTIVES* monthly publication of the FINANCIAL EXECUTIVES INSTITUTE (FEI) (www.financialexecutives.org). It is directed toward corporate financial executives and covers all aspects of financial management.

**FINANCIAL EXECUTIVES INSTITUTE (FEI)** (www.financial executives.org) organization primarily of controllers and treasurers as well as other executives involved in the accounting and financial functions. Its Corporate Reporting Committee represents the organization before authoritative accounting bodies. Research publications are supported and published by the Financial Executives Research Foundation.

**FINANCIAL FORECAST** *see* FINANCIAL PROJECTION.

**FINANCIAL FUTURE** contract to buy or sell a financial instrument at a specific price in a specified future month. There is a relationship between the price of the contract and the interest rate the underlying instrument bears; the contract's value decreases as market interest rates increase and vice versa. Some types of financial instruments used in financial futures contracts are Treasury bills, Treasury notes, Ginnie Maes, and certificates of deposit. Futures contracts are used to speculate on interest rate changes and to hedge investment portfolios against adverse movements in interest rates. Currency futures, a form of financial futures, are used to speculate on foreign exchange rates and to hedge currency values. These contracts are supervised by the Commodities Futures Trading Commission.

**FINANCIAL HIGHLIGHT** section of corporate annual reports that summarizes key financial data on a comparative basis. Sales, earnings per share (primary and after dilution), and dividends are always highlighted along with other information the company considers noteworthy.

**FINANCIAL INDUSTRY REGULATORY AUTHORITY (FINRA)** created in 1987 as a result of the merger of the National Association of Securities Dealers (NASD) and the regulation Committee of the New York Stock Exchange. The goal of FINRA, a not-for-profit organization, is to protect investors by establishing and enforcing ethical standards. *See also* NATIONAL ASSOCIATION OF SECURITIES DEALERS (NASD).

**FINANCIAL INFORMATION SYSTEM** term for a system that accumulates and analyzes financial data in order to make good financial management decisions in running the business. The basic objective of the financial information system is to meet the firm's financial obligations as they come due, using the minimal amount of financial resources consistent with an established margin of safety. Outputs generated by the system include accounting reports, operating and capital budgets, working capital reports, cash flow forecast, and various WHAT-IF ANALYSIS reports. The evaluation of financial data may be performed through ratio analysis, trend evaluation, and financial planning modeling. Financial planning and forecasting are facilitated if used in conjunction with a DECISION SUPPORT SYSTEM (DSS).

**FINANCIAL LEVERAGE** portion of a firm's assets financed with debt instead of equity. It involves contractual interest and principal obligations. Financial leverage benefits common stockholders as long as the borrowed funds generate a return in excess of the cost of borrowing, although the increased risk can offset the general cost of capital. For this reason, financial leverage is popularly called TRADING ON EQUITY. Financial leverage is measured by the DEBT-EQUITY RATIO.

**FINANCIAL MODEL** functional branch of a general CORPORATE PLANNING MODEL. It is used essentially to generate PRO FORMA financial statements and financial ratios. A financial model is a mathematical model describing the interrelationships among financial variables of the firm. It is the basic tool for budgeting and budget planning. Also, it is used for risk analysis and WHAT-IF experiments. Many financial models use spreadsheet programs such as EXCEL and LOTUS 1-2-3. *See also* CORPORATE PLANNING MODEL.

**FINANCIAL PLANNER** professional engaged in providing PERSONAL FINANCIAL PLANNING services to individuals. A financial planner assists a client in the following ways: (1) assesses a client's financial history, such as tax returns, investments, retirement plan, wills, and insurance policies; (2) helps decide on a financial plan, based on personal and financial goals, history, and preferences; (3) identifies financial areas where a client may need help, such as building up retirement income or improving investment return; (4) prepares a financial plan based on the individual situation and discusses it thoroughly; (5) helps implement the financial plan, including referring the client to specialists, such as lawyers or accountants, if necessary; and (6) reviews the situation and financial plan periodically and suggests changes when needed. Financial planners come from a variety of backgrounds and, therefore, may hold a variety of degrees and licenses. They include such credentials as Certified Financial Planner (CFP), Chartered Financial Consultant (ChFC), lawyer (JD), and Certified Public Accountant (CPA).

**FINANCIAL PLANNING MODELS** *see* FINANCIAL MODEL.

**FINANCIAL PLANNING SOFTWARE** personal finance computer programs that keep track of income and expenses by budget category, reconcile accounts, store tax records, figure net worth, track stocks and bonds, and print checks and financial reports. Some programs are sophisticated enough to generate a detailed, long-term personal financial plan covering planning for college education, investment, and retirement. Examples of financial planning software are *Quicken* and *Managing Your Money*.

**FINANCIAL PROJECTION** essential element of planning that is the basis for budgeting activities and estimating future financing needs of a firm. Financial projections (forecasts) begin with forecasting sales and their related expenses. The basic steps in financial forecasting are: (1) project the firm's sales; (2) project variables such as expenses and assets; (3) estimate the level of investment in current and fixed assets that is required to support the projected sales; and (4) calculate the firm's financing needs. The basic tools for financial forecasting include the percent-of-sales-method, REGRESSION ANALYSIS, and financial modeling.

**FINANCIAL RATIO** mathematical relationship between one quantity and another. There are many categories of ratios such as those that evaluate a business entity's liquidity, solvency, return on investment, operating performance, asset utilization, and market measures. An example of a ratio is the earnings yield that equals dividends per share divided by market price per share. Whereas the computation of a ratio is a basic arithmetic operation, its analytical interpretation is more complex. A financial ratio should be computed only if the relationship between accounts or categories has significance. The financial ratio may provide the accountant with clues and symptoms of underlying financial condition. To be meaningful, a given financial ratio of a company for a given year must be compared with (1) prior years to examine the trend, (2) industry norm, and (3) competing companies. *See also* FINANCIAL STATEMENT ANALYSIS.

**FINANCIAL RATIO ANALYSIS** *see* FINANCIAL STATEMENT ANALYSIS.

**FINANCIAL REPORTING** presenting financial data of a company's position, operating performance, and funds flow for an accounting period. Financial statements along with related information may be contained in various forms for external party use such as in the annual report, SEC Form 10-K, and prospectus.

**FINANCIAL REPORTING FRAMEWORK FOR SMALL- AND MEDIUM-SIZED ENTITIES (FRF FOR SMEs)** represents an accounting option for the preparation of financial statements for privately held, owner-managed businesses that are not required to follow U.S. GENERALLY ACCEPTED ACCOUNTING PRINCIPLES (GAAP). FRF FOR SMEs, which was developed by the American Institute of Certified Public Accountants, is not considered to be authoritative.

**FINANCIAL RISK** portion of total corporate risk, over and above basic BUSINESS RISK, that results from using debt. Business risk is caused by fluctuations of earnings before interest and taxes (operating income). Business risk depends on variability in demand, sales price, input prices, and amount of OPERATING LEVERAGE. Financial risk includes DEFAULT risk, which is the risk that the borrower will be unable to make interest payments or principal repayments on debt. The greater the firm's FINANCIAL LEVERAGE, the higher is its financial risk.

**FINANCIAL STATEMENT** report containing financial information about an organization. The required financial statements are balance sheet, income statement, and statement of changes in financial position. They may be combined with a supplementary statement to depict the financial status or performance of the organization. An example of a supplementary statement is an inflation-adjusted financial statement. Some supplementary material is required only for publicly held companies.

**FINANCIAL STATEMENT ANALYSIS** method used by interested parties such as investors, creditors, and management to evaluate the past, current, and projected conditions and performance of the firm. Ratio analysis is the most common form of financial analysis. It provides relative measures of the firm's conditions and performance. HORIZONTAL ANALYSIS and VERTICAL ANALYSIS are also popular forms. Horizontal analysis is used to evaluate the trend in the accounts over the years, while vertical analysis, also called a COMMON SIZE FINANCIAL STATEMENT, discloses the internal structure of the firm. It indicates the existing relationship between sales and each income statement account. It shows the mix of assets that produce income and the mix of the sources of capital, whether by current or long-term debt or by equity funding. When using the financial ratios, a financial analyst makes two types of comparisons:

(1) *Industry comparison.* The ratios of a firm are compared with those of similar firms or with industry averages or norms to determine how the company is faring relative to its competitors. Industry average ratios are available from a number of sources, including: (a) Dun & Bradstreet. Dun & Bradstreet computes 14 ratios for each of 125 lines of business. They are published in *Dun's Review* and *Key Business Ratios*. (b) Risk Management Association (RMA). This association of bank loan officers publishes *Annual Statement Studies*. Sixteen ratios are computed for more than 300 lines of business, as well as a percentage distribution of items on the balance sheet and income statement (*common size financial statements*).

(2) *Trend analysis.* A firm's present ratio is compared with its past and expected future ratios to determine whether the company's financial condition is improving or deteriorating over time.

After completing the financial statement analysis, the firm's financial analyst will consult with management to discuss plans and prospects, any problem areas identified in the analysis, and possible solutions. Given below is a list of widely used financial ratios.

## Financial Statement Analysis: List of Ratios

### Liquidity

| | |
|---|---|
| Net Working Capital | Current Assets – Current Liabilities |
| Current Ratio | $\dfrac{\text{Current Assets}}{\text{Current Liabilities}}$ |
| Quick Ratio | $\dfrac{\text{Cash} + \text{Marketable Securities} + \text{Receivables}}{\text{Current Liabilities}}$ |

### Activity

| | |
|---|---|
| Accounts Receivable Turnover | $\dfrac{\text{Net Credit Sales}}{\text{Average Accounts Receivable}}$ |
| Average Collection Period | $\dfrac{365}{\text{Accounts Receivable Turnover}}$ |
| Inventory Turnover | $\dfrac{\text{Cost Of Goods Sold}}{\text{Average Inventory}}$ |
| Average Age of Inventory | $\dfrac{365}{\text{Inventory Turnover}}$ |
| Total Asset Turnover | $\dfrac{\text{Net Sales}}{\text{Average Total Assets}}$ |

### Leverage

Debt Ratio

$$\frac{\text{Total Debt}}{\text{Total Assets}}$$

Debt/Equity Ratio

$$\frac{\text{Total Liabilities}}{\text{Stockholders' Equity}}$$

Times Interest Earned

$$\frac{\text{Earnings Before Interest \& Taxes}}{\text{Interest Expense}}$$

### Profitability

Gross Profit Margin

$$\frac{\text{Gross Profit}}{\text{Net Sales}}$$

Profit Margin

$$\frac{\text{Net Income}}{\text{Net Sales}}$$

Return On Total Assets

$$\frac{\text{Net Income}}{\text{Average Total Assets}}$$

Return On Common Equity

$$\frac{\text{Net Income}}{\text{Common Equity}}$$

### Market Value

Earnings Per Share

$$\frac{\text{Net Income} - \text{Preferred Dividends}}{\text{Common Stock Outstanding}}$$

Price/Earnings Ratio

$$\frac{\text{Market Price Per Share}}{\text{Earnings Per Share}}$$

Book Value Per Share

$$\frac{\text{Stockholders' Equity} - \text{Preferred Stock}}{\text{Common Stock Outstanding}}$$

Dividend Yield

$$\frac{\text{Dividends Per Share}}{\text{Market Price Per Share}}$$

Dividend Payout

$$\frac{\text{Dividends Per Share}}{\text{Earnings Per Share}}$$

**FINANCIAL STATEMENT AUDIT** one performed by a CPA for the purpose of expressing an opinion as to the fairness of the information contained in the financial statements. The audit work is conducted in accordance with GENERALLY ACCEPTED AUDITING STANDARDS (GAAS) and includes those reviews of internal controls, tests, and verification of data and other activities deemed necessary by the auditor. Typically, annual financial statements are subject to audit while interim statements are not.

**FINANCING ACTIVITIES** transactions including the distribution, acquisition, movement, and management of money, in accordance with some overall objective, policy, or goal.

**FINANCING LEASE** *see* CAPITAL LEASE.

**FINISHED GOODS INVENTORY** amount of manufactured product on hand that awaits sale to customers. Finished goods inventory represents a current asset in the balance sheet. The income statement shows both beginning finished goods and ending finished goods only if cost of goods sold is calculated. When goods that were in process are completed, the entry is to debit finished goods and credit work-in-process. When merchandise is sold, the entry is to debit cost of goods sold and credit finished goods. The difference between the sales and cost of goods sold is the gross profit.

**FIREWALL** a program used to protect a private network from other networks. The firewall application analyzes data packets and determines whether they should be allowed through to the protected network.

**FIRST-IN, FIRST-OUT (FIFO)** method of inventory valuation that assumes merchandise is sold in the order of its receipt. The first-price in is the first-price out. Hence cost of sales is based on older dollars. Ending inventory is reflected at the most recent prices. Assume the following data regarding inventory during the year:

| | | |
|---|---|---|
| Jan. 1 Inventory | 150 units @ $ 8 | = $1,200 |
| Feb. 20 Purchases | 200 units @ $ 9 | = 1,800 |
| Apr. 12 Purchases | 250 units @ $10 | = 2,500 |
| Sept. 20 Purchases | 200 units @ $11 | = 2,200 |
| Goods Available | 800 | $7,700 |

Assume physical inventory on December 31 is 430 units. The year-end inventory valuation is:

| | | |
|---|---|---|
| Last purchase (Sept. 20) | 200 units @ $11 | = $2,200 |
| Next most recent purchase | 230 units @ $10 | = 2,300 |
| (Apr. 12) | | |
| Total | 430 | $4,500 |

*See also* LAST-IN, FIRST-OUT (LIFO).

**FIRST-IN, FIRST-OUT (FIFO) COSTING** procedure for computing the unit costs of a process by which beginning work-in-process inventory costs are separated from added costs applied in the current period. Thus, there are two unit costs for the period: (1) beginning work-in-process units completed and (2) started and completed in the same period. Under FIFO, the beginning WORK-IN-PROCESS is assumed to be completed and transferred first. Equivalent units under FIFO costing may be computed as follows:

Units completed + [Ending work-in-process × degree of completion (%)] – [Beginning work-in-process × degree of completion (%)]

To illustrate, the following data relate to the activities of Department A during the month of January:

|  | Units |
|---|---|
| Beginning work-in-process (100% complete as to materials; 2/3 complete as to conversion) | 1,500 |
| Started this period | 5,000 |
| Completed and transferred | 5,500 |
| Ending work-in-process (100% complete as to materials; 6/10 complete as to conversion) | 1,000 |

Equivalent production in Department A for the month is computed, using FIFO costing, as follows:

|  | Materials | Conversion Costs |
|---|---|---|
| Units completed and transferred | $5,500 | $5,500 |
| Ending work-in-process |  |  |
| Materials (100%) | 1,000 |  |
| Conversion costs (60%) |  | 600 |
| Equivalent production | $6,500 | $6,100 |
| Minus: Beginning work-in-process |  |  |
| Materials (100%) | 1,500 |  |
| Conversion costs (2/3) |  | 1,000 |
| Equivalent production for FIFO | $5,000 | $5,100 |

*See also* WEIGHTED AVERAGE COSTING.

**FIRST-STAGE ALLOCATION** *see* RESOURCE COST ASSIGNMENT.

**FISCAL YEAR**
1. Twelve consecutive months used by a business entity to account for and report on its business operations. Typically, businesses use a fiscal year ending December 31. However, many entities use the natural business year, referring to a year ending at the annual low point in business activity or at the end of a season. For example, governmental units often end their fiscal year on June 30.
2. in taxation, 12-month period ending other than December 31 (calendar year).

**FISHBONE DIAGRAMS** way of determining likely root causes of a problem, often called cause-and-effect diagrams; also called *an Ishikawa diagram.*

**FIXED ASSET** item that has physical substance and a life in excess of one year. It is bought for use in the operation of the business and *not* intended for resale to customers. Examples are building, machinery, auto, and land. Fixed assets with the exception of land are subject to

DEPRECIATION. Fixed assets are usually referred to as property, plant, and equipment.

**FIXED ASSET-TO-EQUITY CAPITAL RATIO** computation that indicates the company's ability to satisfy long-term debt. The ratio equals fixed assets divided by equity capital. A ratio greater than 1 means that some of the fixed assets are financed by debt.

**FIXED ASSET TURNOVER** measurement that reflects the productivity and efficiency of property, plant, and equipment in generating revenue. A high turnover reflects positively on the company's ability to utilize its fixed assets in business operations properly. The turnover equals sales divided by fixed assets.

**FIXED ASSET UNIT** element making up the fixed asset account. An example is a specific machine within the machinery account.

**FIXED BUDGET** *see* STATIC (FIXED) BUDGET.

**FIXED CHARGE** *see* SETUP COST.

**FIXED-CHARGE-COVERAGE RATIO** equation that indicates whether the company is able to meet its fixed commitments (i.e., interest) from its profits. A high ratio reflects favorably upon the firm's ability to refinance obligations as they mature. The ratio equals earnings available to meet fixed charges divided by fixed charges. Fixed charges include rent and interest. The ratio is:

$$\frac{\text{Net Income Before Taxes and Fixed Charges}}{\text{Fixed Charges}}$$

**FIXED COST** expenses that remain constant in total regardless of changes in activity within a *relevant* range. Examples are rent, insurance, and taxes. Fixed cost *per unit* changes as volume changes. *See also* VARIABLE COSTS.

**FIXED DISK** *see* HARD DISK.

**FIXED (FACTORY) OVERHEAD** portion of total factory overhead that remains constant over a given time period without regard to changes in the volume of activity. Examples of fixed overhead are depreciation, rent, property taxes, insurance, and salaries of production supervisors.

**FIXED OVERHEAD SPENDING (BUDGET) VARIANCE** difference between actual fixed overhead incurred and fixed overhead budgeted. This variance is not affected by the level of production.

Fixed Overhead Spending Variance
$$= \text{Actual Fixed Overhead} - \text{Budgeted Fixed Overhead}$$
or $= \text{Actual Overhead} - (\text{Fixed Overhead Standard Rate} \times \text{Budgeted Hours})$

For example, assume actual fixed overhead costs were $31,000. Assume that the denominator activity in machine-hours was 5,000 and the fixed overhead applied rate is $6. The budgeted fixed overhead costs are then $30,000 (5,000 denominator hours × $6). The fixed overhead spending variance is $31,000 − $30,000 = $1,000, which is unfavorable possibly due to events such as unexpected changes in rents, insurance, and property taxes.

**FIXED OVERHEAD VARIANCE** difference between actual fixed overhead incurred and fixed overhead applied to production.

Fixed Overhead Variance $= \text{Fixed Overhead Incurred} - \text{Fixed Overhead Applied}$
$= \text{Fixed Overhead Incurred} - (\text{Fixed Overhead Standard Rate} \times \text{Standard Inputs Allowed for Actual Production})$

The total fixed overhead variance is divided into two specific variances: VOLUME VARIANCE and FIXED OVERHEAD SPENDING (BUDGET) VARIANCE.

**FIXED OVERHEAD VOLUME (DENOMINATOR) VARIANCE** measure of utilization of plant facilities. It results when the actual activity level is measured in direct labor-hours, machine-hours, and so on. Differs from the budgeted (denominator) quantity used in determining the fixed overhead standard rate.

Fixed Overhead Volume Variance
$$= \text{Budgeted Fixed Overhead} - \text{Fixed Overhead Applied}$$
or
$$= (\text{Denominator Hours} - \text{Standard Hours Allowed}) \times \text{Fixed Overhead Standard Rate}$$

The variance is unfavorable if the denominator hours exceed the standard hours allowed; it is favorable in the opposite case. For example, assume actual fixed overhead costs were $31,000. The denominator activity in machine-hours was 5,000 and the fixed overhead applied rate is $6. The budgeted fixed overhead costs are then $30,000 (5,000 denominator hours × $6). The standard machine-hours allowed was 4,000. The fixed overhead volume variance is (5,000 – 4,000) × $6 = $6,000, which is unfavorable because of the company's failure to operate at the budgeted (denominator) activity level. This may be caused by machine breakdowns, poor production scheduling, or failure to meet sales goals.

**FIXED PRICE**
1. price that serves as a standard for the valuation of certain inventory accounts (i.e., raw materials, work-in-process, and finished goods) in STANDARD COSTing.
2. price that must be charged under a contract regardless of production costs.
3. economic concept utilized by governmental units establishing a fixed price for a price floor (below which the price is not legally allowed to fall) and price ceilings (above which the price is not legally allowed to rise) on certain regulated goods and services.
4. price at which INVESTMENT BANKERS agree to sell the issue to the investing public in a public offering of new security issues.

**FIXTURE** fixed asset whose utility is derived from its physical attachment to a property and that usually cannot be removed without causing loss of value or damage. An example is a lighting fixture. A fixture under the terms of a lease or other agreement can be detached. A fixture is classified as a FIXED ASSET.

**FLASH REPORT** one providing highlights of key information promptly to the responsible managerial accountant; also called EXCEPTION REPORT. An example is an exception report such as PERFORMANCE REPORTS that highlight favorable or unfavorable variances. A flash report allows managers to take a corrective action for an unfavorable variance. *See also* PERFORMANCE REPORT.

**FLAT TAX** one in which the income tax rate is the same for all income levels. It is a proportional tax. A pure flat tax would eliminate all deductions, exemptions, and loopholes, and tax all income at the same low tax rate. The tax would also make the tax system less complex and more equitable.

**FLEXIBLE BUDGET FORMULA** *see* COST-VOLUME FORMULA.

**FLEXIBLE BUDGETING** *see* FLEXIBLE (VARIABLE) BUDGET.

**FLEXIBLE BUDGET VARIANCE** *see* BUDGET VARIANCE.

**FLEXIBLE FACTORY** objective of a flexible factory is to provide a wide range of services across many product lines in a timely manner. An example is a fabrication plant with several integrated manufacturing cells that can perform many functions for unrelated product lines with relatively short lead times.

**FLEXIBLE MANUFACTURING SYSTEM (FMS)** computer-controlled process technology suitable for producing a moderate variety of products in moderate, flexible volumes. This system reduces setup or changeover times and facilitates the production of differentiated products in small numbers. The shift in emphasis is from mass production of a few products to a job-shop environment in which customized orders are manufactured. Automation allows for better quality and scheduling, rapid changes in product lines, and lower inventories and costs. *See also* COMPUTER INTEGRATED MANUFACTURING (CIM).

**FLEXIBLE (VARIABLE) BUDGET** one based on different levels of activity. It is an extremely useful tool for comparing the actual cost incurred to the cost allowable for the activity level achieved. It is dynamic in nature rather than static. By using the COST-VOLUME FORMULA (or FLEXIBLE BUDGET FORMULA), a series of budgets can be developed easily for various levels of activity. A STATIC (FIXED) BUDGET is geared for only one level of activity and has problems in cost control. Flexible budgeting distinguishes between fixed and variable costs, thus allowing for a budget that can be automatically adjusted (via changes in variable cost totals) to the particular level of activity *actually* attained. Thus variances between actual costs and budgeted costs are adjusted for volume ups and downs before differences due to price and quantity factors are computed. The primary use of the flexible budget is for accurate measure of performance by comparing actual costs for a given output with the budgeted costs for the *same level of output*.

**FLEXTIME** scheduling concept that allows for nontraditional work hours to be employed on a systematic basis. Hours can be arranged for different times or periods of time to accommodate such aspects as efficiency, traffic, motherhood, disabilities, continuous operations, etc.

**FLIPPING** buying an investment—such as real estate or stock in an initial public offering (IPO)—in anticipation of reselling it quickly as a profit. Analysts argue that a period of growing popularity of flipping in a rising housing or stock market can signal that a downturn is near.

**FLOAT**
1. amount of funds represented by checks that have been issued but not yet collected.
2. time between the deposit of checks in a bank and payment. Due to the time difference, many firms are able to "play the float," that is, to write checks against money not presently in the firm's bank account.
3. to issue new securities, usually through an underwriter.

**FLOATING CAPITAL** net working capital or that part of capital that is invested in current assets of the organization (net of current liabilities) as opposed to its fixed or other capital assets.

**FLOATING (FLEXIBLE) EXCHANGE RATE** international monetary exchange system in which the prices of currencies are determined by competitive market forces; after 1971 exchange rates between the dollar and other foreign currencies were allowed to float. Under this system, rates, which are determined by the supply and demand for foreign exchange, can change from moment to moment.

**FLOPPY DISK** *see* DISKETTE.

**FLOTATION COST** cost of issuing new securities in the market. It consists of (1) the INVESTMENT BANKER'S compensation representing the price the issuer receives versus the price the public pays (commonly referred to as the underwriting spread) and (2) expenses incurred by the issuer such as for legal, accounting, and printing fees. Flotation costs are usually higher for stocks than for bonds. Also, it is a higher percentage of gross proceeds for smaller issues than larger ones.

**FLOWCHART** traditional method of representing in schematic form the flow of data in a system. The flowchart shows the points of input and output, the logic or sequence of the various processing steps in the system, and the relationship of one element of the system to the other parts of the system or to other information systems.

**FLOW OF COSTS** cost passing through various classifications within an organization. See the following exhibit for a summary of *product* and *period* cost flows.

FLOW OF COSTS EXHIBIT

Raw Material

Direct Labor

Factory Overhead Applied

Work-in-Process

Finished Goods

Cost of Goods Sold

**FLOW PROCESS CHART** description of the sequence of operations in a production process. These generally are operation, inspection, movement, storage, and delay.

**FLOW STATEMENT** *see* CASH FLOW STATEMENT.

**FOCUSED FACTORY** objective of a focused factory is to organize around a specific set of resources to provide low cost and high throughput over a narrow range of products.

**FOLIO NUMBER** manner of referring in a journal or ledger to the origination or disposition of the item. For example, if in the CASH DISBURSEMENTS JOURNAL a debit was made to rent expense having the account number 523, then the number 523 would be put in the folio reference column of the journal.

**FOOTING** summary of the debits (left side of any account) and credits (right side of any account) to obtain a new balance. An example follows:

<table>
<tr><td colspan="2" align="center">Cash</td></tr>
<tr><td align="right">1,000</td><td align="right">2,000</td></tr>
<tr><td align="right">500</td><td align="right">400</td></tr>
<tr><td align="right">3,000</td><td></td></tr>
<tr><td align="right">4,500</td><td align="right">2,400</td></tr>
<tr><td align="right">2,100</td><td></td></tr>
</table>

The side that has the largest amount of balance ($4,500) is not moved while the smaller side ($2,400) is brought over and subtracted. The new balance ($2,100) remains on the side that has the larger balance.

**FOOTNOTE** explanatory data that follows the financial statements and is integrally related to them. Footnotes help the user understand financial statement figures and any other matters essential in gauging a company's financial position. Examples of footnotes are disclosure of accounting policies, lawsuits, pension plan particulars, and tax considerations.

**FORCING ALLOCATION** costs of a sustaining activity to a cost object even though that cost object may not clearly consume or causally relate to that activity. Allocating a plant-level activity (such as heating) to product units using an activity driver such as direct labor-hours, for example, forces the cost of this activity to the product. *See also* SUSTAINING ACTIVITY COST.

**FORECAST**
1. projection or estimate of future sales, revenue, earnings, or costs. *See also* SALES FORECASTING.
2. projection of future financial position and operating results of an organization. *See also* FINANCIAL PROJECTION.

**FORECLOSURE** the forced sale of mortgaged property by the holder of a MORTGAGE to satisfy the indebtedness of the mortgagee. Foreclosure of residential property usually results when a mortgagee stops making payments on a mortgage because the principal balance of the mortgage exceeds the fair value of the property.

**FOREIGN CORPORATION**
1. corporation that is chartered under state law and resides in a particular state of the union or other country, which is considered a foreign corporation to the remaining states.
2. corporation formed under the laws of a foreign country.

**FOREIGN CORRUPT PRACTICES ACT** legislation enacted in 1977 to amend the SECURITIES EXCHANGE ACT OF 1934. It provides penalties for certain corrupt practices, such as bribes made to foreign officials, and defines standards relating to internal accounting controls. Management must submit to external audit procedures so the SEC can verify that such internal controls are in place.

**FOREIGN CURRENCY FUTURES** contracts representing a commitment to buy or sell a specific amount of foreign currency at a later date at a specified rate of exchange. They are used to speculate on currency movements and to hedge currency values.

**FOREIGN CURRENCY TRANSACTION** one that requires settlement in a currency other than the entity's FUNCTIONAL CURRENCY. A foreign currency transaction gain or loss is produced from redeeming receivables/payables that are fixed in terms of amounts of foreign currency received/paid. That is, a business (1) buys or sells on credit goods or services whose prices are denominated in a foreign currency or (2) borrows or lends funds whose amounts payable or receivable are denominated in a foreign currency. Gain or loss results from changes in exchange rates between the functional currency and the foreign currency in which the transaction is denominated. Foreign transaction gains or losses are typically included in the INCOME STATEMENT for the period in which the exchange rate changes. Gains or losses on foreign currency transactions deemed to be hedges and intercompany transactions of a long-term investment nature (settlement is not anticipated in the foreseeable future) are *not* included in net income but are considered as gain or loss on FOREIGN CURRENCY TRANSLATION shown in the stockholders' equity section.

Assume merchandise is bought by a company in Country X for 100,000 euros. Assume the exchange rate is 0.7 euros = $1. The journal entry is to debit purchases and credit accounts payable for $142,857 (100,000/.7). When the merchandise is paid for, the exchange rate is .8 euros = $1. The cash payment is therefore $125,000. The journal entry is to debit accounts payable for $142,857 and credit cash for $125,000 and foreign exchange gain for $17,857.

**FOREIGN CURRENCY TRANSACTION GAIN OR LOSS** *see* FOREIGN CURRENCY TRANSACTION.

**FOREIGN CURRENCY TRANSLATION** process of expressing amounts denominated in one currency in terms of a second currency, by using the exchange rate between the currencies. Assets and liabilities are translated at the current exchange rate at the balance sheet date. Income statement items are typically translated at the weighted-average exchange rate for the period. Cumulative (total) translation gains and losses are reported separately as a component of STOCKHOLDERS' EQUITY under "Accumulated Other Comprehensive Income." They are *not* included in net income unless there is a sale or liquidation of the investment in the foreign entity. *See also* FOREIGN CURRENCY TRANSACTION.

**FOREIGN PERSONAL HOLDING COMPANY** in taxation, foreign corporation in which more than 50% of the total combined voting power of all classes of voting stock or the total value of the stock is owned by or for no more than five U.S. citizens or residents.

**FOREIGN SALES CORPORATION (FSC)** tax term for a company incorporated in a foreign country that the United States qualifies as a host country. A country qualifies by entering into an exchange of information agreement of the type that allows tax benefits, such as the Caribbean Basin Initiative. Nonexempt income and certain foreign trade income, which would be taxable on a distribution, are subject to ordinary income treatment. There is a 100% dividends-received deduction for distributions from earnings attributable to foreign trade income of an FSC. There is also an 85% deductible for dividends from earnings attributable to qualified interest and carrying charges derived from a transaction resulting in foreign trade income. *See also* DOMESTIC INTERNATIONAL SALES CORPORATION (DISC).

**FOREIGN TAX** levy imposed by a foreign government on United States individuals or corporate taxpayers. The tax code generally allows a deduction for these taxes if they were incurred in a trade of business or for the production of income.

**FOREIGN TAX CREDIT** credit allowed against U.S. income taxes for foreign taxes paid. The credit can be used only to lower U.S. taxes on *income earned overseas.* A foreign tax credit limitation is computed by multiplying the U.S. tax liability prior to the credit by the ratio of foreign taxable income to total taxable income (U.S. and foreign). For example, a taxpayer earns $120,000, half in the U.S. and half in a foreign country. The U.S. tax prior to the tax credit is $40,800 ($120,000 × .34). The foreign tax credit limitation is $20,400 ($60,000/$120,000 × $40,800). Assume foreign taxes paid were $10,000 on the $60,000 income. Thus the foreign tax credit is $10,000. The U.S. tax on the foreign earnings is therefore $10,400 ($20,400 – $10,000).

**FORENSIC ACCOUNTING** a science (i.e., a department of system-ized knowledge) dealing with the application of accounting facts gathered through auditing methods and procedures to resolve legal problems. Forensic accounting is much different from traditional auditing. Forensic accounting is a specialty requiring the integration of investigative, accounting, and auditing skills. The forensic accountant looks at documents and financial and other data in a critical manner in order to draw conclusions and calculate values and to identify irregular patterns and/or suspicious transactions. A forensic accountant does not merely look at the numbers but rather looks *behind* the numbers.

**FORFEITURE**
1. losing a right or deposit because of the nonoccurrence of an event or action. An example is where one party makes a deposit on property that is later not used, resulting in a loss of the deposit. The recipient of the forfeiture accounts for it as revenue.
2. as per tax law, reallocating a forfeiture in a money purchase plan to other participants under a nondiscriminatory formula or reducing future employer contributions.

**FORGERY** act of fabricating or producing something falsely. Signing someone else's name on a check and cashing it is a common example.

**FORMAT**
1. type or version of format used on the storage medium.
2. process of initializing or preparing a disk or form of computer data storage medium, by recording a special pattern of data over the medium's reactive surface, thereby allowing a computer operating system the ability to store and retrieve data.

**FORM OF BALANCE SHEET** presentation form of a balance sheet, which generally follows one of two formats: (1) the traditional form called the account form, which presents assets on the left and liabilities and owner's equity on the right; and (2) the report form, which presents assets above, liabilities and stockholders' equity below. Both types of format are widely used.

**FORTRAN (*FORMULA TRANSLATION*)** first high-level programming language, developed by IBM in the late 1950s. It allows programmers to describe calculations by means of mathematical formulas.

**FORWARD ACCOUNTING** type of accounting that reflects aspects of judgment, PRO FORMA numbers, projections, budgets, and standard costs, as they may affect the future operating environment. Forward costs are distinguished from *historical accounting,* which accounts for past, historical financial activities. MANAGERIAL ACCOUNTING, which involves the use of accounting data for forward planning, control, and decision making, is part of *forward accounting.*

**FORWARD CONTRACT** a contract similar to a futures contract. However, forward contracts are not uniform or standardized. They are not traded on exchanges. In such a contract, goods are actually delivered at a future date or settlement may be in cash. Forward contracts may be on commodities or instruments. The contract fixes the quantity, price, and date of purchase or sale.

**FORWARD EXCHANGE CONTRACT** agreement to exchange at a given future date currencies of different countries at a specified rate (forward rate). A forward contract is a FOREIGN CURRENCY TRANSACTION. The gain or loss on the contract is typically included in determining net income. The amount of gain or loss, except on a speculative forward contract (designed as a risky investment rather than as a hedge), is computed by multiplying the foreign currency amount of the forward contract by the difference between the spot rate at the balance sheet date and the spot rate at the date of inception of the contract.

**FORWARD FINANCIAL STATEMENT** projective and detailed estimate of an organization's financial position. An income statement, balance sheet, and funds flow may be prepared based upon the assumptions in FORWARD ACCOUNTING. These statements are primarily prepared for comparative analysis purposes to evaluate current and future courses of action.

**FORWARD RATE** price at which two currencies are to be exchanged at some future date.

**401(K) PLAN** employee investment plan; also called *salary reduction plan.* It allows employees to defer part of their gross salary and to invest the amount in stocks, bonds, or money market funds. The amount is indexed for inflation, using the CONSUMER PRICE INDEX (CPI). Employee contributions and all earnings arising from them go tax-free until withdrawn at the request of the employee or until the employee retires or leaves the company. Usually the employer provides a choice of investment vehicles into which the funds may be placed while earning tax-deferred returns. Furthermore, many employers offer matching contributions. The limitation of annual deferrals to 401(k) plans applies only to an employee's elective deferrals—not the employer's matching funds. These contributions, plus the current reduction in income taxes, make 401(k) salary reduction plans an excellent long-term investment.

**FRACTIONAL SHARE** unit of stock that is less than one full share. For example, under a dividend reinvestment program, the dividend amount is insufficient to purchase one full share at the present market price of stock. In this case, the stockholder is credited with the fractional share; when there has been an accumulation of sufficient dividends for one share, it will be issued.

**FRAMEWORK** integrated computer software developed by Ashton-Tate that combines a spreadsheet, a database manager, a word processor, a graphics program, and communications.

**FRANCHISE**
1. privilege granted by a franchisor to a franchisee permitting the latter to operate using the franchisor's name. The franchisee must pay a franchise fee for such right. In addition, the franchisee is typically

required to use the franchisor's products. The franchisee usually receives other benefits from the franchisor, such as advertising.

2. government right granted to an entity giving it a monopolistic advantage (e.g., public utility). *See also* FRANCHISE FEE REVENUE.

**FRANCHISE FEE REVENUE** revenue obtained by a company that allows an *independent party* to operate a business using its name, merchandise, and supplies. Franchise fee revenue from the initial sale of a franchise is recognized by the franchisor *only* when all material services or conditions applicable to the sale have been *substantially performed*. Substantial performance is indicated by: (1) absence of intent to refund cash received or forgive any unpaid balance; (2) performance of substantially all initial services; and (3) nonexistence of other material conditions related to performance. Commencement of operations by the franchise is presumed to be the earliest possible time at which substantial performance occurs. If the initial fee is deferred, related expenses for later MATCHING against revenue must also be deferred. Continuing franchise fees are recognized as earned. An estimated uncollectible account expense provision should be made. *See also* DEFERRED CREDIT.

**FRAUD**
1. deliberate action by individual or entity to cheat another, causing damage. There is typically a *misrepresentation* to deceive, or purposeful withholding of material data needed for a proper decision. An example of fraud is when a BOOKKEEPER falsifies records in order to steal money. *See also* NEGLIGENCE.
2. falsification of a tax return by an individual. Examples of tax fraud are intentionally not reporting taxable income or overstating expenses. Tax fraud is a criminal act.

**FRAUD RISK FACTORS** conditions that typically exist when fraud occurs; namely, incentive/pressure (i.e., a reason to commit fraud), opportunity (i.e., ineffective internal controls), and rationalization/attitude (i.e., justification for committing fraud).

**FREE CASH FLOW** amount of cash that remains after deducting the funds a company must commit to continue operating at its planned level; net cash flows from operating activities, minus dividends, minus net capital expenditures.

**FREE ON BOARD (FOB)** term indicating delivery will be made on board or into a carrier by the shipper without charge. The abbreviation FOB is followed by a shipping point or destination. The invoice price includes delivery at seller's expense and seller's risk to the specified location. For example, "FOB our warehouse in Duluth, Minnesota," means to a buyer requesting New York City delivery that the seller who might have its headquarters and billing office in Chicago, will pay shipping costs from Duluth to New York. Title usually passes from seller to buyer at the FOB point.

**FREIGHT-IN** transportation charge the company pays when it receives goods from a supplier. It is a separate account that is added to purchases in determining the cost of goods and ending inventory. *See also* FREIGHT-OUT.

**FREIGHT-OUT** cost of transporting goods to a customer. It is a selling expense. When the freight is included in the selling price, it is deducted from sales. *See also* FREIGHT-IN.

**FREQUENCY DISTRIBUTION** schedule showing the number of times each observation in the data occurs. Data collected need to be organized in some fashion. One method of summarizing a population or sample is to organize the data in terms of their frequency.

For example, assume that a sales slip can have 0, 1, 2, or 3 errors after it is filled out. Fifty sales slips are randomly selected with the following results: 10 had no errors, 20 had only one error, 12 had two errors, and 8 had three errors. These results can be constructed in a tabular format as follows:

| Number of Errors | Frequency |
|:----------------:|:---------:|
| 0 | 10 |
| 1 | 20 |
| 2 | 12 |
| 3 | 8 |
|   | 50 |

**FRINGE BENEFIT** compensation or other benefit provided by the employer to the employee at no charge that is above and beyond salary or wages. Examples include health plans, CAFETERIA PLANS, and life insurance.

**FRONT-END LOADING** practice of investment houses and mutual funds in which administrative, selling, brokerage, and other fees are deducted from the initial deposit or installment.

**F-TEST** ratio of two mean squares (variances); often can be used to test the significance of some item of interest. For example, in regression, the ratio of the mean square due to the regression to the mean square due to error can be used to test the overall significance of the regression model. By looking up F-tables, the degree of significance of the computed F-value can be determined.

**FULL COSTING** *see* ABSORPTION COSTING.

**FULL COST METHOD** accounting method used by some extractive industries, particularly oil and gas companies, in which *all* exploration costs are capitalized whether the projects are successful or unsuccessful. The capitalized cost is then amortized into expense as the total reserves are produced. *See also* SUCCESSFUL EFFORTS ACCOUNTING.

**FULL-COST-PLUS PRICING** method in which the cost base is the full manufacturing cost per unit. Selling and administrative costs are provided for through the markup that is added to this base. *See also* COST PLUS PRICING.

**FULL COST PROFIT MARGIN** difference between total revenue and total costs traceable to a work cell or product.

**FULL DISCLOSURE** comprehensively and understandably presenting all material facts in the footnotes to the financial statements so that financial statement users are properly informed. Standards of disclosure are formulated by the FASB and SEC. *See also* DISCLOSURE.

**FULL FAITH AND CREDIT** backing of the debt of a government entity with all the resources of the entity, including its taxing and borrowing power. Bonds backed up by the full faith and credit of the issuer are called GENERAL OBLIGATION BONDS.

**FULL PRODUCT COST** cost that includes not only the costs of direct materials and direct labor, but also the costs of all production and nonproduction activities required to satisfy the customer.

**FULLY VESTED** term describing an employee who will be *completely* entitled to pension plan benefits at retirement. *See also* VESTED.

**FUNCTIONAL ACCOUNTING** accounting and reporting by activity. It aids in conforming organizational performance to plan so that proper budgetary and operational controls can be maintained.

**FUNCTIONAL CLASSIFICATION** system under which costs are classified according to the function they perform within the business; for example, manufacturing, selling, general and administrative, or financial costs. The *traditional approach* to the income statement, which is required for external reporting, uses this classification of costs. There are different ways of classifying costs. For example, costs are classified by behavior, as variable or fixed according to their response to changes in levels of activity.

**FUNCTIONAL CURRENCY** legal tender of the primary economic environment in which a company operates. Usually, it is the country where a company generates and expends most of its cash. For example, if a company in Italy (as an independent entity) generated its cash and incurred related expenses in Italy, the Italian currency would be the functional currency. However, if the Italian company was an extension of a Greek parent company, the functional currency would be the Greek currency. *See also* REPORTING CURRENCY.

**FUNCTIONAL DECOMPOSITION** identification of the activities performed in the organization. It yields a hierarchical representation of the organization and shows the relationship between the different levels of the organization and its activities. For example, a hierarchy may start with the division and move down through the plant, function, process, activity, and task levels.

**FUNCTIONAL GAMES** *see* MANAGEMENT GAME.

**FUNCTIONAL REPORTING OF EXPENSES** presenting expenses by major activity. Functional reporting is used by not-for-profit entities other than governmental units and hospitals. Under functional reporting, expenses are accumulated according to program purpose (e.g., research) rather than by object of expenditure. By contrast, under object reporting, items are accounted for according to their natural classification (e.g., salaries expense). Functional classification is also used for profit operations: manufacturing, selling, and administrative.

**FUNCTION COST** classification showing the nature of the output for which costs are incurred, such as product packaging, sales promotion, or other such specific activities.

**FUNCTION KEY** group of keys on the computer keyboard (i.e., F1-F12) whose function depends on the particular program being run at the time. For example, the F1 function key may mean Help for one software program and quite another thing in another software package. Programmable function keys may be used as the equivalent of a combination of other keys.

**FUND**
1. cash, securities, or other assets designated for a specified purpose such as in a SINKING FUND.
2. in GOVERNMENT ACCOUNTING, fiscal and accounting entity with a self-balancing set of accounts recording cash and other financial resources, together with related liabilities and residual equities or balances, and changes therein. Funds are segregated for the purpose of conducting specific activities or attaining certain objectives in accordance with special regulations, restrictions, or limitations. An example is the SPECIAL REVENUE FUND. *See also* FUND ACCOUNTING.
3. as a verb, to finance, using long-term debt, usually bonds.

**FUND ACCOUNTING** system used by nonprofit organizations, particularly governments. Because there is no profit motive, ACCOUNTABILITY is measured instead of profitability. The main purpose is stewardship of financial resources received and expended in compliance with legal requirements. Financial reporting is directed at the public rather than investors. The accounting equation is Assets = Restrictions on Assets. Funds are established to ensure accountability and expenditure for designated purposes. Revenues must be raised and expended in accordance with special regulations and restrictions. Budgets are adopted and recorded in the accounts of the related fund. Contractual obligations are given effect in some funds.

**FUNDAMENTAL ANALYSIS** evaluation of a company's stock based on an examination of the firm's financial statements. It is distinguished from TECHNICAL ANALYSIS, which attempts to predict the market price of a company's stock based on historical price performance and overall stock market trends. It considers overall financial health, economic and political conditions, industry factors, marketing aspects, management quality, and future outlook of the company. The analysis attempts to ascertain whether stock is overpriced, underpriced, or priced in proportion to its market value. Fundamental analysis provides much of the data needed to forecast earnings and dividends. Fundamental analysis tools include HORIZONTAL ANALYSIS, VERTICAL ANALYSIS, and RATIO ANALYSIS, which give a relative measure of the operating performance and financial condition of the company. The following figure summarizes various factors that will go into your investment decision-making process, ranging from economics and the external environment surrounding the investment vehicle to the company's performance measures.

Economic Analysis
(Assessing the Future Performance
of the Overall Economy)

Business Cycles: Monetary Fiscal Policy,
Economic Indicators, Government Policy,
World Events and Foreign Trade, Public
Attitudes of Optimism or Pessimism,
Domestic Legislation, Inflation, GNP
Growth, Unemployment, Productivity,
Capacity Utilization, Interest Rates, and More

Industry Analysis
(Based on the Economic and Market
Analysis, Determining the Business Cycle's
Impact on Specific Industries and
Evaluating Industry Characteristics)

Business Cycle Exposure, Industry Structure,
Growth of the Industry, Competition, Product
Quality, Cost Elements, Government Regulations,
Labor Position, Technological Development,
and Financial Norms and Standards

Company Analysis
(Analyzing How Specific Companies
Perform in Terms of Their Operating and
Financial Features Given Industry
Changes and the Economy)

Growth of Sales, Earnings, Dividends,
Quality of Earnings, Position in the Industry,
Discount Rates, Fundamental Analysis
(Balance Sheet Analysis, Income Statement
Analysis, Cash Flow Analysis), Analysis of
Accounting Policy and Footnotes, Management,
Research and Development, Return and Risk,
Brands, Patents, Goodwill, and Diversification

**FUNDED DEBT** long-term debt of a business. Long-term debt may consist of long-term notes of banks or other lending institutions, but the term funded usually connotes bonds.

**FUNDED PENSION PLAN** one in which the employer contributes pension funds to a trustee who manages the fund and pays employees from the fund when they retire. *See also* ACTUARIAL GAINS, LOSSES; DEFINED BENEFIT PENSION PLAN; DEFINED CONTRIBUTION PENSION PLAN; PENSION PLAN; VESTED.

**FUNDS-FLOW-ADEQUACY RATIO** computation showing the extent to which a company can generate sufficient funds from operations to meet budgeted capital expenditures, increase in inventories, and cash dividends. Typically, a five-year total is used to eliminate cyclical and other distortions. The ratio equals:

$$\frac{\text{Five-Year Sum of Sources of Funds From Operations}}{\text{Five-Year Sum of Capital Expenditures, Inventory Additions, and Cash Dividends}}$$

A ratio of 1 shows the business has covered its needs based on attained levels of growth without having to resort to external financing. If the ratio is less than 1, there may be inadequate internally generated funds to maintain dividends and current operating growth levels.

**FUNDS-FLOW-FIXED-CHARGE COVERAGE** ratio of funds provided by operations plus fixed charges to fixed charges. This ratio indicates whether a company can satisfy its annual fixed charges from funds flow. Fixed charges remain constant under varying rates of production and are often contractual. Examples of fixed charges are rent, lease payments, insurance, and interest. Funds flow can be expressed as working capital from operations or cash flow from operations. Assume funds provided by operations before tax is $2,000,000, which includes a deduction of fixed charges for $300,000. The ratio is thus $2,300,000 divided by $300,000, or 7.67.

**FUND THEORY** system applied to governmental and nonprofit entities (e.g., colleges, charities, hospitals). The fund includes a group of assets and liabilities and restrictions representing specific economic functions or activities. Each fund has its assets restricted for designated purposes. The equation is:

$$\text{Assets} = \text{Restrictions of Assets}$$

Assets are future services to the fund or operational unit. Liabilities are restrictions against those assets. *See also* FUND ACCOUNTING.

**FURNITURE AND FIXTURES** noncurrent depreciable asset consisting of office or store equipment (e.g., desks), lighting, and showroom items.

**FUTURES CONTRACT** agreement to buy or sell a given amount of a commodity or financial instrument at a specified price in a specified future month. The seller of a futures contract agrees to deliver the item to the buyer of the contract, who agrees to purchase the item. The contract specifies the amount, valuation, method, quality, month and means of delivery, and commodity exchange to be traded in. The month of delivery is the expiration date when the commodity or financial instrument must be delivered. *See also* COMMODITIES FUTURES; FINANCIAL FUTURE.

**FUTURE VALUE** amount to which an investment will grow at a future time if it earns a specified interest that is compounded annually. The process of calculating future values is called *compounding*. Let us define:

$$
\begin{aligned}
F_n &= \text{future value} = \text{the amount of money at the end of year } n \\
P &= \text{principal} \\
i &= \text{annual interest rate} \\
n &= \text{number of years}
\end{aligned}
$$

$$
\begin{aligned}
\text{Then } F_1 &= \text{the amount of money at the end of year one} \\
&= \text{principal and interest} = P + iP = P(1 + i) \\
F_2 &= \text{the amount of money at the end of year 2} \\
&= F_1(1 + i) = P(1 + i)(1 + i) = P(1 + i)^2
\end{aligned}
$$

The future value of an investment compounded annually at rate 1 for $n$ years is $F_n = P(1 + i)^n = P\ FVIF(i,n)$ where $FVIF(i,n)$ is the future value of \$1 and can be found in table 1 in the back of the book.

For example, assume that Mr. A placed \$1,000 in a savings account earning 8% interest compounded annually. How much will he have in the account at the end of four years? Then $F_4 = \$1,000(1 + 0.08)^4$.

From table 1 in the back of the book, the $FVIF$(8%, four years) = 1.361. Therefore,

$$
F_4 = \$1,000(1.3605) = \$1,361.
$$

**FUTURE VALUE OF AN ANNUITY** compound annuity in which an equal sum of money is deposited at the end of each year for a certain number of years and allowed to grow.

Let $S_n$ = the future value of an $n$-year annuity and $A$ = the amount of an annuity. Then $S_n$ can be found from using table 2 in the back of the book as follows:

$$
S_n = A\ FVIFA\ (i,n)
$$

where $FVIFA(i,n)$ is the future value of an annuity of \$1 and can be found in table 2 in the back of the book. For example, assume Mrs. A wishes to determine the sum of money she will have in her savings account at the end of six years by depositing \$1,000 at the end of each year for the next six years. The annual interest rate is 8%. The $FVIFA$(8%, six years) is given in table 2 as 7.336. Therefore, $S_6 = \$1,000(7.336) = \$7336$.

# G

**GAAP** *see* GENERALLY ACCEPTED ACCOUNTING PRINCIPLES (GAAP).

**GAAP CODIFICATION** *see* FASB ACCOUNTING STANDARDS CODIFICATION™.

**GAIN** excess of money or fair value of property received on sale or exchange over the carrying value of the item. An example is the sale of a fixed asset when cash received exceeds book value. Gains also occur when the cash payment to eliminate a debt is less than the liability's carrying value. An example is retiring debt before maturity at a price below book value. Gains relate to *incidental* and nonrecurring transactions of the business. *See also* LOSS.

**GAIN CONTINGENCY** potential or pending development that may result in a future gain to the company, such as a successful lawsuit against another company. Conservative accounting practice dictates that gain contingencies should not be booked, although footnote disclosure of the particulars may be made. *See also* LOSS CONTINGENCY.

**GAME THEORY** analytical approach to competitive situations where two or more participants pursue conflicting objectives. The theory attempts to offer a solution that resolves the conflict among the participants. In games, the participants are competitors; the success of one is usually at the expense of the other. Each person selects and executes those strategies that he believes will result in "winning the game." Game theory attempts to provide a guideline for a variety of game situations.

**GANTT CHART** graphical representation of a project schedule used to plan or monitor progress.

**GARNISHMENT** the legal process that requires a third party in possession of a debtor's money or property to turn it over to a CREDITOR of the DEBTOR. A third party becomes liable for the value of the property if it fails to turn over the property.

**GENERAL ACCOUNTING OFFICE (GAO)** a legislative branch (www.gao.gov), headed by the Comptroller General, that was established to assist the Congress in its oversight of the executive branch and to serve as the independent legislative auditor of the federal government. Among the other roles of the GAO are: (1) prescribing principles and standards for federal agency accounting systems; (2) assisting agencies in accounting system design; and (3) reporting to Congress on the status of agency accounting systems.

**GENERAL AGREEMENT ON TARIFFS AND TRADE (GATT)** an agreement between noncommunist nations with economic interests in international trade relations. It is dedicated to encouraging mutually beneficial bilateral agreements that focus upon reducing tariffs, restrictions, and barriers. Established in 1948, GATT also acts as international arbitrator with respect to trade agreement abrogation.

**GENERAL AND ADMINISTRATIVE EXPENSES** all expenses incurred in connection with performing general and administrative activities. Examples are executives' salaries and legal expenses. General and administrative expenses are shown under OPERATING EXPENSES in the income statement.

**GENERAL BALANCE SHEET** presentation form of the balance sheet of institutions such as governmental, religious, charitable, educational, and social entities, prepared in the usual standard commercial form.

**GENERAL BUSINESS CREDIT** credit directly reducing tax applicable to low-income housing and targeted jobs.

**GENERAL CONTINGENCY RESERVE** appropriation of retained earnings for *general* purposes rather than for a specific item of future loss or expense. In effect, it is a reserve for unspecified possible events.

**GENERAL FIXED ASSET ACCOUNT GROUP** in GOVERNMENT ACCOUNTING, self-balancing set of accounts to account for the general fixed assets of a governmental unit. The account group is *not* a fund. It provides double-entry control in *memorandum* fashion of fixed assets that are not accounted for specifically in a fund (e.g., proprietary fund). *See also* GENERAL LONG-TERM DEBT ACCOUNT GROUP.

**GENERAL FUND** in GOVERNMENTAL ACCOUNT, fund used to account for all assets and liabilities of a nonprofit entity except those particularly assigned for other purposes in another more specialized fund. It is the primary operating fund of a governmental unit. Much of the usual activities of a municipality are supported by the general fund. Examples are the purchase of supplies and meeting operating expenditures. An example of a specialized fund, on the other hand, is the capital projects fund that accounts for financial resources used for the acquisition or construction of major capital facilities. *See also* FUND.

**GENERAL JOURNAL** simplest type of journal. It is used when *no special journal exists* to record a transaction, usually when a transaction occurs infrequently. Examples are the declaration of a dividend, correction of an accounting error, and an appropriation of retained earnings. It has only two money columns, one for debits, the other for credits.

**GENERAL LEDGER** record of a business entity's accounts. The general ledger contains the accounts that make up the entity's financial statements. Separate accounts exist for individual assets, liabilities, stockholders' equity, revenue, and expenses. In some cases, control accounts summarize detail appearing in a SUBSIDIARY LEDGER (e.g., individual customer accounts tying into the accounts receivable account). A trial balance is prepared of the general ledger accounts at the end of the accounting period to assure that total debits equal total credits. The general ledger may be in bound or loose-leaf form, magnetic tape, in computer memory, or other form. *See also* LEDGER.

**GENERAL LONG-TERM DEBT ACCOUNT GROUP** GOVERNMENT ACCOUNTING term. Grouping is used to account for the outstanding principal on all long-term debt except that payable from a special assessment, proprietary, or trust fund. At maturity, the funds are transferred to the debt service fund. *See also* GENERAL FIXED ASSET ACCOUNT GROUP.

**GENERAL OBLIGATION BOND** security whose payment is unconditionally promised by a governmental unit that has the power to levy taxes. Many state, county, city, town, and school district obligation bonds are of this type. General obligation bonds are backed by the FULL FAITH AND CREDIT (and taxing power) of the issuing government, whether it be the U.S. or a municipality.

**GENERAL PARTNER**
1. member of a partnership who is jointly and severally liable for all debts incurred by the PARTNERSHIP—that is, a partner who does not have LIMITED LIABILITY.
2. managing partner of a limited partnership who is in charge of its operations. A general partner has unlimited liability. *See also* LIMITED PARTNER.

**GENERAL PRICE INDEX** measure of change in the general level of prices of goods and services. The general indexes gauge the change in the purchasing power of the dollar. Widely used indexes of price change are calculated regularly by U.S. Government agencies. Examples are the Gross Domestic Product Implicit Price Deflator, Consumer Price Index (CPI) for Urban Consumers, and the Producer Price Index. For example, the Consumer Price Index reflects the average change in the retail prices of a broad but select "basket" of consumer goods. The Consumer Price Index is required by the accounting profession for use in CONSTANT DOLLAR ACCOUNTING. It is reported monthly by the U.S. Department of Labor.

**GENERAL PRICE LEVEL ACCOUNTING** restating financial statements in terms of general purchasing power by using a GENERAL PRICE INDEX. *See also* CONSTANT DOLLAR ACCOUNTING.

**GENERAL-PURPOSE FINANCIAL STATEMENT** statement prepared to meet the needs of *all* financial statement users as opposed to meeting the needs of only a particular group such as investors, creditors, management, or regulatory bodies. This is the purpose of financial statements based on GAAP. *See also* SPECIAL-PURPOSE FINANCIAL STATEMENT.

**GENERAL REVENUE SHARING** unrestricted funds provided by the federal government to the fifty states and to cities, towns, counties, etc., under the State and Local Fiscal Assistance Act of 1972, which expired in 1987. These funds could be used for any purpose by the recipient governments.

**GENERAL USE REPORT** any auditor's report that is not intended only for specified parties. Auditor's reports based on financial statement audits are considered general use reports because they are not restricted as to use.

**GENERALIZED AUDIT SOFTWARE (GAS)** used to select and apply audit routines to electronic data. GAS is the most commonly used COMPUTER ASSSISTED AUDIT TECHNIQUE (CAAT).

**GENERALIZED AUDIT SOFTWARE PACKAGE (GASP)** software used by an auditor to (1) access an entity's computerized accounting files, and (2) analyze and test data.

**GENERALLY ACCEPTED ACCOUNTING PRINCIPLES (GAAP)** standards, conventions, and rules accountants follow in recording and summarizing transactions, and in the preparation of financial statements. GAAP derive, in order of importance, from: (1) issuances from an authoritative body designated by the AICPA Council (for example, the FASB Statements, AICPA APB Opinions, and AICPA Accounting Research Bulletins); (2) other AICPA issuances such as AICPA Industry Guides; (3) industry practice; and (4) accounting literature in the form of books and articles. Principles also derive from tradition, such as the concept of matching. In the audit report, the CPA must indicate that the client has followed GAAP on a consistent basis.

**GENERALLY ACCEPTED AUDITING STANDARDS (GAAS)** broad rules and guidelines promulgated by the AICPA's *Auditing Standards Board*. CPAs employ GAAS in preparing for and performing audits of a client's financial statements. The guidelines include references to the auditor's qualifications, audit field work, and reporting the audit results. The broad standards are backed by detailed interpretative literature. An auditor unable to express an opinion on the financial statements must give reasons. A CPA who does not conduct an examination in accordance with GAAS can be held in violation of the AICPA's Code of Professional Ethics and face legal action by affected parties. *See also* STATEMENTS ON AUDITING STANDARDS (SAS).

**GENERATION SKIPPING TRANSFER TAX** may result when an individual attempts to avoid gift and estate tax by transferring money or property to beneficiaries more than one generation below the transferor's generation. For example, the generation skipping transfer tax might apply to transfers directly to a decedent's grandchildren, rather than first making transfers to a decedent's children. If imposed, the rate of tax is equal to the maximum gift and estate tax rate.

**GIFT TAX** tax levied on the transfer of property or money made without adequate legal consideration. This tax is imposed on the donor of a gift and is based upon the fair market value of the property as of the date of transfer. Under the law, each parent may give each recipient $13,000 a year ($26,000 for parents electing *gift-splitting*) without gift tax consequences. Also, gifts between spouses are untaxed.

**GOAL CONGRUENCE** term used when the same goals are shared by top managers and their subordinates. This is one of the many criteria used to judge the performance of an accounting system. The system can achieve its goal more effectively and perform better when organizational goals can be well aligned with the personal and group goals of subordinates and superiors. The goals of the company should be the same as the goals of the individual business segments. Corporate goals can be communicated by budgets, organization charts, and job descriptions.

**GOAL PROGRAMMING** form of LINEAR PROGRAMMING that considers multiple goals that are often in conflict with each other. With multiple goals, all goals usually cannot be realized exactly. For example, the twin goals of an investor who desires investments with maximum return and with minimum risk are generally incompatible and therefore unachievable. Other examples of multiple conflicting objectives can be found in organizations that want to: (1) maximize profits and increase wages; (2) upgrade product quality and reduce product cost; (3) pay larger dividends to stockholders and retain earnings for growth; and (4) reduce credit losses and increase sales. Goal programming does not attempt to maximize or minimize a single objective function as does the linear programming model. Rather, it seeks to minimize the deviations among the desired goals and the actual results according to the priorities assigned. The objective function of a goal programming model is expressed in terms of the deviations from the target goals.

**GOAL SEEKING** situation in which a manager wishes to determine what change would have to take place in the value of a specified variable in a specified time period to achieve a specified value for another variable. For example, a manager can ask the following "goal seeking" question: "What would the unit sales price have to be for the project to achieve a target return on investment of 20%?" Software such as MYSTRATEGY and EXCEL can help answer this type of question.

**GOING CONCERN** *see* CONTINUITY.

**GOING-CONCERN VALUE** worth of a business to another company or person. Going-concern value less asset value (liquidating value) is the entity's value as differentiated from the value of its assets. In a business combination accounted for under the purchase method, going-concern value less liquidation value is referred to as GOODWILL. For example, if Company A pays $5 million cash for Company B, which has net assets worth $4 million, $1 million represents goodwill.

**GOING PUBLIC** process by which shares of common stock are first offered for sale in the public markets (through the organized exchanges or over-the-counter); also called an *initial public offering*. The advantages of going public must be weighed against the disadvantages. Going public may give the company and major stockholders greater access to funds, as well as additional prestige and wealth. It also means that shares assume a market value—a value placed on expected future earnings. On the other hand, the company must open its books to the public through SEC and state filings and put up with pressure for short-term performance by security analysts and large institutional investors.

**GOLDEN HANDCUFFS** contractual agreement almost virtually assuring that the stockbroker will stay with the brokerage firm for a specified time period. The incentive may be in the form of high commission rates, bonuses, participation in a forthcoming initial public offering (IPO) of the brokerage firm itself, or other attractive fringe benefits. The contract may specify a penalty the broker will incur such as forfeiting past commissions if he or she leaves the brokerage firm before a specified date.

**GOLDEN HANDSHAKE** a clause in executive employment contracts that provides the executives with lucrative severance packages in the event of their termination. May include a continuation of salary, bonus, and/or certain benefits and perquisites, as well as accelerated vesting of stock options.

**GOLDEN PARACHUTE AGREEMENT** highly lucrative contract giving a senior corporate executive monetary or other benefits if his or her job is lost in a merger or acquisition. Examples of benefits are severance pay, bonus, and stock option.

**GOODNESS-OF-FIT** degree to which a model fits the observed data. In a REGRESSION ANALYSIS, the goodness-of-fit is measured by the COEFFICIENT OF DETERMINATION ($r$-squared).

**GOODS** items of merchandise, finished products, supplies, or raw materials. Sometimes the term is extended to cover all inventoriable items or assets such as cash, supplies, and fixed assets.

**GOODS AND SERVICES** revenue sources of businesses. *See also* GOODS; SERVICES.

**GOODS-IN-PROCESS INVENTORY** *see* WORK-IN-PROCESS.

**GOODWILL** theoretically, the present value of future excess earnings of a company over other companies in the industry. In other words, it is the value of the company's name and reputation, its customer relations, and other factors that, although intangible, give a concern its competitive edge and produce better-than-typical future earnings. It can only be recorded in a business combination accounted for under the PURCHASE (ACCOUNTING) METHOD. Goodwill equals the purchase price less the book value of the acquired company's net assets less the amount by which the acquired company's depreciable assets are written up to their fair market value. The fair market value of the total going concern should be equal to the purchase price. For example, if XYZ Company paid $3,000,000 for the net assets of ABC Company having a fair value of $2,800,000, the excess of $200,000 represents goodwill. Goodwill is an intangible asset subject to an annual impairment test.

## GOOGLE

1. The most widely used search engine on the Web. Its search engine is known for providing relevant search results using a simple and clean interface. Most of Google's services are free to the public. Google makes money through highly targeted, unobtrusive Internet advertisement.
2. The term "google" is also used as a verb to describe the process of doing a Web search.

**GOVERNMENT ACCOUNTING** principles and procedures in accounting for federal, state, and local governmental units. The National Council on Governmental Accounting establishes rules. There is also a governmental group in the FASB. Unlike commercial accounting for corporations, encumbrances and budgets are recorded in the accounts. Assets of a governmental unit are restricted for designated purposes. *See also* MODIFIED ACCRUAL.

**GOVERNMENT ACCOUNTING STANDARDS BOARD (GASB)** organization that formulates accounting standards for governmental units. It is under the auspices of the FINANCIAL ACCOUNTING FOUNDATION and replaced the National Council on Government Accounting.

**GOVERNMENTAL BUDGETING** financial plan and a basis for evaluating performance and an expression of public policy and a form of control having the force of law. Thus, a governmental budget is a legal document adopted in accordance with procedures specified by applicable laws. A governmental budget must be complied with by the administrators of the governmental unit for which the budget is prepared. By law, the administrators cannot exceed the budget without a formally approved budget amendment. Moreover, because the effectiveness and efficiency of governmental efforts are difficult to measure in the absence of the profit-centered activity that characterizes business operations, the use of budgets in the appropriation process is of major importance. Accordingly, budgetary accounts may be incorporated into the formal accounting systems of governments, and a budgetary comparison statement must be issued.

**GOVERNMENT FUND** term used in GOVERNMENT ACCOUNTING to apply to all funds except for the profit and loss funds (e.g., enterprise fund, internal service fund, and trust and agency fund). Examples of government funds are the general fund, special assessment fund, and capital projects fund. Governmental funds use the MODIFIED ACCRUAL accounting method.

**GRANT-IN-AID** contribution or donation by a superior governmental entity to a local government for a specified purpose. Grants for specified categories are termed *categorical grants*; grants for general purposes, *block grants*.

**GRANULARITY** decomposition of an activity or process.

**GRAPHICAL METHOD** technique used to find graphically the break-even point and highlight the cost-volume-profit relationships over a wide range of activity. The graphical method requires preparation of a BREAK-EVEN CHART. *See also* BREAK-EVEN ANALYSIS; COST-VOLUME-PROFIT (CVP) ANALYSIS; PROFIT-VOLUME (PV) CHART.

**GRAPHICAL METHOD OF LP** solution procedure used when a LINEAR PROGRAMMING (LP) problem has two (or at most three) decision variables. The graphical method follows these steps:
(1) Change inequalities to equalities.
(2) Graph the equalities.
(3) Identify the correct side for the original inequalities.
(4) Then identify the *feasible region*, the area of FEASIBLE SOLUTION.
(5) Determine the CONTRIBUTION MARGIN (CM) or cost at each of the *corner points* (*basic feasible solutions*) of the feasible region.
(6) Pick either the most profitable or least cost combination, which is an OPTIMAL SOLUTION.

For example, suppose that our LP model is:

$$\text{Maximize CM} = \$25A + \$40B$$
$$\text{Subject to: } 2A + 4B \leq 100 \text{ hours}$$
$$3A + 2B \leq 90$$
$$A \geq 0, B \geq 0$$

After going through steps 1 through 4, the feasible region (shaded area) is obtained, as shown in the following exhibit. Then all the corner points in the feasible region are evaluated in terms of their CM as follows:

LINEAR PROGRAMMING GRAPH

| Corner Points | | CM |
|---|---|---|
| A | B | $25A + $40B |
| (a) 30 | 0 | $25(30) + $40(0) = $750 |
| (b) 20 | 15 | $25(20) + $40(15) = $1,100 |
| (c) 0 | 25 | $25(0) + $40(25) = $1,000 |
| (d) 0 | 0 | $25(0) + $40(0) = $0 |

The corner 20A, 15B produces the most profitable solution.

**GRAPHICAL USER INTERFACE (GUI)** relies on windows, menus, icons, and other graphics for interaction between a human and a computer. Interaction generally takes place using a touch screen, mouse, or keyboard. In contrast, a command line interface (CLI) relies exclusively on text, and interaction is only by a keyboard.

**GRAPHIC SOFTWARE** program for depicting accounting information in graphic form, including charts, diagrams, and signs. This enhances understanding of financial statement accounts, trends, and relationships.

**GREENMAIL PAYMENT** payoff given to a potential acquirer by a company targeted for a takeover. In most cases, the targeted company buys back its shares at a significantly higher price. In reciprocation for selling the shares back, the suitor agrees to end the attempted takeover.

**GROSS DOMESTIC PRODUCT (GDP)** an economic indicator that measures the value of all goods and services produced by the economy within its boundaries and is the nation's broadest gauge of economic health. GDP is divided among personal consumption, investment, net exports, and government spending. Consumption makes up roughly two-thirds of the total. GDP is normally stated in annual terms, though data are compiled and released quarterly. The U.S. Bureau of Economic Analysis releases an advance estimate of quarterly GDP, followed by a "preliminary" estimate and a "final" figure. It is reported as a "real" figure, that is, economic growth minus the impact of inflation. The figure is tabulated on a quarterly basis, coming out in the month after a quarter has ended. It is then revised at least twice, with those revisions being reported once in each of the months following the original release. Changes in the GDP of the United States are calculated quarterly and announced in annualized terms (what the annual change would be if the quarter's pace of growth or contraction continued for a year). GDP reports appear in most daily newspapers and online at services like America Online. Also visit the federal government statistics Web site on the Internet at www.bea. gov/bea/newsrel/gdpnewsrelease.htm, www.fedstats.gov/, or www. economicindicators.gov. GDP is often a measure of the state of the economy. For example, many economists speak of recession when there has been a decline in GDP for two consecutive quarters. The GDP in dollars and real terms is a useful economic indicator.

**GROSS INCOME** amount of money earned (which is collected or will be collected) from the sale of goods minus the cost of the goods sold; also called GROSS PROFIT or *gross margin*. For example, if sales total $4,000 and the cost of goods sold is $1,200, the gross income is $2,800 ($4,000 – $1,200). Gross profit less operating expenses equals net income.

**GROSS MARGIN** *see* GROSS PROFIT.

**GROSS MARGIN PRICING** cost-based pricing approach in which the price is computed using a markup percentage based on a product's total production costs.

**GROSS MARGIN RATIO** percentage of each sales dollar remaining after a firm has paid for its goods; also called *gross profit margin*. It is calculated by dividing gross income (profits) by net sales. For example, assume that net sales are $80,000 and gross profit is $30,000. The gross margin ratio is 0.38 ($30,000/$80,000).

**GROSS PRICE METHOD** accounting procedure in which the purchase of merchandise is recorded at the gross amount of the invoice, without regard for the cash discount being offered. *See also* NET PRICE METHOD.

**GROSS PROFIT** sales minus cost of sales; also called *gross margin*.

**GROSS PROFIT ANALYSIS** analysis of the profit variance that constitutes the departure between actual profit and the previous year's income or the budgeted figure; also called *profit variance analysis*. The primary goal of profit variance analysis is to improve performance and profitability.

**GROSS PROFIT MARGIN** *see* GROSS MARGIN RATIO.

**GROSS PROFIT METHOD** system used to estimate inventory at the end of an interim period (e.g., quarter) when preparing INTERIM FINANCIAL STATEMENTS. However, estimating inventory for annual reporting is not acceptable. The method can be used to estimate what the inventory was at the date of a loss (e.g., fire, theft, other type of casualty loss) for insurance reimbursement. Under the method, the expected GROSS-PROFIT RATIO is used. The ending inventory can be computed by preparing a partial income statement starting with sales and ending with gross profit. Assume beginning inventory is $15,000, purchases are $90,000, sales are $200,000, and the gross profit rate is 60%.

| | | |
|---|---:|---:|
| Sales | | $200,000 |
| Less: Cost of goods sold | | |
|    Beginning inventory | $ 15,000 | |
|    Purchases | 90,000 | |
|    Cost of goods available | $105,000 | |
|    Less: Ending inventory | ? | |
| Cost of goods sold | | 80,000 |
| Gross profit (60% × $200,000) | | $120,000 |

The ending inventory must be $25,000 ($105,000 – 80,000).

**GROSS-PROFIT RATIO** gross profit divided by net sales. High ratios are favorable in that they indicate the business is earning a good return on the sale of its merchandise, although that may also invite competition. *See also* GROSS PROFIT.

**GROSS SALES** total sales *before* sales discounts and sales returns and allowances. It equals total unit sales times the selling price per unit. For example, if total units sold are 20,000 and the selling price is $5, gross sales are $100,000.

**GROUP AUDIT** the audit of group financial statements.

**GROUP DEPRECIATION** method for depreciating multiple-asset accounts using one rate. It is used to depreciate a collection of assets that are *similar* in nature and have approximately the same useful lives such as equipment. The method approximates a single unit cost procedure since the dispersion from the average is not significant. The method of computation and journal entries are basically the same as that of the COMPOSITE DEPRECIATION method.

**GROUP FINANCIAL STATEMENTS** financial statements that include financial information of two or more components. For example, consolidated financial statements of a parent corporation and its subsidiaries are considered to be group financial statements. *See also* COMPONENT.

**GROWTH RATE** amount of change in some financial characteristic of a company.
1. percentage change in earnings per share, dividends per share, revenue, market price of stock, or total assets compared to a base year amount.
   For example, growth in earnings per share equals:

$$\frac{\text{EPS (end of period)} - \text{EPS (beginning of period)}}{\text{EPS (beginning of period)}}$$

2. percentage change in an item such as net income considering the time value of money. Here, a future value of $1 table must be used. Assume net income in 2010 is $300,000 and in 2014 is $500,000. The future value of $1 table factor is 1.667 ($500,000/$300,000). The future value of $1 table indicates that the intersection of $n =$ four years and a factor of 1.667 is about 14%, as evidenced here:

**Partial Future Value of $1 Table [FVIF (i, n)]**

| Periods | 10% | 12% | 14% |
|---------|-------|-------|-------|
| 4 | 1.464 | 1.574 | 1.689 |

3. change in retained earnings divided by beginning stockholders' equity.
4. net income less dividends divided by common stockholders' equity. A high ratio reflects a company's ability to generate internal funds, and thus it does not have to rely on external sources.

**GROWTH STOCKS** said of shares of young companies with little or no earnings history. They are valued on the basis of anticipated future earnings and thus have high price-earnings ratios. They generally grow faster than the economy as a whole and also faster than the industry of which they are a part. They are risky because capital gains are speculative, especially in the case of young companies in new industries. An example of a growth stock is a high-tech company.

**G7** a group of the largest industrial nations, which includes all G6 nations and Canada.

**G6** a group that includes the six countries with the largest industrial economies. G6 currently includes the United States, the United Kingdom, Japan, France, Italy, and Germany.

**GUARANTEED BOND**
1. debt issued by one party with payment guaranteed by another party. A considerable number of railroad bonds have been guaranteed by firms other than the debtors. Some of the guaranties assure payment of both principal and interest; some assure interest only.
2. bonds issued by *subsidiaries* and guaranteed by *parent companies* or *affiliates*.

**GUARANTEED PAYMENTS TO PARTNERS** payments made to partners without regard to the partnership's income or loss. Guaranteed payments are deductible by a partnership, because they are typically considered wages paid to a partner who has performed services for the partnership.

# H

**HACKER** very knowledgeable computer user who attempts to break into and corrupt a computer system.

**HALF-YEAR CONVENTION** a tax rule assuming that a newly acquired asset is in service for one-half of the taxable year regardless of when it is actually placed in service.

**HARD COPY** computer term for output printed directly on paper. The user types commands, instructions, or data on a keyboard. The computer's responses, as well as the information entered, are printed on paper, which gives the user a permanent copy of the input.

**HARD DISK** a device for storing computer data. Internally, it consists of a set of electromagnetic disks on which data is stored. A standard hard disk is capable of storing several terrabytes (TB) of data; it can also access its data in milliseconds.

**HARDWARE** the "computer name" given to all the electronic and mechanical devices that make up a computer, as opposed to software, which refers to programs.

**HASHING** technique used to find an accounting record within a computer file. The key field of the record is the input. A mathematical process leads to the approximate location of the desired accounting data within the file.

**HASH TOTAL** summation of numbers having no practical meaning as a control precaution; used by auditors primarily in a computer application. The purpose is to identify whether a record has been lost or omitted from processing. For example, check numbers may be summed to get a hash total. If the total of the check numbers processed does not agree with the hash total, a discrepancy exists, and investigation is required to uncover the error.

**HEAD OF HOUSEHOLD** FILING STATUS category of a taxpaying entity. The head of household is an unmarried individual who maintains a household for another and satisfies the following conditions: (1) the taxpayer maintains a home in which a dependent relative lives for the whole year; (2) the taxpayer pays more than 50% of the cost of maintaining the home; and (3) the taxpayer is either a U.S. citizen or a resident alien.

## HEDGE

1. process of protecting oneself against unfavorable changes in prices. Thus one may enter into an offsetting purchase or sale agreement for the express purpose of balancing out any unfavorable changes in an already consummated agreement due to price fluctuations. Hedge transactions are commonly used to protect positions in (1) foreign currency, (2) commodities, and (3) securities.
2. financing an asset with a liability of similar maturity.

**HEDGE FUND**
1. a limited partnership of investors that invests in speculative stocks.
2. a mutual fund that seeks to make money betting on a particular bond market, currency movements, or directional movements based on certain events such as mergers and acquisitions. It attempts to hedge in order to minimize an exposure to currency risk. In general, international short-term bond funds usually hedge most of the currency risk, while longer-term funds have substantial exposure. Funds use currency options, futures, convertible bond arbitrage, merger arbitrage, and elaborate cross currency hedges, but the most effective hedges are expensive. Among the most successful hedge fund strategies in recent years has been convertible bond arbitrage. Hedge funds buy convertible bonds, which carry a low coupon but can be exchanged for equity at a certain price. They then take short position against the company's stock, trading on the relationship between the company's stock and bond prices.
3. a mutual fund that hedges its risk by buying or selling options to protect its position against market risk. For example, a fund specializing in government debt securities may hedge its position by selling call options against its position to protect it against downside risk. Contrary to popular opinion, a hedge fund constructively uses options to protect investment positions and pursues an extremely conservative investment philosophy.

**HELD-TO-MATURITY SECURITIES** debt securities for which an investor has the positive intent and ability to hold until maturity. Held-to-maturity securities should be reported at amortized cost, which takes into account amortization of premium or discount.

**HETEROGENEITY** *see* DIVERSITY SEGMENTATION.

**HETEROSCEDASTICITY** condition in which the variance of the error term is not constant in REGRESSION (LEAST SQUARES) ANALYSIS.

**HIDDEN RESERVE** understatement of owners' equity or net worth. This understatement can arise either from the undervaluation of assets or from a complimentary overaccrual of liabilities. For purposes of published financial statements, full disclosure must be made with respect to this departure from standard reporting practices. The ultimate effect of putting up a hidden reserve is that in a future period net income will be inflated by the amount of hidden asset value converted to cash.

**HIERARCHY OF COST** approach to group activity costs as they vary with external end-unit volume, internal volumes, batch-related volumes, and cost object diversity-sensitivity.

**HIERARCHY OF GAAP** the sources of accounting principles and the framework for selecting them in preparing financial statements in conformity with GAAP, identified by FASB Statement No. 168, *The*

*FASB Accounting Standards Codification,* and Accounting Standards Codification (ASC) 105, *Generally Accepted Accounting Principles.* The hierarchy consists of authoritative and nonauthoritative guidance:

- Authoritative Guidance includes FASB Statements, Interpretations, Technical Bulletins, Staff Positions, Staff Implementation Guides, EITF Abstracts, Accounting Principles Board (APB) Opinions, Accounting Research Bulletins, Accounting Interpretations, AICPA Statements of Positions, Audit and Accounting Guides, and Practice Bulletins.
- Nonauthoritative Guidance includes FASB Concepts Statements, AICPA Issues Papers, Technical Practice Aids, IFRS, and widely recognized industry accounting practices.

**HIGHLIGHT** *see* FINANCIAL HIGHLIGHT.

**HIGH-LOW METHOD** algebraic procedure used to separate a SEMI-VARIABLE COST or MIXED COST into the fixed and the variable components. The high-low method, as the name indicates, uses two extreme data points to determine the values of $a$ (the fixed cost portion) and $b$ (the variable rate) in the COST-VOLUME FORMULA $y = a + bx$. The extreme data points are the highest and lowest $x - y$ pairs.

**HISTORICAL COST** acquisition of an asset less discounts plus all *normal* incidental costs necessary to bring the asset into existing use and location. Note that the list price is often higher than the acquisition price. Examples of incidental costs are taxes, transportation, installation, and insurance; also called *cost principle*. If an asset is acquired for the incurrence of a long-term liability rather than cash payment, it is recorded at the PRESENT VALUE of the future payments. An asset acquired in exchange for stock is recorded at the fair market value of the stock issued. If the fair value of the stock is not known, then the fair value of the asset received is used.

**HISTORICAL COST ACCOUNTING** financial accounting based on the original cost of an item *ignoring* inflationary increases. It is the only allowable method of preparing the primary financial statements that appear in the annual report. However, inventory and investments in securities are reflected at the lower of cost or market value. *See also* CONSTANT DOLLAR ACCOUNTING; CURRENT COST ACCOUNTING.

**HISTORICAL SUMMARY** supplemental section appearing in the corporate annual report to stockholders in which significant items such as income, revenues, expenses, assets, liabilities, equity, earnings per share, and dividends are presented, usually over a period of at least five years (legal requirement).

**HOLDERS OF RECORD** owners of a firm's shares on the DATE OF RECORD indicated on the firm's *stock ledger*. Holders of record receive STOCK RIGHTS or DIVIDENDS when they are announced. Because of the time needed to make bookkeeping entries when a stock is traded, the stock will sell EX-DIVIDEND for four business days prior to the date of record.

**HOLDING COMPANY** corporation owning enough voting stock in another company to control its policies and management. Advantages of holding companies include: (1) the ability to control sizable operations with fractional ownership; (2) the isolation and diversification of risks through subsidiaries; and (3) the fact that approval of stock purchases by the stockholders of the acquired company is not required. Disadvantages of holding companies include: (1) partial multiple taxation when less than 80% of a subsidiary is owned; (2) the ease of enforced dissolution by the U.S. Department of Justice; and (3) the risks of negative leverage effects in excessive pyramiding.

**HOLDING COSTS** *see* CARRYING COSTS.

**HOLDING GAIN, LOSS** increment or decrement in the value of an asset or liability for an accounting period. They may be realized or unrealized depending upon whether the asset or liability has been exchanged or is still held. Realized gains or losses are recognized in the financial statements. Only in a few cases are unrealized losses recognized, such as with marketable securities and inventory applying the lower of cost or market value rule. However, permanent declines in the value of assets such as obsolete machinery should be reflected in the accounts. It should be noted that if current cost financial statements are prepared, holding gains and losses would be reflected.

**HOLDING PERIOD** time interval that property has been owned by the entity.

**HOME OFFICE DEDUCTION** deduction allowed for income tax purposes if certain requirements are met for maintaining an office in the home. Requirements are that the portion of a home is exclusively used on a regular basis as a principal place of business, or as a place for meeting with clients or customers in the normal course of the taxpayer's business. An additional requirement for employees holds that the office must be maintained only for the convenience of the employer.

**HOMOGENEITY** cost of an activity that has a similar cause-and-effect relationship with a cost object. Occurs when all the cost elements in an activity's cost pool are consumed in the same proportion by all cost objects. *See also* COST ELEMENT; ACTIVITY COST POOL; ACTIVITY COST DRIVER.

**HOMOGENEOUS COST POOL** a group of overhead costs associated with activities that can use the same COST DRIVER.

**HOMOSCEDASTICITY** condition found in a type of scatter graph; also known as *constant variance*. It is one of the assumptions required in a REGRESSION ANALYSIS in order to make valid statistical inferences about population relationships. Homoscedasticity requires that the standard deviation and variance of the error terms ($\mu$) are constant for all $x$ (see graphs below), and that the error terms are drawn from the same population. This indicates that there is a uniform scatter or dispersion of data points about the regression line. If the assumption does not hold (see graphs below), the accuracy of the $b$ coefficient is open to question.

**HORIZONTAL ANALYSIS** time series analysis of financial statements covering more than one accounting period; also called TREND ANALYSIS. It looks at the percentage change in an account over time. The percentage change equals the change over the prior year. For example, if sales in 20X0 are $100,000 and in 20X1 are $300,000, there is a 200% increase ($200,000/$100,000). By examining the magnitude of direction of a financial statement item over time, the analyst can evaluate its reasonableness. *See also* VERTICAL ANALYSIS.

CONSTANT VARIANCE OF $\mu$          NON-CONSTANT VARIANCE OF M
   (HOMOSCEDASTICITY)

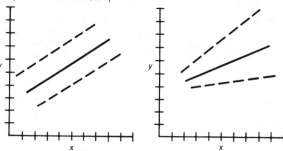

**HORIZONTAL AUDIT** technique used by the CPA to observe the client's accounting procedures to assure that the system of internal controls is running smoothly. An example is testing whether goods received from a vendor have been properly ordered, are of suitable type and quality as per inspection, and have been properly accounted for in the records.

**HORIZONTAL MERGER** a merger of competing entities.

**HOT SITE** is a backup location/site, from where an organization's data center can operate for the duration of a disaster. An organization may have three types of backup locations: a COLD SITE, a WARM SITE, or a hot site. A hot backup site is generally the most expensive of the three options. Everything needed to restore operations is in place. All hardware and software has already been acquired; generally the only thing needed to begin the recovery process is a copy of the latest data backup. Data center function can be restored to full operation without any significant delay.

**HOTSPOT** a location where Wi-Fi network access is available. Hotspots work through wireless access point devices and provide access to the INTERNET and other devices, such as networked printers or networked storage devices. Users generally connect to a hotspot network by knowing network name. *See also* SSID.

**H.R. 10 PLAN** *see* KEOGH PLAN.

**HUB** connection point between the server and the workstation in a LAN.

**HUMAN RESOURCE ACCOUNTING** method that recognizes a variety of human resources and shows them on a company's balance sheet. Under human resource accounting, a value is placed on people based on such factors as experience, education, and psychological traits, and, most importantly, future earning power (benefit) to the company. The idea has been well received by human-resource-oriented firms, such as those engaged in accounting, law, and consulting. Practical application is limited, however, primarily because of difficulty and the lack of uniform, consistent methods of quantifying the values of human resources. *See also* BEHAVIORAL ACCOUNTING.

**HURDLE RATE** term used in capital budgeting. Hurdle rate is the *required rate of return* on a long-term investment opportunity. A proposal would be accepted when the expected rate of return exceeds the hurdle rate. The hurdle rate should equal the incremental cost of capital. *See also* COST OF CAPITAL.

**HYPERLINK** *see* HYPERTEXT.

**HYPERTEXT** database approach linking related data, programs, and pictures. A hypertext document has highlighted words, called hyperlinks, which when clicked on will direct one to more information about the word.

**HYPERTEXT MARKUP LANGUAGE (HTML)** consists of a set of tags or codes that are applied to text to create Web pages. The HTML tags tell the Web browsers how to display the text or images on a Web page. HTML is a formal recommendation by the World Wide Web Consortium (W3C), and major browsers generally, but not always, adhere to these standards. The current version of HTML is known as HTML 5. It is an extensible form of HTML called Extensible Hypertext Markup Language (XHTML).

**HYPOTHESES TESTING** use of a statistical test to discriminate between two hypotheses at two specific risk (or probability) levels. They are called the null ($H_0$) and the alternative ($H_1$) hypotheses. These two hypotheses are usually stated in terms of (anticipated) population parameters—for example:

$$H_0 : \mu = \$100$$
$$H_1 : \mu \neq \$100$$

Statistics (e.g., $\bar{x}$) from the random sample may serve as estimators of the population parameters. For example, in auditing, two commonly used alternative hypotheses are:

$H_0$: The financial statement amount (e.g., book value) is correct.
$H_1$: The financial statement amount is materially in error.

The risk levels, symbolized as $\alpha$ and $\beta$ are specified for two types of errors — TYPE I and TYPE II, respectively — that can occur in the decision process. A Type I error occurs when the null hypothesis ($H_0$) is rejected when it is, in fact, true (i.e., the book value is correct, but the sample results lead you to believe otherwise). A Type II error occurs when the null hypothesis is accepted when it is, in fact, false (i.e., $H_1$ is true).

The decision to accept or reject the null hypothesis is based on (1) statistics computed from the random sample and (2) the probability of obtaining such values (determined from the underlying sampling distribution).

# I

**ICA** *see* INTERNATIONAL CONGRESS OF ACCOUNTANTS (ICA).

**IDEA** *see* INTERACTIVE DATA ELECTRONIC APPLICATION (IDEA).

**ICFA** *see* INSTITUTE OF CHARTERED FINANCIAL ANALYSTS (ICFA).

**IDEAL CAPACITY** largest volume of output possible if a facility maintained continuous operation at optimum efficiency, allowing for no losses of any kind, even those deemed normal or unavoidable; also called *maximum capacity, theoretical capacity*, or *engineered capacity*. Since it is impossible to obtain ideal capacity, unfavorable variances will result if it is used to apply fixed cost. *See also* CAPACITY.

**IDLE CAPACITY**
1. presence of unused capacity together with insufficient raw materials or skilled labor. When idle capacity exists, a firm can take on an incremental order without increasing the fixed costs.
2. economic situation in which the market will not absorb all of the maximum possible output at a price exceeding the variable cost of production. *See also* CAPACITY.
3. capacity that is potentially available but not currently being used, perhaps due to market pressures from competition, distribution constraints, or management policy (such as union contract laws, holidays, overtime rules); also called *excess capacity*. On the other hand, increased idle capacity may represent the rewards and evidence of improved productivity and efficiencies by operations.

**IDLE CAPACITY VARIANCE** measure of utilization of plant facilities. The variance results when a plant is underutilized (idle), and actual production falls below the expected, budgeted, or normal activity, known as DENOMINATOR ACTIVITY.

$$\begin{pmatrix} \text{Fixed Overhead} \\ \text{Idle Capacity} \\ \text{Variance} \end{pmatrix} = \left[ \begin{pmatrix} \text{Denominator} \\ \text{Hours} \end{pmatrix} - \begin{pmatrix} \text{Actual} \\ \text{Hours} \\ \text{Allowed} \end{pmatrix} \right] \times \begin{pmatrix} \text{Fixed Overhead} \\ \text{Standard} \\ \text{Rate} \end{pmatrix}$$

The variance is unfavorable if the denominator hours exceed the actual hours allowed; otherwise, it is favorable.

For example, assume that the denominator activity in machine-hours was 5,000 and the fixed overhead applied rate is \$6. The actual hours used were 4,200. The idle capacity variance is $(5,000 - 4,200) \times \$6 = \$4,800$, an unfavorable variance because the company's plant was underutilized.

**IDLE TIME** cost of direct labor for employees unable to perform their assigned tasks because of machine breakdowns, shortage of materials, power failure, sloppy production scheduling, and the like. The cost of idle time is treated as part of factory overhead—that is, as part of indirect manufacturing costs that should be spread over all the production of a period.

**IEEE 802.11 PROTOCOL** a family of specifications developed by the U.S. Institute of Electrical and Electronics Engineers (IEEE). There are currently three specifications in the family (802.11a, 802.11b, and 802.11g), with more being developed. The 802.11b standard often referred to as Wi-Fi is currently more widespread. However, hardware manufacturers are increasingly offering multi-standard equipment that can work with various standards.

**IF-CONVERTED METHOD** method used to determine the dilution of convertible securities that are *not* common stock equivalents entering into the computation of fully diluted earnings per share. The method assumes convertible securities are converted at the beginning of the year or at issuance date, if later. The TREASURY STOCK METHOD is used to account for any cash received from convertible securities when the if-converted method is used. However, theoretical stock acquisitions are assumed only if the market price of the stock is greater than the exercise price.

**ILLEGAL ACT** violation of law or governmental regulations by an audited entity or its management or employees acting on behalf of the entity.

**ILLIQUID**
1. unable to convert an investment to cash in a short period of time with a minimum capital loss.
2. lacking cash (or working capital) or having a low current ratio. *See also* LIQUID.

**IMPACT STATEMENT** document that analyzes the projected effects of a contemplated project. A primary reference point within this statement concerns probable externalities (e.g., negative implications to the environment). An example would be the proposal of a large industrial corporation located on an upriver site to dump some level of pollutants into the air and streams. The proposal would lead to an environmental impact statement about the effects upon health.

**IMPAIRMENT OF CAPITAL**
1. amount by which stated capital has been decreased by distributions such as dividends or losses.
2. legal restriction enacted to protect creditors by limiting payments of dividends to retained earnings.
3. excess of liabilities over assets due to losses.

**IMPAIRMENT OF VALUE** permanent decline in the value of an asset. The entry is to debit the loss account and credit the asset for the reduction in utility. Recovery of the asset's cost or book value is not a realistic expectation.

**IMPERFECT MARKET** one where imperfect competition exists. Imperfect competition includes monopoly and oligopoly with one or more sellers controlling the market price. *See also* PERFECT MARKETS.

**IMPLEMENTATION, BOTTOM UP APPROACH** approach to implementing ABC with emphasis on achieving operational improvements. Activities and cost objects are disaggregated for high resolution; accuracy requirements are high.

**IMPLICIT COST** *see* IMPUTED COST.

**IMPOUND**
1. to take custody of and seize property or money by some legal action (e.g., court mandate).
2. in GOVERNMENT ACCOUNTING, to reduce authority to incur debt by withholding some portion or all of an APPROPRIATION.

**IMPREST FUND** *see* PETTY-CASH FUND.

**IMPROVEMENT** capitalized expenditure usually extending the useful life of an asset or improving it in some manner over and above the original asset. Thus if an expenditure adds years to an asset or improves its rate of output, it would be considered an improvement that is capitalized. In contrast, a maintenance or repair expense is not capitalized.

**IMPUTED COST** cost that is implied but not reflected in the financial reports of the firm; also called *implicit cost*. Imputed costs consist of the OPPORTUNITY COSTS of time and capital that the manager has invested in producing the given quantity of production and the opportunity costs of making a particular choice among the alternatives being considered.

**IMPUTED INTEREST** interest assumed on a noninterest-bearing note, including discounted or zero-coupon instruments, or on a note with an unrealistically low interest rate. It applies to both notes payable and notes receivable. The imputed interest rate is the one the borrower would normally incur in a similar transaction. Assume a $10,000 one-year noninterest-bearing note payable was issued on 1/1/2014. It would be unrealistic to believe that someone would take a one-year note without interest. Thus, interest must be imputed, to arrive at the present value of the note on 1/1/2015. If we use a 10% imputed interest rate, the present value of the note is $9,091 ($10,000/1.10). Hence, the note consists of a principal portion of $9,091 and an imputed interest portion of $909.

**INADEQUACY** loss or expense that is incurred by virtue of lost or reduced capacity, technological obsolescence, and/or abnormal wear and tear and that requires premature replacement or abandonment.

**INCENTIVE STOCK OPTION (ISO)** stock option granted employees under an option plan that provides a more favorable tax effect than

QUALIFIED STOCK OPTIONS. With incentive stock options, employees receive the right to purchase a specified number of shares of company stock at a specified price during a specified period. ISOs are not taxable at the time of grant or at the time of exercise. Only when the stock is sold are the gains subject to federal taxation. Gains from incentive stock options will be taxed at an ordinary income tax rate. There is a cap on capital gain tax at 28%. Options may be exercised in any order. Also, an employer may not grant an employee more than $100,000 in stock options that first become exercisable in any one year.

**IN-CHARGE ACCOUNTANT** *see* ACCOUNTANT IN CHARGE.

**INCOME**

1. money earned during an accounting period that results in an increase in total assets.
2. items such as rents, interest, gifts, and commissions.
3. revenues arising from sales of goods and services.
4. excess of revenues over expenses and losses for an accounting period (i.e., net income).

*See also* GROSS INCOME; INCOME REALIZATION; NET INCOME; REVENUE.

**INCOME ACCOUNT** term used for revenue and expense accounts.

**INCOME BOND** bond on which the payment of interest is required only when earnings are available. Typically, interest that is bypassed does *not* accumulate. Income bonds are commonly used during the reorganization of a failing or failed business firm.

**INCOME DEDUCTION** nonoperating expenses of an organization that are listed in the final section of the income statement before arriving at net income. These costs, not usually subject to management control of day-to-day operations, are necessarily incurred in the operation of an ongoing enterprise and include interest expense, income taxes, and amortization of bond discount.

**INCOME EXCLUSION RULE** gross income not subject to tax, including: (1) interest on municipal securities; and (2) annuities and pensions that are returns of capital.

**INCOME FROM CONTINUING OPERATIONS** revenues and expenses after tax arising from the *ongoing* operations of the business for the accounting period. In arriving at income from continuing operations, NONRECURRING gains and losses are *included*. *After* income from continuing operations the following separate line items appear: INCOME FROM DISCONTINUED OPERATIONS, EXTRAORDINARY ITEMS, and cumulative effect of a CHANGE IN ACCOUNTING PRINCIPLE.

**INCOME FROM DISCONTINUED OPERATIONS** the results of operations of a component classified as held for sale are reported in the results of operations in the year(s) in which they *occur*. That is, phase-out losses are not accrued. In general, gain or loss from operations of the discontinued component should include operating gains or losses incurred and the gain or loss on disposal of a component incurred in the current period. Gains shall not be recognized until the year actually realized. The results of operations of a *component* of a company that either has been disposed of or is classified as being held for sale are reported in discontinued operations only if *both* of the following conditions are met: (1) the operations and cash flows of the component have been (or will be) eliminated from the ongoing operations as a result of the disposal decision, and (2) the company will not have any significant continuing involvement in the operations of the component after the disposal decision.

**INCOME IN RESPECT OF A DECEDENT** any income that a decedent earned or was entitled to receive prior to dying. Income in respect of a decedent is generally taxable to the survivor who receives the income, as in the case of pension income received by a decedent's widow.

**INCOME REALIZATION** recognition of income at the time of sale or the rendering of the service. The transfer of title in an ARM'S LENGTH TRANSACTION makes the process of earning income complete, as does the delivery of a service.

**INCOME SMOOTHING** form of income management that reflects economic results, not as they are, but rather as management wishes them to look. This results in lower earnings quality since net income does not representatively portray the economic performance of the business entity for the period. Income smoothing relies not on falsehoods and distortions but on the wide leeway existing in alternatively accepted accounting principles and their interpretations. It is conducted within the structure of GAAP. In effect, it redistributes income statement credits and charges among periods. The prime objective is to moderate income variability over the years by shifting income from good years to bad years. Future income may be shifted to the present year or vice versa. In a similar vein, income variability can be modified by shifting expenses or losses from period to period. An example is reducing a DISCRETIONARY COST (e.g., advertising expense, research and development expense) in the current year to improve current period earnings. In the next year, the discretionary cost will be increased.

For analytical purposes, the analyst should restate net income for profit increases or decreases due to income smoothing attempts.

**INCOME SPLITTING** shifting income from one member of a family to another. This, of course, is done to reduce the tax effects of a person in a higher marginal tax bracket, by diverting, allocating, or assigning income to a person in a lower tax bracket. A parent in a higher tax bracket could, for example, give money or property to a child. Income generated by that gift would be taxed at the child's lower rate.

**INCOME STATEMENT** form showing the elements used in arriving at a company's NET INCOME for the accounting period; also called *profit and loss statement*. It must be included in the annual report. An illustrative condensed income statement follows:

Sales
Less: Cost of sales
Gross Margin
Less: Operating expenses (including selling expenses and
   general & administrative expenses)
Income from operations
Add or Less: Other income and expenses
Income before tax
Less: Provision for income taxes
Income from continuing operations
Add or Less: Income from discontinued operations (net of tax)
Income before extraordinary items and cumulative effect
Add or Less: Extraordinary items (net of tax)
Add or Less: Cumulative effect of a change in accounting principle
   (net of tax)
Net income

**INCOME SUMMARY** temporary account in which revenues and expenses are closed at the end of the year. Income summary shows the net income or net loss for the year since total revenue and total expenses have been closed to it. The resulting profit or loss is then transferred to retained earnings. *See also* CLOSING ENTRY.

**INCOME TAX** government levy on the net earnings of an individual, corporation, or other taxable unit. The tax rate is usually a graduated one as earnings go from one tax bracket to another. Tax rates for individuals also depend on the status of the taxpayer (e.g., single, married). Income tax may include an addition to the regular tax such as a surtax. The income tax provision is shown as an expense in the income statement.

**INCORPORATED** legal state of existence signifying that a corporate entity has been recognized; that is, a legal entity has been authorized by a state or other political authority to operate according to the entity's approved articles of incorporation or charter. Incorporated entities share basic attributes: an exclusive name, continued and independent existence from shareholders or members, paid-in capital, and limited liability.

**INCREMENTAL ANALYSIS** decision-making method that utilizes the concept of RELEVANT COSTS; also known as *relevant cost approach* or *differential analysis*. Under this method, the decision involves the following steps: (1) gather all costs associated with each alternative; (2) drop the SUNK COSTS; (3) drop those costs that do not differ between alternatives; and (4) select the best alternative based on the remaining cost data.

For example, assume the ABC Company is planning to expand its productive capacity. The plan consists of purchasing a new machine for $50,000 and disposing of the old machine without receiving anything for it. The new machine has a five-year life. The old machine has a five-year remaining life and a book value of $12,500. The new machine will reduce variable operating costs from $35,000 per year to $20,000 per year. Annual sales and other operating costs are shown as follows:

|  | Present Machine | New Machine |
|---|---|---|
| Sales | $60,000 | $60,000 |
| Variable costs | 35,000 | 20,000 |
| Fixed costs: |  |  |
| Depreciation (straight-line) | 2,500 | 10,000 |
| Insurance, taxes, etc. | 4,000 | 4,000 |
| Net income | $18,500 | $26,000 |

At first glance, it appears that the new machine provides an increase in net income of $7,500 per year. The book value of the present machine, however, is a sunk cost and is irrelevant in this decision. Furthermore, sales and fixed costs such as insurance and taxes are also irrelevant since they do not differ between the two alternatives being considered. Eliminating all the irrelevant costs leaves us with only the incremental costs, as follows:

| | | |
|---|---|---|
| Savings in variable costs | $15,000 | |
| Less: Increase in fixed costs | 10,000 | (a $2,500 sunk cost is irrelevant) |
| Net annual cash savings arising from the new machine | $ 5,000 | |

**INCREMENTAL BACKUP** *see* DIFFERENTIAL BACKUP.

**INCREMENTAL COST-ALLOCATION METHOD** variation of the stand-alone technique, establishes a priority among users and allocates common costs to the primary party up to the amount of that user's stand-alone costs. The remaining common costs are then allocated to the incremental party or parties.

**INCREMENTAL (DIFFERENTIAL) COST**
1. difference in costs between two or more alternatives. This is equivalent to the marginal cost concept but involves multiple changes in output and discrete output choices, rather than a single-unit change. For example, consider the two alternatives A and B, whose costs are as follows:

|                  | A         | B         | Incremental Costs (B – A) |
|------------------|-----------|-----------|---------------------------|
| Direct Materials | $10,000   | $10,000   | $ 0                       |
| Direct Labor     | 10,000    | $15,000   | 5,000                     |

The incremental costs are simply B – A (or A – B) as shown in the last column.

**2.** cost associated with increasing the output of an activity or project above some base level.

**3.** cost associated with increasing the quantity of a cost driver; also known as *differential cost*.

**INCREMENTAL REVENUE ALLOCATION** allocation method establishing priorities among the items in a bundle. The primary product is assigned 100% of its stand-alone revenue, with the remaining revenue from the bundle assigned sequentially to the other items.

**INDEFINITE REVERSAL** condition in which INTERPERIOD INCOME TAX ALLOCATION is not required for the undistributed earnings of a foreign subsidiary when there is sufficient evidence that those earnings will be undistributed *indefinitely*. A footnote is needed declaring the intention to reinvest the earnings indefinitely and the cumulative amount of the undistributed profits. When there is a change in circumstances and earnings will be remitted back to the U.S. parent, tax allocation is required.

**INDEMNIFICATION** reimbursement provided to a party to compensate for loss or damage.

**INDENTURE** legal document that specifically states the conditions under which a bond has been issued, the rights of the bondholders, and the duties of the issuing corporation; also called BOND INDENTURE; *deed of trust*. An indenture normally contains a number of standard and restrictive provisions (COVENANTS), including a sinking fund requirement, a minimum debt-equity ratio to be maintained, and an identification of the collateral if the bond is secured. It also covers redemption rights and call provisions. The indenture provides for the appointment of a trustee to act on behalf of bondholders.

**INDEPENDENCE** condition of accountant having no bias and being neutral regarding the client or another party in performing the audit function. Some independence guidelines for an auditor engaged in the attest function include: (1) no family relationship with the client's executives; (2) no financial interest in the company; and (3) no contingent fee based on the type of audit opinion rendered. The external auditor must furnish an impartial opinion on the client's financial position and operating performance. The audit opinion is based solely on the evidence found while conducting proper auditing procedures.

Independence is created and maintained to enable the auditor to establish credibility for the audit opinion that financial statement users rely upon. *See also* INDEPENDENT ACCOUNTANT.

**INDEPENDENT** *see* INDEPENDENCE.

**INDEPENDENT AUDITOR'S REPORT ON INTERNAL CONTROL OVER FINANCIAL REPORTING** the auditor's opinion on the effectiveness of the company's internal control over financial reporting.

**INDEPENDENT ACCOUNTANT** CERTIFIED PUBLIC ACCOUNTANT (CPA) in public practice having no financial or other interest in the client whose financial statements are being examined. The CPA must be completely objective and impartial to conduct the attest function properly. Note that the term applies to an external auditor as distinguished from an internal auditor on the client's staff. An external auditor who has been involved with the client as an underwriter, promoter, trustee, or officer is *not* independent. *See also* INDEPENDENCE.

**INDEPENDENT (OUTSIDE) DIRECTOR** member of the Board of Directors of an entity who is an outsider, meaning he or she is not an employee of that entity. An example is a broker sitting on the Board of a client company. Such directors are important because they bring unbiased opinions regarding the company's decisions and diverse experience to the company's decision-making process. In order not to have a conflict of interest, independent directors should not participate on the boards of directly competing businesses. Directors are typically compensated based on a standard fee for each board meeting.

**INDEPENDENT VARIABLE** one that may take on any value in a relationship; for example, in $y = f(x)$, $x$ is the independent variable. For example, independent variables that influence sales are advertising and price. *See also* DEPENDENT VARIABLE.

**INDEXATION** feature of a contract or agreement designed to adjust its value for general price-level changes. An example is a COST-OF-LIVING ADJUSTMENT (COLA) in a labor contract.

**INDEXED BOND** obligation with interest payments tied to an inflation index. If price levels rise, the rate of bond interest is adjusted accordingly. *See also* INDEXATION.

**INDEX FUND** a mutual fund that has as its primary objective the matching of the performance of a particular stock index such as the S&P 500 index. The beauty of index funds is twofold: (1) they minimize costs. All the fund company has to do is construct a portfolio out of the stocks in a chosen index. The fund is passively managed, with changes being made only to fine-tune the fund's performance to match more closely the index's results. The alternative is an actively managed fund, which even sounds more expensive. (2) The index funds eliminate your need to work so hard and worry too much. You can be fairly assured that your performance will be as good—or as bad—as the overall performance of the market or markets you select. A drawback to index funds is that since the index is made up of the stocks of large, well-known, and highly regarded companies, they can miss out on the opportunity of superior stock-price appreciation that some small companies often provide.

**INDEXING** *see* INDEXATION.

**INDEX-NUMBER TREND SERIES** method recommended when a comparison of financial statements covering more than two years is involved. In computing a series of index numbers, a base year must be selected and 100% assigned to it. The base year should be the one that is most typical or normal. Assume that the base year is 20X0. On 12/31/20X0 the cash balance of $8,000 is assigned 100%. The cash balances are $10,000 at 12/31/20X1 and $14,000 on 12/31/20X2. The index number for 20X1 is 125% ($10,000/$8,000) and for 20X2 is 175% ($14,000/$8,000).

**INDEX OPTIONS** calls and puts on indexes of stocks. There are "broad" indexes applying to a wide range of firms and industries. There are also "narrow-based" indexes relating to one industry or economic sector. An advantage of investing in an index option is that an interest in many companies is possible with a limited investment. It should be noted, however, that options have a limited life, are used to speculate or to hedge, and are settled in cash. In other words, if an index option is exercised (not normally done), the investor would not receive (or pay) the underlying stock, but would, rather, settle in cash.

**INDIRECT COST** expense that is difficult to trace directly to a specific costing object; also called COMMON COST. National advertising that benefits more than one product and sales territory is an example of an indirect cost. Fixed factory overhead is another example. *See also* DIRECT COST.

**INDIRECT LABOR** labor *not* directly involved in production but essential to the manufacturing process, such as supervisory personnel and janitors. It is classified as part of FACTORY OVERHEAD.

**INDIRECT LIABILITY**
1. situation in which responsibility for payment or satisfaction may arise in the future. An example is cosigning a loan for another party.
2. potential obligation, one that may eventually occur depending on some future event beyond the control of the company; also called CONTINGENT LIABILITY. Contingent liabilities may originate with such events as lawsuits, credit guarantee, and contested income tax assessments.

**INDIRECT MANUFACTURING EXPENSES** *see* FACTORY OVERHEAD.

**INDIRECT MATERIAL** primarily supplies, including glue, nails, and other minor items. They are classified as part of FACTORY OVERHEAD.

**INDIRECT METHOD** the method used in preparing an entity's statement of cash flows that involves reconciling NET INCOME to net cash flows from operating activities.

**INDIRECT TAX** one levied on a certain entity but not borne by that entity. For example, the retail sales tax is usually paid by the consumer in the form of an increase in price on goods or services—the retailer collects and passes on a tax actually borne by the consumer.

**INDIVIDUAL RETIREMENT ACCOUNT (IRA)** personal account that an employee can set up with a deposit that is tax deductible up to $5,000 a year (if 50 years or older, the contribution is $6,000). A working taxpayer *not* covered by another retirement plan may deduct IRA contributions. Also a taxpayer may deduct IRA contributions if ADJUSTED GROSS INCOME (AGI) is less than a certain amount. IRA funds are available to their depositors, penalty-free, at the age of 59½—or sooner in cases of death or disability. Early withdrawal of deductible contributions for any other reason will cost the taxpayer a penalty.

**INDUSTRIAL DEVELOPMENT BOND (IDB)** debt issued by a municipality to finance plants and facilities that are then leased to private industrial businesses; also called *industrial revenue bond*. The subsequent lease payments are used to service the bonds. The intent of IDBs is to attract private industry to promote local economic development. IDBs appealed to investors because they were exempt from federal income taxes. Exemption for IDBs is being phased out. A new category of tax-exempt bonds, called *qualified redevelopment bonds*, is to be used to finance land acquisition and redevelopment in blighted areas.

**INDUSTRIAL ENGINEER** professional who is engaged in the following activities: (1) product design and quality specification; (2) facilities design and layout; (3) design of production processes and machine systems; (4) work measurements; (5) quality control; and (6) scheduling and maintenance.

**INDUSTRIAL REVENUE BOND** *see* INDUSTRIAL DEVELOPMENT BOND (IDB).

**INDUSTRY RATIOS** mean or median financial ratios for a particular industry. The computed ratios for a company being analyzed should be compared to the industry average to form a basis of comparison. To what extent is the company better or worse than typical? Industry ratios are published by financial information services such as Dun & Bradstreet.

**INDUSTRY STANDARDS** in FINANCIAL RATIO ANALYSIS, industry average ratios used as standards to test whether ratios of a particular firm are normal. There are many widely used sources of industry standards. The Risk Management Association (RMA) (www.rmahq. org), the national association of banks and credit officers, computes a set of 16 key ratios for more than 300 lines of business. These ratios are published in *Annual Statement Studies. See also* FINANCIAL STATEMENT ANALYSIS.

**INFLATION** general rise in the price level. When inflation is present, a dollar today can buy more than a dollar in the future. In the presence of hyperinflation, with prices rising at 100% a year or more, there is a tendency for people to prefer hard assets (such as real estate and precious metals) to financial assets (stocks and bonds) in their investment choices.

**INFLATION ACCOUNTING** method of reporting that allows for the financial effects of changes in the price level. Two possible means of taking inflation into account are CONSTANT DOLLAR ACCOUNTING and CURRENT COST ACCOUNTING.

**INFORMATION AND COMMUNICATION SYSTEMS** the component of internal control concerned with (1) the methods and records used to identify and record business transactions, and (2) ensuring that employees understand their individual roles and responsibilities in connection with internal control over financial reporting.

**INFORMATION PROCESSING** transformation of data by classifying, sorting, merging, recording, retrieving, transmitting, or reporting. DATA PROCESSING is any operation or combination of operations that transforms data into useful information, whereas information processing goes one step further to include information generation and INFORMATION RETRIEVAL.

**INFORMATION RETRIEVAL** utilization of micrographics or computer storage for filing, storing, and retrieving information. Micrographics includes microfilm and microfiche that can be indexed for later retrieval on special orders.

**INFORMATION RETURN** return filed with the Internal Revenue Service for which no tax liability is imposed. Examples of such returns are Form 1065 (partnership return), Form W-2, and Form 1099. The law charges a penalty for each failure to file an information return with the IRS and for each failure on the part of businesses to supply a copy of the information return to the taxpayer. The law also adds a penalty for each information return submitted to the IRS, or the taxpayer, that contains incorrect information.

**INFORMATION SYSTEM** system of transforming raw data into useful information for a decision maker. *See* MANAGEMENT INFORMATION SYSTEM (MIS).

**INHERENT LIMITATIONS OF INTERNAL CONTROL** "built-in" limitations that result in limited assurance, rather than absolute assurance, that an entity's INTERNAL CONTROL objectives will be achieved. Inherent limitations include potential collusion, management override of controls, human error, and lack of segregation of duties.

**INHERENT RISK** the "built-in" susceptibility of an assertion to material misstatement presuming no related internal controls. Inherent risk is a component of the risk of material misstatement and exists independently of the audit. Neither management nor the auditor can limit inherent risk.

**INHERITANCE TAX** state tax levied upon the cash or fair market value of property received through inheritance. This tax is borne by the receiver of such property and not by the estate, as in federal ESTATE TAX.

**INITIAL PUBLIC OFFERING** *see* GOING PUBLIC.

**INITIATION DATE** *see* AUTONOMOUS.

**INPUT COST** cost of DIRECT MATERIAL, DIRECT LABOR, and other overhead items devoted to the production of a good or service.

**INPUT-OUTPUT ANALYSIS** study of linear production processes with fixed input coefficients. It attempts to develop a matrix relationship between the flow of goods and services from industries or branches of an economic system. The RECIPROCAL ALLOCATION METHOD that is used to allocate service department costs to production departments is an application of input-output analysis in accounting.

**INQUIRY** request for information; investigation. The auditor in conducting the examination seeks to obtain audit evidence by asking pertinent questions of client personnel or third parties. Answers obtained from such questions typically require corroboration. For example, the auditor may ask an employee why promotion expense is so high for the period, and the reply may be that some of it represents nonbusiness items. The propriety of the promotion expense account must then be evaluated by examining source documents. Another example is that of an auditor asking an employee where a given asset is located so that the asset can be visually corroborated. The question-asking aspect of the auditor with regard to third parties may be in such form as confirmations and legal letters.

**INSIDE DIRECTOR** individual on the board of directors who is an employee of the company. *See also* OUTSIDE DIRECTOR.

**INSIDE INFORMATION** privileged information obtained regarding material business results and pending security transactions that will not be made public until a certain date. Taking advantage of inside information for the purpose of making a profit is illegal.

**INSIDER** as defined by the *Securities Exchange Act of 1934*, corporate director, officer, or shareholder with more than 10% of a registered security, who through influence of position obtains knowledge that may be used primarily for unfair personal gain to the detriment of others. The definition has been extended to include relatives and others in a position to capitalize on inside information.

## INSIDER TRADING

1. the buying and selling of the company's securities based on material information relating to the company that has not been made public. Insider trading according to this definition is against the law in most countries.

2. the buying and selling of shares of a public company by its officers, directors, and stockholders who own more than 10% of the company's stock. In the United States, such transactions must be reported monthly to the SEC under Section 16 of the Securities Exchange Act of 1934: reporting rules for similar trading may also exist in different countries or markets.

**INSOLVENCY** failure of a company to meet its obligations as they become due. An analysis of insolvency concentrates on the operating and capital structure of the business. The proportion of long-term debt in the capital structure must also be considered. *See also* BANKRUPTCY.

**INSOURCING** the opposite of OUTSOURCING.

**INSPECTION TIME** time spent either looking for product flaws or reworking defective units.

**INSPECTOR GENERAL** federal office that performs audit and investigative activities with a focus upon the independent review and appraisal of the activities of some federal agencies. The office is generally required to make periodic reports to Congress, and specifically to the secretary or undersecretary of certain federal agencies. The office was created by the Inspector General Act of 1978.

**INSTABILITY INDEX OF EARNINGS** deviation between actual income and trend income. The higher the index, the more instability associated with a firm's profitability. The index equals:

$$I = \sqrt{\frac{\Sigma\,(y^T - y)^2}{n}}$$

where $y$ = reported net income

$y^T$ = trend income

A simple TREND EQUATION solved by computer is used to determine trend income.

## INSTALLMENT SALE

1. sale made on the installment basis. Many business firms—such as TV dealers, furniture stores, and appliance dealers—make installment sales. Typically, a customer purchases merchandise by sign-

ing an installment contract in which the customer agrees to a down payment plus installment payments of a fixed amount over a specified period. The installment receivable so created by the contract is usually classified as a current asset.

2. transaction with a predetermined contract price in which payments are made on an installment basis over a period of time.

**INSTALLMENT (SALES) METHOD** manner of recognizing revenue when cash is collected. That is, when each payment is received from the customer, a portion of gross profit on the sale (and the gain) is recognized (based on the gross profit percentage in the year of the sale), so that by the final payment the entire gross profit is recorded. For example, ABC Company reports income on the installment basis, and the following information is available:

| Year of Sale | Gross Profit % | Collected During 2014 |
|---|---|---|
| 2013 | 46% | $60,000 |
| 2014 | 40% | 80,000 |

The realized gross profit on installment sales is computed as follows:

| | |
|---|---|
| 2013 | 46% × $60,000 = $27,600 |
| 2014 | 40% × 80,000 = 32,000 |

Promulgated GAAP prohibit accounting for sales by any form of installment accounting except under exceptional circumstances where collectibility cannot be reasonably estimated or assured. The doubtfulness of collectibility can be caused by the length of an extended collection period or because no basis of estimation can be established. In such cases a company can use either the installment (sales) method or the COST-RECOVERY METHOD.

A taxpayer can elect *not* to use the installment method. The election is made by reporting on a timely filed tax return the gain computed by the taxpayer's usual method of accounting (cash or accrual).

**INSTITUTE FOR SUPPLY MANAGEMENT'S INDEX** the index, based on a survey of 375 companies in 17 industries, which measure new orders, inventories, exports, and employment in the service sector. Services account for five-sixths of the $10 trillion U.S. economy and include industries such as entertainment, utilities, health care, farming, insurance, retail, restaurants, and zoos.

**INSTITUTE OF CHARTERED ACCOUNTANTS IN ENGLAND AND WALES** large and influential accountancy association in the British Isles. It issues guidelines for practitioners, evaluates credentials of prospective members, and holds summer school every year. The institute puts out numerous publications, including two journals, *Accountancy* and *Accounting and Business Research*.

**INSTITUTE OF CHARTERED ACCOUNTANTS IN SCOTLAND** collective organization made up of the Edinburgh Society and similar societies in Glasgow and Aberdeen. It dates in its original form to 1854. This institute issues guidance to practitioners, evaluates candidates for membership, and holds annual summer schools. It publishes *THE ACCOUNTANT'S MAGAZINE.*

**INSTITUTE OF INTERNAL AUDITORS (IIA)** (www.theiia.org) professional organization that was established to develop the status of internal auditing. It administers and confers the CERTIFIED INTERNAL AUDITOR (CIA) designation.

**INSTITUTE OF MANAGEMENT ACCOUNTING (IMA)** *see* CERTIFICATE IN MANAGEMENT ACCOUNTING (CMA).

**INSTITUTIONAL INVESTOR** entity that trades large volumes of securities, such as banks, pension funds, insurance companies, mutual funds, labor unions, and corporate profit-sharing and pension plans. A very high percentage of daily trading on the stock exchange results from purchases and sales by institutional investors.

**INSURANCE** agreement through an insurance contract, termed a *policy*, that one party, for an agreed premium, will provide insurance or pay the insured a specified sum of money, contingent upon the specified conditions within the insurance contract, such as loss of life or property of the insured. Employers provide many types of insurance for employees, including health, disability, and life insurance.

**INSURE** to provide or obtain INSURANCE for reimbursement against loss to minimize risk.

**INTANGIBLE ASSET** item lacking physical substance (e.g., goodwill) or representing a right granted by the government (e.g., patent, trademark) or by another company (e.g., franchise). Intangibles have a life in excess of one year. Limited life intangible assets are amortized into expense over the period benefitted. Unlimited life intangibles are subject to a yearly impairment test.

**INTANGIBLE DRILLING COST (IDC)** all necessary intangible expenditures incurred in drilling from the surface to the natural resource deposit. An oil or gas deposit has the option of either capitalizing (and depleting) or immediately expensing certain intangible drilling costs. Among the qualifying intangible costs are labor, taxes, repairs, supplies, power, and equipment rentals.

**INTANGIBLE VALUE** total value of an organization as a going concern less the total value of its net tangible assets, leaving the residual intangible value. This residual value may represent PATENTS, TRADEMARKS, SECRETS, GOODWILL, and the like. In theoretical terms, intangible value is the present value of excess earning power of an entity over the normal rate of return.

**INTEGRATED AUDIT** involves auditing financial statements and internal control over financial reporting concurrently. All issuers (i.e., publicly traded entities) are required to undergo an annual integrated audit. The objective of an integrated audit is to enable an auditor to express opinions on the (1) fairness of the financial statement presentation, and (2) the effectiveness of internal control over financial reporting.

**INTERACTIVE DATA ELECTRONIC APPLICATION (IDEA)** a system that will replace Edgar. IDEA is a different approach from EDGAR. IDEA will initially supplement EDGAR but ultimately will replace it. IDEA provides investors with easier and quicker access to financial information about public companies. IDEA uses data-tagging software akin to bar codes for financial data. The technology is based on the extensible business reporting language (XBRL). It allows for fast comparisons of different business entities or different time periods. The information will be available at no cost on the Internet.

**INTEGER PROGRAMMING** mathematical approach maintaining that solutions to mathematical problems should appear in whole numbers (integers). For example, quantities like 12⅔ chairs, 34½ tables, 4.25 cars, or 2.75 persons may be unrealistic; yet simply rounding off the LINEAR PROGRAMMING solution to the nearest whole numbers may not produce a feasible solution. The integer programming method allows one to find the optimal *integer* solution to a problem without violating any of the constraints.

**INTEGRATED SOFTWARE** software package that combines many applications in one program. Previously, the accountant needed a utility program to load the data from one program into another program. Now there are integrated programs of two or more modules that interact. Integrated packages can move data among several programs utilizing common commands and file structures. In effect, there are multiple applications in memory simultaneously. An integrated package is recommended when identical source information is to be used for varying purposes and activities. For example, *MS Office* lets the accountant do word processing, outlining, telecommunications, graphics, data base, and spreadsheets and save each as a frame that can be integrated with the other frames.

**INTEGRATED TEST FACILITY** test using simulated transactions and dummy master records within a client's master file so that test data are processed simultaneously with actual input. The objective is to substantiate control reliability.

**INTENSITY** cost consumed by each unit of the activity driver. It is assumed that the intensity of each unit of the activity driver for a single activity is equal. Unequal intensity means that the activity should be broken into smaller activities or that a different activity driver should be chosen. *See also* DIVERSITY.

**INTER-AMERICAN ACCOUNTING ASSOCIATION (IAAA)** professional organization that meets every two to three years in different countries comprising the Americas. Technical aspects of the accounting profession are discussed at these meetings. Mexico City serves as the location for the secretariat of the organization.

**INTERCEPT** in a coordinate system, the distance from the origin to the point at which a line or curve intersects an axis. For example, the y-intercept is the value $a$ of the dependent variable $y$ in the formula $y = a + bx$ when $x$ is zero. In a COST-VOLUME FORMULA, $a$ is interpreted as the fixed cost portion of a mixed cost. *See also* COST FUNCTION.

**INTERCOMPANY ACCOUNT** general ledger account recording a transaction between related companies (e.g., affiliates). Typically, intercompany accounts are reciprocal records between the entities in their general ledgers. Examples are intercompany receivables and payables, and intercompany sales and purchases. In preparing combining or CONSOLIDATED FINANCIAL STATEMENTS, intercompany account balances must be eliminated.

**INTERCOMPANY ELIMINATION** deduction of intercompany items when preparing the combining or consolidated balance sheet and income statement. Examples are intercompany loans and intercompany investments between the parent and subsidiary. In the case of extensive eliminations, an eliminations ledger may be used.

**INTERCOMPANY PROFIT** excess of sales over cost of sales for merchandise or revenue minus related expenses for services to a related company when consolidated financial statements are being prepared. Intercompany profit is *fully* eliminated irrespective of the MINORITY INTEREST. Thus only earnings applicable to the outside are reflected as being realized.

**INTEREST**
1. amount charged by a lender to a borrower for the use of funds. The interest rate is typically expressed on an annual basis. Interest equals principal $\times$ interest rate $\times$ period of time. For example, the interest on a $10,000, 8% loan for 9 months is: $10,000 $\times$ 8% $\times$ 9/12 = $600.
2. equity ownership of an individual or other entity in a business or property expressed in percentage terms or in dollars. For example, if an investor company owns 50,000 shares of the investee company's 150,000 outstanding shares, the investor has a 33½% ownership *interest*.

**INTEREST COVERAGE RATIO** ratio that equals income before interest and taxes, divided by interest; also called *times-interest-earned ratio*. The ratio reveals the number of times interest is covered by earnings. A potential creditor would like to see a high ratio because it indicates that the company is able to meet its interest obligations with room to spare.

## INTEREST DEDUCTION

**Individual:** itemized interest deduction on Schedule A of Form 1040. Interest can be only for the taxpayer's own debt and not for that of another individual. The taxpayer can deduct interest on a home mortgage for the principal residence and, within limits, for a second residence. Interest on a margin account with a broker is also deductible to the extent it offsets investment income.

**Corporation:** interest expense for business purposes that is tax deductible. Prepaid interest, however, is not deductible in the year of payment but has to be allocated over the period to which the interest amounts relate, irrespective of whether the cash basis or accrual basis is used.

**INTEREST EXPENSE** current period cost of borrowing funds that is shown as a financial expense in the income statement. Assume that on 11/1/2014 a $6000, one-year, 10% note is taken out. An accrual for interest expense is needed on 12/31/2014 for $100 ($6000 × 10% × 2/12).

**INTEREST METHOD** manner of determining interest expense or interest revenue. The effective interest rate is multiplied by the carrying value of the related debt or receivable at the beginning of the accounting period. The method results in a constant rate of interest but different dollar amounts each period. It is a preferred method over the straight-line method to amortize bond discount or premium. The amount of amortization equals the difference between the debit to interest expense (effective interest rate × carrying value of bond at beginning of year) and the cash payment (nominal interest rate × face value). Assume that on 1/1/2014 a $500,000, 10% bond is issued at 94%. The effective interest rate is 12%. The computation on 12/31/2014 for the bond discount is:

| | |
|---|---|
| Interest expense (12% × $470,000) | $56,400 |
| Cash (10% × $500,000) | $50,000 |
| Bond discount (for difference) | $ 6,400 |

**INTEREST ON INVESTMENT** actual return earned or expected to be earned on a debt instrument. *See also* OPPORTUNITY COST.

**INTEREST RATE** rate, usually expressed as a percentage per annum charged on money borrowed or lent. The interest rate may be variable or fixed. *See also* VARIABLE RATE LOAN.

The various types of interest rates are:

(1) *prime (interest) rate*: rate charged on business loans to the most credit-worthy customers by the nation's leading banks. The prime rate fluctuates with changing supply and demand relationships for short-term funds.

(2) *nominal* or *stated interest rate*: predetermined loan rate. The stated interest rate often differs from the effective interest rate. If the interest is paid when a loan matures, the actual rate of interest paid is equal to the stated interest rate. However, if the interest is paid in advance, it is deducted from the loan, so that the borrower actually receives

less money than requested, which will raise the interest rate above the stated rate. The actual rate thus paid is called the EFFECTIVE INTEREST RATE, or YIELD. It is computed by dividing the dollar interest paid by the amount of loan proceeds available to the borrower. For example, for a $1,000 loan with an annual interest of 10% with a provision of interest paid in advance, the effective rate is 11.11% [$100/($1,000 minus $100) = $100/$900]. In bonds the BOND YIELD usually differs from the nominal (coupon) interest rate.

(3) *discount rate*: rate the Federal Reserve charges member banks for loans. It is also the interest rate used in determining the present value of future cash flows. *See also* DISCOUNT RATE.

**INTEREST RATE FUTURES** contracts where the holder agrees to take delivery of a given amount of the related debt security at a later date (usually no more than three years). Futures may be in Treasury bills and notes, certificates of deposit, commercial paper, or GNMA certificates, etc. Interest rate futures are stated as a percentage of the par value of the applicable debt security. The value of interest rate futures contracts is directly tied to interest rates. For example, as interest rates decrease, the value of the contract increases. As the price or quote of the contract goes up, the purchaser of the contract has the gain, while the seller loses. A change of one basis point in interest rates causes a price change. Those who trade in interest rate futures do not usually take possession of the financial instrument. In essence, the contract is used either to hedge or to speculate on future interest rates and security prices. For example, a pension fund manager might use interest rate futures to hedge the bond portfolio position. Speculators find financial futures attractive because of their potentially large return on a small investment due to the low deposit requirement. However, significant risk exists.

**INTEREST RATE RISK** possibility that the value of an asset will change adversely as interest rates change. For example, when market interest rates rise, fixed-income bond prices fall.

**INTERGOVERNMENTAL REVENUE** revenue received from other governmental agencies and municipalities. An example is grants.

**INTERIM AUDIT**
   1. part of an audit carried out while the accounting period of the full audit is still in process. During interim audit work periods, the work scheduled may be confirmations, inventory observation, or other audit steps that will be concluded during the final phase of the annual audit.
   2. audit of an interim period (e.g., of quarterly statements).

**INTERIM FINANCIAL STATEMENT** statement issued for an accounting period of less than one year, such as quarterly or monthly. Interim financial statements should be based on the accounting principles employed in the previous year's annual report unless a change has been adopted in the current year. Interim financial statements are typically unaudited. Footnote disclosure is given of seasonality effects. If a fourth quarter is not presented, any significant adjustments to it must be commented upon in the annual report.

**INTERIM REPORT** *see* INTERIM FINANCIAL STATEMENT.

**INTERNAL AUDIT** auditing procedures and techniques conducted by INTERNAL AUDITORS primarily concentrating on adherence to management policies, existence of proper internal controls, uncovering misappropriation of funds (i.e., fraud), existence of proper record keeping, and effective operations of the business.

**INTERNAL AUDITOR** employee of the organization who is conducting an internal audit. The internal auditor works independently of the accounting and other departments and is concerned with financial and/or operational activities of the organization. The internal auditor attempts to assure the accuracy of business records, uncover internal control problems, and identify operational difficulties. The internal auditor's opinion on the company's financial records does not have the same acceptance as that of a CPA doing the same work. *See also* EXTERNAL AUDITOR.

**INTERNAL AUDITOR, THE** bimonthly publication of the INSTITUTE OF INTERNAL AUDITORS (IIA). Readership includes internal auditors, controllers, treasurers, CPAs, EDP auditors, managers, and financial managers. Subject matter includes internal auditing, internal control, information systems auditing, professional ethics, and financial management.

**INTERNAL CHECK** accounting procedure or physical control to safeguard assets against loss due to fraud or other irregularities. Internal check is an element of INTERNAL CONTROL. Weak internal check mechanisms mandate a greater degree of auditing procedures. An example of internal control is segregating the record keeping for an asset and its physical custody, such as in the case with inventory and cash. No one individual should have complete control over a transaction from beginning to end. Internal checks make it difficult for an employee to steal cash or other assets and concurrently cover up by entering corresponding amounts in the accounts. An example of internal check is the establishment of input and output controls within a data processing department. A group or person has the responsibility of checking control totals provided by the user department with those generated during the processing of the data. Examples of physical controls are guards and gates to restrict access.

**INTERNAL CONTROL** plan of organization and all the methods and measures used by a business to monitor assets, prevent fraud, minimize errors, verify the correctness and reliability of accounting data, promote operational efficiency, and ensure that established managerial policies are followed. Internal control extends to functions beyond the accounting and financial departments. Accounting controls encompass safeguarding assets and the accuracy of financial records. They are designed to give assurance that transactions are properly authorized and are recorded to allow for financial statement preparation in accordance with GAAP. Further, accounting controls deal with maintaining accountability for assets, proper authorization to access assets, and periodic reconciliations between recorded assets on the books and the physical assets that exist. Administrative or managerial controls deal with operational efficiency, adherence to managerial policies, and management's authorization of transactions. Examples are quality control and employee performance reports. Accounting and administrative controls are not mutually exclusive since some procedures and records falling under accounting control may also be used for administrative control. An essential ingredient in maintaining internal control is the internal audit function. The CPA reports on the adequacy of existing controls within the entity. The external auditor must carefully evaluate the internal control system as a basis to determine the degree of audit procedures necessary in the circumstances.

**INTERNAL CONTROL OVER FINANCIAL REPORTING** a process designed and maintained by management to provide reasonable assurance regarding the reliability of financial reporting and the preparation of the financial statements for external purposes in accordance with United States GAAP.

**INTERNAL DOCUMENT** record made up and kept *within* the entity in connection with its accounting records. It does not go to or come from external parties. Examples are employee time sheets, employee W-2s, inventory receiving reports, and duplicate purchase invoices. The auditor puts much more reliance on external documents than internal ones since they are derived from outside independent parties. Internal documents do not serve as very reliable evidence in the CPA's examination of a client's records. *See also* EXTERNAL DOCUMENT.

**INTERNAL FAILURE COSTS** category of QUALITY COSTS incurred because products and services fail to conform to requirements prior to external sale, such as scrap and rework; a cost of nonconformance.

**INTERNAL RATE OF RETURN (IRR)** rate earned on a proposal. It is the rate of interest that equates the initial investment ($I$) with the present value ($PV$) of future cash inflows. That is, at IRR, $I = PV$, or $NPV$ (net present value) = 0. Under the internal rate of return method, the decision rule is: accept the project if IRR exceeds the cost of capital; otherwise, reject the proposal.

For example, consider the following data:

| | |
|---|---|
| Initial investment | $16,200 |
| Estimated life | 10 years |
| Annual cash inflows | $ 3,000 |
| Cost of capital (minimum required of return) | 10% |

Set up the following equality ($I = PV$):

$$\$16,200 = \$3,000 \times PV$$

Then $PV = \$16,200/\$3,000 = 5.400$, which stands somewhere between 12% and 14% in the 10-year line of table 4 in the back of the book. Because the investment's IRR (13.15%) is greater than the cost of capital (10%), the investment should be accepted.

The IRR method is easy to use as long as cash inflows are even from year to year. Where cash flows are uneven, the IRR can be determined by using Excel.

Excel has a function IRR(*values, guess*). Excel considers negative numbers as cash outflows such as the initial investment, and positive numbers as cash inflows. Many financial calculators have similar features. Suppose you want to calculate the IRR of a $12,950 investment (the value "–12,950" entered in year 0, followed by 10 monthly cash inflows of $3,000). Using a guess of 12% (the value of 0.12), which is in effect the cost of capital, your formula would be @IRR(values, 0.12) and Excel would return 19.15%, as shown below.

| Year 0 | 1 | 2 | 3 | 4 | 5 | 6 | 7 | 8 | 9 | 10 |
|---|---|---|---|---|---|---|---|---|---|---|
| –12,950 | 3,000 | 3,000 | 3,000 | 3,000 | 3,000 | 3,000 | 3,000 | 3,000 | 3,000 | 3,000 |

IRR = 19.15%

An advantage of the IRR method is that it considers the TIME VALUE OF MONEY and is therefore more exact and realistic than ACCOUNTING RATE OF RETURN (ARR). Disadvantages are: (1) it fails to recognize the varying size of investment in competing projects and their respective dollar profitabilities, and (2) in limited cases, where there are multiple reversals in the cash-flow streams, the project could yield more than one internal rate of return.

**INTERNAL REPORTING** financial data or other information accumulated by one individual to be communicated to another within the business entity. The information assists others in the managerial decision-making process. Examples are expense reports, capital budgeting analysis, and other reports designed to guide management rather than inform outsiders.

**INTERNAL REVENUE CODE** federal tax law of the United States that comprises the rules and regulations to be followed by taxpayers. The Internal Revenue Code of 1954 is being followed, including subsequent amendments and revisions.

**INTERNAL REVENUE SERVICE (IRS)** (www.irs.gov) branch of the federal government in charge of collecting most types of taxes, such as personal, corporate, gift, estate, and excise. Some taxes are collected by other agencies, such as custom duties, tobacco, and alcohol. The IRS administers tax rules and regulations, and investigates tax improprieties.

Criminal prosecution may be made by the IRS for tax fraud through the U.S. Tax Court. Examinations of tax returns can involve: (1) simple matters that are resolved by mail; (2) IRS office examination concentrating on additional verification by the taxpayer of selected items; or (3) field examination at the taxpayer's office or representative's office. A field audit is typically broader in scope than an office audit, covering many items on a tax return, and often for more than one year.

**INTERNAL SERVICE FUND** in GOVERNMENT ACCOUNTING, fund used to account for goods or services given to one department by another on a cost reimbursement basis. The fund is profit and loss oriented and hence follows accrual accounting.

**INTERNATIONAL ACCOUNTING STANDARDS (IAS)** a set of international accounting and reporting standards that will help to harmonize company financial information, improve the transparency of accounting, and ensure that investors receive more accurate and consistent reports. Statements of International Accounting Standards issued by the Board of the INTERNATIONAL ACCOUNTING STANDARDS COMMITTEE (IASC) between 1973 and 2001 are designated International Accounting Standards. The INTERNATIONAL ACCOUNTING STANDARDS BOARD (IASB) announed in April 2001 that its accounting standards would be designated INTERNATIONAL FINANCIAL REPORTING STANDARDS (IFRS). Also in April 2001, the IASB announced that it would adopt all of the International Accounting Standards issued by the IASC.

**INTERNATIONAL ACCOUNTING STANDARDS BOARD (IASB)** (www.iasb.org) an independent regulatory body, based in the United Kingdom, that aims to develop a single set of global accounting standards. Board members come from nine countries and have a variety of functional backgrounds. The Board is committed to developing, in the public interest, a single set of high-quality, understandable, and enforceable global accounting standards that require transparent and comparable information in general-purpose financial statements. In addition, the Board cooperates with national accounting standard-setters to achieve convergence in accounting standards around the world.

**INTERNATIONAL ACCOUNTING STANDARDS COMMITTEE (IASC)** group consisting of members from influential accounting bodies in the U.S., England, West Germany, France, Canada, Japan, and other countries. The organization proposes internationally accepted accounting standards and issues discussion papers, drafts, and formal statements on important accounting issues. A major purpose of the committee is to aid comparability of financial reporting among countries.

**INTERNATIONAL AUDITING PRACTICES COMMITTEE (IAPC)** panel of the INTERNATIONAL FEDERATION OF ACCOUNTANTS (IFA) that gives guidance to auditors in various countries.

**INTERNATIONAL BANK FOR RECONSTRUCTION AND DEVELOPMENT (IBRD)** organization that assists less-developed countries in strengthening their economies; also called *World Bank*. The IBRD makes loans to countries or firms for such purposes as roads, irrigation projects, and electric-generating plants.

**INTERNATIONAL CONGRESS OF ACCOUNTANTS (ICA)** body whose aim is to present and resolve international accounting and auditing issues to encourage uniformity, congruity, and international cooperation. This congress meets every five years.

**INTERNATIONAL FEDERATION OF ACCOUNTANTS (IFA)** organization of international representatives whose purpose is to develop and enhance concordance with respect to standards and accounting practices on a worldwide basis. It was formed in 1977.

**INTERNATIONAL FINANCIAL REPORTING STANDARDS (IFRS)** standards and interpretations adopted by the International Accounting Standards Board (IASB). Many of the standards forming part of IFRS are known by the older name of International Accounting Standards (IAS). IFRS are sometimes confused with IAS, which are the older standards that IFRS replaced. IAS was issued from 1973 to 2000. The implementation in 2005 of IFRS as the reporting language for all listed companies in the European Union and for many others around the world has been one of the biggest revolutions in the accounting world for a generation. The Financial Accounting Standards Board (FASB) and International Accounting Standards Board (IASB) are committed to crafting one set of accounting standards. The goal of the convergence project is to unify accounting standards, which in turn should improve comparability of financial statements across national jurisdictions.

**INTERNATIONAL MONETARY FUND (IMF)** organization created at the close of World War II to supervise the international financial system, to lend official reserves to nations with temporary payments deficits, and to decide when exchange rate adjustments are needed to correct chronic payments deficits.

**INTERNET** a worldwide network of computers that utilizes TCP/IP technology for communication. The Internet is decentralized in design, and no one organization owns it. Most individuals get access to the Internet through a commercial Internet Service Provider (ISP).

**INTERPERIOD INCOME TAX ALLOCATION** temporary difference between years in which a transaction affects taxable income and accounting (book) income. Temporary differences originate in one period and subsequently reverse in another. The differences result from four types of transactions, as follows: (1) income included in taxable income after being included in book income (e.g., installment sale); (2) expenses deducted for taxable income subsequent to accounting income (e.g., warranty expense is deducted for book purposes in the year of sale but for tax purposes when paid); (3) income recognized for tax purposes prior to being included for accounting purposes (e.g., rental received in advance); and (4) expenses subtracted for taxable income before being deducted for accounting purposes (e.g., accelerated depreciation method for tax and straight-line depreciation for books). *See also* INTRAPERIOD TAX ALLOCATION; PERMANENT DIFFERENCE.

**INTERPOLATION** process used to estimate an unknown value between two known values by utilizing a common mathematical relation (e.g., proportion, function, linear, or logarithmic). Interpolation is commonly needed when consulting present value tables in which a present value interest factor is desired for a given period and unlisted interest rate. One would use the two closest listed interest rates, above and below the given interest rate, to estimate the present value factor needed for a given computation. Interpolation is more than likely used to find the INTERNAL RATE OF RETURN on an investment project.

**INTERPRETATION** opinion regarding a set of facts. A degree of subjectivity is involved on the part of the individual, based on his or her experience, personality, and biases. For example, after performing a detailed analysis of the financial statements of a company, two financial analysts may differ in their perceptions of what the market price of the company's stock should be.

**INTRANET** private network used within the company. An intranet serves the internal needs of the business entity. Intranet users are able to access the Internet, but firewalls keep outsiders from accessing confidential data. It makes use of the infrastructure and standards of the Internet and the Web. Intranets use low-cost Internet tools, are easy to install, and offer flexibility. Intranets have already been established by virtually all Fortune 500 companies and many other organizations.

**INTRAPERIOD TAX ALLOCATION** distribution of tax for the *current year* in different parts of the financial statements. For example, tax expense is shown on income before tax, cumulative effect of a change in principle net of tax, extraordinary items net of tax, and prior period adjustments net of tax. *See also* INTERPERIOD INCOME TAX ALLOCATION.

**INVENTORIABLE COST** *see* PRODUCT COST.

**INVENTORY** merchandise or supplies on hand or in transit at a particular point in time. The three types of inventory for a manufacturing company are raw materials, work-in-process, and finished goods. Included in inventory are (1) goods in transit for which title has been received and (2) goods out on consignment. Inventory is recorded in the accounting records typically at the lower of cost or market value. An inventory count usually occurs at year-end to assure that the physical quantity equals the quantity per books. At the end of the accounting period, beginning and ending inventories are presented in the income statement in the cost-of-goods-sold calculation, and ending inventory is shown in the balance sheet under current assets.

**INVENTORY CONTROL** monitoring the supplies, raw materials, work-in-process, and finished goods by various accounting and reporting methods. Some controls are the maintenance of detailed stock records showing receipts and issuances; inventory ledger showing quantities and dollars; and written policies regarding purchasing, receiving, inspection, and handling. Periodic inventory counts should occur to verify that the inventory amounts per books physically exist. A good system of inventory control assists in reducing inventory ordering and carrying costs. *See also* ABC METHOD.

**INVENTORY MODELS** quantitative models designed to control inventory costs by determining the optimal time to place an order (or begin production) and the optimal order quantity (or production run). The timing of an order can be periodic (placing an order every X days) or perpetual (placing an order whenever the inventory declines to X units).

**INVENTORY OBSERVATION** observation by an auditor, as part of the examination, of the taking of a company's physical inventory by the client staff. The auditor also checks on a sample basis the count arrived at by the employees to assure it is being done accurately. A review is also made of the client's written policies regarding the inventory counting process.

**INVENTORY PROFIT** unrealized profit derived from holding inventory during a price rise. One measure of inventory profit is the difference between the original cost and the higher current replacement cost. Another measure is the increased value arising from the increase in the CONSUMER PRICE INDEX (CPI) since the acquisition date. Assume that on 1/1/2014, inventory was bought for $50,000. On 12/31/2014, the replacement cost is $54,000. The inventory profit is $4,000.

**INVENTORY RESERVE**
1. appropriation of retained earnings to reflect *future* declines in price of inventory.
2. archaic term relating to the allowance account to reduce inventory from cost to market value in applying the lower of cost or market value rule. The reserve amount is usually calculated from inventory sheets for the specific items.
3. reserve for temporary liquidation of the LAST-IN, FIRST-OUT (LIFO) base, used in interim reporting; the LIFO base that is expected to be replenished by year end. Assume that the original cost of the liquidated LIFO base is $10,000 and its replacement cost is $12,000. The entry at the interim period is to debit cost of sales $12,000, credit inventory $10,000, and reserve for liquidation of LIFO base $2,000.

**INVENTORY STATUS FILE** file indicating how much inventory is on hand or on order.

**INVENTORY TURNOVER** equation that equals the cost of goods sold divided by the average inventory. Average inventory equals beginning inventory plus ending inventory divided by 2. A low turnover rate may point to overstocking, obsolescence, or deficiencies in the product line or marketing effort. However, in some instances a low rate may be appropriate, such as where higher inventory levels occur in anticipation of rapidly rising prices or shortages. A high turnover rate may indicate inadequate inventory levels, which may lead to a loss in business. Assume cost of sales is $70,000, beginning inventory is $10,000, and ending inventory is $9,000. The inventory turnover equals 7.37 times ($70,000/$9,500). It should be noted that some compilers of industry data (e.g., Dun & Bradstreet) use sales as the numerator instead of cost of sales. Cost of sales yields a more realistic turnover figure, but it is often necessary to use sales for purposes of comparative analysis.

**INVENTORY VALUATION** determination of the cost assigned to raw materials inventory, work-in-process, finished goods, and any other inventory item. Various methods are allowed in valuing inventory including LAST-IN, FIRST-OUT (LIFO), FIRST-IN, FIRST-OUT (FIFO), and WEIGHTED AVERAGE. Inventory is valued at the lower of cost or market value applied on either an item-by-item basis, a category basis, or a total basis.

**INVESTING ACTIVITIES** business activities that involve the acquiring and selling of long-term assets, the acquiring and selling of equity or debt securities other than trading, and the making and collecting of loans.

**INVESTMENT**
1. *see* CAPITAL ASSET.
2. expenditure to acquire property, equipment, and other capital assets that produce revenue.
3. securities of other companies held for the long term, called *long-term investments* and shown in the noncurrent asset section of the balance sheet.
4. securities of other companies held for a very short term (short-term investments). They are shown as a MARKETABLE SECURITY in the current asset section of the balance sheet.

**INVESTMENT ADVISOR** financial professional who specializes in making portfolio recommendations for clients. The advisor recommends a mix of investments (i.e., stocks, bonds, real estate) based on the particular needs of the client (i.e., tax rate, risk preferences, liquidity requirements). The investment advisor may also recommend specific companies in which to invest.

**INVESTMENT BANKER** intermediary between an issuer of new securities and the investor. The investment banker buys new securities and then sells them to the public at a higher price, earning a profit on the spread. Depending on the arrangement with the issuing company, the investment banker may perform the functions of underwriting, distribution of securities, and advice and counsel.

**INVESTMENT CAPITAL** *see* CAPITAL ASSET.

**INVESTMENT CENTER** responsibility center within an organization that has control over revenue, cost, and investment funds. It is a profit center whose performance is evaluated on the basis of the return earned on invested capital. The corporate headquarters or division in a large decentralized organization would be an example of an investment center. RETURN ON INVESTMENT and RESIDUAL INCOME are two key performance measures of an investment center.

**INVESTMENT SOFTWARE** computer program that tracks investments in shares, cost, and revenue. Some investment software includes price and dividend histories of securities. Comparisons can be made with major market indicators. Automatic valuation of securities, including current value, unrealized gain or loss, and daily price change, can be made. Tax ramifications of investment decisions can be analyzed by some packages.

**INVESTMENT TURNOVER** return earned on capital invested in a business. It equals:

$$\frac{\text{Sales}}{\text{Net Worth} + \text{Long-Term Liabilities}}$$

A higher ratio indicates good use of the funds placed into the business.

**INVOICE** bill prepared by a seller of goods or services and submitted to the buyer. The invoice describes such items as date, customer, vendor, quantities, prices, freight, and credit terms of a transaction.

**INVOLUNTARY BANKRUPTCY** financial failure that is legally and formally declared by petition of the debtor's creditors, and not by the debtor. *See also* CHAPTER 11; CHAPTER 7.

**INVOLUNTARY CONVERSION** sudden loss of an asset that does not occur in the ordinary course of business, such as destruction by fire or condemnation by a governmental agency. The difference between the cash received from the insurance company and the carrying value of the destroyed asset (or portion thereof) represents a loss or gain for financial reporting purposes. Under the INTERNAL REVENUE CODE, the loss on an involuntary conversion is recognized, but the gain is reflected only to the degree that the proceeds are *not* reinvested in similar property within two or three years subsequent to the conversion.

**IP (INTERNET PROTOCOL) ADDRESS** consists of a series of four numbers of up to three digits, separated by decimal points. All computers and devices connected to the Internet have an IP (Internet Protocol) address.

**IRRELEVANT COSTS** costs that may be either sunk costs or costs that do not differ among alternatives.

**iSHARES** index funds that trade like stocks on stock markets. Each share represents a proportion of ownership in each stock that makes up an index. iShares are a great way for smaller investors to get the diversification of 50 or more companies without having to buy each individual stock.

**ISO** 9000 certification standards developed by the International Organization for Standardization (ISO) that serve as a basis for quality standards for global manufacturers.

**ISSUED CAPITAL STOCK** authorized shares that have been issued for cash, services, or other property. Included in issued shares are TREASURY SHARES. *See also* OUTSTANDING CAPITAL STOCK.

**ISSUERS** publicly traded entities that are subject to the rules of the PUBLIC COMPANY ACCOUNTING OVERSIGHT BOARD (PCAOB).

**ITEMIZED DEDUCTION** subtraction from adjusted gross income for individual taxpayers. Examples of allowable deductions are mortgage interest, certain casualty losses, medical expenses, contributions, real estate taxes, and state and local government income taxes.

# J

**JAVA** a highly popular, fast, secure, and reliable computer programming language that is used everywhere from computers to game consoles to cell phones to the INTERNET.

**JOB ORDER** customer order for a specific number of specially designed, made-to-order products.

**JOB ORDER COSTING** accumulation of costs by specific jobs, contracts, or orders. This costing method is appropriate when direct costs can be identified with specific units of production. Job order costing is widely used by custom manufacturers such as printing, aircraft, construction, auto repair, and professional services. Job order costing keeps track of costs as follows: (1) direct material and direct labor are traced to a particular job; (2) costs not directly traceable—factory overhead—are applied to individual jobs, using a *predetermined overhead rate*. The overhead rate is equal to the budgeted annual overhead divided by the budgeted annual activity units (direct labor-hours, machine-hours, etc.). At the end of the year, the difference between actual overhead and overhead applied is closed to cost of goods sold, if there is an immaterial difference. On the other hand, if a material difference exists, work-in-process, finished goods, and cost of goods sold are adjusted on a proportionate basis based on units or dollars at year-end for the deviation between actual and applied overhead.

**JOB (ORDER) COST SHEET** subsidiary record for work-in-process inventory under a job order production system. A separate cost sheet is kept for each identifiable job, accumulating the direct materials, direct labor, and factory overhead assigned to that job as it moves through production. The form varies according to the needs of the company. A sample job cost sheet follows:

## JOB COST SHEET

Job No. _____

For Stock _____ Customer _____

Product _____ Date Started _____ Date Completed _____

| Direct Material | | | Direct Labor | | | Overhead | |
|---|---|---|---|---|---|---|---|
| Date | Reference | Amount | Date | Reference | Amount | Date | Amount |
| | (Stores Requisition Number) | | | (Work Ticket Number) | | | (Based on Predetermined Overhead Rate) |

Summary of Costs

| | |
|---|---|
| Direct Materials | x x |
| Direct Labor | x x |
| Factory Overhead Applied _____ | x x |
| Total | x x x |

**JOB PROJECT-PERFORMANCE COST VARIANCE** used in controlling job projects, the difference between the actual cost of work performed (CWP) and the budgeted CWP. This variance may further be divided into price and efficiency variances. It measures cost overruns or underruns.

**JOB PROJECT-SCHEDULE COST VARIANCE** difference between the budgeted cost of work performed and the budgeted cost of work scheduled. It measures the extent to which the project is ahead of or behind schedule.

**JOINT AND SEVERAL LIABILITY** legal concept in which two or more persons have an obligation that can be enforced against them by joint action, against all members, and against themselves as individuals, hence several liability or responsibility.

**JOINT COSTS** common manufacturing costs incurred prior to the point, referred to as the SPLIT-OFF POINT, where JOINT PRODUCTS are identified as individual products. There are several methods of allocating joint costs to the joint products, including sales value and volume. *See also* COMMON COST; SELL-OR-PROCESS-FURTHER DECISION.

**JOINT PRODUCTS** items that have a relatively significant sales value when two or more types are produced simultaneously from the same input by a joint process. For example, gasoline, fuel oil, kerosene, and paraffin are the joint products produced from crude oil. *See also* SELL-OR-PROCESS FURTHER DECISION.

**JOINT RETURN** income tax return that effectively provides that income earned by a husband and wife will be treated as though it had been earned by both equally. This is allowed even though one spouse may not have income or deductions. A joint return usually provides a favorable tax effect compared to the filing of a non-joint return.

**JOINT STOCK COMPANY** assemblage of individuals formed to start and operate a business organization. A joint stock company generally shares the same characteristics as a corporation, but it does not provide limited liability, and in many states it lacks formal and official authorization. Once popular because of the ease of formation under the common law, joint stock companies are not seen as much today because it has become easier to form limited liability corporations under state authorization.

**JOINT TENANCY** two or more persons to whom real or personal property is deeded or who together own an undivided interest in such property as a whole. Upon the death of one of the joint tenants, the deceased's property goes to the survivor without becoming an element of the estate of the deceased; also called *joint tenancy with right of survivorship.*

**JOINT TENANCY WITH RIGHT OF SURVIVORSHIP** *see* JOINT TENANCY.

**JOINT VENTURE** joining together of two or more business entities or persons in order to undertake a specific business venture. A joint venture is not a continuing relationship such as a partnership but may be treated as a partnership for income tax purposes.

**JOURNAL** book or place where business transactions are first recorded in chronological order before being posted to the general ledger accounts. The general journal is used to record miscellaneous transactions that do not fit into SPECIAL JOURNALS (sales, purchases, cash receipts, cash disbursements, and payroll journals). A general journal will help link together debit and credit parts of transactions.

**JOURNAL ENTRY** record of the accounting information for a business transaction. The entry is made in a journal and then posted to the ledger. The journal entry has a date, account(s) debited, and account(s) credited. If there is more than one debit or credit, it is referred to as a compound entry. Total debits must equal total credits. The journal entry is accompanied by a short explanation.

**JOURNAL OF GOVERNMENT FINANCIAL MANAGEMENT** formerly, *Government Accountants Journal*, quarterly journal of the Association of Government Accountants (AGA). Subject matter includes all aspects of accounting and financial management relating to government.

**JOURNALIZE** to make an entry for a transaction in the JOURNAL (book of original entry). For example, if rent is paid with cash, this transaction would be entered in the journal. Rent Expense is debited and Cash is credited. Transactions are entered on a daily basis in chronological order. Debits and credits are listed along with their appropriate explanations. Thus the journal reflects in one place all information about a transaction.

*JOURNAL OF ACCOUNTANCY* monthly publication of the AMERICAN INSTITUTE OF CERTIFIED PUBLIC ACCOUNTANTS (AICPA) (www.aicpa.org). Its readership includes practicing CPAs, controllers, treasurers, private accountants, and academicians. All aspects of accounting appear in the *Journal of Accountancy* including auditing, management advisory services, financial accounting applications, international accounting, computer applications, professional ethics, and taxation.

*JOURNAL OF ACCOUNTING RESEARCH* semiannual publication of the Graduate School of Business of the University of Chicago. It is one of the leading academic journals. It includes an annual supplement containing papers presented at conferences held at the university. Subject matter concentrates on empirical, analytical, and experimental research in all areas of accounting.

**JOURNAL VOUCHER** one that documents and authorizes a business transaction. It will lead to a journal entry in a journal.

**JUDGMENT**

1. accountant's opinion regarding a set of facts or evidence. Besides interpreting the meaning of the situation, the accountant must also determine its perceived implications. For example, the degree of audit testing required in a given situation depends on the auditor's judgment of the quality of the internal control system.
2. court order to pay money.

**JUDGMENT SAMPLE** determination by an auditor, based on personal experience and familiarity with the client, of the number of items, as well as the particular items, to be examined in a population. This function allows the accountant to maintain objectivity and thoroughness in testing the sampled items for accuracy. A judgmental sample may be appropriate when only a specific area within the universe is under auditor scrutiny or timely information is required. The sampling is *not* done on a random basis. Furthermore, there is no determination of a sampling error, nor any statistical conclusions about precision or confidence levels. *See also* RANDOM SAMPLE.

**JUNIOR ACCOUNTANT** public accounting firm employee who has duties and responsibilities associated with the early years of professional practice and works under the close supervision of a senior accountant.

**JUNIOR STOCK** shares, issued to employees, that are usually subordinate to regular common stock. The subordination may apply to voting rights, dividends, or liquidation rights. Junior stock may be converted to common stock when the employees meet certain performance requirements.

**JUST-IN-TIME (JIT)** the idea that inventory is manufactured (or acquired) only as the need for it arises or in time to be sold (or used). A major goal is to cut down on inventory investment.

**JUST-IN-TIME (JIT) MANUFACTURING** a "demand-pull" approach that produces only what is necessary to satisfy the demand of the ensuing manufacturing process.

**JUST-IN-TIME (JIT) PRODUCTION SYSTEMS** demand pull system. Purchases of materials and output depend on actual customer demand. Inventories are reduced greatly or eliminated, a few suppliers must reliably deliver small amounts on a frequent basis, plant layouts must become more efficient, a zero defects policy is established, and workers must be able to perform multiple tasks, including continuous monitoring of quality.

# K

**KAIZEN** Japanese term for CONTINUOUS IMPROVEMENT. Kaizen budgeting incorporates expectations for continuous improvement into budgetary estimates. Kaizen costing determines target cost reductions for a period, such as a month. Thus, variances are the differences between actual and targeted cost reduction. The objective is to reduce actual costs below standard costs. The cost-reduction activities associated with the Kaizen approach minimize costs throughout the entire product life cycle. Therefore, it has the advantage of being closely related to the entity's profit-planning procedures. *See* TARGET COST.

**KANBAN** Japanese word for *card* or *ticket*. It is essentially a Japanese information system for coordinating production orders and withdrawals from in-process inventory to realize just-in-time production. Originated from the use of cards to indicate a work station's need for additional parts. A basic kanban system includes a *withdrawal kanban* that states the quantity that a later process should withdraw from its predecessor, a *production kanban* that states the output of the preceding process, and a *vendor kanban* that tells a vendor what, how much, where, and when to deliver.

**KEOGH PLAN** tax-deferred retirement plan for self-employed individuals meeting certain requirements; also called *H.R. 10 plan.* Self-employed individuals can contribute to their Keogh plan up to 25% of earnings, subject to annual limitations that are periodically adjusted for inflation.

**KEYLOGGER** a software used for surveillance. It records every keystroke of a user to a log file. Keylogger may be used by an organization to ensure employees are performing only authorized tasks. Keyloggers can sometimes be embedded in spyware, allowing an organization's information to be compromised.

**KIDDIE TAX** a tax imposed on a child's unearned income (e.g., interest and dividends) in excess of an amount that is determined annually (based on inflation) by the Department of the Treasury. The Kiddie Tax is imposed at the parents' highest rate of tax. The Kiddie Tax is only applicable if a child (1) is under the age of 18, or (2) is age 18 or 19 to 23 and is a full-time student who has earned income not in excess of one-half of his or her support.

**KITING** illegal practice in which a cash shortage is concealed by exploiting the time required for a check to clear. Assume XYZ Company has its home office on Long Island and a branch office in Chicago. The company has accounts with Long Island and Chicago banks. There is a shortage of $50,000 in the Long Island bank. The corporate bookkeeper covers this shortage by drawing a check on December 30, 2014, on the Chicago bank and depositing it to the account in the Long Island bank on the same day. The check is not entered as a cash disbursement in the current year. Rather, the transaction is recorded on January 2, 2015, and the check clears the Chicago bank on January 3, 2015. Unless the discrepancy is found, the Long Island bank balance and book balance reconcile on December 31, 2014, but do not reconcile on January 2, 2015. The auditor can uncover this irregularity by examining bank transfers prior to and after year-end to ascertain that the entry on the books is recorded in the same accounting period as the check is dated and the deposit in the Long Island bank is made. A schedule of interbank transfers should be made showing transfers of funds between bank accounts for several days before and after year-end. Included in the schedule are the dates of withdrawal and deposit per books and per bank. The CPA should trace transfer checks in transit at the balance sheet date to outstanding checks and deposits in transit in the respective bank reconciliations. The accountant should verify the deposit date of all transfers by tracing the deposit to the cutoff bank statement for the receiving bank.

**KNOWLEDGE MANAGEMENT (KM)** the process of connecting people to people and people to information to create a competitive advantage.

# L

**LABOR EFFICIENCY VARIANCE** difference between the amount of labor time that should have been used and the labor that was actually used, multiplied by the standard rate. For example, assume that the standard cost of direct labor per unit of product A is 2.5 hours $\times$ $14 = $35. Assume further that during the month of March the company recorded 4,500 hours of direct labor time. The actual cost of this labor time was $64,800, or an average of $14.40 per hour. The company produced 2,000 units of product A during the month. The labor efficiency variance is $(4,500 - 5,000) \times \$14 = \$7,000$, where 5,000 hours = 2.5 hours $\times$ 2,000 units of output. This variance is favorable since the actual hours used are less than the standard hours allowed. This may be the result of efficient use of labor time due to automation or the use of improved production methods.

**LABOR INTENSIVE** industry or company where labor costs are more important than capital costs. Labor intensive companies generally have greater earnings stability than CAPITAL INTENSIVE ones, because the former have a higher percentage of variable costs, while the latter have a higher percentage of fixed costs. However, labor intensive firms may experience difficulty during inflation due to employee discontent resulting from the decline in real earnings. But higher wage rates would be passed on in higher prices.

**LABOR LAW** legislation enacted to protect workers' rights and the working environment. Significant labor laws were enacted with the *National Labor Relations Act of 1935 (Wagner Act)* and the *Taft Hartley Act of 1948.*

**LABOR RATE (PRICE) VARIANCE** any deviation from standard in the average hourly rate paid to workers:

$$\text{Labor Rate Variance} = (\text{Actual Rate} - \text{Standard Rate}) \times \text{Actual Hours of Labor Used}$$

For example, assume that the standard cost of direct labor per unit of product A is 2.5 hours $\times$ $14 = $35. Assume further that during the month of March the company recorded 4,500 hours of direct labor time. The actual cost of this labor time was $64,800, or an average of $14.40 per hour. The company produced 2,000 units of product A during the month. The labor rate variance is $(\$14.40 - \$14.00) \times 4,500$ hours = $1,800, which is unfavorable since the actual hourly rate exceeded the standard rate. This may be the result of unavoidable increases in labor rates, or it may reflect excessive labor costs due to use of higher skilled labor commanding higher wages.

**LABOR STANDARD** efficiency standard that is often set via time and motion studies and laboratory experiments regarding the various labor operations needed to produce the finished good. The standard time

must incorporate allowances for normal loss of time due to rest periods, machine downtime, and fatigue. It may be computed as follows:

| | |
|---|---:|
| Basic labor time per unit (in hours) | 2.0 |
| Allowance for breaks, fatigue, and machine downtime | .4 |
| Allowance for rejects | .3 |
| Standard hours per unit | 2.7 |

**LABOR VARIANCE** difference between the actual costs and the standard costs of direct labor. Labor variance is divided into two specific
variances: LABOR RATE (PRICE) VARIANCE and LABOR EFFICIENCY
VARIANCE. This breakdown is needed from a control standpoint.

**LAGGARD INDUSTRY** one that lags behind the rest of the economy
in output, employment, and contributions to the gross national product
(GNP). A laggard industry in one nation may not be one in another
nation.

**LAGGING INDICATORS** series of indicators that follow or trail
behind aggregate economic activity. Six lagging indicators are currently published by the government: unemployment rate, business
expenditures, labor cost per unit, loans outstanding, bank interest
rates, and book value of manufacturing and trade inventories. *See also*
LEADING INDICATORS.

**LAND** real estate held for productive use or investment. Land is
recorded at the acquisition price plus incidental costs including real
estate commissions, attorney's fees, escrow fees, title and recording
fees, delinquent taxes paid by the buyer, surveying costs, draining, and
grading of the property.

The cost of knocking down an old building to clear the land to
construct a new building is charged to the land account. Amounts
received from selling materials salvaged from the old building reduces
the cost of the land.

Land is usually presented under the property, plant, and equipment
section of the balance sheet. However, land bought for investment purposes or as a future plant site is classified under investments. If land is
held by a real estate business for resale, it is shown as inventory.

Land is *not* subject to depreciation because it is not a wasting asset.

**LAND IMPROVEMENTS** items having limited lives, such as walk-
ways, driveways, fences, and parking lots. The land improvement
account is subject to depreciation over the estimated lives of the
improvements. It is a different account than land.

**LAPPING** concealing a shortage by delaying the recording of cash
receipts. For example, cash received from customer X is withheld by
the cashier, and a subsequent cash receipt from customer Y is entered
as a credit to X's account. Customer Y's account will not be credited
until a collection is received from customer Z. If the money taken by

the cashier is not replaced, there is an overstatement in total accounts receivable. However, by carefully shifting the overstatement from one customer to another the bookkeeper averts customer complaints when the monthly statements are received. Cashiers with access to the general accounting records have been known to transfer shortages to inventory or other accounts for temporary concealment. Lapping is possible when the bookkeeper receiving customer collections also records transactions to customer accounts. To prevent lapping, the accountant should prepare a control listing of cash receipts by a department not having access to the accounting records. But even without the control listing, it is difficult for the bookkeeper to have agreement between the detail of daily entries in the books and daily bank deposits. It should be noted that duplicate deposit tickets may be altered. The CPA should compare the duplicate copy with the original retained at the bank. In conclusion, the auditor should compare entries in the cash receipts journal and postings to customers' accounts to mailroom listings and daily deposit slips.

**LAPSE** termination or forfeiture of an item—for example, when coverage under an insurance contract expires because of nonrenewal.

**LAPSING SCHEDULE** specific accounting data regarding fixed assets. Included in the Schedule are the original purchase cost of each asset, additions to the assets, sales of the assets, accumulated depreciation, and depreciation expense. This type of worksheet aids in control over fixed assets by keeping detailed track of each fixed asset.

**LAST-IN, FIRST-OUT (LIFO)** inventory method in which it is assumed that goods are sold in the reverse order of their acquisition. Thus cost of sales is based upon the most recent costs. Ending inventory is based upon the costs of the earliest purchase made. During a period of inflation, net income is lower under LIFO than under FIRST IN, FIRST-OUT (FIFO) because current costs are being matched against revenue. However, the ending inventory figure in the balance sheet will be lower under LIFO than FIFO, because inventory is being stated in older dollars. A company can increase or decrease its earnings through the timing of inventory acquisitions. *See also* DOLLAR VALUE LIFO.

**LATEST FINISH TIME** in PROGRAM EVALUATION AND REVIEW TECHNIQUE (PERT), latest time at which an activity must be completed without holding up the complete project.

**LATEST START TIME** in PROGRAM EVALUATION AND REVIEW TECHNIQUE (PERT), latest time at which an activity must begin without holding up the complete project.

**LATEST TIME (LT)** in PROGRAM EVALUATION AND REVIEW TECHNIQUE (PERT), latest time at which an activity can be completed without extending the completion time of the project.

**LATTICE-BASED MODEL** also called *lattice model,* an option pricing mode model that divides time between now and the option's expiration into N discrete periods. *See also* BINOMIAL MODEL.

**LEADING INDICATORS** series of indicators that tend to predict future changes in economic activity; officially called *Composite Index of 11 Leading Indicators.* This series is published monthly by the U.S. Department of Commerce and includes average work week, average weekly initial claims, index of net business formation, new orders, and stock prices. The index of leading indicators, the components of which are adjusted for inflation, has an excellent track record of forecasting ups and downs in the business cycle. *See also* LAGGING INDICATORS.

**LEAD TIME** interval between placing an order and receiving delivery. For example, if it will take two weeks to receive a new delivery, the lead time is two weeks. *See also* REORDER POINT.

**LEARNING CURVE** chart line representing the efficiencies gained from experience. Basically, it is a curve describing the relationship between the consecutive number of units produced ($x$-axis) and the time per unit produced ($y$-axis). More specifically, it is based on the statistical findings that as the cumulative output doubles, the cumulative average labor input time required per unit will be reduced by some constant percentage, ranging between 10% and 40%. The curve is usually designated by its complement. For example, if the rate of reduction is 20%, the curve is referred to as an *80% learning curve.*

Applications of the learning curve theory include (1) pricing decisions, based on the estimates of expected costs; (2) requirements for scheduling labor; (3) capital budgeting decisions; and (4) setting incentive wage rates.

The following data illustrate the 80% learning curve relationship:

| Quantity (in Units) | | Time (in Hours) | |
|---|---|---|---|
| Per Lot | Cumulative | Total (Cumulative) | Average Time per Unit |
| 15 | 15 | 600 | 40.0 |
| 15 | 30 | 960 | 32.0 (40.0 × 0.8) |
| 30 | 60 | 1,536 | 25.6 (32.0 × 0.8) |
| 60 | 120 | 2,460 | 20.5 (25.6 × 0.8) |
| 120 | 240 | 3,936 | 16.4 (20.5 × 0.8) |

As can be seen, as production quantities double, the average time per unit decreases by 20% of its immediate previous time. It can be graphed as seen in the illustration on the next page.

LEARNING CURVE

**LEASE** legal agreement whereby the lessee uses real or personal property of the lessor for a rental charge. The contract may provide for the time period of lease, designated purposes, and restrictions. *See also* CAPITAL LEASE; DIRECT FINANCING LEASE; OPERATING LEASE; SALES TYPE LEASE.

**LEASEBACK** *see* SALE AND LEASEBACK.

**LEASEHOLD** agreement between the lessee and lessor specifying the lessee's rights to use the leased property for a given time at a specified rental payment. As rental payments are made, rent expense is charged. When the rental is paid in advance, a prepaid rent account (prepaid expense) that has to be allocated into expense over the rental period is recorded. If the prepayment is for a long-term lease, however, it is recorded as a deferred charge and then amortized. The amortization entry for a long-term lease is to charge rent expense and credit leasehold. *See also* LEASEHOLD IMPROVEMENT.

**LEASEHOLD IMPROVEMENT** upgrading made by a lessee to leased property. Examples are paneling and wallpapering. These improvements revert to the lessor at the expiration of the lease term. As improvement costs are incurred under an operating lease, the leasehold improvement account is charged. The leasehold improvement is amortized to expense over the shorter of the life of the improvement or the remaining lease term. If there is a lease renewal option and the prospect of renewal cannot be predicted with certainty, the amortization period should be the original lease term rather than the longer possible term. However, the amortization expense on a leasehold improvement is not tax deductible. Leasehold improvement is usually considered an INTANGIBLE ASSET, because the lessee does not own the leased property. However, some companies show it under the property, plant, and equipment section of the balance sheet.

**LEAST-SQUARES ANALYSIS** *see* LEAST-SQUARES METHOD.

**LEAST-SQUARES METHOD** widely used statistical technique employed to study trends in revenue, costs, production, and other data and to investigate the relationships among accounting and financial variables. It fits a straight line through a set of points in such a way that the sum of the squared distances from the data points to the line is minimized. The least-squares method involves the following steps:

(1) Define the distance from the data point from the line, denoted by $u$, as follows:

$$u = (y - y')$$

*where* $y$ = observed value and $y'$ = estimated value base on the line $y' = a + bx$ (see the following figure).

(2) Minimize the sum of the squared distances:

$$\text{Min } u^2 = (y - y')^2 = (y - (a + bx))^2$$

Using differential calculus yields the following equations, called NORMAL EQUATIONS:

$$y = na + bx$$

$$xy = ax + bx^2$$

Solving the equation for $b$ and $a$ yields:

$$b = \frac{nxy - (x)(y)}{nx^2 - (x)^2}$$

$$a = \bar{y} - b\bar{x} \text{ where } \bar{y} = y/n \text{ and } \bar{x} = x/n$$

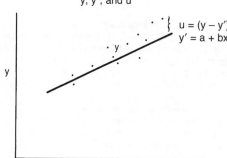

LEAST SQUARES
y, y', and u

$u = (y - y')$
$y' = a + bx$

To illustrate the computations of $b$ and $a$, refer to the following data. All the sums required are computed and shown here:

| Direct Labor-Hours ($x$) | Factory Overhead ($y$) | $xy$ | $x^2$ |
|---|---|---|---|
| 9 hours | $ 15 | 135 | 81 |
| 19 | 20 | 380 | 361 |
| 11 | 14 | 154 | 121 |
| 14 | 16 | 224 | 196 |
| 23 | 25 | 575 | 529 |
| 12 | 20 | 240 | 144 |
| 12 | 20 | 240 | 144 |
| 22 | 23 | 506 | 484 |
| 7 | 14 | 98 | 49 |
| 13 | 22 | 286 | 169 |
| 15 | 18 | 270 | 225 |
| 17 | 18 | 306 | 289 |
| 174 hours | $225 | 3,414 | 2,792 |

From the table above:

$x = 174$   $y = 225$   $xy = 3,414$   $x^2 = 2,792$
$\bar{x} = x/n = 174/12 = 14.5$   $\bar{y} = y/n = 225/12 = 18.75$

Substituting these values into the formula for $b$ first:

$$b = \frac{n xy - (x)(y)}{n x^2 - (x)^2}$$

$$= \frac{(12)(3,414) - (174)(225)}{(12)(2,792) - (174)^2} = \frac{1,818}{3,228} = \underline{0.5632}$$

$$a = \bar{y} - b\bar{x}$$
$$= (18.75) - (0.5632)(14.5) = 18.75 - 8.1664 = \underline{10.5836}$$

Therefore, $y' = 10.5836 + 0.5632 x$

**LEDGER** book in which all accounts of the business are kept. In effect, the ledger is a classification and summarization of financial transactions and the basis for the preparation of the balance sheet and income statement. The ledger also allows one to see the balance in a given account at a particular time. For example, the cash balance at the end of the month can be seen to determine whether the business has a cash problem. Also revealed in looking at the cash account are the cash receipts and cash disbursements for the period.

In a computerized environment, accounts may be stored on magnetic tape or disks instead of in a ledger binder. The accounting principles are, of course, still the same.

**LEGAL CAPITAL** amount of stockholders' equity that cannot be reduced by the payment of dividends. It is defined by the par value of par-value issued stock or the stated value of no-par issued stock. *See also* PAR VALUE; STATED VALUE.

**LEGAL EXCHANGE INFORMATION SERVICE (LEXIS)** online database containing laws, legal cases, and tax regulations of interest to practitioners.

**LEGAL LIABILITY**
   **1.** obligation with specified terms and conditions by which a defined payment amount in money, goods, or services is to be paid within a defined time period in return for a current benefit.
   **2.** responsibility of the accountant to the client and third parties relying on the accountant's work. Accountants can be sued for fraud and negligence in performance of duties.

**LESSEE** individual paying a rental fee to the LESSOR for the right to use real or personal property. The two methods used to account for leases by the lessee are the CAPITAL LEASE and the OPERATING LEASE.

**LESSOR** owner of real or personal property who gives another the right to use it in return for rental payments. The three types of leases for the lessor are the DIRECT FINANCING LEASE, the SALES-TYPE LEASE, and the OPERATING LEASE. *See also* LESSEE.

**LETTER OF CREDIT (L/C)** financial instrument normally issued by the buyer's bank in which the bank promises to pay money up to a stated amount for a specified period for merchandise when delivered. It substitutes the bank's credit for the buyer's and eliminates the seller's risk. It is used in international trade.

**LETTER OF RECOMMENDATION** auditor's letter addressed to the client. It contains the public accountant's conclusions regarding the company's accounting policies and procedures, internal controls, and operating policies. An evaluation is made of the present system, pointing out problem areas. Recommendations for improvement are cited.

**LETTER OF REPRESENTATION** client's letter addressed to the CPA on the audit engagement. It is usually signed by an officer of the company but may be signed by the corporate attorney. The letter states that the financial statements are the responsibility of management and that management's statements to the auditor during the audit process are true. Examples of representations include information regarding a subsequent event occurring after year-end and the existence of off-balance sheet contingencies. As per GENERALLY ACCEPTED AUDITING STANDARDS (GAAS), this letter is mandatory on an audit.

**LEVERAGE** term commonly used in finance and accounting to describe the ability of fixed costs to magnify returns to a firm's owners. OPERATING LEVERAGE, a measure of operating risk, refers to the fixed operating costs found in the firm's income statement. FINANCIAL

LEVERAGE, a measure of financial risk, refers to financing a portion of the firm's assets, bearing fixed financing charges in hopes of increasing the return to its owners. *Total leverage* is a measure of total risk. The way to measure total leverage is to determine how EARNINGS PER SHARE (EPS) is affected by a change in sales.

**LEVERAGED BUYOUT** acquisition of one company by another, typically with borrowed funds. Usually, the acquired company's assets are used as collateral for the loans of the acquiring company. The loans are paid back from the acquired company's cash flow. Another possible form of leveraged buyout occurs when investors borrow from banks, using their own assets as collateral to acquire the other company. Typically, public stockholders receive an amount in excess of the current market value for their shares.

**LEVERAGED LEASE**
1. lease arrangement of property financed by someone other than the lessee or lessor. A long-term creditor finances the lease, and recourse in the event of default is generally not available to the creditor via the lessor.
2. special lease arrangement involving a creditor, lessor, and lessee. A creditor finances most of the cost to acquire an asset, while the lessor puts in a small amount of cash and acquires the asset, using it as security. The asset is then leased to the lessee on a noncancellable basis, and periodic payments to the lessor service the debt. The lessor, having borrowed most of the funds to acquire the asset, has "leveraged" himself, while having both the rewards and the risks of the lease.

**LEVY** imposition or collection, usually by legal or governmental authority, of an assessment of a specified amount. An example is a tax assessment.

**LIABILITY** amount payable in dollars (e.g., accounts payable) or future services to be rendered (e.g., warranties payable). The party having the liability is referred to as the debtor. There are various types of liabilities. An *actual liability* actually exists and has a stated amount (e.g., bonds payable). An ESTIMATED LIABILITY also actually exists, but the amount has to be predicted (e.g., estimated tax liability). These liabilities are booked and are shown in the balance sheet as credit balances under current or noncurrent liabilities, depending upon whether they will be paid in a period of more or less than one year. A CONTINGENT LIABILITY is one that may or may not become due (e.g., notes receivable discounted; a pending lawsuit). A contingent liability is usually footnoted in the financial statement.

**LIABILITY DIVIDEND** dividend in the form of notes payable when the company is short of cash but has adequate retained earnings; also called SCRIP DIVIDEND. The cash payment for the dividend will take place in the future. The recipient of the liability dividend may hold it until the due date to collect funds or may be able to discount it before the maturity date to obtain immediate cash. The entry at the declaration date is to debit retained earnings and credit the liability scrip dividend payable. When paid, scrip dividend payable is debited and cash credited. In the case where the liability involves interest, the interest part of the cash payment is charged to interest expense with the principal portion being debited to scrip dividend payable.

**LIABILITY TAX ALLOCATION METHOD** method of computing deferred taxes based on the estimated tax rates to be in effect when the temporary difference reverses itself. The tax rate is adjusted for rate changes. The method is the only one allowed for financial reporting purposes and is balance-sheet oriented. *See also* DEFERRED TAX ALLOCATION METHOD; NET OF TAX METHOD.

**LIEN** right of a party, typically a creditor, to hold, keep possession of, or control the property of another to satisfy a debt, duty, or liability. A mortgage would create such a security interest or lien upon property in the event of default.

**LIFE CYCLE** movement of a firm or its product through stages of development, growth, expansion, maturity, saturation, and decline. Not all products go through such a life cycle. For example, paper clips, nails, knives, drinking glasses, and wooden pencils do not seem to exhibit such a life cycle; most new products seem to, however. Some current examples include high-tech items such as computers, VCRs, CDs, and DVDs.

PRODUCT LIFE CYCLE

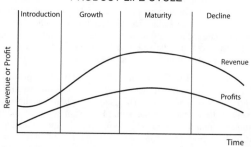

**LIFE-CYCLE ANALYSIS** forecasts of new product growth based on S-curves. Central to the analysis are the phases of product acceptance by the various groups such as innovators, early adapters, early majority, late majority, and laggards.

**LIFE-CYCLE BUDGET** estimates of a product's revenues and expenses over its entire life cycle beginning with research and development, proceeding through the introduction and growth stages, into the maturity stage, and finally into the harvest or decline stage. Life-cycle budgeting adopts a LIFE-CYCLE COST approach. It is intended to account for the costs at all stages of the VALUE CHAIN (R&D, design, production, marketing, distribution, and customer service). This information is important for pricing decisions because revenues must cover costs incurred in each stage of the value chain, not just production. Life-cycle budgeting emphasizes the relationships among costs incurred at different value-chain stages, for example, the effect of reduced design costs on future customer-service costs.

**LIFE-CYCLE COSTING** estimates of a product's revenues and expenses over its expected life cycle. The result is to highlight upstream and downstream costs in the cost planning process that often receive insufficient attention. Emphasis is on the need to price products to cover all costs, not just production costs.

**LIFE INSURANCE** policy taken out by the insured to pay the beneficiary a certain amount upon the insured's death. Proceeds on the death of the policyholder are includable in his or her gross estate under two sets of circumstances: (1) the insurance is payable to his or her estate and (2) the decedent possessed at least one incident of ownership in the policy. The latter means that the decedent either owned the policy until death, or transferred it but retained the right to change the beneficiary, borrow on the policy, and cancel it. To accomplish estate tax *exclusion*, transfer of the policy must occur more than three years prior to death.

**LIFETIME LEARNING CREDIT** may be claimed by individuals and is equal to 20% of up to $10,000 of qualified education expenses (i.e., tuition and fees). The maximum credit of $2,000 is phased out ratably based on the taxpayer's modified adjusted gross income. The phaseout ranges are indexed annually based on inflation. Unlike the AMERICAN OPPORTUNITY CREDIT, the Lifetime Learning Credit is not limited to the first four years of undergraduate education.

**LIKE-KIND EXCHANGE** involves the swapping of property used for business or investment purposes (but not including securities) for property of a similar nature. The grade or quality of the properties exchanged do not have be the same. For example, an exchange of a building for undeveloped land qualifies for like-kind exchange treatment because both properties are real property. Realized gain on the exchange qualifies for tax-deferred treatment, but only to the extent that dissimilar property is not received.

**LIMITED AUDIT** audit of only *specific* accounts or transactions.

**LIMITED LIABILITY** one that does not go beyond the owner's investment in a business. A CORPORATION and LIMITED PARTNERS enjoy this particular feature. The stockholders of a corporation usually have limited liability; they risk only their investment in the business. Sole

PROPRIETORS and *general partners* have unlimited liability. *See also* PARTNERSHIP; UNLIMITED LIABILITY.

**LIMITED LIABILITY COMPANY (LLC)** business form that provides limited personal liability, as a corporation does. Owners, who are called members, can be other corporations. The members run the company unless they hire an outside management group. The LLC can choose whether to be taxed as a regular corporation or as a pass through to members. Profits and losses can be split among members any way they choose. The LLC rules vary by state.

**LIMITED LIABILITY PARTNERSHIP (LLP)** a form of organization in which the individual partners are protected from the liabilities of the other partners. These entities are considered partnerships for both federal and state tax purposes.

**LIMITED PARTNER** member of a partnership whose liability for partnership obligations is limited to the investment in the partnership. A limited partner is not allowed to take active part in the management of the partnership. Limited partnerships have always been useful for tax shelters. However, limited partnerships are ruled *passive investments* and their tax benefits are severely limited. GENERAL PARTNERS have unlimited joint and several liability, and manage the partnership.

**LIMITED REVIEW** CPA engagement consisting of procedures and inquiries that provide a reasonable basis to express limited assurance that no material changes are needed to the financial statements to bring them into conformity with GAAP. *See also* AUDIT; COMPILATION.

**LIMIT ORDER** instruction to execute an order for a stock only at a specified price or better. The broker continues the order until a specified date or until the customer terminates it. Assume an investor places a limit order to buy at $10 or less a stock now selling at $11. If the stock goes up to $20, the broker will not execute a buy order; if it falls to $10, the broker will execute a buy order immediately. Note that the broker does *not* buy a stock for the broker's own account. The broker brings a buyer and seller together and executes a transaction for a commission. Only a dealer (or a broker-dealer acting in its capacity as a dealer) ever actually buys or sells—i.e., takes an inventory position.

**LINE AND STAFF** typical categorical classifications in which authority and personnel structure are organized in a company. Line personnel usually are defined as deriving from direct operational activities such as financing, distribution, leadership, and strategic decision making. A manager is a line person. Staff personnel are usually advisory and facilitative in nature for the line personnel. An accountant is a staff person to upper management because accounting advice is given. Thus line personnel contribute directly to the firm's objectives, while staff contribute indirectly to the accomplishment of these objectives by advising and facilitating the execution of such objectives.

# LINEARITY

1. in LINEAR PROGRAMMING (LP), the requirement that the measure of effectiveness, such as contribution margin or cost and resource usage, must be proportional to the level of each activity conducted individually. For example, each unit of a resource must make the same contribution to the objective function that every other unit of that resource makes.

2. in LINEAR REGRESSION, the requirement that the relationship between a mixed cost and an activity variable such as machine-hours is straight line in the form of $y = a + bx$. This means that the variable portion changes by a *constant* amount per hour no matter how many hours are used.

**LINEAR PROGRAMMING (LP)** mathematical approach to the problem of allocating limited resources among competing activities in an optimal manner. Specifically, it is a technique used to maximize revenue, CONTRIBUTION MARGIN (CM), or profit function *or* to minimize a cost function, subject to constraints. Linear programming consists of two important ingredients: (1) objective function and (2) constraints, both of which are *linear*. In formulating the LP problem, the first step is to define the *decision variables* that one is trying to solve. The next step is to formulate the objective function and constraints in terms of these decision variables. For example, assume a firm produces two products, A and B. Both products require time in two processing departments, assembly and finishing. Data on the two products are as follows:

|  | Products | | Available |
|---|---|---|---|
|  | A | B |  |
| Assembly (hours) | 2 | 4 | 100 |
| Finishing (hours) | 3 | 2 | 90 |
| CM/unit | $25 | $40 |  |

The firm wants to find the most profitable mix of these products. First, define the decision variables as follows:

$A$ = the number of units of product A to be produced
$B$ = the number of units of product B to be produced

Then, express the objective function, which is to maximize total contribution margin (TCM), as:

$$TCM = \$25A + \$40B$$

Formulate the constraints as inequalities:

$$2A + 4B \leq 100$$
$$3A + 2B \leq 90$$

and do not forget to add the non-negative constraints:

$$A \geq 0, B \geq 0$$

**LINEAR REGRESSION** method dealing with a straight-line relationship between variables. It is in the form of $y = a + bx$, whereas nonlinear regression involves curvilinear relationships such as exponential and quadratic functions. *See also* LINEARITY; REGRESSION ANALYSIS.

**LINE AUTHORITY** power to give orders to subordinates. It contrasts with STAFF AUTHORITY, which is the authority to advise but not command others. Line managers are responsible for attaining the organization's goals as efficiently as possible. Production and sales managers typically exercise line authority.

**LINE ITEM BUDGET** budget typically used by governmental entities in which budgeted financial statement elements are grouped by administrative entities and object. These budget item groups are usually presented in an incremental fashion that is in comparison to previous periods. Line item budgets are used also in private industry for the comparison and budgeting of selected object groups and their previous and future estimated expenditure levels within an organization.

**LINE OF BUSINESS REPORTING** *see* SEGMENTED REPORTING.

**LINE OF CREDIT** bank's moral commitment to make loans to a company for a specified maximum amount for a given period of time, typically one year. There is usually *no* commitment fee charged on the unused line. However, a compensating balance requirement often exists.

**LIQUID** having cash or assets readily convertible into cash. A business entity is said to be liquid when it has cash or near-cash assets that are adequate to satisfy short-term liabilities when due.

**LIQUID ASSET** cash asset (e.g., cash or an unrestricted bank account) or readily marketable security. A liquid asset can be converted into cash in a short time period without a material concession in price. Excluded from this definition are accounts receivable and inventory.

**LIQUIDATING DIVIDEND** return of capital rather than a distribution of retained earnings. Such a dividend may occur with a natural resource company having wasting assets (e.g., oil, coal) or when a company in a state of liquidation desires to distribute cash or other assets on a pro rata basis to its owners. The journal entry is to debit paid-in capital and credit cash. Because the distribution to stockholders is from capital rather than earnings, no tax is paid on it.

**LIQUIDATION** process of closing a business entity, including selling or disposing of the assets, paying the liabilities, and having whatever is left over returned to the owners.

**LIQUIDATION BASIS OF ACCOUNTING** must be used when preparing an entity's financial statements when liquidation is imminent (i.e., a plan for liquidation is in effect and there is a remote likelihood that the entity will return from liquidation). Under the liquidation basis of accounting, assets should be valued at the estimated amount of cash or other consideration expected to be received upon disposition of the assets. Liabilities should be valued under the normal rules of GENERALLY ACCEPTED ACCOUNTING PRINCIPLES (GAAP).

**LIQUIDATION VALUE** cash price or other consideration that can be received in a forced-sale of assets, such as that occurring when a firm is in the process of going out of business. Typically, the liquidation value is less than what could be received from selling assets in the ordinary course of business.

## LIQUIDITY

1. ability of current assets to meet current liabilities when due. The degree of liquidity of an asset is the period of time anticipated to elapse until the asset is realized or is otherwise converted into cash. A liquid company has less risk of being unable to meet debt than an illiquid one. Also, a liquid business generally has more financial flexibility to take on new investment opportunities.
2. immediate convertibility into cash without significant loss of value. For example, marketable securities are more liquid than fixed assets, because securities are actively traded in an organized market.

**LIQUIDITY INDEX** guideline showing the number of days in which current assets are removed from cash. The fewer the days removed, the better the entity's liquidity. An illustrative computation follows:

|  | Amount | × | Days Away from Cash | = Total |
|---|---|---|---|---|
| Cash | $ 20,000 | × | – |  |
| Accounts Receivable | 50,000 | × | 30 | $1,500,000 |
| Inventory | 80,000 | × | 50 | 4,000,000 |
|  | $150,000 |  |  | $5,500,000 |

$$\text{Index} = \frac{\$5,500,000}{\$150,000} = 36.7 \text{ days}$$

**LIQUIDITY RATIO** measurement of a business entity's LIQUIDITY, such as the CURRENT RATIO, ACID-TEST RATIO, ACCOUNTS RECEIVABLE TURNOVER, and INVENTORY TURNOVER.

**LISTED SECURITIES** stocks and bonds traded on an organized security exchange such as the NEW YORK STOCK EXCHANGE (NYSE) and the American Stock Exchange (AMEX). They are distinguished from unlisted securities, which are traded in the OVER-THE-COUNTER (OTC) MARKET. The organized exchanges have certain requirements that firms must meet before their stock can be listed. Among the requirements are size of the company, number of years in business, earnings record, number of shares outstanding, and market value of shares.

**LOAN** agreement by which an owner of property (the lender) allows another party (the borrower) to use the property for a specified time period, and in return the borrower will pay the lender a payment (usually interest), and return the property (usually cash) at the end of the time period. A loan is usually evidenced by a PROMISSORY NOTE. Examples are commercial, consumer, mortgage, and auto loan.

**LOAN CAPITAL** short- and long-term liabilities that have a due date and provide for interest.

**LOAN FUND** available for loans. Such funds may be restricted in the sense that only the income generated from the fund may be used for making loans; in this case, the principal is placed in an endowment fund. In cases where both principal and income may be available, all funds are placed in the loan fund group.

**LOAN MODIFICATION PROGRAM** also called the *"Making Home Affordable" initiative,* a new program designed to help homeowners avoid foreclosure. Under this plan, borrowers will have to provide their most recent tax return and two pay stubs, as well as an "affidavit of financial hardship" to qualify for the $75 billion loan modification program, which runs through 2012. Borrowers are allowed to have their loans modified only once, and the program applies only to loans made on January 1, 2009, or earlier.

**LOCAL AREA NETWORK (LAN)** linking of microcomputers within a limited area or a common environment. An example is a network within a building. A LAN improves the client's efficiency and timeliness through the sharing of files, data, and messages. The system comprises hardware and software. A network operating system, network programs, and application programs for a shared environment are required.

**LOCKBOX** box in a U.S. Postal Service facility, used to facilitate collection of customer remittances. The use of a lockbox also reduces processing float. The recipient's local bank collects from these boxes periodically during the day and deposits the funds in the appropriate corporate account. The bank also furnishes the company with a computer listing of payments received by account, together with a daily total. Because the lockbox arrangement has significant per-item cost, it is most cost-effective with low-volume, high-dollar payments.

**LODGING** facility where one sleeps away from home (e.g., hotel, apartment). For tax years beginning in 1987, lodging expenses are deductible by individuals as employee business expenses only if the aggregate amount of miscellaneous deductions exceeds 2% of the taxpayer's adjusted gross income. Further, the tax law establishes rules for including in income qualified campus lodging provided by a school to an employee. In general, gross income does *not* include the value of qualified campus lodging. However, it is included to the extent the rent paid is less than the lesser of 5% of the appraised value of the lodging or the average rentals paid (by persons other than employees and students) to the school for comparable housing.

**LOG** record kept of the use of an item, often for internal control purposes. For example, in a computer application, a log may be kept of those using data files, programs, or hardware devices. The log may include information about data, time-in and time-out, the use of the item, and the reason for use.

**LOGISTIC INFORMATION SYSTEM** one that facilitates shipping, transportation, and warehousing activities. It aims to ensure customer service by getting adequate quantities of the finished product to the proper place in a cost- and time-efficient manner.

**LONG-FORM REPORT** detailed report by an external auditor about the examination of a client's financial statements. It may add to, replace, or include the SHORT-FORM REPORT. The long-form report may contain the audit scope, auditor opinions regarding the financial position and operating performance of the client, percentage change in accounts, evaluation of financial status, and recommendations for client improvement in its accounting system.

**LONG-LIVED ASSET** one whose future benefit is expected for a number of years; also called *long-term asset*. It includes such noncurrent assets as building, equipment, and intangibles.

**LONG-RANGE BUDGET** projections that cover more than one fiscal year; also called *strategic budgeting*. The five-year budget plan is most commonly used. *See also* ANNUAL BUDGET.

**LONG-TERM ASSET** *see* LONG-LIVED ASSET.

**LONG-TERM DEBT** monies owed for a period exceeding one year. Examples are bonds payable and long-term notes payable. The major features of the debt (i.e., interest rate, maturity date) are disclosed in the financial statements, usually in footnotes. Long-term liabilities are distinguished from long-term debt because the former include obligations requiring the rendering of future services (e.g., unearned revenue).

**LONG-TERM LIABILITY** obligation payable in money, goods, or services for a period in excess of one year. It is presented under noncurrent liabilities in the balance sheet. Examples are mortgage payable and the noncurrent portion of warranties payable.

**LOSS**
1. decrease in net assets for which no revenue is obtained and which arises from incidental transactions. Examples are the loss on the sale of a fixed asset, a catastrophe loss (e.g., fire loss, hurricane

damage, flood loss), and a loss on the early extinguishment of debt. A loss is usually unanticipated and nonrecurring.

**2.** excess of expenses over revenue resulting in a net loss.

**LOSS CARRYBACK** offsetting the current year's net loss against net income of the previous years (currently three years) for tax purposes. For financial reporting purposes, the tax effects of a loss carryback should be allocated to the loss period and a refund in taxes should be obtained. *See also* LOSS CARRYFORWARD.

**LOSS CARRYFORWARD** offsetting the current year's net operating loss against future years' net income for tax purposes, assuming that a LOSS CARRYBACK is not possible in whole or in part. For financial reporting purposes, the tax effects of a loss carryforward should not be recognized until the year in which the tax liability is reduced unless earlier realization is assured beyond any reasonable doubt. This assurance is indicated when the entity has been profitable, future earnings are assured, and the loss results from a nonrecurring event.

**LOSS CONTINGENCY** posting of a future loss that may result from some event or happening (e.g., probable damages from a lawsuit). Loss contingencies that are probable should be booked by a charge to the loss account and a credit to the estimated liability. In addition, there should be footnote references to the nature of the contingency. *See also* CONTINGENT LIABILITY; GAIN CONTINGENCY.

**LOSS OF UTILITY** decline in usefulness and hence value of an asset. Loss of utility is the reason to write down the asset. An example is writing down an investment in securities for a permanent decline from cost to market value. Theoretically, an asset should be written down when the present value of its future cash flows is less than its historical cost.

**LOWER OF COST OR MARKET** valuation rule based on CONSERVA-TISM. Certain accounts are shown at the *lower* of their historical cost or current replacement cost reflecting an unrealized loss in the financial statements. In the opposite case (unrealized gain), *no* accounting recognition is given. For example, inventory is reflected at the lower of cost or market on an item-by-item, category, or total basis. In applying the rule, however, market cannot exceed the ceiling (net realizable value = selling price less costs to complete and dispose) nor can market be less than the floor (net realizable value less normal profit margin).

**LP** *see* LINEAR PROGRAMMING (LP).

**LUMP-SUM PURCHASE** acquisition of a group of assets for a single price. The cost should be allocated to the assets based on their fair market values. Assume $75,000 is paid to acquire land, building, and equipment having the fair market values of $40,000, $25,000, and $35,000, respectively. The allocated cost is shown below:

|  | Fair Market Value | Allocated Cost |
|---|---|---|
| Land | $ 40,000 | $30,000 |
| Building | 25,000 | 18,750 |
| Equipment | 35,000 | 26,250 |
| Total | $100,000 | $ 75,000 |

For example, the allocated cost assigned to the land account is arrived at as follows:

$$\frac{\$40,000}{\$100,000} \times \$75,000 = \$30,000$$

# M

**MAC (MEDIA ACCESS CONTROL) ADDRESS** a unique identifier of each node of a network.

**MACHINE-HOUR** cost allocation base that provides a systematic and contemporaneous method of applying overhead costs to work-in-process inventory. An overhead rate of cost per hour of work expended by a machine is applied to the work-in-process. With respect to modern mechanized production, such machine-hour-based rates produce more accurate application of overhead than rates based on direct labor-hours.

**MACRO ACCOUNTING** *see* MICRO ACCOUNTING.

**MACROS** technique that allows the user to combine several keystrokes into one. Macros are simply miniprograms that allow the user to design a menu to include in a TEMPLATE.

**MACRS** *see* MODIFIED ACCELERATED COST RECOVERY SYSTEM.

**MAINFRAME** large computer that may support 100–500 users at one time. Typically, mainframes have a word length of 64 bits and are significantly faster and have greater capacity than the minicomputer and the microcomputer. Mainframes are recommended when vast amounts of data must be processed.

**MAINTENANCE** periodic expenditures undertaken to preserve or retain an asset's operational status for its originally intended use. These expenditures do not improve or extend the life of the asset. An example is the cost of a tune-up for an automobile. Maintenance is an expense and is distinguished from CAPITAL IMPROVEMENTS, which are capitalized.

**MAKE-OR-BUY (OUTSOURCE) DECISION** determination whether to produce a component part internally or to buy it from an outside supplier. This decision involves both qualitative and quantitative factors. Qualitative considerations include product quality and the necessity for long-run business relationships with subcontractors. Quantitative factors deal with cost. The quantitative effects of the make-or-buy decision are best seen through the RELEVANT COST APPROACH. For example, assume a firm has prepared the following cost estimates for the manufacture of a subassembly component based on an annual production of 8000 units:

|                                      | Per Unit | Total     |
|--------------------------------------|----------|-----------|
| Direct materials                     | $ 5      | $ 40,000  |
| Direct labor                         | 4        | 32,000    |
| Variable overhead applied            | 4        | 32,000    |
| Fixed overhead applied               |          |           |
| (150% of direct labor cost)          | 6        | 48,000    |
| Total cost                           | $19      | $152,000  |

The supplier has offered the subassembly at a price of $16 each. Two-thirds of fixed factory overhead, which represents executive salaries, rent, depreciation, and taxes, continue regardless of the decision. Should the company buy or make the product? The key to the decision lies in the investigation of those relevant costs that change between the make or buy alternatives. Assuming that the productive capacity will be idle if not used to produce the subassembly, we can make the following analysis:

|  | Per Unit | | Total of 8000 units | |
|---|---|---|---|---|
|  | Make | Buy | Make | Buy |
| Purchase price |  | $16 |  | $128,000 |
| Direct materials | $ 5 |  | $ 40,000 |  |
| Direct labor | 4 |  | 32,000 |  |
| Variable overhead | 4 |  | 32,000 |  |
| Fixed overhead that can be avoided by *not* making | 2 |  | 16,000 |  |
| Total relevant costs | $15 | $16 | $120,000 | $128,000 |
| Difference in favor of making | $ 1 |  | $8,000 |  |

The make-or-buy decision must be investigated in the broader perspective of available facilities. The alternatives are: (1) leaving facilities idle; (2) buying the parts and renting out idle facilities; or (3) buying the parts and using unused facilities for other products.

**MALWARE** viruses, worms, Trojan horses, spyware, and adware.

**MALPRACTICE INSURANCE** liability insurance for the accountant against legal action in connection with professional services rendered. Insurance coverage varies but may include attorney fees and awarded damages. The accounting practitioner may be sued by clients and third parties (i.e., creditors, investors) relying on his or her work. The increasing cost of obtaining malpractice insurance is a problem of both accounting and other professions.

**MANAGED COST** *see* DISCRETIONARY COST.

**MANAGED EARNINGS** manipulating (pumping up or down) earnings to shed a more favorable light on companies. All companies have flexibility in how they account for some revenues and costs. For example, they can depreciate a capital cost (say, a fleet of cars) in one year or over several years. If they take it in one chunk, their earnings look lower that year and larger every year after that. If they report it in many smaller pieces, they avoid the big hit in the first year. Even though earnings are not perfect, investors' love affair with earnings is here to stay.

**MANAGED (FIXED) COST** *see* DISCRETIONARY (FIXED) COST.

**MANAGEMENT ACCOUNTING** *see* MANAGERIAL (MANAGEMENT) ACCOUNTING.

**MANAGEMENT ADVISORY SERVICES (MAS)** consulting services performed by CPA firms to improve client efficiency and effectiveness. Within the CPA firms, MAS departments are kept independent of other departments such as audit and tax. Examples of MAS services include IT installation and use, marketing, and financial planning.

**MANAGEMENT AUDIT** examination and appraisal of the efficiency and effectiveness of management in carrying out its activities. Areas of auditor interest include the nature and quality of management decisions, operating results achieved, and risks undertaken. *See also* OPERATIONAL AUDIT.

**MANAGEMENT BY EXCEPTION** concept or policy by which management devotes its time to investigating only those situations in which actual results differ significantly from planned results. The idea is that management should spend its valuable time concentrating on the more important items (such as shaping the company's future strategic course). Attention is given only to material deviations requiring investigation. The tools that facilitate use of this concept include DECISION SUPPORT SYSTEM (DSS); EXPERT SYSTEM; PERFORMANCE REPORT.

**MANAGEMENT BY OBJECTIVE (MBO)** system of performance appraisal having the following characteristics: (1) each manager is required to take certain prescribed actions and to complete certain written documents; and (2) the manager and subordinates discuss the subordinate's job description, agree to short-term performance targets, discuss the progress made towards meeting these targets, and periodically evaluate the performance and provide the feedback.

**MANAGEMENT CONSULTING SERVICE** broad service area covering aspects of organizational management, such as planning, finance, inventory, computers, and personnel. These services may include the design and implementation of MANAGEMENT INFORMATION SYSTEMS (MIS), strategic planning, DATA PROCESSING, hardware and software evaluation, data privacy and security, evaluation of management, and suggestions for improvement. Public accounting firms have expanded their services into management consulting. Some critics have expressed concerns that this may weaken auditor independence.

**MANAGEMENT CONTROL SYSTEM** plan assuring that resources are obtained and used effectively and efficiently in the accomplishment of the organization's goals. Major characteristics of a management control system are: (1) it focuses on programs and RESPONSIBILITY CENTERS; (2) it is a total system in that it encompasses all aspects of a firm's operation; (3) it is usually built around a financial and accounting structure; and (4) it uses two types of information for managerial control, *planned data* (such as budgets, standards, and projections) and *actual data*.

**MANAGEMENT DECISION CYCLE** five steps managers take in making decisions and following up on them. The five steps are: (1) the discovery of a problem or need; (2) alternative courses of action to solve the problem or meet the need are identified; (3) a complete analysis to determine the effects of each alternative on business operations is prepared; (4) with the supporting data, the decision maker chooses the best alternative; and (5) after the decision has been carried out, the accountant conducts a post decision review to see if the decision was correct or if other needs have arisen. Any data that relates to future costs, revenues, or uses of resources and that will differ among alternative courses of action are considered relevant decision information.

**MANAGEMENT GAME** form of simulation used in management training. Both SIMULATION and management games are mathematical models, but they differ in purpose and mode of use. Simulation models are designed to simulate a system and to generate a series of financial and operating results regarding system operations. Games do the same thing except that in games human beings play a significant part; that is, participants make decisions at various stages. The major goals of the management game are:

(1) To improve decision-making and analytical skills.

(2) To develop awareness of the need to make decisions lacking complete information.

(3) To develop an understanding of the interrelationships of the various functions of business (accounting, finance, marketing, production, etc.) within the firm and how these interactions affect overall performance.

(4) To develop the ability to function cooperatively and effectively in a small group situation.

Management games offer a unique means of training accountants and have been used successfully as an executive training device. These games generally fall into two categories: executive and functional. *Executive games* are general management games and cover all functional areas of business and their interactions and dynamics. Executive games are designed to train general executives. *Functional games*, on the other hand, focus on middle management decisions and emphasize particular functional areas of the firm. Examples of executive games in wide use include XGAME, COGITATE, and IMAGINIT. Examples of functional games include MARKSIM, FINSIM, and PERT-SIM.

**MANAGEMENT INFORMATION SYSTEM (MIS)** computer-based or manual system that transforms data into information useful in the support of decision making. MIS can be classified as performing three functions:

(1) To generate reports—for example, financial statements, inventory status reports, or performance reports needed for routine or nonroutine purposes.

(2) To answer what-if questions asked by management. For example, questions such as "What would happen to cash flow if the

company changes its credit term for its customers?" can be answered by MIS. This type of MIS can be called SIMULATION.

(3) To support decision making. This type of MIS is appropriately called DECISION SUPPORT SYSTEM (DSS). DSS attempts to integrate the decision maker, the database, and the quantitative models being used.

**MANAGEMENT LETTER** *see* LETTER OF RECOMMENDATION.

**MANAGEMENT REPRESENTATION LETTER** a letter written by management to an auditor at the end of an audit. The purpose of the letter is to confirm explicit and implicit management assertions (representations) made during the course of the audit. The letter is typically signed by the entity's CEO and CFO.

**MANAGEMENT REVIEW** analysis and evaluation by the external auditor of management's performance, including an analysis of the quality of decision making, efficiency of operations, profitability, corporate policies, internal controls, personnel relations, social responsibility, marketing factors, and ability to keep up-to-date technologically, as well as factoring economic and political considerations into decisions among other criteria.

**MANAGEMENT SCIENCE** *see* QUANTITATIVE METHODS (MODELS).

**MANAGEMENT'S DISCUSSION AND ANALYSIS OF EARNINGS** section in FORM 10-K and in the ANNUAL REPORT to stockholders that is required by SEC *Accounting Series Release* No. 159. Management must summarize the reasons for changes in results of operations, capital resources, and liquidity, among others. The section is designed to help investors understand the extent to which accounting changes, as well as changes in business activity, have affected the comparability of year-to-year data. Investors will then be in a better position to assess the source and probability of recurrence in earnings. Examples of subjects to be discussed by management include material changes in discretionary costs, material changes in assumptions underlying deferred costs, and significant changes in product mix or in the relative profitability of lines of business.

**MANAGEMENT'S REPORT** management's assessment of the effectiveness of the company's internal control over financial reporting.

**MANAGER**
1. executive whose function is to plan, organize, and control, and to make decisions in order to achieve organizational objectives.
2. in a public accounting firm, person in charge of an audit engagement. The manager is responsible for all aspects of the engagement, from initiation to closing and rendering an opinion.

**MANAGERIAL EFFORT** extent to which a manager attempts to accomplish a goal. Managerial effort may include psychological as well as physical commitment to accomplish a goal. Motivation is the desire of managers to attain a specific goal (GOAL CONGRUENCE) and the commitment to accomplish the goal (managerial effort).

**MANAGERIAL (MANAGEMENT) ACCOUNTING** process of identification, measurement, accumulation, analysis, preparation, interpretation, and communication of financial information that is used by management to plan, evaluate, and control within an organization. It is the accounting used for the planning, control, and decision-making activities of an organization. Managerial accounting is concerned with providing information to internal managers who are charged with directing, planning, and controlling operations and making a variety of management decisions. Managerial accounting can be contrasted with FINANCIAL ACCOUNTING, which is concerned with providing information, via financial statements, to stockholders, creditors, and others *outside* the organization. More specifically, the differences between financial and managerial accounting are summarized here:

| Financial Accounting | Managerial Accounting |
|---|---|
| (1) Provides data for *external* users. | (1) Provides data for *internal* use. |
| (2) Is required by FASB. | (2) Is not mandated by FASB. |
| (3) Is subject to GAAP. | (3) Is not subject to GAAP. |
| (4) Must generate accurate and timely data. | (4) Emphasizes relevance and flexibility of data. |
| (5) Emphasizes the past. | (5) Has more emphasis on the future. |
| (6) Looks at the business as a whole. | (6) Focuses on parts as well. |
| (7) Primarily stands by itself. | (7) Draws heavily from other disciplines such as finance, economics, and operations research. |
| (8) Is an end in itself. | (8) Is a means to an end. |

**MANAGERIAL MOTIVATION** a combination of managerial effort and goal congruence.

**MANUFACTURING AND PRODUCTION SYSTEM** plan that either creates goods or provides services (or both). Manufacturing and production systems produce output that ranges from highly standardized to highly customized. Depending on the type of system used, an appropriate cost accounting system can be designed. For example, a JOB ORDER costing system is used by custom manufacturers such as shipbuilders, aircraft manufacturers, and printers, whereas a process costing system is used by processing industries such as refineries and chemical manufacturers.

**MANUFACTURING CELLS** plant layout in a lean JIT production environment. Cells are sets of machines, often grouped in semicircles, that produce a given product or product type. Each worker in a cell must be able to operate all machines and, possibly, to perform support tasks, such as setup activities, preventive maintenance, movement of work-in-process within the cell, and quality inspection. In a pull system, workers might often be idle if they are not multi-skilled. Hence, central support departments are reduced or eliminated, space is saved, fewer and smaller factories may be required, and materials and tools are bought close to the point of use. Manufacturing cycle time and setup time are reduced. As a result, on-time delivery performance and response to changes in markets are enhanced, and production of customized goods in small lots becomes feasible.

**MANUFACTURING COST FLOW** flow of manufacturing costs (direct materials, direct labor, and manufacturing overhead) from when incurred through the direct materials inventory, work-in-process inventory, and finished goods inventory accounts to the cost of goods sold account.

**MANUFACTURING COSTS** expenses associated with the manufacturing activities of the company. They consist of three categories: direct materials, direct labor, and factory overhead.

**MANUFACTURING CYCLE EFFICIENCY (MCE)** quotient of the time required for value-added production divided by TOTAL CYCLE TIME. It is a measure of how well a company's manufacturing capabilities use time resources.

**MANUFACTURING CYCLE TIME** delay from the moment the order is ready for setup to its completion. Sometimes called manufacturing lead time or throughput time.

**MANUFACTURING EXPENSE** *see* MANUFACTURING COSTS.

**MANUFACTURING LEAD TIME** *see* MANUFACTURING CYCLE TIME.

**MANUFACTURING OVERHEAD** *see* FACTORY OVERHEAD.

**MANUFACTURING OVERHEAD VOLUME VARIANCE** difference between the manufacturing overhead costs budgeted for the level of production achieved and the manufacturing overhead cost applied to production using the standard variable and fixed manufacturing overhead rates.

**MANUFACTURING RESOURCE PLANNING (MRP-II)** integrated information system that steps beyond first-generation MRP to synchronize all aspects (not just manufacturing) of the business, including production, sales, inventories, schedules, and cash flows. MRP-II uses an MPS (master production schedule), which is a statement of the anticipated manufacturing schedule for selected items for selected periods. MRP also uses the MPS. Thus, MRP is a component of an MRP-II system.

## MARGIN

1. *see* GROSS MARGIN; PROFIT MARGIN.

2. partial payment made by an investor to a broker for securities purchased, with the remainder on credit. The broker retains the securities as collateral and charges the investor interest on the money owed. The Federal Reserve Board determines margin requirements. The margin requirement for stocks is higher than that for convertible bonds because of greater risk. Assume that with a margin requirement of 50% (present requirement), 100 shares of XYZ stock are bought at $100 per share. The actual amount invested is $5000, with a margin of $5000 on credit.

3. in commodities trading, *deposits* required by commodities exchanges.

4. in accounting, a reference to revenue or profitability. Examples are gross profit margin (gross profit/sales) and profit margin (net income/sales).

**MARGINAL ANALYSIS** approach utilizing such concepts as marginal revenue, marginal cost, and marginal profit for economic decision making. For example, decisions for allocating scarce resources are typically expressed in terms of the marginal condition(s) that must be satisfied in order to attain an optimal solution. The familiar profit-maximizing rule of setting production or sales volume at the point where "marginal revenue equals marginal cost" is one such example.

**MARGINAL COST** calculation showing the change in total cost as a result of a change in volume. For example, if one more unit of output causes an increase in total cost of $40, the $40 is the marginal cost. It is useful to calculate marginal cost to determine whether the rate of production should be changed. In general, as activity increases, economies of scale (LEARNING CURVE principle) set in because of greater experience and manufacturing efficiency. Eventually, however, a point is reached where diseconomies of scale (e.g., increased management supervision) occur, causing marginal costs to rise. When a company is at an optimum output level, marginal cost coincides with average total unit cost. The marginal cost curve is usually shown as a U-shape on a graph.

**MARGINAL COSTING** *see* DIRECT COSTING.

**MARGINAL INCOME** *see* CONTRIBUTION MARGIN (CM).

**MARGINAL INCOME RATIO** *see* CONTRIBUTION MARGIN (CM) RATIO.

**MARGINAL REVENUE** change of the total revenue of a business resulting when an extra unit is sold.

MARGINAL COST

**MARGINAL TAX RATE** rate paid on the last dollar of taxable income. For example, assume for married couples filing jointly that there are two tax brackets:

15% on taxable income equal to or below $29,750
28% on taxable income in excess of this amount

If income adds up to $50,000, total taxes paid will be $10,132.50:

| | | |
|---|---|---|
| First $29,750 of taxable income at 15% | = | $ 4,462.50 |
| Remaining $20,250 at 28% | = | $ 5,670.00 |
| | | $10,132.50 |

The 15% and 28% are marginal tax rates, while the average tax rate is a little over 20% ($10,132.50/$50,000).

**MARGIN OF SAFETY** difference between the actual level of sales and BREAK-EVEN SALES. It is the amount by which sales revenue may drop before losses begin and is often expressed as a percentage of budgeted sales:

$$\text{Margin of Safety} = \frac{\text{Budgeted Sales} - \text{Break-Even Sales}}{\text{Budgeted Sales}}$$

The margin of safety is often used as a measure of OPERATING RISK. The larger the ratio, the safer the situation is since there is less risk of reaching the break-even point.

**MARITAL DEDUCTION** tax deduction allowed upon the transfer of property from one spouse to another. This deduction is allowed under the federal gift tax for lifetime transfers or under the federal estate tax for testamentary transfers of a decedent.

## MARK-TO-MARKET

1. the daily adjustment of margin accounts to reflect profits and losses. At the end of each day, the futures contracts are settled and the resulting profits or losses paid.
2. valuing a trading security or available-for-sale security at its market value at the end of the reporting period. The security is presented at its market value whether it is below or above cost. Also called *fair value*.

## MARKDOWN

1. reduction of the original selling price. It may be due to any of several reasons, such as a decline in overall prices of goods, excessive competition, special sale, damaged merchandise, or excess supply. In *markdown cancellation*, the markdown is partially offset at a subsequent date by increases in the prices of goods that had been marked down below the original selling price. *See also* MARKUP.
2. dealer markdowns in securities trading.

## MARKETABLE SECURITY
readily tradable equity or debt security with quoted prices, including commercial paper and Treasury bills. It is a near-cash asset and is classified under current assets. Marketable securities are initially recorded at cost, which consists of the market price and incidental costs to acquire, including brokerage commissions and taxes. Some types of securities, such as restricted stock, are *not* marketable. At year-end, marketable securities are valued at market value.

## MARKET CAP (MARKET CAPITALIZATION)
value of a business entity equal to its outstanding shares multiplied by the current market price per share. For example, if 5,000,000 shares are issued and outstanding and the market price per share is $10, the company's market capitalization is $50,000,000. Institutional investors including insurance companies and pension plans will not invest in a company unless its market capitalization is a minimum amount (e.g., $100 million) predetermined by them. Higher market capitalization reflects a larger and higher quality company, which is probably more widely held and actively traded. *See also* BOOK VALUE.

## MARKET INDEX OF STOCK PRICES
aggregate of prices of stock of a certain type on one of the stock exchanges. Stock market indexes show how the market is doing and may assist the investor in picking the right type stocks at the proper time. For example, Standard & Poor's has several common stock indexes, such as the S&P 500.

## MARKETING EXPENSE *see* SELLING EXPENSE.

## MARKET PRICE

1. price at which the seller and the buyer agree to trade on the open market.
2. in TRANSFER PRICING, best transfer price (i.e., the price that will maximize the profits of the company as a whole), under the following conditions: (1) a competitive market price exists; and (2)

divisions are independent of each other. If divisions are free to buy and sell outside the company, the use of market prices preserves divisional autonomy and leads divisions to act in a manner that maximizes the profits of the company as a whole.

**MARKET RISK PREMIUM** amount above the risk-free rate required to induce average investors to enter the market.

**MARKET SHARE VARIANCE** difference between the actual market share percentage and the budgeted market share percentage, times the actual market size in units, times the budgeted weighted average unit contribution margin.

**MARKET SIZE VARIANCE** budgeted market share percentage, times the difference between the actual market size in units, times the budgeted weighted average UCM. One of the two components of SALES QUANTITY VARIANCE.

## MARKET TIMING

1. an abusive practice where big stock market traders move in or out of funds at the end of the trading day, exploiting stale price data. The practice is not illegal, but it can be damaging to the interests of other investors in the funds. Regulators are currently studying ways to thwart timing-related trades in mutual fund shares.
2. an ideal investing strategy of switching into stocks before they rise and switching out of them before they decline.

## MARKET TRANSFER PRICE *see* MARKET PRICE.

## MARKET VALUE

1. typically, price at which an item could be sold.
2. as used in the LOWER OF COST OR MARKET rule for inventory valuation, replacement cost subject to ceiling and floor limits.

*See also* FAIR MARKET VALUE.

## MARKET VALUE METHOD

1. method used to account for a BOND CONVERSION. The credit to common stock and premium on common stock may be based either on the market value of the bond or the market value of the stock issued. The difference between the book value of the bond and the market value credited to equity represents a gain or loss. *See also* BOOK VALUE METHOD.
2. valuation of inventory at its market value whether above or below cost recognizing an unrealized (holding) loss or gain. This method is not acceptable because to show inventory in *excess* of cost is not conservative.
3. method to account for trading (shown under current assets) and available-for-sale (shown under noncurrent assets) equity and debt securities at their market value at the end of the reporting period. The difference between the cost and market value of the securities portfolio is presented as an unrealized loss or gain. For trading securities,

the unrealized loss or gain is reported in the income statement. For available-for-sale securities, the unrealized loss or gain for the current year is reported under "other comprehensive income" in the income statement and the cumulative amount is reported under stockholders' equity in the balance sheet classified as "accumulated other comprehensive income."

**MARKOV ANALYSIS** method of analyzing the current behavior of some variable to predict its future behavior. One important application of this method in accounting is the estimation of that portion of the accounts receivable that will eventually become uncollectible.

**MARKUP**
1. increase on the original selling price. It is associated primarily with the pricing of items for sale in a retail or wholesale environment. *Markup cancellation* is a reduction on the price of merchandise that has been marked up on the original retail price. *See also* MARKDOWN.
2. amount added to the cost of an item to arrive at a selling price. Markup may be expressed as a percentage of cost or in dollars. For example, if an item costing $20 has a profit markup on cost of 30%, the selling price will be $26 ($20 + $6).
3. dealer markups in securities trading.

**MAS90, MAS200, MAS500** accounting, distribution, and light manufacturing software, developed by Sage Software, ideal for medium-sized companies that can benefit from an outstanding combination of high performance, breadth of application, complete modularity, and exceptional ease of use (www.sagemas.com).

**MASQUERADING** an attack that relies on a fake identity, such as stolen passwords, to gain unauthorized access to an IT system. Essentially, the attacker pretends to be an authorized user in a masquerading attack.

**MASTER (COMPREHENSIVE) BUDGET** plan of activities expressed in monetary terms of the assets, equities, revenues, and costs that will be involved in carrying out the plans. Simply put, a master budget is a set of projected or planned financial statements. It consists basically of a PRO FORMA INCOME STATEMENT, PRO FORMA BALANCE SHEET, and CASH BUDGET. A budget is a tool used for both planning and control. At the beginning of the period, the budget is a plan or standard; at the end of the period, it serves as a control device to help management measure its performance against the plan so that future performance may be improved.

**MATCHING** process of reporting expense on a cause-effect basis against the reported revenue it relates to. Net income is measured by the difference between revenue over associated expenses during the same period. Expenses are incurred in order to obtain that revenue. An example is the matching of sales commission expense to sales.

**MATCHING GRANT** contingent grant awarded only if the receiving entity is able to put up (or independently raise) a sum equal to the amount provided by the granting entity.

**MATERIAL**
1. raw material, direct or indirect. An example is steel to make a car. Usually accounted for separately by a debit to materials (stores control) and a credit to accounts payable or cash. When materials are transferred to work-in-process, inventory is credited.
2. relatively important and significant in dollar amounts. *See also* MATERIALITY.

**MATERIALITY** magnitude of an omission or misstatement of accounting data that misleads financial statement readers. Materiality is judged both by relative amount and by the nature of the item. For example, even a small theft by the president of a company is material. Unfortunately, the FINANCIAL ACCOUNTING STANDARDS BOARD (FASB) has no specific criteria as to what is or is not material. If an item is material, it should be disclosed in the body of the financial statements or footnotes. Some CPA firms use a 5% test for materiality. The SEC in *Accounting Series Release* No. 159 provides that an item is material if it changed by 10% or more relative to the prior year.

**MATERIAL MIX** relative combination (or proportion) of components when a manufacturing process requires several different types of materials. The combination is not necessarily the standard. In many industries, such as chemicals, petroleum products, steel, and food, it is quite possible to vary the material mix and end up with essentially the same product. For example, in the textile industry, different mixes of fibers can produce the same quality of yarn.

**MATERIAL MIX VARIANCE** effect on material costs of a deviation from the expected or standard mix of materials. *See also* PRODUCTION MIX VARIANCE.

**MATERIAL PARTICIPATION** participation in an activity that involves a taxpayer's regular, continuous, and substantial participation. One condition for material participation is performance of more than 500 hours of service during the year. A taxpayer who materially participates in an activity will not be subject to the passive activity rules and, accordingly, may fully deduct an activity's loss against ordinary income.

**MATERIAL REQUIREMENT PLANNING (MRP)** computer-based information system designed to handle ordering and scheduling of dependent-demand inventories (such as raw materials, component parts, and subassemblies that will be used in the production of a finished product). MRP is designed to answer three questions: *what* is needed, *how much* is needed, and *when* is it needed. The primary inputs of MRP are a *bill of materials*, which tells what goes into a finished product; a *master schedule*, which tells how much finished product is desired and when; and an *inventory-records file*, which tells how much inventory is on hand or on order. This information is processed, using various computer programs to determine the net requirements for each period of the planning horizon. Outputs from the process include planned-order schedules, order releases, changes, performance-control reports, planning reports, and exception reports.

**MATERIAL REQUISITIONS** *see* STORES REQUISITIONS.

**MATERIAL WEAKNESS** a deficiency in internal control or a combination of deficiencies in internal control that results in a reasonable possibility that a material misstatement of the annual or interim financial statements will not be prevented or detected (and corrected in the case of a nonissuer) on a timely basis. It does not mean that a material misstatement has occurred or that it will occur, but that it could occur. *See also* DEFICIENCY IN INTERNAL CONTROL; SIGNIFICANT DEFICIENCY.

**MATERIALS PRICE VARIANCE** difference between what is paid for a given quantity of materials and what should have been paid, multiplied by the actual quantity of materials used: Materials price variance = (actual price – standard price) × actual quantity. In reality, since material price variances are isolated at the time of purchase, it is customary to multiply the difference between the actual price and the standard price by the actual quantity *purchased* rather than used. It is more often called *materials purchase price variance*.

**MATERIALS PURCHASE PRICE VARIANCE** *see* MATERIALS PRICE VARIANCE.

**MATERIALS QUANTITY (USAGE) VARIANCE** difference between the actual quantity of materials used in production and the standard quantity of materials allowed for actual production, multiplied by the standard price per unit. Materials quantity variance = (actual quantity – standard quantity) × standard price per unit. The variance is unfavorable if the actual quantity exceeds the standard quantity; it is favorable if the actual quantity is less than the standard.

**MATERIALS VARIANCE** difference between the actual and standard costs of materials. Materials variance is divided into two specific variances: MATERIALS PRICE VARIANCE and MATERIALS QUANTITY (USAGE) VARIANCE. This breakdown is needed from a control standpoint.

**MATHEMATICAL MODEL** mathematical representation of reality that attempts to explain the behavior of some aspect of it. The mathematical model serves the following purposes: (1) to find an optimal solution to a planning or decision problem; (2) to answer a variety of what-if questions; (3) to establish understandings of the relationships among the input data items within a model; and (4) to attempt to extrapolate past data to derive meaning. Mathematical models include techniques such as LINEAR PROGRAMMING (LP), computer simulation,

DECISION THEORY, REGRESSION ANALYSIS, ECONOMIC ORDER QUANTITY (EOQ), and BREAK-EVEN ANALYSIS. *See also* FINANCIAL MODEL; MODEL; QUANTITATIVE METHODS (MODELS); SIMULATION MODELS.

**MATHEMATICAL PROGRAMMING** *see* OPTIMIZATION MODEL.

**MATURITY** due date of a debt at which time the PRINCIPAL must be paid. *See also* MATURITY VALUE.

**MATURITY VALUE** amount to be paid on the maturity date of a financial instrument. It may be a greater amount (i.e., bond issued at a discount) or a lesser amount (i.e., bond issued at a premium) than the initial price. Maturity value is typically the *face value* of a bond or note. Assume that a five-year $20,000 bond is issued at 95—at a discount. The proceeds at issuance are $19,000, but at the due date of the five-year bond, the maturity value will be $20,000.

**MAXIMIZATION** behavior that attempts to maximize such performance measures as revenue, profits, contribution margin, or expected net present value. For example, a marketing manager wishes to maximize sales revenue or market share of the firm's product or service. Profit maximization has been the traditional goal of the firm in classical economic theory.

**MAXIMUM CAPACITY** *see* IDEAL CAPACITY.

**MAXIMUM PRACTICAL CAPACITY** *see* PRACTICAL CAPACITY.

**MAXIMUM TAX** rate that would apply to the various tiers of income subject to tax. As of 2014, the highest federal tax rate for individuals is 39.6%.

**MEAL EXPENSE DEDUCTION** income tax allowance for business meals. It is limited to 50% of the amount on the individual's tax return. Food and beverages are not deductible unless the taxpayer (1) shows the item *directly* applied to the active conduct of the taxpayer's trade or business and (2) sufficient substantiation exists. No deduction is permitted unless business is discussed during, just before, or just after the meal. Further, the meal cannot be *extravagant* as defined by the IRS.

**MEAN** measure of central tendency; also called *average*. Mean and STANDARD DEVIATION are the two most widely used statistical measures that summarize the characteristics of the data. Suppose a new car dealer sells 630 cars during a 30-day period. Then the mean (average) daily sales is obtained by dividing the total number of cars by the number of days as follows:

Mean daily sales per day = 630/30 = 21 per day

Symbolically,

$$\bar{x} = \Sigma x_i / n$$

where $\bar{x}$ = the mean, $x_i$ = the values in the data, $\Sigma$ (read as sigma) is the summation sign, and $n$ = the number of observations in the data.

**MEAN-PER-UNIT (MPU) ESTIMATION** a technique used in statistical sampling that projects the average value of the items in the sample to estimate the value of the population.

**MEDIAN** value of the midpoint variable when the data are arranged in ascending or descending order. For example, in the following data set: 2, 3, 4, 8, 8, the median is the value of the third variable since there are two variables above it and two variables below it. Therefore, the median of the five variables is 4.

**MEDICAL EXPENSE DEDUCTION** itemized deduction allowed when total medical expenses, less reimbursements from medical insurance plans, exceed the applicable adjusted gross income threshold. The applicable threshold is generally 10% of adjusted gross income. For tax years 2013 through 2016, the threshold is reduced to 7.5% of adjusted gross income for individuals age 65 and older.

**MEDICARE** a health insurance program administered by the federal government covering individuals age 65 and older and those with certain disabilities.

**MEMORY** space within a computer where information and program are stored while being actively worked on; also called *core*. It is expressed in terms of the number of characters (BYTES) that can be retained. The memory of the computer is in the form of *read-only (ROM)* and RAM (RANDOM-ACCESS MEMORY) or read/write memory.

**MERCHANDISE INVENTORY** goods acquired for resale. Merchandise inventory is held by a merchandising concern including wholesalers and retailers. Contrast with FINISHED GOODS INVENTORY.

**MERGER** combination of two or more companies into one, with only one company retaining its identity. Typically, the larger of the two companies is the company whose identity is maintained. It often involves an exchange of stock, which avoids taxes; the *purchase (accounting) method*, where goodwill is recorded, must be used. The merger of two companies can be accomplished in one of two ways. The acquiring company can negotiate with management of the other company, or it can make a TENDER OFFER directly to the stockholders of the company it wants to take over.

**METCALF REPORT** critical report published in 1976 indicating, among other things, that the accounting profession's structure and independence were in need of realignment. It suggested that accounting and auditing standards should be established by the federal government rather than by the profession itself. The actual title of this report, which was prepared by the Subcommittee on Reports, Accounting and Management of the U.S. Senate, is "The Accounting Establishment." Presently, no legislation has resulted from the release of this report.

**MICRO ACCOUNTING** term connoting the accounting for a person, company, or government agency, as distinguished from *macro accounting*, which is the accounting for aggregate economic activities of a nation. Micro accounting also applies to the accounting and reporting of financial information of subunits of the entity.

**MICROPROCESSOR** general, all-purpose circuit, placed on a silicon chip. It is a power source of MICROCOMPUTERS. The microprocessor is at the heart of the micro-electronics revolution. This chip is used in calculators, watches, video games, microwave ovens, and, of course, computers. While a microprocessor is inexpensive, its power is equivalent to that of computers that cost several hundred thousand dollars in the 1960s.

**MIDDLEWARE** a type of software application that allows two or more existing disparate applications to communicate with each other using a messaging service.

**MID-MONTH CONVENTION** used when depreciating real property under the MODIFIED ACCELERATED COST RECOVERY SYSTEM (MACRS) for tax purposes and assumes that the property is placed into service (or disposed of) at the mid-point of the month.

**MID-QUARTER CONVENTION** used when depreciating personal property under the MODIFIED ACCELERATED COST RECOVERY SYSTEM (MACRS) for tax purposes, assumes that the property is placed into service (or disposed of) at the mid-point of the quarter. This convention is applicable to all MACRS property placed into service during the year when more than 40% of the total cost of all property placed into service during the year is placed into service in the last quarter of the year.

**MINICOMPUTER** computer that possesses the same components as large mainframes but has reduced memory and slower processing speeds. Before the advent of the minicomputer industry in the 1960s, companies wishing to automate were forced to use a large mainframe. With the evolution of minicomputers, managers could choose computers with substantially lower costs. During the 1980s, the use of minicomputers declined as microcomputers (also known as personal computers, or PCs) became more powerful and cheaper.

**MINIMIZATION** behavior that attempts to minimize such undesirable factors as cost, time, and inconvenience. Cost minimization is a usual goal of the production department of a firm. For example, a production department manager wishes to find the least cost combination of input materials in order to make a finished product. LINEAR PROGRAMMING (LP) models may be formulated in the format of either profit maximization or cost minimization.

**MINIMUM CASH BALANCE** safety cushion needed to avoid a possible cash shortage. In cash budgeting, projecting cash inflows (such as collections from customers) and cash disbursements (such as purchases and capital spending) is a difficult task. Even though the company attempts to forecast cash flows as accurately as possible, it is always a good idea to keep a certain minimum cash balance on hand.

**MINIMUM LEASE PAYMENTS** regular rental payments excluding EXECUTORY COSTS to be made by the lessee to the lessor in a CAPITAL LEASE. The lessee reports an asset and liability at the discounted value of the future minimum lease payments.

**MINIMUM PENSION LIABILITY** condition that is recognized when the ACCUMULATED BENEFIT OBLIGATION is greater than the fair value of plan assets. However, *no* recognition is given in the opposite case. When an accrued pension liability exists, only an additional liability for the difference between the minimum liability and the accrued pension liability can be recorded. When an additional liability is recorded, it is offset by recognizing an intangible asset not exceeding the amount of unamortized prior service cost. If it does exceed that amount, the excess is shown as a reduction of stockholders' equity in an account called net loss not recognized as pension expense. Assume an accumulated benefit obligation of $500,000, and a fair value of pension plan assets of $400,000, leaving a minimum pension liability of $100,000. If we assume that the accrued pension liability is $40,000, then the additional pension liability is $60,000. The unamortized prior service cost is assumed to be $50,000. The journal entry to record the additional liability is:

| | | |
|---|---|---|
| Intangible Asset – Pension Plan | 50,000 | |
| Minimum Pension Liability Adjustment | 10,000 | |
|    Additional Pension Liability | | 60,000 |

**MINIMUM REQUIRED RATE OF RETURN** *see* COST OF CAPITAL.

**MINIMUM TAX** levy imposed on taxpayers with large income to assure that all pay a fair share of the total tax burden. The traditional minimum tax was replaced by the ALTERNATIVE MINIMUM TAX (AMT) under the Tax Reform Act of 1986. AMT not only replaced the minimum tax, but extended it to corporations. The tax base for minimum tax starts with regular taxable income. This base then is adjusted by recomputing certain deductions and deferrals—such as depreciation, long-term contracts, and installment sales gain—in a manner that offsets to a great extent the reduction that these items generate in regular taxable income. The base then is increased by certain TAX PREFERENCE ITEMS (such as excess of accelerated depreciation over straight line).

**MINORITY INTEREST** ownership interest of those *not* in the consolidated group of companies when consolidated financial statements are prepared. An example is an *outside* group that owns 5% of the shares of a subsidiary, with the parent owning 95%.

**MIS** *see* MANAGEMENT INFORMATION SYSTEM (MIS).

**MISCELLANEOUS EXPENSE** incidental expense of a business, not classified as manufacturing, selling, or general and administrative expenses. It is presented on an income statement after operating income. Miscellaneous expenses are immaterial. A more precise designation or separate accounting for them results in a cost greater than the benefit received.

**MISERY INDEX** an index that tracks economic conditions including inflation and unemployment. It was particularly referred to in the economically depressed period of 1977 through 1981 in the United States. The inflation rate was in the double digits at that time.

Misery Index = Inflation Rate + Unemployment Rate + Prime Rate

The index typically is negatively correlated to the current condition of the stock market. The misery index has little value as a predictor of future stock prices. The index may be found in the Bureau of Labor Statistics publications and *The Wall Street Journal*.

**MISLEADING** pointing to an interpretation that is not factual or is unrealistic. Facts or statements that may be misstated, distorted, augmented, omitted, and arranged in such a manner as to obscure and conceal material aspects of an item are misleading. The accountant carefully prepares, based on the reliance on accepted standards of auditing practice and statement presentation, financial information to avoid misleading inferences.

**MIXED COST** *see* SEMIVARIABLE COSTS.

**MODEL** abstraction of a real-life system used to facilitate understanding and to aid in decision making. It has become a popular device in business. The model can be classified into three popular types: (1) physical model; (2) graphical model; and (3) mathematical model. Examples of physical models are childhood toys such as dolls and toy airplanes. Graphical models are abstractions of lines, symbols, shapes, or charts—for example, a BREAK-EVEN CHART. Mathematical models are the ones that have stimulated most of the recent interest in models for decision making. Any mathematical formula or equation is a model. Mathematical models are used to solve planning and decision problems and to answer various *what-if* scenarios. Examples include the *break-even* model and LINEAR PROGRAMMING.

**MODEM** device that enables one computer to communicate with another over telephone lines. The word modem stands for *modulator/demodulator*. To modulate is to change digital signals to analog, so data can be transmitted by audio tones over telephone lines to another computer whose modem can change the audio tones back to the needed digital (bits). To demodulate, the opposite of modulate, is to change analog to digital.

**MODIFIED ACCELERATED COST RECOVERY SYSTEM (MACRS)** a method of accelerated depreciation permitted by tax codes, as modified by recent changes. It classifies depreciable assets into one of several recovery periods, each of which has a designated pattern of allowable depreciation (double-declining balance, 150% declining balance, or straight-line with a half-year convention). *See also* ACCELERATED COST RECOVERY SYSTEM (ACRS).

**MODIFIED ACCRUAL** governmental accounting method. Revenue is recognized when it becomes available and measurable. Expenditures are typically recognized in the period in which the liability is incurred *except for*: (1) inventories of materials and supplies that may be considered expenditures either when bought or used; (2) interest on general and special assessment long-term debt that is recognized on the date due; and (3) use of encumbrances. Most governmental funds follow the modified accrual method. *See also* ACCRUAL ACCOUNTING.

**MODULAR DESIGN** design of components that can be assembled in a variety of ways to meet individual consumer needs.

**MONETARY ITEM** asset or liability whose amounts are fixed or determinable in dollars without reference to future prices of specific goods or services. Their economic significance depends heavily upon the general purchasing power of money. The two types of monetary items are *monetary assets* and *monetary liabilities*. Monetary assets are those stated in current dollars needing no adjustment in the price-level balance sheet, such as cash, accounts receivable, and marketable securities at market value. Monetary liabilities are obligations payable in dollars requiring no adjustment in the price-level balance sheet, such as accounts payable and bonds payable. However, holding monetary items during a period of inflation will result in a PURCHASING POWER LOSS, GAIN in the price-level income statement. *See also* NONMONETARY ITEM.

**MONEY**
1. cash.
2. term broadly used to refer to a medium of exchange and unit of value.

**MONEY MARKET** market for short-term (less than one year) debt securities. Examples of money market securities include U.S. Treasury bills, federal agency securities, bankers' acceptances, commercial paper, and negotiable certificates of deposit issued by government, business, and financial institutions.

**MONEY ORDER** check issued by a bank to a payee when an individual gives the bank funds in exchange. Payees sometimes require a money order since it is, in effect, guaranteed payment. An example is a person giving ABC Savings Bank $1000 and asking the bank to make out its own check payable to an auto dealer.

**MONITORING** a component of internal control that involves the process of assessing the quality of INTERNAL CONTROL performance over a period of time. An entity's use of internal auditors represents an effective means of monitoring internal controls.

**MONOPOLY** exists when an entity has the total control of specific goods or services in a specific area or market.

**MONTE CARLO SIMULATION** *see* MONTE CARLO TECHNIQUE (METHOD, OR ANALYSIS).

**MONTE CARLO TECHNIQUE (METHOD, OR ANALYSIS)** special type of SIMULATION, where the variables of a given system are subject to uncertainty. The technique gets its name from the famous Mediterranean resort often associated with games of chance. In fact, the chance element is an important aspect of Monte Carlo simulation: the approach can be used only when a system has a *random*, or chance, component. Under this approach, a probability distribution is developed that reflects the random component of the system under study. Random samples taken from this distribution are analogous to observations made on the system itself. As the number of observations increases, the results of the simulation will tend to more closely approximate the random behavior of the real system, provided an appropriate model has been developed. Sampling is accomplished by the use of random numbers. Simulation applications include testing alternative inventory policies and simulating a cash budget.

**MORTGAGE** lien securing a note payable that has as collateral real assets and that requires periodic payments. For personal property, such as machines or equipment, the lien is called a CHATTEL MORTGAGE. Mortgages can be issued to finance the acquisition of assets, construction of plants, and modernization of facilities. The bank will require that the value of the property exceed the mortgage on that property. Mortgages have a number of advantages over other debt instruments, including favorable interest rates, fewer financing restrictions, and extended maturity date for loan repayment.

**MORTGAGE BOND** debt secured by a real asset. There are two types of mortgage bonds: senior mortgages, which have first claim on assets and earnings and junior mortgages, which have a subordinate lien. A mortgage bond may have a closed-end provision that prevents the firm from issuing additional bonds of the same priority against the same property or may be an open-end mortgage that allows the issuance of additional bonds having equal status with the original issue.

**MORTGAGE INTEREST DEDUCTION** federal tax deduction allowed for interest paid or accrued within the taxable year with respect to mortgage indebtedness. Interest is deductible on mortgages secured by principal homes and second homes. A taxpayer may not write off interest on any part of the mortgage that exceeds the original purchase price plus improvements of property, unless the taxpayer uses the money for medical or educational purposes.

**MOST LIKELY TIME** in PROGRAM EVALUATION AND REVIEW TECHNIQUE (PERT), the time that the activity would most likely take if it were repeated time and time again; denoted by *m*. *See also* EXPECTED TIME FOR AN ACTIVITY.

**MOVING AVERAGE** average that is updated as new information is received. With the moving average, an accountant employs the most recent observations to calculate an average, using the result as the forecast for the next period. For example, assume that the accountant has the following cash inflow data:

| Month | Cash Collections (000) |
|-------|------------------------|
| May | 20 |
| June | 24 |
| July | 22 |
| August | 26 |
| Sept. | 25 |

Using a four-period moving average, the accountant computes the predicted cash collection for October as follows:

$$\frac{(24 + 22 + 26 + 25)}{4} = \frac{97}{4} = 24.25, \text{ or } \$24,250.$$

**MOVING AVERAGE INVENTORY METHOD** method used under a PERPETUAL INVENTORY SYSTEM, which requires that a new weighted average cost must be calculated after *each* purchase. The new weighted average is computed in the same way as in the WEIGHTED AVERAGE INVENTORY METHOD; that is, the average cost is the cost of the units available for sale after the purchase divided by the number of units available for sale at that time. This average cost is used to determine the cost of each sale made prior to the next purchase.

For example, assume the following inventory data for Company J:

| | | |
|---|---|---|
| Inventory, March 1 | 100 units @ $10 per unit | $1,000 |
| Purchases, March 10 | 80 units @ $11 per unit | 880 |
| Purchases, March 20 | 70 units @ $12 per unit | 840 |
| Goods available for sale | 250 units | $2,720 |
| Sales, March 18 | 90 units | |
| Sales, March 27 | 50 units | |
| | 140 units | |
| Inventory, March 31 | 110 units | |

The moving average costs are computed as follows:

| | | | |
|---|---|---|---|
| March 1, beginning inventory | 100 units @ $10 | | $1,000 |
| March 10, purchases | 80 | @ $11 | 880 |
| March 10, balance | 180 | @ $10.44 | $1,880 |
| March 18, sales | 90 | @ $10.44 | 940 |
| March 18, balance | 90 | @ $10.44 | $ 940 |
| March 20, purchases | 70 | @ $12 | 840 |
| March 20, balance | 160 | @ $11.125 | $1,780 |
| March 27, sales | 50 | @ $11.125 | 556 |
| March 30, balance | 110 | @ $11.125 | $1,224 |

Cost of goods sold (140 units) $940 + $556     $1,496

Ending inventory (110 units @ $11.125)     $1,224

**MOVING EXPENSE DEDUCTION** deduction allowed in computing adjusted gross income of employees and self-employed individuals who paid or incurred moving costs. Two major requirements must be satisfied before a deduction is allowed: minimum distance moved and minimum period of employment. Allowable expenses are transportation and storage of household goods and personal effects, as well as travel (including lodging) from the old residence to the new residence. The cost of meals, however, is not deductible.

**MOVING TIME** time spent moving a product from one operation or department to another.

**MRP** *see* MATERIAL REQUIREMENT PLANNING (MRP).

**MULTICOLLINEARITY** condition that exists when independent variables are highly correlated with each other. In the presence of multicollinearity, the estimated REGRESSION COEFFICIENTS may be unreliable. The presence of multicollinearity can be tested by investigating the correlation ($r$) between the independent variables.

**MULTIPLE DISCRIMINANT ANALYSIS (MDA)** statistical classificatory technique similar to regression analysis that can be used to evaluate financial ratios.

**MULTIPLE OVERHEAD RATES** manner of measuring product costs. A different predetermined overhead rate is set for each department of a factory, rather than having a single predetermined rate for the entire factory. When products are heterogeneous, receiving uneven attention and effort as they move through various departments, departmental rates are necessary to achieve more accurate and equitable product costs. For example, if department A is labor intensive, application of overhead costs could be done more equitably on a basis of direct labor-hours or labor cost. If department B is machine oriented, allocation should be based on machine hours. *See also* PLANTWIDE OVERHEAD RATE; PREDETERMINED OVERHEAD RATE.

**MULTIPLE RECORDING OF TRANSACTIONS** in GOVERNMENTAL ACCOUNTING, entries made in more then one fund, when two or more funds each have authority over the same transaction. For example, the general fund may expend money to acquire fixed assets; however, the fund does not capitalize fixed assets. Thus the entry in the general fund is to debit expenditures and credit vouchers payable, and a memo entry is made in the general fixed asset account group to show the fixed asset.

**MULTIPLE REGRESSION** *see* MULTIPLE REGRESSION ANALYSIS.

**MULTIPLE REGRESSION ANALYSIS** statistical procedure that attempts to assess the relationship between a dependent variable and *two* or more independent variables. Examples: Total factory overhead (the dependent variable) is related to both labor-hours and machine-hours (the independent variables). Sales of a popular soft drink (the dependent variable) is a function of various factors, such as its price, advertising, taste, and the prices of its major competitors (the independent variables). *See also* REGRESSION ANALYSIS.

**MULTI-STEP COST REASSIGNMENT** reassignment of resource costs requiring one or more intermediate activity cost reassignments prior to cost assignment into the final cost objects.

**MULTIPLE-STEP INCOME STATEMENT** one providing multiple classifications and multiple intermediate differences. The multiple-step format reports amounts for the following income captions: (1) gross margin, (2) income from continuing operations, (3) income before extraordinary items, and (4) net income. An illustrative multiple-step income statement follows:

Sales
Less: Sales returns and allowances
Net sales
Less: Cost of sales
Gross margin
Less: Operating expenses
Income from continuing operations
Add: Other revenue and expenses
Less: Other expenses and losses
Income before tax and extraordinary items
Less: Provision for taxes
Income before extraordinary items
Add or Less: Extraordinary items (net of tax)
Net income

**MULTITASKING** simultaneous execution of two or more computer functions.

**MUNICIPAL BOND** *see* TAX-EXEMPT BOND.

**MUNICIPAL FINANCE OFFICERS ASSOCIATION (MFOA)** organization of financial officers working for municipalities. The goal of MFOA is to bring together representatives of various groups concerned with municipal accounting and to put into effect sound principles of accounting, budgeting, and reporting.

**MUTUAL FUND** portfolio of securities professionally managed by the sponsoring *management company* or *investment company* that issues shares to investors. A no-load fund does not charge a sales commission to buy shares, whereas a load fund does charge one. Mutual funds also charge management fees. The major advantages of mutual funds are diversification, professional management, and ownership of a variety of securities with a minimal capital investment. Further, dividend reinvestment and check-writing options may exist. Mutual funds are also convenient because recordkeeping is done by the fund. There are several drawbacks, however. Mutual funds may be costly to acquire because of sizable commissions and professional management fees. Traditionally, mutual fund performance on average has not outperformed the market as a whole. Quotations for mutual funds are stated in dollars and cents. The sale price is known as the NAV or net asset value. An illustrative quote for XYZ Stock Growth Fund follows:

|                        | NAV   | Offer Price | NAV Change |
|------------------------|-------|-------------|------------|
| XYZ Stock Growth Fund  | 11.22 | 12.26       | +.02       |

The quotation tells us that a share in the fund on a particular day could be sold for $11.22—the NAV. On the same date, a share could be bought for $12.26. The difference between the sale price and the purchase price is due to the commission charged on the purchase transaction. The NAV change value of + .02 indicates that the sale price (NAV) increased by 2 cents a share from the preceding day.

Mutual funds may be classified into types, according to organization, fees charged, methods of trading funds, and investment objectives. In open-end funds, investors buy from and sell their shares back to the fund itself. Closed-end funds operate with a fixed number of shares outstanding. These shares are traded like common stocks among individuals in secondary markets. Closed-end funds, although a variation of the investment company, have quite different investment characteristics from open-end funds. For example, they may sell at discounts or premiums to NAV and have variations within the category (e.g., dual-purpose funds).

Many different types of mutual funds exist, including growth stock funds, bond funds, money market funds, and tax-free security funds. A mutual fund family, which offers many various types of funds, typically allows its investors switching privileges at no cost or at a nominal fee.

**MUTUALLY EXCLUSIVE INVESTMENTS** group of CAPITAL BUD-GET projects that compete with one another in such a way that the acceptance of one automatically excludes all others from further consideration. Analysis of competing projects using the NET PRESENT VALUE (NPV) and INTERNAL RATE OF RETURN (IRR) methods may give decision results contradictory to each other. From a practical standpoint, the NPV method generally gives correct ranking to mutually exclusive projects.

**MySQL** the most popular open-source database. It is cost effective, high performance, highly reliable, and scalable.

# N

**NAA** *see* NATIONAL ASSOCIATION OF ACCOUNTANTS (NAA).

**NASDAQ** *see* NATIONAL ASSOCIATION OF SECURITIES DEALERS (NASD).

**NATIONAL ASSOCIATION OF ACCOUNTANTS (NAA)** organization made up mostly of non-CPAs. It has made significant contributions over the years to the development of management accounting principles. It has created the Institute of Management Accounting, which offers a program leading to the CERTIFICATE IN MANAGEMENT ACCOUNTING (CMA).

**NATIONAL ASSOCIATION OF SECURITIES DEALERS (NASD)** self-policing organization of brokers and dealers who handle OVER-THE-COUNTER (OTC) MARKET securities. The NASD functions principally along five lines: (1) it has developed a written code of fair practices dealing with such matters as the appropriateness of prices quoted to customers; (2) it has promulgated standard procedures in transactions between members; (3) it has improved the quality of service that the OTC market gives the investing public; (4) it undertakes to investigate and arbitrate disputes between parties and to take disciplinary measures when justified; and (5) it undertakes to study and make recommendations on pending legislation in the security field. It also owns and operates a computerized system providing price quotations for OTC and some exchange-listed securities. The system is known as NASDAQ, an acronym for *National Association of Securities Dealers Automated Quotations* system. In 2007, NASD merged with the regulation committee of the New York Stock Exchange, effectively creating the Financial Industry Regulatory Authority (FINRA).

**NATIONAL ASSOCIATION OF STATE BOARDS OF ACCOUNTANCY (NASBA)** national organization representing the 54 state licensing boards/agencies that regulate the CPA profession in all states and four U.S. territories.

**NATIONAL AUTOMATED ACCOUNTING RESEARCH SYSTEM (NAARS)** AMERICAN INSTITUTE OF CERTIFIED PUBLIC ACCOUNTANTS' (AICPA) online database containing recommended accounting practices and footnote references. It answers practice questions and gives proper accounting for a transaction or event. In accessing NAARS, a key word or group of words is used to describe the question or problem, and relevant references are obtained.

**NATIONAL COMMISSION ON FRAUDULENT FINANCIAL REPORTING (TREADWAY COMMISSION)** has as its purpose to determine how fraudulent financial reporting practices can be constrained. This commission defined fraudulent financial reporting as "intentional or reckless conduct, whether act or omission, that results in materially misleading financial statements."

**NATIONAL DO NOT CALL REGISTRY** managed by the Federal Trade Commission (FTC), the government's consumer protection agency, the registry limits the telemarketing calls you receive. Telemarketers are required to remove the numbers on the registry from their call lists.

**NATIONAL FEDERATION OF INDEPENDENT BUSINESS (NFIB)** (www.nfib.com) the largest advocacy organization representing small and independent businesses in Washington, D.C., and all 50 state capitals. NFIB was ranked the most influential business organization (and third overall) in "Washington's Power 25" survey conducted by *Fortune* magazine. NFIB's purpose is to impact public policy at the state and federal level and be a key business resource for small and independent business in America. NFIB also gives its members a power in the marketplace. By pooling the purchasing power of its 600,000 members, the National Federation of Independent Business gives members access to many business products and services at discounted costs. NFIB also provides timely information designed to help small businesses succeed. The NFIB's well-known small-business optimism index is based on responses from 1,221 member firms.

**NATIONAL INCOME ACCOUNTING** necessary step in learning how macroeconomic variables—such as the economy's total output, the price level, the level of employment, interest rates, and other variables are determined. The national income accounts provide regular estimates of GROSS DOMESTIC PRODUCT (GDP), the basic measure of the performance of the economy in producing goods and services. They are also useful because they provide a conceptual framework for describing the relationships among three key macroeconomic variables: output, income, and spending.

**NATURAL BUSINESS YEAR** *see* FISCAL YEAR.

**NEGATIVE ASSURANCE** method used by the CERTIFIED PUBLIC ACCOUNTANT to assure various parties, such as bankers and stockbrokers, that financial data under review by them is correct. Negative assurance tells the data user that nothing has come to the CPA's attention of an adverse nature or character regarding the financial data reviewed. This type of assurance is normally given to investment bankers and the SEC when the financial data are being used for stock and bond issuance. In addition, this assurance is given whenever a CPA is asked to comment on financial statements upon which a previous AUDIT OPINION has been rendered. (This type of assurance is unacceptable for the basic financial statements on which a certifying audit has been performed.) Further, negative assurance comments are made on unaudited financial statements and subsequent changes, indicating that nothing came to the auditor's attention that suggests the statements do not comply with applicable accounting requirements; are not fairly presented in conformity with GAAP applied on a consistent basis; or do not fairly present information shown therein. Negative assurance is given because the auditor has not made an examination in conformity with GENERALLY ACCEPTED AUDITING STANDARDS (GAAS). Negative assurance is not appropriate unless the CPA has made an examination in accordance with GAAS for the accounting period before the current one. This is due to the fact that the auditor needs evidence that can be related to COMFORT LETTER procedures. For negative assurance to be permissible, the evidence must have been gathered directly by the CPA giving the assurance, and not by another CPA.

**NEGATIVE CONFIRMATION** written request by the external auditor sent to a party having a financial relationship with the client and asking for a reply only in the case of disagreement. For example, a company may mail a form on behalf of the CPA firm to sampled customers requesting them to notify the auditor only if a discrepancy in the account balance exists. *See also* POSITIVE CONFIRMATION.

**NEGATIVE GOODWILL** term used in a business combination. Negative goodwill is accounted for under the PURCHASE (ACCOUNTING) METHOD when the fair market value of the net assets of the acquired company exceeds the purchase price paid. The credit difference reduces certain assets acquired. If any remaining credit exists, it is accounted for as an extraordinary gain.

**NEGLIGENCE** accountant's failure to conduct an audit with "due care." *Ordinary negligence* applies to judgment errors resulting from a lack of experience, training, or oversight: it is unintentional. *Gross negligence* results when the accountant recklessly disregards established accounting, reporting, and auditing standards. *See also* GENERALLY ACCEPTED ACCOUNTING PRINCIPLES (GAAP).

**NEGOTIATED PRICE** *transfer* price that is established through meetings between the buying and supplying divisions. Negotiated transfer prices, like *market price*-based transfer prices, are believed to preserve divisional autonomy. In case divisions cannot agree on a transfer price, some companies establish arbitrary procedures to help settle disputes. However, intervention by an arbitrator reduces divisional autonomy.

**NEGOTIATED TRANSFER PRICE** *see* NEGOTIATED PRICE.

**NET**
1. gross amount reduced by applicable reductions. For example, net sales equals gross sales less sales returns and allowances and sales discounts. Another example is net purchases that equal gross purchases less purchase returns and allowances and purchase discounts.
2. (informal) net profit after taxes.

**NET ASSETS** total assets less total liabilities. *See also* NET WORTH.

**NET CASH INFLOW** balance of increases in cash receipts over increases in cash payments resulting from a proposed capital investment.

**NET INCOME** revenue less all expenses; also called *net profit*. Other elements involved in computing net income include extraordinary items (net of tax) and cumulative effect of a change in accounting principle (net of tax). *See also* INCOME STATEMENT.

**NET LOSS** amount by which total costs and expenses exceed total revenue for the accounting period. *See also* NET INCOME.

**NET OF TAX** term used when certain items presented in the financial statements have been adjusted for all income tax effects. Some examples of financial statement items shown net of tax in the income statement are *extraordinary gains and losses*, cumulative effect of a CHANGE IN ACCOUNTING PRINCIPLE, and INCOME FROM DISCONTINUED OPERATIONS. In the retained earnings section of the balance sheet, PRIOR PERIOD ADJUSTMENTS are presented net of tax.

**NET OF TAX METHOD** unacceptable method of handling the effects of deferred taxes when temporary differences exist. Deferred taxes caused by temporary differences adjust the specific assets and liabilities to which they apply as well as the related revenues and expenses. *See also* DEFERRED TAX ALLOCATION METHOD; LIABILITY TAX ALLOCATION METHOD.

**NET OPERATING LOSS (NOL)** excess of operating expenses over operating revenues. It excludes income statement items that do not relate to normal business activities, such as extraordinary gains or losses. It also excludes financial expenses and revenue (i.e., interest expense, dividend income). *See also* LOSS CARRYBACK; LOSS CARRYFORWARD.

**NET PRESENT VALUE (NPV)** difference between the PRESENT VALUE (PV) of cash inflows generated by the project and the amount of the initial investment (*I*). The present value of future cash flows is computed using the COST OF CAPITAL (*minimum desired rate of return*, or HURDLE RATE) as the discount rate. *See also* NET PRESENT VALUE METHOD.

**NET PRESENT VALUE METHOD** widely used approach for evaluating an investment project. Under the net present value method, the present value (*PV*) of all cash inflows from the project is compared against the initial investment (*I*). The NET PRESENT VALUE (NPV), which is the difference between the present value and the initial investment (i.e., $NPV = PV - I$), determines whether the project is an acceptable investment. To compute the present value of cash inflows, a rate called the COST OF CAPITAL is used for discounting. Under the method, if the net present value is positive ($NPV > 0$ or $PV > I$), the project should be accepted.

**NET PRICE METHOD** accounting procedure in which purchases are recorded at the net price after cash discounts rather than at the gross amount. When discounts are not taken, the amount paid in excess of the recorded purchase price is charged to a discounts lost account. *See also* GROSS PRICE METHOD.

**NET PROCEEDS**
1. amount received from the sale or disposal of property less all relevant deductions (direct costs associated with the sale or disposal).
2. amount received from the issuance of securities less FLOATATION COSTS.

**NET PROFIT** *see* NET INCOME.

**NET PURCHASE** net cost of purchases, which is purchases *minus* purchase returns and allowances and purchase discounts *plus* transportation. This calculation appears in the cost of goods sold section of the income statement.

**NET REALIZABLE VALUE**
1. expected selling price of an inventory item less expected costs to complete and dispose. This is the ceiling amount in applying the LOWER OF COST OR MARKET rule to inventory valuation.
2. gross accounts receivable less allowance for doubtful accounts, representing the expected collectibility of those receivables.

**NET SALES** gross sales less sales returns and allowances and sales discounts.

**NETWORK**
1. foundation for a PROGRAM EVALUATION AND REVIEW TECHNIQUE (PERT) or CRITICAL PATH METHOD (CPM) analysis. It (1) visualizes all of the individual tasks to complete a given job or program; (2) points out interrelationships; and (3) comprises arrows linking circles (nodes).
2. system used as a complement to multiprogramming, time sharing, and satellite transmission of computer data and programs. Accounting, auditing, and tax practitioners may benefit from the linking of microcomputers through LOCAL AREA NETWORKS (LANS). LANs allow for data exchange, electronic mail, and pooling of data files.

**NET WORKING CAPITAL** *see* WORKING CAPITAL.

**NETWORK INTERFACE CARD (NIC)** a circuit board used to connect a computer to a network. A NIC is also referred to as an Ethernet card or a network adapter.

**NET WORTH** total assets less total liabilities. Net worth, for an individual, is equal to his or her personal equity. In a business, net worth represents the stockholders' equity. *See also* OWNERS' EQUITY.

**NEURAL NETWORKS** technology in which computers actually try to learn from the data base and operator what the right answer is to a question. The system gets positive or negative response to output from the operator and stores that data so that it will make a better decision the next time. While still in its infancy, this technology shows promise for use in accounting, fraud detection, economic forecasting, and risk appraisals. The idea behind this software is to convert the order-taking computer into a "thinking" problem solver.

**NEUTRALITY** absence of bias. For example, financial information should be neutral and is not intended to favor an investor over a creditor. Neutrality is one of the ingredients of RELIABILITY.

**NEW ECONOMY** the new, digital economy driven by industrial information technology, much of which is related to telecommunications such as the Internet—a technology that, many argue, has a huge potential to transform the engineering industry. In the new economy, production and distribution systems are automated, computer-based systems. The old economy, classical or traditional, is undergoing sweeping changes through the speed and efficiency brought by applications of information technology and the Internet.

**NEW YORK STOCK EXCHANGE (NYSE)** national stock exchange that is located at the corner of Broad and Wall Streets in New York City; often called the *Big Board*. It has a central trading location where securities are bought and sold in an auction market by brokers acting as agents for the buyer and seller. It is governed by a board of directors consisting of one-half exchange members and one-half public members. The NYSE is the largest exchange and generates the most dollar volume in large, well-known companies. Its listing requirements are the most restrictive. For a company to be listed on the NYSE for the first time, for example, the corporation must have at least 2000 stockholders owning 100 shares, and its aggregate market value must be $18 million or more.

**NEXT-IN, FIRST-OUT (NIFO)** inventory valuation method whereby the cost of sale of the item is based on the cost to replace it rather than on historical cost. For example, an item costing $10 with a replacement cost of $12 is sold for $20. Under NIFO, gross profit is $8 ($20 minus $12). This method is *not* GAAP. However, during inflationary periods a company may want to price ahead of inflation by establishing its selling price on a replacement-cost basis and would thus use NIFO as a basis for pricing.

**NODAL COST FLOW NETWORK** network view of ABC in which the sources of the cost reassignments and downstream cost objects are thought of as "sending" and "receiving" nodes in a closed-system network.

**NODE** in PROGRAM EVALUATION AND REVIEW TECHNIQUE (PERT), circle in a network representing the beginning and ending of activities. A node symbolizes an event.

**NOMINAL ACCOUNT** income statement account (revenue and expense) that is closed out at the end of the year. *See also* CLOSING ENTRY; REAL ACCOUNT.

**NOMINAL CAPITAL** par or stated value of a company's issued capital stock.

**NOMINAL INTEREST RATE** stated interest rate on the face of a debt security or loan. For example, if a bond having a face value of $100,000 has a coupon interest rate of 8%, the nominal interest is $8,000, which will be paid each year. The terms *nominal interest rate* and COUPON RATE are synonymous in discussing bonds; the latter term is still commonly used even though it is rare these days for bonds to be issued with physical coupons. *See also* EFFECTIVE INTEREST RATE.

**NONBUSINESS EXPENSE DEDUCTION** broad category of deductions, such as state and local sales taxes and certain miscellaneous deductions. Individuals cannot take an itemized deduction for state and local sales taxes. Also, no deduction is allowed for expenses related to attending a convention, seminar, or similar meeting unless such expenses are connected with a trade or business. Thus expenses for a convention, or for a meeting in connection with investments, financial planning, or other income-producing activity, will no longer be deductible. Certain miscellaneous itemized deductions, including unreimbursed employee business expenses, are deductible by individuals only if the aggregate amount of the deductions exceeds two percent of the taxpayer's ADJUSTED GROSS INCOME (AGI).

**NONCASH EXPENSE** expense that did not require a cash outlay during the period under review.

**NONCASH INVESTING AND FINANCING TRANSACTIONS** significant investing and financing transactions that do not involve an actual cash inflow or outflow. They involve only long-term assets, long-term liabilities, or stockholders' equity, such as the exchange of a long-term asset for a long-term liability or the settlement of a debt by issuing capital stock.

**NONCONFORMANCE COSTS** a category of QUALITY COSTS, including internal failure costs (a financial measure of internal performance) and external failure costs (a financial measure of customer satisfaction).

**NONCONTROLLABLE COST** cost not subject to influence at a given level of managerial supervision. For instance, a manager's salary is not within the control of the manager himself. Rent of the factory building is another example. *See also* CONTROLLABLE COST.

**NONCONTROLLABLE INTEREST** *see* MINORITY INTEREST.

**NONCONTROLLABLE RISK** *see* SYSTEMATIC RISK.

**NONDEDUCTIBLE TAX** tax paid but not allowed as a deduction. An example is for state and local sales taxes, making them examples of *nondeductible taxes*.

**NONDIVERSIFIABLE RISK** *see* SYSTEMATIC RISK.

**NONINTEREST-BEARING NOTE** note receivable or note payable that does not provide for interest. In this unrealistic case, IMPUTED INTEREST on the note is required. Until tax reform, such notes were commonly used in transactions between parents and children (e.g., crown loans) and are still permitted under limited circumstances. The term *interest-bearing* is also used in contradistinction to *discount* or *zero-coupon instruments*.

**NONINVENTORIABLE COST** *see* PERIOD COST.

**NONISSUER** an entity whose equity or debt securities are *not* publicly traded on a stock exchange or in the over-the-counter market; it is not required to file financial statements with the SEC. Nonissuers are *exempted* from numerous accounting requirements (i.e., SEGMENT REPORTING) and are sometimes referred to as nonpublic companies.

**NONLINEARITY** situation where the relationship between variables is not directly proportional. For example, a per unit cost may decrease as production increases, because of economies of scale. The following diagram shows a comparison between a linear and a nonlinear cost function. *See also* LINEARITY.

LINEAR RELATIONSHIP    NONLINEAR RELATIONSHIP

**NONMANUFACTURING EXPENSES** *see* OPERATING EXPENSES.

**NONMONETARY EXCHANGE** method of handling an exchange between one business entity and another that results in the acquisition of assets or services or the satisfaction of liabilities by surrendering cash assets (boot) or services or issuing other obligations. If the transaction has commercial substance, all gains and losses are recognized. If the nonmonetary transaction lacks commercial substance, then none of the gain is recognized but all of the loss is recognized. If boot is received and the amount of boot is less than 25% of the fair market value of the asset, then a partial gain is recognized. The gain recognized equals the total potential gain times the ratio of the boot to the total fair market value of the assets plus the boot. If the boot received is equal to or more than 25%, the boot is ignored and the full gain or loss is recognized.

**NONMONETARY ITEM** item stated in *older* dollars and therefore requiring direct adjustment in the price-level financial statements. It is any financial statement item that is not classified as a MONETARY ITEM. Examples of nonmonetary assets are land, buildings, and autos. Nonmonetary liabilities are obligations not payable in money, such as those payable in services (i.e., warranties payable) or those that will adjust an expense (i.e., deferred income tax credit). Stockholders' equity accounts are also considered nonmonetary. Examples of nonmonetary income statement accounts are depreciation and amortization.

**NONPARAMETRIC STATISTICS** type of statistics applied to problems for which rank order is known, but the specific distribution is not; also known as *distribution-free statistics*. Thus, various metals may be ranked in order of hardness without having any measure of hardness.

**NONPRODUCTIVE CAPACITY** capacity that is useable but is temporarily in a nonproductive state due to setups, scheduled downtime, unscheduled downtime or rework (repeating production because the first run came out wrong, or discarding materials rendered unusable after an unsuccessful run).

**NONPROFIT ACCOUNTING** accounting policies, procedures, and techniques employed by NONPROFIT ORGANIZATIONS. Nonprofit accounting is somewhat different for governmental units than for nongovernmental units (i.e., colleges, hospitals, voluntary health and welfare organizations, and charities). Governmental units employ *fund accounting*, which measures ACCOUNTABILITY rather than profitability. The MODIFIED ACCRUAL basis is typically employed by governmental funds. Nongovernmental units use the *accrual* basis.

**NONPROFIT ORGANIZATION** group, institution, or corporation formed for the purpose of providing goods and services under a policy where no individual (e.g., stockholder, trustee) will share in any profits or losses of the organization. Profit is *not* the primary goal of nonprofit entities. Profit may develop, however, under a different name (e.g., surplus, increase in fund balance). Assets are typically provided by sources that do not expect repayment or economic return. Usually, there are restrictions on resources obtained. Examples of nonprofit organizations are governments, charities, universities, religious institutions, and some hospitals. Most nonprofit organizations have been granted exemption from federal taxes by the Internal Revenue Service. Many of these organizations refer to themselves according to the IRS Code section under which they receive exempt status (i.e., 502(c)(3) organization). This identification lets donors know that their contributions to this organization may be deductible for income tax purposes.

**NONRECIPROCAL TRANSFER**
1. transfer of assets or services from a business to its owners or to another entity, or vice versa.
2. exchange of dissimilar assets in a nonmonetary transaction. *See also* NONMONETARY EXCHANGE.

**NONRECURRING** income statement item that is either unusual in nature or infrequent in occurrence. An example is the gain or loss on the sale of a fixed asset. Nonrecurring items are shown before arriving at income from continuing operations. They are *not* shown with a tax or earnings per share effect. *See also* EXTRAORDINARY ITEM.

**NONROUTINE DECISION** short-term, nonrecurring decision such as the following: (1) to accept or reject a special order; (2) to make or buy a certain part; (3) to sell or process further; or (4) to keep or drop a certain product line or division. In these types of decisions, a choice is typically made considering the RELEVANT COSTS and CONTRIBUTION MARGIN.

**NONSAMPLING RISK** any component of audit risk that is not associated with sampling. Nonsampling risk includes applying an audit procedure that does not fit an audit objective, misinterpretation of test results, and the outright failure to detect a material misstatement.

**NONSTATISTICAL SAMPLING** any sampling plan that is based on judgment rather than on probability theory. Nonstatistical and statistical sampling may result in the same sample size and evaluation of test results.

**NONTAXABLE GROSS INCOME** income received by the taxpayer that is not taxable, such as a gift.

**NONTAXABLE INVESTMENT INCOME** income such as interest on a tax-free municipal bond that is not included in taxable income when preparing the federal tax return.

**NONVALUE-ADDED ACTIVITY** activity that increases the time spent on a product or service but does not increase its worth to the customer. The designation "nonvalue-added" reflects a belief that the activity can be redesigned, reduced, or eliminated without reducing the quantity, responsiveness, or quality of the output required by the customer or the organization. *See also* CUSTOMER VALUE and VALUE ANALYSIS.

**NONVALUE-ADDING COST** cost of an operating activity that adds cost to a product or service, but, from a customer's perspective, does not increase its market value.

**NO-PAR-VALUE CAPITAL STOCK** shares designated in the charter that do not have a par or assigned value printed on the stock certificate. However, some states authorize the issuance of no-par stock with a stated value. When no-par stock is issued, the entry is to debit cash and credit capital stock for the total proceeds received. No premium is required on the capital stock account. An advantage of no-par stock is that it avoids a contingent liability to stockholders in the case of a stock discount. One of the original reasons for no-par stock was to avoid state taxes based on par value, but states will sometimes tax no-par stock as if it had par value. A disadvantage of no-par stock is that inept directors may lower the value of outstanding shares by accepting minimal prices on new issues.

**NORMAL ABSORPTION COSTING** method of product costing. It includes actual costs of direct material and direct labor plus factory overhead applied by using predetermined overhead rates times actual units of inputs (such as direct labor hours, machine hours, direct material dollars, or direct labor cost). This method smoothes fluctuations in overhead costs that occur during the year. It also provides timely costing information that would not be available if the firm waited until year-end to determine the actual rates. *See also* EXTENDED NORMAL COSTING.

**NORMAL ACTIVITY** level of production that will satisfy average demand by consumers over a time span (often five years) that includes trend, seasonal, and cyclical factors. It is a long-run average expected activity that is a basis for developing the factory overhead application rate.

**NORMAL CAPACITY** *see* CAPACITY.

**NORMAL COSTING** *see* NORMAL ABSORPTION COSTING.

**NORMAL COSTS**
1. annual average of product costs, not actual product costs that are affected by month-to-month fluctuations in production volume and by erratic or seasonal behavior of many overhead costs. Typical examples of erratic behavior include repairs and maintenance, fuel, air-conditioning costs, vacation and holiday pay, and the employer's share of Social Security taxes. All the costs that distort monthly overhead rates are collected in the annual overhead pool along with the kinds of overhead that do have uniform behavior patterns. In summary, normal costs are the sum of actual direct materials, actual direct labor, and applied factory overhead.
2. pension plan costs incurred during an accounting period for services performed during the period. *See also* NORMAL PENSION COST.

**NORMAL DISTRIBUTION** probability distribution. It has the following important characteristics: (1) the curve has a single peak; (2) it is bell-shaped; (3) the mean (average) lies at the center of the distribution, and the distribution is symmetrical around the mean; (4) the two tails of the distribution extend indefinitely and never touch the horizontal axis; (5) the shape of the distribution is determined by its MEAN ($\mu$) and STANDARD DEVIATION ($\sigma$).

## NORMAL DISTRIBUTION

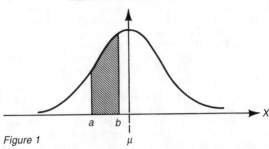

*Figure 1*

As with any continuous probability function, the area under the curve must equal 1, and the area between two values of $X$ (say, $a$ and $b$) represents the probability that $X$ lies between $a$ and $b$ as illustrated on *Figure 1*. Further, since the normal is a symmetric distribution, it has the nice property that a known percentage of all possible values of $X$ lie within ± a certain number of standard deviations of the mean, as illustrated by *Figure 2*. For example, 68.27% of the values of any normally distributed variable lie within the interval $(\mu - 1, \mu + 1)$.

### STANDARD DEVIATION OF THE MEAN

*Figure 2*

| Percent | 99.73% | 99% | 95.45% | 95% | 90% | 80% | 68.27% |
|---------|--------|-----|--------|-----|-----|-----|--------|
| No. of ± 's | 3.00 | 2.58 | 2.00 | 1.96 | 1.645 | 1.28 | 1.00 |

The probability of the normal as given above is difficult to work with in determining areas under the curve, and each set of $X$ values generates another curve as long as the means and standard deviations are translated to a new axis, a $Z$-axis, with the translation defined as

$$Z = \frac{X - \mu}{\sigma}$$

The resulting values, called Z-values, are the values of a new variable called the *standard normal variate*, Z. The translation process is depicted in *Figure 3*.

STANDARD NORMAL VARIATE

The Translation of X to Z by the Transformation $Z = (X - \mu)/\sigma$

*Figure 3*

The new variable Z is normally distributed with a mean of zero and a standard deviation of 1. Tables of areas under this standard normal distribution have been compiled and widely published so that areas under any normal distribution can be found by translating the X values to Z values and then using the tables for the standardized normal. For example, assume the total book value of an inventory is normally distributed with $\mu = \$8,000$ and $\sigma = \$1,000$. What percent of the population lies between \$6,000 and \$10,000? To answer, first translate these two X-values to Z-values using the Z formula:

$$Z_1 = (\$6,000 - \$8,000)/\$1,000 \qquad Z_2 = (\$10,000 - \$8,000)/\$1,000$$
$$= -2 \qquad\qquad\qquad\qquad = +2$$

Referring to *Figure 2*, note that 95.45% of the population lies between these two values. Interpreted as a probability, the statement can be made that total book value will lie between \$6,000 and \$10,000, with a probability of .9545.

**NORMAL EQUATIONS** ones obtained via the LEAST-SQUARES METHOD, which minimizes the sum of squares of the deviations of the actual points from the line $y = a + bx$. The idea is to obtain the line of best fit. The normal equations are:

$$\Sigma y = na + b \, \Sigma x$$
$$\Sigma xy = a \, \Sigma x + bx^2$$

where $\Sigma$ denotes summation over all $n$ observations. *See also* REGRESSION ANALYSIS.

**NORMAL PENSION COST** actuarial present value of benefits attributed by the pension formula to employee service performed during the current year; also called *service cost*. Normal pension cost is funded dollar for dollar. *See also* PRIOR SERVICE PENSION COST.

**NORMAL SPOILAGE** product deterioration that is expected even under the best operating conditions. It is inherent and unavoidable in the short run. Costs of normal spoilage are allocated to the remaining good units in inventory. Management establishes a *normal spoilage rate* that is acceptable under a given combination of production factors. Normal spoilage is a cost of goods produced. *See also* ABNORMAL SPOILAGE.

**NORMAL STOCK METHOD** *see* BASE STOCK METHOD.

**NOTE PAYABLE** written promise to pay money at a future date. The payment consists of principal and usually interest. For example, a $10,000 three-month 6% note will require a payment at maturity of $10,150 ($10,000 principal plus $150 interest). The interest of $150 equals $10,000 × 6% × 3/12. A note payable may be classified as either a current or a noncurrent liability, depending on whether the note is due within one year or less. A note payable may be issued either to make a purchase, to refinance an open account payable, or to borrow from the bank. *See also* NOTE RECEIVABLE.

**NOTE RECEIVABLE** written promise to receive money at a future date, comprising principal and usually interest. Depending on whether the note is for one year or less, it can be classified as either a current or a noncurrent asset. Interest earned on the note is credited to the interest income account. *See also* NOTE PAYABLE.

**NOTE RECEIVABLE DISCOUNTED** discounted proceeds from a note, received by the holder of a customer's note, from a third party, usually a bank or finance company, prior to its maturity date. The proceeds received by the holder equal the maturity value less the bank discount (interest charge). The bank discount is based upon (1) the time period the bank will be holding the note and (2) the note's interest rate. The interest rate charged by the bank is usually higher than the interest rate on the note. The maturity value of the note equals the face value of the note plus interest. The bank discount equals the maturity value times the discount rate times the period the note is held by the bank. The net proceeds received by the payee at the time of discounting equals the maturity value less the bank discount. Note that notes receivable discounted represents a contingent liability to be footnoted.

**NOT-FOR-PROFIT ORGANIZATION** *see* NONPROFIT ORGANIZATION.

**NOT-SUFFICIENT-FUNDS CHECK (NSF CHECK)** check not covered by sufficient bank balance. In preparing its BANK RECONCILIATION, the depositing entity must deduct the NSF check from the cash book balance.

**NUMBER OF DAYS INVENTORY IS HELD** *see* DAYS TO SELL INVENTORY.

# O

**OBJECTIVE FUNCTION** *see* LINEAR PROGRAMMING (LP).

**OBJECTIVE PROBABILITY** characteristic obtained as a result of repeated experiments or repeated trials rather than on the basis of subjective estimates. It is useful in estimating dollar value, quantity, or other characteristics of a given universe for purposes of making statistical decisions.

**OBJECTIVES OF FINANCIAL REPORTING** goal of presenting useful information to financial statement users so that proper decisions can be made. Data presented should be comprehensive so that a good understanding of the entity's activities is possible. Financial information should aid in the evaluation of the amounts, timing, and uncertainties of cash flows. Also, financial reporting should furnish information about the firm's economic resources, claims against those resources, owners' equity, and changes in resources and claims. Financial reporting should provide information about financial performance during a period and management's discharge of its stewardship responsibility to owners. It should likewise be useful to the managers and directors themselves in making decisions on behalf of the owners.

**OBJECTIVES OF FINANCIAL STATEMENTS** goals financial statements are supposed to accomplish. The intent of financial statements is to provide information useful in economic decision making. In particular, the data should be useful in making investment and credit decisions. Financial statements should provide a reliable indication of a company's financial position, operating results, and changes in financial position. Also, statement components and categories should aid in decisions. Financial statements may provide information in addition to that specified by authoritative requirements and regulatory groups. Inasmuch as management knows the most about the business, it is encouraged to identify certain circumstances and explain their financial effects on the enterprise. Note that the FINANCIAL ACCOUNTING STANDARDS BOARD (FASB) Statement of Financial Accounting Concepts No. 1, "Objectives of Financial Statements," provides reporting goals.

**OBJECTIVITY** freedom from subjective valuation and bias in making an accounting decision. Objectivity applies to a measurement having supporting evidence. Verifiability exists in that two accountants working independently of each other will come up with similar answers. An example of objectivity is recognizing revenue at time of sale because it emanates from an independent external transaction.

**OBSERVATION TEST** physical and visual verification by inspection of financial statement items or activities. The external auditor observes and evaluates how company employees conduct a variety of accounting related tasks such as documenting the existence and valuation of assets, safeguarding assets, approving expense accounts, and counting inventory. Observation tests may be conducted for *substantive* reasons, such as observing inventory, and for *compliance* purposes, such as the segregation of duties. However, an observation test does not require *detailed* physical inspection or examination of documentation. Depending on what is being tested and the method being used, the observation test may be performed by other than accounting personnel.

**OBSOLESCENCE** major factor in depreciation, resulting from technological or market changes. Wear and tear from use and natural deterioration through interaction of the elements are other factors that cause depreciation in assets. It is also a big factor in inventory risk.

**OCCUPATIONAL SAFETY AND HEALTH ACT (OSHA)** federal law concerned primarily with the regulation of working conditions in commerce and industry. It contains guidelines and regulations issued by the Department of Labor that mandate standards with respect to occupational safety and health of workers involved in interstate commerce.

**OCR** *see* OPTICAL CHARACTER RECOGNITION (OCR).

**ODD-LOT** any exception to the standard trading unit of a security. For example, with minor exceptions a standard or round-lot of stock is 100 shares, so any amount other than 100 shares or multiples thereof would be an odd-lot. The commission rate on an odd-lot transaction usually includes an *odd-lot differential*, typically 1/8th of a point. Thus the commission rate on an odd-lot transaction is relatively higher than on a round-lot transaction.

**OFF-BALANCE SHEET ASSET** item representing a resource of the entity or something expected to have future economic benefit. It is a positive sign of financial position even though it is not shown in the balance sheet. A going concern is assumed here, since in liquidation unrecorded assets would generally not be realizable. Unrecorded assets include a tax loss carryforward benefit, a purchase contract for an item at a price significantly less than the going rate, anticipated rebates, and a contingent asset (as when the entity may receive a payment if a certain event occurs).

**OFF-BALANCE SHEET FINANCING** manner of obtaining funds, often through a long-term, noncancelable lease accounted for as an operating lease. Since the lease does not meet any of the four criteria for a CAPITAL LEASE, the present value of the lease obligation is not presented on the lessee's balance sheet.

**OFF-BALANCE SHEET LIABILITY** item not reported in the body of the financial statements as a liability but possibly requiring future payment or services. These items include litigation, guarantees of future performance, and renegotiation of claims under a government contract.

**OFFICE OF MANAGEMENT AND BUDGET (OMB)** agency within the Executive Office of the President. The OMB has broad financial management power as well as the responsibility of preparing the executive budget. Among the other duties assigned OMB are: (1) to study and recommend to the president changes relative to the existing organizational structure of the agencies, their activities and methods of business, etc.; (2) to apportion appropriations among the agencies and establish reserves in anticipation of cost savings, contingencies, etc.; and (3) to develop programs and regulations for improved data gathering pertaining to the government and its agencies.

**OFFSET ACCOUNT** one that reduces the gross amount of another account to derive a net balance. Accumulated depreciation, which is a contra account to fixed assets to obtain book value, is an example of an offset account. Discount on note payable, which is a reduction of notes payable to derive the carrying value, is another example.

**OFFSETTING ERROR** error that cancels out another error; also called *counterbalancing error*. For example, if an accountant charged an expense to 20X1 when it should have been charged to 20X2, the effects of the two errors are cancelled out in 20X3. This occurs because in 20X1 the expense is overstated and the profit is understated whereas in 20X2 the expense is understated and profit overstated. Thus the beginning balance of retained earnings on 1/1/20X3 will be properly stated, since the effects of the errors offset each other. Thus over a period of two years, the effects of the errors in expense will counterbalance, and the total net income for the two years together will be the same as if the errors had not occurred. However, it should be noted that the yearly net income figures for 20X1 and 20X2 are still misstated, so the trend in earnings is distorted.

## ON ACCOUNT
1. purchase or sale on credit. For example, the journal entry for a sale on account is to debit accounts receivable and credit sales.
2. partial payment on an obligation.

**100% APPORTIONED COST DRIVER** type of cost driver that relies entirely on an informed estimator's judgment of how much cost should be traced to each cost object and to which cost objects. Does not provide rates per unit of the cost driver (for predictive planning).

**ONE-YEAR TREASURY CONSTANT MATURITY INDEX** an index of rates on U.S. Treasury borrowings that determines the changes in many adjustable-rate mortgages. The index is released by the Federal Reserve Board, which recalculates yields on a variety of Treasury securities as if each would mature in one year.

## ONLINE
1. computer equipment under the control of the central processing unit (CPU). Examples are disk drives and printers.

    **2.** Linking up one computer to another computer in a remote location through the use of the INTERNET.

**ONLINE PROCESSING** term used to refer to equipment that operates under control of the central processing unit (CPU). Online processing equipment can be placed in the same location as the CPU or in a remote location. Generally, online processing refers to processing using a terminal (input) that is remote from the CPU.

**ONLINE SEARCHING** using a computer retrieval system to obtain information from a database such as on the Internet.

**OPEN ACCOUNT**
    **1.** account that has a nonzero credit or debit balance.
    **2.** credit or charge account—that is, an account initiated by a creditor on the basis of credit standing. It may also refer to a balance currently owing due to a credit sale, under mutually agreed-upon terms (such as method of payment, trade discounts, delivery date, and quantities).

**OPEN BOOK MANAGEMENT** management philosophy that gets all employees involved in increasing financial performance and ensures that all workers have access to operational and financial information necessary to accomplishing performance improvements.

**OPEN-END MUTUAL FUND** one that issues new shares and stands ready to buy shares back at net asset value. There is usually no restriction on the amount of money that can be invested in a fund although management companies may decide at some point that the fund has gotten too large and may stop issuing new shares. The fact that there are no fixed number of shares outstanding distinguishes open-end funds from CLOSED-END MUTUAL FUNDS. *See also* MUTUAL FUND.

**OPENING ENTRY** one or a series of entries usually undertaken upon forming a new enterprise, or new accounts, or a new accounting period. A new enterprise requires opening entries with respect to the owner's interests, assets, and liabilities on the books.

**OPERATING ACTIVITIES** business activities that involve the cash effects of transactions and other events that enter into the determination of net income.

**OPERATING BUDGET** *see* OPERATIONAL (OPERATING) BUDGET.

**OPERATING BUDGET SEQUENCE** part of the master budget process that begins with the sales budget and culminates in the pro forma income statement. Its emphasis is on obtaining and using resources.

**OPERATING CAPACITY** *see* CAPACITY.

**OPERATING CYCLE** average time period between buying inventory and receiving cash proceeds from its eventual sale. It is determined by adding the *number of days inventory is held* and the COLLECTION

PERIOD for accounts receivable. Some industries, such as distillery and lumber, have a long operating cycle.

**OPERATING DECISIONS** decisions that involve routine tasks, such as planning production and sales, scheduling personnel and equipment, adjusting production rates, and controlling the quality of production.

**OPERATING ENVIRONMENT** shell program surrounding the *Disk Operating System* (DOS) of a personal computer. It turns the display into a desk-top that is basically a menu from which one selects and runs PC applications. A shell program is a software package with an integration capability. This is created when the resident operating system and application programs are surrounded with a superimposed "shell" of command structures and menus. Microsoft Windows, Linux, and IBM's OS/2, different examples of operating environments, do away with the DOS prompt. An alternative operating environment allows switching of programs, windowing, and cut-and-paste capabilities. Windowing is the capability to accommodate more than one program if the accountant wants the main memory partitioned to handle the programs. For each program in memory, a separate window is displayed on the screen.

**OPERATING EXPENSES** costs associated with the selling and administrative activities of the company; also called *nonmanufacturing expenses*. They represent a PERIOD COST related to time rather than to the product. They are subdivided into SELLING EXPENSES and GENERAL AND ADMINISTRATIVE EXPENSES.

**OPERATING INCOME** revenue less cost of goods sold and related operating expenses applying to the normal business activities of the entity. It excludes financial related items (i.e., interest income, dividend income, interest expense), extraordinary items, taxes, and other peripheral activities. *See also* OPERATING LOSS.

**OPERATING LEASE** rental of property between the lessee and lessor for a fee. An operating lease does *not* meet the criteria for a CAPITAL LEASE. An example is renting of an apartment or automobile. The lessee debits rental expense and credits cash. Rental expense should be recognized on a straight-line basis, unless another systematic and rational basis is more representative of the time pattern in which benefit use is derived. The lessee shows nothing about the lease on the balance sheet. Lessee footnote disclosure includes future minimum lease payments in aggregate and for each of the five succeeding fiscal years, contingent rentals, and sublease rentals. The lessor, upon receipt of rental payments, debits cash and credits rental revenue. The lessor also records depreciation expense on the leased item and any expenses related to the leased property, such as maintenance expense. Normal accrual basis accounting techniques are followed for the recognition of income and expense. The lessor reports on his balance sheet the leased asset less accumulated depreciation. Footnote disclosure by the lessor includes the cost of property on lease or held for leasing by major class, minimum future rentals in the aggregate and for each of the five succeeding years, and contingent rentals. *See also* DIRECT FINANCING LEASE; SALES TYPE LEASE.

**OPERATING LEVERAGE** measure of fixed costs in a company's operating structure. High operating leverage magnifies changes in earnings so that small changes in sales lead to earnings instability. Operating leverage can be measured through the following ratios: (1) fixed costs to total costs; (2) percentage change in operating income to the percentage change in sales volume; and (3) net income to fixed charges. An increase in (1) and (2) or a decrease in (3) shows higher fixed charges, resulting in greater instability.

**OPERATING LOSS** amount by which the cost of goods sold plus operating expenses exceeds operating revenues. The net loss from operations applies only to the normal business activities of the entity. Excluded are financial revenue and expense items and ancillary operations of the firm (i.e., extraordinary items). However, interest would be an includable expense in calculating NET OPERATING LOSS for carryforward purposes. *See also* OPERATING INCOME.

**OPERATING PERFORMANCE RATIO** measure of profitability to sales to determine the return earned on the revenue generated. Some operating performance ratios are the profit margin (net income to sales), gross margin ratio (gross margin to sales), and operating profit margin (operating income to sales). The higher these ratios, the better the profitability earned on the company's sales.

**OPERATING REVENUE** net sales plus other regular income sources related to the normal business operations of the entity (e.g., lease income if a major activity).

**OPERATING RISK** one caused by fluctuations of operating income. This type of risk depends on variability in demand, sales price, input prices, and amount of OPERATING LEVERAGE. A business with a high degree of risk in its operations will have greater instability, often resulting in lower market price of stock and increased cost of financing.

**OPERATING SYSTEM** computer program that allows users to enter and run their software packages. The operating system allows the machine to recognize and carry out the accountant's command. Further, there are built-in routines permitting the user's software to conduct input-output operations without specifying the exact hardware configuration. The operating system normally consists of the job control program, the input/output control system, and the processing program. If a computer operates under one system, it cannot use programs designated for a different operating system.

**OPERATIONAL AUDIT** evaluation made of management's performance and conformity with policies and budgets. The organization and its operations are analyzed, including appraisal of structure, controls, procedures, and processes. The objective is to appraise the effectiveness and efficiency of a division, activity, or operation of the entity in meeting organizational goals. Recommendations to improve performance are also made. The primary user of an operational audit is management. However, an operational audit is slightly different from a MANAGEMENT AUDIT since it concentrates on the organization. Many companies maintain internal audit staffs for the sole purpose of performing operational audits on a recurring basis. For each review, management receives a report from the audit team that will indicate how well the activities are performed, suggest improvements, and offer other conclusions drawn from the work.

**OPERATIONAL COST DRIVER** higher order of an activity cost driver. Usually thought of as the driver of a business process.

**OPERATIONAL (OPERATING) BUDGET** one that embraces the impacts of operating decisions. It contains forecasts of sales, net income, the cost of goods sold, selling and administrative expenses, and other expenses. The cornerstone of an operational budget is forecasted sales. Therefore, the SALES BUDGET is the basic building block for the operational budget. Once the sales budget is prepared, then the PRODUCTION BUDGET can be formulated. The operational budget also consists of the ending inventory budget, direct material budget, direct labor budget, factory overhead budget, selling and administrative budget, and budgeted income statement.

**OPERATION COSTING** hybrid of job-order and process cost systems. Companies that manufacture goods that undergo some similar and some dissimilar processes use this system. Operation costing accumulates total conversion costs and determines a unit conversion cost for each operation. However, direct material costs are charged specifically to products as in job-order systems.

**OPERATIONS** set of all activities associated with the production of goods and services.

**OPERATIONS RESEARCH (OR)** *see* QUANTITATIVE METHODS (MODELS).

**OPERATIONS STRATEGY** strategy specifying how the firm will employ its production capabilities to support its corporate strategy.

**OPINION**
1. AUDIT OPINION.
2. APB OPINION.
3. accountant's judgment regarding a set of facts. For example, the auditor must formulate an opinion on the adequacy of a client's internal control system to determine the degree of audit testing required.

**OPPORTUNITY COST** revenue forfeited by rejecting an alternative use of time or facilities. For example, assume a company has a choice of using its capacity to produce an extra 10,000 units or renting it out for $20,000. The opportunity cost of using that capacity is $20,000. A further example is the return lost by having money tied up in accounts receivable because of a collection problem. If the extra funds tied up in receivables for a three-month period were $400,000, on which the firm could earn 10% per annum, the opportunity cost is $10,000 ($400,000 × 3/12 × 10%).

**OPPORTUNITY COST APPROACH** method in which the concept of OPPORTUNITY COST is applied to solve a short-term, nonroutine decision problem. Opportunity cost represents the net benefit lost by rejecting some alternative course of action. Its significance in decision making is that the best decision is always sought, since it considers the cost of the best available alternative *not* taken. The opportunity cost does not appear on formal accounting statements. *See also* INCREMENTAL ANALYSIS.

**OPTICAL CHARACTER RECOGNITION (OCR)** computer tool that recognizes typed or printed characters (alphabetic and numeric) on paper so they can be recorded on disk or magnetic tape. Optical character recognition can also read foreign characters (e.g., Japanese).

**OPTIMAL CAPITAL STRUCTURE** capital structure with a minimum weighted-average cost of capital and thereby maximizes the value of the firm's stock, but it does not maximize earnings per share (EPS). Greater leverage maximizes EPS but also increases risk. Thus, the highest stock price is not reached by maximizing EPS. The optimal capital structure usually involves some debt, but not 100% debt. Ordinarily, some firms cannot identify this optimal point precisely, but they should attempt to find an optimal range for the capital structure. The required rate of return on equity capital (R) can be estimated in various ways, for example, by adding a percentage to the firm's long-term cost of debt. Another method is the CAPITAL ASSET PRICING MODEL (CAPM).

**OPTIMAL (OPTIMUM) SOLUTION** either the most profitable or the least costly solution that simultaneously satisfies all the constraints of a LINEAR PROGRAMMING (LP) problem. There are two important general properties of an optimal solution: (1) The optimal solution lies on the boundary of the feasible region; the implication of this property is that one can ignore the (infinitely many) interior points of the feasible solution region when searching for an optimal solution. (2) The optimal solution occurs at one of the corner points of the region; this property reduces even further the magnitude of the search procedure for an optimal solution. *See also* BASIC FEASIBLE SOLUTION; FEASIBLE SOLUTION; GRAPHICAL METHOD.

**OPTIMAL PRICE** typically profit maximizing price.

**OPTIMISTIC TIME** in PROGRAM EVALUATION AND REVIEW TECHNIQUE (PERT), the shortest possible time in which an activity is likely to be completed, symbolized as *a*. *See also* EXPECTED TIME FOR AN ACTIVITY.

**OPTIMIZATION** maximization or minimization of a special goal.

**OPTIMIZATION MODEL** type of mathematical model that attempts to optimize (maximize or minimize) an *objective function* without violating resource constraints; also known as *mathematical programming*. Optimization models include LINEAR PROGRAMMING (LP), INTEGER PROGRAMMING, and ZERO-ONE PROGRAMMING.

**OPTION**
1. ability or right to choose a certain alternative.
2. right to buy or sell something at a specified price within a specified period of time. If the right is not exercised within the specified time, the option expires.

A PUT option on a security (such as stock, commodity, or stock index) is an option to sell 100 shares of the underlying security at a specified price for a given period of time, for which the option buyer pays the seller (writer) a price, termed a *premium*. A CALL is the opposite of a put and allows the owner the right to buy 100 shares of the underlying security from the option writer at a specified price for a given period of time.

An *Employee Stock Option* is the option granted to key employees to buy company stock at a below-market price.

**OPTIONS BACKDATING** as an incentive for executives to improve their firms' performance and share price, companies routinely issue stock options, giving executives the right to buy shares later at the price of the stock on the date of the grant. Recently, many companies have sweetened the pot by "backdating" options to dates when share prices were especially low.

**ORDER ENTRY**
1. recording of an order placed or received.
2. initial input system of the order processing system. Marketing is responsible for taking orders. Accounting is responsible for billing the customer and collecting payments.

**ORDERING COSTS** all costs associated with preparing a purchase order. These include the cost of preparing a purchase invoice, telephone, salaries of purchasing clerks, and stationery.

**ORDER RECEIPT TIME** delay between the placement of an order and its readiness for setup.

**ORDINARY ANNUITY** *see* ANNUITY.

## ORDINARY INCOME

1. earnings attributable to the nominal and recurring business operations of the entity.
2. in taxation, income on the sale of an investment held for 6 months or less.

**ORGANIZATIONAL STRUCTURE** *see* CENTRALIZATION; DECENTRALIZATION.

**ORGANIZATION CHART** visual diagram of an organization's structure that depicts formal lines of reporting, communication, and responsibility among managers. Below is a sample organization chart of the controllership.

ORGANIZATION CHART

**ORGANIZATION COSTS** expenditures incurred in launching a business. They include attorney's fees, various registration fees paid to state governments, and other start-up costs. These costs are expensed as incurred.

**ORGANIZATION FOR ECONOMIC COOPERATION AND DEVELOPMENT (OECD)** (www.oecd.org) a forum set up to discuss, develop, and refine economic and social policies. It is an international organization that encourages economic growth, high employment, and financial stability among its members.

**ORIGINAL COST** initial amount recorded for an asset excluding any adjustments to the account subsequent to the initial acquisition date (e.g., betterments, additions). Original cost equals the price paid or present value of liability incurred or fair value of stock issued plus normal incidental costs necessary to put the asset into its initial use (i.e., installation, freight).

**ORIGINAL ENTRY** recording a business transaction in a journal. An explanation is given below the entry describing the particulars. The explanation may refer to supporting data (i.e., voucher) as the basis for the entry.

**OTHER ASSETS** balance sheet category for minor assets not classified under the typical headings (e.g., current assets, intangible assets, and long-term investments). This type of asset may be immaterial in amount relative to total assets. An example is obsolete machinery to be sold.

**OTHER COMPREHENSIVE BASIS OF ACCOUNTING (OCBOA)** a basis of accounting, other than GAAP, that an entity uses to report its assets, liabilities, equity, revenues, and expenses. Examples of OCBOA include income tax basis and cash basis of accounting.

**OTHER COMPREHENSIVE INCOME** any gains and losses that are included in comprehensive income but are not included in net income. Examples include unrealized gains and losses attributable to available-for-sale securities and adjustments pertaining to foreign currency translation.

**OUTGO** *see* OUTLAY.

**OUTLAY** *expenditure*; also called *outgo*. For example, in CAPITAL BUD-GETING, initial cash outlay for a machine is the amount of the purchase price and the normal incidental costs to put it into operation, such as charges for delivery, taxes, installation, and flooring.

**OUTLAY COST** expenditure by cash. *See also* OUTLAY.

**OUT-OF-POCKET COST** actual cash outlays made during the period for payroll, advertising, and other operating expenses. Depreciation is not an out-of-pocket cost, since it involves no current cash expenditure.

**OUTSIDE DIRECTOR** member of the board of directors of an entity who is not an employee of that entity. An example is a banker sitting on the board of a client company. Such directors are important because they bring unbiased opinions regarding the company's decisions and diverse experience to the company's decision-making process. *See also* INSIDE DIRECTOR.

**OUTSOURCING** acquisition of products and services from sources outside the organization instead of producing them internally.

**OUTSTANDING CAPITAL STOCK** shares in the hands of stock-holders. Outstanding shares are issued shares minus treasury shares. Dividends are based on outstanding shares. *See also* TREASURY STOCK.

**OUTSTANDING CHECK** one issued by the company but not yet cleared by the bank. It is listed in the cash payments journal for the month but is not included on the bank statement for that month. In preparing the bank reconciliation, it is deducted from the bank balance. The exception is an uncleared CERTIFIED CHECK, which is not considered outstanding since both parties, the company and the bank, know about it and have subtracted it.

**OVERABSORPTION** credit balance in the Factory Overhead account that arises when the overhead costs applied to WORK-IN-PROCESS exceed the overhead costs incurred during a period. *Underabsorption* results if there is a debit balance. *See also* OVERAPPLIED OVERHEAD.

**OVERAPPLIED OVERHEAD** amount by which the factory overhead added to work-in-process inventory at a predetermined overhead rate (and credited to factory overhead applied) exceeds the actual overhead shown in factory overhead control. *See also* PREDETERMINED OVERHEAD RATE; UNDERAPPLIED OVERHEAD.

**OVERDRAFT**
1. situation where a borrower draws money against a previously established line of credit. The basic cost to the borrower is the interest rate levied on the daily overdraft balance. The borrower typically pays interest only on funds used, since there is no compensating balance requirement, and only for the period in days for which the funds are taken. For this reason, the effective interest cost of an overdraft "loan" is the nominal or stated interest rate paid on the overdraft balance.
2. negative balance in a checking account caused by payment of checks drawn against insufficient funds.

**OVERHEAD APPLICATION** *see* PREDETERMINED OVERHEAD RATE.

**OVERHEAD COST** *see* FACTORY OVERHEAD.

**OVERHEAD RATE** *see* PREDETERMINED OVERHEAD RATE.

**OVERHEAD VARIANCE** *see* FACTORY OVERHEAD.

**OVER-THE-COUNTER (OTC) MARKET** market for buying and selling securities not listed on organized stock exchanges. The OTC is typically a telephone market, with most business conducted by phone or, now, electronic device. Dealers, called *market makers*, stand ready to buy or sell specific securities for their own accounts. These dealers will buy at a bid price and sell at an asked price that reflects the competitive market conditions. The OTC market is the largest of all markets in the United States in dollar terms.

**OWNERS' EQUITY** interest of the owners in the assets of the business represented by capital contributions and retained earnings. *See also* CREDITORS' EQUITY; NET WORTH.

# P

**PACIOLI, LUCA** author of the first statement and commentary on double-entry bookkeeping. This treatise, published in Venice in 1494, was part of a work *Summa de Arithmetica, Geometria Proportioni et Proportionalita*. His treatise had great influence in Europe.

**PAID-IN CAPITAL** section of stockholders' equity that shows: (1) amount of stock a corporation has issued; (2) the premiums or discounts that have resulted from selling stock (paid-in capital in excess of par or stated value); (3) stock received from donations; and (4) the resale of TREASURY STOCK. Stockholders' equity consists of paid-in or contributed capital and retained earnings.

**PAID-IN SURPLUS** PAID-IN CAPITAL in excess of par or stated value. It is the result of selling capital stock (or issuing stock) at a price greater than par or stated value.

**PAPER PROFIT** *unrealized gain* from holding an item while its market value has increased. The amount equals the difference between the current market price and the initial cost. Examples are appreciation in value of inventory or securities. Paper profits are realized profits at the time of sale, at which point income statement recognition is given to them.

**PARALLEL PROCESSING** simultaneous performance of two or more tasks by a computer. For example, parallel processing takes place when one instruction is being run while another instruction is being read from memory.

**PARAMETER**
1. constant or coefficient of a variable in an equation or a system of equations. For example, in a COST-VOLUME FORMULA of the form $y = a + bx$, the constant $a$ and the slope $b$ are parameters. The total fixed costs, the unit variable cost, and the unit selling price are examples of parameters.
2. numerical characteristic of a population computed using every element in the population. For example, the mean and the mode are parameters of a population.

**PARENT COMPANY**
1. owner of a SUBSIDIARY COMPANY. *See also* CONSOLIDATION.
2. HOLDING COMPANY that is not engaged in a trade or business.

**PARETO ANALYSIS** analysis used to differentiate between *the vital few* and *the trial many*. It is based on the concept that about 80 percent of the problems come from 20 percent of the items. Pareto analysis can be used to identify cost drivers or activity drivers that are responsible for the majority of cost incurred by ranking the cost drivers in order of value. *See also* COST DRIVER ANALYSIS; ACTIVITY DRIVER ANALYSIS.

**PARITY**

**Computers:** number that is odd or even. Usually when bits (1's and 0's) are transferred or stored, there is an extra bit added so that the total number of 1's is always odd (alternatively, always even). This is referred to as the parity of the data. Since a transmission error has a one-half chance of altering the parity, frequent errors will warn the receiver of the data of possible errors.

**Economics:** term designating a constant spread between prices; for example, having a constant relationship between domestic and world sugar prices.

**Labor law:** salary equality among workers such as policemen and firemen.

**PARITY CHECK** test conducted by checking a unit of data (e.g., a word or a BYTE) for even or odd parity to ascertain whether a mistake has taken place in reading, writing, or transmitting information. For instance, if data is written, the computed parity bit is compared to the parity bit already appended to the data. If these match, it indicates the data are correct. If they do not agree, a parity error exists.

**PARITY PRICE** measuring device for price levels in terms of an index number of 100. The price of a commodity or service is linked to another price or a cumulative average of prices determined from a historical base period. Subsequent changes in both price levels are reflected in an index number on a scale of 100. Parity price devices are employed frequently by the federal government for social and economic objectives. Farm price support programs are examples of such uses.

**PARTIALLY AMORTIZED LOANS** *see* BALLOON.

**PARTIAL PRODUCTIVITY** output divided by a single input factor. Factors of production may include direct materials, direct labor, overhead, or capital (for example, use of machinery instead of direct labor). A partial productivity measure comparing results over time determines whether the actual relationship between inputs and outputs has improved or deteriorated. A disadvantage of a partial productivity measure is that it relates output to a single factor of production and, therefore, fails to consider tradeoffs among input factors.

**PARTICIPATING PREFERRED STOCK** rarely issued type of preferred stock. In addition to receiving the regular specified dividend, preferred stockholders will "participate" with common stockholders in any extra dividends paid. There are two types of participating preferred stock, partially participating and fully participating. If partially participating, preferred stockholders participate above the preferential rate on a pro rata basis with common stockholders, but only up to an additional rate specified on the stock certificate. For instance, on a 7% preferred stock issue, the allowed participation may be up to 10%. Thus the participating privilege is limited to an additional 3%. With fully participating preferred stock, preferred stockholders enjoy a preference for the current year at the preference rate (plus any cumulative preference) and they share on a pro rata basis in any dividends above the preference rate. For example, a 6% fully participating preferred stock receives its 6% preference rate plus a pro rata share based on the total par value of the common stock and preferred stock of excess dividends after common stockholders have received their matching 6% of par of the common stock.

**PARTICIPATIVE BUDGETING** system enabling key employees in a department to provide input into the budgetary process. Thus the accountant receives useful budgeting information from those affected by the budget. Participative budgeting is a good motivational tool because the people participating may work harder to accomplish the budgeting goals, cooperation is facilitated, and more realistic budgeting figures are obtained.

**PARTNERSHIP** form of business organization created by an agreement between two or more persons who contribute capital and/or their services to the organization. Advantages are: (1) it is easily established with minimal organizational effort and costs; and (2) it is free from special government regulation. Disadvantages are: (1) it carries unlimited liability for the individual partners (firms organized as co-partnerships do not dissolve with the death or withdrawal of a partner); (2) it is dissolved upon the withdrawal or death of any of the partners; and (3) its ability to raise large amounts of capital is limited. GENERAL PARTNERS are those who are responsible for the day-to-day operations of the partnership and who are responsible for the partnership's total liabilities, while LIMITED PARTNERS are those who contribute only money, who are not involved in management decisions, and whose liability is limited to their investment.

**PAR VALUE** amount arbitrarily assigned by the corporate charter to one share of stock and printed on the stock certificate. The par value represents the legal capital per share. There can be no dividend declared that would cause the stockholders' equity to go below the par value of the outstanding shares. Par value may be a minimum cushion of equity capital existing for creditor protection. The par value is the amount per share entered in the capital stock account. It is usually significantly lower than the market price per share.

**PASSIVE ACTIVITY** any activity in which the taxpayer does not materially participate. Passive activities include all limited partnership investments as well as rentals of REAL PROPERTY. In general, losses from passive activities may only be used to offset gains from passive activities.

**PASSWORD** secret character string that is required before one can log onto a computer system, thus preventing unauthorized persons from obtaining access to the computer. The primary reason for using a password is to protect confidential information from modification, destruction, misuse, and other security-related dangers by unauthorized persons.

**PAST COSTS** *see* SUNK COST.

**PATENT** exclusive right given by the government to the company to use, manufacture, and sell a product or process for a nonrenewable 20-year period without interference or infringement by other parties. Patent is classified as an intangible asset. Costs such as registration fees and attorney costs incurred in obtaining the patent are capitalized. Research and development costs applicable to developing the product, process, or idea are immediately expensed. Legal costs of a *successful* defense of a patent are capitalized and amortized over the remaining life. If the patent right is lost in court it should be written off and shown as an extraordinary charge. The cost of a patent purchased from an outsider is deferred and amortized. If the *sole* purpose of buying the outsider patent is to eliminate the competition, the amortization period is the *remaining* life of the company's patent that is being protected. The patent is amortized on a straight-line basis over its 20-year life, or its economic life, if less. As a practical matter, often the useful life is less than 20 years due to changes in the marketplace and new technology. If a patent is assigned to others, royalties obtained are accrued as revenue is earned.

**PAYABLE** amount owed to another party. It is presented as a liability in the balance sheet. A payable is an item that is unpaid, whether or not due. If a payable is due in one year or less (e.g., accounts payable), it is a current liability. If it is to be paid in more than one year, it is shown as a long-term liability. One type of payable is accrued expenses payable (e.g., salaries payable). The failure to satisfy a payable on the due date may result in a penalty (interest) charge, creditor action against the firm (e.g., lawsuit), or in an extreme case, bankruptcy.

**PAYBACK PERIOD** length of time required to recover the initial amount of a capital investment. If the cash inflows occur at a uniform rate, it is the ratio of the amount of initial investment over expected annual cash inflows, or:

$$\text{Payback Period} = \text{Initial Investment/Annual Cash Inflows}$$

For example, assume projected annual cash inflows are expected to be $6,000 a year for five years from an investment of $18,000. The payback period on this proposal is three years, which is calculated as follows: Payback period = $18,000/$6,000 = 3 years. If annual cash inflows are not even, the payback period would have to be determined by trial and error. Assume instead that the cash inflows are $4,000 in the first year, $5,000 in the second year, $6,000 in the third year, $6,000 in the fourth year, and $8,000 in the fifth year. The payback period would be 3.5 years. In three years, all but $3,000 has been recovered. It takes one-half year ($3,000/ $6,000) to recover the balance. When two or more projects are considered, the rule for making a selection decision is as follows: Choose the project with the shorter payback period. The rationale behind this is that the shorter the payback period, the greater the liquidity, and the less risky the project. Advantages of the method include (1) it is simple to compute and easy to understand and (2) it handles investment risk effectively. Disadvantages of the method include (1) it does not recognize the TIME VALUE OF MONEY and (2) it ignores profitability of an investment.

**PAYBACK RECIPROCAL** 1 divided by the PAYBACK PERIOD (i.e., the reciprocal of the payback time). This often gives a quick, accurate estimate of the INTERNAL RATE OF RETURN (IRR) on an investment when the project life is *more* than twice the payback period and the cash inflows are uniform during every period. For example, XYZ Company is contemplating three projects, each of which would require an initial investment of $10,000, and each of which is expected to generate a cash inflow of $2,000 per year. The payback period is five years ($10,000/$2,000), and the payback reciprocal is 1/5, or 20%. The table of the present value of an annuity of $1 shows that the factor of 5.00 applies to the following useful lives and internal rates of return:

| Useful Life (Years) | IRR (%) |
|---|---|
| 10 | 15 |
| 15 | 18 |
| 20 | 19 |

It can be observed that the payback reciprocal is 20% as compared with the IRR of 18% when the life is 15 years, and 20% as compared with the IRR of 19% when the life is 20 years. This shows that the payback reciprocal gives a reasonable approximation of the IRR if the useful life of the project is at least twice the payback period.

**PAYMENT IN KIND** settlement of a charge for goods or services or satisfaction of liabilities with similar or identical mediums of exchange and value (e.g., money for money, goods for goods, and services for services). It also connotes a transaction where one medium of exchange is satisfied with another. For example, a carpenter fixes a lawyer's roof. The value of the work is $200, which is paid with one hour's worth of legal services.

**PAYOFF** *see* DECISION THEORY.

**PAYOFF TABLE** *see* DECISION THEORY.

**PAYOUT RATIO** ratio of cash dividends declared to earnings for the period. It equals dividends per share divided by earnings per share. Stockholders investing for income favor a higher ratio. Stockholders looking for capital gains tolerate low ratios when earnings are being reinvested to finance corporate growth. Assume cash dividends of

$100,000, net income of $400,000, and outstanding shares of 200,000. The payout ratio equals 25% ($.50/$2.00).

**PAYROLL COSTS** employer costs incurred for employees' services. Payroll costs consist of the actual cash paid to the employees and the withheld amounts (liabilities) for employee's federal income taxes, FICA, and various voluntary health and benefit plans. Employer's payroll costs also consist of its matching share of employee's FICA taxes and contributions to the state and federal unemployment insurance programs.

**PAYROLL REGISTER** form with many columns that contains and summarizes payroll information (amount of money paid to employees less deductions). Information includes employee's name, regular hours, sick hours, overtime hours, federal income taxes withheld, medical insurance deductions, union dues, gross pay, and net pay. The payroll register may be used as a supplementary record or as a special journal.

**PAYROLL TAX** taxes levied on employee's salaries or net income of self-employed individuals. Social Security taxes are imposed upon employees; self-employed individuals and employers are responsible for a matching amount. Unemployment taxes are levied only upon the employer.

**PDCA** *see* PLAN-DO-CHECK ACT CYCLE.

**PEACHTREE SOFTWARE** accounting system programs developed by Peachtree Software of Norcross, Georgia (www.peachtree.com).

**PEER REVIEW** review of the work of one CPA or CPA firm by another CPA or CPA firm. The purpose of peer review is to assure that quality controls are being applied in conformity with AMERICAN INSTITUTE OF CERTIFIED PUBLIC ACCOUNTANTS (AICPA) Quality Control Standards. The review process includes looking at working papers and accounting procedures followed. Mandatory peer review applies to a CPA firm's accounting and auditing services but not to tax and management advisory services. The following is involved in the peer review process when appraising a CPA firm's quality control policies and procedures: (1) reviewing each organizational or functional level within the firm; (2) reviewing selected engagement working paper files and reports; and (3) reviewing documentation indicating the firm's compliance with membership requirements. At the completion of the peer review, the reviewer discusses the findings with the reviewee and issues a report. Sanctions may be imposed on deficient CPA firms including continuing professional education (CPE) training, censures and reprimands, fines, and suspension from membership.

**PEER-TO-PEER NETWORKING** networking that allows all computers to communicate and share resources as equals. Music-file sharing, instant messaging, and other applications rely on P2P technology.

**PENETRATION PRICING** method of pricing a standard product. It sets a low initial price for a product in order to gain quick acceptance in a broad portion of the market. It calls for a sacrifice of short-term profits in order to establish a certain amount of market share. One objective is to obtain a committed customer. *See also* SKIMMING PRICING.

**PENNY STOCK** low priced, highly speculative stock. A penny stock is usually traded on the OVER-THE-COUNTER (OTC) MARKET, but the New York and American stock exchanges also list penny stocks. Penny stock is issued by a company with a short life or with past instability in operations. These stocks typically experience volatility in price relative to the stock of established companies on the major stock exchanges.

**PENSION FUND** resources set aside on a periodic basis by the employee and/or employer that will earn a return so that the accumulated principal and interest will be sufficient to meet employee retirement benefits. The pension fund money is retained by a trustee who directly pays the employees at retirement. Annuity payments to employees will be made from pension fund assets. The administration of the fund may be done by the employing company, a trustee, or an insurance company or other similar organization. *See also* DEFINED BENEFIT PENSION PLAN; DEFINED CONTRIBUTION PENSION PLAN; KEOGH PLAN.

**PENSION PLAN** contractual arrangement in which the employer provides benefits to employees upon retirement. Many plans include disability and death benefits. A pension plan involves recognizing the employer's cost and the funding of pension benefits. Pension expense is tax-deductible to the employer. The employee is taxed when the pension annuity is received from employer contributions or originally not-taxed employee contributions. The two most common types of plans are DEFINED CONTRIBUTION PENSION PLAN and DEFINED BENEFIT PENSION PLAN. Pension plan provisions vary from company to company. For example, the pension plan may be contributory or noncontributory, meaning the employee may or may not also make payments to the pension plan.

**PENSION PLAN LIABILITY RESERVE** obligation recognized by the employer for the future liability to make annuity payments to employees. The reserve is typically a liability when it results from charging pension expense. However, in a revocable plan, the reserve is considered an appropriation of retained earnings regardless of whether it effects specific assets.

**PENSION-PLAN VESTING** *see* VESTED.

**PERCENTAGE DEPLETION** method of computing depletion for income taxes. It is not allowed on financial statements; only COST DEPLETION is permitted. For tax purposes, the Internal Revenue

Service Code allows businesses to deduct the larger of cost depletion or percentage depletion in computing taxable income. It is computed as a percentage of revenue. Rates allowed vary widely, from 22% for oil and certain minerals to 5% for sand and gravel. Percentage depletion is often greater than cost depletion.

**PERCENTAGE-OF-COMPLETION METHOD** method that recognizes profit on a long-term construction contract as it is earned gradually during the construction period. This approach is preferred over the COMPLETED CONTRACT METHOD because it does a better job of matching revenue and expense in the period of benefit. It should be used when *reliable estimates* of the degree of completion are possible. It is more realistic and levels out the earnings. Under the method, the measure of revenue to be recognized each year is equal to percentage completed × contract price. One approach to estimate the percentage completed is based on the following relationship:

$$\frac{\text{Cost Incurred to Date}}{\text{Total Estimated Costs}} \times \text{Contract Price} = \text{Cumulative Revenue}$$

Any revenue that had been recognized in a prior period is subtracted from the cumulative total in arriving at the current period's income.
   *See also* CONSTRUCTION-IN-PROGRESS; PROGRESS BILLINGS.

**PERCENTAGE STATEMENT** approach by which items in the financial statements are shown as percentages of a total; in the income statement, each item is shown as a percentage of sales; in the balance sheet, each item is shown as a percentage of total assets or equities.
   *See also* COMMON SIZE FINANCIAL STATEMENTS.

**PER DIEM** on a daily basis. The term is used to designate payment on a daily basis; e.g., the daily rate that an accountant charges for services performed.

**PERFECT MARKET** market structure characterized by a very large number of buyers and sellers of a homogeneous (nondifferentiated) product. Entry and exit from the industry is costless, or nearly so. Information is freely available to all market participants, and there is no collusion among firms in the industry. It is difficult to identify a perfect market in reality; however, lumber and agriculture provide close approximations in the United States.

**PERFORMANCE AUDIT** appraisal of how a particular activity is carrying out the company's policies and procedures. Such review may cover any activity within a department, division, or local area. A performance audit can be a review of a program to assure that it is satisfying its objectives. The program may apply to management and accounting procedures, guidelines, or policies. The performance audit may take into account the anticipated benefits of a program relative to the actual performance. Also relevant may be the costs and time associated with the activity. A report of management's abilities is typically prepared to meet particular goals. Included in the report are measures of the effectiveness of internal controls and efficiency of procedures and processes. The performance audit may be initiated by the organization or by external interested parties. However, the performance audit is *not* performed as a means to attest to the financial records and statements of the company. An example of a performance audit is how certain work routines are being conducted.

**PERFORMANCE BUDGET** medium- to short-range budget used in governmental accounting. It is typical of the type incorporated by a PROGRAM PLANNING-BUDGETING SYSTEM (PPBS) but without references to long-range goals.

**PERFORMANCE EVALUATION** cumulative consideration of factors (that may be subjective or objective) to determine a representative indicator or appraisal of an individual or entity's activity, or performance in reference to some subjective (or standard) over some period of time. Factors to consider may include degree of goal attainment, how items are measured, and what standards are to be applied. *See also* COST CENTER; INVESTMENT CENTER; PROFIT CENTER.

**PERFORMANCE MEASUREMENT** quantification of a company's or segment's efficiency or effectiveness in conducting business operations for the accounting period. Some possible measures of performance are revenue center, cost center, profit center, and investment center. In the revenue center approach, a comparison is made between actual revenue and expected revenue. With the cost center method, actual cost is compared to budgeted cost. The profit center is accountable for costs and revenues in deriving net income. It is even better to use an investment center method of performance evaluation because responsibility is placed not only for revenue and costs but also for the investment employed. Two investment center measurements are RETURN ON INVESTMENT and RESIDUAL INCOME.

**PERFORMANCE REPORT** statement that displays measurements of actual results of some person or entity's activity over some time period. These results are ideally compared with budgeted or standard measurements obtained under some conditional assumptions over the same period. Variations from such budget or standards are known as VARIANCES and may be favorable or unfavorable depending upon lower or higher measurements relative to the standards. Corrective action is taken for unfavorable performance.

**PERIOD COST** expense that is *not* inventoriable; it is charged against sales revenue in the period in which the revenue is earned, also called *period expense*. Selling and general and administrative expenses are period costs. *See also* PRODUCT COST.

**PERIOD EXPENSE** *see* PERIOD COST.

**PERIODIC AUDIT**
1. audit for an intermediate period (e.g., one month, three months).
2. audit carried out at specified intervals within the year.

**PERIODIC INCOME** proportional accounting, over time periods, for income already accounted for but not received (deferred revenue), or income already received and accounted for but not earned (prepaid subscriptions), or income receivable in the future and not recorded (interest on fixed-income securities).

**PERIODIC INVENTORY SYSTEM** one that does not require a day-to-day record of inventory changes. Costs of materials used and costs of goods sold cannot be calculated until ending inventories, determined by physical count, are subtracted from the sum of opening inventories and purchases (or costs of goods manufactured in the case of a manufacturer).

For calculating the cost of ending inventory, there are several methods available: LIFO, FIFO, and WEIGHTED AVERAGE.

**PERIODICITY CONCEPT** concept under which each accounting period has an economic activity associated with it, and the activity can be accounted for, measured, and reported.

**PERIODIC ORDER SYSTEMS** places minimal emphasis on record keeping. However, a risk of substantial overstock or understock may arise unless inventories are checked for assurance that the model is still appropriate.

**PERIOD OF BENEFIT** accounting period in which revenue is matched against related expenses (e.g., cost allocation). If an expenditure benefits a future period, it is charged to an asset account. However, if an expenditure benefits the current accounting period or if there is an inability to ascertain the period of benefit, it should be expensed in the current period.

**PERIPHERALS** auxiliary equipment used in computer systems. They include printers, CDs, tape and disk drives, and other input-output and storage devices. Peripherals do not include the central processing unit (CPU).

**PERMANENT DIFFERENCE** difference between book income and taxable income caused by an item that affects one but not the other. The difference will *not* reverse. For example, interest on municipal bonds is included in book income but not in taxable income. Another example: premiums on officers' life insurance that are not deductible for tax purposes but are for financial reporting. Tax expense on the INCOME STATEMENT is based on book income less permanent differences. *See also* INTERPERIOD INCOME TAX ALLOCATION.

**PERMANENT FILE** items to include in the permanent file include copies of long-term contracts and leases, copies of an entity's ARTICLES OF

INCORPORATION and bylaws, and copies of benefit plans. A permanent file is sometimes referred to as a continuing file because it includes documentation that is applicable to future audit engagements and not just the current audit engagement.

**PERMANENTLY RESTRICTED ASSETS** in not-for-profit accounting, assets that are restricted by outside agencies or persons, as contrasted with assets over which the entity has control and discretion. An example of a permanently restricted asset is donated property on which the donor has placed a restriction on its use.

**PERPETUAL INVENTORY SYSTEM** one keeping continual track of additions or deletions in materials, work-in-process, and cost of goods sold on a day-to-day basis. Physical inventory counts are usually taken at least once a year in order to check on the validity of the book records. Cost of goods sold therefore is kept on a day-to-day basis rather than being determined periodically. *See also* PERIODIC INVENTORY SYSTEM.

**PERPETUITY** ANNUITY that goes on indefinitely. An example of a perpetuity is preferred stock that yields a constant dollar dividend indefinitely. The PRESENT VALUE of a perpetuity is $A/i$ where $A$ is the periodic payment (the amount of an annuity) and $i$ is the DISCOUNT RATE per period. For example, assume that a perpetual bond has an $80-per-year interest payment and that the discount rate is 10%. The present value of this perpetuity is $800 ($80/0.10).

**PERSONAL EXEMPTION** amount an individual can exclude from taxable income. The tax law provides a $3,950 exemption for the 2014 tax year. If an individual has dependents and meets the specified definitional requirements, an additional exemption is allowed for each dependent. Personal exemptions are phased out based on adjusted gross income thresholds, which are adjusted annually based on inflation.

**PERSONAL FINANCIAL PLANNING** field of financial planning for individuals. It involves (1) analyzing a client's personal finances; and (2) recommending how to improve the client's financial condition. Personal financial planning covers the following specific areas:

Analysis of current financial position
Investment strategies
Estate planning
Cash flow analysis
Retirement income
Long-term accumulation plans
Life insurance
Tax planning
Disability insurance

*See also* FINANCIAL PLANNER.

**PERSONAL FINANCIAL PLANNING SOFTWARE** computer program assisting users in examining revenue and expenses, comparing actual to budget, monitoring assets and liabilities, goal analysis, investment portfolio analysis, tax planning, and retirement planning. Personal financial planning templates can be used in conjunction with a spreadsheet program. An example of personal planning software is Quicken.

**PERSONAL FINANCIAL SPECIALIST (PFS)** designation in personal financial planning awarded by AICPA to those who have met practice requirements and passed an examination.

**PERSONAL FINANCIAL STATEMENT** document prepared for an individual using the *accrual* basis of accounting rather than the CASH basis. A Statement of Financial Condition shows ASSETS at estimated current values listed by order of liquidity and maturity without classification as current and noncurrent. Business interests that constitute a large part of total assets should be shown separately from other investments. Only the person's interest (amount that person is entitled to) as beneficial owner should be included when assets are jointly owned. *Liabilities* are shown by order of maturity without classification as current or noncurrent. A Statement of Changes in Net Worth is *optional* showing the major sources and uses of net worth. Comparative financial statements are also *optional*. Footnote disclosures should be made of the following: (1) individuals covered by the financial statements; (2) major methods used in determining current value; (3) nature of joint ownership of assets; (4) face amount of life insurance owned; (5) NONFORFEITURE rights that do not qualify for asset inclusion (i.e., pensions based on life expectancy); (6) methods and assumptions used to compute estimated income taxes; (7) maturities and interest rates relating to RECEIVABLES and debt; and (8) noncancellable commitments not reflected under liabilities (i.e., OPERATING LEASE).

**PERT** *see* PROGRAM EVALUATION AND REVIEW TECHNIQUE (PERT).

**PERT/COST** project management system developed by the United States government that measures and controls costs by work packages. In this method, cost estimates must be made for each activity. Then the system monitors dollar expenditures for each activity as well as time expenditures. A variety of analyses can be performed, including the "crashing" of certain activities in the project. *Also see* PROGRAM EVALUATION AND REVIEW TECHNIQUE (PERT).

**PESSIMISTIC TIME** in PROGRAM EVALUATION AND REVIEW TECHNIQUE (PERT), the longest possible time in which an activity is likely to be completed, symbolized *b*. *See also* EXPECTED TIME FOR AN ACTIVITY.

**PETTY-CASH FUND** minimal amount of money kept on hand by a business entity to meet small expenditures (e.g., postage, taxi fare). One individual (custodian) should be responsible for the fund to maintain control. The fund is available currency and is periodically reimbursed, usually monthly. At any point, the fixed amount of the fund consists of the total currency left and the vouchers (receipts) for the expenditures made. The vouchers should be perforated so they will not be used again.

**PHISHING** scams by e-mail.

**PHP** an acronym for "PHP Hypertext Preprocessor," a widely used, server-side open-source scripting language.

**PHYSICAL INVENTORY** determining the quantity of inventory on hand through an inventory count (i.e., quantity, weight). By multiplying the quantity times the unit cost, the total inventory cost is derived. There are three types of physical inventories. One is a continuous inventory to supplement the perpetual inventory records. Another is an inventory count of only specific merchandise on a periodic basis. The third is an annual year-end count. The physical inventory is compared to the book inventory. Discrepancies are noted and investigated. The financial statements must show inventory at the perpetual amount. Assume book inventory is $10,000 and physical inventory is $9,900. The entry for the inventory difference is to debit inventory shortage and credit inventory for $100.

**PHYSICAL VERIFICATION** observation, listing, counting, and measuring of the assets of a company, such as inventory, fixed assets, cash on hand, stocks, or bonds. It also includes other items such as insurance policies and contracts. The auditor typically substantiates the figure as per the financial records by physically determining the existence of the item and examining it. For example, the fixed asset account can be physically verified by inspecting the individual machines, buildings, or other fixed assets. The methods used for verification will depend on the scope of work required and type of asset being verified. With some types of items, the auditor will require the assistance of other professionals familiar with the item—for example, with precious metals, minerals, construction projects, and some manufacturing activities. Standards of auditing require some form of physical verification when inventory is present in the financial statements of a company. The timing of the verification depends upon such factors as method of accounting used for the item, auditor's satisfaction with internal controls associated with the item, size of the item in dollars and physical bulk (gold vs. widgets), and other matters relating to the audit. *See also* INVENTORY CONTROL; INVENTORY OBSERVATION; INVENTORY VALUATION.

**PIECEMEAL OPINION** external auditor's opinion regarding the fairness of presentation of specific financial statement items. A piecemeal opinion is not permitted anymore under GENERALLY ACCEPTED AUDITING STANDARDS (GAAS). It was previously used in some cases where a disclaimer or adverse opinion was involved on the financial statements as a whole.

**PLAINTEXT** ordinary readable text. This term is used in cryptography to describe text that has not yet been encrypted, or text after it has been decrypted. Once plaintext is encrypted, it is called CIPHERTEXT.

**PLAN-DO-CHECK ACT CYCLE (PDCA)** "management by fact" or scientific method approach to continuous improvement (the Deming Wheel). PDCA creates a process-centered environment, because it involves studying the current process, collecting and analyzing data to identify causes of problems, planning for improvement, and deciding how to measure improvement (Plan). The plan is then implemented on a small scale if possible (Do). The next step is to determine what happened (Check). If the experiment was successful, the plan is fully implemented (Act). The cycle is then repeated using what was learned from the preceding cycle.

**PLANNED CAPACITY** *see* CAPACITY.

**PLANNING** selection of short- and long-term objectives and the drawing up of tactical and strategic plans to achieve those objectives. In planning, managers outline the steps to be taken in moving the organization toward its objectives. After deciding on a set of strategies to be followed, the organization needs more specific plans, such as locations, methods of financing, hours of operations, and so on. As these plans are made, they will he communicated throughout the organization. When implemented, the plans will serve to coordinate, or meld together, the efforts of all parts of the organization toward the company's objectives.

**PLANT AND EQUIPMENT** fixed assets used in business operations, including land and buildings; sometimes termed PROPERTY, PLANT, AND EQUIPMENT.

**PLANT ASSET** noncurrent physical asset applicable to manufacturing activities. *See also* FIXED ASSET.

**PLANT LEDGER** SUBSIDIARY LEDGER that consists of supporting accounts to a company's general ledger fixed asset account. The ledger provides the detail of individual assets necessary for proper control, tracking, record keeping, and maintenance. Information concerning a particular asset such as those for acquisitions, additions, replacements, extraordinary repairs, and retirements, is recorded in this account.

**PLANTWIDE OVERHEAD RATE** single predetermined overhead rate used in all departments of a company, rather than having a separate rate for each department. If the company's departments are homogeneous, the use of a single plantwide rate may be adequate as a means of allocating overhead costs to production jobs. *See also* MULTIPLE OVERHEAD RATES; PREDETERMINED OVERHEAD RATE.

**PLEDGED ASSET** one used as collateral to secure a debt obligation or contract. A footnote reference is given of the circumstances surrounding the pledged asset; otherwise, the asset appears as it would ordinarily be classified on the balance sheet and is not presented as an offset under liabilities.

**POINT-OF-SALE (POS)**
1. system that uses a computer terminal located at the point of sales transaction so that the data can be captured immediately by the computer system.
2. general point for revenue recognition. GENERALLY ACCEPTED ACCOUNTING PRINCIPLES (GAAP) require the recognition of revenue in the accounting period in which the sale is deemed to have occurred. For services, the sale is deemed to occur when the service is performed. In the case of merchandise, the sale takes place when the title to the goods transfers from seller to buyer. In many cases, this coincides with the delivery of the merchandise. As a result, accountants usually record revenue when goods are delivered.

**POINTS** a fee paid by a borrower to a lender. Typically, a point is equal to 1% of the amount borrowed. Points paid in connection with the purchase or improvement of a principle residence are fully deductible in the year paid. All other points must be amortized over the life of the loan.

**POOL RATE** the overhead costs for a HOMOGENEOUS COST POOL divided by the appropriate COST DRIVER associated with the pool.

**PONZI SCHEMES** a method of escalating values built on fabricated assets. The most famous of these schemes occurred during the 1920s, perpetrated by Charles Ponzi, in which dividends were paid to early investors out of the payments received from later investors. When no new investors joined the investment scheme, it collapsed. In 2009, two infamous Ponzi schemes surfaced: (1) According to civil charges filed by the SEC, R. Allen Stanford, the Stanford Financial Group and Stanford Capital Management defrauded investors worldwide, resulting in losses of more than $9 billion, using a Ponzi scheme. (2) Bernard Madoff, who served as a non-executive chairman of the NASDAQ stock exchange, pled guilty to an 11-count criminal complaint, admitting to defrauding thousands of investors of billions of dollars. He was convicted of operating a Ponzi scheme that has been called the largest investor fraud ever committed by a single person, resulting in client losses estimated at almost $65 billion. On June 29, 2009, he was sentenced to 150 years in prison, the maximum allowed.

**POPULATION** set of data consisting of all conceivable observations of a certain phenomenon. A SAMPLE contains only part of these observations. Examples of populations are: (1) number of defective and nondefective bolts produced in a factory on a given day; (2) heights and weights of students in a university; and (3) all possible outcomes (heads, tails) in successive tosses of a coin. Population can be finite or infinite. The first two examples are finite and the third example is infinite. Assume the auditor wants to verify promotion and entertainment expense of the company. The *population* is the total expense for the accounting period under examination. A sample can be derived on a random basis to check selected promotion and entertainment documentation so as to derive an inference about the population balance.

**PORTFOLIO** combining securities to reduce risk by diversification. An example of a portfolio is a mutual fund. This is a popular investment vehicle consisting of a variety of securities or assets that are professionally managed. A major advantage of investing in mutual funds is diversification. Investors can own a variety of securities with a minimal capital investment. Since mutual funds are professionally managed, they tend to involve less risk. To reduce risk, securities in a portfolio should have negative or no correlation to each other.

**PORTFOLIO THEORY** idea advanced by H. Markowitz about a well-diversified portfolio. The central theme of the theory, also referred to as modern portfolio theory, is that rational investors behave in a way that reflects their aversion to taking increased risk without being compensated by an adequate increase in expected return. Also, for any given expected return, most investors will prefer a lower risk, and for any given level of risk, they will prefer a higher return to a lower return. Markowitz showed how *quadratic programming* could be used to calculate a set of "efficient" portfolios. An investor then will choose among a set of efficient portfolios the best that is consistent with the risk profile of the investor.

**POS** *see* POINT-OF-SALE (POS).

**POSITION** the financial condition of an entity.

**POSITIVE ASSURANCE** an opinion or affirmative statement made by an auditor that usually results from the performance of an audit of financial statements or other high-level examination engagement.

**POSITIVE CONFIRMATION** written or oral request by the auditor of a party having financial dealings with the client about the accuracy of an item. A response is required whether the particular item is correct or incorrect. A positive confirmation can be sent to customers to verify account balances. *See also* NEGATIVE CONFIRMATION.

**POST** transfer from the journal to the ledger a debit or credit to the given account involved.

**POSTAUDIT**
1. examination of a transaction after its occurrence. A postaudit determines if a company's policies and procedures have been properly followed. The test may be to verify if paid invoices have necessary documentation and approvals. This test verifies internal control procedures and work performed by clerks.
2. in an audit performed by a public accountant, period that exists between the completion of the auditor's field work and the issuance of the report on the financial statements. During this period, the auditor is in constant contact with the client while the audit report is prepared and the final review of the drafted financial statements takes place.

The auditor has a responsibility to disclose subsequent events so that the financial statements are not misleading. *See also* PREAUDIT.

**POST BALANCE-SHEET REVIEW** audit procedures applicable to the interval of time between the date of the financial statements and the completion date of the audit fieldwork. Attention is given to SUBSEQUENT EVENTS materially affecting the fair presentation of the financial statements.

**POST-CLOSING TRIAL BALANCE** one prepared from the general ledger for the end of the accounting period after preparing the *closing entries*. Since revenue and expense accounts have been closed out, the only accounts with balances are balance sheet accounts.

**POST DATE** placing on a document or a check a date that follows the date of initiation or execution. An example is buying something on January 10th and dating the check January 25th, so the check cannot be cashed until later. *See also* ANTEDATE.

**POST-OPTIMALITY ANALYSIS** *see* SENSITIVITY ANALYSIS.

**POSTPONABLE COST** cost being shifted to the future with little effect on the efficiency of current operations. Routine maintenance is an example.

***PRACTICAL ACCOUNTANT, THE*** monthly journal published by Accountants Media Group (www.webcpa.com). The subject matter relates to all aspects of accounting, information systems, and estate planning. The readership is primarily accountants in general practice.

**PRACTICAL CAPACITY** highest activity level at which the factory can operate with an acceptable degree of efficiency, taking into consideration unavoidable losses of productive time (i.e., vacations, holidays, repairs to equipment); also called *maximum practical capacity*. *See also* CAPACITY.

**PREAUDIT** substantiation that proper authorization exists for an act, such as making up a purchase order or entering into a contract. There is also examination of documentation prior to payment of an item, such as an invoice or payroll request. The controller is responsible for conducting preaudits. The internal auditor tests to assure that appropriate preaudit procedures are being carried out.

**PREACQUISITION CONTINGENCY** a contingent asset, liability, or impairment of an asset of the acquired entity that existed before the business combination. It is normally included in the allocation of the purchase price.

**PRECIOUS METALS** valuable commodities (e.g., gold and silver) representing a private store of value. Precious metals are liquid, have international markets, and provide a hedge against inflation, currency risk, and unfavorable political and economic developments. However, they are a volatile investment. Their prices typically increase in difficult periods and decline in good times. Precious metals usually go in the opposite direction of common stock; as common stock returns move down, returns on gold move up. Tax must be paid on the gain when sold. Precious metal ownership has several disadvantages including high storage cost, high transaction cost, and no annual dividend revenue.

**PREDECESSOR AUDITOR** independent CPA who either leaves the client willingly or is terminated and replaced by a SUCCESSOR AUDITOR.

**PREDETERMINED OVERHEAD RATE** rate, based on budgeted factory overhead cost and budgeted activity, that is established before a period begins.

$$\text{Predetermined Overhead Rate} = \frac{\text{Budgeted Yearly Total Factory Overhead Costs}}{\text{Budgeted Yearly Activity (direct labor-hours, etc.)}}$$

Budgeted activity units used in the denominator of the formula, more often called the *denominator level*, are measured in direct labor-hours, machine-hours, direct labor costs, or production units.

**PREDICTION ERRORS** *see* COST OF PREDICTION ERRORS.

**PREEMPTIVE RIGHT** right of a current stockholder to maintain the percentage ownership interest in the company by buying new shares on a pro rata basis before they are issued to the public. It prevents existing stockholders from dilution in value or control. The typical procedure is that each existing stockholder receives a *subscription warrant* indicating how many shares can be bought. Usually, the new shares are issued to the current stockholder at a lower price than the going market price. In addition, brokerage commissions do not have to be paid. For example, if an individual owns 2% of the shares of a company that is coming out with a new issue of 100,000 shares, the individual is entitled to buy 2,000 shares at a favorable price to maintain the proportionate interest.

**PREFERRED CREDITOR** one having priority over another creditor when the company becomes bankrupt. For example, a secured creditor (who has secured assets in support of his claim) has precedence over a general creditor (who has loaned money to the business without collateral).

**PREFERRED STOCK** class of capital stock that has preference over common stock in the event of corporate liquidation and in the distribution of earnings. It usually pays dividends at a fixed rate, but there is also adjustable rate preferred and "Dutch auction" preferred. For example, 6% preferred stock means that the dividend equals 6% of the total par value of the outstanding shares. Except in unusual instances, no voting rights exist. Types include CUMULATIVE PREFERRED STOCK and PARTICIPATING PREFERRED STOCK.

**PRELIMINARY AUDIT**
   1. fieldwork done prior to the end of the accounting period under examination in order to quicken the issuance of the audit report. The preliminary audit includes evaluating internal controls, financial records, and transactions. An analysis of account balances is begun. The CPA determines what audit scope and steps will be required so that an opinion on the financial statements may be rendered. The preliminary audit is different from a periodic audit because it typically involves no audit report and is an element of a regular annual audit.
   2. first engagement with a client, examining the overall business and its accounting system and operations before deciding on the extent of audit procedures that will be necessary.

**PREMIUM**
   1. excess of the amount received over the par or face value of a security. For example, if a $1,000 bond is issued at 102, the premium on the bond is $20 ($1,000 × 2%).
   2. price paid for a contract.
   3. periodic payment made on an insurance policy.
   4. promotion item given away in a marketing effort.
   5. excess paid over a typical expense item, such as a bonus above employee's regular salary.
   6. extra payment made for incentive purposes.
   7. price a call or put buyer pays to the writer (seller) for an option contract.
   8. amount in excess of market value paid in a TENDER OFFER.

**PREMIUM ON CAPITAL STOCK** excess received over the par value of stock issued. The premium account is shown under the paid-in capital section of stockholders' equity because it resulted from the issuance of stock. It is *not* an income statement account since the company earns profit by selling goods and services to outsiders, *not* by issuing shares of stock to owners.

**PREPAID EXPENSE** expenditures paid for in one accounting period but not completely used or consumed until the next accounting period. Examples of expenses paid in advance are insurance, advertising, and rent. Prepaid expenses are often of a recurring nature. They are shown under current assets.

**PREREQUISITE** event or action that has to be satisfied before the next event or action can occur. For example, an accounting student must take intermediate accounting before advanced accounting.

**PRESENT FAIRLY** term used in the *auditor's report* where there exists adequate disclosure, reasonable detail, and absence of bias. Adequate disclosure requires all management information necessary to interpret financial statements. Reasonable detail requires that certain particulars of broad statement classifications be presented, such as intangible assets that are broken down into types. Absence of bias means that the auditor is independent and impartial and does not favor one party over another (i.e., STOCKHOLDER over *investor*).

**PRESENT VALUE** current worth of future sums of money. The process of calculating present value, or *discounting*, is actually the opposite of finding the compounded future value. Recall from FUTURE VALUE that $F_n = P(1 + i)^n$. Therefore, $P = F_n/ [(1 + i)^n] = F_n[1/(1 + i)^n] =$ PVIF$(i,n)$ where PVIF$(i,n)$ is the present value of $1 and is given in table 3 in back of book.

For example, assume Mr. B has been given an opportunity to receive $20,000 six years from now. If he can earn 10% on his investment, what is the most he should pay for this opportunity? To answer this question we need to find the present worth of $20,000 to be received six years from now. The PVIF(10%, 6 years) is in table 3—0.564. Therefore,

$$P = \$20,000(0.564) = \$11,280$$

This means that Mr. B could be indifferent to the choice between receiving $11,280 now or $20,000 six years from now since the amounts are time equivalent at 10%.

**PREVENTIVE COSTS** a category of QUALITY COSTS incurred to prevent defects of products and services, such as quality training programs and quality circles.

**PRICE DISCOUNT** *see* TRADE DISCOUNT.

**PRICE-EARNINGS RATIO (P/E RATIO)** statistic that equals market price per share divided by earnings per share. It is a good ratio to use in evaluating the investment possibility of a company. A steady decrease in the P/E ratio reflects decreasing investor confidence in the growth potential of the entity. Some companies have high P/E multiples reflecting high earnings growth expectations. Young, fast-growing companies often have high P/E stocks with multiples over 20. A company's P/E ratio depends on many factors such as risk, earnings trend, quality of management, industry conditions, and economic factors.

**PRICE LEVEL ACCOUNTING** method of measuring the impact of changes in general purchasing power of the dollar. Inflation is measured and reported in the financial statements. Balance sheet and income statement accounts are restated to average current year dollars using the Consumer Price Index. *Purchasing power gains and losses* on MONETARY ITEMS are reflected in the price-level income statement. *See also* CONSTANT DOLLAR ACCOUNTING; CURRENT VALUE ACCOUNTING.

**PRICE-TO-BOOK RATIO** market price per share divided by book value (tangible assets less all liabilities) per share. It is a measure of stock valuation relative to net assets.

**PRICE-TO-SALES RATIO** the current price divided by the sales per share for the trailing twelve months. If there is a preliminary earnings announcement for a quarter that has recently ended, the revenue (sales) values from this announcement will be used in calculating the trailing twelve month revenue per share.

**PRICE VARIANCE** difference between actual unit price and standard unit price, multiplied by actual quantity of input used. It reflects a change between the expected price and actual price of input.

Price Variance = (Actual Price − Standard Price) × Actual Quantity

where a positive result indicates an increase in costs (i.e., an unfavorable variance), while a negative result means a reduction in costs (i.e., a favorable variance). *See also* LABOR RATE (PRICE) VARIANCE; MATERIALS PRICE VARIANCE; SALES PRICE VARIANCE.

**PRICING DECISIONS** decisions faced by top management and marketing managers. How much to charge for a product or service depends on a multitude of factors such as competition, cost, advertising, and sales promotion. Economic theory suggests that the best price for a product or service is the one that maximizes the difference between total revenue and total costs. However, in reality, the price charged is usually some form of cost-plus, which is later adjusted for market conditions and competition.

**PRIME COST** in manufacturing, DIRECT MATERIAL plus DIRECT LABOR. It excludes overhead. *See also* CONVERSION COST.

**PRIME RATE** interest rate charged by banks to their most financially sound customers. The prime rate is a reference point for other interest rates—some are lower than the published prime, most are higher. For example, the interest rate on commercial paper is less than the prime interest rate. Most companies have to borrow from financial institutions at a rate in excess of the prime rate. The rate is influenced by the cost of funds to the bank and the rates borrowers will accept.

**PRINCIPAL**
1. face amount of a financial instrument on which interest accrues. For example, a $25,000, 8%, one-year note has a principal portion of $25,000 and an interest portion of $2,000.
2. carrying value of an obligation (i.e., bonds payable).
3. amount invested, excluding return on investment.
4. high-level individual (i.e., partner) in a CPA firm having major authority and responsibilities.
5. owner, especially one with executive authority, of a business firm.

**PRIOR PERIOD ADJUSTMENT** revenue or expenses applicable to a previous period. The beginning balance of retained earnings is adjusted for the prior period adjustment (net of tax). An illustrative retained earnings section of the balance sheet follows:

Retained Earnings 1/1/2014 – Unadjusted
Add or Deduct: Prior Period Adjustment
Retained Earnings 1/1/2014 – Adjusted
Add: Net Income
Less: Dividends
Retained Earnings 12/31/2014

The *only* two examples of prior period adjustments are: (1) the correction of an error made in a prior year; and (2) the recognition of a tax LOSS CARRYFORWARD benefit arising from a purchased subsidiary.

**PRIOR SERVICE PENSION COST** retroactive benefits cost for services rendered in *periods prior* to the initiation of a pension plan or an amendment to a plan. The cost of these retroactive benefits is the resulting increase in the projected benefit obligation. It involves the allocation of equal amounts to future years of service for active employees. *See also* NORMAL PENSION COST.

**PRIVATE ACCOUNTANT** individual employed only by one organization as distinguished from an individual working for an independent accounting firm that serves many clients. The private accountant is an internal accountant reporting to the managers of the entity. A private accountant may be involved in preparing internal management reports for decision making such as capital budgeting, budgeting, and segmental performance analysis.

**PRIVATE ACTIVITY BOND** a bond issued by a state or local government, the proceeds of which are used to finance the facilities of an entity other than the government issuing the bond. Private activity bonds may be used, for example, to finance airports, docks and wharves, and qualified educational facilities. Interest received by the holder of qualified private activity bonds is tax-exempt for regular tax purposes, but is considered to be an adjustment when calculating the ALTERNATIVE MINIMUM TAX.

**PRIVATE COMPANIES PRACTICE SECTION (PCPS)** division of the AMERICAN INSTITUTE OF CERTIFIED PUBLIC ACCOUNTANTS (AICPA) for CPA firms serving nonpublic companies. Member CPA firms participate in PEER REVIEW. The other section is the SEC practice section.

**PRIVATE COMPANY COUNCIL (PCC)** created by the Financial Accounting Foundation to work with the FINANCIAL ACCOUNTING STANDARDS BOARD (FASB) in order to establish alternatives to GENERALLY ACCEPTED ACCOUNTING PRINCIPLES (GAAP) for private entities.

**PRIVATE CORPORATION** *see* PRIVATELY HELD COMPANY.

**PRIVATE EQUITY** money raised from big investors such as pension funds and college endowments. Private equity companies buy companies with the goal of eventually reselling the takeover targets for a profit.

**PRIVATE OFFERING** *see* PRIVATE PLACEMENT.

**PRIVATELY HELD COMPANY** firm owned by a few people. It is distinguished from a PUBLICLY HELD COMPANY, which is also a private company, but whose shares are traded in the public market; also called a *closed corporation* or *private corporation*. A publicly held company can either be closely held (meaning most of the public shares are owned or controlled by a few people) or widely held, as with a company whose shares are listed on a national stock exchange. A privately held company is typically referred to as a NONISSUER.

**PRIVATE PLACEMENT** sale of securities by the issuing company directly to an investor (generally a large institutional investor) rather than an offering through the public exchange markets. A private placement does not have to be registered with the SEC, as a PUBLIC OFFERING does, if the securities are not purchased for resale.

**PRIVILEGED COMMUNICATION** confidential communication, such as that between a client and his attorney. The receiver of the information (attorney) is not legally required to disclose it. Common-law privileged communication between the client and the CPA exists only in a few states where it is permitted by statute.

**PRIZES AND AWARDS** items received for winning a contest or in recognition of an activity. Cash prizes or awards generally must be included in taxable income. The prize or award can be excluded from taxable income *only* when the taxpayer assigns it to a charitable organization.

**PROBABILITY** degree of likelihood that something will happen. Probabilities are expressed as fractions (½, ¼, ¾), as decimals (.5, .25, .75), or as percentages (50%, 25%, 75%) between 0 and 1. For example, a probability of 0 means that something can never happen; a probability of 1 means that something will *always* happen. The probability of an event is calculated as follows:

$$p(a) = \frac{\text{Number of Outcomes Favorable to the Occurrence of the Event}}{\text{Total Number of Possible Outcomes}}$$

The probability of getting heads in one toss is: $p(\text{heads}) = 1/(1 + 1) = ½$.

**PROBABILITY DISTRIBUTION** table or graph showing the *relative frequency* of each of various outcomes. Widely known probability distributions include the binomial distribution and the NORMAL DISTRIBUTION. A probability distribution of a possible number of tails from two tosses of a fair coin may look like this:

| Number of Tails | Probability of This Outcome |
|:---:|:---:|
| 0 | .25 |
| 1 | .50 |
| 2 | .25 |

**PROBABILITY SAMPLE** *see* RANDOM SAMPLE.

**PROCEDURAL AUDIT** evaluation of internal controls, accounting policies, and other procedures of a business entity by an independent CPA. Recommendations for improvement in procedures or activities in the system are made. An overall appraisal may be made of the entire business, or the audit may be directed to a particular business segment. At the conclusion of the audit, management receives a report that will list the findings. These audits are normally performed by the internal audit staff in many companies and take place during the entire year. Where a company does not have an internal audit staff, it may hire the auditor that certifies its financial statements to perform a procedural review as part of the annual audit. When such an arrangement is made, management expects to receive a separate report on this review, offering its findings with recommendations.

**PROCEEDS** funds received from the sale of assets or issuance of securities such as capital stock or bonds.

**PROCESS** sequence or arterial network of logically related and time-based work activities to provide a specific output for an internal or external customer. For example, the assembly of a television set or the paying of a bill or claim entails several linked activities. *See also* BUSINESS PROCESS.

**PROCESS-BASED MANAGEMENT** managing business processes to achieve a desired result.

**PROCESS BENCHMARKING** *see* BENCHMARKING.

**PROCESS COST** cost assigned to a business process based on the cost of the activities that compose the process.

**PROCESS COSTING** method that aggregates manufacturing costs by departments or by production processes. Total manufacturing costs are accumulated by major categories—direct materials, direct labor, and factory overhead applied. Unit cost is determined by dividing the total costs charged to a cost center by the output of that cost center. Process costing is appropriate for companies that produce a continuous mass of like units through a series of operations or processes—generally used in such industries as petroleum, chemicals, oil refinery, textiles, and food processing. A COST OF PRODUCTION REPORT is a cost sheet used for process costing that summarizes the total cost charged to a department and the allocation between the ending work-in-process inventory and the units completed and transferred to the next department or finished goods inventory. The output of a processing department during a given period is measured in terms of *equivalent units* of production which is the expression of the physical units of output in terms of doses or amount of work applied thereto. In computing the unit cost for a processing center, when a beginning inventory of work-in-process exists, two specific assumptions about the flow of cost are used—WEIGHTED AVERAGE and

FIFO. Under weighted average, the costs in the beginning inventory are averaged with the current period's costs to determine one average unit cost for all units passing through the cost center in a given month. Under FIFO, costs in the beginning inventory are not mingled with the current period's costs but transferred out as a separate batch of goods at a different unit cost than units started and completed during the period.

**PROCESS COST REPORT** set of three schedules that help managers track and analyze costs in a process costing system; it consists of the schedule of equivalent production, the unit cost analysis schedule, and the cost summary schedule.

**PROCESSING COSTS** *see* CONVERSION COST.

**PROCESSING TIME** actual amount of time spent working on a product.

**PROCESSOR**
1. device that can perform operations on data. Examples are the central processing unit (CPU) and a front-end processor. For instance, the CPU directs data and instructions to and from other devices in the computer system, like the computer's memory and input devices. It also interprets programs.
2. language processor, such as an assembler, compiler, or interpreter.

**PROCESS REENGINEERING** analysis of business processes resulting in radical change rather than incremental improvement. Redesign of processes is intended to result in the elimination of unnecessary steps, reduction of circumstances in which mistakes can occur, cost minimization, quicker response time, and better quality.

**PROCESS VALUE ANALYSIS (PVA)** analytical method of identifying all activities and relating them to the events that cause or drive the need for the activities and the resources consumed.

**PRODUCER'S RISK** probability of rejecting a good quality lot.

**PRODUCT COST** cost of inventory on hand, also called *inventoriable cost*. They are assets until the products are sold. Once they are sold, they become expenses, i.e., *cost of goods sold*. All manufacturing costs are product costs. Examples are DIRECT MATERIAL, DIRECT LABOR, and FACTORY OVERHEAD.

**PRODUCT COSTING SYSTEM** set of procedures that accounts for an organization's product costs and provides timely and accurate unit cost information for pricing, planning and control, inventory valuation, and financial statement preparation.

**PRODUCT DEVELOPMENT TIME** performance measure of competitive strategy. A company that is first in the market with a new product has obvious advantages. Reducing development time is also important because product life cycles are becoming shorter, and organizations need to respond quickly and flexibly to new technology, changes in consumer tastes, and other competitive challenges. One financial measure of product development is BREAKEVEN TIME. CUSTOMER RESPONSE TIME is another crucial competitive factor.

**PRODUCT FAMILY** group of products or services that have a defined relationship because of physical and production similarities. The term PRODUCT LINE is used interchangeably.

**PRODUCT FINANCING ARRANGEMENT** agreement to finance the acquisition of a product through debt. Another entity may buy a product on behalf of the purchaser. At the time of acquisition, the purchaser debits inventory and credits a liability for the amount owed to the other entity. When payment of the obligation is made, the liability is debited for the principal, interest expense is debited for the interest, and cash is paid for the total amount.

**PRODUCT LIFE CYCLE** *see* LIFE CYCLE.

**PRODUCTION BUDGET** schedule for expected units to be produced. It sets forth the units expected to be manufactured to satisfy budgeted sales and inventory requirements. Expected production volume is determined by adding desired ending inventory to planned sales and then subtracting beginning inventory.

**PRODUCTION COST** *see* MANUFACTURING COST.

**PRODUCTION CYCLE TIME** time it takes for production personnel to make the product available for shipment to the customer.

**PRODUCTION MIX VARIANCE** cost variance that arises if the actual production mix deviates from the standard or budgeted mix. In a multi-product, multi-input situation, the mix variances explain the portion of the *quantity (usage, or efficiency) variance* caused by using inputs (direct materials and direct labor) in ratios different from standard proportions, thus helping to determine how efficiently mixing operations are performed. The MATERIAL MIX VARIANCE indicates the impact on material costs of the deviation from the budgeted mix. The *labor mix variance* measures the impact of changes in the labor mix on labor costs.

$$\begin{array}{l} \text{Material} \\ \text{Mix} \\ \text{Variance} \end{array} = \left( \begin{array}{l} \text{Actual Units} \\ \text{Used at} \\ \text{Standard Mix} \end{array} - \begin{array}{l} \text{Actual Units} \\ \text{Used at} \\ \text{Actual Mix} \end{array} \right) \times \begin{array}{l} \text{Standard} \\ \text{Unit} \\ \text{Price} \end{array}$$

$$\begin{array}{l} \text{Labor} \\ \text{Mix} \\ \text{Variance} \end{array} = \left( \begin{array}{l} \text{Actual Hours} \\ \text{Used at} \\ \text{Standard Mix} \end{array} - \begin{array}{l} \text{Actual Hours} \\ \text{Used at} \\ \text{Actual Mix} \end{array} \right) \times \begin{array}{l} \text{Standard} \\ \text{Hourly} \\ \text{Rate} \end{array}$$

Probable causes of unfavorable production mix variances are as follows: (1) substitution forced by capacity restraints; (2) poor production scheduling; (3) lack of certain types of labor; and (4) certain materials in short supply.

**PRODUCTION RUN MODEL** *see* ECONOMIC PRODUCTION RUN SIZE MODEL.

**PRODUCTION VOLUME VARIANCE** *see* VOLUME VARIANCE.

**PRODUCTION YIELD VARIANCE** difference between the actual yield and the standard yield. YIELD is a measure of productivity. In other words, it is a measure of output from a given amount of input. For example, in the production of potato chips, a certain yield such as 40% or 40 pounds of chips for 100 pounds of potatoes might be expected. If the actual yield is less than the expected or standard yield for a given level of input, the yield variance is unfavorable. A yield variance is computed for labor as well as materials. A *labor yield variance* is considered the result of the quantity and/or the quality of labor used. The yield variance explains the remaining portion of the QUANTITY VARIANCE and is caused by a yield of finished product that does not correspond with the quantity that actual inputs should have produced. When there is no mix variance, the yield variance equals the quantity variance.

$$\begin{matrix} \text{Material} \\ \text{Yield} \\ \text{Variance} \end{matrix} = \left( \begin{matrix} \text{Actual Units} \\ \text{Used at} \\ \text{Standard Mix} \end{matrix} - \begin{matrix} \text{Actual Output} \\ \text{Units Used at} \\ \text{Standard Mix} \end{matrix} \right) \times \begin{matrix} \text{Standard} \\ \text{Unit} \\ \text{Price} \end{matrix}$$

$$\begin{matrix} \text{Labor} \\ \text{Yield} \\ \text{Variance} \end{matrix} = \left( \begin{matrix} \text{Actual Hours} \\ \text{Used at} \\ \text{Standard Mix} \end{matrix} - \begin{matrix} \text{Actual Output} \\ \text{Hours Used at} \\ \text{Standard Mix} \end{matrix} \right) \times \begin{matrix} \text{Standard} \\ \text{Hourly} \\ \text{Rate} \end{matrix}$$

Probable causes of unfavorable production yield variances are: (1) use of low quality materials and/or labor; (2) existence of faulty equipment; (3) use of improper production methods; and (4) improper or costly mix of materials and/or labor.

**PRODUCTIVITY** ratio of outputs to inputs.

**PRODUCTIVITY MEASURES** related to the efficiency, mix, and yield variances. They can be developed for both manufacturing and service entities, although the latter may sometimes find that output is difficult to measure. Productivity is the relationship between outputs and inputs (including the mix of inputs). The higher this ratio, the greater the productivity. Improvements in productivity depend on technical efficiency and input trade-off efficiency. A process becomes more technically efficient when, for any set of inputs that will produce a given output, nonvalue-added activities are eliminated and value-added activities use the minimum resources needed to produce the given output.

**PRODUCT LEVEL ACTIVITIES** activities performed to support the diversity of products in a manufacturing plant.

**PRODUCT LIFE CYCLE** period that starts with the initial product specification and ends with the withdrawal of the product from the marketplace. A product life cycle is characterized by certain defined stages, including research, development, introduction, maturity, decline, and abandonment. *See* LIFE CYCLE.

**PRODUCT LINE** *see* PRODUCT FAMILY.

**PRODUCT MIX** *see* SALES MIX.

**PRODUCT MIX DECISIONS** decisions that concern the relative amounts of each type of product or service that, given demand and resource constraints, will maximize total profits. For example, if the firm can sell as much as it can produce and has a single resource constraint, the decision rule is to maximize the contribution margin per unit of the constrained resource. However, given multiple constraints, the decision is more difficult and more sophisticated techniques must be used, such as linear programming for example.

**PRODUCT UNIT COST** manufacturing cost of a single unit of product; total cost of direct materials, direct labor, and manufacturing overhead for the units produced divided by the total units produced.

**PROFESSIONAL ETHICS** moral principles and standards of conduct guiding CPAs in performing their functions. Codes of professional ethics are established by organizations of CPAs, such as the American Institute of CPAs and state societies. A violation of professional ethics will make the accountant subject to disciplinary action. The accountant's professional ethics affect the reputation of the profession and the confidence of the public. Some of the professional ethic requirements follow. The CPA should be *independent* of clients served so that objectivity and integrity are maintained. For example, independence is violated if the CPA has a financial interest in the client, or is connected with the enterprise as an underwriter or director. The CPA must be professionally *competent*, exercise *due professional care*, properly *plan and supervise* the engagement, and *obtain adequate data* to form a conclusion about an engagement. CPAs cannot have their names associated with forecasts in such a way as to have users believe they vouch for the achievability. The CPA must follow GAAS in the pursuance of the audit function and may not express an unqualified opinion on financial statements if they depart from GAAP. The CPA must keep confidential information obtained from the client in the course of a professional engagement. Further, professional services cannot be offered on a contingent fee based on findings or results of services. A CPA in public practice shall not engage in an incompatible occupation creating a conflict of interest.

**PROFITABILITY** ability of a business entity to generate net income. Potential investors closely analyze a firm's current and prospective profitability since they affect dividends and market price of stock. *See also* PRICE-EARNINGS RATIO (P/E RATIO).

**PROFITABILITY ACCOUNTING** *see* RESPONSIBILITY ACCOUNTING.

**PROFITABILITY INDEX** ratio of the total present value (PV) of future cash inflows to the initial investment (I). That is, PV/I. This index is primarily used as a means of ranking projects in descending order of attractiveness. In a single project case, if the index is greater than 1, the project should be accepted. For example, consider the following data:

| | |
|---|---|
| Initial investment | $12,950 |
| Estimated life | 10 years |
| Annual cash inflows | $ 3,000 |
| Cost of capital (minimum required of return) | 12% |

The profitability index is 1.31 (*PV/I* = $16,950/$12,950). Note *PV* = $3,000 × *PV* of an annuity of $1 for 10 years and 12% = $3,000 × 5.65 = $16,950. Since this project generates $1.31 for each dollar invested (or its index is greater than 1), it should be accepted.

**PROFITABILITY OBJECT** level cost accumulation at which revenues are matched to cost consumption to analyze profitability.

**PROFIT AND LOSS STATEMENT** *see* INCOME STATEMENT.

**PROFIT CENTER** responsibility unit that measures the performance of a division, product line, geographic area, or other measurable unit. Divisional profit figures are *best* obtained by subtracting from revenue only the costs the division manager can control (direct division costs) and eliminating allocated costs common to all divisions (e.g., an allocated share of company image advertising that benefits all divisions but is not controlled by division managers). Profit is a very often used method to evaluate a division's financial success as well as the performance of its manager. In determining divisional profit, a TRANSFER PRICE may have to be derived. The divisional profit center allows for decentralization. as each division is treated as a separate business entity with responsibility for making its own profit. *See also* RESPONSIBILITY ACCOUNTING; RESPONSIBILITY CENTER.

**PROFIT MARGIN** ratio of income to sales. (1) net profit margin equals net income divided by net sales. It indicates the entity's ability to generate earnings at a particular sales level. By examining a company's profit margin relative to previous years and to industry norms, one can evaluate the company's operating efficiency and pricing strategy as well as its competitive status with other companies in the industry. (2) gross profit margin equals gross profit divided by net sales. A high profit margin is desirable since it indicates the company is earning a good return over the cost of its merchandise sold.

**PROFIT MAXIMIZATION** hypothesis that the goal of a firm is to maximize its profit.

**PROFIT PLANNING** process of developing a profit plan that outlines the planned sales revenues and expenses and the net income or loss for a time period. Profit planning requires preparation of a MASTER BUDGET and various analyses for risk and *what-if* scenarios. Tools for profit planning include the COST-VOLUME-PROFIT (CVP) ANALYSIS and *budgeting*.

**PROFIT-SHARING PLAN** plan by which corporate executives and employees receive a share of the company's net income on some equitable basis. Such basis may relate to salary level and service years. The maximum amount that an employer can deduct in any one year for the profit-sharing plan is 15% of compensation. Two or more profit-sharing plans are treated as one plan for purposes of limiting employer deductions. Under the present tax law, employer contributions are *not* limited to the employer's current or accumulated earnings.

**PROFIT VARIANCE** difference between actual profit and budgeted profit. Profit, whether it is GROSS PROFIT in ABSORPTION COSTING or CONTRIBUTION MARGIN in DIRECT COSTING, is affected by three basic items: sales price, sales volume, and costs. In a multi-product firm, if all products are not equally profitable, profit is also affected by the mix of products sold. If actual profit is greater than budgeted profit, the total profit variance is favorable and credited; otherwise, it is unfavorable and debited. *See also* CONTRIBUTION MARGIN (CM) VARIANCE; SALES PRICE VARIANCE.

**PROFIT VARIANCE ANALYSIS** *see* GROSS PROFIT ANALYSIS.

**PROFIT-VOLUME (PV) CHART** one that determines how profits vary with changes in volume. Profits are plotted on the vertical axis and units of output are shown on the horizontal axis. See the sample chart below.

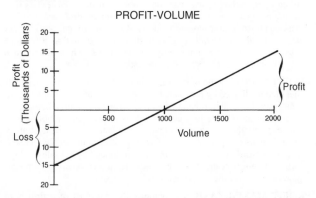

PROFIT-VOLUME

**PRO FORMA** financial statement with amounts or other information that are fully or partially assumed. The assumptions underlying these amounts are also typically given. For example, pro forma disclosure is required for a change in accounting principle in the current year of what earnings would have been in the prior year if the new principle had been used in the previous period. In this case, the pro forma disclosure is at the bottom of the income statement.

**PRO FORMA BALANCE SHEET** *see* BUDGETED BALANCE SHEET.

**PRO FORMA INCOME STATEMENT** *see* BUDGETED INCOME STATEMENT.

**PRO FORMA STATEMENT** *see* FINANCIAL MODEL; PRO FORMA.

**PRO FORMA STATEMENT OF CASH FLOWS** projected statement of cash flows. As with the regular statement, it classifies cash receipts and disbursements depending on whether they are from operating, investing, or financing activities. The direct presentation reports the major classes of gross cash operating receipts and payments and the difference between them. The indirect presentation reconciles net income with net operating cash flow. The reconciliation requires balance sheet data, such as the changes in accounts receivable, accounts payable, and inventory, as well as net income. Thus, all the pro forma statements are interrelated. For example, the pro forma cash flow statement will include anticipated borrowing. The interest on this borrowing will appear in the pro forma income statement.

**PROGRAM** set of instructions written in a computer language directing operations to be performed. A utility program is a standard program that conducts routine tasks like merging files and sorting.

**PROGRAM EVALUATION AND REVIEW TECHNIQUE (PERT)** useful management tool for planning, coordinating, and controlling large, complex projects such as formulation of a MASTER BUDGET, construction of buildings, installation of computers, and scheduling of the closing of books. The development and initial application of PERT dates to the construction of the Polaris submarine by the U.S. Navy in the late 1950s. The PERT technique involves the diagrammatic representation of the sequence of activities comprising a project by means of a network consisting of arrows and circles (nodes), as shown in *Figure 1. Arrows* represent "tasks" or "*activities*," which are distinct segments of the project requiring time and resources. *Nodes (circles)* symbolize "*events*," or milestone points in the project representing the completion of one or more activities and/or the initiation of one or more subsequent activities. An event is a point in time and does not consume any time in itself as does an activity. An important aspect of PERT is the CRITICAL PATH METHOD (CPM). A path is a sequence of connected activities. In *Figure 1*, 2-3-4-6 is an example of a path. The CRITICAL PATH for a project is the path that takes the greatest amount of time. This is the minimum amount of time needed for the completion of the project. Thus, activities along this path must be shortened in order to speed up the project. To compute this, calculate the *earliest time (ET)* and the *latest time (LT)* for each event.

CRITICAL PATH

*Figure 1*

The earliest time is the time an event will occur if all preceding activities are started as early as possible. Thus, for event 4 in *Figure 2*, the earliest time is 19.3 (i.e., 13 + 6.3). The latest time is the time an event can occur without delaying the project beyond the deadline. The earliest time for the entire project is 49.5. Working backward from event 6 (finish) it is seen that the latest time for event 4 is 35.5. The SLACK for an event is the difference between the latest time and earliest time. For event 4 the slack is 35.5 − 19.3 = 16.2. This is the amount of time event 4 can be delayed without delaying the entire project beyond its due date. Finally, the *critical path* for the network is the path leading to the terminal event so that all events on the path have zero path. *Figure 2* shows the earliest and latest times for each event.

CRITICAL PATH

*Figure 2*

| Event | Earliest Time | Latest Time | Slack |
|-------|---------------|-------------|-------|
| 1 | 0 | 6.3 | 6.3 |
| 2 | 0 | 0 | 0 |
| 3 | 13 | 13 | 0 |
| 4 | 19.3 | 35.5 | 16.2 |
| 5 | 37 | 37 | 0 |
| 6 | 49.5 | 49.5 | 0 |

The path 2-3-5-6 is the critical path.

In a real-world application of PERT to a complex project, the estimates of completion time for activities will seldom be certain.

To cope with the uncertainty in activity time estimates, proceed with three time estimates: an *optimistic time* (labeled $a$), a *most likely time* ($m$), and a *pessimistic time* ($b$). A weighted average of these three time estimates is then calculated to establish the *expected time* for the activity. The formula is: $(a + 4m + b)/6$. For example, given three time estimates, $a = 1$, $m = 3$, and $b = 5$, the expected time is $[1 + 4(3) + 5]/6 = 3$.

**PROGRAMMED (FIXED) COSTS** *see* DISCRETIONARY (FIXED) COST.

**PROGRAMMING** process of writing instructions for a computer. The program has to be turned into machine-readable form and put into the computer. The program must be tested to assure accuracy, and supporting documentation prepared.

**PROGRAM-PLANNING-BUDGETING SYSTEM (PPBS)** planning-oriented approach to developing a program budget. A program budget is a budget in which expenditures are based primarily on programs of work and secondarily on character and object. It is a transitional type of budget between the traditional character and object budget, on the one hand, and the performance budget on the other. The major contribution of PPBS lies in the planning process, i.e., the process of making program policy decisions that lead to a specific budget and specific multi-year plans.

**PROGRESS BILLINGS** interim billings for construction work or government contract work. The entry is to debit progress billings receivable and credit progress billings on construction in progress. Progress billings is a contra account to CONSTRUCTION-IN-PROGRESS. *See also* BILLINGS ON LONG-TERM CONTRACTS.

**PROGRESSIVE TAX** levy that requires a higher percentage payment on higher income. The personal income tax structure in the United States with its multiple brackets has been traditionally an example of a progressive tax. *See also* TAX RATE SCHEDULE.

**PROJECT** broad, complex, multidisciplinary approach to the production of a good or service.

**PROJECT COSTING** cost system that collects information on activities and costs associated with a specific activity, project, or program.

**PROJECTED BALANCE SHEET** *see* BUDGETED BALANCE SHEET.

**PROJECTED BENEFIT OBLIGATION (PBO)** actuarial present value as of a date of all benefits attributed by the pension benefit formula to employee service performed before that date. It is measured using assumptions as to *future* compensation levels if the pension benefit formula is based on those future salary levels (e.g., pay-related, final-pay). *See also* ACCUMULATED BENEFIT OBLIGATION (ABO); VESTED BENEFIT OBLIGATION (VBO).

**PROJECTED INCOME STATEMENT** *see* BUDGETED INCOME STATEMENT.

**PROJECT PLANNING** making planning decisions for capital investments, many of which may extend over long periods. For example, the decision to buy a particular piece of machinery and equipment is the result of project planning. Project planning has long-term effects on the company's future profitability. CAPITAL EXPENDITURE *analysis* or COST-BENEFIT ANALYSIS is a technique needed for project planning. *See also* CAPITAL BUDGETING.

**PROJECT SELECTION** choosing the best among alternative proposals on the basis of cost-benefit analysis. *See also* CAPITAL BUDGETING.

**PROMISSORY NOTE** formal unconditional promise in writing to pay on demand or at a future date a definite sum of money. The person who signs the note and promises to pay is called the maker of the note. The person to whom payment is to be made is called the payee of the note.

**PROMOTION EXPENSE** cost of samples or promotional items made available to the public at large. Promotion expense is fully tax deductible. Examples are distributed merchandise samples and tickets to a show offered as a customer prize.

**PROPERTY DIVIDEND** one paid in property. The dividend is recorded on the declaration date at the market value of the property.

**PROPERTY, PLANT, AND EQUIPMENT** long-lived *fixed productive assets* used in business activities. It is a noncurrent asset balance sheet classification. Property, plant, and equipment are shown at their book values. Examples are buildings and machinery. *See also* PLANT AND EQUIPMENT.

**PROPRIETARY FUND** in governmental accounting, one having profit and loss aspects; therefore it uses the *accrual* rather than modified accrual accounting method. The two types of proprietary funds are the ENTERPRISE FUND and the INTERNAL SERVICE FUND.

**PROPRIETARY THEORY** theory that assets are owned by the proprietor and liabilities are owed by him. The accounting equation is:

$$Assets - Liabilities = Capital$$

Capital is the net value of the business to the owner.

Under the proprietary theory, revenues increase capital, while expenses reduce it. Net income belongs to the owner, representing an increase in the proprietor's capital.

The proprietary theory best applies to single proprietorship entities because there exists a personal relationship between the management of the business and the owner. Often, in fact, they are the same person.

It also applies to a partnership where net income is added each period to the partners' capital accounts.

## PROPRIETORSHIP

**1.** assets minus liabilities of an organization. It equals contributed capital plus accumulated earnings.

**2.** form of business organization. *See also* SOLE PROPRIETOR.

**PRO RATA** basis for allocating an amount proportionately to the items involved. An amount may be proportionately distributed to assets, expenses, funds, and so forth. For example, at year end, underapplied overhead may be allocated to work-in-process, finished goods, and cost of sales based on the dollars or units applicable to those accounts. Assume underapplied overhead is $1,000, work-in-process is $4,000, finished goods is $5,000, and cost of sales is $1,000. The pro rata charge to work-in-process, for instance, would be $400 ($4,000/$10,000 × $1,000). The journal entry is:

| | | |
|---|---|---|
| Work-in-process | 400 | |
| Finished goods | 500 | |
| Cost of sales | 100 | |
| Factory overhead | | 1,000 |

**PRORATION** allocating or assigning an amount in proportion to some base to an activity, department, or product. Service costs are frequently allocated to user departments based on the base allocation formula/procedure (e.g., number of employees, machine hours spent). *See also* ALLOCATION.

**PROSPECTUS** document that must accompany a new issue of securities. It contains the same information appearing in the registration statement, such as a list of directors and officers, financial reports certified by a CPA, underwriters, the purpose and use for the funds, and other reasonable information that prospective buyers of a security need to know. A preliminary prospectus, RED-HERRING (so named because of a red stamp indicating the tentative nature of the document during the period in which it is being reviewed for fraudulent or misleading statements by the SECURITIES AND EXCHANGE COMMISSION (SEC)), is issued prior to the *final, statutory* prospectus, which also contains offering instructions.

**PROTOCOL** guidelines and principles associated with the workings of a network. Rules surround data and electrical signals on the network, the manner of information transmissions, the way in which the network is accessed, and the processing of applications on the network.

## PROVISION

**1.** amount of an expense that must be recognized currently when the exact amount of the expense is uncertain. An example is an expense such as provision for income taxes.

2. contra asset account such as allowance for bad debts and allowance to reduce securities from cost to market value.
3. making an appropriation of retained earnings for a specified purpose.

**PROXY**
1. power of attorney by which the holder of stock transfers the voting rights to another party. Sometimes PROXY FIGHTS erupt with outside groups competing in the solicitation of proxies that would give them voting control.
2. short for *proxy statement,* a written document that the SEC requires to be provided to shareholders before they vote by proxy on corporate matters. It typically contains proposed members of the BOARD OF DIRECTORS, INSIDE DIRECTORS' salaries, and any resolutions of minority stockholders and of management.

**PROXY FIGHTS** competition that erupts when outsiders attempt to gain control of a company's management. This requires soliciting a sufficient number of votes by proxy to unseat the existing management. The fights (battles) generally occur when the present management is performing poorly; however, the odds of outsiders winning a proxy fight are generally slim.

**PROXY STATEMENT** *see* PROXY.

**PRUDENT INVESTMENT**
1. investment made prudently and intelligently. A reasonable degree of safety and return are expected. *See also* FIDUCIARY.
2. rule that allows an uninstructed trustee considerable discretionary authority to purchase investments of any type that an ordinarily prudent person would find suitable in the case at hand.

**P2P** *see* PEER-TO-PEER NETWORKING.

**PUBLIC ACCOUNTANT (PA)** one performing professional accounting services for the public. The public accountant is licensed by a state to use the PA designation. Licensing requirements for a PA are significantly less than for a CERTIFIED PUBLIC ACCOUNTANT.

**PUBLIC ACCOUNTING** profession that public accountants are engaged in. Independent public accountants perform many functions, including auditing financial statements, designing financial accounting systems, assisting in the managerial accounting function, providing managerial advisory services, and tax preparation. The public accountant may perform services for corporations, partnerships, individuals, and other organizations. The certified public accountant is regulated by state law and must meet stringent technical and ethical requirements. These requirements include passing the CPA examination, satisfying experience requirements (e.g., two years in New York), and abiding by the American Institute of CPA's Code of Professional Ethics.

**PUBLIC COMPANY ACCOUNTING OVERSIGHT BOARD (PCAOB)** (www.pcaobus.org) a private sector, nonprofit corporation, created by the Sarbanes-Oxley Act of 2002, to oversee the auditors of public companies in order to protect the interests of investors and further the public interest in the preparation of informative, fair, and independent audit reports. All accounting firms auditing public companies must register with the PCAOB.

**PUBLIC INTEREST ACCOUNTING** *see* ACCOUNTANTS FOR THE PUBLIC INTEREST (API).

**PUBLICLY HELD COMPANY** enterprise whose ownership is held by the general public, including individuals, officers, employees, and institutional investors. A publicly held company has stock listed on an exchange and must file financial statements and reports with the SEC. *See also* PRIVATELY HELD COMPANY.

**PUBLIC OFFERING** presenting new securities to the investing public, after registration requirements have been filed with the SEC. The securities are usually made available to the public at large by a managing investment banker and its underwriting syndicate. In the public offering, unlike PRIVATE PLACEMENT, the corporation does not deal directly with the ultimate buyers of the securities. The public market is an impersonal one.

**PUBLIC OVERSIGHT BOARD (POB)** group consisting mostly of nonaccountants that oversees activities of CPA firms belonging to the AICPA's SEC practice section. The POB's objective is to assure quality professional services.

**PULL-THROUGH PRODUCTION** production system in which a customer's order triggers the purchase of materials and the scheduling of production for the required products.

**PURCHASE (ACCOUNTING) METHOD** manner of accounting for a business combination. Under the purchase method, the acquiring corporation records the net assets acquired at the fair market value of the consideration given. Any excess of the purchase price over the fair market value of the net identifiable assets is recorded as goodwill. The acquiring corporation then records periodic charges to income for the depreciation of the excess price over book value of net identifiable assets. Goodwill is subject to an annual impairment test. Note that goodwill already on the books of the acquired company is not brought forth. Net income of the acquired company is brought forth from the acquisition date to year-end. Direct costs of the purchase reduce the fair value of securities issued. Indirect costs are expensed.

**PURCHASE DISCOUNT** reduction given under the heading CASH DISCOUNT or TRADE DISCOUNT. A cash discount is intended for prompt payments by the purchaser, whereas a trade discount represents a reduction in list price in return for quantity purchases.

**PURCHASE GROUP** *see* SYNDICATE.

**PURCHASE ORDER** form used by the purchasing department to order goods or merchandise. Several copies are usually prepared, each on a different color paper. The original is sent to the supplier; this purchase order is an authorization to deliver the merchandise and to submit a bill based on the prices listed. Carbon copies of the purchase order are usually routed to the purchasing department, accounting department, receiving department, and finance department.

**PURCHASE ORDER LEAD TIME** time it takes for raw materials and parts to be ordered and received so that production can begin.

**PURCHASE PRICE VARIANCE** *see* MATERIAL PRICE VARIANCE.

**PURCHASE REQUISITION** a document used by a user department to request the acquisition of goods or services. An approved purchase requisition is sent to the purchasing department and serves as the basis for the preparation of a PURCHASE ORDER.

**PURCHASING POWER LOSS (OR GAIN)** event that occurs when holding MONETARY ITEMS during a period of inflation or deflation. A purchasing power loss occurs on holding monetary assets during inflation because of the decline in purchasing power of the dollar. A purchasing power gain arises, from a borrowing company's standpoint, on monetary liabilities in an inflationary environment, because the company will be paying back in *cheaper dollars*. Purchasing power gains or losses are shown in the price-level adjusted income statement. Assume that on 1/1/20X9 net monetary assets are $55,000, and during 20X9 the increase in net monetary assets is $6,000. The relevant Consumer Price Indices are: 1/1/20X9 212.9, average for 20X9 220.9, and 12/31/20X9 243.5. The computation of the purchasing power loss for 20X9 follows:

| | Historical Cost | | Conversion Factor | Average 20X9 Dollars |
|---|---|---|---|---|
| 1/1/20X9 | $55,000 | × | $\frac{220.9}{212.9}$ | $57,067 |
| Increase in monetary items | 6,000 | × | $\frac{220.9}{220.9}$ | 6,000 |
| | | | | $63,067 |
| 12/31/20X9 | $61,000 | × | $\frac{220.9}{243.5}$ | $55,338 |
| Purchasing Power Loss | | | | $ 7,729 |

*See also* CONSTANT-DOLLAR ACCOUNTING.

**PURCHASING SYSTEM** procedures, manual or computerized, followed by an organization to achieve the following basic objectives: (1) to determine the quality and quantity needed and the time when an item is needed; (2) to obtain the best possible price; and (3) to maintain information on sources of supply. The system should utilize such concepts as ECONOMIC ORDER QUANTITY (EOQ), *optimal reorder point*, QUANTITY DISCOUNTS, and MATERIAL REQUIREMENT PLANNING (MRP).

**PUSH-DOWN ACCOUNTING** method of accounting in which the financial statements of a subsidiary are presented to reflect the costs incurred by the parent company in buying the subsidiary instead of the subsidiary's historical costs. The purchase costs of the parent company are shown in the subsidiary's statements.

**PUSH-THROUGH METHOD** production system in which products are manufactured in long production runs and stored in anticipation of customers' orders.

**PUT**
1. option to sell a specific security at a specified price within a designated period for which the option buyer pays the seller (writer) a premium or option price. Contracts on listed puts (and CALLS) have been standardized at date of issue for periods of three, six, and nine months, although as these contracts approach expiration, they may be purchased with a much shorter life.
2. bondholder's right to redeem a bond prior to maturity.

**PV CHART** *see* PROFIT-VOLUME (PV) CHART.

# Q

**Q RATIO** the market value of all securities (not just equity) divided by the replacement cost (not book value) of all assets. The Q ratio reflects the market's valuation of new investment. A ratio greater than one means that a firm is earning returns greater than the amount invested. For this reason, a company with a ratio exceeding one should attract new resources and competition; also called *Tobin's Q*. The higher the Q ratio, the greater the industry attractiveness and/ or competitive advantage. The notion of this ratio holds that a firm's market value ultimately equals the replacement cost of its tangible assets. Some argue that calculating the replacement cost of assets is subject to enormous measurement errors; thus, the Q ratio is useless as a valuation tool.

**QUALIFICATION**
1. reference in the audit report to a material limitation placed on the auditor's examination or to uncertainty regarding a specific item in the financial statements. *See also* QUALIFIED OPINION.
2. reservation in a proposed agreement making the agreement unenforceable unless a specified condition is met.
3. technical competence to perform a particular job, such as passing the CPA examination and meeting experience requirements in order to be licensed as a certified public accountant.

**QUALIFIED OPINION** judgment by the CPA in the AUDIT REPORT that "except for" something, the financial statements fairly present the financial position and operating results of the firm. An "EXCEPT FOR" OPINION relates to a limitation placed on the scope of the audit. The result of the limitation is the failure of the CPA to obtain sufficient objective and verifiable evidence in support of business transactions of the company being audited.

**QUALIFIED STOCK OPTION** plan granting an employee the right to purchase company stock at a later date at a specified option price that will most always be lower than the market price; also called *incentive stock option*. If the stock price goes below the option price, the company can issue the executive a second incentive option with a lower exercise price. There is a $100,000 per employee ceiling on the value of stock covered by options that are exercisable in any one calendar year. Another advantage to the corporate executive of an incentive stock option is that no tax is paid until the stock bought with the option is sold.

**QUALITATIVE FACTORS** considerations in decision making, in addition to the quantitative or financial factors highlighted by INCREMENTAL ANALYSIS. They are the factors relevant to a decision that are difficult to measure in terms of money. Qualitative factors may include: (1) effect on employee morale, schedules, and other internal elements; (2)

relationships with and commitments to suppliers; (3) effect on present and future customers; and (4) long-term future effect on profitability. In some decision-making situations, qualitative aspects are more important than immediate financial benefit from a decision.

**QUALITY** measure of conformance of a product or service to certain specifications or standards. *See also* TOTAL QUALITY MANAGEMENT; APPRAISAL COSTS; INTERNAL FAILURE COSTS; EXTERNAL FAILURE COSTS; PREVENTIVE COSTS.

**QUALITY ASSURANCE** all of the activities necessary to ensure that the customer receives satisfactory performance.

**QUALITY AT THE SOURCE** responsibility of every employee, work group, department, or supplier to inspect the work.

**QUALITY CONTROL**
1. procedures to establish an optimal level of audit performance by practitioners. Included are proper supervision over field work, evaluation of internal control, and employment of generally accepted auditing standards. The monitoring of a CPA firm's system of quality control by a peer reviewer involves consideration of the adequacy and relevance of the CPA firm's procedures, practices, and compliance thereto, effectiveness of professional development, and quality of the CPA firm's practice aids.
2. policies and techniques used to assure that some level of performance has been achieved. Included are controls in design and inspection. Variances from established norms are identified and rectified.
3. in manufacturing, procedures to achieve a desired level of satisfaction of the operation or product being produced. A number of tests and measurements may be required to determine that a part meets required specifications.

**QUALITY CONTROL CHART** graph sometimes used in analyzing deviations of actual results from standards, known as VARIANCES. Measurements of actual results are shown on the graph and compared with measurements of the expected mean and upper and lower control limits, which are established by using statistical procedures. In statistical quality control charts, the upper and lower control limits are set three STANDARD DEVIATIONS from the mean. *See also* THREE-SIGMA LIMITS.

QUALITY CONTROL CHART

**QUALITY COSTS** costs incurred because poor quality cost may exist or actually does exist.

**QUALITY OF EARNINGS** extent that net income is realistic in portraying the operating performance of a business—that reported results have not intentionally been overstated or understated by management. In appraising net income, quantitative techniques, such as ratio analysis, can be employed.

**QUALITY REVIEW** evaluation by one accounting firm or accountant of the soundness of the practices of another accounting firm or accountant. A professional organization may also be engaged to examine the audit functions performed by a CPA firm. The quality review will include an appraisal of such areas as working paper preparation, audit programs, internal control, audit reports, staff functions, scheduling, supervision, client relations, and training. *See also* PEER REVIEW.

**QUALITY TRAINING** familiarizing all employees with the means for preventing, detecting, and eliminating nonquality. The educational processes are tailored to the appropriate groups.

**QUANTIFICATION** expression of economic activity in monetary units. Thus financial statement items are typically expressed in numbers comprising monetary units, such as dollars.

**QUANTITATIVE FACTORS** considerations relevant to a decision that can be measured in terms of money or quantitative units. Examples are incremental revenue, added cost, and initial outlay. *See also* QUALITATIVE FACTORS.

**QUANTITATIVE METHODS (MODELS)** collection of mathematical and statistical methods used in the solution of managerial and decision-making problems, also called *operations research* (OR) and *management science*. There are numerous tools available under these headings such as LINEAR PROGRAMMING (LP), ECONOMIC ORDER QUANTITY (EOQ), LEARNING CURVE THEORY, PERT, and REGRESSION ANALYSIS.

**QUANTITY DISCOUNT** *see* TRADE DISCOUNT.

**QUANTITY DISCOUNT MODEL** form of an economic order quantity (EOQ) model that takes into account quantity discounts. Quantity discounts are price reductions designed to induce large orders. If quantity discounts are offered, the buyer must weigh the potential benefits of reduced purchase price and fewer orders against the increase in carrying costs caused by higher average inventories. Hence, the buyer's goal in this case is to select the order quantity that will minimize total costs, where total cost is the sum of carrying cost, ordering cost, *and* purchase cost.

**QUANTITY (USAGE) VARIANCE** efficiency variance for direct materials. *See also* EFFICIENCY VARIANCE.

**QUARTERLY REPORT** financial report issued every three months between annual reports. It includes unaudited financial statements consisting of the balance sheet, income statement, and statement of changes in financial position along with related footnotes. Also, typically there is a narrative overview of business operations. *See also* INTERIM FINANCIAL STATEMENT.

**QUASI CONTRACT** legal duty or obligation to pay for a benefit received as though a contract had actually been made. This will be done in a limited number of situations in order to attain an equitable or just result. For example, when a homeowner permits repairs to be made with the knowledge that they are being made by a stranger who would expect to be paid for such repairs, there is *quasi-contractual duty* to pay for the reasonable value of the improvement, i.e., in order to avoid the homeowner's unjust enrichment at the expense of the person making the repair.

**QUASI-REORGANIZATION** procedure used to eliminate a retained earnings deficit by restating certain assets, liabilities, and capital accounts. It allows a company a fresh start when it appears that operations can be turned around. It permits the company to proceed on much the same basis as if it had been legally reorganized, without the difficulty and expense generally connected with such a legal reorganization. Stockholders and creditors must agree to it. The following steps are taken: (1) assets are written down to fair market value; (2) capital stock is restated, creating additional paid-in capital by reducing par value; and (3) a zero balance in retained earnings is created by eliminating the deficit in retained earnings by transferring part of capital to the account. Retained earnings bear the date of the quasi-reorganization.

**QUATTRO PRO** spreadsheet software offered by Corel.

**QUERY LANGUAGE** used to request data from a database table. An example of a query language is SQL.

**QUESTIONABLE PAYMENT** improper and often illegal monies given to obtain favorable treatment by another party. An example is a bribe made to a government official or buyer of goods in another company.

**QUEUE** waiting line that forms wherever there is more than one user of a limited resource.

**QUEUE DISCIPLINE** rules that determine the order in which arrivals are serviced.

**QUEUING THEORY (WAITING LINE THEORY)** quantitative technique for balancing services available with services required. It evaluates the ability of service facilities to handle capacity and load at different times during the day. It is useful in problems of balancing cost and service level, such as determining the number of toll booths on a highway and the number of tellers in a bank.

**QUICK ASSET** current asset that can be converted into cash in a short period of time. Examples are cash, marketable securities, and accounts receivable. Certain current assets, such as inventory and prepaid expenses, are excluded.

**QUICKBOOKS PRO** leader in accounting software for small business, brings complete financial management capabilities to small business owners who do not want to deal with the hassle of trying to understand accounting jargon or debit/credit accounting. QuickBooks (www.quickbooks.com) users can easily set up their business with QuickBooks, making it easy to create custom invoices, enter sales, perform electronic banking and bill payment, track customer contracts, track time, perform job costing, manage inventory, handle payroll, and even prepare for tax time.

**QUICKEN** personal finance software by Intuit, Inc. (www.quicken. com).

**QUICK RATIO** *see* ACID TEST RATIO.

**QUOTED PRICE** price of the last transaction of a listed security or commodity. In over-the-counter trading, *quote* means bid and asked.

# R

*r see* CORRELATION COEFFICIENT (*r*).

**RAM (RANDOM-ACCESS MEMORY)** computer's main memory where programs, application software, and data are stored. The size of the RAM (measured by kilobytes) is an important indicator of the capacity of the computer; also called *read/write memory*.

**RANDOM ACCESS** *see* DIRECT ACCESS.

**RANDOM ACCESS FILE** file constructed in a manner in which records may be placed in a random order; also called *direct access file*. Each record in a random access file has associated with it a relative index number. Whenever a record is read from a random access file, a computer program must produce a relative index number for this record in order to locate the record in the file. This type of file design offers the following advantages: (1) it provides rapid access to the desired information. In a decision-making environment where information is needed quickly, random access is a requisite to rapid retrieval; (2) it is efficient for retrieving a relatively few records at a time; and (3) it provides a method of keeping files up to date as transactions or events occur. *See also* DIRECT ACCESS.

**RANDOM SAMPLE** one allowing for the equal probability that each item will be chosen. To assure this, identification numbers are assigned to each item in a group and a table of random numbers is used to determine the sample members.

**RANDOM VARIANCES** differences that are due to chance, also called *chance variances*. The identification of random variances avoids unnecessary investigations of variances and eliminates frequent changes in a process or an operation. Statistical control charts are often used to distinguish random variances from variances that need investigation. *See also* STATISTICAL QUALITY CONTROL.

**RANDOM WALK** theory that stock prices behave in an unpredictable fashion because the stock market is efficient. The market price of a stock goes randomly around real (intrinsic) value. Current security prices are independent of prior prices. Thus historical prices are not a reliable predictor of future ones.

According to random walk, financial information significant enough to affect future value is available to knowledgable investors. Thus new data affecting stock prices are immediately reflected in market value. At any given time, the price of a stock is the optimum estimate of its value including all available information. *See also* EFFICIENT MARKET HYPOTHESIS.

**RAPID APPLICATION DEVELOPMENT (RAD)** a software development process that allows software to be developed in a short time, often with compromises. RAD is achieved by taking advantage of modern automated tools and techniques that significantly reduce development times.

**RATE EARNED ON COMMON STOCKHOLDERS' EQUITY** ratio indicating the earnings on the common stockholders' investment. It equals net income minus preferred dividends divided by average common stockholders' equity. Assume net income of $50,000, preferred dividends of $10,000, and average common stockholders' equity of $200,000. The ratio is 20% ($40,000/$200,000).

**RATE EARNED ON STOCKHOLDERS' EQUITY** statistic reflecting profit to the owners of the business. It equals net income divided by average owners' equity. Assume net income of $60,000, stockholders' equity at the beginning of the year of $700,000, and stockholders' equity at the end of the year of $500,000. The return rate is 10% ($60,000/$600,000).

**RATE EARNED ON TOTAL ASSETS** *see* RETURN ON INVESTMENT (ROI).

**RATE OF EXCHANGE** term used for the rate at which one currency (or commodity) can be exchanged for another. For example, one British pound may be equivalent to $1.80 in U.S. dollars. One Japanese Yen may equal $.0065 in American currency.

**RATE OF RETURN ON INVESTMENT** annual percentage return after taxes that actually occurs or is anticipated on an investment. For example, if $100,000 is invested in a stock and the after-tax return on it for the year is $8000, the rate of return is 8%. *See also* RETURN ON INVESTMENT (ROI).

**RATE VARIANCE** *see* LABOR RATE (PRICE) VARIANCE.

**RATIO** relationship of one amount to another. Ratios may compare balance sheet items, income statement items, or balance sheet items to income statement items. In effect, they relate financial statement components to each other. They are used to evaluate the company's financial health, operating results, and growth prospects. For example, ACCOUNTS RECEIVABLE TURNOVER will reveal collection problems with customers. *See also* RATIO ANALYSIS.

**RATIO ANALYSIS** study undertaken by financial statement preparers and users to evaluate the financial strength or weakness of a company and its operating trend. Various *ratios* are computed, depending upon the objective of the user analyzing the financial statements. Short-term creditors are primarily concerned with a company's ability to meet short-term debt from current assets, so they concentrate on the LIQUIDITY RATIOS emphasizing cash flow. Long-term creditors want to be paid back in the long term, so they look to solvency ratios such as total debt to total stockholders' equity. Potential investors are interested in dividends and appreciation in market price of stock, so they focus on profitability ratios (e.g., profit margin) and market measures (e.g., price-earnings ratio). Auditors zero in on the going concern of the client by determining its ability to meet debt (e.g., interest coverage ratio). Also, auditors wanting to know where to concentrate their audit attention look for illogical relationships in accounts over time such as the ratio of promotion and entertainment expense to sales. The limitations of financial ratios for analytical purposes must be considered, including: (1) a ratio is static in nature and does not reveal future flows; (2) a ratio does not reveal the amount of its components (e.g., a current ratio figure does not tell you how much is in cash or inventory); (3) a ratio does not reveal the quality of its components (e.g., a high current ratio that is made up of poor quality receivables and obsolete inventory); and (4) a ratio is based on historical cost not taking into account inflation. *See also* SOLVENT; TURNOVER.

**RATIO ESTIMATION** a technique used in statistical sampling that is used to estimate the dollar amount of a population using the ratio of the audit value of a sample to the book value (recorded amount) of a sample. Ratio estimation is an alternative to both DIFFERENCE ESTIMATION and MEAN-PER-UNIT (MPU) ESTIMATION.

**RAW IN PROCESS INVENTORY ACCOUNT** inventory account in the just-in-time operating environment that combines the materials inventory and the work-in-process inventory accounts.

**RAW MATERIALS INVENTORY** beginning or ending balance of raw materials on hand for an accounting period. It represents items that will be a component of a produced good. The beginning and ending balances of raw materials inventory are shown in the income statement when cost of goods sold is presented. The ending balance is reported in the balance sheet. *See also* RAW MATERIALS USED.

**RAW MATERIALS USED** items placed into the production process. They are a cost of making the product. An example is steel used in the manufacture of an automobile.

**REACQUIRED STOCK** *see* TREASURY STOCK.

**READ/WRITE MEMORY** *see* RAM (RANDOM-ACCESS MEMORY).

**REAL ACCOUNT** balance sheet account that is carried forward into the next year. It is a proprietary account. *See also* NOMINAL ACCOUNT.

**REAL ESTATE**
1. real property such as land, land improvements, and building held for business use in the production of income. It is contrasted with personal property.
2. real property held for investment purposes. Increased value in real estate has typically exceeded the rate of inflation. But real estate as an inflation hedge varies from locality to locality. Also, leverage exists with real estate since a high percentage of the investment may be made with debt funds. Down payments are often less than 25%.

However, a large capital investment is usually required. Real estate provides capital appreciation or depreciation. Certain real estate investments, such as residential and commercial property, generate annual income. Directly managed real estate income property provides tax deductions in the form of depreciation expense, interest expense, and property taxes.

**REAL ESTATE INVESTMENT TRUST (REIT)** a type of investment company that invests money (obtained through the sale of its shares to investors) in mortgages and various types of investment in real estate, in order to earn profits for shareholders. Shareholders receive income from the rents received from the properties and receive capital gains as properties are sold at a profit. REITs have been formed by a number of large financial institutions such as banks and insurance companies. The stocks of many of them are traded on security exchanges, thereby providing investors with a marketable interest in a real estate investment portfolio. REITs that distribute all of their income generally pay no entity-level tax. However, in exchange for this special tax treatment, REITs are subject to numerous qualifications and limitations including: (1) Shareholder qualifications. Generally, REITs are not permitted to be closely held and must have a minimum of 100 shareholders. (2) Qualified asset and income tests. REITs are required to have at least 75% of their value represented by qualified real estate assets and to earn at least 75% of their income from real estate investments.

**REALIZATION** recognizing revenue at the time of sale of merchandise if a retail business, or at the time of rendering the service if a service business. At realization, the earnings process is complete because the transaction is consummated, selling price is determinable, cost of sale is known, and future costs can be accurately estimated. Realization also applies to recognizing a gain on the sale of a security.

**REALIZED GAIN, LOSS** difference between the amount received from the sale or disposal of an asset and its carrying value. Realized gains and losses are shown in the income statement. They are also typically included in arriving at taxable income. In some cases, a realized loss can occur even though no sale has taken place. Examples are the write-down of a long-term investment due to a permanent decline in value, and the transfer of a security from long-term to short-term when market value is below cost.

**REAL ECONOMY** economy made up of manufacturing and services sectors as compared with the financial sector.

**REAL PROPERTY** rights, interests, and benefits inherent in the ownership of real estate, as distinguished from *personal property*; frequently thought of as a bundle of rights. Real estate may be loosely defined as land (including air rights) and other properties that are permanently attached to land such as houses, fences, and landscaping. The terms real property and REAL ESTATE are often used interchangeably.

**REAL-TIME SYSTEM** computer term for a system that uses a non-sequential processing method. This differs from batch processing, which employs sequential processing. It provides access to any piece of information and finds that piece of data in the same amount of time as any other piece. Real-time processing systems are more expensive than batch processing but provide decision-making information on a current basis, that is, when the decision needs to be made, or while a customer waits for a response.

**REASONABLENESS TEST** procedure to examine the logic of accounting information. For example, the trend in promotion and entertainment expense for a company can be compared to that of prior years of the same company or to competitive companies, or to industry norms. If the promotion and entertainment expense is relatively high, it will require investigation because it does not appear reasonable.

**REBATE**
1. ABATEMENT.
2. amount paid back or credit allowed because of an overcollection or the return of an object sold, also called *refund*.
3. unearned interest refunded to borrower if the loan is paid off prior to maturity.
4. payment to a customer upon completion of a purchase as an inducement or sales promotion tactic.

**RECAPITALIZATION** process of changing a firm's capital structure by altering the mix of debt and equity financing without changing the total amount of capital. This process often occurs as part of REORGANIZATION under the bankruptcy laws. In DEFEASANCE, the total capital amount can change.

**RECAPTURE OF DEPRECIATION** portion of a capital gain (the amount of a gain on depreciable assets) representing tax benefits previously taken and taxed as ordinary income.

**RECEIPTS**
1. cash or other assets received.
2. evidence substantiating the occurrence of an event. Accounting documents showing receipt include a receiving report of merchandise or a bill for an expenditure incurred (e.g., hotel bill, restaurant check).

**RECEIVABLES** claims held against customers and others for money, goods, or services. If collection is expected in one year or less (or in the normal operating cycle of the business if longer), they are classified as current assets. If not, they are presented as noncurrent assets. Receivables are further classified in the balance sheet as trade or nontrade. Trade receivables are due from customers for merchandise sold or services performed in the ordinary course of business. Trade receivables may either be accounts receivable or notes receivable. Nontrade receivables come into being from other types of transactions and may he written promises to pay monies or deliver services. Examples are advances to employees, claims against other entities (i.e., tax refunds, insurance receipts), deposits, and financial receivables (i.e., interest receivable, dividend receivable).

**RECEIVABLE TURNOVER** *see* ACCOUNTS RECEIVABLE TURNOVER.

**RECEIVING REPORT** document used within a firm, upon receiving the shipment of merchandise to formally record quantities and description.

**RECESSION** downturn in the economy. Many economists speak of recession when there has been a decline in the gross national product for two consecutive quarters.

**RECIPROCAL** result derived from the division of 1 by a given quantity. For example, the reciprocal of 2 is ½.

**RECIPROCAL ALLOCATION METHOD** process of allocating service department costs to production departments, where RECIPROCAL services are allowed between service departments; also known as the *reciprocal* method, the *matrix* method, the *double-distribution* method, the *cross-allocation* method, and *simultaneous equation* method. The method sets up simultaneous equations to determine the allocatable cost of each service department. The data for an example follows:

| | Production Departments | | Service Departments | |
| --- | --- | --- | --- | --- |
| | A Machining | B Assembly | General Plant (GP) | Engineering (E) |
| Overhead costs before allocation | $30,000 | $40,000 | $20,000 | 10,000 |
| Engineering hours by Engineering | 50,000 | 30,000 | 5,000 | 4,000 |
| Direct labor hours by General Plant | 60,000 | 40,000 | 15,000 | 20,000 |

Using the direct method yields:

| Departments | Service Departments | | Production | |
| --- | --- | --- | --- | --- |
| | GP | E | A | B |
| Overhead costs | $ 20,000 | $10,000 | $30,000 | $40,000 |
| Reallocation: | | | | |
| GP(1/2, 1/3, 1/6) | ($20,791)* | 3,465 | 10,396 | 6,930 |
| E(50/85, 30/85, 5/85) | 791 | ($13,465)* | 7,921 | 4,753 |
| | 0 | 0 | $48,317 | $51,683 |

The following equations are set up:

$$GP = \$20,000 + 5/85\ E$$
$$E = \$10,000 + 1/6\ GP$$

Substituting M from the second equation into the first:

$$GP = \$20,000 + 5/85\ (\$10,000 + 1/6\ GP)$$

Solving for GP gives GP = $20,791. Substituting GP = $20,791 into the second equation and solving for E gives E = $13,465.

**RECIPROCAL ARRANGEMENT** agreement in which one party will perform a certain act if the other performs a specified act as well. An example is where Company X agrees to buy certain goods from Company Y if Company Y orders merchandise from some division of Company X.

**RECOGNITION**
1. recording a business occurrence in the accounting records. An example is recognizing an unrealized loss on an investment portfolio at year-end, when aggregate market value is below cost. In this case, the transaction is recognized even though realization (sale) has not occurred.
2. ascertaining the particulars of an item (i.e., amount, timing) before accepting and recording it.

**RECOGNIZED GAIN OR LOSS** the amount of gain or loss on a transaction that is required to be reported for income tax purposes. Recognized gain or loss is not necessarily the amount of the realized gain or loss, which is the economic gain or loss.

**RECONCILIATION** adjusting the difference between two items (i.e., amounts, balances, accounts, or statements) so that the figures agree. The practitioner often has to analyze the deviation between two items, such as in preparing a BANK RECONCILIATION. For example, a reconciliation occurs when comparing the home office books account related to branch transactions with the corresponding account on the branch office books related to home office transactions. These two accounts are adjusted for the reconciling items causing the difference.

**RECORD** collection of related data items. For example, a company may store information regarding each employee in a single record consisting of a FIELD representing the name, a field representing the Social Security number, and so on. A collection of records is called a *file*.

**RECORD DATE** *see* DATE OF RECORD.

**REDEMPTION**
1. right to call or redeem a firm's outstanding preferred stock by paying the preferred stockholders the par value of the stock plus a premium.

**2.** repayment of bonds by a CALL before maturity, usually involving a call premium.

**3.** repayment of mutual funds at *net asset value* when a shareholder's holdings are liquidated.

## RED FLAGS

**1.** signifying a warning and demanding attention, such as unfavorable cost variance.

**2.** internal controls within and outside the accounting information system software that indicate possible suspect transactions.

**RED HERRING** slang term for a preliminary PROSPECTUS that outlines the important features of a new issue. This prospectus contains no selling price information or offering date. It is so named because of the stamped red-ink statement on the first page telling the reader that the document is *not* an official offer to sell the securities. Once the REGISTRATION STATEMENT is approved by the SEC, the *offering circular*, the final, statutory prospectus, is printed and the security can be offered for sale.

**REDISCOUNT RATE** *see* DISCOUNT RATE.

**REDISTRIBUTED COST** reassignment of a cost. For example, rent of the computer department is first assigned to it. Then, the total service cost of the computer department is redistributed on some rational basis (such as space occupied) to other service departments and to production departments. *See also* PRORATION.

**REDUNDANT ARRAYS OF INDEPENDENT DISKS (RAID)** allows an organization to save the same data on multiple hard drives. This usually improves performance and reduces the possibility of data loss by incorporating redundancy in storage.

**REENGINEERING** *see* BUSINESS PROCESS REENGINEERING (BPR).

**REFUND** *see* REBATE.

**REG FD** *see* REGULATION FULL DISCLOSURE.

## REGISTERED SECURITY

**1.** security whose owner is recorded by the issuing corporation or its registrar. In the case of a registered bond, principal of such a bond and interest, if registered as to interest, is paid to the owner of the bond listed on the record of the issuing company. It contrasts with BEARER (*coupon*) BONDS, where detachable coupons must be presented to the issuer for interest payment.

**2.** public issue registered with the SEC.

## REGISTRATION

**1.** act or fact of making an entry of any class of transactions or statements for the purpose of documentation for future reference. Such documentation may be in the form of financial information noted in registers, such as a cash register.

**2.** process set up by the *Securities Exchange Acts of 1933 and 1934* that requires publicly issued securities to be reviewed by the SEC.

**3.** recording of stocks or bonds in the owner's name as opposed to bearer's name.

**REGISTRATION STATEMENT** document that must be submitted to the SEC disclosing all facts relevant to the new securities issue that will permit an investor to make an informed decision. It is a lengthy document containing (1) historical, (2) financial, and (3) administrative facts about the issuing corporation. *See also* PROSPECTUS.

**REGRESSION ANALYSIS** statistical procedure for estimating the average relationship between the dependent variable (sales, for example) and one or more independent variables (price and advertising, for example). It is a popularly used method for estimating the COST-VOLUME FORMULA ($y = a + bx$). SIMPLE REGRESSION involves one independent variable, e.g., direct labor-hours or machine-hours alone, whereas MULTIPLE REGRESSION involves two or more independent variables. Assuming a *linear* relationship, the simple regression model indicates that the relationship is $y = a + bx$, where $a$, and $b$ are unknown constants, called regression coefficients. The multiple regression model is $y = a_0 + a_1x_1 + a_2x_2 + \cdots + a_kx_k$, where $a$'s are coefficients and $x$'s represent the number of independent variables.

In estimating the cost-volume formula, regression analysis attempts to find a line of best fit. To find the line of best fit, a technique called the LEAST-SQUARES METHOD is widely used.

**REGRESSION COEFFICIENT** parameter value in a regression equation. For example, in a LINEAR REGRESSION EQUATION $y = a + bx$, $a$ and $b$ are regression coefficients. Specifically, $a$ is called *y-intercept* or *constant*, while $b$ is called a SLOPE.

**REGRESSION EQUATION (MODEL)** statistical model that relates the dependent variable (sales, for example) to one or more independent variables (advertising and income, for example). *See also* REGRESSION ANALYSIS.

**REGRESSIVE TAX** system in which the percentage of income paid declines as income rises. Under a regressive system, as income rises from \$15,000 to \$100,000, the tax rate would fall from 20% to 10%, for example. In this sense, a regressive tax is the opposite of a PROGRESSIVE TAX. The term is also used generally to refer to any tax system that favors the rich at the expense of the poor. The general sales tax with its fixed rate is considered regressive, because lower income groups tend to spend a higher percentage of their incomes on goods and services than higher income groups.

**REGULATION Q** the Federal Reserve Bank's regulation that sets deposit interest rate ceilings and regulates advertising of interest on savings accounts. This regulation applies to all commercial banks. It is a rule, first instituted in the Banking Act of 1933.

**REGULATION FULL DISCLOSURE** a rule passed by the Securities and Exchange Commission in an effort to prevent selective disclosure by public companies to professionals and certain shareholders. This requires a company to fully disclose any information of a material nature simultaneously to everyone to ensure a level playing field for individual and institutional investors.

**REGULATIONS** authoritative body of rules specifying details of procedure and conduct to be followed in accordance with such criteria as uniformity, efficiency, control, ethics, and legal considerations.

**REGULATION S-X** SECURITIES AND EXCHANGE COMMISSION (SEC) regulation specifying the specific format and content of financial reports. It also requires companies that intend to offer securities to the public to provide adequate disclosure so that the investing community can evaluate the merits of the issue.

**REGULATION T** the Federal Reserve Bank's regulation governing the amount of credit that may be advanced by brokers and dealers to customers for the purchase of securities. *See also* INITIAL MARGIN; MARGIN BUYING.

**REGULATION U** the federal regulation governing the amount of credit that may be advanced by a bank to its customers for the purchase of securities.

**REHABILITATION TAX CREDIT** special tax incentive given for the continued use and rehabilitation of historical buildings and old structures in an effort to arrest urban decay. Developers receive a credit based upon a percentage of the cost they incur rehabilitating these structures.

**REINSURANCE** agreement in which one insurer indemnifies another insurer for all or part of the risk of a policy originally issued and assumed by that other insurer.

**REIT** *see* REAL ESTATE INVESTMENT TRUST (REIT).

**RELATED PARTY TRANSACTION** interaction between two parties, one of whom can exercise control or significant influence over the operating policies of the other. A *special relationship* may exist, for example, between a business enterprise and its principal owners. In related party situations, the following footnote disclosures are required: (1) nature of the relationship; (2) description of the transaction including amounts; (3) amounts due from, or to, related parties at year-end; (4) the effects of any change in terms; and (5) manner of settlement. Even though no transactions occurred between related parties in the current year, disclosure of the nature of the control relationship is still required.

**RELATIONAL DATA BASE** data base consisting of relationships between data items.

**RELATIVE FREQUENCY OF OCCURRENCE** proportion of times that an event occurs in the long run when the conditions are stable, or the observed relative frequency of an event in a very large number of trials. For example, suppose that an accounts receivable manager knows from past data that about 70 of 1,000 accounts usually become uncollectible after 120 days. The manager would estimate the probability of bad debts as 70/1000 = .07 or 7%.

**RELATIVE SALES VALUE METHOD** manner of allocating JOINT COSTS in proportion to relative sales values of joint products. For example, joint products X and Y have a joint cost of $1,200 and X sells for $70 while Y sells for $50. Then X would be allocated $1,200 × ($70/$120) = $700 of the joint cost while Y would be allocated $1,200 × ($50/$120) = $500 of the cost.

**RELEVANCE** item that is capable of making a difference in decision-making. Information is available in a *timely* fashion before it loses its value in decision-making. Data have *predictive value* about outcomes past, present, and future. Information has *feedback value* that provides information about earlier expectations.

**RELEVANT COST APPROACH** *see* INCREMENTAL ANALYSIS.

**RELEVANT COSTS** expected future costs that differ from the alternatives being considered. SUNK COSTS are *not* relevant to the decision at hand, because they are historical costs. *Incremental* or *differential* costs are *relevant* because they are the ones that differ from the alternatives. Since not all costs are of equal importance, managers must identify those that are relevant to a decision. For example, in a decision on whether to replace an existing business with a new one, the cost to be paid for the new venture is relevant. However, the initial cost of the old business is not relevant because it is a sunk cost. *See also* INCREMENTAL ANALYSIS.

**RELEVANT RANGE** span of activity over which a certain cost behavior holds true. It is risky to extrapolate beyond the relevant range because there are no observations outside the range. For example, fixed costs will not change only for a specified range of volume of activity, called the relevant range. Beyond this, fixed costs are not constant. BREAK-EVEN ANALYSIS and analysis of MIXED COSTS are most useful only in this range of activity—that is, the volume zone in which the behavior of variable costs, fixed costs, and selling prices can be predicted with reasonable accuracy.

**RELIABILITY**
1. in auditing, confidence that the financial records have been properly prepared and that accounting procedures and internal controls are correctly functioning.
2. in financial accounting theory, term describing information that is reasonably free from error and bias and accurately presents the

facts. *Verifiability* exists when a reconstruction of financial data, following acceptable accounting practices, results in the same actual results previously attained; further, two accountants working independently will come up with similar results. *Representational faithfulness* exists when there is agreement between a portrayal (description) and the item it is supposed to represent (validity). Information is *neutral* when it does not favor one company over another. *See also* VERIFIABLE.

3. probability that a product or process will perform satisfactorily over a period of time under specified operating conditions.

**REMOTE JOB ENTRY SYSTEM** one commonly found in ONLINE PROCESSING. Online computer processing can be used for BATCH PROCESSING or can be *real time*. When it is used for batch processing, it is generally referred to as real batch processing, or remote job entry.

**RENT EXPENSE** cost to lease an item of property. The rental charge incurred by the lessee may be based on time and/or some other factor (e.g., sales). It is shown in the income statement as an operating expense.

**REORDER POINT** inventory level at which it is appropriate to replenish stock. The calculation is as follows:

Reorder Point =
Average Usage Per Unit of Lead Time × Lead Time + SAFETY STOCK

First, multiply average daily (or weekly) usage by the lead time in days (or weeks) yielding the lead time demand. Then add safety stock to this to provide for the variation in lead time demand to determine the reorder point. If average usage and lead time are both certain, no safety stock is necessary and should be dropped from the formula.

*See also* ECONOMIC ORDER QUANTITY (EOQ) MODEL.

**REORGANIZATION** process of restating company assets to reflect current market value and restating the financial structure downward to reflect reductions on the asset side of the balance sheet. A financially troubled firm usually goes through reorganization. Under a reorganization, the firm continues in existence. Chapter 11 of the BANKRUPTCY law provides for reorganization. Chapter 7 provides for LIQUIDATION.

**REPETITIVE MANUFACTURING** manufacture of identical products (or a family of products) in a continuous flow.

**REPLACEMENT COST**
1. CURRENT COST to replace the service potential of an existing asset. Emphasis is placed on obtaining an asset with identical future service capabilities.
2. current cost to replace property in a particular geographic area.

**REPLACEMENT COST ACCOUNTING** valuing assets and liabilities, at their cost to replace. It is a departure from historical cost accounting. The effect of inflationary changes on items bought and sold is considered. Holding gains and losses arise from a change between the historical cost and the replacement cost. *See also* CURRENT VALUE ACCOUNTING; GENERAL PRICE LEVEL ACCOUNTING.

**REPLACEMENT METHOD OF DEPRECIATION** method in which the current depreciation expense amount, usually determined by the STRAIGHT-LINE DEPRECIATION method, is augmented by a percentage derived from a comparison of the anticipated replacement cost of a depreciable asset with its original cost. This method requires an estimate to be made of the anticipated replacement cost.

**REPLICATION** duplicating methods or processes to gather data to confirm or deny a standing assumption or set of circumstances. Results may be replicated if such methods are employed independently and these results are verified under similar conditions, thus providing two independent checks upon the data gathered and their implied assumptions. An example is when two accountants independently add the total of daily cash receipts and find agreement.

**REPORT FORM**
1. format of an income statement that reads from top to bottom. It begins with sales or revenues at the top leading to net income at the bottom, with significant totals in between. *See also* FORM OF BALANCE SHEET.
2. auditor's report format, either in short or long form.

**REPORT FORM OF BALANCE SHEET** *see* FORM OF BALANCE SHEET.

**REPORTING** periodically furnishing others with financial information to aid in control or decision making. In internal reporting, the internal auditor may provide management with an analysis of operations and internal controls within the company. In external reporting, the CPA may render an audit opinion on the financial statements of a client includable in the annual report and Securities and Exchange Commission filings.

**REPORTING CURRENCY** currency in which a company prepares its financial statements, i.e., U.S. dollars for a U.S. company. *See also* FUNCTIONAL CURRENCY.

**REPORT RELEASE DATE** the date on which an auditor gives permission to a client to use the auditor's report on the financial statements. The report release date typically follows the date of the audit report and serves as the starting point for retention of audit documentation. *See also* RETENTION PERIOD.

**REPRESENTATION LETTER** written confirmation from management to the auditor about the fairness of various financial statement elements. The purpose of the letter is to emphasize that the financial statements are management's representations, and thus management has the primary responsibility for their accuracy. Also, the letter provides supplementary audit evidence of an internal nature by giving formal management replies to auditor questions regarding matters that did not come to the auditor's attention in performing audit procedures. Some auditors request written representations of all financial statement items. All auditors require representations regarding receivables, inventories, plant and equipment, liabilities, and subsequent events. Frequently, all these representations are included in one letter. The letter is required at the completion of the audit fieldwork and prior to issuance of the financial statements with the auditor's opinion. Management acknowledges its responsibilities for running the company, the adequacy of financial policies employed, confirmation of practices observed during the audit, and confirmation to the auditor that management has made full disclosure of all material activities and transactions in its financial records and statements.

**REPRESENTATIVE SAMPLE** random sample that is a good indicator of the accuracy of the items in a population. The sample may or may not have a determinable error.

**REPRODUCTION COST** current cost to replace an asset with an *identical* asset. Typically, there is an allowance for depreciation.

**REQUIRED MINIMUM DISTRIBUTION (RMD)** the minimum amount that must be withdrawn annually from a retirement plan starting with the year in which the account owner reaches 70½ years of age or, if later, the year in which the account owner retires. RMDs must begin once the account holder is age 70½, regardless of whether he or she is retired, in the case of an IRA or a retirement plan in which the account owner is a 5% owner of the business sponsoring the plan. The RMD rules do not apply to Roth IRAs during the lifetime of the owner.

**REQUISITION** written request within an organization for a particular service or good. It typically is issued from one department to another. An example is a request form that must be filled out for office supplies to be released by the storeroom.

**RESEARCH AND DEVELOPMENT (R&D) COSTS** expenditures incurred to discover new knowledge and to develop that knowledge into a design for a new product. R&D costs are usually *expensed* as incurred. However, the following two classes of costs have future use in R&D activities and are capitalized: (1) materials and equipment and (2) intangibles purchased from others. The costs of such assets used or consumed (depreciated) are expensed as R&D costs. Note that R&D costs incurred for others under contract are capitalized.

Costs of computer software to be sold, leased, or otherwise marketed should be charged to expense as R&D costs until technological feasibility has been established through completion of either a detailed program or a working model. When technological feasibility has been established, all software production costs are capitalized and subsequently reported at the lower of unamortized cost or net realizable value. Amortization will start when the product is available for general release to customers. Periodic amortization should be the greater of: (1) the ratio of current revenue to the total current and anticipated future gross revenues from the product or (2) the straight-line method over the remaining economic life of the property.

**RESEARCH AND DEVELOPMENT (R&D) TAX CREDIT** provision of the tax law under which companies can deduct 20% of "increased" qualified expenditures for researching and developing new products. The tax credit reduces taxes due on a dollar-for-dollar basis. The "increased" amount equals the current year R&D expenditure less the average R&D expenditure over the last three years. Assume R&D in 20X9 is $250,000. In the prior years, R&D costs were $150,000 in 20X6, $225,000 in 20X7, and $210,000 in 20X8. The average is thus $195,000. Therefore, the credit equals:

| | |
|---|---:|
| Current year R&D | $250,000 |
| Average 3-year R&D | 195,000 |
| "Increased" R&D | 55,000 |
| Tax credit percent | × .20 |
| Tax credit | $ 11,000 |

The credit significantly aids research-oriented, high-technology businesses. *Excluded* from "qualified" R&D expenses as a basis for the tax credit are efficiency studies, trial production runs, market tests, and management studies. "Qualified" R&D have to be of a technological nature, involve experimentation, and aid in a new or improved product or process.

**RESERVE**

1. appropriation of retained earnings for a designated purpose, such as plant expansion or a bond sinking fund. The purpose of the reserve is to tell stockholders and creditors that part of retained earnings is unavailable for dividends.
2. accrued liability, such as reserve for taxes (outdated usage).
3. contra account to the gross cost of an asset to arrive at the net amount, such as reserve for depreciation or reserve for bad debts. In this use, the term *reserve* is outdated; *accumulated depreciation* and *allowance for bad debts* are used instead.

**RESERVE FOR CONTINGENCIES** appropriated retained earnings for general unspecified contingencies such as possible damage due to Acts of God.

**RESERVE FOR ENCUMBRANCES** in GOVERNMENT ACCOUNTING, account reflecting part of the fund balance that has been committed by a contract, purchase order, salary agreement, travel claim, etc. Therefore, reserve for encumbrances represents a reservation of the fund's equity. Entries for this account occur when an ENCUMBRANCE comes into being and when the actual expenditure is later made.

**RESERVE FOR RETIREMENT OF PREFERRED STOCK** appropriation of RETAINED EARNINGS that has the effect of restricting common dividend declarations. This provides for the gradual reacquisition and cancellation of an organization's PREFERRED STOCK. Upon complete retirement of the preferred stock, the account maintained for preferred stock will cease to exist. Any excess of retirement premium not fully absorbed by the PAID-IN CAPITAL accounts will necessitate a charge to retained earnings. The remaining amount of appropriated retained earnings, if any, constitutes the residual retirement reserve, which is closed to unrestricted retained earnings. The implementation of a reserve is not a necessary action to ensure that the reacquisition of preferred stock will take place. In fact, in a well-run organization this may well be unnecessary. Rather, it serves as a device to allay fears of security holders that liquid assets will be depleted through dividend distributions.

**RESERVE RECOGNITION ACCOUNTING (RRA)** procedural attempt by the SEC to improve the reporting practices of oil and gas companies' valuations of natural resource reserves. Supplemental income statements are required that must exhibit the discounted value of new proven reserves discovered during the year and previously discovered reserves. The SEC specifies the use of a 10% discount rate, which among other difficulties (such as the definition of "proven," estimations of reserve quantities, projected selling prices, and inclusion of foreign reserves with foreign co-ownership), provides a somewhat arbitrary method of accounting for reserves. *See also* DISCOVERY VALUE ACCOUNTING.

**RESIDUAL** synonym for error. It is calculated by subtracting the forecast value from the actual value to give a "residual" or error value for each forecast period.

**RESIDUAL EQUITY THEORY** theory that common stockholders are considered to be the real owners of the business. The residual equity theory is in part the basis for the EARNINGS PER SHARE (EPS) computation that applies only to common stockholders. The purpose of this approach is to furnish better information for common stockholders in making investment decisions and in predicting possible future dividends. The theory lies between the PROPRIETARY THEORY and the ENTITY THEORY. Under it, the accounting equation is:

$$\text{Assets} - \text{Liabilities} - \text{Preferred Stock} = \text{Common Stock}$$

**RESIDUAL INCOME (RI)** operating income that an INVESTMENT CENTER is able to earn above some minimum return on its assets. It is a popular alternative performance measure to RETURN ON INVESTMENT (ROI). RI is computed as:

$$RI = \text{Net Operating Income} - (\text{Minimum Rate of Return on Investment} \times \text{Operating Assets})$$

Residual income, unlike ROI, is an absolute amount of income rather than a rate of return. When RI is used to evaluate divisional performance, the objective is to maximize the total amount of residual income, not to maximize the overall ROI percentage figure. For example, assume that operating assets are $100,000, net operating income is $18,000, and the minimum return on assets is 13%. Residual income is $18,000 – (13% × $100,000) = $18,000 – $13,000 = $5,000. RI is sometimes preferred over ROI as a performance measure because it encourages managers to accept investment opportunities that have rates of return greater than the charge for invested capital. Managers being evaluated using ROI may be reluctant to accept new investments that lower their current ROI, although the investments would be desirable for the entire company. Advantages of using residual income in evaluating divisional performance include: (1) it takes into account the opportunity cost of tying up assets in the division; (2) the minimum rate of return can vary depending on the riskiness of the division; (3) different assets can be required to earn different returns depending on their risk: (4) the same asset may be required to earn the same return regardless of the division it is in; and (5) the effect of maximizing dollars rather than a percentage leads to GOAL CONGRUENCE.

**RESIDUAL TERM** see ERROR TERM.

**RESIDUAL VALUE**
1. value of leased property at the end of the lease term.
2. at any time, the actual or estimated value (that is, proceeds minus disposal costs) of an asset, also called SALVAGE VALUE or SCRAP VALUE.
3. value of a depreciable asset after all allowable depreciation has been taken.

**RESOURCE COST ASSIGNMENT** process by which cost is attached to activities. The process requires the assignment of cost from general ledger accounts to activities using resource drivers. For example, the chart of accounts may list information services at a plant level. It then becomes necessary to trace (assuming that tracing is practical), or to allocate (when tracing is not practical), the cost of information services to the activities that benefit from the information services by means of appropriate resource drivers. It may be necessary to set up intermediate activity cost pools to accumulate related costs from various resources before the assignment can be made. See also ACTIVITY COST POOL; RESOURCE COST DRIVER.

**RESOURCE COST DRIVER** best single measure of the quantity of resources consumed by an activity. An example of a resource cost driver is the percentage of total square feet occupied by an activity. This factor is used to allocate a portion of the cost of operating the facilities to the activity.

**RESOURCE COSTS** costs of economic elements or inputs used to perform activities. They include people's salaries, as well as the cost of materials, supplies, equipment, technologies, and facilities. *See also* COST ELEMENT.

**RESPONSIBILITY** obligation to perform. In the classical view, this obligation formally comes down from a superior position and is inherent in any job (it has its origins in the rights of private property as defined by the appropriate laws). In the behavioral view, responsibility must and should be delegated; a successive dividing and passing down of obligation occurs. The appropriate amount of authority or power must be delegated with the responsibility. However, a higher position can never rid itself of ultimate responsibility.

**RESPONSIBILITY ACCOUNTING** collection, summarization, and reporting of financial information about various decision centers (*responsibility centers*) throughout an organization; also called *activity accounting* or *profitability accounting*. It traces costs, revenues, or profits to the individual managers who are primarily responsible for making decisions about the costs, revenues, or profits in question and taking action about them. Responsibility accounting is appropriate where top management has delegated authority to make decisions. The idea behind responsibility accounting is that each manager's performance should be judged by how well he or she manages those items under his or her control. *See also* RESPONSIBILITY CENTER.

**RESPONSIBILITY CENTER** unit in the organization that has control over costs, revenues, or investment funds. For accounting purposes, responsibility centers are classified as COST CENTERS, REVENUE CENTERS, PROFIT CENTERS, and INVESTMENT CENTERS. A well-designed responsibility accounting system should clearly define *responsibility centers* in order to collect and report revenue and cost information by areas of responsibility.

The following figure illustrates the manners in which responsibility accounting can be used within an organization and highlights profit and cost centers.

**RESPONSIBILITY REPORTING** *see* RESPONSIBILITY ACCOUNTING.

**RESTATEMENT** reiteration or republication of a financial statement or document, such as a balance sheet or income statement, in a manner that incorporates revisions and changes based on accounting principles or policies.

## RESPONSIBILITY CENTERS

**RESTATEMENT OF OVERHEAD RATES** approach implemented at the end of the period to calculate the actual overhead rates and then restate every entry involving overhead. The effect is that job-cost records, the inventory accounts, and cost of sales are accurately stated with respect to actual overhead. This means the disposing of overhead variances is costly but has the advantage of improving the analysis of profitability. If a restatement approach is not taken, the treatment of the balance in the overhead account (over- or underapplied overhead) depends on the materiality of the amount. For example, a manufacturer may write off the amount to cost of goods sold if it is not material. If the amount is material, it should be prorated to work-in-process, finished goods, and costs of goods sold on the basis of the currently applied overhead in each of the accounts. An alternative is to prorate the variance based on the total balances in the accounts. The improvements in information technology and decreases in cost have made *restatement of overhead rates* more appealing.

**RESTRICTED FUND** in not-for-profit accounting, fund whose assets are limited to designated purposes as per donor or grantor request.

**RESTRICTED STOCK OPTION** offerings provided by employers to executives after 1950 and prior to 1964 that were restricted in the sense that the option price had to be a minimum of 85% of the fair market value of the stock on the grant date. Upon exercising and holding the stock for the required time period, long-term capital gain treatment was available. Income was not recognized on the stock options as of the grant date and was also not recognized at the purchase date by virtue of the lower purchase price. Restricted stock options were subsequently replaced by QUALIFIED STOCK OPTIONS with more rigorous requirements in 1964. However, qualified stock options were eliminated in The Economic Recovery Tax Act of 1981, whereupon the INCENTIVE STOCK OPTION was introduced.

**RESTRICTED USE REPORT** any auditor's report that is intended only for specified parties. Restricted use reports include reports on subject matter based on measurement criteria specified in contractual agreements or regulatory provisions, communications on internal control-related matters noted in a financial statement audit, and the auditor's communications with those charged with governance. A restricted use report would include a paragraph indicating the report is not intended to be, and should not be, used by anyone other than the specified parties.

**RESTRUCTURING CHARGES** costs to rearrange facilities and downsize, which are expensed as they are incurred.

**RESTRUCTURING OF DEBT** *see* DEBT RESTRUCTURING.

**RESULT BENCHMARKING** *see* BENCHMARKING.

**RETAIL INVENTORY METHOD** accounting method used for inventory control and formulation of purchasing policy by retail businesses. Both selling price and cost of the inventory are taken into account. A cost/retail ratio is determined that is multiplied by the retail value of the ending inventory to arrive at its cost. The *conventional retail* method approximates the lower of cost or market valuation by the *exclusion of markdowns* and other reductions below original selling price and the *inclusion of markups* in computing the cost/retail ratio. Assume the following: (1) inventory on 1/1/2014 at cost $14,200; (2) inventory on 1/1/2014 at selling price $20,100; (3) purchases at cost $32,600; (4) purchases at selling price $50,000; (5) markups $1,900; (6) markdowns $2,200; and (7) sales $60,000. The computation of conventional retail follows:

| | Cost | Retail |
|---|---|---|
| Beginning inventory | $14,200 | $20,100 |
| Purchases | 32,600 | 50,000 |
| Markups | | 1,900 |
| Available | $46,800 | $72,000 |
| Less: Sales | | (60,000) |
| Markdowns | | ( 2,200) |
| Inventory at retail | | $ 9,800 |
| Cost/retail ratio | 46,800/$72,000 = 65% | |
| Inventory at cost under conventional retail: | | |
| $9,800 × 65% | | $ 6,370 |

Note again that the conventional retail method includes markups but not markdowns in calculating the cost to retail ratio that results in a lower inventory figure. If the retail method was used, markups and markdowns would both be included in calculating the cost/retail ratio, resulting in a higher inventory figure.

**RETAINED EARNINGS** accumulated earnings of a corporation since inception less dividends. Retained earnings is also net of PRIOR PERIOD ADJUSTMENTS and transfers to paid-in capital accounts. Retained earnings is shown as a separate category within the stockholders' equity section of the balance sheet. It typically has a credit balance; a deficit is unusual. Retained earnings is broken down into the following two types: UNAPPROPRIATED RETAINED EARNINGS and APPROPRIATED RETAINED EARNINGS.

**RETAINED EARNINGS STATEMENT** accounting form showing the beginning balance of retained earnings, adjustments to it during the year, and ending balance. The retained earnings statement may be presented separately or in a combined statement of income and retained earnings. An illustrative retained earnings statement follows:

Retained Earnings—Unadjusted beginning balance
Plus or Minus: Prior period adjustments
Retained Earnings—Adjusted beginning balance
Plus: Net income
Minus: Dividends
Retained Earnings—Ending balance

**RETENTION PERIOD** the period of time for which an auditor is required to keep audit documentation. In the case of an audit of a nonissuer, audit documentation should be retained for a period of five years from the report release date; the retention period is extended to seven years in the case of an audit of an issuer.

**RETIREMENT**
1. removal of a fixed asset from operative service with the appropriate adjustments to the fixed asset and accumulated depreciation accounts. Retirement may be due to a variety of reasons such as the asset having reached the end of its useful life or it having been disposed of by sale.
2. repayment of a debt.
3. cancellation of reacquired shares of stock or bonds by a corporation. *See also* REDEMPTION; TREASURY STOCK.
4. permanent withdrawal of an employee from employment.

**RETIREMENT METHOD OF DEPRECIATION** manner of fixed asset accounting under which no depreciation expense entry is recorded until the asset is retired from service. At retirement, depreciation expense is debited and the asset account for the retired asset is credited. If the asset has salvage value, the debit to depreciation expense is reduced by this amount and there is a corresponding debit to cash, receivables, or salvage. This method, once popular among public utilities, is now largely discarded.

**RETIREMENT OF DEBT** elimination of a debt obligation through repayment, conversion, or refunding. *See also* EARLY EXTINGUISHMENT OF DEBT.

**RETROACTIVE ADJUSTMENT**
1. restatement of prior years' financial statements to show financial data on a comparable basis, such as in the case of a CHANGE IN REPORTING ENTITY.
2. PRIOR PERIOD ADJUSTMENT. Retroactive pension benefits should not he recognized as pension expense in the year of adoption or amendment to a pension plan but should be recognized during the service periods of those employees who are expected to receive benefits under the plan. The cost of this retroactive adjustment benefit is the increase in the projected benefit obligation at the amendment date.

**RETROACTIVE APPLICATION** the application of a different accounting principle to prior accounting periods as if that principle had always been used or as the adjustment of previously issued financial statements to reflect a change in the reporting entity.

**RETURN ON ASSETS** net income divided by average total assets. Used to measure the amount earned on each dollar of assets invested. A measure of overall earning power or profitability.

**RETURN ON ASSETS PRICING** pricing method in which the objective of price determination is to earn a profit equal to a specific rate of return on assets employed in the operation.

**RETURN ON EQUITY** a measure of the returns earned on the owners' (both preferred and common stockholders') investment. The return on equity (ROE) is calculated as:

$$\text{ROE} = \frac{\text{Net profit after taxes}}{\text{Stockholders' equity}} = \frac{\text{Net profit after taxes}}{\text{Total assets}} \times \frac{\text{Total assets}}{\text{Stockholders' equity}}$$
$$= \text{ROI} \times \text{Equity multiplier}$$

ROE measures the returns earned on the owners' (both preferred and common stockholders') investment. The use of the equity multiplier to convert the ROI to the ROE reflects the impact of the leverage (use of debt) on the stockholders' return.

$$\text{The equity multiplier} = \frac{\text{Total assets}}{\text{Stockholders' equity}}$$

$$= \frac{\text{Total assets}}{\text{Total assets} - \text{Total liabilities}}$$

$$= \frac{1}{1 - \dfrac{\text{Total liabilities}}{\text{Total assets}}}$$

$$= \frac{1}{(1 - \text{debt ratio})}$$

For example, XYZ Company presents the following financial data:

| | | |
|---|---|---|
| Total assets | = | $100,000 |
| Net profit after taxes | = | 18,000 |
| Stockholders' equity | = | $45,000 |

Then,

$$\text{ROI} = \frac{\text{Net profit after taxes}}{\text{Total assets}} = \frac{\$18,000}{\$100,000} = 18\%$$

Then,

$$\text{equity multiplier} = \frac{\text{Total assets}}{\text{Stockholders' equity}} = \frac{\$100,000}{\$45,000} = 2.22$$

$$= \frac{1}{(1 - \text{debt ratio})} = \frac{1}{(1 - 0.55)} = \frac{1}{0.45} = 2.22$$

$$\text{ROE} = \frac{\text{Net profit after taxes}}{\text{Stockholders' equity}} = \frac{\$18,000}{\$45,000} = 40\%$$

$$\text{ROE} = \text{ROI} \times \text{equity multiplier} = 18\% \times 2.22 = 40\%$$

If the company used only equity, the 18% ROI would equal ROE. However, 55% of the firm's capital is supplied by creditors ($45,000/ $100,000 = 45% is the equity-to-asset ratio; $55,000/$100,000 = 55% is the debt ratio). Because the 18% ROI all goes to stockholders, who put up only 45% of the capital, the ROE is higher than 18%. This example indicates that the company was using leverage (debt) favorably.

The following figure shows the relationship among ROI, ROE, and financial leverage.

ROI, ROE, AND FINANCIAL LEVERAGE

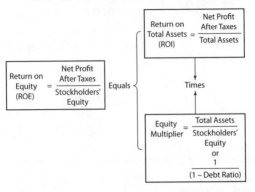

**RETURN ON INVESTMENT (ROI)** measure of the earning power of assets. The ratio reveals the firm's profitability on its business operations and thus serves to measure management's effectiveness. It equals NET INCOME divided by average total assets; also called *rate earned on total assets*. Other versions of ROI exist, such as net income before interest and taxes divided by average total assets. Return on investment is a commonly used measure to evaluate divisional performance. *See also* RESIDUAL INCOME.

**RETURN ON PENSION PLAN ASSETS** deduction in arriving at pension expense. Plan assets (i.e., STOCKS, BONDS, REAL ESTATE) are valued at the MOVING AVERAGE of asset values over a time period. Plan assets include employer and employee contributions. Pension assets have to be segregated in a TRUST or restricted to be deemed plan assets.

**REVALUATION SURPLUS** valuation equity account that is adjusted to a higher level, caused by an upward appraisal of capital assets and a resultant increase in the carrying value of such assets.

**REVENUE**
1. increase in the assets of an organization or the decrease in liabilities during an accounting period, primarily from the organization's operating activities. This may include sales of products (SALES), rendering of services (*revenues*), and earnings from interest, dividends, lease income, and royalties.
2. in GOVERNMENT ACCOUNTING, the gross receipts and receivables from taxes, customs, etc., without consideration of appropriations and allotments.

**REVENUE ANTICIPATION NOTE** term for note issued by a municipality in expectation of future revenues to be received from given sources such as sales taxes. Once funds are obtained from the particular sources, the note is paid off. *See also* TAX ANTICIPATION NOTE (TAN).

**REVENUE BONDS** debt whose principal and interest are payable exclusively from earnings of the project built with proceeds, such as a stadium, toll bridge, hospital or other enterprise. Revenue bonds are issued normally by municipalities. In addition to a pledge of revenues, such bonds sometimes contain a mortgage on the enterprise's property and then are known as mortgage revenue bonds.

**REVENUE CENTER** unit within an organization that is responsible for generating revenues. A revenue center is a PROFIT CENTER since for all practical purposes there is no revenue center that does not incur some costs during the course of generating revenues. A favorable variance occurs when actual revenue exceeds expected revenue.

**REVENUE EXPENDITURE** outlay benefitting *only* the current year. It is treated as an expense to be matched against revenue. An example is a tune-up of a car that has a period of benefit of one year or less. Repairs expense is charged. *See also* CAPITAL EXPENDITURE; MATCHING.

**REVENUE RECOGNITION** process of recording revenue, under one of the various methods, in the accounting period. In the period of revenue recognition, related expenses should be matched to revenue. The most often used method of recognizing revenue is at the time of sale or rendering of service. The cash basis of revenue recognition is also popular among service businesses. Other methods of revenue recognition include during production and at the completion of production. *See also* COMPLETED CONTRACT METHOD; INSTALLMENT (SALES) METHOD; PERCENTAGE-OF-COMPLETION METHOD; REALIZATION.

**REVENUE RULING** rule published by the INTERNAL REVENUE SERVICE (IRS) giving taxpayers guidance in the preparation of their tax returns. A revenue ruling provides an official interpretation of the tax law related to a particular type of transaction.

**REVERSE STOCK SPLIT** a stock split that reduces, rather than increases, the number of shares of stock outstanding, and effectively increases the par value of each share.

**REVERSING ENTRY** bookkeeping technique in which adjusting entries involving subsequent receipts or payments are literally reversed on the first day of the following accounting period. This procedure permits the routine recording of subsequent related receipts and payments without having to recognize the portions that were accrued at an earlier date.

**REVIEW** accounting service providing some assurance to the Board of Directors and interested parties as to the reliability of financial data without the CPA conducting an examination in accordance with generally accepted auditing standards. The AICPA Auditing Standards Board formulates review standards for public companies while the AICPA Accounting and Review Services Committee provides review standards for nonpublic businesses. A review consists primarily of inquiry and ANALYTICAL PROCEDURES. It is *not* an audit nor does it furnish a basis for an opinion since there is no gathering of audit evidence. The review program includes reading minutes of meetings, reading interim financial information to see whether it conforms to GAAP, and obtaining management's written representations as to its responsibility for the information provided. The accountant's report should include: (1) a statement that the review is conducted in accord with appropriate standards for reviews; (2) identification of the interim data reviewed; (3) description of the procedures followed; (4) a statement that a review is much less in scope than an audit in conformity with GENERALLY ACCEPTED AUDITING STANDARDS (GAAS); (5) a statement as to whether material modifications exist to make the information conform with GAAP; and (6) a statement that financial statement information is the representation of management. In a review of financial statements of nonpublic businesses, the objective is to give limited assurance that no significant modifications to the financial statements are needed to make them conform with GAAP. Procedures of a corroborative nature are not necessary. Work should be documented in the working papers indicating the disposition of unusual items. A report should not be issued if the accountant is unable to conduct an appropriate review. If the CPA finds a departure from GAAP in performing the review, the financial statements should be modified. If they are not modified, the CPA should state in the review report the departure and its financial statement effect. *See also* COMPILATION.

**REVOLVING FUND** account that is repeatedly expended, replenished, and then expended again. An *imprest petty-cash fund* is an example. Vouchers are paid daily and the petty-cash fund is usually replenished at the end of each month.

**RIGHT**
1. moral or legal claim. An example is the right of a common stockholder to vote in a corporate election.
2. privilege to subscribe to new stock issues. One right attached to existing shares may provide the opportunity to purchase a fractional share or particular number of shares of a new capital stock issue. A PREEMPTIVE RIGHT allows a shareholder the opportunity of maintaining a proportionate share of the enterprise by subscribing to an appropriate amount of newly issued shares. *See also* RIGHTS OFFERING.

**RIGHT-HAND SIDE**
1. amount of resources or capacities available to a firm for a given period, appearing on the right-hand side of a LINEAR PROGRAMMING (LP) problem.

    **2.** right-hand side of the balance sheet that covers LIABILITIES and STOCKHOLDERS' EQUITY.

**RIGHT OF RETURN** option of purchaser to give goods back to the seller for full credit. The buyer's right to return merchandise precludes revenue recognition by the seller at the time of sale unless all of the following conditions are met: (1) selling price is determinable; (2) buyer's obligation to pay is not contingent on resale of the product; (3) buyer must pay for item if lost; (4) acquisition by buyer has economic substance; (5) future performance by seller is not required for resale by buyer; and (6) future returns may be reasonably estimated. If these conditions are not satisfied, revenue and related expenses must be deferred until the conditions are met or the right of return has expired.

**RIGHTS AND OBLIGATIONS** an assertion in an entity's financial statements made by management that (1) the entity has legal title to recorded assets, and (2) recorded liabilities represent legal obligations to be paid.

**RIGHTS OFFERING** issue of rights to current stockholders to buy new common shares in the company at a specified subscription price that is less than what the offering price to the public will be. It enables existing stockholders to maintain their proportionate ownership in the company when the new issues are made, called PREEMPTIVE RIGHTS.

**RISK**
    **1.** state in which each alternative leads to one of a set of specific outcomes, each outcome occurring with a probability that is known to a decision maker.
    **2.** variation in earnings, sales, or other financial variable.
    **3.** probability of a financial problem affecting the company's operational performance or financial position, such as economic risk, political uncertainties, and industry problems. *See also* UNCERTAINTY.

**RISK ADJUSTED DISCOUNT RATE** riskless rate plus a risk premium. It is a rate adjusted upward as the investment becomes riskier. By increasing the discount rate from 10% to 15%, for example, the expected flow from the investment must be relatively larger or the increased discount rate will generate a negative NPV, and the proposed acquisition/investment will be rejected. Although difficult to apply in extreme cases, this technique has much intuitive value.

**RISK ANALYSIS** process of measuring and analyzing the RISK associated with financial and investment decisions. Risk refers to the variability of expected returns (earnings or cash flows). Statistics such as STANDARD DEVIATION and COEFFICIENT OF VARIATION are used to measure various risks. BETA coefficient is used to measure a stock's relative volatility in relation to the market and to analyze a portfolio risk. *Risk analysis* is important in making capital investment decisions because of the large amount of capital involved and the long-term nature of the investments being considered. The higher the risk associated with a proposed project, the greater the return that must be earned to compensate for that risk. There are several methods for the analysis of risk, including: *risk-adjusted discount rate*, CERTAINTY EQUIVALENT, MONTE CARLO SIMULATION, SENSITIVITY ANALYSIS, and DECISION TREES.

**RISK ASSESSMENT** the component of INTERNAL CONTROL concerned with the identification and analysis of the risks that management may not achieve its objectives. Management is responsible for performing risk assessment.

**RISK ASSESSMENT PROCEDURES** the procedures performed during an audit to obtain an understanding of the entity and its environment, including its INTERNAL CONTROL. Risk assessment procedures, which include inquiries and analytical procedures (e.g., ratio analysis), enable an auditor to identify changes from the prior period that might represent the risk of material financial statement misstatement. The performance of risk assessment procedures is mandatory in a financial statement audit.

**RISK MANAGEMENT**
1. the analysis of and planning for potential risks and their subsequent losses. The objective of risk management is to try to minimize the financial consequence of random losses.
2. the business activity that assesses the risks a company is faced with and a plan for the potential coverage or payment of those risks.

**RISK MEASURES** quantitative measures of risk. They attempt to assess the degree of variation or uncertainty about earnings or return. There are several measures, including the standard deviation, coefficient of variation, and beta. The standard deviation is a statistical measure of dispersion of the probability distribution of possible returns. The smaller the deviation, the tighter the distribution and, thus, the lower the riskiness of the investment. One must be careful in using the standard deviation to compare risk since it is only an absolute measure of dispersion (risk) and does not consider the dispersion of outcomes in relationship to an expected return. In comparisons of securities with differing expected returns, we commonly use the *coefficient of variation*. The coefficient of variation (CV) is computed simply by dividing the standard deviation for a security by its expected value. The higher the coefficient, the more risky the security. Beta measures a stock's or mutual fund's volatility relative to the general market.

**RISK OF ASSESSING CONTROL RISK TOO HIGH** in audit sampling, the chance, when performing a test of controls, that a sample indicates a higher rate of deviation from a prescribed control than the true deviation rate in the population. Since this may result in the performance of unnecessary additional substantive procedures, risk of assessing control risk too high relates to the inefficiency of the audit.

**RISK OF ASSESSING CONTROL RISK TOO LOW** in audit sampling, the chance, when performing a test of controls, that a sample indicates a lower rate of deviation from a prescribed control than the true deviation rate in the population. Since this may result in a reduction of substantive procedures, the auditor might ultimately express an incorrect opinion on the financial statement presentation. Accordingly, risk of assessing control risk too low relates to ineffectiveness of the audit.

**RISK OF INCORRECT ACCEPTANCE** in audit sampling, the chance, when performing a substantive procedure, that a sample indicates no material misstatement in a recorded account balance when in fact it is materially misstated. Ultimately, this could cause an auditor to express an incorrect opinion on the financial statement presentation. Accordingly, risk of incorrect acceptance relates to ineffectiveness of the audit.

**RISK OF INCORRECT REJECTION** in audit sampling, the chance, when performing a substantive procedure, that a sample indicates material misstatement in a recorded account balance when in fact it is not materially misstated. Since this may result in the performance of unnecessary additional substantive procedures, risk of incorrect rejection relates to the inefficiency of the audit.

**RISK OF MATERIAL MISSTATEMENT (RMM)** the chance that financial statements may include material misstatement. The risk of material misstatement is a combination of inherent risk and control risk. An auditor is required to assess the risk of material misstatement in every audit. The product of RMM and detection risk is equal to audit risk.

**RISK PREMIUM** amount by which the required return on an asset or security exceeds the *risk-free rate*, $r_f$. In terms of the CAPITAL ASSET PRICING MODEL (CAPM), it can be expressed as $b(r_m - r_f)$, where $b$ is the security's BETA coefficient, a measure of SYSTEMATIC RISK, and $r_m$ is the required return on the market portfolio. The risk premium is the additional return required to compensate investors for assuming a given level of risk. The higher this premium, the more risky the security and vice versa.

**RISK-RETURN TRADE-OFF** the concept that the higher the return or yield, the larger the risk; or vice versa. All financial decisions involve some sort of risk-return trade-off. The greater the risk associated with any financial decision, the greater the return expected from it. Proper assessment and balance of the various risk-return trade-offs available is part of creating a sound financial and investment plan. For example, the less inventory a firm keeps, the higher the expected return (since less of the firm's current assets is tied up). But there is also a greater risk of running out of stock and thus losing potential revenue. In an investment arena, you must compare the expected return from a given investment with the risk associated with it. Generally speaking, the higher the risk undertaken, the more ample the return; conversely, the lower the risk, the more modest the return. In the case of investing in stock, you would demand higher return from a speculative stock to compensate for the higher level of risk. On the other hand, U.S. T-bills have minimal risk so a low return is appropriate. The proper assessment and balance of the various risk-return trade-offs is part of creating a sound investment plan.

The following figure illustrates a risk-return trade-off.

### RISK-RETURN TRADE-OFF CHART

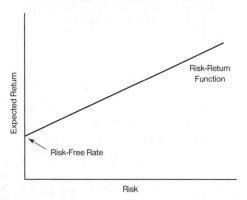

**RISK TAKER** a person who is not fearful of uncertainty and may even enjoy risky, speculative situations. He or she is a person who will take a chance or gamble in hopes of winning.

**ROBINSON-PATMAN ACT** legislation that forbids quoting different prices to competing customers unless such price discrimination is justified by differences in costs of manufacturing, sales, or delivery.

**ROBUST QUALITY** quality control concept, its goal is to reach the target value in every case for the reason that hidden quality costs occur when output varies from the target even though the units are within specifications.

**ROLLING FORWARD BUDGET** *see* CONTINUOUS BUDGET.

**ROLLOVER**
1. renewal of a short-term obligation by mutual agreement of debtor and creditor. This short-term debt appears under current liabilities.

Footnote disclosure of the arrangement is made along with major provisions.

2. movement of funds from one investment to another. For example, when a certificate of deposit or bond matures, the funds may be rolled over into another certificate of deposit or bond.

**ROM (READ-ONLY MEMORY)** computer memory containing instructions that do not need to be altered; the permanent memory of the computer put in by the manufacturers. The computer can read instructions out of ROM, but no data can be stored there.

**ROOT CAUSE ANALYSIS** identification of the underlying cause(s) of specific areas of deficiency in business processes.

**ROTH IRA** an IRA to which nondeductible contributions may be made. Earnings on and distributions from a Roth IRA are not taxable. Contributions to a Roth IRA are subject to income limitations, which are adjusted periodically for inflation. The RMD rules do not apply to Roth IRAs during the lifetime of the owner. *See also* REQUIRED MINIMUM DISTRIBUTION (RMD).

**ROUND-LOT** unit of trading on a securities exchange. For example, a round-lot on the NEW YORK STOCK EXCHANGE (NYSE) is 100 shares of stock or one $1000-face-value bond (although brokers may have their own higher round-lot requirements in the case of bonds). Inactive stocks have a 10-share round-lot. *See also* ODD-LOT.

**ROUTER** used to forward data packets along a network. A router is used to connect two networks: often a local area network and a wide area/Internet Service Provider network is connected using a router.

**ROYALTY** monies paid to use property, such as the use of copyrighted materials and natural resource extractions. The royalty payment is usually based upon some percentage of the income or fee for substances generated from the use of such property.

***R*-SQUARED (*r*-SQUARED)** *see* COEFFICIENT OF DETERMINATION.

**RULE**
1. statement governing procedures, interpretations, or inferences belonging to sets of operations or decisions. *See* DECISION RULE.
2. directive, instruction, or order detailing something to be done. Requiring the cash receipts to be counted at the end of the day to assure that the physical cash received agrees with the recorded book amount is an example of rule.

**RULE OF 72** a rule of thumb method used to determine how many years it takes to double investment money at a given growth or interest rate. Under the method, dividing the number 72 by the fixed rate of return equals the number of years it takes for annual earnings from the investment to double. That is, $72/r$ (in percent). For example, if you bought a share of ADR yielding an annual return of 25%, the invest-ment will double in less than three years: 72/25 = 2.88 years. The rule can be reversed, too. For example, if you know that your money doubled in four years, you can divide 72 by 4. You will see that you earned roughly 18% per year.

*Note:* The Rule of 72 does not work, however, when dealing with extreme numbers. For example, dividing 72 by a 72% return indicates that you expect to double your money in one year. It is not true. It would rather take a 100% return. Furthermore, it is more accurate when dealing with somewhat higher returns to use 76, not 72.

**RULE OF 69** very similar to the rule of 72, a rule stating that an amount of money invested at $r$ percent per period will double in $69/r$ (in percent) + .35 periods. For example, if you bought a share of ADR yielding an annual return of 25%, the investment will double in a little over three years. $69/25 + .35 = 2.76 + .35 = 3.11$ years

**RULE OFF** physical underscoring of a total or amount in a ledger to indicate that it should not be disturbed or altered because it represents a cumulative significant figure. Bookkeepers frequently rule off to indicate the balancing or closing of accounts.

**RULINGS** official interpretation by the INTERNAL REVENUE SERVICE (IRS) of the tax law as applied to specific situations; also called REVENUE RULING. Unlike a Treasury Department regulation, the IRS interpretation does not have complete authoritative significance and, as such, is more limited in application. Letter rulings of interest to the general public have been published subsequent to 1976 and are avail-able as references to taxpayers.

**RUSSELL 2000/3000** two useful indexes of small cap stocks, calculated by Frank Russell Co. of Seattle (www.russell.com). The Russell 2000 consists of smaller capitalization stocks. The Russell 3000 consists of the largest 3,000 publicly traded stocks of U.S. domiciled corpora-tions and includes large, medium, and small capitalization stocks. It represents about 98% of the total capitalization of the New York, American, and NASDAQ markets.

# S

**SAAS (SECURITY AS A SERVICE)** outsourcing of security management to another entity that delivers e-mail, Web, and network protection through the cloud. Outsourcing security provides numerous benefits, including easier administration and automatic updates of the security system. SaaS product vendors include Cisco, McAfee, Symantec, Trend Micro, and VeriSign.

**SAFARI** Apple Inc.'s default Web browser that is available for Macintosh, iPhone, and iPad devices.

**SAFEGUARDING OF ASSETS** protecting the firm's assets through a good internal control system. The objective is to guard against loss of assets because of theft, accidental destruction, and errors. Assurance must exist that transactions related to assets have been properly processed and that appropriate physical handling and control over assets exist.

**SAFE HARBOR RULE** tax provision enacted as part of the Economic Tax Recovery Act of 1981 to guarantee *sale/leaseback* treatment to certain transactions if specific requirements are met. The purpose of this provision was to make it easier for loss companies to "sell" their tax benefits accruing on new asset purchases by entering into sale/leaseback transactions with profitable companies. The intent was to generate an immediate cash flow for such loss companies, rather than deferring the benefits through carryover provisions.

**SAFETY MARGIN** excess of actual sales over break-even sales. If the break-even point is 3,000 units and actual sales volume is 3,400 units, a safety margin of 400 units exists. Thus sales can decrease by 400 units before the company would incur a loss. *See also* BREAK-EVEN POINT.

**SAFETY STOCK** extra units of inventory carried as protection against possible stockouts. The safety stock must be carried when the firm is not sure about either the demand for the product or *lead time* or both. In the case where demand is uncertain, safety stock is the difference between the maximum usage and the average usage multiplied by the lead time. For example, assume that a store is faced with an uncertain usage for its baseballs. Lead time is constant at two weeks. Normal weekly usage is 700 dozen but it can go as high as 850 dozen. The store would compute the safety stock as follows:

| | |
|---|---|
| Maximum weekly usage | 850 dozen |
| Average weekly usage | 700 |
| Excess | 150 |
| Lead time | × 2 weeks |
| Safety stock | 300 dozen |

*See also* REORDER POINT.

**SALARY REDUCTION PLAN** *see* 401(K) PLAN.

**SALE**
1. revenue recognition from the delivery of merchandise or from rendering a service in exchange for consideration. Consideration may be in the form of cash, cash equivalent, or other property. Revenue can be recognized at the time of sale because an exchange has taken place, selling price is determinable, and expenses are known.
2. in retailing, temporary reduction of prices to move inventory and raise cash.

**SALE AND LEASEBACK**  sale of property by the owner to a purchaser who then leases it to the former owner. The net effect of this transaction is similar to a loan to the former owner with the property serving as collateral. Any profit or loss on the sale is deferred and amortized in proportion to the amortization expense on the leased asset if a CAPITAL LEASE, or in proportion to the rental payments if this is an OPERATING LEASE. However, when the fair value of the property at the time of the transaction is less than its book value, a loss will be recognized immediately, up to the amount of the difference between undepreciated cost and fair value.

**SALES ALLOWANCE** reduction in the selling price of goods because of a particular problem (e.g., breakage, quality deficiency, incorrect quantity). Sales allowance is a deduction from gross sales to arrive at net sales. It is a contra revenue account.

**SALES BUDGET** operating plan for a period expressed in terms of sales volume and selling prices for each class of product or service. Preparation of a sales budget is the starting point in budgeting since sales volume influences nearly all other items.

**SALES DISCOUNT** cash given by the seller to the purchaser for early payment of the account due. For example, assume that the credit terms of a sale are 1/10, net/30. This means that if the customer pays in 10 days, 1% off the invoice price is granted. However, the customer must pay for the goods no later than 30 days after the date of sale. Note that if the customer remits after 10 days (but before 30 days), no cash discount is obtained.

Sales discount is subtracted from gross sales in arriving at net sales. It is a contra revenue account.

Another common term of sale is giving a percentage discount when the customer pays within a specified time period after the end of the month (EOM) of sale. An example is a discount of 2% if payment is received within 20 days after the month of sale.

**SALES FORECASTING** projection or prediction of future sales. It is the foundation for the quantification of the entire business plan and a MASTER (COMPREHENSIVE) BUDGET. Sales forecasts serve as a basis for planning. They are the basis for capacity planning, budgeting, production and inventory planning, manpower planning, and purchasing planning. There are two primary approaches to sales forecasting: qualitative and quantitative. Qualitative approaches include salespeople polls and consumer surveys. Quantitative methods include MOVING AVERAGE, EXPONENTIAL SMOOTHING, TREND ANALYSIS, and REGRESSION ANALYSIS.

**SALES JOURNAL** special book in which credit sales are recorded. The total columns of the sales journal are posted as a debit to accounts receivable and a credit to sales. Separate columns may exist to classify sales by category (e.g., product line).

**SALES MIX** relative proportions of the product sold. For example, a company has three products and their respective sales are as follows:

|       | A        | B        | C        | TOTAL     |
|-------|----------|----------|----------|-----------|
| Sales | $30,000  | $60,000  | $10,000  | $100,000  |

Then the sales mix ratios for A, B, and C are 30%, 60%, and 10%, respectively.

**SALES MIX VARIANCE** effect on profit of selling a different proportionate mix of products than had been budgeted. This variance arises when different products have different CONTRIBUTION MARGINS. The sales mix variance shows how well the department has done in terms of selling the more profitable products while the SALES VOLUME VARIANCE measures how well the firm has done in terms of its sales volume.

$$\begin{matrix} \text{Sales} \\ \text{Mix} \\ \text{Variance} \end{matrix} = \begin{pmatrix} \text{Actual Sales} & \text{Actual Sales} \\ \text{at Budgeted} & - & \text{at Actual Mix} \\ \text{Mix} \end{pmatrix} \times \begin{matrix} \text{Budgeted} \\ \text{Contribution} \\ \text{Margin per Unit} \end{matrix}$$

**SALES ORDER** a document, essential for effective internal control, that includes the details of an approved customer's order, formatted to meet the needs of the seller. A sales order typically includes the buyer's name and address, a description of the goods ordered, the quantity ordered, and any special terms of the sale.

**SALES PRICE VARIANCE** difference between actual selling price per unit and the budgeted selling price per unit, multiplied by the actual number of units sold.

Sales Price Variance = (Actual Price – Budgeted Price) × Actual Sales

If the actual price is greater than the budgeted price, a variance is favorable; otherwise, it is unfavorable.
    *See also* SALES VOLUME VARIANCE.

**SALES QUANTITY VARIANCE** *see* SALES VOLUME VARIANCE.

**SALES RETURN** merchandise given back to the seller because of defects. Sales returns reduce the seller's gross sales. Sales return is a contra revenue account.

**SALES TAX** state or local tax based on a percentage of the selling price of the goods or service that the buyer must pay. It is not revenue to the seller, who simply collects it and passes it onto the state or local government. Assume credit sales of $30,000 are made with a sales tax rate of 8%. The entry to record the sale is:

| Accounts receivable | 32,400 | |
| Sales | | 30,000 |
| Sales tax payable | | 2,400 |

The purchaser cannot deduct sales tax as an itemized deduction.

**SALES TYPE LEASE** accounting by LESSOR in which one or more of the four criteria required for a CAPITAL LEASE are met and both of the following criteria are satisfied: (1) collectibility of minimum lease payments is predictable and (2) no important uncertainties surround the amount of unreimbursable costs yet to be incurred. A sales type lease gives rise to a manufacturer's or dealer's profit or loss on the assumed sale of the item in the year of lease as well as interest income over the life of the lease. Lease payments receivable is recorded representing the minimum lease payments (net of amounts, if any, including executory costs with any profit thereon) plus the unguaranteed residual value accruing to the benefit of the lessor. The difference between lease payments receivable and the discounted value of the payments is recorded as unearned interest income. The DISCOUNT RATE used to determine the present value of lease payments is the lessor's implicit rate. Assume a sales type lease is entered into on 1/1/2014. Six year-end annual lease payments of $20,000 are to be received. The discount rate is 5%. The present value of an ORDINARY ANNUITY for $n = 6$, $i = 5\%$ is 5.0757. The cost of the leased item is $85,000. Initial direct costs of the lease are $4,000. Appropriate journal entries for 2014 and 2015 follow:

| 1/1/2014 | | |
| Receivable | 120,000 | |
| Sales | | 101,514 |
| Unearned Interest Revenue | | 18,486 |
| $20,000 \times 5.0757 = 101,514$ | | |
| Cost of Sales | 85,000 | |
| Inventory | | 85,000 |
| Direct Expenses | 4,000 | |
| Cash | | 4,000 |
| 12/31/2014 | | |
| Cash | 20,000 | |
| Receivable | | 20,000 |
| Unearned Interest Revenue | 5,076 | |
| Interest Revenue | | 5,076 |
| $5\% \times 101,514 = 5076$ | | |

```
12/31/2015
Cash                              20,000
   Receivable                                        20,000
Unearned Interest Revenue         4,330
   Interest Revenue                                   4,330
5% × 86,590 = 4330
```

*See also* DIRECT FINANCING LEASE.

**SALES VOLUME VARIANCE** difference between the actual number of units sold and the budgeted number, multiplied by the budgeted selling price per unit; also called *sales quantity variance*.

Sales Price Variance = (Actual Sales – Budgeted Sales) × Budgeted Price

If the actual sales are greater than the budgeted sales, a variance is favorable; otherwise, it is unfavorable. For example, ABC Shops sold 50,000 units of product A for $21 each, in comparison with the budgeted 60,000 units at $22. The sales volume variance is (60,000 – 50,000) × $22 = $220,000. Since the actual sales were lower than the budgeted sales, the sales volume variance is unfavorable. *See also* SALES PRICE VARIANCE.

**SALVAGE VALUE** expected price for a fixed asset no longer needed in business operations; also called SCRAP VALUE. In determining depreciation expense, salvage value is deducted from cost (except when the double-declining-balance method of accelerated depreciation is used).

**SAMPLE** selected items in a POPULATION. It is often impossible or impractical to observe a population if it is large. A decision maker relies on a sample of it, then tries to draw conclusions or make inferences about the population.

**SAMPLING** process of selecting items from a POPULATION to reach a conclusion about the population. For example, counting selected inventory items in performing an audit to verify the total inventory balance. *See also* STATISTICAL SAMPLING.

**SAMPLING DISTRIBUTION** giving the probability of each possible value of a statistic. It is computed from a sample of $n$ items, for all possible samples of size $n$ from a particular population. For example, compute a statistic such as the mean, standard deviation, and so on, which will vary from sample to sample. In this manner, a distribution is obtained of a statistic that is its sampling distribution.

**SAMPLING ERROR** difference between the value obtained by sampling and the value that would have been obtained if the entire population had been investigated. The auditor is concerned that sampling error is minimized.

**SAMPLING RISK** percentage likelihood that a sample result is not representative of the population. An allowance for sampling risk refers to the difference between the achieved upper precision limit (UPL) and the actual sample deviation rate.

**SARBANES-OXLEY (SARBOX) ACT** (www.sarbanes-oxley.com) wide-ranging U.S. corporate reform legislation, coauthored by the Democrat in charge of the Senate Banking Committee, Paul Sarbanes, and Republican Congressman Michael Oxley. The Act, which became law in July 2002, lays down stringent procedures regarding the accuracy and reliability of corporate disclosures, places restrictions on auditors providing non-audit services, and obliges top executives to verify their accounts personally. Each issuer's annual report must include an internal control report containing an assessment of the effectiveness of the internal control structure and procedures.

**SAS** *see* STATEMENT ON AUDITING STANDARDS (SAS); STATISTICAL ANALYSIS SYSTEM (SAS).

$S_b$ *see* STANDARD ERROR OF THE REGRESSION COEFFICIENT.

**SCALABILITY** the ability of a system to expand or contract to meet business needs without modifying the application software. Scalability is achieved by adding or upgrading hardware.

**SCAN** to read through a document rather hastily. In a *desk-top publishing computer system*, a document can be quickly passed through a *scanner* and subsequently edited on-screen.

**SCATTERGRAPH METHOD** graphical procedure used to separate a SEMIVARIABLE EXPENSE (or mixed cost) into the fixed and the variable cost portion. In this method, a semivariable expense is plotted on the vertical axis (or *y*-axis) and activity measure is plotted on the horizontal axis (or *x*-axis). Then a *regression* line is fitted by visual inspection of the plotted data, as shown in the following graph. The scattergraph method is relatively easy to use and simple to understand. However, it should be applied with extreme caution, because it does not provide an objective test for assuring that the regression line drawn is the most accurate fit for the underlying observations.

SEMIVARIABLE COST

**SCHEDULE**
1. supporting set of calculations, data, information, or analysis that shows or amplifies how figures in primary statements are derived. An example is a schedule for an aging of accounts.
2. auditor's set of working papers for an audit.
3. to prioritize, arrange, or position with respect to a finite time period.
4. assignment of work to a facility and the specification of the sequence and timing of the work.

**SCHEDULE OF EQUIVALENT PRODUCTION** process costing schedule in which a period's equivalent units are computed for both material costs and conversion costs.

**SCIENTER** refers to knowledge or intent of malfeasance (wrongdoing). In order to be guilty of securities fraud under Section 10(b) of the Securities Exchange Act of 1934, a defendant must have acted with scienter.

**SCIENTIFIC AMORTIZATION** *see* EFFECTIVE INTEREST METHOD.

**SCOPE** aspects of an audit concerning the procedures employed, the extent of what was done, and the financial items examined.

**SCOPE LIMITATION** situation that may include client-imposed restrictions upon the audit, restrictions beyond the client's control, or the existence of other conditions precluding necessary auditing procedures. Client-imposed restrictions commonly limit the observation of inventories and the confirmation of accounts receivable. Time elements, geographical distances, and disappearances of evidence may prevent audit observation. All of these limitations in the scope of the audit may hamper the statement of an auditor's unqualified (unmodified) opinion as to the financial state of the enterprise.

**SCRAP VALUE** sales value of scrap. Scrap is residue from manufacturing operations that has relatively minor recovery value. In accounting for scrap, the sales value of scrap is treated as an offset to factory overhead. However, in some job order situations, the sales value of scrap is credited to the particular job that produced the scrap.

**SCRIP DIVIDEND** *see* LIABILITY DIVIDEND.

**SCROLL** movement of the WINDOW up or down relative to the contents of a computer file in order to reach parts not originally seen on the screen.

**S$_e$** *see* STANDARD ERROR OF THE ESTIMATE.

**SEARCH** to seek a particular sequence of characters by working through a file on the screen. It is a function of an *editor*, which is a computer program that enables the user to sit at a terminal or a keyboard, view the contents of a file, SCROLL, add material, or make other changes.

**SEARCH ENGINE** *see* WEB SEARCH ENGINE.

**SEARCH ENGINE OPTIMIZATION (SEO)** consists of a set of strategies and techniques to naturally or organically increase the number of visitors to a Web site by obtaining a top ranking in the results of a search engine. SEO techniques ensure that a Web site will be found and indexed by search engines.

**SEASONALITY** seasonal variation in business or economic activity that takes place on a recurring basis. Seasonality may be caused by various factors, such as weather, vacation, and holidays. In appraising a company's financial statements at a particular time, the accountant or analyst must consider the seasonal effects upon them and make appropriate seasonal adjustments.

**SEC EDGAR DATABASE** database that contains electronic copies of SEC filings by publicly traded companies (www.edgar-online.com and www.tenkwizard.com).

**SECONDARY DISTRIBUTION** "off the board" offering of a previously issued security from an investment institution, acting as underwriter or as selling investor, to other members of the exchange on which the security is listed. Sales of this nature are usually block sales. Allowing such a sale to take place on the exchange floor might severely lower the price of the stock. Certain block dispositions require SEC sanction.

**SECRET RESERVE** *see* HIDDEN RESERVE.

**SECTION 404(a) OF SARBANES-OXLEY ACT** applicable to all publicly traded entities and requires annual reports filed with the SEC to include a report prepared by management that includes its (1) acknowledgment of its responsibility for establishing and maintaining adequate INTERNAL CONTROL, and (2) assessment about the effectiveness of its internal control.

**SECTION 404(b) OF SARBANES-OXLEY ACT** applicable to publicly traded entities with a market capitalization in excess of $75,000,000. It requires the independent auditor to audit internal control and express an opinion as to its effectiveness.

**SECTION 906 OF THE SARBANES-OXLEY ACT** a section that requires the CEO and the CFO to certify each periodic report that includes financial statements. The certification, which is separate from the Section 302 certification, may state that the periodic report fully complies with the requirements of the Securities Exchange Act of 1934 and that "information contained in the periodic report fairly presents, in all material respects, the financial condition and results of operations of the issuer."

**SECTION 179 EXPENSE ELECTION** an election by a taxpayer to deduct the cost of tangible depreciable personal property used in a trade or business. The deduction under Section 179 is in lieu of depreciating the property. The Section 179 expense deduction is claimed on Form 4562, and is subject to certain limitations that vary from year to year.

**SECTION 302(A) OF THE SARBANES-OXLEY ACT** a section that requires a company's CEO and CFO to certify each quarterly and annual report. They are required to certify that the financial statements and other financial information included in the report are fairly presented in all material respects.

**SECTION 1250 ASSETS** depreciable real property, subject to depreciation recapture upon disposition.

**SECTION 1245 ASSETS** depreciable personal property, subject to depreciation recapture upon disposition.

**SECTION 1231 ASSETS** assets used in a trade or business that are held for more than one year and include depreciable tangible and intangible personal property and depreciable and non-depreciable real property (e.g., land).

**SECURE SOCKETS LAYER (SSL)** a protocol to provide a secure communication channel between two devices operating over the Internet or Intranet. Data is encrypted/decrypted using two keys: a public key and a private key. It is a transparent protocol and does not require much from the end user when establishing a connection; the end user simply establishes a connection using https rather than http.

**SECURED LIABILITY** obligation secured by a pledge of assets that can be sold, if necessary, to ensure payment.

**SECURITIES ACT OF 1933** landmark legislation that provided governmental regulation over the initial issuance of securities. It covered *registration* and disclosure. The Securities Exchange Act of 1934 dealt with the trading of already outstanding securities. It covered enforcement. The regulating body set up to enforce and promulgate regulations, as well as mandate policies and standards within the accounting and auditing disciplines is the SECURITIES AND EXCHANGE COMMISSION (SEC).

**SECURITIES AND EXCHANGE COMMISSION (SEC)** federal government agency monitoring and regulating corporate financial reporting and disclosure, use of accounting principles, auditing practices, and trading activities. Its ACCOUNTING SERIES RELEASES (ASRS) and STAFF ACCOUNTING BULLETIN (SAB) apply to publicly held companies. SEC requirements promote full disclosure to protect investor interests. For the most part, the SEC follows the accounting and auditing pronouncements of bodies organized by the public accounting profession. It therefore relies on the FINANCIAL ACCOUNTING

STANDARDS BOARD (FASB), the *Committee on Auditing Procedure*, and the AUDITING STANDARDS BOARD (ASB).

**SECURITIES EXCHANGE ACT OF 1934** *see* SECURITIES ACT OF 1933.

**SECURITY**

  1. financial instrument that shows ownership, such as an equity item (e.g., stock), debt instrument (e.g., bond, note), or right (e.g., option).
  2. collateral in support of debt. An example is real estate that serves as security for a bank loan.

**SEED MONEY** funds put up by venture capitalists to finance a *new* business. Often, seed money involves a loan or investment in preferred stock or convertible bonds. A major purpose of seed money is to form a basis for additional financing to aid in the firm's growth.

**SEGMENT** functional or responsibility area within a business that can be reported upon separately. The assets, revenue, and earnings of a segment are operationally distinguishable. Examples of business segments are division, department, product line, and geographic area. *See also* SEGMENT REPORTING.

**SEGMENTED REPORTING** process of reporting activities of various segments of an organization such as divisions, product lines, or sales territories; also called *line of business reporting*. The *contribution approach* is valuable for segmented reporting because it emphasizes cost behavior patterns and controllability of costs. The contribution approach is based on the theses that: (1) fixed costs are much less controllable than variable costs; (2) *direct fixed costs* and *common fixed costs* must be clearly distinguished. Direct fixed costs are those that can be identified directly with a particular segment of an organization, whereas common fixed costs are those that cannot be identified directly with the segment; and (3) common fixed costs should be clearly identified as *unallocated* in the contribution income statement by segments. Any attempt to allocate these types of costs, on some arbitrary basis, to the segments of the organization can destroy the value of responsibility accounting. It would lead to unfair evaluation of performance and misleading managerial decisions.

**SEGMENT MARGIN** profitability measure used to evaluate the financial performance of a business segment (i.e., division, territory, product line). It equals segmental revenue less related product costs and traceable operating expenses attributable to that segment. In preparing a contribution margin income statement, segment margin equals net revenues less variable manufacturing and selling costs less controllable fixed costs by the segment manager and others. Segment earnings do not include common costs—those costs not logically or practically assigned to the business segment (i.e., president's salary, interest expense).

**SEGMENT REPORTING** presentation required in the ANNUAL REPORT when a reportable segment meets one or more of the following tests: (1) revenue is 10% or more of combined revenue; (2) operating profit is 10% or more of combined operating profit (operating profit excludes unallocable general corporate revenue and expenses, interest expense, and income taxes); or (3) identifiable assets are 10% or more of the combined identifiable assets; also called *line of business reporting*. FASB Statement No. 131 requires that financial statements include information about operations in different industries, foreign operations, export sales, major customers, and government contracts. The disclosures provide data useful in evaluating a segment's profit potential and riskiness. A significant segment in the past that is expected to be so again should be reported even though it failed the 10% test in the current year. Segments shall represent a substantial portion (at least 75%) of the company's total revenue to unaffiliated customers. As a matter of practicality, however, no more than 10 segments should be shown. While intersegment sales or transfers are eliminated in consolidated financial statements, they are included for purposes of segment disclosure in determining the 10% and 75% rules. The DISCLOSURES are not required for an enterprise that derives 90% or more of its revenues from one industry. The segmental disclosures may be presented in the body of the financial statements, footnotes, or a separate schedule. The disclosure requirements are not applicable to nonpublic companies or in interim reports.

**SEGREGATION OF DUTIES** internal control concept in which individuals do not have responsibility for incompatible activities. For example, the record-keeping or authorization function should be divorced from the physical custody of the asset to guard against misuse. The person who approves invoices for payment should not be responsible for writing and signing checks. An auditor should note situations where one individual's responsibility extends improperly over related areas, i.e., the person maintaining inventory records has physical possession of the merchandise. Segregation of duties assists in detecting errors and deterring improper activities. The smaller the organization, the more difficult this practice becomes.

**SELF-BALANCING** term referring to an equality of debits and credits, such as in the case of the general ledger.

**SELF-CONSTRUCTED ASSET** entity that makes its own asset (e.g., manufactures the asset rather than buying it from outside). Such an asset is recorded at the incremental costs to build (material, labor, and overhead), assuming idle capacity. Fixed overhead is excluded unless it increases because of the construction effort. However, self-constructed assets should not be recorded at an amount exceeding the outside price.

*Example:* Incremental costs to self-construct equipment are $40,000. The equipment could be bought from outside at $37,000.

The journal entry is:

| | | |
|---|---|---|
| Equipment | 37,000 | |
| Loss | 3,000 | |
| Cash | | 40,000 |

**SELF-EMPLOYMENT INCOME** net taxable income of a self-employed individual. The income is reported on Schedule C of Form 1040. If there is more than one business, self-employment income is the total earnings of all businesses. A loss in one business is deductible from the profits of another. A self-employed individual pays a higher social security tax than a regular employee.

**SELF-EMPLOYMENT TAX** paid by self-employed individuals and consists of social security and Medicare taxes. The self-employment tax is based on net earnings from self-employment, as opposed to TAXABLE INCOME.

**SELF-INSURANCE** coverage borne by the person or company itself against the risk of loss that may occur if property is destroyed or damaged from some cause (e.g., fire). A company that self-insures cannot establish an estimated liability. It can appropriate retained earnings and footnote the nature of the self-insurance.

**SELF-LIQUIDATING LOAN** seasonal loan that is used to pay for a temporary increase in accounts receivable or inventory. As soon as cash is realized from the assets, the loan is repaid. The borrowed money is used to acquire resources that are combined for later sale, and the proceeds from the sale are used to repay the loan. Most short-term unsecured loans are self-liquidating. This kind of loan is recommended for companies with excellent credit ratings for financing projects that have quick cash flows.

**SELLING AND ADMINISTRATIVE EXPENSE BUDGET** detailed plan of operating expenses, other than those of the production function, needed to support the sales and overall operations of the organization for a future period.

**SELLING EXPENSE** cost incurred to sell (e.g., advertising, salesperson commission) or distribute (e.g., FREIGHT-OUT) merchandise. It is one of the types of operating expenses and is a period cost. *See also* GENERAL AND ADMINISTRATIVE EXPENSES.

**SELLING GROUP** *see* SELLING SYNDICATE.

**SELLING SHORT** selling securities (or commodities futures contracts) not owned by the seller. The investor (seller) earns a profit when the market price of the security declines, and loses money when the purchase price is higher than the original selling price. To make a short sale, the broker borrows stock and loans it to the investor. Later on, hopefully when the market price is lower, the investor buys the shares to repay the lending broker. Assume an investor sells short 50 shares of stock having a market price of $25, for a total of $1250. The broker borrows the shares and holds onto the proceeds of the short sale to secure the loan and satisfy margin requirements. Later on, the investor buys the stock at $20 a share, repays the 50 shares, earning a per share profit of $5, or a total of $250.

Investors "sell short against the box" when they sell short shares they actually own (*not* borrowed shares). Short sales against the box may occur so that a loss is minimized or the tax consequences of a long sale may be postponed to a subsequent tax year.

**SELLING SYNDICATE** security dealers or brokers united for the purpose of distributing a new or secondary security issue to the public; also called *selling group*. The group is chosen by a syndicate manager (managing underwriter). This group usually has an established reputation for the disposition of the type of securities to be issued. If the disposition of securities comes under the supervision of the SEC, then the appointment of such a group does not occur until filing and SEC confirmation takes place. A member of the selling syndicate may have to take a position in securities that have not yet been resold to the public.

**SELL-OR-PROCESS-FURTHER DECISION** short-term, nonroutine decision about whether to sell a product at a particular stage of production or to process it further in the hope of obtaining additional revenue. When two or more products are produced simultaneously from the same input by a joint process, these products are called JOINT PRODUCTS. The term JOINT COSTS is used to describe all the manufacturing costs incurred prior to the point where the joint products are identified as individual products, referred to as the SPLIT-OFF POINT. At the split-off point some of the joint products are in final form and salable to the consumer, whereas others require additional processing. In many cases, the company might have the option to sell the products at the split-off point or process them further for increased revenue. In connection with this type of decision, joint costs are considered irrelevant, since the joint costs have already been incurred at the time of the decision, and therefore are SUNK COSTS. The decision will rely exclusively on additional revenue compared to the additional costs incurred due to further processing.

**SEMI-FIXED COST** *see* SEMIVARIABLE COST.

**SEMIVARIABLE COST** one that varies with changes in volume but, unlike a variable cost, does not vary in direct proportion; also called *mixed cost*. In other words, this cost contains both a variable and fixed component. Examples are the rental of a delivery truck, where a fixed rental fee plus a variable charge based on mileage is made; and power costs, where the expense consists of a fixed amount plus a variable charge based on consumption. A further example is a total factory overhead, which is a mixture of fixed overhead and variable overhead.

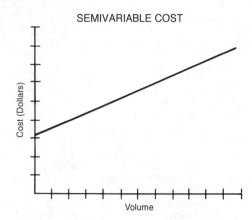

SEMIVARIABLE COST

**SENIOR ACCOUNTANT** staff accountant, employed by a CPA firm, who supervises a client engagement. Functions performed by the senior accountant include preparing an audit program and the audit of the client's financial statements. A senior accountant is below the manager level.

**SENIOR DEBT** debt that a company must repay first if it goes out of business. If a company goes out of business, senior debt holders are paid before junior debt holders. It is one of the safest forms of financing from the perspective of the debt holder.

**SENIOR SECURITY** one that in liquidation has preference over other securities in a company's capital structure. For example, bonds and preferred stock rank ahead of common stock in the distribution of earnings or in liquidation. Note that bonds are senior to preferred stock, which is senior to common stock.

## SENSITIVITY ANALYSIS

1. in LINEAR PROGRAMMING (LP), a technique for determining how the optimal solution to a linear programming problem changes if the problem data such as objective function coefficients or right-hand side values change; also called *post-optimality analysis*. To an alert accountant, the optimal solution not only provides answers—given assumptions about resources, capacities, and prices in the problem formulation—but should raise questions about what would happen *if* conditions should change. Some of these changes might be imposed by the environment, such as changes in resource costs and market conditions. Some, however, represent changes that the manager can initiate, such as enlarging capacities or adding new activities.

2. form of SIMULATION that enables decision makers to experiment with decision alternatives using a what-if approach. The manager

might wish to evaluate alternative policies and assumptions about the external environment by asking a series of what-if questions.

**SEPARABLE COSTS** costs incurred beyond the split-off point and identifiable with specific products.

**SEPARATELY MANAGED ACCOUNTS (SMAs)** managed accounts with customized investment products in search of a performance edge or just the ability to brag about having a personal money manager. The allure of SMAs stems from their flexibility and transparency. Don't like semiconductor stocks? No problem. Your religious beliefs ban owning "sin stocks"? They're out. As for transparency, you get a list of this week's trades and the Web site address and password so you can check up on your holdings. SMAs can be pricey, especially for smaller investors. U.S. stock mutual funds charge an average 1.4% in fees, and SMA fees can top 3%. There is disagreement on the point at which they become "fee-efficient."

**SEPARATE RETURN** tax return filed by married individuals who chose to state their own income and deductions, exemptions and credits. A return filed in this manner forces both individuals to itemize deductions. Tax rates are generally unfavorable in comparison to joint return rates. *See also* FILING STATUS.

**SEQUENTIAL ACCESS** storing of records based upon some sequence determination, such as alphabetic or numeric order. Direct access file processing requires a direct access device such as magnetic disk unit, where retrieval time can be in milliseconds as compared with several seconds or even minutes in a sequential file utilizing a tape unit. A majority of today's computerized information systems that use the direct access method also use sequential processing for some portion of the processing activities in the same information system.

**SEQUENTIALITY** recognition that activity costs are governed by a logical order that mirrors how work is performed.

**SEQUENTIAL METHOD** *see* STEP ALLOCATION METHOD.

**SERIAL BONDS** bonds that mature in installments rather than at one maturity date. They are typically issued by a municipality. Each bond certificate has a given redemption date. *See also* BOND.

**SERIAL CORRELATION** *see* AUTOCORRELATION.

**SERVER** computer that houses the LAN operating system as well as shared files and programs.

**SERVICE AUDITOR** an independent auditor of a service organiza-tion's internal controls. A service auditor typically issues one of two types of reports: (1) a Type 1 report, which covers management's description of the service organization's internal controls as well as the suitability of the design of the controls, and (2) a Type 2 report, which covers matters covered in a Type 1 report and the operating effectiveness of the service organization's internal controls. In order to assess control risk at below the maximum level for the internal controls at the service organization, the service auditor should generally obtain a Type 2 report.

**SERVICE CENTER** *see* SERVICE DEPARTMENT.

**SERVICE COST** *see* NORMAL PENSION COST.

**SERVICE DEPARTMENT** responsibility center within a factory that performs a class of service distinct from operating departments of the factory. Examples are purchasing, building and ground personnel, and power departments. All of these activities are necessary parts of the manufacturing process and primarily supportive of production departments. SERVICE DEPARTMENT COSTS must be allocated to production departments before *factory overhead rates* are determined.

**SERVICE DEPARTMENT COSTS** costs incurred in rendering service to production departments and to other service departments. Service department costs are factory overhead costs. Since the production departments are directly benefitted by service departments, the costs of a service department should be allocated to the appropriate production departments (as part of factory overhead costs).

**SERVICE LEVEL** percentage of time in which a company can satisfy all orders arriving during the reorder period. It is computed as 1 minus the probability of being out of stock. For example, assume that a company establishes the acceptable probability of being out of stock as 5%. Then the service level is 95%.

**SERVICE LIFE** time an asset will provide benefit to the business. The depreciation expense calculation requires an estimate of years of usefulness. The service life of an asset may be less than its physical life due to obsolescence or future lack of need.

**SERVICE ORGANIZATION** an entity that provides processing services to other entities, commonly referred to as user entities. For example, a service organization may process payroll transactions for a user entity.

**SERVICE-ORIENTED ARCHITECTURE (SOA)** defined by the World Wide Web Consortium (W3C) as "a set of components which can be invoked, and whose interface descriptions can be published and discovered." SOA is an approach to developing software that has its origins in middleware. Middleware is software that allows two or more independent software systems to interact and exchange data. SOA utilizes modular software services to interact within a system, as well as between systems. SOA systems are flexible and capable of expanding or evolving over time.

**SERVICE POTENTIAL** anticipated future benefits to be obtained from an asset.

**SERVICE RATE** number of customers or units that can be serviced by one server in a given period of time.

**SERVICES** useful labor performed by an individual or organization on behalf of others. Doctors, lawyers, interior decorators, etc., provide services for which they are paid by their clients. *See also* GOODS.

**SET OF ACCOUNTS** group of ledger accounts that a particular firm adopts. Ledger accounts are customarily sequenced and numbered in the order in which they will appear in the financial statements. Listed first are the balance sheet accounts—assets, liabilities, and stockholders' equity, in that order. The income statement accounts—revenue and expenses—follow. Of course, the more complex the operation, the greater the number of ledger accounts required. Each specific account has its own number. A listing of account names and numbers is called the CHART OF ACCOUNTS.

**SETTLEMENT DATE** time at which a security transaction must be paid by the buyer and the securities delivered by the seller. Stocks and bonds have a settlement date of *three* business days subsequent to the TRADE DATE. Listed options and government securities must be settled by the next business day.

**SETTLEMENT IN PENSION PLAN** discharge of all or a portion of an employer's pension benefit obligation. Any excess plan assets revert to the company. A settlement must satisfy *all* of the following criteria: (1) it is irrevocable; (2) it relieves responsibility for a pension benefit obligation; and (3) it eliminates significant risk applicable to the obligation. An example is giving a lump-sum payment to employees in exchange for pension rights. There is immediate recognition of the gain or loss arising from the settlement. *See also* CURTAILMENT IN PENSION PLAN; TERMINATION IN PENSION PLANS.

**SETUP COST** expenses incurred each time a batch is produced. It consists of engineering cost of setting up the production runs or machines, paperwork cost of processing the work order, and ordering cost to provide raw materials for the batch.

**SHADOW PRICE** maximum price that management is willing to pay for an extra unit of a given limited resource. Management may wish to know whether it pays to add capacity in a particular department. It would be interested in the monetary value to the firm of adding, say, an hour per week of assembly time. This monetary value is usually the additional CONTRIBUTION MARGIN (CM) that could be earned. This amount is the shadow price. A shadow price is, in a way, an OPPORTUNITY COST—the CM that would be lost by not adding an additional hour of capacity. To justify a decision in favor of a short-term capacity decision, the decision maker must be sure that the shadow price exceeds the actual price of that expansion. For example, suppose that the shadow price of an hour of the assembly capacity is $8.75 while the actual market price is $9.50. That means it does not pay to obtain an additional hour of the assembly capacity.

**SHARE** one unit of ownership interest in a company, mutual fund, limited partnership, etc. For example, the owner of 1000 shares of a company's common stock that has 100,000 shares outstanding has a 1% equity interest.

**SHAREHOLDER** *see* STOCKHOLDER.

**SHAREHOLDERS' EQUITY** *see* STOCKHOLDERS' EQUITY.

**SHAREPOINT** a Microsoft product that allows an entity to create Web sites. SharePoint allows an organization to securely store, organize, share, and access information from any PC, tablet, or smartphone. SharePoint Online is available as a cloud-based service for organizations that do not want to install and deploy SharePoint servers on premises.

**SHARPE RATIO** *see* SHARPE'S RISK-ADJUSTED RETURN.

**SHARPE'S RISK-ADJUSTED RETURN** risk-adjusted grades that compare five-year, risk-adjusted return, developed by Nobel Laureate William Sharpe. The fund manager is thus able to view his excess returns per unit of risk. This measure combines standard deviation and mean total return to show a risk-adjusted measure of the fund's performance. The higher this number is, the better. *Note:* As a rule of thumb, a Sharpe ratio of more than 1.00 is pretty good.

**SHERMAN ANTITRUST ACT** legislation, passed in 1890, after a series of major corporate mergers. It outlaws any form of monopoly. It also outlaws acts or contracts to create monopoly and any attempt to acquire monopoly power. *See also* ANTITRUST LAWS.

**SHIPPING DOCUMENT** *See* BILL OF LADING.

**SHORT ACCOUNT** one used in short sales of securities or commodities. The short seller makes a profit if the price of the security or commodity declines because the securities or commodities purchased to repay the lender of the stock or contracts borrowed to cover the short sale have a lower price than that recorded in the sale. *See also* SELLING SHORT.

**SHORT FORM MERGER** the merger of companies by a simplified procedure in which one company owns 90% of the stock of another.

**SHORTAGE COSTS** costs incurred when an item is out of stock; also called *stockout costs*. These costs include the lost CONTRIBUTION MARGIN (CM) on sales plus lost customer goodwill.

**SHORT-RUN PERFORMANCE MARGIN** contribution margin minus controllable (discretionary) fixed costs. Discretionary costs are characterized by uncertainty about the relationship between input (the costs) and the value of the related output. Examples are advertising and research costs.

**SHORT SELLING (SALE)** a trading technique in which one sells a security he or she does not own (by borrowing it from a broker) and later buying a like amount of the same security. This technique is used to make a profit from a fall in stock price. The rationale behind short selling goes as follows: The simplest way to make money in the stock market is to buy a stock at a low price and sell it later at a higher one. In a short-selling situation, investors are reversing the sequence; they are selling high, promising to buy back the stock later at what they hope will be a lower price. If the stock price falls, they make money. If it rises and they have to buy back their stocks for more than they sold them for, they lose money.

**SHORT-TERM DEBT** money payable by the debtor to the creditor within one year. It is a current liability. Short-term debt includes the portion of a long-term liability payable within the year.

**SHORT-TERM DEBT RATIO** calculation of debt payable within one year to total debt. The ratio indicates whether a firm will be able to satisfy its immediate financial obligations. A high ratio points to a lack of liquidity since most of the corporate debt will have to be met in the current year.

**SHORT-TERM INVESTMENT** funds placed in securities that are expected to be held for one year or less. Examples include *marketable securities*, commodities, money market instruments, and options. The return on short-term investments may come in the form of financial income (i.e., dividend income, interest income) and/or capital appreciation.

**SHORT-TERM (SHORT-RUN) DECISIONS** decisions usually involving idle capacity, a time period of one year or less during which certain factors of production are fixed and cannot be changed. *See also* NONROUTINE DECISIONS; SPECIAL-ORDER DECISIONS.

**SHRINKAGE** excess of inventory shown on the books over actual quantities on hand. It can result from theft, evaporation, or general wear and tear. *See also* WASTE.

**SIGHT DRAFT** order signed by the drawer asking the drawee to pay the amount due the payee upon demand. In many cases the drawer and payee are the same. *See also* TIME DRAFT.

**SIGNIFICANT** important, essential, distinctive, or of sufficient nature to warrant special notice relative to a standard or norm. The deviation may be of such magnitude that its occurrence is probably not due to chance. Significant events often require disclosure in the body or footnote to the financial statements.

**SIGNIFICANT DEFICIENCY** a deficiency in internal control or a combination of deficiencies in internal control that is less severe than a material weakness, yet is important enough to warrant attention by those charged with governance (in the case of a nonissuer) or those individuals in the client organization having financial statement oversight responsibility (in the case of an issuer). It does not mean that a material misstatement has occurred or that it will occur, but that it could occur. *See also* DEFICIENCY IN INTERNAL CONTROL and MATERIAL WEAKNESS.

**SIGNIFICANT TESTING** methodology incorporating probability theory to investigate the possible outcomes of events or population parameters to determine whether or not their occurrence is associated with chance. A popular approach entails the use of the null hypothesis (i.e., there is no difference between groups or variables). At a chosen *level of significance* (ALPHA), a sample statistic is compared with the specified population. If there is found to be a difference, the null hypothesis is rejected and the finding is significant at the given alpha level. If the null hypothesis is retained, the relationship is referred to as nonsignificant. *See also* HYPOTHESIS TESTING; T-TEST.

**SIMPLE CAPITAL STRUCTURE** capital structure having no COMMON STOCK EQUIVALENTS. There are no securities outstanding that are potentially dilutive. *See also* COMPLEX CAPITAL STRUCTURE.

**SIMPLE INTEREST** computations based only on the original principal. COMPOUND INTEREST is applied to the original principal and accumulated interest. For example, $100 deposited in a savings account at 10% simple interest would yield the interest of $10 *per year* (10% of $100).

**SIMPLE RATE OF RETURN** measure of profitability obtained by dividing the expected future annual net income by the required investment; also called ACCOUNTING RATE OF RETURN or *unadjusted rate of return*. Sometimes the *average* investment rather than the original initial investment is used as the required investment, which is called *average rate of return*. For example, consider the following investment:

| Initial investment | $6,500 |
| Estimated life | 20 years |
| Expected annual net income | $675 |

Then the simple rate of return is $675/$6,500 = 10.4%. Using the average investment, which is usually assumed to be one-half of the original investment, the average rate of return will be doubled as follows:

$$\frac{\$675}{\$6,500/2} = \frac{\$675}{\$3,250} = 20.8\%$$

**SIMPLE REGRESSION** regression analysis that involves *one* independent variable. For example, total factory overhead is related to one activity variable (either direct labor-hours or machine-hours). Also, the demand for automobiles is a function of its price only. *See also* MULTIPLE REGRESSION ANALYSIS; REGRESSION ANALYSIS.

**SIMPLEX METHOD** technique most commonly used to solve a LIN-EAR PROGRAMMING (LP) problem. It is an algorithm, a step-by-step procedure for moving from corner point to corner point of the feasible region in such a manner that successfully larger (smaller) values of the objective function in a maximization (minimization) problem are obtained at each step. The procedure is guaranteed to yield the optimal solution in a finite number of steps.

**SIMPLE YIELD** return equal to the nominal dollar interest divided by the MARKET VALUE (price) of the bond. It is an approximate, simplified rate reflecting the cost to the debtor and the return to the holder of a debt instrument. The *yield maturity* is a much more accurate measure. Assume a $100,000, 8%, five-year bond is issued at 93%. The simple yield is:

$$\frac{\text{Nominal Interest}}{\text{Market Value}} = \frac{8\% \times \$10,000}{93\% \times \$10,000} = \frac{\$800}{\$9,300} = 8.6\%$$

*See also* YIELD TO MATURITY.

**SIMPLIFIED EMPLOYEE PENSION (SEP)** a type of retirement plan that enables an employer to make deductible contributions on behalf of its employees. Amounts deducted by the employer are excludible from the employee's gross income. Deductible contributions are generally limited to 25% of the employee's compensation and may not exceed the annual defined contribution plan limit. In essence, a SEP is an individual retirement account established by an employer.

**SIMULATION** attempt to represent a real-life system with a MODEL to determine how a change in one or more variables affects the rest of the system, also called *what-if analysis*. Simulation will not provide optimization except by trial and error. It will provide comparisons of alternative systems or how a particular system works under specified conditions. It is a technique used for what-if scenarios. The advantages of simulation are: (1) when a model has been constructed, it may be used over and over to analyze different kinds of situations; (2) it allows modeling of systems whose solutions are too complex to express by one or several mathematical relationships; (3) it requires a much lower level of mathematical skill than do OPTIMIZATION MODELS.

**SIMULATION MODELS** what-if models that attempt to simulate the effects of alternative management policies and assumptions about the firm's external environment. They are basically a tool for management's laboratory. It is a detailed representation of the real world. Most financial models are simulation models that are designed primarily for generating projected financial statements, budgets, and special reports, and for performing a variety of what-if analyses in an effort to find the best course of action for the company. Due to technological advances in computers (such as spreadsheets, financial modeling languages, graphics, data base management systems, and networking), more and more companies are building and using modeling for their planning and decision-making efforts. Another version of simulation is MONTE CARLO SIMULATION that is used when a system has a random, or chance, component.

**SIMULTANEOUS EQUATION METHOD** *see* RECIPROCAL ALLOCATION METHOD.

**SINGLE AUDIT ACT OF 1984** consists of uniform audit requirements for state and local governments that are the recipients of federal financial assistance programs. Under the act, an entity is required to undergo a Single Audit (also known as an OMB A-133 audit) if it expends at least $500,000 of federal financial assistance. A single audit is concerned with both financial and compliance aspects.

**SINGLE-CHANNEL LINE** waiting line with only one server.

**SINGLE ENTRY BOOKKEEPING** simple bookkeeping system in which transactions are recorded in a single record. An example is a checkbook showing expenditures. For example, an accounts payable listing may represent purchases on account; no journal entries are made or ledgers kept. It is an incomplete form of DOUBLE ENTRY BOOKKEEPING because it does not rely on equal debits and credits. Although financial statements cannot readily be prepared in a single entry system, they are usually derived from inspection or count and comparison of beginning and ending totals. Plugging is usually necessary to derive owner's equity for the balance sheet.

**SINGLE-STEP INCOME STATEMENT** income statement format that eliminates most intermediate subtotals such as GROSS INCOME and OPERATING INCOME by accumulating and showing first all ordinary revenue and gain items and then all ordinary expense and loss items. Net income is then displayed as their difference plus considerations for discontinued operations and extraordinary gains and losses. *See also* MULTIPLE-STEP INCOME STATEMENT.

**SINKING FUND** fund set aside for periodic payments, aimed at reducing or amortizing a financial obligation. A bond with a sinking fund provision is an example. The issuer makes periodic payments to the trustee, who can retire part of the issue by purchasing the bonds in the open market. The trustee can invest the cash deposited periodically in the sinking fund in income-producing securities. The objective is to accumulate investments and investment income sufficient to retire the bonds at their maturity. A sinking fund may be established for other purposes such as for plant expansion.

**SINKING FUND METHOD OF DEPRECIATION** a method of depreciation under which the depreciation expense is an amount of an ANNUITY so that the amount of the annuity at the end of the useful life would equal the ACQUISITION COST of the asset. Theoretically, the depreciation charge should include interest on accumulated depreciation at the beginning of the period. This method is rarely used in practice.

**SKIMMING PRICING** strategy used when a new product is introduced. It involves setting a high initial price primarily to recoup research and development investments; the price is progressively lowered as time passes and competition sets in. The objective is to maximize short-term profits. *See also* PENETRATION PRICING.

**SLACK** in PROGRAM EVALUATION AND REVIEW TECHNIQUE (PERT), free time in a network. The slack for an event is the difference between the *latest time (LT)* and the *earliest time (ET)*. It is the length of time an activity can be delayed without interfering with the project completion.

**SLACK PATH** in PROGRAM EVALUATION AND REVIEW TECHNIQUE (PERT), a path representing a series of activities that require less time than the CRITICAL PATH.

**SLIDE** error caused by misplacing a decimal point. 35.9750 recorded incorrectly as 3597.50 is an example of a slide.

**SLOPE** tangent of the angle between a given straight line and the $x$-axis. It is equal to $(y_2 - y_1) / (x_2 - x_1)$ when $(x_1, y_1)$ and $(x_2, y_2)$ are two distinct points on a nonvertical line. The slope indicates generally the steepness and direction of the line. More specifically, the slope is the change in $y$ for every unit change in $x$. Slope is a necessary parameter for utilization of LINEAR REGRESSION models. It is $b$ in the COST-VOLUME FORMULA $y = a + bx$.

## SMALL BUSINESS CORPORATION

1. under Internal Revenue Code section 1244, corporation that enables shareholders to claim an ordinary loss (rather than a capital loss).
2. SUBCHAPTER S CORPORATION. For legal purposes, an S corporation is no different than other corporations. For tax purposes, however, an S corporation is a PARTNERSHIP. That is, corporate income and losses pass through the shareholders' individual tax returns. To qualify as an S corporation, a company must meet the following requirements: (1) it cannot have more than 100 shareholders; (2) it cannot have more than one class of stock; (3) it cannot have any nonresident foreigners as shareholders; and (4) it must properly elect S corporation status.

**SMART CARD** small plastic card resembling a credit card with a unique embedment of an integrated circuit of electronic data. It provides security on who uses it, how it is used, and what data are contained or stored on it.

**SMARTPHONE** a mobile phone offering advanced computer capabilities, such as e-mail and Web access. Most smartphones run on Apple's iOS or Google's Android operating system. Smartphones allow one to install "apps," or application software, to do just about anything from staying organized to playing games.

**SMISHING** the sending of text messages that trick you into loading viruses onto your cell phone.

**SOCIAL ACCOUNTING** application of DOUBLE ENTRY BOOKKEEPING system to macro-economic analysis; also called NATIONAL INCOME ACCOUNTING. It is a tool used to measure economic performance of a nation. It is concerned with the determination, estimation, and analysis of such economic welfare factors as national income and GROSS DOMESTIC PRODUCT (GDP). Social accounting also involves such areas as health and education, and their measurement by a double entry system.

**SOCIAL AUDIT** review of the public-interest, nonprofit, and social activities of a business. These audits usually are performed primarily for internal benefit and typically are not released to the public. The social audit may be performed routinely by internal or external consulting groups, as part of regular internal audits. These evaluations consider social and environmental impacts of business activities.

**SOCIAL IMPACT STATEMENT** evaluative and detailed report to assess the effect and consequences of the public-interest, nonprofit activities of an entity (such as a corporation, region, or even society) upon an area of specified social concern.

**SOCIAL SECURITY TAX** levy on employers and employees on a stated percentage of salary charged by the federal government to fund the social security program and other benefits that permit payments to eligible retired persons or their survivors. The social security tax is withheld from the employee's pay, and with the employer's payroll tax share, is remitted to the government periodically. *See also* FEDERAL INSURANCE CONTRIBUTION ACT (FICA).

**SOFT LANDING** term used to describe the economy slowing enough to eliminate the need for the Fed to further raise interest rates to dampen activity—but not enough to threaten a recession, which is what results when the economy contracts instead of expands. Hard landing, on the hand, could mean a recession.

**SOFTWARE** computer instructions. A collection of instructions for a particular function is a program. A collection of programs to carry out a specific task is referred to as a package. The term *software* applies to applications programs, specialized system programs, or operating system utilities (which relates to operating the computer system). Software packages are available for many accounting-related applications, including bookkeeping, tax preparation and planning, management advisory services, audit, spreadsheets, database management, preparing formal reports and documents, and practice administration (i.e., time and billing).

**SOFTWARE AS A SERVICE** business model whereby companies (such as Google, eBay, and Amazon.com) provide services based on their software, rather than providing software as a product (such as Microsoft Office). *See also* WEB 2.0.

**SOFTWARE THINKING PROGRAMS** computer software used by accountants preparing written reports for clients, including management letters and specialized analyses of operations. Writing skills (e.g., clarity, organization) can be greatly enhanced through the use of thinking software. Idea (outline) programs enable CPAs to create a logical outline from a random set of ideas entered into the microcomputer in nonlogical order. The information is labeled, organized, and structured. A given information set can be a major category, while other pieces are identified as subordinates.

**SOLE PROPRIETOR** unincorporated business with one owner having all the net worth. In the event the business fails, the owner is *personally* liable for all debts incurred.

**SOLID STATE STORAGE DEVICES** devices that store data on flash memory. Unlike traditional hard drives, these devices have no moving parts. The data is stored in an array of semiconductor memory using integrated circuits, rather than on magnetic or optical media. Data access time is much faster on solid state storage devices.

**SOLVENT** condition of a company able to satisfy its debt obligations when due. Various financial ratios can be computed to measure a company's degree of solvency, such as the DEBT-EQUITY RATIO and the INTEREST COVERAGE RATIO. Solvency partly depends on corporate earning power because a company sustaining losses will sooner or later become insolvent. The going-concern assumption lies on the premise of a solvent business. *See also* INSOLVENCY.

**SOURCE DOCUMENT** basic evidence needed to record an accounting transaction. Journal entries, financial records, and accounting reports are eventually derived from source documents. Examples of source documents are purchase orders, sales invoices, and time cards.

**SOURCES OF EVIDENCE** supporting documentation, financial records, and written and oral statements from external and internal people to the organization, gathered by the auditor in order to formulate an audit opinion on a company's financial statements.

**SPAM** a computer term for unwanted e-mail. In a Monty Python television skit, a group of Vikings in a restaurant sing about the meat product, "Spam, spam, spam, spam, spam, spam, spam, spam, lovely spam! Wonderful spam!" until told to shut up. As a result, something that keeps being repeated to great annoyance was called spam, and computer programmers picked up on it.

**SPECIAL ASSESSMENT FUND** in GOVERNMENT ACCOUNTING, fund used to account for the financing of public improvements or services from the issuance of bonds or assessments levied against the properties benefitted.

**SPECIAL AUDIT** one with a restricted, narrow scope to conform with a governmental agency's regulatory requirements. *See also* LIMITED AUDIT.

**SPECIALIST** the work of a specialist may be used in the performance of an audit. A specialist has special knowledge in a field other than accounting, such as actuarial science, appraisal, or environment. The auditor will typically use the work of the specialist unless the auditor's procedures lead to the belief that the specialist's findings are unreasonable. The auditor should test any data provided to the specialist considering the auditor's assessment of control risk. In general, the auditor should not refer to the specialist's findings in an unqualified (unmodified) opinion.

**SPECIALIZED INDUSTRY** one having its own unique methods of accounting and reporting. An example is the uniform system of accounts mandated by the Interstate Commerce Commission for railroads.

**SPECIAL JOURNAL** records of original entry other than the general journal that are designed for recording specific types of transactions of similar nature. Advantages of special journals are threefold: (1) their use permits a division of labor; (2) they save time in posting from the journals to the general ledgers; and (3) they reduce recording time and errors. Most firms use at least the following special journals:

| Special Journal | Special Transactions Recorded |
| --- | --- |
| Sales journal | Sales on credit terms |
| Purchase journal | Purchase on account |
| Cash receipts journal | Receipt of cash |
| Cash disbursements journal | Payment of cash |
| Payroll journal | Payroll |

**SPECIAL-ORDER DECISIONS** short-term and nonroutine decisions such as whether to accept a production order at an offered price that is below the normal selling price, or what price to charge for a product that could be produced with otherwise idle facilities. *See also* CONTRIBUTION APPROACH TO PRICING.

**SPECIAL-PURPOSE FINANCIAL REPORTING FRAMEWORKS** include (1) cash basis, (2) income tax basis, (3) regulatory basis, and (4) compliance basis. The PUBLIC COMPANY ACCOUNTING OVERSIGHT BOARD (PCAOB) refers to the first three bases as "other comprehensive bases of accounting."

**SPECIAL-PURPOSE FINANCIAL STATEMENT** one having usefulness only to *limited* users. Some companies may accompany certified GENERAL PURPOSE FINANCIAL STATEMENTS with special-purpose statements. Further, these specialized statements are typically seen when companies file information to be used for governmental and trade statistics.

**SPECIAL PURPOSE VEHICLE/ENTITY (SPV/SPE)** a type of corporate entity or limited partnership created for a specific transaction or business, especially one unrelated to a company's main business. Their losses and risks generally are not recorded on a company's balance sheet. The SPV/SPE is usually a subsidiary company with an asset/liability structure and legal status that makes its obligations secure even if the parent company goes bankrupt. A company can use such an entity to finance a large project without placing the entire firm at risk. The problem is that, due to accounting loopholes, these vehicles became a way for companies to conceal debt. Essentially, it looks like the company has no liability when they really do. As the Enron bankruptcy showed, if things go wrong, the results can be devastating.

**SPECIAL REPORT** type of auditor's report that is prepared in accordance with GENERALLY ACCEPTED AUDITING STANDARDS (GAAS). It attempts to elaborate, explain, or exhibit in a prescribed fashion certain sections, accounts, or items of a financial statement. Examples of such reports are cash receipts/disbursements reports, proposed acquisitions, and tax basis financial statements. Financial statements may be prepared in accordance with rules other than GAAP, such as insurance regulatory requirements.

**SPECIAL REVENUE FUND** in GOVERNMENT ACCOUNTING, fund used to account for the proceeds of special revenue sources (other than special assessments, expendable trusts, or major capital projects) that are legally restricted to expenditure for specified purposes. Examples of special revenue funds are those established for the purpose of financing schools, parks, or libraries.

**SPECIAL SITUATION** unusual occurrence or event requiring special accounting or legal treatment because of its importance.

**SPECIFIC IDENTIFICATION** inventory valuation in which ending inventory items are identified in some manner, such as by serial number and purchase date. Assume the following items were purchased during the year:

| | | |
|---|---|---|
| Purchase invoice #102 (Feb. 20) | 180 units @ $ 9 | = $1,620 |
| Purchase invoice #129 (Apr. 12) | 130 units @ $10 | =  1,300 |
| Purchase invoice #165 (Sept. 20) | 120 units @ $11 | =  1,320 |
| Total | 430 units | $4,240 |

Assume the ending inventory is 145 units consisting of 85 units from the Feb. 20 purchase and 60 units from the Sept. 20 purchase.

The ending inventory valuation is:

| Feb. 20 | 85 units @ $ 9 | $ 765 |
|---------|----------------|-------|
| Sept. 20 | 60 units @ $11 | 660 |
| Total | 145 units | $1,425 |

*See also* AVERAGE COST FLOW ASSUMPTION; FIRST-IN, FIRST-OUT (FIFO); LAST-IN, FIRST-OUT (LIFO).

**SPECIFIC PERFORMANCE** when ordered by a court, requires the performance of a specific act, which is usually stated in a contract. Specific performance is normally not enforced if (1) the contract is unconscionable or terminable at will by either party, (2) severe hardship would result, or (3) personal services are involved.

**SPECIFIC PRICE INDEX** one reflecting the price change of a particular type item (i.e., goods, services) or of related groups of items. It is computed at a given date and compared to a base date. *See also* GENERAL PRICE INDEX.

**SPECIFIC PRICE-LEVEL CHANGE** difference in the replacement cost or market price of a particular good or service, or a related group of products or services. It differs from a general price-level change that applies to a broad base of goods and services. *See also* SPECIFIC PRICE INDEX.

**SPECULATION** placing funds in a high-risk investment, such as an option or futures contract. Risk is measured by variability of outcome and the probability distribution of those outcomes. A speculative investment has predictable results, but over a wide range of possible outcomes and with high probabilities of the extremes occurring. Speculation is basically short-term trading with the hope of obtaining a higher profit in the form of capital gain but with greater risk. The potential loss on a speculative investment can be limited by employing a HEDGE.

**SPEECH RECOGNITION SOFTWARE** program in which verbal commands activate the MICROCOMPUTER to perform functions such as WORD PROCESSING, SPREADSHEET, or DATA BASE MANAGEMENT SYSTEM (DBMS). For instance, hardware (boards) and software exist so the accountant can input data by talking to the computer, moving the cursor, and filling in the details of a spreadsheet.

**SPEECH SYNTHESIS** software program that allows a microcomputer with a speech chip to speak in an understandable voice.

**SPENDING VARIANCE** *see* FIXED OVERHEAD SPENDING (BUDGET) VARIANCE; VARIABLE OVERHEAD SPENDING VARIANCE.

**SPINOFF** type of corporate reorganization in which the original corporation transfers some of its assets to a newly formed corporation. In exchange for the assets, the original corporation receives all of the new corporation's capital stock, which it then distributes to its shareholders as a property dividend.

**SPLIT** *see* STOCK SPLIT.

**SPLIT-OFF POINT** juncture of production where JOINT PRODUCTS become individually identifiable. A diagram follows on the next page. *See also* SELL-OR-PROCESS-FURTHER DECISION.

SPLIT-OFF POINT DIAGRAM

**SPOILAGE** production that does not result in good finished products. The amount of spoilage can be considered either normal or abnormal. Spoilage can be classified into the following categories: (1) Spoiled goods—goods that do not meet production standards and are either sold for their salvage value or discarded; (2) Defective units—goods that do not meet standards and are sold at a reduced price or reworked and sold at the regular or a reduced price; (3) Waste—material that is lost in the manufacturing process by shrinkage, evaporation, etc.; and (4) Scrap—by-product of the manufacturing process that has a minor market value.

**SPOOFING** a technique to mask one's identity. For example, e-mail spoofing (or "fooling") is used by spammers to modify the e-mail header so that the message appears to have originated from someone other than the actual source.

**SPREADSHEET** a computer program for displaying and analyzing data in a tabular form. Computer spreadsheet programs evolved from manual paper-based worksheets, where calculations could be tedious, time-consuming, and error-prone. Spreadsheet programs are excellent for performing simulations, financial projections, and various accounting applications. Microsoft Excel is the most widely used spreadsheet program in the market today.

**SPREADSHEET PROGRAMS** *see* SPREADSHEET.

**SPYDERS** *see* STANDARD & POOR'S DEPOSITARY RECEIPT (SPDR).

**SPYWARE** any technology that aids in gathering information about a person or organization without their knowledge. Spyware can get into a computer as a software virus or as the result of installing a new program.

**SSID (SERVICE SET IDENTIFIER)** used to differentiate one WLAN (wireless local area network) from another. SSID is a 32 alphanumeric character unique identifier that is attached to the header of each data packet that is sent over a WLAN.

***STAFF ACCOUNTING BULLETIN* (SAB)** detailed and technical publication from the Office of the Chief Accountant of the SEC that suggests how the various ACCOUNTING SERIES RELEASES (ASRS) should be applied in practice. A substantial amount of the SAB deals with the implementation of REPLACEMENT-COST ACCOUNTING, as required by ASR No. 190. The SABs were begun in 1975.

**STAFF AUDITOR**
1. external auditor employed by a public accounting firm that examines a client's financial records.
2. internal auditor working for the company to assure corporate accounting policies are being carried out, internal controls are adequate, and operating activities are running smoothly.

**STAFF AUTHORITY** power to give advice, support, and service to line departments. Staff managers do not command others. Examples of staff authority are found in personnel, purchasing, engineering, and finance. The management accounting function is usually "staff" with responsibility for providing line managers and also other staff people with a specialized service. The service includes budgeting, controlling, pricing, and special decisions. *See also* LINE AUTHORITY.

**STAND-ALONE COST METHOD** method that allocates a portion of common costs to each user by applying a ratio equal to the stand-alone cost of providing benefits to that user divided by the sum of the stand-alone costs for all users. A variation of the stand-alone technique is the INCREMENTAL COST-ALLOCATION METHOD.

**STAND-ALONE REVENUE ALLOCATION** weighting scheme based on unit selling prices, for example, average actual prices, which is the theoretically preferable method; unit costs; or physical units in the bundle. A variation of the stand-alone revenue allocation technique is the INCREMENTAL REVENUE ALLOCATION.

**STANDARD** quantitative expression of a performance objective, such as standard hours of labor allowed for actual production or a standard purchase price of materials per unit. Sometimes the terms *standard* and *budget* are used interchangeably. For example, budgeted sales revenue could be used as a standard in evaluating the performance of the marketing department. A standard is set for the following three reasons: (1) to measure performance of a responsibility center; (2) to simplify recordkeeping; and (3) to improve performance by taking appropriate remedial action on an unfavorable deviation from the standard.

**STANDARD & POOR'S DEPOSITARY RECEIPT (SPDR)** shares of a security designed to track the value of the S&P 500; also called *SPDRs* or *Spyders*. Spyders trade on the American Stock Exchange under the symbol SPY. One SPDR unit is valued at approximately one-tenth of the value of the S&P 500. Dividends are distributed quarterly and are based on the accumulated stock dividends held in trust, less any expenses of the trust.

**STANDARD BILL OF MATERIALS** listing of the standard quantity per unit of each item of material going into a unit of finished product. It should be adjusted for unavoidable waste, spoilage, and other normal inefficiencies.

**STANDARD COST** production or operating cost that is carefully predetermined. A standard cost is a target cost that *should be* attained. The standard cost is compared with the actual cost in order to measure the performance of a given costing department or operation. *Variances*, which are the differences between actual costs and standard costs, may indicate inefficiencies that have to be investigated. Corrective action may have to be taken.

**STANDARD COST SYSTEM** process by which production activities are recorded at standard costs and variances from actual costs are isolated. Standard costs are carefully predetermined target costs that should be attained under efficient operating conditions. A standard cost system is designed to aid management in judging performance of a responsibility center in an organization. The standard costing system is designed to facilitate: (1) planning and controlling costs; (2) judgment of performance; (3) budget preparation; (4) inventory valuation; and (5) employee motivation. The analysis of variances that are the differences between standard and actual costs is the key in a standard cost system. This reveals the causes of deviations between actual and standard costs. This feedback aids in planning future goals, controlling costs, and measuring performance.

**STANDARD COST VARIANCE** *see* VARIANCE.

**STANDARD DEDUCTION** amount allowed to an individual taxpayer who does not elect to itemize deductions. This standard deduction is incorporated into the tax rate and table schedules. A taxpayer who elects to itemize deductions may deduct only the excess over the standard deduction amount to determine taxable income.

**STANDARD DEVIATION**
1. statistic that measures the tendency of data to be spread out. Accountants can make important inferences from past data with this measure. The standard deviation, denoted with $\Sigma$ and read as *sigma*, is defined as follows:

$$\sigma = \sqrt{\frac{\Sigma(x - \bar{x})^2}{n - 1}}$$

where $\bar{x}$ is the mean.

For example, one-and-one-half years of quarterly returns for XYZ stock follow:

| Time Period | x | $(x - \bar{x})$ | $(x - \bar{x})^2$ |
|---|---|---|---|
| 1 | 10% | 0 | 0 |
| 2 | 15 | 5 | 25 |
| 3 | 20 | 10 | 100 |
| 4 | 5 | -5 | 25 |
| 5 | -10 | -20 | 400 |
| 6 | <u>20</u> | 10 | <u>100</u> |
|  | 60 |  | <u>650</u> |

From the preceding table, note that

$$\bar{x} = 60/6 = 10\%$$

$$= \sqrt{\Sigma(x - \bar{x})^2/n - 1} = \sqrt{650/(6-1)} = \sqrt{130} = \underline{11.40\%}$$

The XYZ stock has returned on the average 10% over the last six quarters and the variability about its average return was 11.40%. The high standard deviation (11.40%) relative to the average return of 10% indicates that the stock is very risky,

2. measure of the dispersion of a probability distribution. It is the square root of the mean of the squared deviations from the EXPECTED VALUE $E(x)$.

$$\sigma = \sqrt{\Sigma(x_i - E(x))^2 \; p_i}$$

It is commonly used as an absolute measure of risk. The higher the standard deviation, the higher the risk.

For example, consider two investment proposals, A and B, with the following probability distribution of cash flows in each of the next five years:

|  | Cash Inflows | | | |
|---|---|---|---|---|
| Probability | (.2) | (.3) | (.4) | (.1) |
| A | $ 50 | 200 | 300 | 400 |
| B | $100 | 150 | 250 | 850 |

The expected value of the cash inflow in proposal A is:

$$\$50(.2) + 200(.3) + 300(.4) + 400(.1) = \underline{\$230}$$

The expected value of the cash inflow in proposal B is:

$$\$100(.2) + 150(.3) + 250(.4) + 850(.1) = \underline{\$250}$$

The standard deviations of proposals A and B are computed as follows:

For A:

$$\sqrt{\begin{array}{l}(\$50 - 230)\,(.2) + (200 - 230)\,(.3) + (300 - 230)\,(.4) \\ + \;(400 - 230)\,(.1)\end{array}} = \underline{\$107.70}$$

For B:

$$\sqrt{\begin{array}{l}(\$100-250)(.2)+(150-250)(.3)+(250-250)(.4)\\+\ (850-250)(.1)\end{array}} = \underline{\underline{\$208.57}}$$

Proposal B is more risky than proposal A, since its standard deviation is greater.

**STANDARD DIRECT LABOR COSTS** standard hours of direct labor multiplied by the standard wage for direct labor.

**STANDARD DIRECT MATERIALS COST** standard price for direct materials multiplied by the standard quantity for direct materials.

**STANDARD ERROR OF THE ESTIMATE** measure of the scatter of the actual observations above the regression line; designated $S_e$. It is computed as

$$S_e = \sqrt{\Sigma(y-y')^2/(n-k-1)}$$

where $k$ is the number of independent variables in the regression equation. The statistic can be used to gain some idea of the accuracy of our predictions.

**STANDARD ERROR OF THE REGRESSION COEFFICIENT** measure of the amount of sampling error in a REGRESSION COEFFICIENT; designated $S_b$. It is computed as

$$S_b = \frac{S_e}{\sqrt{(x-\overline{x})^2}}$$

where $S_e$ is the standard error of the estimate. *See also* STANDARD ERROR OF THE ESTIMATE.

**STANDARD FIXED MANUFACTURING OVERHEAD RATE** total budgeted fixed manufacturing overhead costs divided by an expression of capacity, usually normal capacity in terms of standard hours or units.

**STANDARD HOURS ALLOWED** time that should have been used to manufacture actual units of output during a period. It is obtained by multiplying actual units of production by the standard labor time. For example, a company actually produced 2000 units during the month of March. The standard labor time required to produce one unit of output was 3 hours. The standard hours allowed for actual production is 2000 units $\times$ 3 hours = 6000 hours.

**STANDARD LABOR RATE** direct labor rate that should be paid for each hour of labor time. It includes not only base wages earned but also an allowance for fringe benefits and other labor-related costs. For example, it can be determined as follows:

| | |
|---|---|
| Wage rate per hour | $9.00 |
| Payroll taxes at 10% | .90 |
| Fringe benefits at 30% | 2.70 |
| Standard rate per hour | $12.60 |

**STANDARD MANUFACTURING OVERHEAD COST** sum of the estimates for variable and fixed manufacturing overhead costs in the next accounting period.

**STANDARD MATERIAL PRICE** per unit price for direct materials that should be paid for a single unit of materials. It reflects the final, delivered cost of the materials, net of any discounts taken. It may be determined as follows:

| | |
|---|---|
| Purchase price per pound | $ 5.00 |
| Freight by truck | .35 |
| Receiving and handling | .10 |
| Less: purchase discount | (.50) |
| Standard price per pound | $ 4.95 |

**STANDARD OF COMPARISON** standard used in relating a base or typical item to a current one. For example, budgeted sales may be compared to actual sales, with deviations noted. Corrective action can then be taken. Also, the trend in a financial statement item may be examined for a percentage change. If sales last year were $100,000 and this year are $150,000, the percentage increase is 50%. A comparison can also be made of a company's financial statement figures to those of other companies in the industry as well as to industry norms.

**STANDARD OPINION** judgment rendered by a CPA who is satisfied that the company's financial statements are fairly presented in conformity with U.S. GAAP. Further, it means that excessive uncertainty does not exist with regard to material transactions or events. Financial statements with standard opinions can normally be relied upon in making business judgments concerning the company.

**STANDARD QUANTITY ALLOWED** amount of materials that should have been used to manufacture units of output during a period. It is obtained by multiplying actual units of production by the standard material quantity per unit. For example, a company actually produced 2000 units during the month of March. The standard material quantity required to produce one unit of output was 5 pounds. The standard quantity allowed for actual production is 2000 units $\times$ 5 pounds = 10,000 pounds.

**STANDARD VARIABLE MANUFACTURING OVERHEAD RATE** total budgeted variable manufacturing overhead costs divided by an expression of capacity, such as the expected number of standard machine-hours or standard direct labor-hours.

**STARTUP COSTS** pre-opening one-time expenditures incurred to open a new facility, introduce a new product or service, conduct business in a new territory, start business with a new customer class, or begin some new operation. All startup costs are expensed as incurred.

## STATED CAPITAL
1. amount of capital contributed by stockholders of a corporation. It may also refer to the method of valuating no-par-value stock where the portion of the amount contributed is credited to the capital stock account and the balance is credited to PAID-IN CAPITAL.
2. LEGAL CAPITAL of a company.

**STATED LIABILITY** amounts listed under liabilities in the various financial records and statements without audit or verification. They are subject to future adjustment or correction. It is basically a face value observation of liabilities.

**STATED VALUE** per share value sometimes assigned to no-par stock by the corporation. It defines the legal capital of the corporation. It is the amount credited to the no-par capital stock account. A typical journal entry made for the issuance of stated value stock is given below:

|                                          | Dr. | Cr. |
|------------------------------------------|-----|-----|
| Cash (or other assets)                   | XX  |     |
| Capital stock (at stated value)          |     | XX  |
| Paid-in capital in excess of stated value|     | XX  |

## STATEMENT
1. formal document presenting the financial condition and operating performance of an enterprise. These include the income statement, balance sheet, and statement of changes in financial position. Also included may be documents for internal use such as performance appraisals, budgets, and so on.
2. summary statement documenting terms, conditions, or status of an account. An example is a statement of retail credit account status.
3. verbal utterance or proposition.

**STATEMENT OF ACCOUNT** report indicating the account status of an agreement between creditor and debtor. The statement is usually issued by the creditor indicating details such as the unpaid balance due and payment history. An example of such a statement is that of a department store credit account or MasterCard billing statement.

**STATEMENT OF AFFAIRS** financial report showing assets and liabilities at expected liquidation values and stockholders' equity. The statement is prepared primarily when an actual or pending BANKRUPTCY exists. Or a creditor may want to see pessimistic figures for a company facing severe financial problems. This is a worst-case scenario.

**STATEMENT OF CASH FLOWS** statement that provides information about an entity's cash receipts and cash disbursements for a period as they apply to operating, investing, and financing activities. The statement is required in the annual report. Cash flows from operating activities comprise the first section of the statement. These apply to transactions impacting net income. Examples of cash inflows from operating activities are cash sales, customer collections on account, interest income, and dividend income. Examples of cash outflows from operating activities are paying suppliers of merchandise, paying suppliers of operating expense items, employee wages, interest expense, and taxes. Investing activities relate to the purchase or sale of equity and debt securities of other entities and the acquisition or sale of property, plant, and equipment. The financing section appears last in the statement of cash flows. Financing activities relate to obtaining equity capital, dividend payments to stockholders, debt issuance, and repayment of bonds.

When a cash receipt or cash payment is for more than one activity, classification is based on the activity that is the prime reason for that cash flow. For instance, the purchase and sale of equipment to be used by the company is often deemed as an investing purpose.

Emphasis is placed on explaining the change in cash and cash equivalents for the year. In general, a cash equivalent is a very liquid short-term investment that has an initial maturity date of three months or less.

The statement cash flows for the company would be presented as follows:

### Liverpool Sugar Corporation
### Statement of Cash Flows
### for the Year Ended December 31, 20X9

| | |
|---|---:|
| Cash flows from operating activities: | |
| Cash received from customers | $1,004,000 |
| Cash payment for acquisition of materials | (469,000) |
| Cash payment for interest and dividends | (12,000) |
| Cash payment for taxes | (136,000) |
| Net cash provided by operating activities | $ 387,000 |
| Cash flows from investing activities: | |
| Cash paid to purchase plant and equipment | $(676,000) |
| Sale of long-term investment | 100,000 |
| Net cash provided by investing activities | (576,000) |
| Cash flows from financing activities: | |
| Sale of bonds | $ 300,000 |
| Cash paid for dividends | (36,000) |
| Net cash used in financing activities | 264,000 |
| Net decrease in cash and cash equivalents | $(75,000) |
| Cash and cash equivalents at the beginning of the year. | 198,000 |
| Cash and cash equivalents at the end of the year | $273,000 |

**STATEMENT OF CASH RECEIPTS AND DISBURSEMENTS** *see* CASH-FLOW STATEMENT.

**STATEMENT OF CHANGES IN NET WORTH** reflects the revenue and expenses of an individual as well as increases and decreases in estimated current values of an individual's assets and liabilities.

**STATEMENT OF CHANGES IN STOCKHOLDERS' EQUITY** details specific changes in an entity's main equity components, which include retained earnings, stock, additional paid-in-capital, and, if applicable, comprehensive income. In essence, this statement reconciles beginning and ending balances of accounts in the stockholder's equity section of an entity's balance sheet.

**STATEMENT OF COSTS OF GOODS MANUFACTURED** *see* COSTS OF GOODS MANUFACTURED SCHEDULE.

**STATEMENT OF FINANCIAL POSITION** *see* BALANCE SHEET.

**STATEMENT OF REALIZATION AND LIQUIDATION** presentation prepared by an enterprise going out of business. It is a summary type presentation of the realization (receipts from asset disposals) and the liquidation (retirement and settlement of liabilities) and operating statement of enumerated revenues, losses, and expenses of the liquidator.

**STATEMENT OF RETAINED EARNINGS** one that accompanies the balance sheet and shows the beginning balance of retained earnings, adjustments to it during the year, and the final balance. An illustrative statement format follows:

Retained Earnings—1/1 Unadjusted
Plus or Minus: Prior Period Adjustments
Retained Earnings—1/1 Adjusted
Plus: Net Income
Minus: Dividends Declared
Retained Earnings—12/31

**STATEMENT OF STOCKHOLDERS' EQUITY** statement included in the annual report presenting the individual components of STOCK-HOLDERS' EQUITY and the changes therein during the last year. The major elements of stockholders' equity include capital stock, paid-in capital, retained earnings, treasury stock, unrealized loss on long-term investments, and foreign currency translation gains and losses.

**STATEMENTS OF FINANCIAL ACCOUNTING CONCEPTS (SFAC)** reports issued by the FINANCIAL ACCOUNTING STANDARDS BOARD (FASB) to indicate the fundamental concepts of financial accounting, reporting, and disclosure. They reflect the objectives of financial statements. Included in the Financial Accounting Concepts are fundamental theories and practices underlying financial accounting. The elements of financial statements of business enterprises are presented, as well as financial reporting objectives of nonbusiness organizations.

**STATEMENTS OF FINANCIAL ACCOUNTING STANDARDS (SFAS)** accounting, reporting, and disclosure requirements of the FINANCIAL ACCOUNTING STANDARDS BOARD (FASB). They are rules to be followed by accountants in accumulating financial data and preparing financial statements. The standards are, in effect, GENER-ALLY ACCEPTED ACCOUNTING PRINCIPLES (GAAP). They cover diverse subjects, such as leases, pensions, and income statement presentation.

**STATEMENTS OF POSITION (SOPs)** recommendations, rather than requirements, issued by the ACCOUNTING STANDARDS EXECU-TIVE COMMITTEE of the AMERICAN INSTITUTE OF CERTIFIED PUBLIC ACCOUNTANTS (AICPA) concerning specialized accounting policies practiced in given industries. They are issued in the public interest. For instance, one Statement of Position covers the accounting and reporting for universities. The FASB is currently promulgating special-ized accounting principles that were previously dealt with by the SOPs.

**STATEMENTS OF REVENUES AND EXPENDITURES** in GOV-ERNMENT ACCOUNTING, statements showing revenues obtained less expenditures incurred. The difference represents the change in fund balance.

**STATEMENTS ON AUDITING PROCEDURE (SAP)** name for auditing pronouncements before 1972. Since then, STATEMENTS ON AUDITING STANDARDS (SAS) have been issued.

**STATEMENTS ON AUDITING STANDARDS (SAS)** reports issued by the AICPA's AUDITING STANDARDS EXECUTIVE COMMITTEE that represent preferable auditing standards and practices. *See also* AUDIT-ING STANDARDS BOARD (ASB).

**STATEMENTS ON STANDARDS FOR ACCOUNTING AND REVIEW SERVICES (SSARS)** name for pronouncements issued by the AMERICAN INSTITUTE OF CERTIFIED PUBLIC ACCOUNTANTS (AICPA) applicable to compilations and reviews of financial statements of non-issuers (i.e., nonpublic entities).

**STATEMENTS ON STANDARDS FOR ATTESTATION ENGAGEMENTS (SSAE)** name for pronouncements issued by the AICPA applicable to attest engagements concerning subject matter or assertions about subject matter. *See also* ATTESTATION (ATTEST) ENGAGEMENT.

**STATEMENTS ON STANDARDS FOR TAX SERVICES (SSTS)** name for pronouncements issued by the AICPA that include enforce-able standards of tax practice. While SSTS are applicable to AICPA members, they parallel the responsibilities specified by the INTERNAL

REVENUE SERVICE. These standards are designed to protect the profession, the public, and the government.

**STATES OF NATURE** conditions that are likely to occur and over which the decision maker has no control. *See also* DECISION THEORY.

**STATE UNEMPLOYMENT COMPENSATION** money paid to eligible unemployed individuals. It is financed by a payroll tax levied on employers by the various states. Some variation exists as to the filing and payment requirements among different states.

**STATIC (FIXED) BUDGET** one based on a single level of activity (e.g., a particular volume of sales or production). It has two characteristics: (1) it is geared toward only one level of activity; (2) actual results are compared against budgeted (standard) costs only at the original budget activity level. A FLEXIBLE (VARIABLE) BUDGET differs from a static budget on both scores. First, it is not geared to only one activity level, but rather, toward a *range* of activity. Second, actual results are not compared against budgeted costs at the original budget activity level. Managers look at what activity level was attained during a period and then turn to the flexible budget to determine what costs should have been at that actual level of activity.

**STATISTIC** numerical characteristic of a sample (taken from a population) computed using only the elements of a sample of the population. For example, the mean and the mode are statistics of the sample.

**STATISTICAL ANALYSIS SYSTEM (SAS)** statistical software package, developed by the SAS Institute, Inc., Cary, North Carolina. The SAS package aids in extensive statistical analyses, including descriptive statistics, REGRESSION ANALYSIS, and data graphing of statistical information.

**STATISTICAL COST CONTROL** procedure for distinguishing between random and other types of cost variances. Decisions to investigate variances are frequently based on THREE-SIGMA LIMITS rather than on a formal analysis of expected costs. Statistical cost control utilizes the control chart that helps distinguish random (chance) variances from variances that need investigation. The analysis of the latter helps to obtain improvements in production and processes. The identification of chance variances avoids unnecessary investigations of variances and eliminates frequent changes. A process or production method is said to be in statistical control if the variances are within three-sigma limits of the control chart.

**STATISTICAL CURVE FITTING** methodology commonly used as a quantitative forecasting technique. Many different types of curves can be used in fitting historical data for predicting such variables as sales and costs—linear, exponential, and others. For example, some form of curve fitting is often done to approximate the basic *trend* component of a time series. The trend can be linear (straight line) or curvilinear. The problem is to determine which form of curve will best fit the available data and provide the basis for an accurate forecast of the future. Statistics such as *r-squared* (COEFFICIENT OF DETERMINATION) can be of tremendous help for this purpose.

**STATISTICAL QUALITY CONTROL** method of quality control that uses statistical sampling of units produced by a production process. These are checked for defectives (variances) to determine whether or not the process is in control. If not, corrective action is taken. In the field of statistical quality control, the statistical control chart is used as a basic tool to formally distinguish between normal and abnormal variances. Control charts help distinguish RANDOM VARIANCES from variances that need managerial investigation. The analysis of the latter helps to obtain improvements in products and processes. The identification of chance variances avoids unnecessary investigations of variances and eliminates frequent changes. *Three-sigma control limits* are most popularly used to decide whether a process (operation) is in a state of statistical control.

A process is said to be in a state of statistical control if the sample variations stay within the limits. If the process is out of control, it is important to locate specific causes for the variation and take a corrective action. *See also* THREE-SIGMA LIMITS.

**STATISTICAL SAMPLING** method based on the assumption that, within a given confidence level and allowance for sampling risk, a randomly selected sample of items from a population will reflect the same characteristics that occur in the population. For example, auditors may draw conclusions based on data derived from a relatively small sample of the total population.

**STATISTICAL SOFTWARE** computer programs that perform functions helpful to accountants, particularly managerial accountants, such as determining STANDARD DEVIATION, multiple regression analysis, CORRELATION, VARIANCE ANALYSIS, and FREQUENCY DISTRIBUTION. A model base management system produces mathematical models and can change and store components. Examples are SPSS, SAS, and Minitab.

**STATISTICS** field of study concerning information calculated from sample data. The field is divided into two categories: DESCRIPTIVE STATISTICS and INFERENTIAL STATISTICS. Both are widely used in business.

**STATUTE OF FRAUDS** requires certain types of contracts to be in the form of a signed document in order to be enforceable. In general, contracts subject to the statute of frauds include contracts that (1) cannot be performed within one year, (2) involve the transfer of interest in land, and (3) involve the sale of goods totaling at least $500.

**STATUTORY AUDIT** one conducted to meet the particular requirements of a governmental agency. Where such audits take place, the scope and audit programs are set by the governmental body. Banks, insurance companies, and brokerage firms have statutory audits. Since the auditor's report must conform to standards required by the governing agency, the statements and other financial data generated from these audits may not conform to GAAP.

**STATUTORY CONSOLIDATION** a merger in which a new corporate entity is created from the two merging companies, which cease to exist. *See also* STATUTORY MERGER.

**STATUTORY MERGER** a merger in which one of the merging companies continues to exist as a legal entity, rather than being replaced by the new entity. *See also* STATUTORY CONSOLIDATION.

**STEP ALLOCATION METHOD** manner of allocating services rendered by service departments to other service departments using a sequence of allocation; also called the *step-down method* and the *sequential method.* The sequence normally begins with the department that renders service to the greatest number of other service departments; the sequence continues in step-by-step fashion and ends with the allocation of costs of service departments that provide the least amount of service. But no *reciprocal* service is considered.

**STEP COSTS** costs that are approximately fixed over a small volume range, but are variable over a large volume range. For example, supervision costs are fixed for a given range of production volume, but increased production often requires additional work shifts leading to added supervisory costs in a lump-sum fashion. The figure below illustrates this.

STEP COSTS

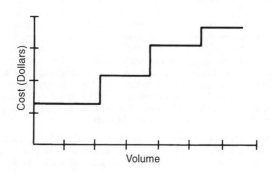

**STEP-DOWN METHOD** *see* STEP ALLOCATION METHOD.

**STEP FUNCTION COSTS** *see* STEP COSTS.

## STOCK

1. evidence of ownership in a company and a claim against a company's assets and earnings. It is the legal capital of the entity divided into shares. Two types of stock are COMMON STOCK and PREFERRED STOCK. *See also* CAPITAL STOCK; CUMULATIVE PREFERRED STOCK; PARTICIPATING PREFERRED STOCK; STOCK CERTIFICATE.
2. inventory available for sale.

**STOCK APPRECIATION RIGHTS** awards entitling employees to receive cash or stock, in any combination thereof (determined at grant date or when exercised), in an amount equivalent to the excess of market price on a specified number of shares of the corporation's stock above an option price.

**STOCK BONUS PLAN** plan similar to a PROFIT-SHARING PLAN except that contributions do not necessarily depend on profitability, and benefits are distributable in the employer's stock. The maximum amount that an employer may deduct for tax purposes in any one year is 15% of compensation. The only exception is for limitation carryforwards accumulated for tax years beginning before 1987. Two or more stock bonus plans are treated as one plan for purposes of limiting employer deductions.

**STOCK CERTIFICATE** document showing stockholder's ownership in the company. The certificate shows the number of shares, par value, class of stock (e.g., common stock), and voting rights. When endorsed, stock certificates are negotiable.

**STOCK COMPANY** firm whose capital is in the form of shares with transferable ownership rights.

**STOCK DIVIDEND** pro rata distribution of additional shares of a corporation's own stock to its stockholders. A stock dividend may be declared when the cash position of the firm is inadequate and/or when the company wishes to prompt more trading by reducing the market price of stock. A *small* stock dividend (less than 20%–25% of the shares outstanding at the date of declaration) decreases retained earnings and increases the capital accounts (capital stock and paid-in capital) for an amount equal to the fair value of the shares issued. A *large* stock dividend (in excess of 20%–25% of shares outstanding) decreases retained earnings and increases capital stock at the par or stated value only. *See also* CASH DIVIDEND.

**STOCKHOLDER** individual or business that owns shares in a corporation. A STOCK CERTIFICATE is evidence of ownership. The stockholder's return comes from DIVIDENDS and appreciation of the stock in the MARKET PRICE.

**STOCKHOLDERS' EQUITY** ownership interest of stockholders in the corporation; also called *shareholders' equity*, OWNERS' EQUITY, and NET WORTH. Stockholders' equity is the difference between total assets less total liabilities. The components of the stockholders' equity section of the balance sheet are:

Capital Stock
Plus: Paid-in capital
Plus: Retained earnings
     Unappropriated
     Appropriated
Plus or Minus: Foreign currency translation gain or loss
Minus: Unrealized loss on long-term investment portfolio
Total
Minus: Treasury stock
Total Stockholders' Equity

**STOCKHOLDERS OF RECORD** holders of stock as of the DATE OF RECORD who are entitled to receive a cash dividend already declared. For example, on January 8, the board of directors of a company declared a $.30 per share cash dividend on its common stock payable on February 18 to *stockholders of record* on January 20. The common stockholders who are on the company's records on January 20 will receive the $.30 dividend per share on February 18 (*date of payment*). Stockholders of record are also entitled to rights, voting privileges, and dividends other than cash.

**STOCK INDEX FUTURES** contract to buy or sell a broad stock market index. Introduced in 1982, futures contracts at the present time are available on the S&P 500 Stock Index, the New York Stock Exchange Composite Stock Index, and the Value Line Composite Stock Index. Smaller investors can avail themselves of the S&P 100 futures contract, which involves a smaller margin deposit. Stock index futures allow the investor to buy and sell the "market as a whole" rather than a specific security. An investor anticipating a bull market but unsure which particular stock will rise might buy (long position) a stock-index future. Another investor, seeking to hedge the portfolio against loss of value in a bear market might, on the other hand, sell a stock-index future.

**STOCK OPTION** right given the holder to buy a specified number of shares of stock at a certain price by a particular date. Stock option plans are often used to compensate corporate officers and other employees for specific services. Under a compensatory stock option plan, compensation should be expensed in the periods in which the related services are actually performed. Compensation is measured by the quoted market price of the stock at the *measurement date* less the option price the employee is to pay. The measurement date is the earliest date on which both the number of shares to be issued and the option price are known. Assume 2,000 shares are under option, market price at measurement date of 1/1/2014 is $15, option price is $10, par value is $6, and there is a four-year benefit period. Deferred compensation equals $10,000 (2,000 shares × $5). The entry at the measurement date is:

| 1/1/2014 | Deferred compensation | 10,000 | |
|---|---|---|---|
| | Stock options | | 10,000 |

On 12/31/2014, the entry is:

| 12/31/2014 | Compensation expense | 2,500 | |
|---|---|---|---|
| | Deferred compensation | | 2,500 |

Deferred Compensation is a contra account to stock options in the capital stock section of stockholders' equity, shown as follows on 12/31/2014:

| Stock options | $10,000 |
|---|---|
| Less: Deferred compensation | 7,500 |
| Balance | $ 2,500 |

If the market price of stock on the exercise date exceeds the option price, the employee will exercise. Otherwise, the employee will not. Assume the market price is $23 a share upon exercise of the options. The entry is:

| Cash ($10 × 2000) | 20,000 | |
|---|---|---|
| Stock options | 10,000 | |
| Common stock (2000 × 6) | | 12,000 |
| Paid-in capital | | 18,000 |

Note the employee pays only $10 (option price), not the current market price of $23. Footnote disclosures in a stock option plan include the number of shares under option, option price, number of shares exercisable, and shares issued under the option during the year.

**STOCK-OUT COSTS** *see* SHORTAGE COSTS.

**STOCK OUTSTANDING** *see* OUTSTANDING CAPITAL STOCK.

**STOCK REGISTER** record of the particulars related to the issuance of stock certificates to stockholders. Included are the shares issued, par value, name and address of owner, date of issuance, shares returned, cancelled shares, and other pertinent information.

**STOCK RIGHT** privilege giving current stockholders the first right to buy shares in a new offering, thus maintaining their proportionate ownership interest; also called PREEMPTIVE RIGHT. Suppose the investor owns 3% of XYZ Company. If the company issues 5,000 additional shares, the investor may receive a stock rights offering—a chance to buy 3%, or 150 shares, of the new issue. This right enables the investor to purchase new common stock at a subscription price for a short time, usually no more than several weeks. The subscription price (exercise price) is lower than the public offering price of the stock. A single right is the privilege applicable to one old share of capital stock to purchase a certain number of shares of new capital stock. When the rights are exercised, the issuing company makes a journal entry to record the proceeds received, and the common shares are issued.

**STOCK SPLIT** issuance of a substantial amount of additional shares, thus reducing the par value of the stock on a proportionate basis. No journal entry need be made, because the company's accounts do not change. However, there should be a memorandum entry describing the stock split. A stock split is often prompted by a desire to reduce the market price per share in order to stimulate investor buying. Assume XYZ Company has 1000 shares of $20 par value common stock. The total par value is thus $20,000. A two-for-one stock split is issued. There will now be 2,000 shares at a $10 par value. The total par value remains at $20,000. Typically, the market price per share of the stock should also drop to one-half of what it was before the split.

**STOCK SUBSCRIPTION** agreement to purchase a given number of shares at a specified price at a later date. Often, a down payment is required, and typically the payments are on an installment basis. It is a legal contract that is reflected in a debit owner's equity contra account. Subscribed stock is credited as the capital is contributed. *See also* CAPITAL STOCK SUBSCRIBED.

**STOCK WARRANT** option to purchase a certain number of shares at a stated price for a specified time period at a subscription price that is higher than the current market price (properly called *subscription warrant*). A warrant may or may not come in a one-to-one ratio with the stock already owned. Unlike a put or call option, a warrant is usually good for several years; some, in fact, have no maturity date and are known as *perpetual warrants*. Warrants are often given as sweeteners for a bond issue (e.g., to lower the interest rate or enhance the marketability). Warrants included with a bond may also exist in a merger when the acquiring company offers cash plus warrants in exchange for voting common stock of the acquired business. Generally, warrants are detachable from the bond and have a market life of their own. Warrants pay no dividends nor do they have voting rights. The warrant enables the holder to take part indirectly in price appreciation. *See also* DETACHABLE STOCK WARRANT; UNDETACHABLE STOCK WARRANT.

**STOP-LOSS ORDER** direction given to a broker to buy or sell a stock when it rises to or drops below a certain price. Assume an investor owns XYZ Company stock, having a current market price of $50 per share. The investor gives the broker a stop-loss order to sell this stock if it slips down to $46 a share. By selling the shares at a predetermined price, the investor is protected from further stock price declines.

**STOP-OR-GO SAMPLING** also referred to as sequential sampling, a technique that may enable an auditor to form conclusions when testing less than the full sample size.

**STOP PAYMENT** instruction to the bank not to honor a check when presented. As long as the check has not been cashed, the maker has up to six months to present a stop payment notice. However, a stop payment right does not apply to electronic funds transfers.

**STORAGE TIME** time a product spends in materials storage, work-in-process inventory, or finished goods inventory.

**STORE CARDS** perpetual-inventory records that are subsidiary ledger accounts for Stores (Control). All purchases of materials and supplies are charged to Stores (Control) as purchased because the storekeeper is accountable for them. At a minimum, these cards contain quantity columns for receipts, issuances, and balance. A sample store card follows.

STORE CARD

| Item _____ | | | | | | | | | |
|---|---|---|---|---|---|---|---|---|---|
| | | Received | | | | Issued | | | Balance |
| Date | Reference | Quantity | Unit Cost | Total Cost | Quanity | Unit Cost | Total Cost | | |

**STORES**
1. raw materials, supplies, and parts.
2. control account for all purchases of materials and supplies. All purchases of materials, parts, and supplies are charged to Stores as purchased because the storekeeper is accountable for them. The Stores Control account is supported by an underlying subsidiary ledger, called STORE CARDS.
3. retail outlets.

**STORES REQUISITIONS** forms used to keep track of materials charged to a particular job or department. The form contains such items as job number, department, description of the material, quantity, unit cost, and dollar amount. A sample form follows.

STORES REQUISITION

| Job No. _____ | | Date _____ | |
|---|---|---|---|
| Department _____ | | | |
| Debit Account _____ | | | |
| Authorized By _____ | | | |
| Description | Quantity | Unit Cost | Amount |
| | | | |

**STRADDLE** to combine a CALL and PUT on the identical stock with the same expiration date and strike price. It is employed to take advantage of significant variability in stock price. High BETA (a measure of volatility) stocks might be most suited for this. A significant price movement on one side will cover the cost of obtaining the options.

**STRAIGHT-LINE DEPRECIATION** method providing equal depreciation charges for each period because it assumes *constant* benefit from the asset. It is the easiest and most popular method of computing depreciation expense. Straight-line depreciation expense equals cost less salvage value divided by life. Assume an auto having a five-year life was acquired for $13,000, with salvage value of $1,000. Depreciation expense per year is $2,400 [($13,000 − $1,000)/5].

**STRATEGIC ALLIANCE** agreement of two or more companies with complementary core competencies to jointly contribute to the VALUE CHAIN.

**STRATEGIC BUDGETING** *see* LONG-RANGE BUDGET.

**STRATEGIC COST MANAGEMENT** managerial use of cost information for the purpose(s) of establishing organizational strategy, controlling the success methods to achieve the strategies, and evaluating the level of success in meeting the proclaimed strategies.

*STRATEGIC FINANCE* a monthly publication (www.strategicfinancemag.com), published by the Institute of Management Accountants (IMA), dealing with leadership strategies in accounting, finance, and information management.

**STRATEGIC PLANNING** implementing an organization's objectives. In any organization, strategic planning occurs in two phases: (1) deciding on the products to produce and/or the services to render; (2) deciding on the marketing and/or manufacturing strategy to follow in getting the intended product or service to the proper audience. Strategic planning decisions will have long-term impacts on the organization while operational decisions are day-to-day in nature.

**STRATIFIED SAMPLING** method used to divide a population into homogeneous subgroups (strata). Each stratum is then sampled individually. The auditor may separately evaluate the sample results or may combine them to furnish an estimate of the characteristics of the total population. When very high- or low-value items are segregated into separate populations, each population is more homogeneous. A more representative sample can be derived from a relatively homogeneous population. Hence, fewer items need to be examined when several strata are examined separately than when the entire population is evaluated. Stratification improves the sampling process and enables auditors to relate sample selection to the materiality and turnover of items. Various audit procedures may be applied to each stratum, depending on the circumstances. An example of stratified sampling occurs when total accounts receivable (population) is divided into groups based on dollar balances for confirmation purposes. An illustration follows:

| Stratum | Method of Selection Used | Type of Confirmation |
|---|---|---|
| 1. All accounts of $100,000 or more | 100% confirmed | Positive |
| 2. All other accounts under $100,000 | Random number table selection | Positive |

Stratification may not be by dollar amount only but also by type of transaction and by transaction frequency. Stratification is suggested when the characteristic under audit examination varies materially within different portions of the population. This approach is employed typically in variables sampling and often in attributes sampling.

**STREET NAME** term used when securities are held in the name of a broker or other nominee rather than the investor. Because the broker is holding the securities, it is easier to make a transfer of them at the time of sale. If the stock were registered in the investor's name and physically held by him or her, transfer of shares would take longer.

**STRIKE PRICE** *see* EXERCISE PRICE.

**STRUCTURED QUERY LANGUAGE (SQL)** a programming language that is used for creating, updating, deleting, and reading data from a database. SQL is the standard database query language for virtually all databases, including Oracle, Microsoft SQL Server, Microsoft Access, and MySQL.

**SUBCHAPTER S CORPORATION** form of corporation whose stockholders may be taxed as partners. That is, income is taxed as direct income of the shareholders, regardless of whether it is actually distributed to them. To qualify as an S corporation, a company cannot have more than 100 shareholders; it cannot have more than one class of stock; it cannot have any nonresident foreigners as shareholders; and it must properly elect S corporation status. The key advantage of this form of organization is that the shareholders receive all the organizational benefit of a corporation while escaping the double taxation of a corporation.

**SUBJECTIVE PROBABILITY** estimate of the *relative frequency* of each of various future outcomes, based on the intuition or experience of the accountant making the estimate. Subjective probability is used in many business situations (i.e., estimating rates and/or dollar returns on investment decisions). Based on his or her experience, assume a treasurer is considering possible interest rates the company can expect to pay on bonds it intends to issue next week. The treasurer feels that interest rates can have only four possible values. The subjective assessment is as follows:

| Interest Rate | Probability This Will Happen |
|---------------|------------------------------|
| 9% | .2 |
| 9¼% | .3 |
| 9½% | .4 |
| 9¾% | .1 |

**SUBJECT MATTER** includes historical or prospective performance or condition (e.g., financial forecasts and projections), physical characteristics (e.g., square footage of a building), historical events (e.g., price of an item at a specified date), analyses (e.g., break-even analyses), systems or processes (e.g., internal control over financial reporting), and behavior (e.g., compliance with laws and regulations). *See also* ATTESTATION(ATTEST) ENGAGEMENTS.

**SUBLEASE** agreement in which the lessee contracts with a third party allowing the latter to use the lessee's right to the leased property. An example is the sublease of an apartment by the tenant to another party. If the lessee accounts under the operating lease method, the sublessee would also account under this method.

**SUBOPTIMIZATION** optimization of the goals of different departments of the entire organization. Suboptimization occurs when different subunits each attempt to reach a solution that is optimal for that unit, but that may not be optimum for the organization as a whole.

For example, the quality control department of a factory may want to introduce a program that will guarantee that every bulb that is produced is perfect. However, the higher cost and the resulting high price would lead to a disaster for the overall company in the form of lower sales.

**SUBORDINATED DEBT** securities that have a claim on the firm's assets only after the claims of holders of senior debt have been satisfied. The subordinated debt holder is in a much riskier position than the senior debt holders.

**SUBORDINATED SECURITY** *see* SUBORDINATED DEBT.

**SUBPRIME MORTGAGES** mortgages for people with credit scores that are under 620; also called *non-prime mortgages*. Many such homeowners found themselves unable to pay off their mortgages as interest rates rose and house values sank. *See also* TOXIC ASSETS.

**SUBSCRIBED STOCK** *see* CAPITAL STOCK SUBSCRIBED.

**SUBSCRIPTION**
1. agreement to purchase a security.
2. pledge to give a contribution to an organization for a cause (e.g., charity).

**SUBSEQUENT ACTIVITY** activity that receives service from another activity.

**SUBSEQUENT DISCOVERY OF FACTS** identification of matters after the issuance of an audit report. If the matters existed at the date of the audit report and are significant, the auditor should advise the client that the financial statements need to be recalled and modified. If the client refuses to do so, the auditor should take the appropriate legal action to recall the financial statements and advise actual and potential users of the financial statements that the audit report can no longer be relied upon.

**SUBSEQUENT EVENT** material happening occurring after the date of the financial statements but before the audit report is issued. Footnote disclosure is required so that financial statement users are properly informed. The subsequent event typically has a significant impact on financial position or earning capacity. Examples of subsequent events requiring disclosure are lawsuits, impairment of assets, and permanent decline in price of securities.

**SUBSIDIARY ACCOUNT** one of the accounts in a particular SUBSIDIARY LEDGER. The balance of all the subsidiary accounts should agree with the control account in the GENERAL LEDGER. An example is an individual customer's account (i.e., Mr. X) in the accounts receivable ledger of a department store. All the customer accounts should agree with the accounts receivable account in the general ledger.

**SUBSIDIARY COMPANY** firm in which a controlling interest is owned by another company, called the PARENT COMPANY. After acquisition, the parent company accounts for its investment in the subsidiary company including intercompany eliminations. *See also* CONSOLIDATION.

**SUBSIDIARY COMPANY ACCOUNTING** method undertaken by a subsidiary for the recording of its transactions with the parent. Subsidiary companies have separate books or accounting records. In theory, transactions between the subsidiary and parent should be accounted for in *arm's-length* terms. Even though each is a separate incorporated entity, consolidated financial statements are usually prepared for financial presentation purposes. Consequently, the subsidiary's assets and liabilities are combined with the parent. The common ownership aspect presents many difficulties in the fair and informative presentation of a consolidated entity's financial condition for reporting and tax purposes.

**SUBSIDIARY LEDGER** supporting ledger of related accounts that in total equals the control account appearing in the GENERAL LEDGER. Examples are individual creditor accounts agreeing with accounts payable (creditors' ledger) and individual factory overhead items such as factory rent and factory insurance agreeing with the factory overhead account (factory overhead ledger).

**SUBSTANTIVE PROCEDURES** performed by an auditor in order to identify material misstatements in financial statement amounts and disclosures. Substantive procedures enable an auditor to obtain the sufficient appropriate audit evidence needed to provide the auditor with a reasonable basis for his or her opinion about the fairness of the financial statement presentation. The two types of substantive procedures are (1) tests of details of account balances, classes of transactions, and disclosure items, and (2) substantive analytical procedures. The first type of substantive procedures is required in an audit, while the second type is discretionary. Tests of details of transactions may be performed continually throughout the year under audit or at or close to the balance sheet date. When the CPA traces a sales invoice from the sales journal to the ledger for correctness, it is considered a test of details of transactions. When the CPA compares the book balance (i.e., recorded amount) of cash to the bank reconciliation, it is considered a test of details of account balances. Comparing recorded interest expense to recorded corporate debt is an example of a substantive analytical procedure. *See also* TESTS OF DETAILS.

**SUBSYSTEM** component of a larger system. For example, the financial, marketing, accounting, and production systems are subsystems or components of a MANAGEMENT INFORMATION SYSTEM (MIS).

**SUCCESSFUL EFFORTS ACCOUNTING** method of accounting for exploration costs by companies in the extractive industries, especially oil and gas. Expenditures for successful projects are deferred while those for unsuccessful ones are immediately expensed. Capitalized costs applicable to producing properties are amortized based on the reserves produced. *See also* FULL COST METHOD.

**SUCCESSOR AUDITOR** external auditor of a company who displaces the PREDECESSOR AUDITOR.

**SUMMARY FINANCIAL STATEMENTS** derived from audited financial statements, but include less detail. An auditor may express an opinion on summary financial statements provided the auditor did not issue an adverse opinion or disclaimer of opinion on the audited financial statements. Also referred to as *condensed financial statements*.

**SUMMARY OF SIGNIFICANT ACCOUNTING POLICIES** a required description of all significant accounting policies used by the entity. The summary is typically the first or second note to the financial statements. Alternatively, the summary may be placed after the basic financial statements and before the notes to the financial statements.

**SUM-OF-THE-YEARS'-DIGITS (SYD) METHOD** accelerated depreciation method in which the amounts recognized in the early periods of an asset's useful life are greater than those recognized in the later periods. The SYD is found by estimating an asset's useful life in years, assigning consecutive numbers to each year, and totaling these numbers. For $n$ years, the short-cut formula for summing these numbers is $SYD = n(n + 1)/2$. The yearly depreciation is then calculated by multiplying the total depreciable amount for the asset's useful life by a fraction whose numerator is the remaining useful life and whose denominator is the SYD. Thus annual depreciation equals

$$(\text{Original Cost} - \text{Salvage Value}) \times \frac{\text{Remaining Useful Life}}{\text{SYD}}$$

For example, assume that an asset costs $1000 and has an estimated useful life of five years. The estimated salvage value at the end of the five-year period is $100. The SYD is $5(5 + 1)/2 = 15$. The calculations for this example are shown below:

| Year | Fraction | | | Depreciation |
|------|----------|---|---|--------------|
| 1 | 5/15 | × | $900 = | $300 |
| 2 | 4/15 | × | 900 = | 240 |
| 3 | 3/15 | × | 900 = | 180 |
| 4 | 2/15 | × | 900 = | 120 |
| 5 | 1/15 | × | 900 = | 60 |
| | | | Total | $900 |

**SUNK COST** costs incurred in the past whose total will not be affected by any decision made now or in the future. Sunk costs are usually past or historical costs. For example, suppose a machine acquired for $50,000 three years ago has a book value of $20,000. The $20,000 book value is a sunk cost that does not affect a future decision involving its replacement.

**SUPERABSORPTION COSTING** costing method treating costs from all links in the value chain as an inventory cost.

**SUPERCOMPUTER** data processing machine designed to be significantly larger and/or faster than the typical mainframe computer. It can process both scalar and vector quantities. It handles many thousands of operations simultaneously. Supercomputers can perform billions of additions per second. An example is the Cyberplus parallel processor.

**SUPERVARIABLE COSTING** treats only direct materials as the only variable cost.

**SUPPLEMENTARY STATEMENT** schedules or statements that amplify, elaborate on, or detail the income statement, balance sheet, and statement of changes in financial position. An example is inflation-adjusted statements.

**SUPPLIERS' MANAGEMENT** the careful selection of suppliers and the cultivation of long-term relationships based on the consistent ability to meet mutual expectations.

**SUPPLY CHAIN** interdependent collection of organizations that supply materials, products, or services to a customer.

**SUPPLY CHAIN MANAGEMENT** managing the "virtual" enterprise composed of suppliers and customers. Collaborative behavior will lead to streamlined business processes and mutual benefits.

**SUPPLY CHAIN MANAGEMENT (SCM) SOFTWARE** software that facilitates supply chain management function seamlessly. SCM is the organization of activities between a company and its suppliers in an effort to provide for the profitable development, production, and delivery of goods to customers. As a result of information sharing, production lead times and inventory holding costs have been reduced, and on-time deliveries to customers have been improved. SCM software systems support the planning of the best way to fill orders and help tracking of products and components among companies in the supply chain.

**SUPPORT COSTS** costs of activities not directly associated with production. Examples are the costs of process engineering and purchasing.

**SURETY** a promise by one party to assume responsibility for the debt of a borrower in the event of the borrower's default. The party that provides this promise is also known as a surety or guarantor.

**SURPLUS**
1. earned surplus or RETAINED EARNINGS reflecting the accumulated net income less dividend distributions.
2. CAPITAL SURPLUS, the stockholders' equity in a corporation in excess of par or stated value of capital stock.

**SURROGATE ACTIVITY DRIVER** activity driver that is not descriptive of an activity, but that is closely correlated to the performance of the activity. The use of a surrogate activity driver should reduce measurement costs without significantly increasing the costing bias. The number of production runs, for example, is not descriptive of the material-disbursing activity, but the number of production runs may be used as an activity driver if material disbursements coincide with production runs.

**SURROGATE COST DRIVER** acceptable substitute for a cost driver. It is used because the driver cannot be easily measured.

**SURTAX** additional tax applied to income above some specified figure resulting in a higher effective tax rate. *See also* MAXIMUM TAX.

**SURVIVING COMPANY** in a BUSINESS COMBINATION, the one that acquires the net assets and continues the operations of the predecessor company. The surviving company may be a newly organized entity or a previously existing business.

**SURVIVING SPOUSE** wife or husband who survives the other. A surviving spouse is entitled to the income-splitting advantages permitted on joint tax returns if the spouse died during either of the two taxable years before the current taxable year. Also, the surviving spouse must have a dependent child at home and not have remarried. All amounts paid to a beneficiary of a life insurance policy at a date after the insured's death (i.e., an annuity) are included in gross income to the degree the amount is greater than the amount payable as a death benefit.

**SUSPENSE ACCOUNT** temporary account (i.e., not included in the financial statements) for recording part of a transaction, such as those involving receipts or disbursements, prior to final analysis or identification of that transaction.

**SUSTAINING ACTIVITY COST** cost of an activity that benefits the organization but is not caused by any specific supplier, product, service, or customer cost object. Examples of such activities are preparation of financial statements, plant management, and support of community programs.

**SWAP CONTRACT** involves an agreement between two parties to exchange future cash payments. Swap contracts may involve interest rate swaps, currency swaps, commodity swaps, or equity swaps.

**SWING LOAN** *see* BRIDGE LOAN.

**SYNDICATE** temporary association of investment bankers brought together for the purpose of selling securities; also called *purchase group*. One investment banker in the group, usually the originating house, is selected to manage the syndicate. There are two types of underwriting syndicates, divided and undivided. In a *divided* account, the liability of each member investment banker is limited in terms of participation. Once a member sells the securities assigned, that investment banker has no additional liability regardless of whether the other members are able to sell their portion of the security or not. In an *undivided* account, each member is liable for unsold securities up to the amount of its percentage participation irrespective of the number of securities that investment banker has sold. Most syndicates are based on the undivided account arrangement.

**SYSTEMATIC RANDOM SELECTION** *see* SYSTEMATIC SAMPLING.

**SYSTEMATIC SAMPLING** sampling approach used in auditing. In a population of $n$ units and a desired sample of $s$ units, the auditor selects every $r$th unit ($n/s$) systematically beginning at a random point among the first $r$ units in the population. In the case where a population is not in numerical sequence, it is easier to choose a systematic random sample instead of a pure random sample. If documents or transactions are unnumbered, no need exists with this approach to number them physically, as would be the case with random number table selection. Instead, with systematic sampling the auditor counts off the sampling interval to choose the documents. Some audit software packages have routines for systematic selection purposes. A problem with this sampling approach is that every $r$th unit may correspond to an existing sequence in the population, so sample items are continually selected from the same part of a recurring pattern. Assume the auditor is examining 500 paid checks from a total population of 15,000 checks. One random starting point is used. The auditor will select every 30th check (15,000/500). So that 500 checks may be chosen, the auditor goes upward or downward from their random starting point. Assume a random starting point of check number 80. Therefore, check numbers 50 (80 − 30) and 20 (80 − 60) are includable in the sample, as well as every 30th check number subsequent to number 80 (i.e., 110, 140, etc.). If the auditor chose 10 random starting points, 50 checks (500/10) would be chosen from each random start. Hence, the auditor would pick every 300th check number (15,000/50) prior to and subsequent to each of the random starting points.

**SYSTEMIC RISK** the risk that an entire financial system could collapse. Systemic risk might be based on an economic crisis that results in financial system instability.

**SYSTEM PROGRAM** product of the computer manufacturer to aid the user in easily and productively operating the system. *See also* OPERATING SYSTEM.

**SYSTEMS ANALYST** one who is engaged in systems analysis involving identification, measurement, and recommendation of system alternatives to management for final selection. After an intensive investigation of the information needs of the different levels of management, the systems analyst should identify the available system alternatives. These include: (1) acquisition of a new system; (2) modification of the old system; and (3) use of a third party's services, such as a timeshare outside service bureau, which could eliminate or continue the use of the old system. For each available alternative, feasibility studies should be conducted before a recommendation is made to management for final selection.

**SYSTEM WEAKNESS** inadequate internal controls in the client's accounting system resulting in a higher risk environment. The auditor must expand the audit procedures and techniques when internal control is weak.

**SYSTRUST** a type of trust service that addresses the risks and opportunities of an information technology system. Systrust engagements are governed by STATEMENTS ON STANDARDS FOR ATTESTATION ENGAGEMENTS (SSAE).

# T

**T-ACCOUNT** common accounting form in the shape of the capital letter T. It has the following components: (1) a title describing the particular financial statement item (e.g., sales revenue), (2) a left side referred to as a DEBIT, and (3) a right side called a CREDIT. There is a separate T-account for each item in the ledger. A T-account looks as follows:

**Account Name**

| Debit | Credit |
|-------|--------|

**TAG** in markup languages such as HTML and XML, notation used to define a data element for display or other purposes.

**TAGUCHI METHOD OF QUALITY CONTROL** a method of controlling quality, developed by Genich Taguchi, a past winner of the Deming Award, that emphasizes robust quality design and the *quality loss function* (QLF). Taguchi claims that quality is greatly determined at the design level. In addition to quality control in production, he emphasizes quality control in four other functions: (1) product planning, (2) product design, (3) process design, and (4) production service after purchase. Further, Taguchi's QLF quantitatively measures the success or failure of quality control. The traditional view is that any product that measures within the upper and lower specification limits is "good," and a product outside the limits is "bad." In contrast, the QLF presumes that *any* deviation from the target specification is important because it means economic losses for the customer. Furthermore, the economic losses increase quadratically as the actual value deviates from the target value.

**TAKE-HOME PAY** *see* DISPOSABLE INCOME.

**TAKEOVER** form of acquisition usually followed by a merger. Takeover can be hostile or friendly. The public TENDER OFFER is a means of acquiring a target firm against the wishes of management. In a friendly takeover the acquiring firm negotiates with the targeted company, and common agreement is reached in an amiable atmosphere for subsequent approval by shareholders. *See also* MERGER; PROXY FIGHTS (BATTLES).

**TALF PROGRAM** *see* TERM ASSET-BACKED LOAN FACILITY (TALF) PROGRAM.

**TAKEOVER TAX TREATMENT** implications based on the terms of a takeover by one company of another. The tax effects will differ depending on the method used to account for the business combination.

**TANGIBLE ASSET** one having physical substance and a life greater than one year. It is not held for resale in the ordinary course of business. Examples are machinery, furniture, and building.

**TARGET COST** *see* STANDARD COST.

**TARGET COSTING** method used in the analysis of product design that involves estimating a target cost, via a desired profit and sales price, and then designing the product/service to meet that cost. This method precedes KAIZEN costing. The Japanese concept of Kaizen is relevant to target costing. A policy of seeking continuous improvement in all phases of company activities facilitates cost reduction, often through numerous minor changes.

**TARGET INCOME** amount of income an organization is trying to achieve during a particular period. The specification of target income may be based upon a desired rate of return on invested money (for example, 20% return on investment) or a growth in earnings per share (EPS). The target income may be also specified as a percentage of sales (for example, 15% of sales).

**TARGET INCOME SALES** amount required to attain a particular income level or target net income. TARGET INCOME sales volume is computed as:

$$\text{Target Income Sales Volume} = \frac{\text{Fixed Costs} + \text{Target Income}}{\text{Unit Contribution Margin}}$$

For example, assume that unit contribution margin is $15, fixed costs are $15,000, and target income is $15,000. Target income sales volume = ($15,000 + $15,000)/$15 = 2,000 units. This means that 2,000 units need to be sold to make $15,000 profit.

**TARGET PRICE** expected market price for a product, given the company's knowledge of its customers and competitors.

**TARGET PRICING** a pricing method that involves (1) identifying the price at which a product will be competitive in the marketplace, (2) defining the desired profit to be made on the product, and (3) computing the target cost for the product by subtracting the desired profit from the competitive market price. The formula

$$\text{Target Price} - \text{Desired Profit} = \text{Target Cost}$$

Target cost is then given to the engineers and product designers, who use it as the maximum cost to be incurred for the materials and other resources needed to design and manufacture the product. It is their responsibility to create the product at or below its target cost.

**TARIFF**
1. tax on imports or exports, most often calculated as a percent of the price charged for the good by the foreign supplier. The money collected is *duty*. A tariff may be imposed as a source of revenue for the government. A more common purpose of tariffs is protection against foreign competition. By raising prices of imported goods

relative to the prices of domestic goods, tariffs encourage consumers to buy domestic rather than foreign products.

**2.** schedule of rates or fares in the transportation industry.

**TARP** *see* TROUBLED ASSET RELIEF PROGRAM (TARP).

**TAX** charge imposed by a governmental body on personal income, corporate income, estates, gifts, or other sources to obtain revenue for the public good. Tax filing and payment are legally enforceable.

**TAXABLE INCOME**
**Individual:** ADJUSTED GROSS INCOME (AGI) less itemized deductions and PERSONAL EXEMPTIONS. After taxable income is derived, the tax to be paid can be determined by looking at the tax rate schedules.
**Corporation:** gross income less allowable business deductions.

*TAX ADVISOR, THE* monthly journal published by the AMERICAN INSTITUTE OF CERTIFIED PUBLIC ACCOUNTANTS (AICPA) designed primarily for CPAs, attorneys, and tax executives. All major areas of taxation of interest to practitioners are covered including their practical applications. Theoretical discussion of federal tax law sometimes appears.

**TAX ALLOCATION** *see* INTERPERIOD INCOME TAX ALLOCATION.

**TAX ANTICIPATION BILL (TAB)** short-term obligation issued by the U.S. Treasury to raise funds during a period when tax receipts are not large enough to cover current disbursements. TABs mature approximately one week after quarterly corporate tax payments are due. The attractiveness of TABs is that the government will accept them in payment for taxes at their face value.

**TAX ANTICIPATION NOTE (TAN)** short-term debt instrument issued by a municipality in order to raise funds to cover shortages prior to tax receipts. TAN debt is retired once individual and corporate tax revenues are received.

**TAX AVOIDANCE** payment of the least tax possible by using legal tax planning opportunities such as estate planning. Engaging in tax avoidance measures is not in any way construed as betraying or shirking a public or patriotic duty. In fact, a majority of court decisions have supported this assertion. TAX EVASION, in contrast, utilizes illegal methods to achieve this end.

**TAX BENEFIT RULE** Internal Revenue Service provision stating that amounts received in one period, representing a recovery of an amount deducted in a prior year, are to be included in income to the extent that the prior deduction resulted in a decrease in taxable income in that year.

**TAX COURT** U.S. administrative court where judges handle cases of dispute between the taxpayer and the Internal Revenue Service. No jury trials are available. Taxpayers must file a petition to the court within 90 days of receiving a statutory deficiency notice. Areas decided on by the court include estate, gift, and federal income taxes. The court findings are reported generally in writing and are open to public inspection.

**TAX CREDIT** reduction in taxes payable to the Internal Revenue Service or local government. A tax credit is more beneficial to the taxpayer than an itemized deduction because it reduces taxes on a dollar-for-dollar basis.

**TAX DEED** document evidencing the passage of title to a purchaser of property sold for taxes. The tax deed is issued upon foreclosure of the property lien. Typically, there is a grace time period permitting the owner to make good on the delinquent taxes in order to redeem the property.

**TAX EFFECT**
1. general term describing the consequences of a specific tax scenario with respect to a particular tax-paying entity. Many factors are considered such as time elements, projections and estimates of revenues, expenses, deductions, acquisitions, disposals, and the like and their relationship upon present and future tax liability.
2. impact on taxes of a taxable revenue or expense item. For instance, an interest expense itemized deduction of $2,000 will result in tax savings of $560 at the 28% tax bracket.

**TAX ELECTION** choice of an option or options with respect to tax treatments of specified situations, transactions, report form, and timing of reports. Some elections must have the Commissioner's approval, such as certain changes in accounting method, and some may be done without approval, on an annual basis, such as the filing of a joint tax return.

**TAX EQUITY AND FISCAL RESPONSIBILITY ACT OF 1982 (TEFRA)** legislation notably involving accelerating estimated tax payments by corporations, restricting the medical deduction, and establishing 10% withholding on interest and dividends. The Act repealed *safe-harbor* leasing.

**TAX EVASION** failure to pay taxes legally due a governmental agency. Examples are failure to report income received and claiming of fictitious deductions. There is a penalty for tax fraud based on the underpayment of tax. Criminal prosecution also may apply. *See also* TAX AVOIDANCE.

**TAX-EXEMPT BOND** security whose interest is not subject to federal or local tax in the state of the issuer. Though often called a *municipal bond*, it may also be issued by a county, state, or state agency. For example, a New York City resident does not pay federal, state, or city tax on the interest received from a New York City obligation. It is triple tax-free, though this is not necessarily true of other states. An investor in a mutual fund that invests solely in tax-exempt bonds often pays no tax on interest earned. However, some states tax fund dividends. The return on a tax-exempt bond is equivalent to a higher return on a taxable corporate bond because of the tax savings. The dollar advantage of a tax-exempt security increases as the tax rate rises. Assume a taxpayer in the 35% tax bracket receives 6% on a tax-exempt bond. The equivalent taxable yield on a corporate bond is 9.23% (6%/.65). It should be noted, however, that the holder of a tax-exempt security *does* have to pay tax on the gain at the time of sale representing the difference between the cost and the selling price. For example: An investor buys a $1,000, 5% tax-exempt bond for 90%. The cost is therefore $900. The taxpayer will be taxed on the gain of $100 in the year the bond is redeemed.

**TAX-FREE EXCHANGE** transfers of assets or property from one taxpayer to another that are specifically exempted from federal income tax consequences. Examples are exchanges of property or assets to certain corporate entities in which ownership of transferred assets are still maintained; a controlled corporation (Section 351) or like-kind exchanges under Section 1031. In the year of exchange, there is no recognized gain or loss. However, there is an adjustment to basis of the assets received in the transfer, in effect deferring the gain upon future disposition.

**TAX HAVEN** foreign country providing significant, permanent tax breaks to individuals and companies operating within it. In a tax haven country, foreigners may receive income or own assets and pay very low taxes. Many companies are situated or have subsidiaries in tax havens for TAX AVOIDANCE reasons. There are two objectives for establishing a subsidiary in a tax haven: (1) a subsidiary can operate as a legitimate operation and generate profits while simultaneously enjoying the tax advantages; and (2) a parent may establish a subsidiary in a tax haven for the purpose of tax avoidance only. The major purpose is to shift income from a country with high taxes to a tax haven country by using a subsidiary as an intermediary.

**TAX INDEXING** method using a form of INDEXATION to decrease the overall impact of the erosion of purchasing power in periods of inflation and subsequent "bracket creep."

**TAX LIEN** governmental agency claim to a taxpayer's property for delinquent or overdue taxes. Tax assessment, demand, and refusal to pay effectively create the lien. The tax lien may on occasion attach to property held by a third-party transferee. When full taxes are paid, the lien ceases.

**TAX ON SCHOLARSHIPS OR FELLOWSHIPS** charges levied on grants received by a degree candidate at a university. An exclusion is available only for amounts used for tuition, fees, and course-related costs. This exclusion does *not* apply to amounts paid for teaching, research, or other related services. Thus funds received for scholarships and fellowships are includable in gross income for tax purposes except for those directly related to pursuing a degree.

**TAX PLANNING** systematic analysis of differing tax options aimed at the minimization of tax liability in current and future tax periods. Whether to file jointly or separately, the timing of a sale of an asset, ascertaining over how many years to withdraw retirement funds, when to receive income, when to pay expenditures, the timing and amounts of gifts to be made, and ESTATE PLANNING are examples of tax planning. TAX SOFTWARE can be used for tax-planning purposes.

**TAX PREFERENCE ITEM** certain items defined under Section 57 of the Internal Revenue Code that may result in the imposition of the ALTERNATIVE MINIMUM TAX (AMT). These items of otherwise exempt income or deductions or of special tax benefit were targeted to ensure that taxpayers who benefit should pay at least a minimum amount of tax. Items include tax-exempt interest on nonessential municipal bonds and contributions of appreciated property.

**TAX RATE** amount of tax to be paid based on taxable income. The tax rate typically changes as the unit of the tax base changes.
**Individual:** tax rate depends on whether the tax return is for a single filer, joint filer, or head of household.
**Corporation:** the maximum tax rate is 35%.

**TAX RATE SCHEDULE** schedule used to determine the tax on a given taxable income. The marginal tax rate typically increases as the taxable income rises.

**TAX REFORM** federal law making changes to the tax provisions, including filing requirements, income reporting, allowable deductions, tax credits, and tax rates.

**TAX RETURN** general name of the form used to file taxes payable to a federal or local government. Included on the tax return are such items as gross income, allowable deductions, tax credits, and tax due. Individual taxpayers file on a calendar-year basis using Form 1040, which is due 3½ months after the tax year. Corporations can file Form 1120 on a calendar-year or fiscal-year basis. It is due 2½ months after the tax year. Tax returns are also prepared for partnerships (Form 1065), estates (Form 706), and gifts (Form 709).

**TAX SHELTER** investments, typically in limited partnerships, that can protect or defer (shelter) a portion of income from current taxes. Passive losses can be applied only to passive income. Usually, a significant amount of capital along with a very high amount of debt is necessary. Allowable deductions are generally permitted only to the amount *at-risk*. A tax shelter is desired by taxpayers in high tax brackets so they can take the losses from it to reduce their taxable income. Examples of tax shelters are real estate and oil and gas. Other permissible tax shelters are tax-exempt municipal obligations and single-premium life insurance policies. For failing to register a tax shelter there is a penalty of 1% of the aggregate amount invested, with no maximum. Failure to report a tax shelter identification number is $250. Penalties for shelters deemed abusive can be staggering. Tax shelters have been *greatly restricted*. *See also* AT-RISK RULES.

**TAX SHIELD** deductions that result in a reduction of income tax payments. The tax shield is computed by multiplying the deduction by the tax rate itself. For example, assume an annual depreciation deduction is $3,000 and the tax rate is 40%; the tax shield, or tax savings on depreciation is $3,000 × .4 = $1,200. The company saves $1,200 annually in taxes from the depreciation deduction. The higher the deduction, the larger the tax shield. Therefore, an accelerated depreciation method produces higher tax savings than the straight line method. Note that the term applies to other non-cash charges (e.g., amortization and depletion) as well.

**TAX SOFTWARE** tax modules that prepare federal and state returns and TAX PLANNING modules for corporations, partnerships, individuals, and estates and trusts. A microcomputer—with its ability to store large amounts of data that can be manipulated at tremendous rates of speed—performs many of the mechanical and repetitive tasks involved in income tax return preparation. For example, Turbo Tax prepares individual, corporate, partnership, fiduciary, and deferred compensation tax returns. Tax-planning software essentially performs spreadsheet *what-if* tax scenarios.

**TAX YEAR** period that a tax return covers. Taxpayers file on a calendar-year basis unless another accounting period has been chosen. A fiscal-year basis referring to any other one-year interval can also be selected. If a tax year is to be changed, approval must be received from the Internal Revenue Service. A new company or estate may employ any allowable tax year, but a new partnership has to use the same period employed by the major partners.

**TCP/IP** *see* TRANSFER CONTROL PROTOCOL/INTERNET PROTOCOL.

**TECHNICAL ANALYSIS** means of predicting stock prices based on historical price and trading patterns; it is not concerned with the financial statistics that are the focus of FUNDAMENTAL ANALYSIS. It uses charts (e.g., head and shoulders, rising bottoms) to identify trends in the market or individual securities. Technical analysts believe the market can be predicted in terms of direction and magnitude. Stock prices tend to move with the market because they react to various demand and supply forces. An attempt is made to uncover a consistent pattern in prices or a relationship between stock price changes and other market data. Technical analysts try to predict short-term price changes and then recommend the timing of a purchase or sale. A sample company stock chart follows:

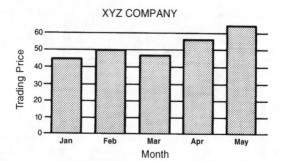

**XYZ COMPANY**

**TECHNOLOGY COSTS** category of cost associated with the development, acquisition, implementation, and maintenance of technology assets. It can include costs such as the depreciation of research equipment, tooling amortization, maintenance, and software development.

**TEFRA** *see* TAX EQUITY AND FISCAL RESPONSIBILITY ACT OF 1982 (TEFRA).

**TELECOMMUNICATIONS** transmission of data between computers at different locations. Data are typically sent over telephone lines, but radio waves and satellites are also used. A computer with a communications board (RS-232C Serial Port), telecommunications software, and modem are needed for communication; a terminal may also be used. Software is required to communicate between computers within the firm, for time-sharing situations, and for accessing commercial databases. Software also aids in the manipulation of information coming over the modem. Communications packages usually reserve some of the computer memory as a buffer. Information is placed in the capture buffer, awaiting future disposition (saving to disk or printing the information). Alternatively, one can load data from a disk into the buffer for uploading to another computer in ASCII if a synchronous communication is used. Information handling functions are the core of the telecommunications program. Some communications programs do error checking of information received (i.e., XModem Protocol). Communications software permits CPAs in different geographic areas to communicate with each other by electronic mail or to transfer data files and documents between offices. Bulletin boards can be established by CPAs to share up-to-date accounting and auditing information with their clients.

**TEMPLATE**
1. mechanical aid in drawing flowcharts and flowchart symbols.
2. worksheet that includes the relevant formulas for a particular application but not the data. It is a blank worksheet on which data are saved and filled in as needed for a future accounting application. Templates are guides for preparing the spreadsheet. They are predefined files, including cell formulas and row or column labels for

specific applications. In effect, they are worksheet models designed to solve specific types of problems. Templates allow for the referencing of cells and formulations of interrelated formulas and functions. They are reused to analyze similar transactions.

**TEMPORARILY RESTRICTED NET ASSETS** funds whose use is restricted by outside parties until some event occurs. For example, a not-for-profit organization may have received donated assets that are restricted by the donor until some time period has elapsed.

**TEMPORARY ACCOUNT** account that does not appear on the balance sheet; also called NOMINAL ACCOUNT. Revenue and expense accounts, along with income distribution accounts (such as dividend) are temporary accounts. The balances in all temporary accounts are transferred to the capital or the retained earnings account, leaving the temporary accounts with zero balances. This procedure, called *closing*, is necessary to determine a periodic net income (or loss) and prepare books for the next period.

**TEMPORARY DIFFERENCE** *see* INTERPERIOD INCOME TAX ALLOCATION.

**TEMPORARY INVESTMENTS** strategy of using seasonal excess of cash to invest in marketable securities that the company intends to convert back into cash within one year. The investments produce dividend and/or interest income as well as possible capital appreciation for the company. Temporary investments are considered short-term investments and are classified as current assets under the MARKETABLE SECURITY heading on the balance sheet.

**TENDER OFFER** bid to buy the stock of a firm at a specified price (usually at a premium over the market price). The objective of a tender offer is to take control of the *target company*. Sometimes the offer is submitted for approval to the board of directors of the target company, or the offer may be made directly to the shareholders of the company. The SEC requires that any corporate suitor accumulating 5% or more of a target company make disclosures to the SEC, the target company, and the pertaining exchange. *See also* TAKEOVER.

**10-K** annual filing with the SECURITIES AND EXCHANGE COMMISSION (SEC) for publicly traded companies. Financial statements and supporting details are provided. Form 10-K typically contains more financial information than the annual report to stockholders. Audited basic financial statements are included. Examples of disclosures are sales, operating income, segmental sales by major line of business for the last five years, and general business information.

**10-Q** quarterly filing with the SECURITIES AND EXCHANGE COMMISSION (SEC) by publicly traded companies. It contains interim financial statements and related disclosures and may cover one particular quarter or be cumulative. It should present comparative figures for the same period of the prior year. The statements may or may not be audited. Form 10-Q is less comprehensive than Form 10-K.

**TERM ASSET-BACKED LOAN FACILITY (TALF) PROGRAM** a program created by the U.S. Federal Reserve Board, announced on November 25, 2008. The facility will support the issuance of asset-backed securities (ABS) collateralized by student loans, auto loans, credit card loans, and loans guaranteed by the Small Business Administration (SBA). Under the TALF, the Federal Reserve Bank of New York (FRBNY) will lend up to $1 trillion on a non-recourse basis to holders of certain AAA-rated ABS backed by newly and recently originated consumer and small business loans.

**TERM BOND** issue whose component bonds mature at the same time. *See also* SERIAL BONDS.

**TERMINATION BENEFITS** amounts due employees who cease to work for the employer. The amount of the termination benefit may be in the form of an ANNUITY or *lump-sum payment*. The termination benefit may arise from lay-off of TERMINATION IN PENSION PLANS.

**TERMINATION IN PENSION PLAN** termination benefits may either be special, offered only for a short time period, or contractual, required by the terms of the plan in a specific event such as a plant closing. Loss and liability should be recognized for special termination benefits when employees accept the offer and the amount can be reasonably estimated. The entry when "early retirement payoff" occurs is to debit loss and credit estimated liability equal to the current payment plus discounted value of termination benefits. *See also* CURTAILMENT IN PENSION PLAN; SETTLEMENT IN PENSION PLAN.

**TERM LOANS** intermediate- to long-term (typically, two- to ten-year) business loans with provisions for systematic repayments (amortization during the life of the loan). The repayment or amortization schedule is a particularly important feature of such loans. Amortization protects both the lender and borrower against the possibility that the borrower will not make adequate provisions for retirement of the loan during its life. The term loan sometimes ends with a *balloon* payment.

**TESTCHECK** substantiation of certain items in an account or financial record so the auditor can form an opinion as to the accuracy of the entire account or financial record. The items examined can be based on a representative sample. An example is testchecking every fifth entertainment expense voucher for supporting documentation and approval.

**TESTDECK** in computer applications, body of test data processed by a program that compares computerized results with predetermined manual results. If the two agree, computer processing of information is being performed properly. If not, the program has not been implemented in accordance with the documentation. The testdeck procedure is an audit control mechanism.

**TEST OF TRANSACTION** auditing procedure related to examining specified transactions and supporting documentation. It is part of the testing process used by the auditor to check internal-controls reliability. It is undertaken to gather evidence so that an audit opinion can be rendered as to the fairness of financial statement presentation. Included in such a test is verifying transaction amounts and tracing transactions to accounts in the financial statements. Transaction tests are of a much more limited scope than ANALYTICAL REVIEW. In transaction tests, a selected number of specific transactions are tested to see if controls are performing properly. A resulting error rate for complying with the procedures is established. Based on the rate of error, auditors determine if they can rely on the information developed from posting or recording transactions. The test helps auditors determine the scope of audit work. *See also* COMPLIANCE TEST; SUBSTANTIVE TEST.

**TESTS OF CONTROLS** procedures performed by an auditor to evaluate the effectiveness of the operation of an entity's internal controls. When performing tests of controls, an auditor is concerned with how controls were performed, when controls were performed, by whom controls were performed, and how consistently controls were performed. Tests of controls include inquiry, observation, inspection, and transaction walkthroughs. Tests of controls are required in (1) integrated audits of issuers, and (2) audits of nonissuers when the auditor wants to base the risk of material misstatement on effective internal controls.

**TESTS OF CONTROLS THROUGH THE COMPUTER** test of a client's controls over internal control may take the form of the test data (deck) method or the parallel simulation method. In the former, the auditor uses test data to examine the controls and procedures embodied in the client's program. Here, the auditor is not testing the client's data files. Under the parallel simulation method, the auditor uses parallel simulation as part of testing the controls related to internal control. Actual client data are reprocessed with the auditor's simulation of the client program. It creates a simulated client output. The major purpose of parallel simulation is to insure that unauthorized changes have not been made by the client's program.

**TESTS OF DETAILS** the type of substantive procedures applied to account balances, classes of transactions, and disclosure items to obtain audit evidence that the amounts and disclosures in the financial statements are fairly stated.

**THEORETICAL CAPACITY** *see* CAPACITY; IDEAL CAPACITY.

**THEORETICAL SUBSTANCE** theory in which substance rules over legal form in financial accounting; also called *substance over form*. Examples are the inclusion of common stock equivalents in the earnings-per-share calculation even though such securities are not legally common stock at the present time, and treating a CAPITAL LEASE as an asset even though the property is not legally owned by the lessee.

**THEORY OF CONSTRAINTS** approach to continuous improvement (reducing operating expenses and inventory and increasing throughput) based on a five-step procedure: (1) identifying constraints, (2) exploiting the binding constraints, (3) subordinating everything else to the decisions made in the second step, (4) increasing capacity of the binding constraints, and (5) repeating the process when new binding constraints are identified. It seeks to identify a company's constraints or bottlenecks and exploit them so that throughput is maximized and inventories and operating costs are minimized.

**THOSE CHARGED WITH GOVERNANCE** the individuals who are responsible for overseeing the strategic direction and obligations of an entity, including the financial reporting process. Those charged with governance include the audit committee and the board of directors.

**THREE-SIGMA LIMITS** three STANDARD DEVIATIONS from the mean, used as the upper and lower control limits, in STATISTICAL QUALITY CONTROL charts. There are about three chances in one thousand that a variation that falls outside the control limits will be only random in character.

**THREE-WAY ANALYSIS** computation of three variances for factory overhead: *spending, efficiency*, and *volume* variances. The budget variance in the TWO-WAY ANALYSIS is separated into spending and efficiency variances. When an analysis of historical costs permits the estimation of variable and fixed overhead, but the accounting records do not allow the separation of actual overhead costs into their variable and fixed elements, this three-way analysis of overhead variance is used. The three-way analysis provides the following reconciliation between actual and applied overhead:

| Actual (1) | Flexible (2) budget | Flexible (3) budget | Applied (4) costs |
|---|---|---|---|
| Actual Factory Overhead Costs | (AH × SR) for Variable + Budgeted Fixed Overhead Costs | (SH × SR) for Variable + Budgeted Fixed Overhead Costs | (SH × SR) for Variable + Fixed Overhead Rate × Activity Allowed |
| | Spending Variances (1–2) | Efficiency Variances (2–3) | Volume Variances (3–4) |
| | Budget Variance (1–3) | | Volume Variance (3–4) |

where AH = actual hours used, SH = standard hours allowed, and SR = standard overhead rate.

**THROUGHPUT** rate of production of a defined process over a stated period of time. Throughput can be measured in either financial or nonfinancial terms (for example, cash flows generated from selling products or services to customers, units of products, batches produced, dollar turnover, or other meaningful measurements. Components of throughput include MANUFACTURING CYCLE EFFICIENCY, process productivity, and process quality yield.

$$\text{Throughput} = \begin{matrix}\text{Manufacturing} \\ \text{Cycle Efficiency}\end{matrix} \times \begin{matrix}\text{Process} \\ \text{Productivity}\end{matrix} \times \begin{matrix}\text{Process} \\ \text{Quality Yield}\end{matrix}$$

$$\frac{\text{Good Units}}{\text{Total Time}} = \frac{\begin{matrix}\text{Value-Added}\\\text{Processing Time}\end{matrix}}{\text{Total Time}} \times \frac{\text{Total Units}}{\begin{matrix}\text{Value-Added}\\\text{Processing Time}\end{matrix}} \times \frac{\text{Good Units}}{\text{Total Units}}$$

**TICK MARK** symbol, usually a check mark or asterisk, that the auditor places next to work completed on items being audited. WORK PAPERS will have tick marks next to individual functions performed. Different tick marks can be used to signify different things. An explanation of the tick mark appears somewhere within the work papers. For instance, a certain mark may be placed beside the total of promotion and entertainment expense. The commentary to the mark may be something like "verified supporting documentation for promotion and entertainment expenditure."

**TIME-ADJUSTED RATE OF RETURN (TARR)** *see* INTERNAL RATE OF RETURN (IRR).

**TIME AND BILLING SOFTWARE** computer program that tracks hours spent by function and chargeable expenses of staff accountants for a given client. Sources are hourly rates, time sheets, practice and time management reports, and accounting reports. At the end of a period, a bill based on expenses, time spent, and hourly rates is sent. When billing on a flat-fee basis, hourly information is useful to the practitioner in evaluating staff accountants' proficiency. Hourly rates of staff accountants can be varied, depending on the client serviced. Time and billing programs also furnish projected fees to present and prospective clients. Client payment history—when payments were made, last time fees were increased—can be part of the report.

**TIME AND MATERIALS PRICING** approach to pricing used by service businesses in which the total billing is composed of actual direct materials and parts cost, actual direct labor cost, plus a percentage markup of each to cover overhead costs, and a profit factor.

**TIME AND MOTION STUDY** systematic study of the time and human motions used to perform an operation. The purpose is to eliminate unnecessary motions and to identify the best sequence of motions for maximum efficiency. Therefore, time and motion study can be an important source of productivity improvements. For example, a time and motion study analyzing the functioning of tellers in a bank might be conducted in an effort to effect savings in costs and processing time.

**TIME-BASED MANAGEMENT** using time as a strategic weapon by identifying market opportunities, responding to customers' needs, and eliminating waste.

**TIME CARD** *see* WORK TICKET.

**TIME DEPOSIT** savings account at a financial institution that earns interest but is not legally subject to withdrawal on demand or transfer by check. The depositor can withdraw only by giving notice. A CERTIFICATE OF DEPOSIT (CD) is a special type of time deposit. Should the CD depositor wish to withdraw funds prior to the date of maturity, the financial institution imposes a substantial penalty.

**TIME DRAFT** written order to be paid at a given future time after the drawee accepts it. It differs from a SIGHT DRAFT, which is payable on demand. *See also* ACCEPTANCE.

**TIME SERIES ANALYSIS** considers the fact that data points taken over time may have an internal structure, such as autocorrelation, trend, or seasonal variation, that should be accounted for when analyzing data.

**TIME SHARING**
1. information system that services many users from one computer; these users are served simultaneously until the volume of work to be processed forms a waiting line. Time sharing is a multiuser environment whereby many terminals are usually logged-on to a mainframe computer. All of the users are able to access the computer to upload information, to download information, obtain electronic mail, use programs on the computer, and so on.
2. in real estate, division of ownership or use of a resort unit or apartment on the basis of time periods.

**TIMES-INTEREST-EARNED RATIO** *see* INTEREST COVERAGE RATIO.

**TIME SOFTWARE** computer program that tracks hours worked by employees by function, operation, or activity. It prepares an analysis of the variance between budgeted and actual hours as well as prepares trends in actual hours over a stated time period (e.g., quarterly comparisons).

**TIME STANDARD** amount of time required to perform a task by a trained operator working at a normal pace and using a prescribed method.

**TIME STUDY** development of standards through stopwatch observation.

**TIME VALUE OF MONEY** concept that a dollar one has today is worth more than a dollar tomorrow. The reason: today's dollar can earn interest by putting it in a savings account or placing it in an investment. The longer it takes to get $1, the less it is worth today because interest is being lost. *See also* FUTURE VALUE; PRESENT VALUE.

**TOLERABLE**
1. In cost accounting, acceptable variance between actual and standard cost or revenue.
2. In auditing, degree of acceptable misstatement in substantive testing without materially misstating the financial statements. A tolerable rate is the maximum deviation rate in tests of controls that is acceptable by the auditor in his or her assessment of control risk.

**TOLERABLE DEVIATION RATE** in audit sampling, the maximum population deviation rate from a prescribed INTERNAL CONTROL that an auditor is willing to accept or tolerate without having to alter his or her planned reliance on the control.

**TOLERABLE MISSTATEMENT** in audit sampling, the maximum dollar amount of misstatement in an account balance or class of transactions that an auditor is willing to accept or tolerate and still be able to conclude that there is no material misstatement.

**TOP-DOWN APPROACH** in an integrated audit, the approach to be used in selecting internal controls to be tested. An auditor should first evaluate overall risks at the financial statement level and then risks at the entity level. Finally, an auditor should focus on account balances, disclosure items, and assertions for which material misstatement is a reasonable possibility.

**TOTAL COST** sum of the various costs incurred. For example, total manufacturing costs are the sum of direct materials, direct labor, and factory overhead. By management function, the total costs of a manufacturing business are the sum of manufacturing costs and selling and administrative expenses. By behavior in relation to fluctuations in activity, total costs are the sum of variable costs and fixed cost. *See also* UNIT COST.

**TOTAL COST OWNERSHIP (TCO)** tracing costs to a person or organization responsible for costs related to their designated products, services, and/or customers.

**TOTAL DIRECT LABOR COST VARIANCE** difference between standard direct labor cost for the good units produced and the actual direct labor costs incurred.

**TOTAL DIRECT MATERIALS COST VARIANCE** difference between standard cost for direct materials and the actual cost incurred for those items.

**TOTAL FACTOR PRODUCTIVITY** *see* TOTAL PRODUCTIVITY.

**TOTAL FIXED COSTS** costs that remain constant in total regardless of changes in activity.

**TOTAL MANUFACTURING COSTS** total costs of direct materials, direct labor, and manufacturing overhead incurred and charged to production during an accounting period.

**TOTAL MANUFACTURING OVERHEAD VARIANCE** difference between the actual manufacturing overhead costs incurred and the standard manufacturing overhead costs applied to production using the standard variable and fixed manufacturing overhead rates.

**TOTAL PRODUCTIVITY (TOTAL FACTOR PRODUCTIVITY)** quantity of output divided by the cost of all inputs.

**TOTAL PROJECT APPROACH** method that looks at all the items of revenue and cost data under two alternatives and compares the net income or contribution margin results; also called *comparative statement approach*. It differs from the INCREMENTAL ANALYSIS approach. For example, assume the ABC Company is planning to expand its productive capacity. The plans consist of purchasing a new machine for $50,000 and disposing of the old machine without receiving anything. The new machine has a five-year life. The old machine has a five-year remaining life and a book value of $12,500. The new machine will reduce variable operating costs from $35,000 per year to $20,000 per year. Annual sales and other operating costs follow:

|  | **Present Machine** | **New Machine** |
| --- | --- | --- |
| Sales | $60,000 | $60,000 |
| Variable costs | 35,000 | 20,000 |
| Fixed costs: |  |  |
| Depreciation (straight-line) | 2,500* | 10,000 |
| Insurance, taxes, etc. | 4,000 | 4,000 |

*Note that the depreciation expense of the old machine is irrelevant because it is a SUNK COST.

The total project approach results in the following:

|  | **Present Machine** | **New Machine** | **Increment (or Difference)** |
| --- | --- | --- | --- |
| Sales | $60,000 | $60,000 | — |
| Less: VC | 35,000 | 20,000 | ($15,000) |
| CONTRIBUTION MARGIN | $25,000 | $40,000 | $15,000 |
| Less: FC |  |  |  |
| Depreciation | — | $10,000 | $10,000 |
| Other | 4,000 | 4,000 | — |
| Net income | $21,000 | $26,000 | $ 5,000 |

The schedule for the total project approach shows an increase in profit of $5,000 with the purchase of the new machine.

**TOTAL QUALITY CONTROL (TQC)** philosophy that aggressively strives for a defect-free manufacturing process.

**TOTAL QUALITY MANAGEMENT (TQM)** approach to quality that emphasizes continuous improvement, a philosophy of "doing it right the first time" and striving for zero defects and elimination of all waste. It is a concept of using quality methods and techniques to strategic advantage within firms.

A comparison between TQM and BUSINESS PROCESS REENGINEER-ING (BPR) is presented below.

|  | *TQM* | *BPR* |
|---|---|---|
| Goals | Small-scale improve-ments at all levels of management with cumulative effects | Outrageous |
| Case for action | Assumed to be necessary | Compelling |
| Scope and focus | Attention to tasks, steps, and processes across the board | Select but broad business processes |
| Degree of change | Incremental, evolutionary, and continual | Order of magnitude and periodic; revolutionary |
| Role of information technology (IT) | Incidental | Cornerstone |
| Senior management involvement | Important up front | Intensive throughout |

**TOTAL VARIABLE COSTS** costs that vary in total in direct proportion to changes in activity.

**TOXIC ASSETS** worthless assets such as subprime mortgages, bad mortgages, or bad stocks, so-called because there is no market for them.

**TQM** *see* TOTAL QUALITY MANAGEMENT.

**TRACE** to determine if a financial statement item has been handled according to proper corporate or accounting policy. For example, if the auditor wants to trace the balance in the travel expense account, he will trace account postings from the ledger to the journal they came from. The auditor will then trace from the journal transaction to the source document to assure that proper backup exists.

**TRACEABILITY** ability to assign a cost directly to an activity or a cost object in an economically feasible way by means of a causal relationship. *See also* TRACING.

**TRACEABLE COST** one directly assigned to a given item or function. For example, costs may be identified to a given department, process, product-line, geographic area, industry segment, class of customer, etc. An example is advertising expense that is applicable to a particular product.

**TRACING** assignment of cost to an activity or a cost object using an observable measure of the consumption of resources by an activity. Tracing is generally preferred to allocation if the data exists or can be obtained at a reasonable cost. For example, if a company's cost accounting system captures the cost of supplies according to which activities use the supplies, the costs may be traced (as opposed to allocated) to the appropriate activities. Tracing is also called direct tracing. The 1998 draft also defines cost tracing broadly as the ability to assign a cost to a cost object. Thus, it treats assignment and tracing as synonymous.

**TRACK**
1. reference or supporting computation for a particular item, such as an account balance or entry. Tracking an item will reveal how it was obtained.
2. concentric circle on a computer disk where data are recorded.

**TRACKING STOCK** a stock created by a company to follow, or "track," the performance of one of its divisions—typically one that is in a line of business that is fast-growing and commands a higher industry price-to-earnings ratio than the parent's main business; also called letter stock or targeted stock. The objective is to increase value to shareholders, and thereby lower a company's cost of capital. Some companies distribute tracking stock to their existing shareholders. Others sell tracking stock to the investing public, raising additional cash for themselves. Some companies do both. Tracking stock, however, does not typically provide voting rights. Issuing tracking stock is an increasingly popular corporate-financing technique.

**TRADE CREDIT** type of credit extended by one business to another business, allowing the latter to buy goods from the former without making immediate full payment by check or with cash. It is credit obtained through open-account purchases represented by an ACCOUNTS PAYABLE by the buyer and an ACCOUNTS RECEIVABLE by the seller. Trade credit is an important external source of working capital for a business, although it can be very expensive. For example, a credit of 2/10 net 30 (2% cash discount if paid within 10 days, otherwise due in 30 days) translates into a 37% annual interest rate if the cash discount is foregone.

**TRADE DATE** date a security transaction actually occurs. Typically, the SETTLEMENT DATE is *five* business days after the trade date.

**TRADE DEFICIT** excess of imports of goods (raw materials, agricultural and manufactured products, and capital and consumer products) over the exports of goods, resulting in a negative *balance of trade*. Trade surplus is the reverse. The balance of trade is distinguished from the BALANCE OF PAYMENTS, which consists of the CURRENT ACCOUNT including services as well as merchandise trade and other *invisible items* such as interests and profits earned abroad. Factors that affect a country's balance of trade include the strength or weakness of its currency value in relation to those of the countries with which it trades and the comparative advantage in key manufacturing areas.

**TRADE DISCOUNT** reduction of the list or regular price in return for the purchase of large quantities, also called *quantity discount* or *price discount.*

**TRADEMARK** legal protection afforded names, symbols, and other specific identities assigned to a product. A trademark is generally considered to have no limited term of existence or natural limited life. U.S. Patent Office registration gives legal protection for an indefinite number of renewals for periods of 10 years each. A trademark is deferred and amortized to expense over the benefit period. The costs capitalized include design and registration, as well as the legal costs of successfully defending the trademark in court.

**TRADING ON EQUITY** FINANCIAL LEVERAGE, or the use of borrowed funds, particularly long-term debt, in the capital structure of a firm. Trading *profitably* on the equity, also known as *positive (favorable) financial* leverage, means that the borrowed funds generate a higher rate of return than the interest rate paid for the use of the funds. The excess accrues to the benefit of the owners because it magnifies, or increases, their earnings.

**TRADITIONAL COST ALLOCATIONS** allocating indirect costs without using cost drivers. A cause-and-effect relationship may not exist between the cost and the base used for the allocation.

**TRADITIONAL COST SYSTEM** *see* CONVENTIONAL COST SYSTEM.

**TRANSACTION CYCLE** repetitive flow of the activities of an ongoing enterprise described in terms of three major transaction cycles as follows: (1) *Revenue Cycle*, relating to sales, shipping, receivables, and collections; (2) *Buying Cycle*, referring to purchases, payables, and payments; and (3) *Production Cycle*, relating to manufacturing products and storage.

**TRANSACTION RISK** the risk that future cash transactions will be affected by changing exchange rates.

**TRANSACTIONS** events or happenings in a business that change its financial position and/or earnings. Transactions are recorded in a journal and then posted to a ledger. Examples of business transactions are investing in the business, buying supplies, paying bills, withdrawing money from the business, buying equipment, and paying rent.

**TRANSACTION TEST** *see* TEST OF TRANSACTION.

**TRANSACTION-VOLUME COST DRIVER** type of cost driver that draws on a measurement from a feeder subsystem that not only varies with cost magnitude but proportionately assigns the costs to its cost objects. It yields a per-unit cost.

**TRANSCRIBE**
1. act that serves to transfer an amount from one financial record to another. Transferring an original source document amount to a journal or posting to a ledger is an example of this act.
2. transforming audio representation manually into typed copy.

**TRANSFER AGENT** representative, usually a bank or trust company, designated by a corporation to make legal transfers of stocks and bonds and, in some cases, to distribute dividends. In this event the agent keeps the current stock-transfer books, ledger, and payment lists. Transfer agent and *registrar* duties may be performed by the same agent.

**TRANSFER CONTROL PROTOCOL/INTERNET PROTOCOL (TCP/IP)** protocol explaining the subdivision of information into packets for transmission and the way in which applications involve transmitting e-mail and file transfer.

**TRANSFER PRICE** charge made when one division of a company provides goods or services to another division of the company. A good transfer price will help evaluate the performance of the divisions. *See also* TRANSFER PRICING.

**TRANSFER PRICING** deciding on the price of goods or services that are exchanged between various divisions of a decentralized organization. A major goal of transfer pricing is to enable divisions that exchange goods or services to act as independent businesses. Various transfer pricing schemes are available, such as MARKET PRICE, COST-BASED PRICE, or NEGOTIATED PRICE. Unfortunately, there is no single transfer price that will please everybody—that is, top management, the selling division, and the buying division. Usually the best transfer price is the outside market price less costs saved by dealing within the company (e.g., transportation costs, advertising, salesperson salaries). If the two division managers—buying division and selling division—cannot agree on a price, one will be arbitrated by upper management. When an outside market price is not available, *budgeted* cost plus profit markup may be used so that cost efficiencies at the selling division are still maintained.

**TRANSFERRED-IN COSTS** costs of processing a product or performing a service from a prior department to the current department. The costs usually occur under a PROCESS COSTING system. Consider two processing departments in a chain—Department A and Department B.

Transferred-in costs would be the costs attached to partially completed units transferred in from Department A.

**TRANSFER TAX**
1. state tax levied upon the transfer or sale of a security or property. Some states base the tax on selling price (e.g., New York) while other states base the tax on the par value (e.g., Texas).
2. federal tax on the sale of stocks and bonds.
3. federal tax on gifts made and estate proceeds.

**TRANSLATION RISK** also called ACCOUNTING RISK, the degree to which a firm's finanicial statements are exposed to exchange rate fluctuations.

**TRANSPARENT MARKET** a market in which there is open communication between stockholders, investors, and company officials and current trade and quote information is readily available to the public.

**TRANSPORTATION LP PROBLEM** problem of determining how much to ship from each origin to each destination in order to minimize total shipping costs.

**TRAVEL AND ENTERTAINMENT EXPENSE DEDUCTION** tax allowance for a percentage of business expenses. The rules apply regardless of whether the expense was paid while the taxpayer was away from home overnight or not. A business meal is deductible only if it is *directly related* to the active conduct of the taxpayer's trade or business. *Unreimbursed* employee expenses for business travel and entertainment become miscellaneous itemized deductions subject to a 2% adjusted gross income "floor."

**TRAVELING AUDITOR**
1. company employee who visits branches or subsidiaries or other outlying locations from the home office.
2. CPA firm employee who is primarily involved in auditing clients at distant locations on a continuous basis.

**TREADWAY COMMISSION** popular name for the National Commission on Fraudulent Reporting that has issued a number of recommendations for the prevention of fraud in financial reports, ethics, and effective internal controls.

**TREASURER** person in a firm who deals with financial and money problems. The treasurer is engaged in (1) capital obtainment, (2) investor relations, (3) short-term financing, (4) banking and custody, (5) credits and collections, (6) investments, and (7) insurance and employee benefits. The treasurer's functions are distinguished from those of the CONTROLLER, who supervises the accounting activities of the firm.

**TREASURY BILL** short-term obligation of the federal government, commonly called T-bill. Treasury bills are auctioned weekly through competitive bidding by the Treasury with maturities of 91 days and

182 days. In addition, nine-month and one-year bills are sold periodically. Treasury bills carry no coupon but are sold on a discount basis. Denominations range from $10,000 to $1 million. The yields on T-bills are lower than those on any other marketable securities due to their virtually risk-free nature. The market is very active, and the transaction costs involved in the sale of Treasury bills in the secondary market are small.

**TREASURY BOND**
1. long-term debt instrument issued by the U.S. Treasury department with maturities of 10 years or longer issued in minimum denominations of $1,000.
2. bond issued by a corporation and then repurchased. Such a bond is considered as retired when repurchased.

**TREASURY CERTIFICATE** debt security of the United States government that pays coupon interest and whose maturity date is one year or less from the issuance date.

**TREASURY NOTES** intermediate government obligations with maturities of one to ten years. Denominations range from $1000 to $1 million or more. Due to the existence of a strong secondary market, they are attractive marketable security investments. Like Treasury bills, Treasury notes have a low yield because of their virtually risk-free nature.

**TREASURY STOCK** issued shares that have been reacquired by the company. Treasury shares may be resold or canceled. Dividends are *not* paid on treasury shares nor are voting fights associated with them. The two acceptable methods of accounting for treasury stock are the COST METHOD and PAR VALUE method. Under the cost method, treasury stock is shown at the *cost* to reacquire the shares. Under the par value method, treasury stock is recorded at the par value of the reacquired stock. Treasury stock is shown as a deduction in arriving at stockholders' equity. Under either method, there is an appropriation of retained earnings equal to the cost of the treasury stock held.

**TREASURY STOCK METHOD** procedure for determining the common stock equivalency of options and warrants when computing earnings per share. The treasury method assumes that options or warrants were exercised at the beginning of the period (or at time of issue, if later), and that the funds obtained were used to purchase and retire common stock at the average market price during the period. The number of shares required cannot exceed 20% of the common stock outstanding at year-end. If funds remain, it is assumed that they are used to reduce long-term or short-term debt. If there are any funds remaining after debt is reduced, they are assumed to be invested in U.S. government securities or commercial paper.

**TREASURY WARRANT** order on the U.S. Treasury that a certain dollar amount be paid with a bank check.

**TREND ANALYSIS** forecasting technique that relies primarily on historical time series data to predict the future. The analysis involves searching for a right TREND EQUATION that will suitably describe trend of the data series. The trend may be linear, or it may not. A linear trend can be obtained by using a LEAST SQUARES METHOD. The line has the equation $y = a + bt$ where $t = 1,2,3 \ldots$, $b$ = slope of the line, and $a$ = value of $y$ when $t = 0$. The coefficients of the equation, $a$ and $b$, can be determined using these equations:

$$b = \frac{n\Sigma ty - (\Sigma t)(\Sigma y)}{n\Sigma t^2 - (\Sigma t)^2}$$

$$a = \frac{\Sigma y}{n} - b\frac{\Sigma t}{n}$$

**TREND EQUATION** special case of SIMPLE REGRESSION, where the $x$ variable is a time variable. This equation is used to determine the trend in the variable $y$, which can be used for forecasting. For example, assume the following sales data are given for the last 16 months:

| Time ($t$) | Sales ($y$) |
|:----------:|:-----------:|
| 1  | $6.18 |
| 2  | 5.92 |
| 3  | 6.49 |
| 4  | 6.69 |
| 5  | 7.24 |
| 6  | 7.20 |
| 7  | 7.24 |
| 8  | 7.49 |
| 9  | 7.45 |
| 10 | 7.66 |
| 11 | 7.89 |
| 12 | 7.85 |
| 13 | 7.77 |
| 14 | 8.01 |
| 15 | 8.35 |
| 16 | 8.38 |

Using the NORMAL EQUATIONS of simple regression gives the following result:

$$y = 6.1135 + 0.147014t$$

where $t$ is time $(1,2,3 \ldots)$ and $y$ is sales. The forecasted sales for the next period $(t = 17)$ can be computed as follows:

$$y = 6.1135 + 0.147014t = 6.1135 + 0.147014(17) = 8.6127$$

*See also* TREND ANALYSIS.

## TRIAL BALANCE

1. listing of the account balances from the general ledger, prepared at the end of the accounting period. All accounts are listed in the order in which they appear in the ledger. Total debits must equal total credits; otherwise, an error has been made. Even though the trial balance furnishes arithmetical proof that debits equal credits, it does not detect all errors. For example, a posting to the wrong account may have occurred. The trial balance is a work sheet and *not* a formal financial statement. It serves as a convenient basis for the preparation of the balance sheet and income statement. *See also* POST-CLOSING TRIAL BALANCE.

2. listing of the account balances of a subsidiary ledger (i.e., customer accounts) that must agree with the total of the control account (i.e., accounts receivable) in the general ledger.

**TROUBLED ASSET RELIEF PROGRAM (TARP)** a program of the U.S government to purchase assets and equity from financial institutions to strengthen its financial sector. It is the largest component of the government's measures to curb the ongoing financial and subprime mortgage crisis of 2007–2008. *See also* SUBPRIME MORTGAGE.

**TROUBLED DEBT RESTRUCTURING** situation, defined in Statement of Financial Accounting Standards No. 15, where the DEBTOR has financial difficulties and asks the CREDITOR for some relief from the obligation. The debtor will recognize an extraordinary gain on the restructuring of the payable equal to the difference between the fair value of assets exchanged and the book value of the debt, inclusive of accrued interest. The creditor recognizes a loss on the difference between the fair value of assets received and the book value of his investment. Appropriate footnote disclosure should also be given by the debtor and creditor related to the restructuring terms.

**TRUST** agreement in which the trustee takes title to property (called the *corpus*) owned by the grantor (donor) to protect or conserve it for either the grantor or the trust's beneficiary. The trust is established by the grantor. The trustee is typically given authority to invest the property for a return. Trusts may be revocable or irrevocable.

## TRUSTEE

1. third party to a BOND indenture. The trustee's function is to make sure the issuer lives up to the numerous provisions in the indenture. A trustee is usually a trust department of a commercial bank. The trustee is paid a fee and acts to protect the interests of the bondholders.

2. third party to a BANKRUPTCY proceeding. The trustee's responsibility is to value and recapitalize the firm if it is to be reorganized.

**TRUST FUND** one used to account for a government's fiduciary responsibilities and activities in managing trusts. There are basically three types of trust funds: expendable trust funds, nonexpendable trust funds, and pension trust funds.

**TRUST RECEIPT** instrument acknowledging that the borrower holds specified property in trust for the lender. The lender retains title. This type of financing is used for equipment dealers, automobile dealers, and others involved in durable expensive goods. When the lender receives the sale proceeds, title is given up.

*T*-STATISTIC *see* *T*-VALUE.

*T* **TABLE** table that provides *T*-VALUES for various degrees of freedom and sample sizes. The *t* table is based on the *Student t* probability distribution. See the *t* table (Table 5).

*T*-TEST
1. in REGRESSION ANALYSIS, test of the statistical significance of a regression coefficient. It involves basically two steps: (1) compute the *T*-VALUE of the regression coefficient as follows: *t*-value = coefficient/standard error of the coefficient; (2) compare the value with the *t* table value. High *t*-values enhance confidence in the value of the coefficient as a predictor. Low values (as a rule of thumb, under 2.0) are indications of low reliability of the coefficient as a predictor.
2. general statistical test for hypotheses, based on *t*-distribution, known as a small sample distribution. The *t*-test is used to estimate and test hypotheses about population means, the difference between two means, a population variance, and a comparison of two population variances. For example, an accounting instructor wishes to test to determine if the use of a new and old textbook had anything to do with the difference in performance of the two classes.

**TURNOVER** frequency with which an item (i.e., fixed asset, inventory, accounts receivable, personnel) is replaced during an accounting period. Assume credit sales of $360,000 and average receivables of $60,000. The number of times receivables turned over for the period is 6 ($360,000/$60,000). In Great Britain, turnover means sales.

**TURNOVER RATIO** measure of a particular asset's activity (e.g., sales, cost of sales). The average asset balance for the period is used equal to the beginning balance plus the ending balance divided by 2. A turnover ratio is an *activity* ratio. By looking at the turnover of an asset in terms of generating revenue, the accountant can properly appraise a company's ability to manage assets efficiently. Examples are the turnover in fixed assets (sales/fixed assets), accounts receivable (sales/accounts receivable), and inventory (cost of sales/inventory).

**TURNOVER TAX** indirect tax, typically on an ad valorem basis, applicable to a production process or stage. For example, when manufacturing activity is completed, a tax may be charged on some companies. Sales tax occurs when merchandise has been sold. *See also* AD VALOREM TAX.

*T*-VALUE measure of the statistical significance of an independent variable *b* in explaining the dependent variable *y*. It is determined by dividing the estimated regression coefficient $b$ by its standard error $S_b$. That is

$$t\text{-Value} = b/S_b$$

Thus, the $t$-statistic measures how many standard errors the coefficient is away from zero. Generally, any $t$-value greater than $+2$ or less than $-2$ is acceptable. The higher the $t$-value, the greater the confidence we have in the coefficient as a predictor. Low $t$-values are indications of low reliability of the predictive power of that coefficient.

**TWITTER** a public forum where a user can read, write, and share messages called Tweets. Each Tweet is limited to 140 characters.

**TWO-BIN INVENTORY CONTROL** involving the use of two containers for inventory. Items are withdrawn from the first bin. When its contents are exhausted, it is time to reorder. Sometimes an order card is placed at the bottom of the first bin. The second bin contains stock sufficient to satisfy expected demand during the lead time period and a safety stock that is needed to avoid a possible stockout.

**TWO-WAY ANALYSIS** computation of two variances—*price* and *quantity* variances for direct materials and direct labor and *budget* and *volume* variances for factory overhead. The budget variance is the difference between actual overhead costs and the budget overhead based on standard hours allowed. The volume variance (denominator variance) is the difference between denominator volume and actual volume, multiplied by a predetermined fixed overhead rate. The two-way analysis for factory overhead stops here; it does not break up the budget variance into *spending* and *efficiency* variances. *See also* THREE-WAY ANALYSIS.

**TWO-WAY ANALYSIS OF OVERHEAD VARIANCE** dividing the total overhead variance into two variances: volume and controllable (the latter is sometimes called the budget, total overhead spending, or flexible budget variance). The variable overhead spending and efficiency variances and the fixed overhead budget variance are combined.

**TYPE I ERROR** risk that the sample supports the conclusion that recorded book value (e.g., account balance) is materially misstated when it is, in fact, not; also called *alpha risk*. *See also* HYPOTHESIS TESTING.

**TYPE II ERROR** risk that the sample supports the conclusion that the recorded account balance is not materially misstated when it is, in fact, materially misstated; also known as *beta risk*. *See also* HYPOTHESIS TESTING.

# U

**ULTRA VIRES** an action outside the proper authority or power of a corporation or corporate officer as established in the corporate charter (Latin for "beyond the power").

**UNADJUSTED RATE OF RETURN** *see* SIMPLE RATE OF RETURN.

**UNADJUSTED TRIAL BALANCE** one showing account balances in debit and credit columns prior to preparing an ADJUSTING JOURNAL ENTRY.

**UNAMORTIZED BOND DISCOUNT** balance of the BOND DISCOUNT that remains to be amortized in future years. It is shown as a contra account to bonds payable (bond investment) to arrive at the net liability (asset). (It should be noted that an alternative treatment is to show the bond investment account net of the discount.) When the unamortized bond discount is amortized, interest expense is charged. *See also* UNAMORTIZED BOND PREMIUM.

**UNAMORTIZED BOND PREMIUM** part of the BOND PREMIUM that is to be amortized in later years. It is shown as an addition (deduction) to the maturity value of the bonds payable (bond investment) to arrive at the net balance. The future periodic amortization of unamortized bond premium is credited to interest expense. *See also* UNAMORTIZED BOND DISCOUNT.

**UNAPPROPRIATED RETAINED EARNINGS** part of retained earnings that is "free" or available for dividends. *See also* APPROPRIATED RETAINED EARNINGS.

**UNAUDITED STATEMENT** one in which the auditor prepares or aids in preparing but does not examine in accordance with GENERALLY ACCEPTED AUDITING STANDARDS (GAAS). In effect, the auditor is undertaking an accounting service of accumulating and preparing financial information, but is *not* applying audit procedures as a basis to form an audit opinion. An unaudited statement must be identified as such, and the auditor must issue a disclaimer opinion in which he states that he is not rendering an opinion on it.

**UNAVOIDABLE COSTS** costs to be incurred regardless of the decision to make or buy a certain part or keep or drop a certain product line; these costs cannot be recovered or saved. Much or all of fixed costs in those cases are unavoidable costs, e.g. property taxes and rent.

**UNCERTAINTY** state of knowledge in which one or more alternatives result in a set of possible specific outcomes, but where the probabilities of the outcomes are neither known nor meaningful. Unlike RISK, uncertainty is not objective and does not assume complete knowledge of alternatives. In most practical cases, decision makers tend not to distinguish between uncertainty and risk. *See also* DECISION-MAKING UNDER UNCERTAINTY.

**UNCOLLECTIBLE ACCOUNT** account receivable, note receivable, or other type of receivable that is unlikely to be paid. An example is a customer who is bankrupt or on the verge of default. *See also* ALLOWANCE FOR BAD DEBTS; ALLOWANCE METHOD; BAD DEBT; DIRECT WRITE-OFF METHOD.

**UNCONSOLIDATED SUBSIDIARY** subsidiary showing individual financial statements that are not presented in the CONSOLIDATED FINANCIAL STATEMENTS. The EQUITY METHOD of accounting is used for unconsolidated subsidiaries. A subsidiary is not consolidated even though more than 50% of voting common stock is owned by the parent when one of the following situations exists: (1) parent is not in actual control of subsidiary (i.e., subsidiary is in a politically unstable foreign country); (2) parent has only temporary control of the subsidiary; or (3) the nature of the subsidiary's operations are significantly different than those of the parent.

**UNCONTROLLABLE COSTS** *see* CONTROLLABLE COSTS.

**UNDER- AND OVERAPPLIED** *see* OVERAPPLIED OVERHEAD; UNDERAPPLIED OVERHEAD.

**UNDERAPPLIED OVERHEAD** amount by which the factory overhead added to work-in-process inventory at a predetermined overhead rate (and credited to factory overhead applied) is less than the actual overhead shown in factory overhead control. *See also* OVERAPPLIED OVERHEAD; PREDETERMINED OVERHEAD RATE.

**UNDERSTANDABILITY** term indicating that financial information is stated in terms that enable users to perceive its significance.

**UNDERSTANDING WITH THE CLIENT** SAS Number 83 provides that the auditor should have a written agreement with the client concerning the engagement services so as to avoid misinterpretation. The understanding should cover such areas as the purposes of the engagement, auditors' responsibilities, management's duties, limitations of the engagement, conditions under which access to the audit workpapers may be granted to others, arrangements involving a predecessor auditor, and use of specialists and internal auditors. The understanding should be documented in the working papers.

**UNDERWRITING** acceptance of risk in return for payment. In a new securities issue, the underwriter, known as the INVESTMENT BANKER and his or her syndicate, may perform an underwriting function by purchasing the securities at a fixed price from the issuer, hoping to sell them at a higher offering price and making a profit on the *spread*. Underwriting is the function of investment bankers, who usually form an underwriting group, also called a SYNDICATE, to pool the risk and assure successful distribution of the issue.

**UNDETACHABLE STOCK WARRANT** one issued along with a bond that requires simultaneous exercise of both to obtain stock. If the warrant is *not* detachable, the bond is, in essence, CONVERTIBLE DEBT *only*. No allocation of the proceeds should be to the conversion feature. The reason to account for the issuance only as convertible debt is the inseparability of the debt and conversion option. The excess received on the issuance attributable to the undetachable stock warrants is credited to premium on bonds payable since the issuance is accounted for solely as debt. *See also* DETACHABLE STOCK WARRANT; STOCK WARRANT.

**UNDISTRIBUTED PROFIT** earnings of a business entity such as a syndicate, joint venture, or partnership, preceding the allocation of profit according to the member's profit distribution agreement. *See also* EARNED SURPLUS.

**UNEARNED REVENUE**
1. payment received in advance of providing a good or service. Since an obligation exists on the part of the company to provide goods or services for which the advance payment was received, unearned revenue is a liability. An example is a retainer received by an attorney. When the services are performed, revenue is then earned.
2. in taxation, revenue obtained other than from personal services.

**UNEMPLOYMENT COMPENSATION TAX** *see* FEDERAL UNEMPLOYMENT TAX ACT (FUTA) and STATE UNEMPLOYMENT COMPENSATION.

**UNENCUMBERED BALANCE** in GOVERNMENT ACCOUNTING, balance relating to a portion or the entire amount of an appropriation that has not been encumbered or expended.

**UNEXPIRED COST** all costs, including inventory costs and miscellaneous prepaid or deferred costs, that are associated with the revenue of future periods. Unexpired costs are carried to future periods as assets because they represent future benefits.

**UNFAVORABLE VARIANCE** excess of actual costs over standard costs. Unfavorable variances typically require further investigation for possible causes. *See also* STANDARD COST SYSTEM; VARIANCE.

**UNFUNDED** no funds have been provided for a specified obligation or liability. Such may be the case for a pension plan where part of pension expense has not been funded (cash paid) by the employer. This will result in a deferred pension credit.

**UNIFORM COMMERCIAL CODE (UCC)** legal code that standardizes business law in the United States. The Code was formulated in 1952 by the National Conference of Commissioners on United States Laws. The Code was offered to the state legislatures, and all states except Louisiana adopted it. For example, the Code covers regulations on commercial paper, warranties, uncertified checks, written agency agreements, security agreements, and bankruptcy. The Uniform Commercial Code is followed by practicing lawyers.

**UNIFORMITY** term describing the presentation of financial statements by different companies using the *same* accounting procedures, measurement concepts, classifications, and methods of disclosure. In essence, uniform accounting treatment and disclosures by companies facilitate their comparison. However, strict uniformity is not possible in accounting because of differences in company and industry practices. For example, the same event may be handled differently by competing companies, as in the case when different inventory methods are used. *See also* COMPARABILITY.

**UNIFORM PARTNERSHIP ACT** proposed law prepared by the National Conference of Commissioners on Uniform State Laws to apply to partnerships. Several states have adopted it. According to the Act, a partnership is an association of two or more individuals who carry on as co-owners of a business for profit.

**UNIFORM RESOURCE LOCATOR (URL)** used to specify addresses on the World Wide Web. URLs have the following format: protocol:// hostname. The protocol used for Web resources is HyperText Transfer Protocol (HTTP) or its secure version (HTTPS). Other protocols include FTP and MAILTO, among many others.

**UNISSUED STOCK** shares that have been authorized but have not been issued. Assume authorized shares of 500,000 and issued shares of 200,000. The unissued shares are 300,000.

**UNIT CONTRIBUTION MARGIN** excess of the unit selling price over the unit variable cost. For example, if the sales price is $30 and the unit variable cost is $18, then the unit CONTRIBUTION MARGIN (CM) is $12. This means that each unit sold contributes $12 toward the fixed cost or profit.

**UNIT COST** cost of producing one unit of product or service, usually based on averages. For example, if total manufacturing costs are $100,000 and the production volume for a given period is 10,000 units, the unit production cost is $10 per unit ($100,000/10,000 units). Unit costs may be stated in terms of gallons, feet, tons, individual units, and so on. Unit costs must be available for comparison of varying volumes and amount and for the purpose of establishing unit sales price of the product or service. If volume of activity increases, the variable cost per unit remains the same but the fixed cost per unit drops.

**UNIT COST ANALYSIS SCHEDULE** process costing statement used to accumulate all costs charged to the Work-in-Process Inventory account of each department or production process and to compute cost per equivalent unit for direct material costs and conversion costs.

**UNIT LEVEL ACTIVITIES** activities performed each time a unit is produced; such activities vary with the number of units produced.

**UNIT OF SAMPLING** item in a population that is subject to sampling by the auditor to draw a conclusion regarding the acceptability of the population. The sampling unit may be based on physical, cost, or other characteristic. An example is selecting inventory items to be examined to draw an inference as to whether the inventory account is properly stated. Another example is taking a sample of sales invoices by number to test their mathematical accuracy.

**UNITED STATES SERIES I SAVINGS BOND** a U.S. savings bond designed to protect the purchasing power of your principal and guarantees a real fixed rate of return above inflation for the life of the bond (10 to 30 years). The current series I savings bond, called *I-bond* for short, guarantees 3% above inflation. You can purchase up to $30,000 worth of the bonds each year, you can never lose principal, earnings are free from state and local taxes, and federal taxes are deferred until you redeem the bond. Plus, there are no fees when you buy or sell these bonds. Although you can cash an I-bond 6 months after the issue date, there is a 3-month earnings penalty if you redeem them in less than 5 years. I-bonds are sold in denominations of $50 to $10,000 at most banks and also online at www.savingsbonds.gov.

**UNITS OF PRODUCTION METHOD** procedure in which depreciation is allocated in proportion to the asset's use in operation. First, the depreciation per unit of production is computed by dividing the total depreciable cost by the asset's projected units-of-production capacity. To find periodic depreciation expense, multiply the depreciation per unit of production by the number of units produced during the period.

**UNIX** a powerful, extensively used operating system that has been implemented on a variety of platforms.

**UNLIMITED LIABILITY** in a SOLE PROPRIETORSHIP or a GENERAL PARTNERSHIP, liability of owners not limited to the owner's investment. In a corporation, stockholders usually have LIMITED LIABILITY; they risk their investment in the enterprise but not their personal assets.

**UNQUALIFIED OPINION**
1. auditor's judgment that he or she has no reservation as to the fairness of presentation of a company's financial statements and their conformity with U.S. GENERALLY ACCEPTED ACCOUNTING PRINCIPLES (GAAP); termed an unmodified opinion in the care of nonissuer's financial statements; sometimes referred to as a clean opinion. In the auditor's opinion, the company has presented fairly its financial position, results of operations, and changes in cash flows. However, if there is inconsistency in application of GAAP, there should be disclosure in the auditor's report.

**2.** unqualified opinion on the effectiveness of internal control over financial reporting. It is an opinion that internal control over financial reporting is effective in all material respects as of the assessment date.

**UNREALIZED LOSS, GAIN** change in value of an asset that is still being held. It is distinguished from a REALIZED GAIN, LOSS on the sale of the asset. The term commonly refers to the write-down or write-up of an investment portfolio of trading or available-for-sale securities resulting from applying the market value method on an aggregate basis. On a trading securities portfolio, the unrealized loss or gain is shown on the income statement. On an available-for-sale securities portfolio, the total unrealized loss or gain is presented as a separate item under "Accumulated Other Comprehensive Income" in the stockholders' equity section of the balance sheet. Assume on 12/31/2014 a trading securities portfolio has a cost of $100,000 and a market value of $88,000. The entry is:

| | | |
|---|---|---|
| Unrealized loss | 12,000 | |
| Allowance | | 12,000 |

If on 12/31/2015, the trading securities portfolio in market value goes to $93,000 from $88,000, the entry is:

| | | |
|---|---|---|
| Allowance | 5,000 | |
| Unrealized gain | | 5,000 |

**UNRESTRICTED NET ASSETS** in GOVERNMENT ACCOUNTING, assets with no external restriction as to use or purpose. They can be employed for any purpose designated by the governing board, as distinguished from funds restricted externally for specific purposes.

**UNSECURED LOAN** borrowing that is not secured by a mortgage on a specific property. It is backed only by the borrower's credit rating. Unsecured loans are typically short term. The disadvantages of this kind of loan are that, because it is made for the short term and has no collateral, it carries a higher interest rate than a secured loan, and payment in a lump sum is required.

**UNSYSTEMATIC RISK** one that is unique to a specific security. It is the antithesis of market (or systematic) risk. Thus, as portfolios become more diversified, the unsystematic risk moves to zero because the risks of specific securities cancel each other out. Components of unsystematic risk include economic risk, business risk, financial risk, and accounting risk. *See also* BETA.

**UPLOAD** process of providing data from a microcomputer to a MAINFRAME or MINICOMPUTER or another MICROCOMPUTER. For example, an accountant can upload information from his or her computer to the client's computer system. *See also* DOWNLOAD; TELECOMMUNICATIONS.

**UPPER DEVIATION RATE** sometimes referred to as the *upper occurrence rate*, an auditor's estimate of the population's rate of deviation from a prescribed internal control. The upper deviation rate, which is typically determined using statistical tables, is equal to the sample deviation rate plus an allowance for sampling risk. The upper deviation rate is then compared to the tolerable deviation rate (specified by the auditor) in order to determine whether a prescribed INTERNAL CONTROL may be relied on by the auditor. In turn, reliance on an internal control results in a lower assessment of control risk.

**UPPER LIMIT** *see* CEILING.

**UPTICK** a term used to designate a price higher than that on the preceding transaction in the stock; also called *plus tick*. A stock may be sold short only on an uptick, or on a zero-plus tick. *Zero-plus tick* is a term used for a transaction at the same price as the preceding trade but higher than the preceding different price. Conversely, *down tick,* or *minus tick,* is used to designate a transaction made at a price lower than the preceding trade. A *zero-minus tick* is a transaction made at the same price as the preceding sale but lower than the preceding different price. A plus sign or a minus sign is displayed throughout the day next to the last price of each company's stock traded at each trading post on the floor of the New York Stock Exchange (NYSE).

**UPTICK RULE** SEC rule that prohibits short selling of securities except on an uptick. The rule provides that, subject to certain exceptions, a listed security may be sold short (1) at a price above the price at which the immediately preceding sale was effected (plus tick), or (2) at the last sale price if it is higher than the last different price (zero-plus tick). *See also* UPTICK.

**URL (UNIFORM RESOURCE LOCATOR)** an address system used for the Internet. The http prefix is used for the World Wide Web. For example, www.barnesandnoble.com is the full address for the Barnes & Noble online bookstore.

Some Common Addresses

| | |
|---|---|
| http:// | World Wide Web |
| ftp:// | FTP server |
| Gopher:// | Gopher server |
| mailto:// | e-mail |
| News:// | Newsgroup |
| wais:// | Wide Area Information Server |

**USAGE VARIANCE** *see* EFFICIENCY VARIANCE.

**USEFUL LIFE** typical operating service life of an asset for the purpose it was acquired. The term usually applies to fixed assets. The useful life used for DEPRECIATION ACCOUNTING does not necessarily coincide with the actual physical life or any commonly recognized ECONOMIC LIFE. *See also* DEPRECIABLE LIFE; DEPRECIATION.

**UTILITY**

1. economic and highly subjective term describing satisfaction of a specified want. Utility and usefulness are not necessarily synonymous terms. Artwork may be functionally useless but yet provide great utility to an art lover.
2. value of a certain outcome or payoff to someone; the pleasure or displeasure that person would derive from that outcome.

**UTILITY PROGRAM** software supporting the processing of a computer such as diagnostic and tracing programs.

# V

## VALIDATE
1. attest to the correctness and reliability of a financial item. A validity review or test is required by the ACCOUNTANT to satisfy the legitimacy of the item. An example of validation is the examination and approval of an employee's expense request form by a supervisor. Another example is the counting of petty cash to see that it conforms to the amount in the financial records.
2. make something legal or effective. An example is signing one's name to a bill of sale, which closes the deal. *See also* VALIDITY TEST.

**VALIDITY TEST** audit procedure that ascertains whether a recorded financial statement item is accurately stated. Validity tests are those activities associated with satisfying oneself as to the precision, reliability, relevance, and authorization of transactions recorded in the books of a company. The methods used in the testing activity depend upon the type of transactions or amounts being tested. In testing transactions, the tester may use various methods to select the sample of the transactions and perform selected tests on the transactions. *See also* VALIDATE.

**VALUATION ACCOUNT** item offset against or added to the gross amount of an account to arrive at a *net* balance. Examples are the allowance account that is subtracted from trading securities to reduce cost to market value, allowance for uncollectible accounts that is netted against accounts receivable, accumulated depreciation that is deducted from the fixed asset, or bond premium that is added to bonds payable.

**VALUATION, ALLOCATION, AND ACCURACY** an assertion in an entity's financial statements made by management that account balances, transactions, and disclosure items have been recorded properly at appropriate amounts.

**VALUATION ALLOWANCE** *see* CONTRA ACCOUNT.

## VALUE
1. highly subjective term, usually an expression of monetary worth applied to a particular asset, group of assets, business entity, or services rendered. It should not be confused with the term cost even though it is frequently measured, equated, and identified by it. Thus the term should be used with an appropriate modifying adjective.
2. amounts at which items are stated in financial records and statements. Value is expenditures or amounts deemed to benefit future periods. *See also* BOOK VALUE; MARKET VALUE.
3. represented by the amount of goods, services, or money necessary to complete an exchange for a specific commodity. In economic terms, value of goods equals price multiplied by quantity.

**VALUE ADDED** difference, at each stage of production, between the cost of a product and the cost of all the materials purchased to make the product.

**VALUE-ADDED ACTIVITY** activity that increases the worth of a product or service and for which the customer is willing to pay.

**VALUE-ADDED NETWORK (VAN)** company providing a private network allowing for "store and forward" capabilities associated with electronic data interchange. A TRADING PARTNER can send information to a VAN, which ascertains the intended recipient. The data is then stored in a mailbox until the data is retrieved (forwarded). Benefits of a VAN are improved security, less scheduling difficulties, and less problems associated with protocol and communication.

**VALUE-ADDED TAX (VAT)** indirect percentage tax levied on products or services at various stages of production and distribution. The actual value added to the product, including raw materials, labor, and profit, is determined at each stage or state of production and the tax is computed upon the increase in value. It is basically a tax allocated among the economic units responsible for the production and distribution of goods and services. Because collection of VAT takes place at the product's ultimate destination, VAT is not charged on export sales. VAT is charged on all domestically sold products regardless of the country of origin. Thus VAT is designed to provide an incentive to export and, of course, a disincentive to import.

**VALUE-ADDING COST** cost of an operating activity that increases the market value of a product or service.

**VALUE ANALYSIS** process of trying to reduce product costs by substituting less costly materials, redesigning nonessential parts, and the like.

**VALUE CHAIN** linked set of all value-creating processes or activities that convert basic input materials into products or services for the final consumer.

**VALUE CHAIN COSTING** ACTIVITY-BASED COST model that contains all of the activities in the VALUE-CHAIN (design, procure, produce, market, distribute/render, and post-service a product or service) of one organization.

**VALUE ENGINEERING** means of reaching targeted cost levels. It is a systematic approach to assessing all aspects of the value chain cost of reaching targeted cost levels and the value chain cost buildup for a product: R&D, design of products, design processes, production, marketing, distribution, and customer service. The purpose is to minimize costs without sacrificing customer satisfaction. Value engineering requires distinguishing between incurring costs and locked-in costs. Costs incurred are the actual use of resources, whereas locked-in (designed-in) costs will result in the use of resources in the future as a result of past decisions. Traditional cost accounting focuses on budget comparisons, but value engineering emphasizes controlling costs at the design stage, that is, before they are locked in.

**VALUE IN USE** discounted value of net cash receipts to be obtained from the corporate asset. The present value calculation includes consideration of annual cash inflows plus the disposal value.

**VARIABLE ANNUITY** one whose periodic payments are dependent on some undetermined or uncertain outcome such as the value of a securities portfolio. A contract between an investor and insurance company may take this form and subsequently the periodic payments would change as a function of the changes in applicable securities prices or rates of return. A variable annuity may also consist of payments that vary depending on changes in money market interest rates.

**VARIABLE BUDGET** *see* FLEXIBLE (VARIABLE) BUDGET.

**VARIABLE COSTING** method in which the costs to be *inventoried* include only the *variable* manufacturing costs. Fixed factory overhead is treated as a period cost—it is deducted along with the selling and administrative expenses in the period incurred. That is,

| | |
|---|---|
| Direct materials | $xx |
| Direct labor | xx |
| Variable factory overhead | xx |
| Product cost | $xx |

Fixed factory overhead is treated as a period expense.

Variable costing is used for internal management only. Its uses include: (1) inventory valuation and income determination; (2) relevant cost analysis; (3) BREAK-EVEN and COST-VOLUME-PROFIT (CVP) ANALYSES; and (4) short-term decision-making. Variable costing is, however, not acceptable for external reporting or income tax reporting. Companies that use variable costing for internal reporting must convert to ABSORPTION COSTING for external reporting.

Under absorption costing, the cost to be inventoried includes all manufacturing costs, both variable and fixed. Nonmanufacturing (operating) expenses, i.e., selling and administrative expenses, are treated as period expenses and thus are charged against the current revenue.

| | |
|---|---|
| Direct materials | $xx |
| Direct labor | xx |
| Variable factory overhead | xx |
| Fixed factory overhead | xx |
| Product cost | $xx |

Two important facts are noted: 1. Effects of the two costing methods on net income: (a) When production exceeds sales, a larger net income will be reported under absorption costing. (b) When sales exceed production, a larger net income will be reported under direct costing. (c) When sales and production are equal, net income will be the same under both methods. 2. Reconciliation of the direct and absorption costing net income figures: (a) The difference in net income can be reconciled as follows:

$$\begin{pmatrix} \text{Difference in} \\ \text{net income} \end{pmatrix} = \begin{pmatrix} \text{Change in} \\ \text{inventory} \end{pmatrix} \times \begin{pmatrix} \text{Fixed factory} \\ \text{overhead rate} \end{pmatrix}$$

(b) the above formula works only if the fixed overhead rate per unit does not change between the periods.

**VARIABLE COST PERCENTAGE** figure that equals total variable costs divided by total sales. Labor-intensive companies have a higher variable cost ratio than capital-intensive ones. If product demand declines, it is very difficult to cut the labor and raw materials (variable costs) required to produce each unit of product. It is easier to reduce fixed costs (layoff of a foreman or personnel department employee, etc.). Variable costs per unit are usually reduced through automation (increasing fixed costs). For example, if variable costs are $150 and total sales are $600, the ratio is .25.

**VARIABLE-COST-PLUS PRICING** method in which the unit variable cost is defined as the cost base. Fixed costs are provided for through the markup that is added to this base. *See also* COST PLUS PRICING.

**VARIABLE COST RATIO** relationship showing variable costs as a percentage of sales. It is also 1 minus the CONTRIBUTION MARGIN (CM) ratio. An example follows:

|  | Total | Percentage |
|---|---|---|
| Sales | $37,500 | 100% |
| Less: Variable costs | 15,000 | 40 |
| Contribution margin | $22,500 | 60% |

The variable cost ratio is 40% ($15,000/$37,500). It is also 1 minus the CM ratio, or $1 - .6 = .4 = 40\%$.

**VARIABLE COSTS** expenses that vary *in total* in direct proportion to changes in activities such as machine-hours and labor-hours within a RELEVANT RANGE. Examples are direct materials and gasoline expense based on mileage driven. Variable cost *per unit* is constant. *See also* FIXED COST.

**VARIABLE (FACTORY) OVERHEAD** portion of total factory overhead that varies directly with changes in volume. Examples of variable overhead are indirect materials, supplies, indirect labor, and fuel and power.

TOTAL VARIABLE COST · VARIABLE COST PER UNIT

**VARIABLE INTEREST ENTITY (VIE)** entity whose equity investors do *not* have sufficient equity at risk such that the entity cannot finance its own activities. When a business has a controlling financial interest in a variable interest entity, the assets, liabilities, and profit of that entity must be included in consolidation. The entity that consolidates a variable interest entity is called the *primary beneficiary*. Variable interest is a contractual, ownership, or other interest in an entity that changes as the entity's net assets change. Entity is any legal structure to carry out operations or handle assets such as corporations, partnerships, limited liability companies, and trusts. There are many examples of variable interests such as guarantees, equity investments, written put options, and forward contracts. A business enterprise must consolidate a variable interest entity when that enterprise has a variable interest that will cover most of the entity's expected losses or receive most of the entity's anticipated residual return.

**VARIABLE OVERHEAD EFFICIENCY VARIANCE** difference in actual and budgeted variable overhead costs that results from inefficient use of indirect materials and indirect labor. Variable overhead efficiency variance = (actual labor-hours − standard labor-hours allowed for actual production) × standard variable overhead rate.

For example, assume that the standard cost of direct labor per unit of product A is 2.5 hours × \$3 = \$7.50. Assume further that during the month of March the company recorded 4,500 hours of direct labor time. The actual variable overhead costs were \$13,750. The company produced 2,000 units of product A during the month. The variable overhead efficiency variance is (4,500 − 5,000) × \$3 = \$1,500, which is favorable since the actual hours used is less than the standard hours allowed. This may be the result of efficient use of labor time due to automation, use of superior production methods, or good foreman performance.

**VARIABLE OVERHEAD SPENDING VARIANCE** difference in actual and budgeted variable overhead costs that results from price changes in indirect materials and indirect labor and insufficient control of costs of specific overhead items. Variable overhead spending variance = actual overhead costs − (standard rate × actual hours of labor used).

For example, assume that the standard variable overhead cost per unit of product A is 2.5 hours × $3.00 = $7.50. Assume further that during the month of March the company recorded 4,500 hours of direct labor time. The total actual variable overhead cost for the month was $13,750. The company produced 2,000 units of product A during the month. The variable overhead spending variance is $13,750 − ($3.00 × 4,500 hours) = $250, which is unfavorable since actual overhead spent exceeded the budgeted amount. This may be the result of unavoidable price increases in indirect materials and indirect labor.

**VARIABLE PRICING MODEL** *see* CONTRIBUTION APPROACH TO PRICING.

**VARIABLE RATE LOAN** loan carrying an interest rate that may move up or down, depending on the movements of an outside standard such as the rate paid on U.S. Treasury securities; also called an *adjustable rate loan*. The lender can increase or decrease the interest rate on this type of loan at specified intervals to keep pace with changing market conditions. The frequency of the interest rate changes and the limit, if any, on the amount of change is set by the lender and must be specified in the loan document.

**VARIABLES SAMPLING** sampling designed to predict the value of a given variable for a population. The variables under AUDIT are typically the total population or the arithmetic mean. An example is the CPA's estimation of the cost of a group of inventory components. Initially, the accountant samples a limited number of components, computes the per-item cost, and finally statistically derives the plus or minus range of the total inventory value under examination.

**VARIANCE**
1. in *statistics*, measure of a dispersion of probability distribution. It is the square of the STANDARD DEVIATION. For example, if the standard deviation is 20, the variance is 400.
2. difference of revenues, costs, and profit from the planned amounts. One of the most important phases of responsibility accounting is establishing standards in costs, revenues, and profit and establishing performance by comparing actual amounts with the standard amounts. The differences (variances) are calculated for each responsibility center, analyzed, and unfavorable variances are investigated for possible remedial action.
3. in COST ACCOUNTING, deviation between the actual cost and the standard cost. If actual cost exceeds standard cost, an unfavorable variance exists. A variance can be calculated for different cost items such as manufacturing costs (i.e., direct material, direct labor, and

overhead), selling expenses, and administrative expenses. The reasons for a variance should be identified and corrective action taken. For example, actual production is 80 units. Standard cost per unit is $5 while actual cost per unit is $6. The unfavorable variance equals $80 ($400 vs $480).

**VARIANCE ANALYSIS** *see* ANALYSIS OF VARIANCES.

**VENTURE CAPITAL** financing source for new businesses or turn-around ventures that usually combine much risk with potential for high return. There are various stages of venture capital, such as beginning with seed money and then proceeding to the development stage. Sources of venture capital include wealthy individuals, small business investment companies, and limited partnerships.

**VERIFIABLE** confirming or substantiating an item. The term refers to the ability of accountants to ensure that accounting information is what it purports to be. The term also means that the selected method of measurement has been used without error or bias. An example of verifiability is that of two accountants looking at the same information (e.g., inventory valuation) and coming to similar conclusions.

**VERIFICATION** process of validating a statement, item, or account. The accountant seeks and examines evidence in support of the item. The auditor also attempts to determine accuracy in the amount of the item by conducting auditing tests and procedures. Sometimes assurance need show only that the characteristic is within a prescribed range.

**VERTICAL ANALYSIS** financial statement item that is used as a base value. All other accounts on the financial statement are compared to it. In the balance sheet, for example, total assets equals 100%. Each asset is stated as a percentage of total assets. Similarly, total liabilities and stockholders' equity are assigned 100% with a given liability or equity account stated as a percentage of the total liabilities and stockholders' equity. For the income statement, 100% is assigned to net sales with all revenue and expense accounts related to it. Under vertical analysis, the statements showing the percentages are referred to as COMMON SIZE FINANCIAL STATEMENTS. Common size percentages can be compared from one period to another to identify areas needing attention. An illustration follows:

| | | |
|---|---|---|
| Net Sales | $300,000 | 100% |
| Less: Cost of Sales | 60,000 | 20% |
| Gross Profit | $240,000 | 80% |
| Less: Operating Expenses | 150,000 | 50% |
| Net Income | $ 90,000 | 30% |

*See also* HORIZONTAL ANALYSIS.

**VERTICAL MERGER** combination of a parent firm and the suppliers of its raw materials or purchasers of its finished product. Vertical merger extends the lines of distribution or production, either backward toward the source or forward toward the end-user. A firm controlling the entire production process is considered totally integrated vertically.

**VESTED** term indicating rights to pension benefits that are paid up and therefore not contingent upon the employee's continuing in the service of the employer. The EMPLOYEE RETIREMENT INCOME SECURITY ACT (ERISA) provides that an employee must be at least 25% vested in benefits derived from employer contributions after 5 years of covered service. By the time the employee has 15 years of covered service, vesting must have risen to 100%.

**VESTED BENEFIT OBLIGATION (VBO)** the actuarial present value of vested pension benefits employees have a right to receive regardless of future employment or future salary levels.

**VIRAL MARKETING** a marketing method used in the WEB 2.0 world in which users spread news about products and services to one another.

**VIRTUAL PRIVATE NETWORK (VPN)** basically a virtual version of a secure, physical network. A VPN gives an organization the ability to extend its secure network while using the INTERNET, such as by allowing its employees to remotely access a central server.

**VIRUS** a small software program that is designed to interfere with a computer's normal operations. A computer virus is capable of replicating itself and spreading itself from one computer to another.

**VISUAL C#** modern, high-level, object-oriented, general-purpose programming language for rapidly building both desktop and Web applications.

**VOICE OVER INTERNET PROTOCOL (VOIP)** allows voice/phone calls to be transported over an IP data network. Significant cost savings can be achieved when phone calls travel over an IP data network rather than a phone company's network.

**VOLUME (PRODUCTION VOLUME) VARIANCE** amount of under- or overapplied fixed factory overhead. It is the difference between budgeted fixed factory overhead and the amount applied based on a predetermined rate and the standard input allowed for actual output. It measures the use of capacity rather than specific cost outlays. *See also* FIXED OVERHEAD VOLUME (DENOMINATOR) VARIANCE; IDLE CAPACITY VARIANCE.

**VOLUNTARY HEALTH AND WELFARE ORGANIZATION** entity providing health-related services. It is a not-for-profit organization that follows accrual accounting. The fund groups of a voluntary health and welfare organization include current funds, plant funds, and endowment funds. *Current funds* are used for operations; they are classified as unrestricted or restricted. The restriction may relate to a specific operating objective by reason of gift, grant, etc. *Plant funds* include land, buildings and equipment, and related debt, along with assets to be used for future acquisitions and replacements. *Endowment funds* are used to account for bequests that require principal to be maintained intact.

**VOLUNTARY HOSPITAL** one providing patient services including surgery and testing. It follows not-for-profit accounting and has unrestricted (general) and restricted fund groups. *Unrestricted funds* include: (1) *operating funds* for routine hospital activities, including plant assets and related long-term debt; and (2) *board-designated funds*, representing resources set aside for special users. *Restricted fund* types include: (1) *specific-purpose*, applying to expenses restricted to specific operating purposes; (2) *endowment*, where principal is kept intact, and earnings may or may not be available subject to donor restrictions; and (3) *plant replacement and expansion*, applying to resources restricted for plant and equipment acquisitions.

**VOUCHER** form used in an internal control system to contain and verify all information about a bill to be processed or paid. Usually the original bill is then attached to the voucher. The voucher and bill are filed together until time of payment.

**VOUCHER SYSTEM** type of internal system used to control the cash (checks) being spent (written). The voucher system consists of vouchers, voucher files (paid and unpaid), voucher register that takes the place of the purchase journal, cash register that takes the place of the cash disbursement journal, and the general journal. This system ensures the person paying the bills that the bills are proper and should be paid. On the due date a voucher is removed from the "unpaid" voucher file and forwarded to the firm's disbursing officer for final approval of payment.

**VOUCHING** an audit procedure in which an auditor selects recorded items and then examines documents to support their validity. Vouching enables verification that transactions have occurred and that assets physically exist. Accordingly, vouching is a test for overstatement.

# W

**WAITING LINE THEORY** *see* QUEUING THEORY.

**WALK** theory that stock prices behave in an unpredictable fashion because the stock market is efficient. The market price of a company's stock goes randomly around real (intrinsic) value. Current security prices are independent of prior prices. Thus historical prices are not a reliable predictor of future ones. According to random walk, financial information significant enough to affect future value is available to knowledgeable investors. Thus new data affecting stock price are immediately reflected in market value. At any given time, the price of a stock is the optimum estimate of its value including all available information. *See also* EFFICIENT MARKET HYPOTHESIS.

**WALK-THROUGH TEST** audit procedure used in evaluating the reliability of the client's accounting system. The auditor looks at the supporting documentation for a transaction from its starting point and then proceeds to examine the accounting system steps thereafter until ultimate disposition of the item. The walk-through examination is one of the COMPLIANCE TESTS that the auditor can perform.

**WAREHOUSE RECEIPT** document listing goods or commodities (e.g., gold) stored in a warehouse that shows retention of title to the goods. Warehouse receipts may be negotiable or non-negotiable. Negotiable receipts allow transfer without endorsement and may act as a security for a loan. Non-negotiable receipts must be endorsed upon transfer. Warehouse receipts, regulated by the Uniform Warehouse Receipts Act, allow the sale of goods without having to physically deliver them.

**WARM SITE** is a backup location/site from where an organization's data center can operate for the duration of a disaster. An organization may have three types of backup locations: a COLD SITE, a warm site, or a HOT SITE. A warm backup site is a compromise between a hot and a cold site. A warm site generally has all the hardware needed, though many times on a smaller scale than the original data center. Often, there is some delay in resuming data center function to full operation from a warm backup site.

**WARRANT**
1. *see* STOCK WARRANT.
2. guarantee of the occurrence of something, such as warranting the performance of another party.
3. in GOVERNMENT ACCOUNTING, order drawn authorizing payment to a designated payee.

**WARRANTY** agreement by the seller of goods or services to satisfy for a stated period of time deficiencies in the item's quality or performance. Warranty terms may be included on the buyer's receipt.

The warranty usually provides for repair or replacement of the item in the case of malfunctioning or poor workmanship. Typically, there is no additional charge during the warranty period. The seller records warranty expense and related estimated liability in the year of sale. A warranty percentage is usually based on prior experience. Assume sales for 2014 are $100,000. Estimated warranty cost is 2% of sales. The entry to record warranty expense is:

| 12/31/2014 | Warranty expense | 2,000 | |
|---|---|---|---|
| | Estimated warranty payable | | 2,000 |

If on 1/25/2015, actual warranty services performed cost $500, the entry is:

| | Estimated warranty payable | 500 | |
|---|---|---|---|
| | Cash | | 500 |

## WASH SALE
1. transaction or sale that is nullified by its reversal or offset within a short time of its initiation. Such sales are now forbidden by stock exchange rules.
2. losses on a sale of stock that, for federal income tax purposes, may not be recognized if the same stock is purchased within 30 days preceding or following the date of sale.

**WASTE** term used for shrinkage, evaporation, and so on. The cost of waste from these causes usually is not traced and is not recognized in the accounts. In a standard cost system an allowance for waste may be included in the determination of standard cost. Waste in excess of standard is thus revealed as a quantity or usage variance.

## WASTING ASSET
1. FIXED ASSET with limited life and subject to DEPRECIATION. It therefore excludes land.
2. natural resource such as oil, coal, and timber, having a limited useful life and subject to DEPLETION. Such assets decrease in worth primarily due to the extraction of the valued commodity held by these assets. *See also* INTANGIBLE ASSET.
3. security whose value expires at a specified time in the future. An option contract (PUT or CALL) is an example of a *wasting asset.*

**WATERED STOCK** stock that has been issued for an amount that is below the stock's par value.

**WEB BROWSER** browsers for the World Wide Web (WWW) enabling one to hook up with network servers to obtain HTML documents and Web pages. It provides a linkage among pages and documents. The server may physically be on the Internet or a private network. The browser may contain "help" applications for special files.

**WEBMASTER/WEBMISTRESS** a person responsible for managing a Web site.

**WEB PAGE** a document written with HTML tags that is accessible through a Web browser. A Web page is retrieved through its URL and may contain all types of media, including text, graphics, audio/video, and hyperlinks.

**WEB SEARCH ENGINE** a tool designed to search for information, including accounting-related information, on the World Wide Web. The search results are usually presented in a list and are commonly referred to as hits. The accounting information may consist of accounting association Web sites, images, and other information.

**WEB SERVER** consists of hardware/software to manage and control a Web site. Presently, the two leading Web servers are Apache and Microsoft's Internet Information Server (IIS).

**WEB SERVICE** a standard way of integrating two or more Web applications over the Internet. Web services allow different applications from different sources to communicate with each other using data in EXTENSIBLE MARKUP LANGUAGE (XML) format. Web services do not have a GRAPHICAL USER INTERFACE (GUI), relying instead on a programmatic interface.

**WEB SITE** consists of one or more Web pages served from a single Web domain.

**WEB SITE DEVELOPMENT COSTS** Web site development is segregated into three stages (activities) that have an impact on the accounting treatment for costs incurred. The first stage is planning in which the costs incurred are expensed. Development is the second stage, and Web application and infrastructure as well as graphics development costs are capitalized and then amortized after the Web site is ready. However, costs to develop the content for the site may be capitalized or expensed depending on the circumstances. In the third stage of post-implementation, work is performed after the site is put into service (e.g., administration, training, security). These costs are expensed as incurred. Also in the third stage, there are expenditures for additional upgrades and features after the site is launched. The costs attributable to this are capitalized if the upgrades and enhancements provide *additional functionality*.

**WEB TRUST** a type of trust service that assesses an entity's Web site in terms of transaction integrity, information security, and disclosure of business practices. Web trust engagements are governed by STATEMENTS ON STANDARDS FOR ATTESTATION ENGAGEMENTS (SSAE).

**WEB 2.0** a loose collection of capabilities, technologies, business models, and philosophies that characterizes the new and emerging business uses of the Internet. Software as a service is an example of Web 2.0. Web 2.0 concepts have led to the development and evolution of Web culture communities and hosted services, such as social-networking sites, video sharing sites, wikis, and blogs. The following table compares Web 2.0 with traditional processing. (For some reason, the term *Web 1.0* is not used.)

**COMPARISON OF TRADITIONAL
PROCESSING WITH WEB 2.0**

| Traditional Processing | Web 2.0 Processing |
|---|---|
| Software as product | Software as service |
| Infrequent, controlled releases | Frequent releases of perpetual betas |
| Business model relies on sale of software licenses | Business model relies on advertising or other revenue from use |
| Extensive advertising | Viral marketing |
| Product value fixed | Product value increases with use and users |
| Publishing | Participation |
| Major winners: Microsoft, Oracle, SAP | Major winners: Google, Amazon.com, eBay |

**WEIGHT** relative importance given to an individual item included in forecasting, such as alpha in exponential smoothing. In the method of MOVING AVERAGES all of those past values included in the moving average are given equal weight.

**WEIGHTED AVERAGE** average of observations having different degrees of importance or frequency. The formula for a weighted average is Weighted Average = $\Sigma wx$, where $x$ = the data values and $w$ = relative weight assigned to each observation, expressed as a percentage or relative frequency. For example, assume the XYZ Company uses three grades of labor to produce a finished product as follows:

| Grade of Labor | Labor Hours Per Unit of Labor | Hourly Wages ($x$) |
|---|---|---|
| Skilled | 6 | $10.00 |
| Semiskilled | 3 | 8.00 |
| Unskilled | $\underline{1}$ | 6.00 |
|  | 10 |  |

The weighted average is computed as follows:

Weighted average = $10.00 (6/10) + $8.00(3/10) + $6.00(1/10)
                 = $ 9.00 per hour

Note that the weights equal the proportion of the total labor required to produce the product. A weighted average is calculated in the WEIGHTED AVERAGE INVENTORY METHOD and the COST OF CAPITAL.

**WEIGHTED AVERAGE CONTRIBUTION MARGIN** one in which weights are relative to sales mix. For example, assume that Company Z has two products with the following contribution margin data:

|  | A | B |
|---|---|---|
| Unit CONTRIBUTION MARGIN (CM) | $3 | $5 |
| Sales mix | 60% | 40% |

The weighted average CM per unit is ($3)(0.6) + ($5)(0.4) = $3.80

**WEIGHTED AVERAGE COSTING** procedure for computing the unit cost of a process. Beginning work-in-process inventory costs are added to the costs of the current period, then a weighted average is obtained by dividing the combined costs by equivalent units. Thus there is only one average cost for goods completed. Equivalent units under weighted average costing may be computed as follows:

Units completed + (ending work-in-process × degree of completion (%)). To illustrate, the following data relate to the activities of Department A during the month of January:

|  | Units |
|---|---|
| Beginning work-in-process (100% complete as to materials; 2/3 complete as to conversion) | 1,500 |
| Started this period | 5,000 |
| Completed and transferred | 5,500 |
| Ending work in process (100% complete as to materials; 6/10 complete as to conversion) | 1,000 |

Equivalent production in Department A for the month is computed, using weighted average costing, as follows:

|  | Materials | Conversion Costs |
|---|---|---|
| Units completed and transferred | 5,500 | 5,500 |
| Ending work in process |  |  |
|    Materials (100%) | 1,000 |  |
|    Conversion costs (60%) |  | 600 |
| Equivalent production | 6,500 | 6,100 |

*See also* FIRST-IN, FIRST-OUT (FIFO) COSTING.

**WEIGHTED AVERAGE COST OF CAPITAL** weights the percentage cost of each component by the percentage of that component in the financial structure.

**WEIGHTED AVERAGE INVENTORY METHOD** method in calculation in which the weighted average cost per unit for the period is the cost of the goods available for sale divided by the number of units available for sale. When the perpetual inventory system is used, the weighted average method is called the MOVING AVERAGE method.

**WEIGHTED COST DRIVER** technique of increasing or decreasing the cost consumption intensity of an individual cost object by weighting the measured quantity of the cost driver.

**WEIGHTED MEAN** *see* WEIGHTED AVERAGE.

**WESTLAW** online database of West Publishing containing legal cases and other legal information for practicing attorneys.

**W-4 FORM** form known as the Employee's Withholding Allowance Certificate. It is filled out by a new employee, or an employee who wishes to change the figures in the form, to provide information needed by the employer to calculate an employee's pay net of exemptions and other tax deductions. The W-4 form does not provide information for deductions for union dues, medical insurance, pension, and so on.

**WHAT-IF ANALYSIS** *see* SIMULATION.

**WHITE KNIGHT** a company that an entity prefers to merge with, rather than going through a hostile takeover.

**WHITE PAPER**
1. a government report bound in white; also called a *white book*.
2. an authoritative report on a major issue, as by a team of journalists.
3. a short treatise whose purpose is to educate industry customers.

**WHOLE-LIFE COST** concept closely associated with LIFE-CYCLE COST. Whole-life costs equal life-cycle costs plus after-purchase costs. Attention to the reduction of all whole-life costs through analysis and management of all value-chain activities is a powerful competitive tool because of the potential for increasing customer satisfaction. Life-cycle and whole-life cost concepts are associated with target costing and target pricing. A firm may determine that market conditions require that a product sell at a given target price. Hence, a TARGET COST can be determined by subtracting the desired unit profit margin from the target price. The cost reduction objectives of life-cycle and whole-life cost management can, therefore, be determined using target costing.

**WIDE AREA NETWORK (WAN)** network comprising a large geographic area.

**WI-FI** *see* WIRELESS FIDELITY.

**WIKI** a knowledge base maintained by its users. It is processed on Web sites that allow users to add, remove, and edit content. The most famous wiki is Wikipedia.

**WILLIE SUTTON RULE** reminder to focus on the high-cost activities. The rule is named after bank robber Willie Sutton, who—when asked "why do you rob banks?"—is reputed to have replied "because that's where the money is."

**WILSHIRE 5000 INDEX** the broadest weighted index of all common stock issues on the NYSE, AMEX, and the most active issues on the over-the-counter market. Approximately 85% of the securities are traded on the NYSE. The index's value is in billions of dollars. It includes about 6,000 stocks (not 5,000 as its name would suggest) so it is representative of the overall market.

**WINDFALL PROFITS** earnings of an unexpected nature and generally not due to the efforts and expenditures of the entity that benefits. The Crude Oil Windfall Profits Tax of 1980 placed a tax on such profits on the production and sale of crude oil. The windfall profits figure is derived from complex calculations defined in the code, based on the difference between selling price less state severance taxes and a defined base price.

**WINDOW** portion of a computer display screen. Some programs allow the user to divide the screen into two or more windows, making it possible to work on two different tasks simultaneously.

**WINDOW DRESSING** making a company look better financially than it really is. Assume just before the end of the accounting year current assets are $100,000 and current liabilities are $50,000, representing a current ratio (current assets/current liabilities) of 2:1. To improve its current ratio for the annual report in order to attract prospective lenders, the company window-dresses by paying off $30,000 in current debt. This now makes current assets $70,000 and current liabilities $20,000, resulting in a misleading current ratio of 3.5:1. This current ratio is temporary and deceiving because, most likely, at the beginning of the next accounting year the firm will borrow additional short-term funds that reduce the current ratio.

**WIRELESS FIDELITY (WI-FI)** the popular term for a high-frequency wireless local area network. The consumer-friendly name for the 802.11b/g/n/ac engineering standard. It lets home and office users create wireless local networks, which connect two or more computers to each other and a faster Internet line. This way there is no more poking holes in walls or tripping over bulky Ethernet cables. The Wi-Fi technology is rapidly gaining acceptance as an alternative to a wired local area network (LAN).

**WIRELESS TECHNOLOGY** a variety of technologies to communicate without wires, namely radio transmissions.

**WITHHOLDING TAX** deductions by an employer from employee salaries for the payment of federal and state income taxes. It is paid in a prescribed manner to the taxing authority. Withholding tax is remitted by the employer to the IRS or deposited into the designated bank on a periodic basis as prescribed by the IRS. *See also* FEDERAL INSURANCE CONTRIBUTION ACT (FICA); FEDERAL UNEMPLOYMENT TAX ACT (FUTA).

**WORD** popular word processing software by Microsoft.

**WORDPRESS** the largest self-hosted blogging tool. While WordPress, which is used on millions of sites, started as just a blogging system, it has evolved to be used as a full content management system. Its popularity means that thousands of plug-ins, widgets, and themes are available through which it can be customized.

**WORD PROCESSING** method that involves the use of computerized equipment to automatically produce written letters and documents, reports, memorandums, reminder letters, audit bid proposals, contracts, confirmations, representation letters, and billings. Typically, word processing programs (e.g., WORD) allow the user to insert, delete, rearrange, search and replace, write style sheets, and move text from one document to another. A table of contents may be prepared from headings and subheadings. A glossary and index may also be furnished. Windows can display different portions of the same document or of completely independent but related documents.

**WORK CELL** physical or logical grouping of resources that performs a defined job or task. The work cell may contain more than one.

**WORKERS' COMPENSATION** program providing payments, without regard to a finding of negligence of either party, to workers involved in specific job-related injuries. These laws were enacted so that the employee would not have to go through a long and arduous lawsuit and possibly not recover due to the employer's advantageous financial standing. Payments are specifically exempt from taxation.

**WORKFLOW** sequence of actions accomplishing a business goal. A toolset to proactively analyze, compress, and automate information-based activities.

**WORKING CAPITAL** current assets less current liabilities, properly called *net working capital*. Working capital is a measure of a company's liquidity. Sources of working capital are (1) net income, (2) increase in noncurrent liabilities, (3) increase in stockholders' equity, and (4) decrease in noncurrent assets.

**WORKING CAPITAL TURNOVER** sales divided by average working capital. It reflects the entity's effectiveness in using working capital to obtain revenue. If sales are $100,000, beginning working capital is $20,000, and ending working capital is $30,000, the turnover rate is 4 times ($100,000/$25,000).

**WORK-IN-PROCESS (WIP)** partially completed inventory units at the end of the accounting period. An example is a table without legs; also called *goods-in-process*. In ABSORPTION COSTING, work-in-process is valued at the total cost to process it, including direct material, direct labor, and factory overhead (fixed and variable). In DIRECT COSTING, work-in-process is valued at only the variable costs to produce it, consisting of direct material, direct labor, and variable overhead. Ending work-in-process is shown as a current asset in the balance sheet. Beginning and ending work-in-process units are shown in the cost of goods manufactured schedule of the income statement.

## WORKOUT

1. a range of prices within which a transaction or a series of transactions is likely to take place. For example, a market maker might quote a price range within which he or she would attempt to buy or sell a large order of securities.

2. the process of a debtor's meeting a loan commitment by satisfying altered repayment terms. For example, a firm in Chapter 11 bankruptcy proceedings might reach an agreement with its creditors for ways in which the firm's obligations can be worked out.

**WORK MEASUREMENT** determination of the length of time it should take to complete a job. Job times are vital inputs for manpower planning, estimating labor costs, scheduling, budgeting, and designing incentive systems. In addition, from the workers' standpoint, time standards provide an indication of expected output. *Time standards* used under STANDARD COST SYSTEMS reflect the amount of time it should take an average worker to do a job under typical operating conditions. The standards include expected activity time plus allowances for probable delays. The most commonly used methods of work measurement are: (1) stopwatch time study; (2) historical times; (3) predetermined data; and (4) work sampling.

**WORK PAPERS** documents prepared or obtained by the auditor in performing an examination of a client's financial records. The work papers may be called into court and may be subject to examination by the IRS when they relate to tax pool analysis. Included in the work papers are schedules, analyses, transcriptions, memos, and confirmation results related to balance sheet and income statement items. The work papers serve as the basis of the work performed and support the auditor's opinion. Upon review of the work papers, a reviewer can determine the quality of the work performed.

**WORK SHEET** document or schedule in which an accountant or auditor gathers information to substantiate an opinion concerning an account BALANCE or TEST OF TRANSACTION. Types of work sheets that may be prepared are: (1) test of transaction information showing the sample selected, attributes tested, findings for each item in the sample, and the sample as a whole; (2) BANK RECONCILIATION; (3) schedule of FIXED ASSETS; and (4) analysis of various expenses with conclusions on the findings. A group of assembled work sheets becomes the WORK PAPERS composing the documentation for the audit or review work performed by the accountant. Work sheets may include letters, minutes of meetings, and other items not prepared by the auditor.

**WORK TICKET** form used to charge jobs for direct labor used. This work ticket, sometimes called *time ticket* or *time card*, indicates the time spent on a specific job. An employee who is paid an hourly wage and who operates a lathe will have one *clock card* that is used as a basis for determining individual earnings; but the employee will fill out or punch several work tickets each day when starting and stopping work on particular jobs or operations. A sample form follows.

WORK TICKET

| | | |
|---|---|---|
| Employee No. _____ | Date _____ | Job No. _____ |
| Operation _____ | Account _____ | Dept. _____ |
| | | Pieces: |
| Stop _____ | Rate _____ | Worked _____ |
| | | Rejected _____ |
| Start _____ | Amount _____ | Completed _____ |

**WORLD BANK** *see* INTERNATIONAL BANK FOR RECONSTRUCTION AND DEVELOPMENT (IBRD).

**WORLD TRADE ORGANIZATION (WTO)** an international organization that deals with the rules of trade between nations. The goal of the WTO is to assist producers of goods and services, exporters, and importers in conducting their business.

**WORLD WIDE WEB (WWW)** Internet system for worldwide hypertext linking of multimedia documents, making the relationship of information that is common between documents easily accessible and completely independent of physical location.

**WORM** a program that replicates itself and penetrates a valid computer system. It may also spread within a network.

**WORTHLESS SECURITY** a stock or bond that completely loses its value during the year. In general, a loss on a worthless security is treated as a capital loss.

**WRITE-DOWN** reduction of part of the balance of an asset by charging an expense or loss account. The reason for a write-down is that some economic event has occurred indicating that the asset's value has diminished. An example is the obsolescence of some inventory.

**WRITE-OFF**
  1. transfer of the *entire* balance of an asset account into an expense or loss account. A full reduction in an asset indicates it is not worth anything (has no future benefit) due to some occurrence. An

example is the destruction of a machine in a fire when the company has no insurance and the machine no salvage value.

2. elimination of a specific customer's account balance because of uncollectibility, as in the case of a bankruptcy.

**WRITE-UP** increase in the BOOK VALUE of an asset not due to a cash payment or other asset, issuance of a liability, or issuance of stock. Generally, this is *not* a permitted accounting practice. One exception is the write-up of fixed assets in a purchase method merger. Another exception is the case of a discovery of a natural resource such as oil on the land premises. In this unique situation, land can be charged for this discovery at fair market value as follows:

Land (appraisal increment)
Paid-in capital

The land (appraisal increment) account would then be subject to depletion.

**WRITE-UP SOFTWARE** also called *client write-up software,* accounting software structured exclusively for use by accounting professionals working in the background on a diverse array of clients.

**W-2 FORM** statement used for income tax purposes. Called *Wage and Tax Statement*, it is sent to an employee and shows gross earnings and deductions (such as federal, state, and local income taxes and FICA) for a calendar year. The business sends a copy of the W-2 to the Internal Revenue Service and other tax jurisdictions it covers. The employee attaches a copy of the W-2 to the employee's federal, state, and local income tax returns.

# X

**XBRL** *see* EXTENSIBLE BUSINESS REPORTING LANGUAGE (XBRL).

**XHTML** (Extensible Hypertext Markup Language). *See also* HTML.

**XML (EXTENSIBLE MARKUP LANGUAGE)** a generic language of the World Wide Web Consortium (W3C) for creating new markup languages. Markup languages (such as HTML) are used to represent documents with a nested, treelike structure. XML is a product of W3C and a trademark of MIT.

# Y

**YEAR-END ADJUSTMENT** process of adjusting the entry to an account at the end of the calendar or fiscal year in order to properly state it for financial statement preparation purposes. Types of required adjustments include accrual or deferral of a revenue or expense item, reclassification, adjustments to conform book figures to physical counts (i.e., inventory), and reflecting unusual transactions.

**YELLOW BOOK** the common name for the Generally Accepted Government Auditing Standards published by the U.S. Government Accountability Office. The Yellow Book is used by auditors of government entities and entities that receive government awards.

**YIELD**
1. real rate of return to the investor or effective cost to the issuer of a security for a specified time period. It differs from the NOMINAL INTEREST RATE. *See also* SIMPLE YIELD; YIELD TO MATURITY.
2. return from an asset or service provided.
3. conceding a point to another party.

**YIELD TO MATURITY** effective rate on a BOND; also called the EFFECTIVE INTEREST RATE. It considers the bond's FACE VALUE, market price, NOMINAL INTEREST RATE, and maturity period. If a bond was issued with a yield in excess of the nominal interest rate, it was sold at a DISCOUNT because it is costing the company more than the stated interest rate.

The yield to maturity formula equals:

$$\frac{\left(\text{Nominal Interest} + \dfrac{\text{Discount}}{\text{Years}}\right)}{\left(\dfrac{\text{Present Value} + \text{Maturity Value}}{2}\right)}$$

Note that if the bond was issued at a PREMIUM, the numerator would be:

$$\text{Nominal Interest} - \frac{\text{Premium}}{\text{Years}}$$

Assume a 10%, $100,000 bond was issued at $96,000. The life is five years. The effective rate is:

$$\frac{\left(\$10,000 + \dfrac{\$4,000}{5}\right)}{\left(\dfrac{\$96,000 + \$100,000}{2}\right)} = \frac{\$10,800}{\$98,000} = 11.02\%$$

**YIELD VARIANCE** effect of varying the total input of a factor of production (e.g., direct materials or labor) while holding constant the input mix (the proportions of the types of materials or labor used) and the weighted average unit price of the factor of production. *See also* PRODUCTION YIELD VARIANCE.

# Z

**ZERO-BASE BUDGETING** planning and budgeting tool that uses COST-BENEFIT ANALYSIS of projects and functions to improve resource allocation in an organization. Traditional budgeting tends to concentrate on the incremental change from the previous year. It assumes that the previous year's activities and programs are essential and must be continued. Under zero-base budgeting, however, cost and benefit estimates are built up from scratch, from the zero level, and must be justified.

**ZERO-BRACKET AMOUNT** type of STANDARD (or blanket) DEDUCTION from ADJUSTED GROSS INCOME (AGI) available to taxpayers, whether or not they can itemize nonbusiness expenses in the process of calculating their taxable income. This is the term used prior to the new tax laws.

**ZERO-COUPON BOND** bond, sold at a deep discount, that accrues interest semiannually. Both the principal and the accumulated interest are paid at maturity. Although a fixed rate is implicit in the discount and the specific maturity, they are not fixed income securities in the traditional sense because they provide for no periodic income. Although the interest on the bond is paid at maturity, accrued interest, though not received, is taxable yearly as ordinary income.

**ZERO-ONE PROGRAMMING** term used in a special case of INTEGER PROGRAMMING where all the decision variables are integers and can assume values of either zero or one. The zero-one programming technique has been successfully applied to solve a project selection problem in which projects are *mutually exclusive* and/or technologically interdependent.

**ZERO-SUM GAME** competition in which the total gains of the winner exactly equal the total loss of the loser. For example, if two accounting firms in a small town are competing for a share of a fixed market (i.e., a fixed number of clients) and one can increase a share of the market at the other's expense, the game is *zero-sum*.

**Z SCORE**
1. in statistics, the standard normal variate that standardizes a normal distribution by converting an $x$-scale to a $z$-scale.
2. score produced by Altman's bankruptcy prediction model, which is as follows:

$$Z = 1.2 * X1 + 1.4 * X2 + 3.3 * X3 + 0.6 * X4 + 0.999 * X5$$

where $X1$ = working capital/total assets (%), $X2$ = retained earnings/total assets (%), $X3$ = earnings before interest and taxes/total assets (%), $X4$ = market value of equity/book value of debt (%), and $X5$ = sales/total assets (number of times). The $Z$ score is known to be about 90% accurate in forecasting business failure one year in the future and about 80% accurate in forecasting it two years in the future.

## ABBREVIATIONS

**AAA** American Accounting Association

**ABO** Accumulated Benefit Obligation

**AccSEC** Accounting Standards Executive Committee

**ACRS** Accelerated Cost Recovery System

**ADA** Americans With Disabilities Act

**ADR** Assets Depreciation Range

**AFWA** Accounting and Financial Women's Alliance

**AGA** Association of Government Accountants

**AGI** Adjusted Gross Income

**AI** Artificial Intelligence

**AICPA** American Institute of Certified Public Accountants

**AIS** Accounting Information System

**AISG** Accountants International Study Group

**AMT** Alternative Minimum Tax

**APB** Accounting Principles Board

**API** Accountants for the Public Interest

**ARB** Accounting Research Bulletins

**ASB** Auditing Standards Board

**ASC** FASB Accounting Standards Codification

**ASCII** American Standard Code for Information Interchange

**ASR** Allowance for Sampling Risk

**ASRs** Accounting Series Releases

**AWSCPA** American Women's Society of Certified Public Accountants

**BASIC** Beginners All-Purpose Symbolic Instruction Code

**BCD** Binary Coded Decimal

**BOM** Bill Of Materials

**CA** Chartered Accountant

**CAFR** Comprehensive Annual Financial Report

**CAPM** Capital Asset Pricing Model

**CASB** Cost Accounting Standards Board

**CD** Certificate of Deposit

**CFA** Chartered Financial Analyst

**CFC** Controlled Foreign Corporation

**CFO** Chief Financial Officer

**CFP** Certified Financial Planner

**ChFC** Chartered Financial Consultant

**CIA** Certified Internal Auditor

**CICA** Canadian Institute of Chartered Accountants

**CISA** Certified Information Systems Auditor

**CM** Contribution Margin

**CMA** Certificate in Management Accounting

**COBOL** Common Business Oriented Language

**COLA** Cost-Of-Living Adjustment

**CPA** Certified Public Accountant

**CPE** Continuing Professional Education

**CPI** Consumer Price Index
**CPM** Critical Path Method
**CPU** Central Processing Unit
**CRT** Cathode Ray Tube
**CVP** Cost-Volume-Profit

**DBMS** Data Base Management System
**DCF** Discounted Cash Flow
**DIF** Data Interchange Format
**DISC** Domestic International Sales Corporation
**DSS** Decision Support System
**DUS** Dollar Unit Sampling
**DVD** Digital Versatile Disk; Digital Video Disk

**EBIT** Earnings (Total Income) Before Interest and Taxes
**EDGAR** Electronic Data Gathering, Analysis, and Retrieval
**EFTS** Electronic Fund Transfer System
**EOQ** Economic Order Quantity
**EPS** Earnings Per Share
**ERISA** Employee Retirement Income Security Act of 1974
**ESOP** Employee Stock Ownership Plan
**ET** Earliest Time

**FAF** Financial Accounting Foundation
**FASB** Financial Accounting Standards Board
**FBAR** Report of Foreign Bank and Financial Accounts
**FEI** Financial Executives Institute
**FICA** Federal Insurance Contribution Act
**FIFO** First-In, First-Out
**FINRA** Financial Industry Regulatory Authority

**FLSA** Fair Labor Standards Act
**FOB** Free On Board
**FORTRAN** *For*mula *Tran*slation
**FRF for SMEs** Financial Reporting Framework for Small- and Medium-Sized Entries
**FSC** Foreign Sales Corporation
**FTC** Federal Trade Commission
**FUTA** Federal Unemployment Tax Act

**GAAP** Generally Accepted Accounting Principles
**GAAS** Generally Accepted Auditing Standards
**GAO** General Accounting Office
**GASB** Government Accounting Standards Board
**GASP** Generalized Audit Software Package
**GATT** General Agreement on Tariffs and Trade
**GDP** Gross Domestic Product

**IAAA** Inter-American Accounting Association
**IAPC** International Auditing Practices Committee
**IASC** International Accounting Standards Committee
**IBRD** International Bank for Reconstruction and Development
**ICA** International Congress of Accountants
**ICFA** Institute of Chartered Financial Analysts
**IDEA** Interactive Data Electronic Application
**IDB** Industrial Development Bond
**IDC** Intangible Drilling Cost
**IFA** International Federation of Accountants

**IFPS** Interactive Financial Planning System

**IIA** Institute of Internal Auditors

**IMA** Institute of Management Accounting

**IMF** International Monetary Fund

**IRA** Individual Retirement Account

**IRR** Internal Rate of Return

**IRS** Internal Revenue Service

**ISOs** Incentive Stock Options

**LAN** Local Area Network

**L/C** Letter of Credit

**LDC** Less-Developed Countries

**LEXIS** Legal Exchange Information Service

**LIFO** Last-In, First-Out

**LP** Linear Programming

**LT** Latest Time

**MAS** Management Advisory Services

**MBO** Management By Objective

**MFOA** Municipal Finance Officers Association

**MIS** Management Information System

**MPU** Mean Per Unit Estimation

**MRP** Material Requirement Planning

**NAA** National Association of Accountants

**NAARS** National Automated Accounting Research System

**NASD** National Association of Securities Dealers

**NASDAQ** National Association of Securities Dealers Automated Quotations

**NIFO** Next-In, First-Out

**NOL** Net Operating Loss

**NPV** Net Present Value

**NSF CHECK** Not-Sufficient-Funds Check

**NYSE** New York Stock Exchange

**OCR** Optical Character Recognition

**OMB** Office of Management and Budget

**OR** Operations Research

**OTC** Over-the-Counter

**OSHA** Occupational Safety and Health Act

**PA** Public Accountant

**PBO** Projected Benefit Obligation

**PCAOB** Public Company Accounting Oversight Board

**PCC** Private Company Council

**PCPS** Private Companies Practice Section

**P/E RATIO** Price-Earnings Ratio

**PERT** Program Evaluation and Review Technique

**PHINet** Prentice-Hall's Information Network

**POB** Public Oversight Board

**POS** Point-of-Sale

**PPBS** Program-Planning-Budgeting System

**PV CHART** Profit-Volume Chart

*r* Correlation Coefficient

**R&D** Research and Development

**RAM** Random-Access Memory

**REG FD** Regulation Full Disclosure

**REIT** Real Estate Investment Trust

**RI** Residual Income

**ROI** Return On Investment

**RMD** Required Minimum Distribution

**RMM** Risk of Material Misstatement
**ROM** Read-Only Memory
**RRA** Reserve Recognition Accounting

**SAB** *Staff Accounting Bulletin*
**SAP** Statements on Auditing Procedure
**SAS** Statements on Auditing Standards
**SAS** Statistical Analysis Systems
**S$_b$** Standard Error of the Regression Coefficient
**S$_e$** Standard Error of the Estimate
**SEC** Securities and Exchange Commission
**SFAC** Statements of Financial Accounting Concepts
**SFAS** Statements of Financial Accounting Standards
**SOPs** Statements of Position
**SSAE** Statements on Standards for Attestation Engagements
**SSARS** Statements on Standards for Accounting and Review Services

**SSTS** Statements on Standards for Tax Services
**SYD** Sum-of-the-Years'-Digits

**TAB** Tax Anticipation Bill
**TALF PROGRAM** Term Asset-Backed Loan Facility Program
**TAN** Tax Anticipation Note
**TARP** Troubled Asset Relief Program
**TARR** Time-Adjusted Rate of Return
**TEFRA** Tax Equity and Fiscal Responsibility Act of 1982

**UCC** Uniform Commercial Code
**VAT** Value-Added Tax
**VBO** Vested Benefit Obligation

**WIP** Work-In-Process
**WTO** World Trade Organization

**XBRL** Extensible Business Reporting Language
**XML** Extensible Markup Language

## TABLE 1

### COMPOUNDED VALUE OF $1.00

(Future Value of $1.00)
$$F_n = (1 + i)^n = \text{FVIF}\,(i,\,n)$$

| Periods | 4% | 6% | 8% | 10% | 12% | 14% | 20% |
|---|---|---|---|---|---|---|---|
| 1 | 1.040 | 1.060 | 1.080 | 1.100 | 1.120 | 1.140 | 1.200 |
| 2 | 1.082 | 1.124 | 1.166 | 1.210 | 1.254 | 1.300 | 1.440 |
| 3 | 1.125 | 1.191 | 1.260 | 1.331 | 1.405 | 1.482 | 1.728 |
| 4 | 1.170 | 1.263 | 1.361 | 1.464 | 1.574 | 1.689 | 2.074 |
| 5 | 1.217 | 1.338 | 1.469 | 1.611 | 1.762 | 1.925 | 2.488 |
| 6 | 1.265 | 1.419 | 1.587 | 1.772 | 1.974 | 2.195 | 2.986 |
| 7 | 1.316 | 1.504 | 1.714 | 1.949 | 2.211 | 2.502 | 3.583 |
| 8 | 1.369 | 1.594 | 1.851 | 2.144 | 2.476 | 2.853 | 4.300 |
| 9 | 1.423 | 1.690 | 1.999 | 2.359 | 2.773 | 3.252 | 5.160 |
| 10 | 1.480 | 1.791 | 2.159 | 2.594 | 3.106 | 3.707 | 6.192 |
| 11 | 1.540 | 1.898 | 2.332 | 2.853 | 3.479 | 4.226 | 7.430 |
| 12 | 1.601 | 2.012 | 2.518 | 3.139 | 3.896 | 4.818 | 8.916 |
| 13 | 1.665 | 2.133 | 2.720 | 3.452 | 4.364 | 5.492 | 10.699 |
| 14 | 1.732 | 2.261 | 2.937 | 3.798 | 4.887 | 6.261 | 12.839 |
| 15 | 1.801 | 2.397 | 3.172 | 4.177 | 5.474 | 7.138 | 15.407 |
| 16 | 1.873 | 2.540 | 3.426 | 4.595 | 6.130 | 8.137 | 18.488 |
| 17 | 1.948 | 2.693 | 3.700 | 5.055 | 6.866 | 9.277 | 22.186 |
| 18 | 2.026 | 2.854 | 3.996 | 5.560 | 7.690 | 10.575 | 26.623 |
| 19 | 2.107 | 3.026 | 4.316 | 6.116 | 8.613 | 12.056 | 31.948 |
| 20 | 2.191 | 3.207 | 4.661 | 6.728 | 9.646 | 13.743 | 38.338 |
| 30 | 3.243 | 5.744 | 10.063 | 17.450 | 29.960 | 50.950 | 237.380 |
| 40 | 4.801 | 10.286 | 21.725 | 45.260 | 93.051 | 188.880 | 1469.800 |

**TABLE 2**

**COMPOUNDED VALUE OF ANNUITY OF $1.00**

(Future Value of Annuity)

$$S_n = \frac{(1+i)^n - 1}{i} = \text{FVIFA}\,(i, n)$$

| Periods | 4% | 6% | 8% | 10% | 12% | 14% | 20% |
|---|---|---|---|---|---|---|---|
| 1 | 1.000 | 1.000 | 1.000 | 1.000 | 1.000 | 1.000 | 1.000 |
| 2 | 2.040 | 2.060 | 2.080 | 2.100 | 2.120 | 2.140 | 2.200 |
| 3 | 3.122 | 3.184 | 3.246 | 3.310 | 3.374 | 3.440 | 3.640 |
| 4 | 4.247 | 4.375 | 4.506 | 4.641 | 4.779 | 4.921 | 5.368 |
| 5 | 5.416 | 5.637 | 5.867 | 6.105 | 6.353 | 6.610 | 7.442 |
| 6 | 6.633 | 6.975 | 7.336 | 7.716 | 8.115 | 8.536 | 9.930 |
| 7 | 7.898 | 8.394 | 8.923 | 9.487 | 10.089 | 10.730 | 12.916 |
| 8 | 9.214 | 9.898 | 10.637 | 11.436 | 12.300 | 13.233 | 16.499 |
| 9 | 10.583 | 11.491 | 12.488 | 13.580 | 14.776 | 16.085 | 20.799 |
| 10 | 12.006 | 13.181 | 14.487 | 15.938 | 17.549 | 19.337 | 25.959 |
| 11 | 13.486 | 14.972 | 16.646 | 18.531 | 20.655 | 23.045 | 32.150 |
| 12 | 15.026 | 16.870 | 18.977 | 21.385 | 24.133 | 27.271 | 39.580 |
| 13 | 16.627 | 18.882 | 21.495 | 24.523 | 28.029 | 32.089 | 48.497 |
| 14 | 18.292 | 21.015 | 24.215 | 27.976 | 32.393 | 37.581 | 59.196 |
| 15 | 20.024 | 23.276 | 27.152 | 31.773 | 37.280 | 43.842 | 72.035 |
| 16 | 21.825 | 25.673 | 30.324 | 35.950 | 42.753 | 50.980 | 87.442 |
| 17 | 23.698 | 28.213 | 33.750 | 40.546 | 48.884 | 59.118 | 105.930 |
| 18 | 25.645 | 30.906 | 37.450 | 45.600 | 55.750 | 68.394 | 128.120 |
| 19 | 27.671 | 33.760 | 41.446 | 51.160 | 63.440 | 78.969 | 154.740 |
| 20 | 29.778 | 36.778 | 45.762 | 57.276 | 75.052 | 91.025 | 186.690 |
| 30 | 56.085 | 79.058 | 113.283 | 164.496 | 241.330 | 356.790 | 1181.900 |
| 40 | 95.026 | 154.762 | 259.057 | 442.597 | 767.090 | 1342.000 | 7343.900 |

**TABLE 3**

**PRESENT VALUE OF $1.00**

$$P = 1/(1 + i)^n = \text{PVIF}\,(i,\, n)$$

| Periods | 4% | 6% | 8% | 10% | 12% | 14% | 20% |
|---|---|---|---|---|---|---|---|
| 1 | 0.962 | 0.943 | 0.926 | 0.909 | 0.893 | 0.877 | 0.833 |
| 2 | 0.925 | 0.890 | 0.857 | 0.826 | 0.797 | 0.769 | 0.694 |
| 3 | 0.889 | 0.840 | 0.794 | 0.751 | 0.712 | 0.675 | 0.579 |
| 4 | 0.855 | 0.792 | 0.735 | 0.683 | 0.636 | 0.592 | 0.482 |
| 5 | 0.822 | 0.747 | 0.681 | 0.621 | 0.567 | 0.519 | 0.402 |
| 6 | 0.790 | 0.705 | 0.630 | 0.564 | 0.507 | 0.456 | 0.335 |
| 7 | 0.760 | 0.665 | 0.583 | 0.513 | 0.452 | 0.400 | 0.279 |
| 8 | 0.731 | 0.627 | 0.540 | 0.467 | 0.404 | 0.351 | 0.233 |
| 9 | 0.703 | 0.592 | 0.500 | 0.424 | 0.361 | 0.308 | 0.194 |
| 10 | 0.676 | 0.558 | 0.463 | 0.386 | 0.322 | 0.270 | 0.162 |
| 11 | 0.650 | 0.527 | 0.429 | 0.350 | 0.287 | 0.237 | 0.135 |
| 12 | 0.625 | 0.497 | 0.397 | 0.319 | 0.257 | 0.208 | 0.112 |
| 13 | 0.601 | 0.469 | 0.368 | 0.290 | 0.229 | 0.182 | 0.093 |
| 14 | 0.577 | 0.442 | 0.340 | 0.263 | 0.205 | 0.160 | 0.078 |
| 15 | 0.555 | 0.417 | 0.315 | 0.239 | 0.183 | 0.140 | 0.065 |
| 16 | 0.534 | 0.394 | 0.292 | 0.218 | 0.163 | 0.123 | 0.054 |
| 17 | 0.513 | 0.371 | 0.270 | 0.198 | 0.146 | 0.108 | 0.045 |
| 18 | 0.494 | 0.350 | 0.250 | 0.180 | 0.130 | 0.095 | 0.038 |
| 19 | 0.475 | 0.331 | 0.232 | 0.164 | 0.116 | 0.083 | 0.031 |
| 20 | 0.456 | 0.312 | 0.215 | 0.149 | 0.104 | 0.073 | 0.026 |
| 30 | 0.308 | 0.174 | 0.099 | 0.057 | 0.033 | 0.020 | 0.004 |
| 40 | 0.208 | 0.097 | 0.046 | 0.022 | 0.011 | 0.005 | 0.001 |

**TABLE 4**

**PRESENT VALUE OF ANNUITY OF \$1.00**

$$P_n = \frac{1}{i}\left(1 - \frac{1}{(1+i)^n}\right)$$

| Periods | 4% | 6% | 8% | 10% | 12% | 14% | 20% |
|---------|--------|--------|--------|-------|-------|-------|-------|
| 1 | 0.962 | 0.943 | 0.926 | 0.909 | 0.893 | 0.877 | 0.833 |
| 2 | 1.886 | 1.833 | 1.783 | 1.736 | 1.690 | 1.647 | 1.528 |
| 3 | 2.775 | 2.673 | 2.577 | 2.487 | 2.402 | 2.322 | 2.106 |
| 4 | 3.630 | 3.465 | 3.312 | 3.170 | 3.037 | 2.914 | 2.589 |
| 5 | 4.452 | 4.212 | 3.993 | 3.791 | 3.605 | 3.433 | 2.991 |
| 6 | 5.242 | 4.917 | 4.623 | 4.355 | 4.111 | 3.889 | 3.326 |
| 7 | 6.002 | 5.582 | 5.206 | 4.868 | 4.564 | 4.288 | 3.605 |
| 8 | 6.733 | 6.210 | 5.747 | 5.335 | 4.968 | 4.639 | 3.837 |
| 9 | 7.435 | 6.802 | 6.247 | 5.759 | 5.328 | 4.946 | 4.031 |
| 10 | 8.111 | 7.360 | 6.710 | 6.145 | 5.650 | 5.216 | 4.192 |
| 11 | 8.760 | 7.887 | 7.139 | 6.495 | 5.938 | 5.453 | 4.327 |
| 12 | 9.385 | 8.384 | 7.536 | 6.814 | 6.194 | 5.660 | 4.439 |
| 13 | 9.986 | 8.853 | 7.904 | 7.103 | 6.424 | 5.842 | 4.533 |
| 14 | 10.563 | 9.295 | 8.244 | 7.367 | 6.628 | 6.002 | 4.611 |
| 15 | 11.118 | 9.712 | 8.559 | 7.606 | 6.811 | 6.142 | 4.675 |
| 16 | 11.652 | 10.106 | 8.851 | 7.824 | 6.974 | 6.265 | 4.730 |
| 17 | 12.168 | 10.477 | 9.122 | 8.022 | 7.120 | 6.373 | 4.775 |
| 18 | 12.659 | 10.828 | 9.372 | 8.201 | 7.250 | 6.467 | 4.812 |
| 19 | 13.134 | 11.158 | 9.604 | 8.365 | 7.366 | 6.550 | 4.844 |
| 20 | 13.590 | 11.470 | 9.818 | 8.514 | 7.469 | 6.623 | 4.870 |
| 30 | 17.292 | 13.765 | 11.258 | 9.427 | 8.055 | 7.003 | 4.979 |
| 40 | 19.793 | 15.046 | 11.925 | 9.779 | 8.244 | 7.105 | 4.997 |

## TABLE 5

## VALUES OF $t$

| Degrees of Freedom | $t_{.100}$ | $t_{.050}$ | $t_{.025}$ | $t_{.010}$ | $t_{.005}$ |
|---|---|---|---|---|---|
| 1 | 3.078 | 6.314 | 12.706 | 31.821 | 63.657 |
| 2 | 1.886 | 2.920 | 4.303 | 6.965 | 9.925 |
| 3 | 1.638 | 2.353 | 3.182 | 4.541 | 5.841 |
| 4 | 1.533 | 2.132 | 2.776 | 3.747 | 4.604 |
| 5 | 1.476 | 2.015 | 2.571 | 3.365 | 4.032 |
| 6 | 1.440 | 1.943 | 2.447 | 3.143 | 3.707 |
| 7 | 1.415 | 1.895 | 2.365 | 3.000 | 3.499 |
| 8 | 1.397 | 1.860 | 2.306 | 2.896 | 3.355 |
| 9 | 1.383 | 1.833 | 2.262 | 2.821 | 3.250 |
| 10 | 1.372 | 1.812 | 2.228 | 2.764 | 3.169 |
| 11 | 1.363 | 1.796 | 2.201 | 2.718 | 3.106 |
| 12 | 1.356 | 1.782 | 2.179 | 2.681 | 3.055 |
| 13 | 1.350 | 1.771 | 2.160 | 2.650 | 3.012 |
| 14 | 1.345 | 1.761 | 2.145 | 2.600 | 2.977 |
| 15 | 1.341 | 1.753 | 2.131 | 2.600 | 2.947 |
| 16 | 1.337 | 1.746 | 2.120 | 2.584 | 2.921 |
| 17 | 1.333 | 1.740 | 2.110 | 2.567 | 2.898 |
| 18 | 1.330 | 1.734 | 2.101 | 2.552 | 2.878 |
| 19 | 1.328 | 1.729 | 2.093 | 2.539 | 2.861 |
| 20 | 1.325 | 1.725 | 2.086 | 2.528 | 2.845 |
| 21 | 1.323 | 1.721 | 2.080 | 2.518 | 2.831 |
| 22 | 1.321 | 1.717 | 2.074 | 2.508 | 2.819 |
| 23 | 1.319 | 1.714 | 2.069 | 2.500 | 2.807 |
| 24 | 1.318 | 1.711 | 2.064 | 2.492 | 2.797 |
| 25 | 1.316 | 1.708 | 2.060 | 2.485 | 2.787 |
| 26 | 1.315 | 1.706 | 2.056 | 2.479 | 2.779 |
| 27 | 1.314 | 1.703 | 2.052 | 2.473 | 2.771 |
| 28 | 1.313 | 1.701 | 2.048 | 2.467 | 2.763 |
| 29 | 1.311 | 1.699 | 2.045 | 2.462 | 2.756 |
| 30 | 1.310 | 1.697 | 2.042 | 2.457 | 2.750 |
| 35 | 1.306 | 1.690 | 2.030 | 2.438 | 2.724 |
| 40 | 1.303 | 1.684 | 2.021 | 2.423 | 2.704 |
| 50 | 1.299 | 1.676 | 2.009 | 2.400 | 2.678 |
| 60 | 1.296 | 1.671 | 2.000 | 2.400 | 2.660 |
| 100 | 1.290 | 1.660 | 1.984 | 2.364 | 2.626 |
| 120 | 1.289 | 1.658 | 1.980 | 2.358 | 2.617 |